Verdi in America

Also by George W. Martin

CCB, the Life and Century of Charles C. Burlingham, 1858–1959, New York's First Citizen

Twentieth Century Opera: A Guide

Verdi at the Golden Gate: Opera and San Francisco in the Gold Rush Years

Aspects of Verdi

The Damrosch Dynasty: America's First Family of Music

Madam Secretary, Frances Perkins

Causes and Conflicts: The Centennial History of the Association of the Bar of the City of New York, 1870–1970

The Red Shirt and the Cross of Savoy: The Story of Italy's Risorgimento, 1748–1871

Verdi: His Music, Life and Times

The Battle of the Frogs and the Mice: An Homeric Fable

The Opera Companion

Giuseppe Verdi, b. 10 Oct. 1813, d. 27 Jan. 1901.
From a drawing by Everett Raymond Kinstler, 1963.

Verdi in America

"Oberto" through "Rigoletto"

George W. Martin

 UNIVERSITY OF ROCHESTER PRESS

First published 2011

University of Rochester Press
668 Mt. Hope Avenue, Rochester, NY 14620, USA
www.urpress.com
and Boydell & Brewer Limited
PO Box 9, Woodbridge, Suffolk IP12 3DF, UK
www.boydellandbrewer.com

ISBN-13: 978-1-58046-388-1
ISSN: 1071-9989

Library of Congress Cataloging-in-Publication Data

Martin, George Whitney.
   Verdi in America : Oberto through Rigoletto / George W. Martin.
     p. cm. — (Eastman studies in music, ISSN 1071-9989 ; v. 86)
   Includes bibliographical references and index.
   ISBN 978-1-58046-388-1 (hardcover : alk. paper) 1. Verdi, Giuseppe, 1813–1901—Performances—United States. 2. Opera—United States—19th century. 3. Opera—United States—20th century. I. Title.
   ML410.V4M2663 2011
   782.1092—dc22

                            2011014164

A catalogue record for this title is available from the British Library.

This publication is printed on acid-free paper.
Printed in the United States of America

Per quanta poca esperienza io mi possa avere, vado nonostante in teatro tutto l'anno, e stò attento moltissimo.

[However little experience I may have, I do go to the theater all year long, and I pay a great deal of attention.]

—Verdi, November 15, 1843, to Guglielmo Brenna,
secretary of Venice's Teatro la Fenice,
who was fussing over the structure of *Ernani*

Contents

Illustrations

Preface and Acknowledgments

The introduction deals with the substance of the book; this preface, with its structure along with some technical details and acknowledgments that need stating.

The book's purpose is threefold. First, to describe the differing receptions in the United States of the first seventeen of Verdi's operas, *Oberto* through *Rigoletto*. Ten of these achieved their U.S. premieres promptly, 1847–60, but only one, *Ernani*, had what might be called an easy success. Others, such as *Rigoletto*, won acceptance only slowly; and still others, like *Macbeth*, after disappointing starts, vanished in the mid-nineteenth century but came back strongly in the twentieth. For each I survey how public opinion initially formed and then changed, or did not; and I speculate on the reasons therefore and, with caution, on the likely future of the opera in this country.

The second purpose is related: by recounting how public opinion of many of Verdi's operas altered over time, to show the effect in this country of what is commonly called "the Verdi Renaissance," which began in Germany in the 1920s. That renewed interest in Verdi and, some would say, greater understanding of his works passed slowly from country to country, gained strength in all of them, and in the United States had a stronger impact on the operatic scene of the second half of the twentieth century than sometimes realized. Briefly, the rediscovery of Verdi, particularly of his operas that preceded *Rigoletto*, reached the United States in the 1940s, began to permeate American operatic artists and audiences in the 1950s, and led in the 1960s and subsequent decades to the revivals of many operas long-neglected and to the premieres of seven not previously performed here.

The third and final purpose is, by two transitional chapters (chapters 7 and 12) as well as occasional discussion in the introduction and throughout the text, to provide a context against which critical and audience comment on the operas may be weighed. For as the country grew in population, wealth, and modes of transportation, so, too, did the production of opera in size of orchestra, skill of chorus, ability to tour, and even in audience behavior. Moreover, until about 1890, in all aspects, that growth, though differing from region to region, was remarkably swift, so that in one generation long-lived members saw and heard opera grow from crude beginnings to sophisticated entertainment. And it is against that swiftly changing context that the reception of Verdi's early operas should be considered. This brings us to the book's structure.

First, however, a word about the number of operas Verdi composed, for I refer frequently to the "sixteen" preceding *Rigoletto*. Depending on how many of his revisions one counts as separate operas, they number in all anywhere from twenty-six to thirty-three. In this book, only his revision for Paris of *I Lombardi*, which he titled *Jérusalem*, is treated as a separate work. For it, he worked to a new French libretto, gave the work a new title, revised orchestration, and composed much new music, including a ballet. And though the opera today is seldom staged, in New Orleans in the nineteenth century it was performed some ninety times, not including excerpts on gala occasions and several performances on tour.

A word, too, about the operas' titles. The full title for *I Lombardi*, mentioned above, is *I Lombardi alla prima crociata*, or *The Lombards on the First Crusade*. Cumbersome on tongue and page, it frequently is cut to either *I Lombardi*, or even *Lombardi*; similarly, *I due Foscari*, to *Foscari*; *Un giorno di regno*, to *Un giorno*, *La battaglia di Legnano*, to *La battaglia*; and others. Except as above, at first mention of an opera with a wordy title, I usually give the title in full; thereafter, in the shortened form.

To return now to the introduction in the United States of Verdi's sixteen operas preceding *Rigoletto* and on which the impact of the Verdi Renaissance can most easily be seen: they divide into three groups. First, the six that premiered here in the years 1847–50, four of which were introduced (and a fifth partially) by an Italian company on tour from Havana. This company, bringing its own soloists, orchestra, and chorus, set a new standard for Italian opera in the United States and with its production of *Ernani* stirred audiences in New York, Boston, and Philadelphia to heed a new composer, Verdi.

The second group of operas, four having U.S. premieres in 1850–60, arrived in a different fashion, under different conditions, and are introduced by chapter 7, a transitional chapter that tells how the country and context for producing opera had changed. For example, though still often sung by artists imported from Italy or France, the operas now were staged by resident companies based chiefly in New Orleans or New York, which for the most part recruited their orchestras and choruses locally, a long step forward in the country's musical development. Of the four operas in this second group, *Rigoletto* was by far the most important, but in the United States it had a surprisingly slow start.

In the third and final group are the seven operas not performed here until the latter half of the twentieth century, their introduction being a consequence of the Verdi Renaissance. And they form a group unto themselves, not only because of the late date of their U.S. premieres but also because they were first heard here and judged by ears that knew well Verdi's later works, a quite different experience from hearing them with no knowledge of *Rigoletto*, *Aida*, *Otello*, or *Falstaff*.

A second transitional chapter (chapter 12) precedes this group of seven, pointing to ways in which the country had grown and methods and types of opera production again had changed and increased. For example, these seven "unheard operas" were introduced not by our then well-established companies in the largest cities, New York, Chicago, and San Francisco, but typically either by smaller "regional" companies based elsewhere, or by small ones within the big cities, or by companies presenting "concert opera," sung without scenery or costumes. The influence of these smaller groups has been great, perhaps even in the case of one opera, *Stiffelio*, a cause for a production by the Metropolitan. But how long these seven will continue to be heard is not clear. The operatic world is peculiarly subject to the whims of artists and the public, and a day may come when most of Verdi's operas that preceded *Rigoletto* will sink again into oblivion. But seemingly not all; some such as *Nabucco*, *Macbeth*, and *Luisa Miller* surely have joined the list of those that periodically will reappear.

A word, too, about the period covered. Though for the most part in reporting the reception of any of the seventeen operas, I limit myself to productions staged in the nineteenth and twentieth centuries, I have in a few instances extended that period past the turn of the century in order to round out the twentieth fully. Thus I include some productions conceived in the twentieth century but staged here only later—for example, a Finnish production of *Macbeth* that premiered at Savonlinna in 1993 and came to Philadelphia in 2003. Or sometimes I simply ignore the closing date of 2001 in order to show better the shift in popularity of some opera, and to offer some thoughts on the cause.

Also, I should explain why I end my survey with *Rigoletto* when that opera, in the canonical periods of "early," "middle," and "late" typically assigned to composers, usually is ranked as one of the first of Verdi's "middle period." My reason is that when considered from the point of view of audience response across the country, the opera falls clearly into a first period of only moderate success. With Verdi's next, his eighteenth, *Il trovatore*, he had perhaps the greatest popular success in the United States of any operatic composer and certainly the greatest here of his career. Across the country and in every operatic language *Trovatore* was staged continually, surviving every sort of production, even one where a woman, without transposing the vocal line, sang the tenor's title role. Moreover, weekly or even daily until the early 1920s, in all the country's cities and towns the local bands pounded out the opera's "Miserere" and "Anvil Chorus." Thus Verdi became a household name, and his subsequent operas were received with a different attitude. Hence I limit this book to the operas preceding *Trovatore*, those on which the Verdi Renaissance had the most obvious impact.

As for technical details: Let me first stress that with none of these seventeen operas do I purport to mention every production it has had in the United States. With the least known of them, perhaps *I masnadieri*, I probably have mentioned most if not all of its productions. With the far better-known *Nabucco*, *Ernani*, *Macbeth*, and *Rigoletto*, I have noted or discussed only those productions that I think had influence in their day, or reflected most clearly the current perception of the opera, or deserve mention for having handled onstage some aspect of the opera particularly well or badly, and hence swayed audience response.

Similarly, when I say that in the United States an opera in a certain span of years had no production, how can I, or the reader, be sure? Proving the negative is nigh impossible, but Works Progress Administration performance chronologies exist for several cities, as do histories, statistics, and databases for several important houses, doctoral theses on a number of regions and companies, together with Loewenberg's *Annals* and Kaufman's *Selected Chronology* as well as the latter's many articles and unpublished notes. In the endnotes and Selected Bibliography, I cite many of these sources, and where not one of them reports a performance of the opera within the period, I think we can assume that at the very least no important production of it took place. For a successful production in one city will stir an attempt in others, if only because the singers in one city will take the opera with them to another.

In choosing among contemporary critics and opinion to quote, I have favored in every era those who not only praise or damn the singers, but comment on the context in which they sang, preferring those who to some extent discuss the style and qualities of the music, the size and balance of the orchestra, the number and skills of the chorus, the size, design, and lighting of the theaters, and the expectations and behavior of the audiences. Above all, I have sought to find opinion that recounts the audience's response to the music; what it liked, did not like, and, what is more speculative, the reasons why.

With regard to each opera's U.S. premiere, I have quoted the reviews at length, not only because of their intrinsic interest but also as a base to measure the later shift in critical opinion. Anyone of course can look up these early reviews in the journals where they first appeared, but readers may find it useful to have excerpts gathered under one cover.

In addition to such reviews, to buttress my account of the audience's response to the music, I have also quoted, where possible, statements by audience members in their diaries, by reports of what they chose to sing at home, of what they might buy in music stores (both in sheet music and, in later years, in recordings), and of what they might hear at opera recitals and band concerts. And sometimes for performances in the second half of the twentieth century I have relied on my own impressions of how an audience responded to the opera's music and staging. To paraphrase Verdi, "I go often to opera, and I pay attention."

About the sequence of chapters on the individual operas: In each of the three groups I have put them in order of their world, not U.S., premieres (though the two often coincide). That order may strike some as awkward, but after experimenting with other ways, I thought it best. What should determine order: the first excerpt sung? the first (roughly) full performance? In concert, onstage? Perhaps *I Lombardi*, Verdi's fourth opera but the first to be staged here, should lead off; or perhaps *Ernani*, his fifth, but the first to have an excerpt sung here and the first to have a big success, carrying his name from city to city. Amid all the possibilities, one date was certain and recognized everywhere, the opera's world premiere, and I chose to follow that.

Then: What kind of a performance should count as a presentation of the opera? Not always an easy decision. About *I due Foscari*, for example, I state that through December 2008 it has had only a single performance in Philadelphia. Yet a very small, very valiant Philadelphia-based company, Amici Opera, gave two performances of it on October 2 and 8, 2004, in a church auditorium at Collingswood, New Jersey, a Philadelphia suburb, but across the Delaware River. The performance claimed to be "the first time in this area"—but in Philadelphia, Pennsylvania, or Collingswood, New Jersey? I have heard and seen a number of Amici Opera performances—it has completed a Verdi cycle—and find them hard to characterize. The company plays mostly in church auditoriums with a small stage, charges admission, and generally draws an audience of twenty or thirty, most of whom seem to be the singers' friends. The voices sound like a mix of professional and amateur, at various levels of training, and hence often out of balance. Costumes, scenery, and lighting are simple and unspecific; the orchestra consists of a single (well-played) piano; cuts are many, and often large; choristers number one or two, sometimes adding principals; and the infrequent ballet corps is often a single person who steps about with gestures through a prelude, overture, or some introductory chorus left unsung. Does such a production qualify as a staging of the opera?

Comparing it to productions by the Amato Opera in New York, I ruled it did not. The Amato, albeit in a tiny theater (capacity 107), offered a small orchestra, usually a piano and seven or eight instruments, scenery and costumes pertinent to the opera, fewer cuts (often none), better-trained and -balanced voices, and a chorus of ten or more, not employing principals. Moreover, generally playing to a full house, it scheduled each opera for eight or ten performances, far more rehearsed. Pocket Opera in San Francisco is somewhat similar. Other people, of course, might draw the line differently.

And another line of uncertain placement: my distinction between a reduction of a score and an arrangement. Ears hear differently, but to mine, for these early operas at least, an orchestra of about thirty-two is the smallest that can make Verdi sound like himself. Most Italian orchestras of his time, those in the theaters for which he wrote, had orchestras of fifty or more, and in a performance with an orchestra of thirty-two or less, to my ear, the sound begins to be merely a suggestion, an approximation of Verdi. And I call that scoring an arrangement, but count as a reduction one that, though shrinking of the number of instruments, does not lose the composer's characteristic sound. Of course that sound varies from opera to opera. For example, *Aida* can sound pretty much like itself with an orchestra of forty, but *Don Carlos* cannot.

Eight of the book's chapters, those on *Oberto*, *Un giorno di regno*, *Nabucco*, *Lombardi*, *Ernani*, *Foscari*, *Giovanna d'Arco*, and *Alzira*, first appeared in different guise as articles in the *Opera Quarterly*, published by Oxford University Press. These appeared serially, in the order of Verdi's composing, starting in autumn 2002 and ending in spring 2005. They were also published online by Oxford Press at http://oq.oxfordjournals.org/; and I thank the Oxford Press for permission to reprint them as revised. Also, the two transitional chapters (7 and 12), in quite different form and under the titles "Some Overlooked Operatic History," appeared in the *Yale Review*, January and April 2009 issues. All else appears here for the first time.

In discussing the history of individual operas I have not given synopses of the operas, but limited myself to naming characters when needed and to outlining in any detail only those scenes discussed at some length. Synopses of all of Verdi's operas can be found in many books, including *The New Grove Guide to Verdi and His Operas*, as well as *The New Grove Dictionary of Opera*, and also (often accompanied by a libretto) in recordings, which now exist for all of Verdi's operas. In addition, synopses and librettos for all the operas, and in Italian and English, may be found on the Internet at www.giuseppeverdi.it.

Finally, some acknowledgments. In trying to recreate the context in which Verdi's operas first appeared in the United States, especially the cultural ambience of the country's leading operatic cities, or to clear a confusion, confirm a date, or convert a speculation into fact, I have frequently sought help from today's scholars, archivists, and librarians. The many scholars may be found in the endnotes and bibliography. Among the archivists, those to whom I most frequently turned, were: in New Orleans, Jack Belsom, archivist of the New Orleans Opera Association; in New York, Robert Tuggle and his staff in the Metropolitan Opera Archives; in Philadelphia, Frank Hamilton for his database *Opera in Philadelphia*; and finally, Thomas G. Kaufman for his many chronologies of American opera companies and in particular for his worldwide chronology, *Verdi and His Major Contemporaries*, from which on many occasions he shared his notes with me.

Among the librarians, I particularly wish to thank those at the New York Public Library, in both its music and main divisions; at the New-York Historical Society; and the Boston Athenaeum; also those who by phone, fax, or letter answered my questions put to the Library of Congress, the Boston Public Library, and the collections and museums in New Orleans, San Francisco, and College Park, Maryland. Verily, the writer's best friend is often a librarian!

I also want to mention four others who in different fashion advised, encouraged, and responded to questions with information: E. Thomas Glasow, editor of the *Opera Quarterly*, 1997–2004, who thought the history of opera in the United States needed attention and was always ready to discuss, edit, and perhaps publish articles on it. He died, alas, before I completed this book for which his enthusiasm was partly responsible. The other three are American conductors particularly associated with Verdi, and with whom I frequently consulted about the problems of producing this or that opera onstage: Victor

DeRenzi, Vincent La Selva, and David Lawton—learned men all, and generous with their time and knowledge.

Last, and most important, I thank my niece, Dr. Agnes H. Whitaker, who lives in New York City and whose hospitality over the years made possible continual research in that expensive city. Without her care in all respects, this book would not be.

George W. Martin
Kennett Square, PA
June 2010

Introduction

Verdi, like Shakespeare in our theater, is now so much a part of opera in the United States that we tend to forget that he was not always with us, not always popular, and that many of those hearing him for the first time in the late 1840s felt assaulted by his music. One outraged New York critic, reviewing the U.S. premiere of *Ernani*, wished to have cut on his tombstone, "HE LIKED NOT VERDI,"[1] and a member of a later audience who kept a diary noted, Verdi "keeps up a ceaseless torrent of forcible-feeble emphasis, passion, and vehemence till one is weary of him as of an author who deals only in italics, large capitals, dashes and interjection marks."[2] Yet a critic in Philadelphia remarked, "His sustained style, intensely dramatic situations, grand *finales* and concerted pieces; altogether it was a new experience to us." And in Boston another recorded that with *Ernani* "all recollections of English opera were effaced by this life-breathing, passionate, and effective performance, and from that hour a new ideal of excellence in operatic affairs became fixed and irrevocable."[3]

As the Bostonian implied, opera in the United States in the late 1840s, at least in our eastern seaboard cities, was undergoing a change. English opera, typically songs interspersed with dialogue and played by actors not singers, was slowly giving way to Italian opera, which required more musical skill. Not only were the Italian operas more heavily orchestrated, with larger choruses and more complicated music, arias for songs, sextets for duets, but often their finales continued unbroken by recitative or dialogue for ten minutes or more.

One city, New Orleans, was far ahead in this change. In 1847, the year in which the Italian Opera Company of Havana brought *Ernani* to the United States, New Orleans had the country's only resident opera company, the only theater devoted primarily to opera, the largest theater orchestra, and even, at times, a small ballet corps; and as early as 1829 had started what was probably the country's first, fairly regular, newspaper column of opera news, comment, and criticism.[4] The New Orleans company had toured in six summers, 1827–33, to Boston, New York, Philadelphia, and Baltimore, presenting a total of 251 performances of 61 operas by 24 composers, mostly light French works with much spoken dialogue but all accompanied by better soloists, orchestra, and chorus than those usually heard in the northeast.[5] Yet its impact, though stimulating, ultimately was limited by New Orleans's isolation, four weeks away by sail, and by its small population, in 1850 barely a tenth of the potential, combined audiences of Boston, New York, Philadelphia, and Baltimore. Moreover, because of the city's French cultural heritage, its citizens generally preferred French to Italian opera, Grétry, Boieldieu, or Meyerbeer to Verdi. In New Orleans in the mid-nineteenth century the most popular of Verdi's early operas was not *Ernani* but *Jérusalem*, an 1847 revision of his *I Lombardi* (1843) that he had scored to a new French libretto and more in the style of Meyerbeer.

Yet the future for opera in the United States lay more in the northeast, particularly in New York, which in 1850 had a population of 696,115, roughly five times more than any of the other four cities (see appendix C). And by the mid-1850s New York would have a large theater devoted primarily to opera, the Academy of Music, and several operatic orchestras as large and expert as those in New Orleans. Verdi's operas, however, began to arrive in New York before this transformation was complete.

As late as the 1840s in the country's northeast, unlike New Orleans, many people were still wary of theaters in general and of Italian opera in particular, not sure they liked it or even approved of it for others. Clerics frequently preached against theaters of any kind;[6] Timothy Dwight, a former president of Yale College, in 1824 condemned them in his *Essay on the Stage;*[7] and as late as 1858 a music critic for the *Tribune*, who was himself a composer, William Henry Fry, complained of Mozart: "We presume it would do no good or we might give a homily on the indecency of *Don Giovanni*. . . . How modest American girls can look on in public at the representation of an undisguised scene of seduction, can hear the shrieks of the supposed victim, and see her return to the stage as the conquest of the libertine is a question we leave them and their parents to solve. The whole drift of this drama—the rigamarole of the valet about conquests—is of the same kind of brazen pruriency. The hellfire at the close does not cleanse it a jot."[8] In these years, on the whole, the Creoles in New Orleans brought more knowledge and attention to the musical side of their operatic performances and behaved better in their theaters than their Anglo-Saxon-Scots-Irish cousins in the northeast.

As stated in the preface, the book's purpose is threefold: to describe the reception in the United States during the nineteenth and twentieth centuries of each of Verdi's first seventeen operas, *Oberto* through *Rigoletto*, recounting how opinion of them formed and changed; to show how the so-called Verdi Renaissance of the twentieth century gave new life to some of his operas that previously had failed here while leading seven more to their U.S. premieres; and to provide a context against which the operas' receptions may be gauged.

Of Verdi's later operas, ending with *Falstaff* (1893), only *Trovatore* and *Aida* achieved like *Ernani* an instant, continuing success. Even *Rigoletto* at first failed at the box office and in 1866 was debated in court as an example of lurid immorality.[9] Earlier, in 1861, *Traviata* had been banned briefly in Brooklyn, and an American soprano, Emma Abbott, in the late 1870s refused to sing the leading role because of its immorality (though she later relented).[10] And following *Aida*, Verdi's final operas, *Otello* and *Falstaff*, were so demanding of orchestra, chorus, and soloists that for the most part only the larger companies attempted them.

Undoubtedly, the chief reason for the extraordinary rise in popularity during the mid-twentieth century of all of Verdi's operas was the impact of the "Verdi Renaissance" that started in Germany in the mid-1920s, spread slowly through the world, and for the "earlier" operas reached the United States, onstage at least, in a production of *Macbeth* in 1941. And whereas in the nineteenth century audiences here had viewed that opera as a failure, allowing it to disappear altogether, they now judged it to be, despite some flaws, a masterpiece.

This theme of the Verdi Renaissance bears on each opera discussed, for it was directly responsible not only for the return to the standard repertory of *Nabucco, Luisa Miller,* and *Macbeth* but also for the startling vogue in the late twentieth century for *Attila,* and for the recovery of a "lost" opera, *Stiffelio,* which may prove viable. Like many a "renaissance," however, there is some argument over when, where, and how the "rebirth" began, who was chiefly responsible for it, and how dark for Verdi were the ages preceding it.[11]

To start with the latter: For a long period, roughly 1885–1925, he was in eclipse, dismissed by those of supposedly superior taste as a "hurdy-gurdy" composer of little or no musical value, suited best and perhaps only to barrel organs. In the United States that idea was fostered in part by a tremendous influx of German musicians, who soon dominated our burgeoning music schools, orchestras, and newspaper criticism and by their constant chatter persuaded a generation of young artists and operagoers that the only music dramas worthy of serious listening or study were those of Wagner and his followers. In 1913, for example, W. J. Henderson of the *Sun,* then one of New York's leading critics, dismissed *Ballo in maschera* in part because: "Much of the pungent early style of Verdi—the strident climaxes, the brazen instrumental proclamations, the frequently pretentious and semi-martial vocal utterances—remain in this work."[12]

That attitude was not peculiar to the United States. As the English scholar Francis Toye (1883–1964) noted in the preface to his *Verdi, His Life and Works* (1931), in his youth "Lip service might be paid to the merits of *Otello* and *Falstaff,* otherwise there was the same dreary repetition of the nonsense—for it is nonsense—about the 'guitar-like orchestra' in *La Traviata* or *Rigoletto; Aida* was 'flashy' or 'empty'; *Il Trovatore* just 'absurd.'" The other operas, especially those preceding *Rigoletto,* were remembered, "if at all, by some isolated numbers associated with famous singers." In his book—unique for its day—he gave a full chapter to each of Verdi's twenty-six operas (with some discussion of revisions), yet felt constrained in his preface to open with some "words of explanation" on why he had bothered to write on Verdi and "above all" at such "length."[13]

Many artists of course have gone out of favor for a time after their death, but the scarcity of Verdi in opera houses around the world during the first quarter of the twentieth century is remarkable. Even in Italy. For example, at Bologna's Teatro Comunale, between 1895 and 1912 the company staged only one performance each of *Rigoletto, Traviata,* and *Aida.*[14] And the same dearth of Verdi, sparked chiefly by the current love of Wagner, soon appeared in New York, in the Metropolitan's schedules: In the four seasons 1893 through 1896 Verdi had 42 performances of six operas, and Wagner, 53 of six; and in the five seasons, 1903 through 1907, Verdi had 74 of five operas (*Rigoletto, Trovatore, Traviata, Ballo,* and *Aida*), and Wagner, 156 of ten (with the leaders, *Tannhäuser,* 27, *Parsifal,* 25, and *Lohengrin,* 23). Smaller touring companies, unable to meet the expense of staging Wagner—larger orchestra, chorus, and stronger-voiced soloists—somewhat redressed the balance, for their audiences still flocked to Verdi, but critical talk and attention focused almost exclusively on Wagner.[15]

Occasionally artists or scholars who thought Verdi underrated would try to raise his position. Toscanini in Milan in 1902, against strong opposition, insisted on scheduling a new production of *Trovatore,* offering the opera as a serious drama at a time when many Italians thought it only a hackneyed joke; and he had a startling success.[16] But the next year with a revival of *Luisa Miller,* he failed. Reported the *Mondo artistico,* in an opinion with which many others agreed, "the work which is certainly not one of Verdi's best, bored people." Though Toscanini with his well-conceived, passionate productions proposed a reconsideration of Verdi, he did not carry the Italian musical world with him.[17]

In New York Giulio Gatti-Casazza, the general manager at the Metropolitan, 1908–35, had a somewhat similar mixture of success and failure. He and Toscanini, who came to the house with him, together produced a *Ballo in maschera* in 1913 to celebrate the centenary of Verdi's birth. (The year was also the centenary of Wagner's birth, and in celebration the Met put on a new *Ring,* four operas.) Verdi's *Ballo* had not been heard in nine seasons, and W. J. Henderson of the *Sun,* reported: "To make a suitable selection of unfamiliar Verdi works for such a [celebratory] purpose is by no means as easy as it might seem. *Un ballo in maschera,* despite the manifold absurdities of the libretto, which is even more extraordinary than old-fashioned librettos are wont to be, has its claim because there is musical material in it calling for the services of a strong cast." And in a final dismissive sentence: "It is the kind of music, too, which is beloved of people devoted to the elementary things in art."[18] The production lasted only three seasons (ten performances in the house, three on tour), and the opera was not revived until 1940. But a revival of *Ernani* in 1921, though without Toscanini who had left in 1915, did better, lasting four seasons (fifteen performances in the house and four on tour).

Earlier, in 1918 and 1920, Gatti had staged, for the first time at the Metropolitan, *Forza* and *Don Carlos,* not heard in New York since 1880 and 1877. With Rosa Ponselle making her debut as Leonora, he succeeded with *Forza,* which then entered the Metropolitan's repertory, never to drop out for long; but with *Don Carlos,* though he considered it "a magnificent drama" and in one of its three seasons offered Feodor Chaliapin as King Philip, he failed, at least partially. Most critics harshly dismissed not the performers but Verdi: "the bungling libretto . . . the bubbling bosh of the romantic love episodes . . . this stodgy mess."[19] And after only eleven performances in the house and three on tour, the opera disappeared until 1950, when in a new production it opened the season and was hailed as a masterpiece.

The man primarily responsible for the Verdi Renaissance, however, was neither a critic, conductor, impresario, nor even a professional singer, but a poet, playwright, and novelist, Franz Werfel. Though associated chiefly with Vienna, and during and after World War II with Hollywood, he was born in Prague in 1890 and grew up there in the Jewish quarter. Attending opera, he soon became famous for singing along with the performers and for his love of Verdi, especially those operas from Verdi's so-called middle-period, *Rigoletto* to *Don Carlos*. He considered Verdi's final three, *Aida*, *Otello*, and *Falstaff*, rather ponderous and inflated, and because the low opinion generally held of his favorites irritated him greatly, he set out to change opinion.[20]

A novel is an odd way to start an operatic renaissance, but then *Verdi, A Novel of the Opera* is an unusual work. Werfel imagines Verdi in Venice in 1882 at a time when Wagner is also in the city. Verdi is at the height of his fame in Italy, but has not composed an opera since *Aida* (1871). His inspiration is blocked. He feels oppressed by Wagner, and thinks that perhaps if he met the man, and they talked, the block might shatter. For what happens next, one should read the book, a strange mixture of fact, fiction, and sympathetic imagination that uncovers much about the man and artist. To an astonishing degree it achieves Werfel's desire to stir interest in Verdi. As one American reviewer remarked (for the book was promptly translated into several languages): "Perhaps a little detail will best characterize the intensity of the impression which Verdi [as portrayed] produced on me. I thought quite spontaneously that I must use every opportunity to hear his music. Werfel never praises this music, never extols it at the expense of Wagner; he only shows Verdi's character, and the result is that I yearn to hear everything Verdi ever wrote."[21]

The agreement of most scholars that the Verdi Renaissance began with this novel is quite astonishing,[22] but only part of the story, for Werfel did more. Besides giving speeches and publishing articles on Verdi's artistry, he prepared a German edition of *Forza*, which reportedly had not been heard in Germany since 1878, and this "Werfel edition" was first performed at the Dresden Opera, conducted by Fritz Busch, in March 1926. Thereafter, it went to Vienna, Berlin, Hamburg, Basel, Prague, and to the many smaller German houses, and subsequently, in translation, to Sweden, Hungary, Poland, Lithuania, Bulgaria, Slovenia, and Russia, everywhere stimulating a demand for more of Verdi's operas, not only the four or five best known but also the obscure and unfamiliar. Werfel made new German translations of *Boccanegra* and *Don Carlos*, while others translated *Luisa Miller*, *Macbeth*, and such hitherto forgotten works as

Nabucco, Foscari, and *Masnadieri.* By the spring of 1933, when Busch left Dresden, he was offering seasons with ten Verdi operas in the repertory.[23]

That surge of interest in German-speaking theaters caught the world's attention. Toye, for instance, in his book on Verdi and his works, gives more weight to it than to the Toscanini revivals of Verdi that he heard in the mid-1920s at La Scala—in 1925, for example, *Rigoletto, Trovatore, Traviata, Ballo,* and *Falstaff*—though admitting that some of these productions first inspired him to begin his study. But he states unequivocally that it was the number and range of the German performances, reviving some of Verdi's earliest operas and making popular favorites of them that prompted him "to write a long book instead of a comparatively short one."[24]

Possibly also it was the success in Germany of *Luisa Miller* and *Boccanegra* that encouraged Gatti-Casazza to stage the former for the first time at the Metropolitan, in 1929 with Rosa Ponselle, and the latter for the first time in the United States, in 1931 with Lawrence Tibbett. Again he succeeded with one, *Boccanegra,* which like his previous *Forza* became a Metropolitan staple, expanding Verdi's position in the repertory from five or six operas to seven or eight continually revived, taken on tour, and, after radio broadcasts began in the 1930s, heard across the country.

Meanwhile, in Germany, Hitler and his Nazi party came to power in January 1933, and many of the artists responsible for the Verdi revivals retreated to England, taking their knowledge and experience with them. Among them were the conductor Fritz Busch, the stage designer Caspar Neher, and stage director Carl Ebert. These soon astonished the English musical world and public with a production at Glyndebourne in 1938 and 1939 of one of Verdi's "earlier" operas, *Macbeth,* not heard in England since 1860. And, as described at greater length in this book's chapter on that opera, that production, again conducted by Busch, came to New York and played on Broadway in 1941 and 1942, the first time *Macbeth* had been heard in the United States since 1864.

In the twenty years after World War II, revivals of Verdi's lesser-known operas in the United States slowly accelerated, spurred by the arrival of Rudolf Bing in 1950 to be general manager of the Metropolitan. He had worked with Busch in Germany and England, and also with Neher and Ebert, hence the line back to the German revivals stirred initially by Werfel is direct. At the Metropolitan, Bing reintroduced *Don Carlos* (1950), *Ernani* (1956), and *Luisa Miller* (1967); staged for the first time in the house, *Macbeth* (1958) and *Nabucco* (1960), the latter his only failure; and in a concert performance at a summer festival at Newport, Rhode Island, tested *I vespri Siciliani* (1967), which two seasons after he retired was staged with success in the house in 1973–74. And in the course of these years some of the country's smaller companies began to mount the seven Verdi operas hitherto not heard in the United States.

In searching for reasons to explain the lasting impact of the Verdi Renaissance, some seem clear. After World War I it was, at least in part, a reaction, not so much against Wagner, for his operas continued to be popular, as against the exclusivity of Wagnerism, the constant assertion by admirers that his was the only way; and after World War II, in part because Hitler and the Nazis had identified themselves so closely to him, a reaction against his music. For most people, however, any bias against the music soon lessened. Perhaps more to the point, the "Renaissance" was also in part a reaction against the complexity of opera orchestration developed by Wagner's disciples, such as Richard Strauss and Pfitzner; against the cerebralism of the atonality and serialism that Schoenberg and Berg were introducing; and against the sensationalism of some Russian composers such as Prokofiev and Stravinsky. As a critic noted, after Wagner "the orchestra became the protagonist, and responsibility for dramatic continuity and articulation shifted from the stage to the pit."[25] But the more critics and composers throve on the complexities of harmony and thematic development, and the more intricate and intellectual these complexities became, the more did many among artists and audiences, especially the latter, long for greater simplicity, clarity, and melody. And because no contemporary composer of comparable genius was providing it, they turned back to Verdi.[26]

Tomorrow, interest in Verdi's operas, perhaps now at flood tide, may ebb, but then again, perhaps not. For his operas, like those of all composers, have been aided greatly by the technological revolution in recordings, starting with long-playing records, passing through compact discs into iPods that can carry more than a thousand hours of music in a player smaller than a pocket handkerchief. In addition, we now have videocassettes and discs that offer us both visual and aural records of actual performances, as well as live performances from the Metropolitan playing simultaneously across the country in movie theaters. With each step, the gain for opera has been immense. Many people can read a Shakespeare play and imagine to a great extent how it will sound and play onstage; but few can do as much with an opera's orchestral score. Consequently, by the mid-1940s, except for those who heard the Metropolitan company at home or on tour (and increasingly after 1931 by radio), most people knew well only *Aida*, *Rigoletto*, *Trovatore*, and *Traviata*, with perhaps a slight acquaintance with *Ballo*, *Forza*, or *Otello*.

Today, Verdi's position in our opera repertory—the hundred or so operas reappearing every fifteen or twenty years—is greatly expanded. Gatti-Casazza, for example, had said of Verdi's operas, "six are indispensable to the repertory, and half a dozen others are periodically revived." Twelve in all.[27] Conductors and impresarios today might say that ten are indispensable, another ten periodically revived, and a final ten reserved for anniversary years and cycles of the complete works. In the past fifteen years every one of Verdi's operas has had at least four staged or concert performances in the United States, and all are available in multiple recordings.

Moreover, the public's interest in Verdi has been backed to an extraordinary extent by critics and scholars. The number of books and articles now published annually on Verdi would have astonished Toye, or indeed, anyone in his generation. An Institute for Verdi Studies was founded in Parma in 1960 and a similar institute (the American Institute for Verdi Studies) in New York in 1974, and both have published many books and articles as well as making material available for research. In addition, scholars have lent their skills to start publication of a "critical edition" of all of Verdi's works, beginning in 1983 with a carefully scrubbed orchestral score of *Rigoletto* along with a detailed commentary thereon.[28] To date, similar volumes have appeared on *Trovatore, Traviata,* on nine of the "earlier" operas, on the *Requiem,* and one, *Inni,* on the cantata *Inno delle nazioni* and the *Inno popolare* (*"Suona la tromba"*).[29]

As a result of this scholarly interest combined with public support at the box office, Verdi seems to have attained a position in our opera repertory somewhat like Shakespeare in our theater. I leave to others the reasons for Shakespeare's place, but I will summarize an argument for Verdi's, limiting myself to what seem to be five of his most important characteristics. First, in comparing him to Donizetti, consider a distinction noted as early as 1859 by the Italian scholar Abramo Basevi in his study of Verdi's works then known, *Oberto* through *Ballo in maschera*: "Verdi, as the more passionate, strives more often to agitate and excite the audience; whereas Donizetti strives almost always to delight it."[30] This characteristic of Verdi, at least in the United States in the mid-nineteenth century, often worked against his reception. Audiences used to Donizetti came to the theater to be entertained, to hear favorite songs well sung, and to socialize. Moreover, the mechanics of the opera house favored Donizetti's style: the auditorium, with candles, gas, or oil, remained lit throughout the performance. Singers, in order to have their faces seen, marched to the footlights to sing, and to the modern eye, opera performances would seem much like concerts in costume. Verdi, on the other hand, quite against the custom of the day, wanted to stage his *Macbeth* mostly in the dark, wanted to concentrate on the personalities of his protagonists, on their feelings, hopes, and actions, and sought from the audience more attention than often they were prepared to give. Yet time favored Verdi, for with the arrival of electricity, auditoriums could be darkened during performance and the stage more effectively lit, whereupon social chatter declined, attention focused more on the stage, and perhaps even, with the spread of Freudian ideas, audiences became more interested in the varieties of personalities and their relationships. In sum, drama not concert.

Next, there is Verdi's skill in theatrical pacing. Among those staging or singing his operas one often hears said, however varied the wording: "Verdi plays better onstage than he reads in the score." And this is especially true of his early operas in which some of the vocal lines and their accompaniments, in shape, harmony, and rhythm, are too commonplace, too predictable, too repetitious. Yet even so, he usually manages to imbue each act, particularly toward its close, with a sense of acceleration, ending typically with a concerted finale that vocally blooms and pulls the audience into sympathy and satisfaction.

Then too, all his operas are about humans—no gods, dragons, rings of fire, or scenes in hell or heaven, no drifting through myth into an unreal world, but each opera anchored in common experience.[31] With greater or less success he portrays fellow humans confronting harsh dilemmas, trapped in awkward decisions in which they suffer. And for such stories I think there will always be an audience.

Moreover, in Verdi (as in Shakespeare) the men and women are always responsible for their acts and choices. Though fate may be against them, for each there is an area left for choice, and choose they must. Anyone wanting to hear an opera in which society is blamed for all that happens will not hear it in Verdi. In *Traviata*, perhaps the most frequently performed of his operas, Violetta makes her choice and suffers for it—as do the protagonists in *Trovatore*, *Aida*, *Macbeth*, and in all his other operas. That view of our condition—that we may not be able to control our fate but we can control our response to it, noble or unworthy—will, I suspect, always find an audience.

Lastly, there is his gift for melody, comparable in the opera house to Shakespeare's gift for poetry in the theater. Verdi's contemporary, Saverio Mercadante, in Verdi's early years often could do better in orchestration, and sometimes in rhythmic drive, but where he failed to match Verdi was in the ability to sum up a dramatic situation with a simple, piercing melodic phrase, like Aida's cry, "Numi, pietà."

Melody, as scholars have shown, has a power to subsume its text: thus, once its main thrust is set, be it anger, love, or some other emotion, then even though the text becomes nonsense, the melody alone will continue to deliver its intended message. Thus, in *Trovatore* in the tenor's aria "Ah si, ben mio," when Manrico sings of his love for Leonora, because the text got badly jumbled, for 150 years tenors sang nonsense, yet no one seemed to notice, at least no one objected; the message was clear. As one scholar then observed, "It may be the melody, not the word, that speaks."[32] Or, a less stark example from the same opera, when the baritone Count sings of his love for Leonora, though non Italians may not understand all his words, they know he is declaring his love for her, and as the music swells, so, too, do their hearts. Supertitles often reflect this truth by leaving second verses untranslated, even when sung to new words.

Moreover, in the theater, melody creates a sense of community between stage and audience. The process is mysterious, but the effect is undeniable. When joined with words, melody creates character and drama onstage, and in an audience can fuse a thousand individuals into a single, responsive unit. Verdi was not a songwriter, peddling brief emotions within small, confined forms, but a composer, creating love-and-death dramas through music. His stories can be more or less reasonable, his orchestration better or worse, his melodies sometimes coarse and uninspired, but in all his operas, however successful, he conceived his expression in terms of melody, and for that, too, I think he will always have an audience.

Part One

Six Operas and the Havana Company, 1847–50

Chapter One

Nabucco

Verdi's only Biblical opera, *Nabucodonosor,* but commonly called *Nabucco* and first heard on March 9, 1842, at La Scala, gave that house the greatest success in its history—in the opera's first year, sixty-five performances.[1] And by the close of 1845, at least thirty-two more opera houses in northern and central Italy had staged it, as well as theaters in the principal cities of Austria, Denmark, France, Hanover, Portugal, Prussia, Spain, Turkey, and Wurttemberg. Yet *Nabucco* took almost six years to reach the Western Hemisphere, not arriving until December 4, 1847, when staged in Havana, at the sumptuous Gran Teatro de Tacón.[2] Earlier that year, the Havana company (mostly Italians) had come on a six-month tour to New York, Boston, and Philadelphia during which they mounted three Verdi operas, *I Lombardi, Ernani,* and *I due Foscari*—all composed after *Nabucco.* Of the three, only *Lombardi* had been heard in the United States and only in New York. Thus the Havana company, besides giving *Ernani* and *Foscari* their U.S. premieres, also introduced *Lombardi* to Boston and Philadelphia. But why should those three operas, composed after *Nabucco,* whose success was so notable, have reached the United States before it?

Chance alone, perhaps. But possibly, too, for reasons arising from the opera's special nature as well as the more general difficulties of producing opera in the United States in the 1840s. In Protestant England, for example, where early Victorian custom frowned on Holy Writ put onstage, the opera's story of the Hebrew people taken captive to Babylon was recast into a purely pagan conflict between Assyria and Babylon.[3] Such was not custom in the United States, yet in New York at least one critic complained of the Biblical story and a company in San Francisco, as in England, "secularized" the opera.

In 1824 a retired president of Yale College, in *An Essay on the Stage* (1824), had condemned all theater as "an evil so great, contagious, and extended, [it] ought to meet universal opposition," and called for its "extinction."[4] Even by 1847, though fewer held his view, many still thought theatrical performances of any kind inherently sinful, and in deference to them many cities, especially in the country's northeast, frowned on Biblical subjects put onstage and by law prohibited any theatrical performance on the Sabbath.[5]

Then, too, the leading soprano role of Abigaille, as Verdi composed it, is famously difficult, requiring trills, high notes and low, with runs between, and an energetic delivery alternating with a melting sweetness. But Italian opera in the 1840s had a tradition of changing a soloist's vocal line to suit the singer, and Verdi himself for this reason made changes in the role. More likely the greater obstacles lay in the opera's choral, instrumental, and scenic demands and the difficulties of meeting them in a new country with small theaters and a limited supply of musicians.[6]

Verdi had composed the opera for La Scala's large stage and auditorium (capacity 2,300), its orchestra of seventy or more, and a chorus probably of equal size, for he reportedly had insisted it be strengthened.[7] But in the opera's first years in the United States, squeezed onto smaller stages, with an orchestra and chorus of half the size or even less, it suffered. For example, there were many places for the theatrical staging to stumble. In the first act, Nabucco, preceded by a marching band (first heard offstage and then marching into the Temple ahead of him),[8] was to enter on a horse—for the Hebrews, the ultimate profanation of their Temple. In the second, when Nabucco proclaims himself a god, a thunderbolt is to knock the crown from his head, while in the fourth and final act, in Babylon, to mark the triumph of Jehovah over the Babylonian god Bel, a huge statue of the Idol must shatter. For unaccustomed ears the noise and pace of the spectacle might seem primitive or even barbaric, but when well-rehearsed, the scenes were overwhelming: the Old Testament come to life.

But quite aside from the horse, the bolt, and the Idol, in a small theater with a small chorus, the continual changing of chorister costumes, from Hebrew wigs, cloaks, and weapons to Assyrian, and back again, greatly compound the confusion. And in the orchestra, though Verdi scored six solo cellos to introduce the prophet Zaccaria's prayer, "Vieni, O Levita!" in the United States in the mid-nineteenth century, no opera company, visiting or resident, could muster so many. Even in 1996 the Sarasota company, with an orchestra pit then roughly half the size of today's at La Scala, gave the third solo cello line to a viola, and the sixth, to a double bass.[9]

More important than these scenic and orchestral difficulties, however, are those facing the chorus. The opera is Verdi's only one in which the chorus is a protagonist. In *I Lombardi* and *Ernani*, for instance, though the chorus has music that quickly became popular, in neither is it so essential to the action. In *Nabucco* only half the story tells of a fictitious struggle for the Babylonian throne between Nebuchadnezzar and his adopted daughter Abigaille, the child of slaves.[10] The other half, based on verses of the Bible, tells of the historical destruction of Jerusalem by Nebuchadnezzar in 586 BC, of the Hebrew people's Babylonian Captivity, of their faith in their God, and of their reward for that faith in their liberation. Only by mutilating the opera can their music be cut or skimped.

The opera's most famous chorus, the Hebrews' haunting lament, "Va, pensiero, sull'ali dorate" (Fly, thought on golden wings), is based on Psalm 137: "By the waters of Babylon we sat down and wept, when we remembered thee, O Zion." Though scored for a full chorus of mixed voices, it is essentially an aria for chorus, with most of it sung in unison.[11] The curtain rises on the Hebrew people in place, stationary, and remaining so throughout the scene. Their music, *largo* throughout the chorus, thereafter advances only to *andante più mosso*, with but one change of emotion; thus the scene is almost oratorio— static, easily learned in advance, and requiring little stage rehearsal. Even a chorus made up of local recruits, common in the United States in the 1840s, could sing it.

But the choral numbers for the Hebrews in act I, in the Temple in Jerusalem, are quite different and, for the 1840s, quite unusual. The choral scene that shapes the first third of the act, though starting in vehemence, moves through despair, prayer, panic at news of Nabucco's approach, and then, under the leadership of their prophet Zaccaria, trust in God. Such shifting emotions need some physical response; panic, without movement, is scarcely credible. Moreover, several short scenes for soloists interrupt the chorus and require reaction. So, too, in the last third of the act. For the long choral finale the score's musical and stage directions are *allegro agitatissimo*, the people, in separate small groups, to run onstage *precipitosamente*, singing. They also must respond to soloists, ending in an outburst at Nabucco (who is singing *con gioia feroce*) that starts *presto* and accelerates into a dizzying *più presto*.

Contrast Donizetti's choral numbers for act I of *La favorita* (1840), an opera first heard in the United States in New Orleans, in 1843, and popular across the country for many years thereafter. Donizetti's act 1 curtain rises on a group of monks who, after singing a simple melody up and down the scale of C major— "May our prayer rise to Heaven"—exit, leaving the stage to soloists. And after a change of scene to a garden, the women's chorus sings of "Golden sunbeams, gentle breezes," and soon leaves the stage to soloists.

Verdi's more dynamic choruses, with their frequent shifts from loud to soft, often within a single bar, and then back with accompanying crashes in the orchestra, to ears accustomed to Donizetti might sound jarring and confusing. And in their call for dramatic action onstage they were quite beyond the skills of most choral singers in the United States in 1848.

In the development of opera in the country, the skills and numbers of the chorus always lagged behind the orchestra, the weaker, less-favored sister. In 1825, when the first Italian troupe of thirteen singers had come to New York and had presented, for the first time in the country, Italian opera sung in Italian, of their number six were chorus, four men and two women. And these, according to the *New York American*, "surpassed everyone's expectation."[12] But when local recruits (perhaps ten or twelve) were added to the chorus, they did little well. One critic complained of the nasal quality in the women's voices,[13] and another, of their poor costumes. And a third wrote in the *New York Review and Athaeneum Magazine:* "Two or three of them, who contrive, we scarcely know how, to sing their parts in a wrong key, ought to be dismissed, and they should all be taught to walk off the stage, as well as to walk on. They seldom accomplish their retreat without jostling the other performers, and, in

Tancredi, on one occasion half of them marched with unrelenting feet directly across Amenaide's ample train."[14]

Thirteen years later in New Orleans, then leading New York in opera production, for the local French company had its own house, permanent orchestra, and chorus, the chorus numbered twenty or so, mostly of French heritage and singing all performances in that language. Yet when an Italian company came on tour from Havana, its chorus of six men and three women outsang the French. And an unsigned review in the local, semiweekly *Le Moqueur, Journal des Flâneurs*, in comparing the two groups, offered a glimpse of the home company's current choral skills:

> [The French] sing in unison whereas the Italians sing in parts. To that, we will add that when the Italians sing, they sing boldly, without reserve; then, too, they count themselves actors, and their movements contribute to the vigor of their voices. Whereas our people, perversely, half learn their parts and sing between their teeth, standing with arms crossed, like statues, and instead of working with the scene, amuse themselves by doing little tricks and saying stupid things. Another reason our chorus is so feeble, is that, for economy's sake, we make use of actors in place of singers for the parts.[15]

Coming now to 1848 and the premiere production of *Nabucco* in New York, we have a report on the chorus by the conductor Max Maretzek, who arrived in the country after the premiere but conducted some of the company's later performances of the opera. To introduce himself to the chorus he went to their rehearsal hall, which turned out to be one large room in a storehouse shared with the scenery and costume shops:

> Some of the male members of the chorus on my arrival were occupied in a game of cards . . . a few of the ladies employed in the chorus, were dividing their attention with an impartiality of the most praiseworthy character between an operation commonly called mending their stockings and the study of the parts, while others . . . were engaged in an earnest conversation with two of the tailor-boys, of which I heard enough, to form an idea that it touched upon the stipulations for a private treaty of commerce, in which the purloined silks and calicoes of Mr. Fry [the company's manager] were most certainly destined to play a very prominent part. Some few of the choral-singers . . . were also engaged in the tailoring department, while a tailoress rejoicing in the euphonious name of Valvasori, enjoyed the distinction of being secured, in addition, for the chorus. . . . Being totally unacquainted with the "go-ahead" style in which theatrical matters were carried on in this country, my eyes expanded upon all around me with a purely involuntary amazement![16]

But even by 1861, long after Maretzek managed to impose some discipline and training on the chorus, one of his leading sopranos, Clara Louise Kellogg, complained: "The chorus was made up of Italians who never studied their music, merely learned it at rehearsal, and the rehearsals themselves were often farcical."[17] So it seems fair to doubt that for the *Nabucco* premiere in 1848, the chorus of twenty or so was up to the demands of the opera, a doubt further strengthened by the failure of contemporary reviews to remark on its unusually vigorous choral scenes.

The opera's U.S. premiere, sung in Italian, was presented at New York City's Astor Place Opera House (capacity 1,800) by the house company (with Italian soloists) on April 4, 1848. Likely the company hoped to repeat the Havana company's success the previous year with *Ernani* (see that opera's chapter). But neither the story nor music of *Nabucco* was much admired. A critic for the weekly *Albion*, whose reports were often fuller than those of the daily papers, wrote:

> The house was but thinly attended. . . .
>
> The plot of the Opera is taken from the Bible; how far such a course is permissible we will not now stop to enquire, but we cannot but observe that while there exists so wide a field for Operatic subjects of a secular nature, it would be much better to let the scriptures alone. . . .
>
> The music of this Opera is a facsimile of Verdi's other operas, *I Lombardi* and *Ernani*. Of the three, however, we like *I Lombardi* the most and *Nabucco* the least. . . .
>
> The overture, as a composition [with six of its seven themes taken from choral numbers], is worthless. It is fury vs. sense, and fury carries everything before it. Verdi loves noise, he revels in a row, and everything is sacrificed for bluster and confusion. We see nothing in this music to admire; it is simply a varying of Donizetti, but by no means an improvement. It wants even the little freshness which Donizetti possessed. Some of the choruses have a kind of quaintness, which is not originality, but fantasy run mad. The solos have not the slightest individuality, they are as like each other as peas from the same pod.
>
> The voicing, both for the soloists and chorus, is outrageous; it is tearing to every voice, and is productive of nothing but consumption.[18]

Ten days later the company offered the opera in a concert version at the Broadway Tabernacle (capacity 2,500), built as a Congregational Church and for some therefore a setting less sinful than an opera house. But on second hearing, the *Albion* critic found the music still less appealing: "The programme consisted chiefly of selections from *Nabucco*, which if it was hard to endure on the stage, became positively intolerable in the concert room." Yet he admired the singers, particularly the Abigaille in her aria at the start of act II.[19]

Taking the opera to Boston, the company did not risk a full theatrical performance at the Howard Athenaeum, where it was performing. Rather, on Sunday evening June 4, 1848, at the Melodeon (capacity 1,200), then Boston's chief concert hall, it gave *Nabucco* its local premiere billed as "Verdi's Grand Sacred Drama." The critic for the *Boston Evening Transcript* reported the drama composed "in a spirited style," but felt the piece had been given "in a highly acceptable manner"—a phrase perhaps suggesting cuts. Yet he hoped it would be repeated "on the next Sabbath evening," and it was.[20]

When the opera next appeared, however, it was heard only in excerpts. To employ the Astor Place company during Holy Week, 1849, its new impresario Max Maretzek gave two sacred concerts in the churchlike Tabernacle. In the next few years Maretzek would establish himself as one of the country's most adventurous impresarios, mounting and conducting the U.S. premieres of many of the century's greatest works, including *Rigoletto, Trovatore*, and *Traviata*. But in these Holy Week concerts, on April 5 and 7, he cannot have offered much of *Nabucco*, for he featured as a premiere, a *Miserere* by Donizetti, along with Schubert's *Ave Maria*, and selections from Rossini's *Stabat Mater* and *Mosè*.[21]

The opera's immediate fate was to be shred and parts used in a pastiche, *Judith*, prepared for a touring English soprano, Anna Bishop, whose manager, Robert N. C. Bochsa,[22] reorchestrated some eighteen excerpts from six of Verdi's operas.[23] The *Morning Express* reported, "The splendid spectacle [which had five performances] . . . was most gorgeously set upon the stage; the chorus, costumes, scenery and appointments, including a military band, being each in its way most effective." The *Musical Times* concluded sourly, "The whole thing is nothing but a solo of two hours length for Madame Anna Bishop, with occasional *obbligato* accompaniments of a bass voice and with *refrains* [*sic*] by the chorus"—which suggests the dynamic choruses had been cut.[24]

Four years later, Bishop and Bochsa, then in San Francisco, revived *Judith*, and this time, according to local report, the story line hewed closer to the Biblical saga of Judith and Holofernes with music now taken mostly from *Nabucco*—but still with arias from other operas and a ballet inserted. Bochsa called it a "Grand Biblical Spectacle Opera" in six "tableaux," and it achieved six performances, a long run for San Francisco in 1854.[25] Remarked the *Pioneer Magazine*, "Judith was a mosaic, which would hardly stand before a critical attack. Yet it contained a great deal of most excellent music, and was adapted to the limited power of the company." Likely, that adjustment to talent was the key to success.[26]

Bochsa's *Judith*, however, prepared San Francisco's audience for a visiting Italian company's *Nabucco*, which premiered at the Metropolitan Theatre (capacity 2,000) on November 30, 1854. The company had a good baritone for the title role, a soprano adequate for Abigaille, and was able to hire locally as its conductor George Loder, who in New York had conducted much Verdi and knew the style well.[27] The *Pioneer Magazine* reported:

> *Nabucco* is similar in character to most of Verdi's operas, intricate concerted pieces of great artistic skill, and brilliant instrumentation, with a lack of beauty

Figure 1.1. Todd Thomas in the title role of Verdi's *Nabucco*, in the Sarasota Opera's 1995 production. Photograph by Paul Jeremias. Courtesy of the Sarasota Opera Company.

and melody. It was placed upon the stage with great completeness. . . . The choruses were the best part of this opera, and the triumphant march, played by the military band upon the stage, and the funeral march behind the scenes, had a grand effect. The part of Nabucco, presented by [Alessandro] Lanzoni, was, however, the feature of the opera. In the last scene of the second act, when the king loses his throne and his reason—in the *aria* and prayer in the fourth act and in the last scene and finale of the fourth act, he was truly admirable.[28]

The success was real, for the company repeated the opera twice, which was unusual for a new opera in a city as small as San Francisco (c. 48,000 in 1854).[29] Yet at its second and third performances the audiences and critics reportedly enjoyed it still more, hearing in it musical delights that had previously passed unnoticed, one of them a prayer sung by Nabucco's daughter Fenena as she is led to her execution.[30]

In 1862, another San Francisco company revived the opera under the title *Nino*, with the story changed, as in England, to a conflict between Babylonians and Assyrians. Again the opera had a success. According to the *Daily Evening Bulletin:*

> The music, though occasionally of a noisy character, is often beautiful, and some of it very striking. . . . Among the many fine things that are in the opera may be mentioned the quintet and chorus of the 2nd act, when the impious Nino calls on the people to worship him; the air in the 3rd act where he entreats Abigail to spare the life of Fenena; the grand though simple chorus of the captive Babylonians [originally Hebrews] in the same act; the lament of Fenena when led to martyrdom; and the glorious hymn to Isis (or originally, to the God of Israel) that closes the work. The funeral march in the 4th act, and the short triumphal march on the first appearance of Nino are fine. . . . There is a pleasing introduction, which from its length may almost be called an overture, that contains morsels of the melodies that afterwards occur in the piece.[31]

The opera, as Verdi composed it, ended not with "the glorious hymn" to the God of Israel but with a brief scene for the death of Abigaille, who, repenting of her effort to seize the throne and to kill Fenena, has swallowed poison. More often than not, in the nineteenth century this scene was cut, though Verdi, in his earliest account of the opera's origin, describes the scene as his inspiration, the first text he set to music.[32] In a later, better-known account, however, he describes as the inspirational, first scene composed, the chorus of captive Hebrews lamenting by the waters of Babylon.[33] In any case, he gave the death scene an unusual orchestration, suggesting he deemed it special. The dying Abigaille enters supported by two soldiers, and the orchestra, after the unaccompanied hymn to Jehovah, escorts her onstage with an English horn, harp, solo cello, and bass, a distinctive sound that Verdi later colors with more woodwinds, most prominently the flute.

Some critics admire the scene, others think it superfluous.[34] Why Verdi, at the opera's third performance at La Scala, should have agreed to drop it is speculative. The singer (many years later his second wife) was in wretched voice, but when at the ninth performance a replacement in good voice entered the cast, the scene remained cut. Possibly others at La Scala suggested to Verdi that the opera ended well enough with the chorus, and he, new to success, did not challenge the advice. A study of librettos from Italian performances, 1842–44, suggests that the scene was included in only six of eighty productions.[35]

In the United States the ratio was higher. The scene seems to have been omitted in the opera's premiere production (1848) that played in New York and Boston. But at the opera's second appearance in New York, in May 1860, it probably was included, for it was sung when the reorganized company the next month gave two performances in Boston.[36] It also was sung in the opera's premiere in San Francisco (1854), though dropped in the opera's 1862 revival as *Nino*. And in October 1860, when a company in New York performed the opera, the entire last act was cut, a mutilation that drew strong critical protest to the conductor, who pleaded Italian custom.[37]

In the twentieth century, however, in both Europe and the United States, the death scene almost always was performed. The opera's story, after all, is twofold: the salvation of the Hebrew people (with a model in Rossini's *Mosè*), and the conflict between the warrior princess Abigaille and Nabucco (whose character has precedents in Rossini), original with Verdi and his librettist.[38] Today most musicians and stage directors seem to feel the second story, as much as the first, requires its final scene. In Italy, the Verona Arena in its 1981 production (and perhaps in other years) offered a novel solution: it ended with the chorus to Jehovah but played the death scene immediately before it.[39]

In the nineteenth century, San Francisco was the only U.S. city in which *Nabucco* sustained a success. Aside from its six performances in the guise of *Judith* (1854), it had three in its premiere season as *Nabucco* (1854), three in the spring and two in the late autumn of 1862, followed by three in 1863, two in 1865, and one in 1866—then none until 1961.[40]

One reason for the opera's disappearance may have been the aura of spectacle that clung to it, making it costly to mount. When Max Maretzek, for example, now leading his own New York company, revived it in May 1860 for four performances, the *Herald* reported: "This opera was put on the stage in excellent style, the scenery, costumes and all the appointments, from the Babylonian brass band to the caparisoned steed of Nabucco, being all in complete order. . . . The opera was received with . . . hearty applause." Yet Maretzek, who in these years did not include Verdi in his published list of eleven "good" composers,[41] promptly dropped it from his repertory. Even the immense popularity of the later *Ernani*, *Rigoletto*, *Trovatore*, *Traviata*, and *Aida* could not keep it afloat. Occasionally its overture was played or an aria sung at a concert, but as the nineteenth century waned, though *Nabucco* survived in Italy, in the United States it became a name to which only a few excerpts attached, chiefly the bass Zaccaria's prayer.[42]

After World War I, however, as part of the Verdi Renaissance, interest in it outside of Italy began to revive. In Germany, starting in 1928, the opera had many successful productions, in response in part to Franz Werfel's novel about Verdi, his translation of many Verdi letters with a brief life, and his translations of several Verdi operas.[43] These in turn moved the English critic Toye to write a biography (1931), which offered an essay on every one of the operas. Such detail, at a time when most English-speaking critics were still trumpeting Wagner and counting Verdi for little, was astonishing. And Toye startled colleagues further by concluding: "*Nabucco* is probably the most satisfactory of all the early Verdi operas. There are passages more expressive in *Macbeth* and *Luisa Miller*, but as an entity *Nabucco* stands above them both, and not till *Rigoletto* did the composer produce again an opera so satisfactory as an artistic whole."[44] That judgment jolted readers in England and the United States; for as the introduction to an American reprint of Toye's biography (1946) noted, in the United States even avid operagoers had never seen it staged.[45]

Yet, during World War II, when Tocanini in a radio broadcast from New York, on January 31, 1943, resurrected "Va, pensiero," and then repeated the chorus on May 25, 1944, at a huge Red Cross Concert in Madison Square Garden, thousands of Americans became aware of the opera.[46] Also, on May 12, 1946, they read reports of Toscanini's concert in La Scala, celebrating the theater's reconstruction after the war. The program presented excerpts from Rossini, Verdi, Puccini, and Boito, with two of the four Verdi selections from *Nabucco*, the overture and "Va, pensiero."[47] And on December 26, 1946, when La Scala finally started its first postwar season, the opening night opera was *Nabucco*.[48]

In the next decade in Europe the opera constantly reappeared, reaching the United States in a recording of the complete opera taken from Italian radio in 1951.[49] That was soon followed by many recordings of Verdi's choruses and overtures, almost always including those from *Nabucco*.[50] Meanwhile, those Americans who followed opera in Europe were intrigued with the Welsh National Opera, which, beginning in 1952, annually included *Nabucco* in its repertory (ultimately, for eleven years). If in Wales, why not in the United States?

Finally, on March 5, 1960, the Symphony Society of San Antonio, Texas, as part of its Sixteenth Grand Opera Festival, gave the opera a single performance. The society mistakenly billed its production as "the third" in the United States, but it was, indeed, the first since the 1860s. Mounted in the city's Municipal Auditorium, where it played to an audience of more than five thousand, the production had a first-rate cast, colorful scenery, the society's symphony orchestra, and a large chorus of amateurs who for months had rehearsed almost every night.[51]

The performance drew many people from out of state, including Allen Hughes, usually a *New York Times* critic but now reviewing the production for the *San Antonio Express*. He found it admirable, especially the chorus, whose singing "was reliable and of good tone all the way. It did not have the somewhat strained intensity that routined, assertive, and worn professional chorus singers generally produce." He liked the scenery, especially "the palace courtyard and the Hanging Gardens," and described the opera as "a big, brilliant, and splashy Biblical pageant backed up by a musical score full of rousing tunes, marches, and resounding choruses." The majority of the audience, he surmised, "would willingly return for a repeat performance if they had the chance."[52]

The opera's next performance, only seven months later, was in New York, where, on October 24, it opened the Metropolitan's 1960–61 season. Unfortunately, though the cast was good, the production was not. The *Times* critic, Harold C. Schonberg, wrote:

> It was a new production of very rare opera. Not only is [*Nabucco*] a newcomer to the Metropolitan but also in all likelihood it has not been seen in this city for a hundred years. . . .
>
> The music may be a little crude in spots, but it is full of ideas. . . . *Nabucco* gives the listener of today a chance to hear some remarkable vocal writing, many brilliant choruses, and a type of melodic intensity that no Italian composer except Verdi brought to his music. . . . Thus the revival proved fascinating. One wishes that the same could be said about the production.
>
> The original four acts were compressed into three. This required some heavy cutting in the last two acts. . . . Not only that, but some scenes were transposed. . . . More disturbing were the sets. This production can be considered low-budget *Nabucco* that is also low in imagination.[53]

Schonberg was polite. The scenery, designed by a German prominent in his craft, Teo Otto, was dismal. He provided a few columns to the back, and before them risers and platforms that allowed the chorus to watch the conductor, but, as another critic complained, "did little to provide credible surroundings for the action."[54] Throughout much of the opera, however exciting the music, the chorus stood stock-still. The scenery's colors were predominantly dark reds, purples, brown, black, and from the first night looked dingy. Costumes were no better. From start to finish, the production bored the eye.[55]

It ended, however, with Abigaille's death scene—which the stage director spoiled. As the chorus concluded its hymn to Jehovah, between its banked rows the dying Abigaille dragged herself onstage, alone, unsupported by soldiers. Singing softly, and with bowed head, against the crowd of the chorus she was hard to locate. Probably many in the audience found her only when the scene was half over, and so it seemed utterly superfluous.

The music, for the most part, went better, though not without troubles. For reasons not altogether clear, neither the Abigaille nor the Nabucco were comfortable in their roles. The soprano, Leonie Rysanek, cut the trills, simplified the runs, and fudged the low notes, as many sopranos have done, but sang, as Schonberg wrote, "with vocal intensity, a thrilling top and a good deal of command."[56] The Nabucco, Cornell MacNeil, had the voice but lacked the presence, especially in the last two acts where perhaps too much of his role had been cut to allow him to develop its stature. Moreover, the conductor, Thomas Schippers, a young American coming to the score for the first time, did not fully command its style. Verdi once advised a rehearsal conductor that the opera's "*tempi* should not be slow. They should all move."[57] Schippers took the opera at a fast clip, but perhaps too rigidly; the choral numbers did not gather

Figure 1.2. Act 2, scene 1, of the Metropolitan Opera's 1960 production of
Nabucco. With Leonie Rysanek (Abigaille). Photograph by Louis Mélançon.
Courtesy of the Metropolitan Opera Archives.

momentum, swell, and roll. Audience response was tepid, and after the season's nine performances in the house (including a national radio broadcast),
and five on tour (Philadelphia, Boston, Atlanta, Bloomington, and Detroit),[58]
the Metropolitan shelved the production, attaching to the opera for many a
belief that it was a failure, not worth reviving.

That view was summarized by Paul Henry Lang, critic for the *Herald Tribune:*

> The opera is somewhat static and uneven, the libretto atrocious, but
> *Nabucco* has fine moments and good melodies. Amazingly enough, the

young composer's ensemble technique is remarkably developed; the quartet in the second act is a grand piece. However, while Verdi displays many signs of his future power, his musical ideas have a short breath, reaching a cadence after a few measures, even though some of the tunes have great possibilities. The arias and recitatives are sometimes a little jerky, because they are frequently interrupted by little meaningless coloratura cadenzas that are evidently not part of the melodic design, as they are in Verdi's later operas. There are innumerable holds that slow down everything, the tessitura for the vocal parts is uncomfortably high, and the succession of high notes is often abruptly followed by unmotivated low ones. The characterization is rudimentary—Verdi did not yet know how to create a woman in music—although there are moments when Nabucco himself really comes to life. Nevertheless, *Nabucco* is a significant work, for while Verdi closely observed the operatic conventions of the time, everything, including the Rossinian and Bellinian touches, is imbued with a personal and masculine quality. . . . It is nice to hear *Nabucco* once or twice—it contains clear indications of genius—but I am afraid . . . this opera is not for "foreigners" [non-Italians], at least not as a repertory piece.[59]

Lang's points may be argued, but he states a view of the opera often voiced in the United States in the 1960s. Yet in his conclusion—that the opera could succeed only in Italy—events promptly contradicted him. In the United States interest in *Nabucco* continued to bloom. San Francisco staged an opulent production in 1961, in a style opposed to the Metropolitan's. In San Francisco, wrote one critic, the stage director tumbled "terrified Hebrews from the wings onto the sloping temple floor as the first act battle spilled to the stage."[60] Chicago had a production in 1963, the first in the city's 124-year history—only moderately successful, according to one critic, because the company had borrowed the Metropolitan's stylized scenery and costumes.[61] Like the Metropolitan, the Lyric Opera of Chicago dropped the opera, whereas San Francisco, where *Nabucco* always seemed to find success, revived it in 1964, 1970, 1982 (new production), 1987, and 1999. Meanwhile, around the country smaller companies began to stage the opera, so that in the last thirty years of the century *Nabucco* became increasingly familiar.[62]

In this the opera was aided by a La Scala production brought to the Montreal Exposition in October 1967. Seen by many Americans, including critics and impresarios, this production greatly influenced perceptions of how *Nabucco* should be staged. As Martin Bernheimer, critic for the *Los Angeles Times*, later remarked: "If *Nabucco* is to be revived in the sophisticated 1980s, the production team must make at least one crucial decision. They can pull out the theatrical stops and play the opera—banalities and all!—as a Cecil B. DeMille spectacular; or they can reduce the threat of giddiness by camouflaging the creaky maneuvers with modernistic stylization, simplification or abstraction."[63]

Where the Metropolitan, in 1960, had made a weak case for stylization, La Scala, in 1967, made a strong one for the Hollywood spectacular. Of the La Scala production, *Times* critic Schonberg, though often cool to opera, wrote:

> La Scala presented Verdi's *Nabucco* last night, and it was the performance that all admirers of the company had been waiting for. This was grand opera, this was La Scala. The sets by Nicola Benois were sumptuous and in wonderfully dizzy disregard for archeological accuracy. As a production it out-Russianed the Russians, what with fire, smoke, great idols riven in half and falling with thunder. The rich-looking costumes looked as though they had come directly from the Victor Book of the Opera, 1912 edition. Great. Best of all, a cast of singers all but advanced en masse upon the footlights and sang. I mean, really sang. . . . Volley after volley of tone rang out. . . . The opera is a masterpiece, but makes only half its impact with timid or inferior singers. It needs this kind of 19th-century production, this kind of uninhibited vocal excitement.[64]

The examples of San Antonio, San Francisco, and La Scala seemingly convinced American opera companies that *Nabucco* was best mounted in a style of "banalities and all." That conclusion, however, ensured that it would continue to be hard to produce, particularly for smaller companies with small stages. A recurring disappointment of productions, even in large houses, was a tendency to ease demands on the chorus by allowing it to stand still, tilting the opera toward oratorio. But no American company tried, as did three in England, to add a contemporary shiver to the opera by imposing on it images of modern Jewish history, including the Holocaust.[65]

Even as the music of *Nabucco* has become more familiar, reviews of it have become less interesting, as critics devote more space to praising or damning the singers than to discussing the work. Moreover, journalists and program writers now tend merely to beat old opinions into clichés: describing the opera as mostly choral—forgetting the half that is Abigaille and Nabucco; reciting the difficulties of the role of Abigaille—forgetting the hundreds of sopranos who have sung it with success (albeit with simplifications here and there);[66] and chanting that the opera stands or falls on Abigaille—forgetting that Nabucco is the title role and has some notably interesting and varied music. When well sung, as at the San Francisco premiere in 1854, or in Montreal in 1967, Nabucco dominates the stage, the first of Verdi's great roles for baritones. But in journalism recycled opinion is often the fate of operas that become familiar, and in the United States *Nabucco* rapidly became still better known.

In March 2001, the Metropolitan returned to the opera for the first time in forty years. The new production, scenery, and staging, was a compromise, not entirely happy. The Temple in Jerusalem was a huge pile of sand-brown stone blocks, fit together as if the ruins of some mighty foundation. With steps and landings among the blocks, soloists or chorus members could move up, down,

Figure 1.3. Set model designed by John Napier for act 1 of the Metropolitan Opera's 2001 production of *Nabucco*. Photograph courtesy of the Metropolitan Opera Archives.

or to the side, playing scenes at different levels. The palace in Babylon was the pile turned round, now colored bronze or black, and dominated by a throne beneath a statue of Bel. But the color scheme—light for the Hebrews, dark for the Babylonians—was not followed exactly, and in all acts the pile pushed the action forward, which was good, but also cramped it, so that scenes often more resembled a tableau than a flow of movement. The production, however, played the story straight, without topical themes imposed, even as it stinted on the traditional theatrical coups. In performances in the house the thunderbolt knocking the crown from the head of the blaspheming Nabucco was sometimes fumbled, so that the audience saw him take it off. Though Verdi titled the final act "L'idolo infranto" (The Shattered Idol), and directed exactly when the idol was to crumble, onstage there was no idol, no crumbling, no scenic sign of Jehovah's triumph over Bel. On the other hand, though Nabucco entered the Temple in Jerusalem without a marching band or horse, there were visible and alarming flames as the Babylonians torched it, and Abigaille's death scene was well handled. As the chorus finished its hymn in praise of Jehovah, she entered alone, atop the pile of quarried stone, and as a spotlight picked her out, the chorus turned to look up at her, focusing the audience's attention on her even before she began to sing. Throughout the evening the singers and music carried the opera.

Figure 1.4. Abigaille's death scene in the Metropolitan Opera's 2001 production of *Nabucco*, with soprano Maria Guleghina. Photograph by Winnie Klotz. Courtesy of the Metropolitan Opera Archives.

In all, the production was a great popular success, and at each performance "Va, pensiero," the chorus of Hebrew lament, was encored. An eager public bought out all nine performances (one of them a national radio broadcast), and many, disappointed, consoled themselves with a telecast on March 31. The following season came too soon for the Metropolitan to repeat the opera, but the company revived it in the next three seasons, 2002, 2003, and 2004, for a total of twenty-seven in-house performances including radio broadcasts each year to an audience numbered at eleven million. Finally, in 2005, the Metropolitan released a copy of the televised performance (March 31, 2001) on a DVD recording. Meanwhile, in June 2004, it had offered the opera in four park concerts, in Manhattan (an audience estimated at twenty-five thousand), Queens, Staten Island, and Montclair, New Jersey. By then most opera buffs were thoroughly familiar with the opera, and even casual operagoers had heard it at least once on radio, seen it on television, or bought a recording.[67]

In 1971 Lang of the *Herald Tribune* had surmised that *Nabucco* was not an opera for Americans, "at least not as a repertory piece." In succeeding years, however, Americans declared otherwise.

Chapter Two

I Lombardi alla prima crociata

Though *I Lombardi alla prima crociata* (The Lombards on the First Crusade) was Verdi's fourth opera in order of composition—following two lesser works and *Nabucco*—it was his first to be staged in the United States, at Palmo's Opera House, in New York, on March 3, 1847. But before then, on at least three occasions in New York, excerpts had been sung in concerts. And the earliest of these, on May 12, 1846, was possibly the first public performance of any Verdi music in the United States. At the city's Apollo Theater, the Italian artist Rosina Pico, just back from Havana, where his *Ernani* and *I Lombardi* shortly would receive their hemispheric premieres, introduced the composer to New York audiences by singing "Ernani involami" and, from the last act of *I Lombardi*, Giselda's ecstatic assertion that a vision of her beloved in paradise was not a dream, "Non fu sogno!"[1]

Pico sang the *Lombardi* aria again on May 20 in Castle Garden, at a concert of the New York Philharmonic, which was widely reviewed because it presented in its second part the U.S. premiere of Beethoven's Ninth Symphony. To precede the symphony, the Philharmonic offered not one but three overtures, a piano concerto, and three operatic arias, two by Donizetti and one by Verdi. And Pico with "Non fu sogno!" was reported to have "sung gloriously" and won "a rapturous *encore*"—though the New York lawyer George Templeton Strong, who was present and "sadly disappointed" in the symphony, described the arias in his diary as merely "some *tolerabiles ineptia* from Verdi and Donizetti."[2]

The other selection from *I Lombardi* sung in public before the opera's premiere was the "conversion" trio for soprano, tenor, and bass that closes act 3, "Qui posa il fianco" (Here set yourself down). A young Muslim prince, dying and in love with Giselda, a Christian, for her sake converts and is baptized by a hermit with water from the River Jordan. A solo violin introduces the scene with a miniature concerto—opening statement, three tiny movements, and coda—and, even after the voices enter, the violin continues to interject its message of hope and salvation. In the United States, this trio would surpass even the Crusaders' chorus of lament, "O Signore dal tetto natio," as the opera's most frequently excerpted number.[3]

Its first public performance here apparently was in New York, on January 7, 1847, at a farewell concert given by the Austrian-French composer and pianist Henri Herz. The newspapers, of course, focused their reports on the pianist, leaving unstated whether the trio was presented entire or shorn of its violin introduction. Even Herz's part of the program, however, was mostly operatic.

In addition to his popular Grand Fantasia based on *Lucia di Lammermoor* and his Variations on "The Last Rose of Summer," he introduced two new fantasies on *Semiramide* and *I puritani*, and with fifteen other pianists onstage thumped out an eight-piano, thirty-two-hands version of the Overture to *William Tell*.[4]

The premiere of *I Lombardi*, staged by a group of Italian singers led by Antonio Sanquirico, their basso buffo, followed on March 3 at Palmo's Opera House, one of New York's smaller theaters, seating about 1,100. A former public bath, it stood on Chambers Street, facing City Hall Park and across from the larger, more venerable Park Theatre. Palmo's reconstructed interior, though horseshoe-shaped, was unpretentious: only eight boxes, four to a side; and fronting the stage, a parquet (or orchestra floor), and behind it, a slightly raised parquet circle, above which was a balcony. All seats were boards, uncushioned and without arms. Though the seats were numbered, the numbers were placed too close, so that a board when filled, often held fewer people than numbered seats, and likely much of the seating was treated as unreserved. The house was lit by chandeliers of gas jets designed to resemble candles, and the drop curtain depicted the marriage of Jupiter and Juno. The mixed chorus numbered twenty-four, and the orchestra, led by Michele Rapetti, a resident Italian violinist and leader in the city's musical affairs, thirty-two—such numbers and quality proclaiming a major undertaking.[5]

The size and quality of opera orchestras in the country's northeast had been slowly improving since the Park Theatre in 1825, for the first season of Italian opera sung in Italian in the United States, had increased its house orchestra from fourteen to twenty-five: 7 violins, 2 violas, 3 cellos, 2 basses; 2 flutes, 2 clarinets, 1 bassoon; 2 trumpets, 2 horns, 1 timpani, and a piano. In London, at the King's Theatre, from which the troupe of thirteen singers primarily had come, the orchestra usually numbered fifty.[6]

Of equal importance to the Park's enlarged orchestra, however, was the fact that it played together for an eleven-month season. Led by the pianist, for it had no conductor in the modern sense, it rehearsed and performed nine operas for a total of seventy-nine performances. And though on two nights it lost its way, in *Tancredi* and in the finale to the first act of *Don Giovanni*, it yet had set a new standard in the country's northern cities for skill and sound, bringing them abreast of the French company's orchestra in New Orleans.[7]

In the next twenty years, however, the New Orleans company again surged ahead, and in eight summer tours northward with soloists and a core of its orchestra and chorus swollen by northern recruits again set the standard higher. During its last tour, in the summer of 1845, it staged a repertory of French grand opera, notably *Guillaume Tell, Robert le Diable, Les Huguenots, La Juive*, and *Favorite*, with an orchestra of forty led by a conductor. At the Paris Opéra, for such grand, romantic operas the orchestra typically numbered at least seventy-nine. But in New York, though one critic complained of a paucity of violins and timpani, the majority praised the orchestra, and the *Anglo-American* pronounced its conductor, Eugène Prévost, "the best leader we have ever met with in America."[8] Thus two years later, the Palmo house's orchestra of thirty-two, with a first violinist acting as conductor, while an impressive assembly, was not the largest the city had heard and perhaps not large enough for an opera so grandiose as *The Lombards on the First Crusade*, but then, the house was relatively small, and the balance, reportedly right.[9]

The city's *Albion*, a weekly journal with emphasis on cultural events, reported on the premiere:

> The production of a new opera by a new composer forms quite an era in our musical times, and is therefore worthy of our particular consideration. Verdi, the new composer . . . has attained the highest pitch of popularity in Italy, but in Paris he made several failures, and only succeeded in securing the attention of the connoisseurs of that city by the production of the opera which we are about to notice.
>
> *I Lombardi* succeeded well in Paris not alone on account of its merits as music, but because its plot affords scope for the most magnificent scenery and decoration, and the most gorgeous display of costumes. In short it is at once an opera and a magnificent *spectacle*. . . .
>
> There is, however, undoubtedly much fine music in *I Lombardi*, and much quaintness, which is but too often taken for originality. The melodies do not possess the catching, popular qualities of a Bellini, or a Donizetti, but they are very similar in character and construction; but Verdi's music, or rather his melodies, seem to us as though they were written under restraint, that is, as though they were composed under the most impressive remembrances of the masters of his school who have gone before him. The apparent natural course of the melody is constantly turned aside to avoid similarities, which imparts to such melodies a strained and unsatisfactory character. Verdi, like all the modern Italian writers, is a victim to a passion for instruments of brass and percussion. He is not content with using the whole force and volume of the regular orchestra, but in addition, he produces a powerful military band upon the stage; he is not content with giving them military music solos, but opens their brazen throats in all the fortes, which produces, in our little opera house, a power of sound sufficient to give hearing to the deaf, and to destroy that exquisite sense in those already possessed of it. This love of notes is the curse of our modern writers: with the Italians it is mere noise without substance. It will be a happy day for the cause of music, when writers will return to Mozart's simplicity! . . .
>
> There are several quaint and striking choruses in the first and second acts, besides some concerted pieces of considerable power, but the third act contains more to admire than all the three others combined. The chorus of Pilgrims and Crusaders, with which it opens ["Gerusalem!"] is an admirable piece of writing both for voices and Orchestra. It was exceedingly well executed, the charming passages for the Violoncello, being performed in a masterly manner by Mr. [Alfred] Boucher. The duo between the Soprano and Tenor, which succeeds it, is also a fair sample of Verdi's style while the trio

["Qui posa il fianco"] which concludes the act is a most clever and effective piece of writing, and being sung in excellent style, it has on each representation been honoured by an encore. Taking the Opera as a whole we think it well worthy the consideration of the public.[10]

But if the critic for the *Albion* talked mostly of the opera's musical strengths, his colleague on the *Morning Courier and New-York Enquirer* stressed its flaws:

> Verdi's *I Lombardi* was presented for the first time Monday night. It has been placed upon the stage with great care, and in point of scenery, tasteful decorations—all that addresses the eye—it is as effectively produced as anything could be in so confined a space, and makes a very showy spectacle. The plot, however, is so ill-contrived that the piece is rather a series of disconnected scenes than one having a dramatic interest.
> . . . But if the plot is extravagant and elaborately ill wrought, what shall be said of the music? Simply that the chief excellence of the piece is that it harmonizes with the plot admirably or rather overpowers and outdoes it in its own way, so that the extravagance of the plot becomes merely accessory and subordinate. . . .
> Its melody is unpalatable, not from its peculiar character and force. . . . It has nothing graceful, nothing heart-touching, but all is obtrusively odd, *bizarre*, designed to astonish, and to make an *exhibition* of those qualities which good music should express.
> Its harmony, too, is most strange, intolerable, and outré that ever was heard; it is not possible for one accustomed to classic music to relish it; it is conventional, a fashion that will have its day and die.
> . . . In brief, it is in its whole substance *melo-dramatic*, that is, it is a sort of music we can suffer ourselves to be amused with, but are never moved by directly.[11]

Another person present, one not claiming any musical expertise and liking to present his views to readers as "a plain man's opinions," was Walt Whitman. Only three months earlier in the *Brooklyn Daily Eagle* he had raged against the artificiality of Italian music, "its flourishes, its ridiculous sentimentality, its anti-republican spirit"—but now felt differently.

> The Italian co. in N. Y. have at last produced their long promised opera of *I Lombardi*, or "the first crusade," written by Verdi, and got up theatrically in a very superior manner, its merits as a spectacle almost equal its qualities as a musical performance the scenery being very fine, and also superintended by Italian artists, whereat one might imagine some parts of it to be representations of the fair skied and sunny land. How beautiful, for instance is that moonlight view in Milan! . . . [Ferdinando] Beneventano's voice [bass] in no previous opera has so fully developed its powers: those powers are indeed wonderful, (there can be but few similar specimens in the world,) and in his bursts of musical furor he seems to possess the ability of drowning the

entire orchestra! The music of *I Lombardi* is written in a substantial manner, and every passing note appears to be governed by a profound knowledge of harmony the only objection to which is, that it results in something of a heavy style. Rapetti plays a violin solo in the third act, which alone is worth going from the ninth ward of Brooklyn to hear; and the solo is backed by one of the sweetest songs [Clotilda] Barili ever sang. We would advise all who appreciate the inspiration of true music, to go and hear some of the finest chorus singing, instrumentation, and arias, ever produced in this part of the country.[12]

Finally, the critic for the *Tribune*, reviewing a later performance of the opera and noting that "full benches" were "the best proofs" of public approval, observed:

> *I Lombardi* was performed last evening before a good house . . . [the opera has] won its way from a cool reception to a high place in the favor of the somewhat fastidious audiences. . . . The music is there. . . . A decided improvement was apparent last evening in excluding the band, which has formerly been introduced upon the stage. The thing might answer in a large house, but was decidedly too heavy for Palmo's—The orchestra is fully equal to all that the house will well bear in the way of instrumentation. Rappeti's performance in the opening of the third act is a great feature of the piece as performed here and draws out every evening of its execution, the greatest applause.[13]

Yet, despite this initial success, the opera failed in the United States, in part because haunted always by the complaint of an "ill-contrived" libretto. Verdi and his librettist Temistocle Solera had based their work—Verdi's only opera derived directly from an Italian source—on a monument of Italian romantic poetry, an heroic epic of fifteen cantos, *I Lombardi alla prima crociata* (1826). The author, Tommaso Grossi, was inspired equally by Walter Scott's novel *Ivanhoe* (1819) and by Tasso's epic *Gerusalemme Liberata* (1575), in which the historic Godfrey de Bouillon in 1099 wins Jerusalem from the Muslims. Into Tasso's semihistorical account of the First Crusade, Grossi wove a fictional story of a Lombard family's fraternal feud, with reconciliation between good and bad brother finally achieved in the Holy Land, to which he added a Muslim prince who loves the good brother's daughter and for her sake converts to Christianity, providing the opera with the "conversion" trio for soprano, tenor (the prince), and bass (a hermit).

Rearranging Grossi's time sequence, Verdi and Solera took from the epic eleven scenes, which proved too few to tell a coherent story. Especially in its fictional episodes the opera has many incredible coincidences and unexplained developments. To cite one: Early in act 2 the young Muslim prince, at his first appearance, sings a charming love song ("La mia letizia infondere") to an unidentified lady of different faith imprisoned in the Muslim harem. Apparently, at some earlier time the two had met and fallen in love. In the next scene those in the audience with sharp ears may hear that the daughter of the good Lombard brother has been captured by Muslims, but her identity as the tenor's beloved is still merely implied. Only in the following scene's opening chorus, does it become explicit; but how or when the lovers met is never explained.[14]

In Italy, where audiences knew Grossi's poem, presumably many could fill in the missing background, but in the United States, where the poem was little known, they could not. The critic for the *Courier and Enquirer* was only the first of many to condemn the libretto and complain of "disconnected scenes."

These scenes, however, offered many opportunities for spectacular scenery. The opera opens, for example, in Milan in the piazza of the old and much-loved Lombard cathedral, the Basilica of St. Ambrose, where a prior of Milan announces the First Crusade, fixing the year as 1095. In act 2, three years later, the Crusaders are besieging Antioch, with a chance to portray the Muslim ruler's Council Chamber, full of ambassadors, soldiers, and people, as well as, in a later scene, his harem, soon invaded by Turkish soldiers pursued by Crusaders. In act 3, the scene moves to the Valley of Jehoshaphat with the Mount of Olives looming and Jerusalem in the distance, and "the conversion" scene depicts a hermit's grotto with the River Jordan nearby. In the last act, the audience is taken first to the Crusaders' camp outside Jerusalem's walls, about to be stormed, with the city's towers topped by Muslim crescents. Lastly, inside a Crusader's tent the good Lombard brother forgives the bad, who turns out to have been the baptizing hermit and who, as his dying request, asks to gaze one last time on Jerusalem. The tent's side is pulled back, revealing the Holy City, its walls and towers now draped with banners of the cross and illuminated by rays of the rising sun.[15]

In the large opera houses of Milan, Paris, and London, the spectacle of these holy places, no doubt, was stupendous. In the smaller American theaters the ability of their stage painters to dazzle their audiences, including "plain man" Whitman, speaks well of their skill, for gas lighting in the 1840s could achieve only limited variation, and sets were chiefly painted backdrops and "wings" hung at the sides and protruding onto the stage only a yard or two.

Musically, the opera is uneven, with some scenes said to be better than the best in its predecessor, *Nabucco*, and others, worse than the worst. Possibly, Verdi himself felt the imbalance, for in 1847, when given the chance to revise an opera for Paris, he chose *I Lombardi*, and while tightening the story, refashioned it to a French libretto as *Jérusalem*, substituted French for Italian Crusaders and composed for it a ballet and considerable new music.[16] He also replaced the Muslim prince with a Christian lover, requiring considerable change in the "conversion" trio. Now moved to the opera's last act and no longer concerned with baptism, it became a trio about the restitution of honor, and the violin's miniconcerto and its later interjections, promising salvation, were all dropped. In sum, in place of naiveté, Verdi offered greater suavity, though many had found the naiveté charming (and still do). In French-speaking countries, and in New Orleans, *Jérusalem* (though often with its ballet cut in whole or part) had a great success.[17] Elsewhere *I Lombardi* was preferred.

In New York in the spring of 1847 the Sanquirico company, having had a successful March season at Palmo's, planned another for April,[18] and after taking only a week's vacation, it opened at the same house on the April 7 with Donizetti's *Lucrezia Borgia*. Of the seven operas performed, *Lombardi* proved the most unfortunate and perhaps the least popular. A soprano's illness caused the first two scheduled performances to be canceled, and for the third only the final act was sung, preceding act 2 of Rossini's *Barbiere*. Finally, toward the end of the season the opera achieved three performances, with the audience at the last two reportedly sparse. Then, the coup de grâce: Though Rapetti, the violinist who led the orchestra, had announced *Lombardi* for his benefit night, he later, at the "request of many friends" agreed to substitute *Lucia*.[19]

In another way, too, fate was unkind to the opera. Only a week after the Sanquirico company started its second season, an Italian opera company from Havana, playing at the larger and more comfortable Park Theatre (capacity 2,300), on April 15, opened a season with the U.S. premiere of Verdi's *Ernani*. The occasion also marked the first time in the city's history, and perhaps the country's, that two Italian companies had competed so directly for what was yet a small audience.[20]

The Havana company, however, was the stronger. It arrived with a company of seventy-two artists (soon expanded to eighty-three), which included not only its soloists and chorus, but orchestra, scenery, and costumes: "Everything, save a theatre," exclaimed the *Herald* the day of the opening.[21] The chorus of twenty was small (four sopranos, three altos, six tenors, and seven basses) but better schooled than the Sanquirico chorus. "We have scarcely if ever had such choristers upon our stage," cheered the *Albion*.[22] Similarly, the orchestra, numbering thirty-two and sometimes slightly enlarged by local recruits, was more expert, and it was led by two distinguished musicians, the violinist Luigi Arditi, and, as its codirector, the double bassist Giovanni Bottesini. At the Havana premiere of *I Lombardi*, Arditi as the solo violinist in the "conversion" trio had won five repeats of the miniconcerto;[23] and Bottesini, though the orchestra's sole double bass, was said by the *Albion* critic to be "in himself almost equal to four."[24] Between acts or at the end of operas the two men would play duets they had composed, mostly variations on popular operatic tunes. Though the Havana company, before departing for Boston, gave only three performances, two of *Ernani* and a concert, the excitement over its promised return in June was intense and drained support from the Sanquirico company, which limped to the close of its spring season and disbanded.

But not only did the Havana company set for audiences a new standard of excellence in performance, it also introduced them to *Ernani*, which for forty or so years in the United States would rank second only to *Il trovatore* as Verdi's most popular opera. The company had in its touring repertory, besides *Ernani*, two other Verdi works, *I due Foscari*, and *I Lombardi*, but it performed the latter only in Boston and Philadelphia. The company's ranking of the operas can be seen in its schedule for Philadelphia, where between July 12 and August 6, in a season of eighteen performances of eight operas, it gave *Ernani* five times, *Lombardi* twice, and *Foscari* once.[25] In all three cities *Ernani* was the favorite.

Bottesini, the company's codirector, confessed in a letter to his father, that the "company . . . must thank the virginity of the American eardrums, because otherwise there would be a massacre. If one excepts *Ernani*, the other operas are ruined. Horrendous discords, but always applauded. What luck!"[26] Yet in Boston, as in New York, critics and audiences ignored the defects of the performances in their excitement over the company's virtues. Looking back five years later, Boston's theatrical historian, William W. Clapp, wrote: "Such a combination of brilliancy, effect and vigor, with the sentimental and tender, had never before revealed itself upon the Boston lyric stage."[27] And though perhaps not intending to state a difference between Verdi and Bellini, then an operatic favorite, he suggested one in stressing the new mixture of tenderness with vigor.

In Philadelphia, praise was more muted. A theatrical historian of the day, Charles Durang, devoted only a single sentence to the premiere of *I Lombardi*: "There seemed a great clashing of brass instruments in this opera, expressive of battle music."[28] And Joseph Sill, a merchant who loved opera and kept a diary, recorded of the company: "[I went] to see the opera of 'the Sonnambula,' and was much delighted—more with the completeness of the orchestra and the chorus than with any particular singer." With the company's *Norma* he was less pleased. "As a whole it was about mediocrity; and did not excite much applause."[29] And he left the noisy *Lombardi* unheard.

In late October 1847, the Havana company returned to Cuba, leaving New York to a new local company of chiefly Italian singers, performing in the new and luxurious Astor Place Opera House (capacity 1,500 to 1,800).[30] The company's soloists were less exciting and its orchestra less skilled. According to Max Maretzek, a conductor who soon would take over the company as both manager and its first conductor (and so may be prejudiced in his report), the company had an orchestra

of about thirty-six performers. . . . They had a leader, Signor Lietti . . . who was occupied in playing the first violin part, fully unconscious of the other instruments in the orchestra. But I wrong him. In order to guide them, he was possessed with the monomania of playing more loudly and vigorously upon his fiddle than any of his subordinates. He trampled on the floor as though he had been determined to work a path through the deal planking, and made a series of the most grotesque faces with his nose, mouth and eyes.[31]

Maretzek, who had been brought over from London where he had held a variety of operatic posts, continued to poke fun, but beyond question when he took over the company in the fall of 1848 it gained a first-rate conductor and impresario and improved in all departments. This advance for opera, replacing the first violinist or pianist with a conductor, had earlier been achieved in New Orleans, but in the country's northeast was a step forward.[32]

Before Maretzek's arrival, however, this Astor Place company opened with *Ernani* and then staged *I Lombardi*, the first with great success, the latter, with little. The New York lawyer Strong, echoing the now prevalent view that *Ernani* was the stronger work, after recording in his diary some cautious praise for it, wrote of *Lombardi:* "The opera [is] trash. All Verdi's faults and none of his redeeming traits. The hero experiences religion to a rather pretty *andante* movement in the second act, is baptized by the *basso* (old Rosi) to a stupid *terzetto* in the third, and goes to heaven attended by certain *apterous* [wingless] angels in white satin to a celestial chorus strongly resembling a Sunday school hymn, very shortly afterwards. The plot is unintelligible, the music always rather insipid and meretricious, and the baptizing business decidedly indecent and profane."[33] When this company in February 1848 moved to Philadelphia for twenty-three performances, it took of Verdi only *Ernani*.[34] And when returning to Philadelphia in December of that year for fourteen performances, it presented three of *Ernani* but only two of *Lombardi*, with the latter apparently stirring little interest.[35]

Five years later, on October 17, 1853, this same company, now led by Maretzek, revived *I Lombardi*, and the critic for the weekly *Albion* wrote of the current and previous productions:

> After a five years' absence . . . Verdi's *I Lombardi* re-appeared. . . . It was a failure even then, though produced in a most showy and expensive style, with artists who were then prime favorites, with a large double orchestra, with all other means and appliance to produce success, and with a fashionable *prestige* in its favour. It was *then* a *fiasco*, we say, and it is not to be wondered at, that it did not succeed now.
>
> Although we sympathize with the industrious and energetic manager, we cannot as true lovers of the musical art say that we regret this want of success. It shows that people prefer *music* to show and brassy noises. . . . We speak of *Lombardi, Ernani, Nabucco, Macbeth,* and others, when we say, that such productions are enough to ruin all singers. No young Soprano can possibly, without unnatural and constant straining of the voice, hang through four acts at the skirt of the Piccolo flute, and overtop the noises of all the brass and reed that are brought to bear against her. . . . Of the performance . . . we have but little to say. The Opera gives an opportunity for considerable display of scenery and costumes. . . . The costuming was good; the scenery, however, old and indifferent. Some of the choruses were sung with considerable power and precision, and the Orchestra was a trifle better kept together than on some other recent occasions.[36]

The *Times* began its report by characterizing Verdi as "the best abused composer of the day," and later adding, "he is one of those unfortunate men of genius who fail to excite the sympathy of a general audience." And apparently the revival did not change that opinion. Yet the critic acknowledged that Maretzek, though making cuts in the music, had mounted a good show. "It has been excellently rehearsed. The Chorus, for once, sang with vigor and precision. . . . The Orchestra was perfect. . . . We would suggest, also [to orchestra members], the entire propriety of dressing alike; and not, as at present, in a variety of costumes." Apparently, such was not yet the custom.

For scenery, however, Maretzek had used what the theater, Niblo's Garden, could provide, which according to the critic was: "the same old, dirty, worn-out scenes . . . thrust before the public on every opera night, totally regardless of propriety," and the costumes, too, were a disappointment. "It is a delusion no longer popular, that glazed linen at all resembles sheet armor; it is also usually conceded that steel is of a bluish rather than a brownish tint. Under these circumstances would it not be well for the gallant Crusaders to divest their limbs of the linen integuments with which they are swathed?"[37]

This production, seemingly a musical though not a scenic success, was the opera's last on the country's East Coast until 1886. Out west, in San Francisco, it fared slightly better, with three performances in 1855, three in 1865, and one in each of 1868 and 1873, and then none until the next century.[38] Only in New Orleans, where it played in its French revision, *Jérusalem*, did it find continuing success.[39] Nevertheless, though *I Lombardi* might languish unperformed, its better music was not forgotten and turned up often at concerts and recitals, with preferred excerpts being the tenor's aria "La mia letizia infondere," the soprano's "Non fu sogno," the chorus "O Signore dal tetto natio," and the "conversion" trio.[40]

The 1886 performance in New York, at the Academy of Music, was part of a season primarily devoted to Verdi, particularly his early operas, and produced by a Signor Angelo, of whom everyone seems to have thought ill. Colonel J. H. Mapleson, an impresario for thirty years who staged operas in England and the United States, claimed to have given Angelo (who apparently had no second name) a start in life by hiring him as a servant. In that lowly position, according to Mapleson, Angelo soon amassed considerable wealth by scalping tickets to performances by Adelina Patti and by conducting scams in cheap cigars and vermouth. Plainly, no man hath greater scorn than an impresario facing his own upstart, for "Angelo," wrote Mapleson, "is well known in the United States, chiefly by the unwashed condition of his linen."[41] Be that as it may, Angelo evidently loved Verdi, for he announced a season, opening on October 18, 1886, with Errico Petrella's *Ione* and thereafter offering a cycle of Verdi's early works: *Luisa Miller*, *I Lombardi*, and *I due Foscari* as well as *Un ballo in maschera*.

Wrote the critic of the *New York Post* on what he called "the disinternment of *I Lombardi*":

Such performances, however, as Signor Angelo's opera company perpetrated last evening serve neither the cause of Signor Verdi in particular nor the cause of Italian opera in general. Signora Mathilda Ricci, a new prima donna, made such an utter *fiasco* that her very first aria (which some persons inclined to be friendly had the hardihood to applaud) was roundly hissed by the audience . . . a demonstration of disapproval which may be an every day occurrence in Continental theatres, but which has not happened here in years. . . . Under such circumstances of misrepresentation it would be unfair to judge from present standards of Verdi's opera. It may safely be said, however, that it is one of his very weakest. Nor could it well be otherwise with such a sad, strange medley of a libretto. . . . The scenery again presented the world thoroughly out of joint. It was like a series of geographical nightmares.[42]

The critic for the *Times* was kinder. "The story of *I Lombardi*," he began, "is decidedly complicated," and after devoting five and a half inches of type to unraveling it, he concluded that it was "the most embroiled of imbroglios." But the performance, which he agreed had begun badly, had improved in later acts, and he noted that both "La mia letizia infondere" and "O Signore dal tetto natio" had won encores. The trio had not, presumably because of the soprano's inadequacies, but the critic listed it as one of the opera's better numbers, along with the quintet and finale to act 1, which the previous evening had been "the least impressive of the four." Unhappily for Signor Angelo, the poor performances and reviews cut his season short, the company split in a row over wages, and he slipped from the pages of history.[43]

Still, through its excerpts, some memory of *I Lombardi* continued to survive, and in 1915 on the West Coast, a touring company, National Grand Opera, revived it. On January 21 in Los Angeles, as a feature of the company's three-week season of eleven operas, it gave the opera its local premiere. The critic for the *Evening Herald* called the production "the greatest and most artistic achievement . . . scored so far this season. . . . The orchestra surpassed itself . . . the chorus won an ovation. . . . And another thing that added to the beauty of this most exquisite performance was the new scenery and costumes, which were imported from Italy." Moreover, the critic, who was the director of the local Orpheus Club, thought the opera "a splendid medium to educate Americans who at first cannot appreciate classic opera. It is an opera which through its simplicity should appeal to children and young students."[44]

But unhappily, in San Francisco, despite an opening success with *Rigoletto*, the revival of *Lombardi* did not succeed. Though the *San Francisco Call* reported "a pleasant rendering" of "true Verdian music," the *Chronicle* headlining its review "Ancient Opera Fails to Charm," went on to say: "The company tried to turn back the hands of the clock, and it cannot be done." The reviewer mocked the libretto, and while granting the opera had "many moments of interest as foreshadowing a greater Verdi," complained that "there is none of that contra melody that the real Verdi found when the melody in the orchestra vied in beauty with the melody in the throats of the singers."[45] After several more badly attended performances, caused in part perhaps by competition from the Pan-Pacific International Exposition, the company disbanded, with a chorus member suing the impresario for wages.[46]

Meanwhile, in the Metropolitan's Sunday Evening Concerts, 1883–1946, the first excerpt from *Lombardi* to be sung, on Christmas Eve 1905, was the chorus "O Signore dal tetto natio," and remarkably, it never again appeared. But in the years 1920 through 1930 the "conversion" trio was sung nine times, often by artists such as Rosa Ponselle, Beniamino Gigli, and the bass José Mardones, and apparently always with the violin introduction and *obbligato*.[47] In addition, on New Year's Eve 1930, the Victor Orchestra made a famous recording of the trio with Elisabeth Rethberg, Gigli, and Ezio Pinza, cutting the violin introduction (which would have required a second 78 rpm side) but keeping the violin's later interjections in the singing. Then on January 31, 1943, in New York, Toscanini included the trio (with the violin introduction) in his radio broadcast heard by millions. That rendition was transferred to disc in 1957 as part of a "Verdi and Toscanini" album (33 rpm), which was widely sold. Meanwhile an Italian company issued a recording of the complete opera, one of a series of Verdi's operas recorded during 1951, the fiftieth anniversary of his death, and in the years following, the opera had many productions in Europe, for eight years even achieving repertory status with the Welsh National Opera.[48] Early in 1972 still another complete recording appeared, and as part of the revival of interest in Verdi's early operas, a production in the United States soon seemed likely.[49]

The Opera Orchestra of New York made the first venture with a concert performance in Carnegie Hall on December 7, 1972. For the occasion the company's director, Eve Queler, cast three outstanding principals, Renata Scotto (soprano), José Carreras (tenor), and Paul Plishka (bass), and the performance, without scenery, costumes, or staging, was a triumph. Andrew Porter, writing in the *New Yorker*, expressed the feelings of many who heard it:

> Modern commentators ascribe much of the enthusiasm [for the opera in mid-nineteenth-century Italy] to the patriotic fervor of the time. Like Boito in his review of an 1864 revival at La Scala, they are ready to discern "the marvelous traces, here and there, of eternal beauty," but always there is a note of reserve. The odd thing is that no two writers agree on which passages are splendid and which not. I was not wholehearted about "I Lombardi" myself until, last week, Eve Queler directed a concert performance of the work in Carnegie Hall that swept away all resistance to the piece and made most of the objections to it seem trivial.[50]

Porter ascribed much of the evening's success, as did most critics, to the artistry of Scotto:

Figure 2.1. Eve Queler, music director and conductor of the Opera Orchestra of New York. Photograph by Steve J. Sherman. Photograph courtesy of Opera Orchestera of New York.

> She moved us all to a frenzy of excitement in the second-act finale [in Antioch], that startling scene in which Giselda declares that commercial interest, not morality, has prompted the invasion, and goes on to denounce "the impious holocaust of human corpses" and contradict Urban II's slogan, "*Deus le vault!*" [God wills it!], which launched the First Crusade, with her own cry of "*Dio nol vuole!*" [God does not will it!].[51]

As Peter G. Davis had noticed in reviewing the 1972 recording for *High Fidelity*, "Giselda . . . clearly interested Verdi and virtually every scene in which she participates comes alive."[52] This judgment was borne out by the opera's first staged production in the United States in sixty-four years, when the San Diego Opera, in June 1979, started its Verdi Festival, a proposed cycle of all of Verdi's operas, with three performances of *I Lombardi*.[53]

Attending one of them, Joseph Kerman, an academic critic thought by some to be rather hard-boiled about opera, was quite amazed at how moving the final scene of fraternal reconciliation "becomes on the stage." And further, he found Giselda's two speeches in that scene, first soothing the "bad" brother, her uncle who is dying, and then urging her father to reconcile, among "the earliest examples of Verdi transfixing a drama by means of short but enormously telling lyric phrases." To which he added, in a sentence deliciously designed to show what many think are the vices and virtues of his sort of analytic criticism: "I wept, collecting myself only so far as to observe how the passing modulation to E flat at the end of this C-major chorus echoes the single half-remote passing modulation in the other C-major chorus, 'O Signore, dal tetto natio,' also to E flat, just a few minutes earlier, and how much better it is managed rhythmically."[54]

Yet because, over all, the scenery and costumes, so important to nineteenth-century production of the opera, were exceptionally dreary, for many in the audience the production may have failed. As Martin Bernheimer concluded for the *Los Angeles Times*: "It wasn't much to look at. But much of it was wonderful to listen to."[55]

Then in April 1982, the New York City Opera, in a fit of bad judgment, imported San Diego's scenery and costumes but not its stellar cast, and had an artistic disaster. Without great singing, the scenery was all too noticeable, and according to the critic for the *Wall Street Journal*, the set was "an assortment of unattractive, spackled steps and platforms . . . and every time a scene ended, the turntable stage spun around revealing more steps virtually indistinguishable from the first set and provoking merciless laughter, hisses and finally boos from the audience."[56] The *Times* critic, after noting the audience's disapproval, observed: "The *I Lombardi* production that made its bow last night hit bottom in design and direction, and the singing was rarely more than acceptable."[57] Musically, too, some of the decisions were inartistic. The violin prelude to the "conversion" trio, for instance, was played as an "Entr'acte" between acts 3 and 4, so that it followed rather than preceded the trio, leaving all the violin's interjections into the trio proper without preamble or foundation.

As if to drive home the point that what *I Lombardi* must have, at very least, is good singing, the Opera Orchestra of New York gave it another concert performance in 1986, again well cast and again with success.[58] Imagine then the pleasure with which those who liked the opera greeted the Metropolitan's announcement of a production for its 1993–94 season. At last, a chance to join spectacle—those glamorous settings—with great singing.

In the event, the Metropolitan had an interesting failure, caused in part by bad luck and in part by questionable artistic decisions. The luck concerned the role of Giselda, given to Aprile Millo, who had scored a success with it in the Opera Orchestra's 1986 concert performance. But for the Met, in 1993, Millo was out of voice, and withdrew after the second performance, leaving the role to Lauren Flanigan, who sang it splendidly.[59] Aided by Samuel Ramey as the hermit and evil brother, she, like Scotto, made Giselda's scenes intense and exciting, but unhappily for her and for the opera, the first published reviews were all of the indisposed Millo. Moreover, Flanigan's young and ardent Muslim prince was played by the aging, arthritic Luciano Pavarotti, who despite the efforts of the other two principals sang his scenes as if in a concert performance.

He sang beautifully, and the thousands who had bought tickets to hear him cheered loudly, but likely they left the house without any sense of the opera's drama. (Or they left early, because he had no part in the final scene.) And so, at times, dissimilar readings of the opera seemed to play simultaneously, concert and drama, and to an audience similarly divided in interest.

Other questionable artistic decisions chiefly concerned the scenery, costumes, and stage direction, which seemed often to fight with the score and Verdi's directions for the settings. The critic for the *Times* reported:

> John Conklin's sets cut the opera loose from its historical moorings. Minimal detail is generally combined with gross exaggeration of a scenic element: a giant, crucified Christ hanging in the black space of a church, an enormous red pillar in a harem. When it comes to the River Jordan, the process has been reversed: its baptismal waters are contained in a cologne-size bottle. Dunya Ramicova's costumes are campy; the chorus of assassins looks like a force of foot soldiers from Teen-Age Mutant Ninja Turtles cartoons. . . . The director of this production [Mark Lamos] . . . evidently wanted to emphasize the condemnatory aspect of Verdi's score. He has created an airless, abstract world in which no opportunity is lost to fill the stage with blood-red crosses, which accumulate like grave markers.[60]

Conversely, Paul Griffiths in the *New Yorker* liked the scenery, staging, and costumes:

> The roughness in the piece may be the roughness of a raw . . . creativity, but it's a roughness that fits all too well, almost sinisterly well, with the dramatic proceedings as realized by Mr. Lamos. Several of the Holy Land scenes are dominated by ranks of coarse-cut crosses, covered with the scarlet loss of new blood—and we remember that the priests of the Sant'Ambrogio scene were also vested in brilliant scarlet. What we have here is a portrayal of the Church Militant as the Church Barbaric. The tableau of crosses, an image that's repeated until the very end of the opera, comes on each time seeming more threatening, in an appalling crescendo that's thoroughly in keeping with the music. Nastiness on this scale may not be what Verdi intended, but it's the way he sounds, and in making the nastiness functional—in fixing it on the crusaders—Mr. Lamos puts a little power into the dramatic shambles of the score. He also provides—faint praise though this must be—the most thought-provoking new production at this theatre in a couple of seasons.[61]

Griffiths opened, without closing, some interesting questions. Should we ignore the composer's clear intent? Can we, without injury to the opera? In what way, as Griffiths claims, does Verdi's music speak counter to his stated intent? In the opera's famous third-act chorus, for instance, "Gerusalem! la grande, la promessa città," crusaders and bare-headed pilgrims (men and women) enter in

Figure 2.2. Act 3, scene 1, of the Metropolitan Opera's 1993 production of *I Lombardi*: "Gerusalem! La grande, la promessa città." Photograph by Winnie Klotz. Courtesy of the Metropolitan Opera Archives.

a procession, singing of Jerusalem in hushed, awed tones, and the music (slow march time), despite some words about "blood well spent" and "a God terrible in war," and despite some loud phrases, never becomes aggressive, fiery, or triumphant. Rather, it is yearning and reverent, and, as the procession passes, it ends softly, with a repeated: "Gerusalem!" Verdi, in his stage directions stated that "in the distance can be seen Jerusalem." But at the Metropolitan, instead of the distant city, the audience saw, hanging directly over the heads of the crusaders and pilgrims, a blizzard of blood-red crosses that called into question the crusaders' purpose and the pilgrims' religious spirit.

Similarly, in the opera's final scene, when the good and the evil brother (the hermit) are reconciled and to satisfy the latter's request the tent's side is opened, Verdi directed that we should see Jerusalem, now close to, in the morning light, with Christian banners flying. At the Metropolitan, however, the reconciliation, the hermit's dying, and the final chorus to music of majestic affirmation all played out beneath a huge crucifix, with a Christ suffering not the usual single gash in his side but a multitude of wounds added by the crusade. Observed Manuela Hoelterhoff, in the *Wall Street Journal*, "The opera ends with the brothers reunited under a plastic crucifix so hideous I was surprised they didn't chuck their weapons and convert to Islam on the spot."[62] Again, musically, scenically the Metropolitan offered conflicting conceptions of the opera, each undercutting the other.

In October 2005, in Florence, Italy, another company pushed this divided view of the opera still further. As Stephen Hastings of *Opera News* reported, it "attempted to update the opera as a denunciation of present-day 'crusades' in the Middle East. The opening scene evoked Ground Zero rather than the Basilica of Sant'Ambrogio in Milan, and the episodes in the Holy Land emerged as a critical commentary on the war in Iraq." Julian Budden, for *Opera*, wrote: "Costumes were modern, with only the crusaders allowed martial gear, so the struggle with the Muslims was unequal from the start (it probably was so in 1099). More questionable was a series of vignettes, obtained from sliding panels, of individual acts of brutality (some of them culled from today's newspapers) committed on the unarmed infidel by crusading soldiery during the battle interlude." Neither critic thought the concept a success, and both thought the evening saved by good singing. Budden even remarked that the singing "may have led many of us to view the work more kindly than before."[63]

The Metropolitan presented its 1993–94 production for ten performances in the home house, including national radio and television broadcasts, and in the spring gave a single concert performance in Frankfurt, Germany, where the trio was encored. Then the production was dropped, and not as yet (2009) revived. Compared to the company's achievement with *Macbeth* and later with *Nabucco*, its effort over *Lombardi*, despite its superb orchestral sound and solo violin, was confused and failed. It neither built an enthusiastic audience in New York nor stirred companies elsewhere to try the opera.

Alex Ross, in the *New Yorker*, may have had this production in mind in writing "Verdi's Grip, Why the Shakespeare of Grand Opera Resists Radical Staging." "Many of the directors who now dominate the opera scene do not know what they are doing. . . . Chances are, any Verdi opera you saw this year took the form of a revisionist production that was at odds with the composer's raging sincerity. One prominent director has been quoted as saying, 'Nobody comes to Verdi for the plots.' More likely, people come to Verdi because he meant every word."[64] In this respect, despite simple scenery and costumes, the New York Grand Opera in its 1995 summer production, though with little-known singers, smaller orchestra, and outdoors in Central Park, by accepting the opera's naiveté did better by it than the Metropolitan.[65]

Figure 2.3. Act 4, final scene of the Metropolitan Opera's 1993 production of *I Lombardi*. Photograph by Winnie Klotz. Courtesy of the Metropolitan Opera Archives.

Figure 2.4. Act 4 of the New York Grand Opera's 1995 production of *I Lombardi*, with Cynthia Springsteen (left, as Giselda); Gerard Powers (center, as Alvino), and Valentin Peytchinov (right, as Pagano). Photograph by Zulema Morin. Courtesy of the New York Grand Opera Company.

Yes, Giselda "clearly interested Verdi" and so her scenes come "alive." But in her most powerful scene, her condemnation of the crusade, she rails as against God's will only the military side of the crusade. She does not question her own faith or a general belief in Christian doctrine, as witness later her sincere participation in the conversion trio and her effort to reconcile in forgiveness her father and her uncle. And until stage directors and designers are willing to accept Verdi's view of the first crusade—the military force arguably wrong but the pilgrims' faith, yearning for Jerusalem, and doctrine of forgiveness, essentially right—*I Lombardi* may resist revival.

Chapter Three

Ernani

When the Italian Opera Company of Havana came on tour to the United States in April 1847, it surpassed all expectations. It not only at once set higher standards for vocal and instrumental performance, but on opening night in New York had a triumph with new music, the U.S. premiere of Verdi's *Ernani* (1844). The company was the creation of the immensely rich Marty y Torrens, who had used his fortune (based on a monopoly of the sale of fish in Cuba) to build an opera house in Havana, the opulent Gran Teatro de Tacón (capacity 3,000), and to staff it with Italian artists. In the summers of 1837 and 1842, its predecessor company in Havana had played short seasons in New Orleans, but in 1843, after reorganization by Marty, it had made a tour to seven of the country's southern and eastern cities.[1] Now, four years later, it came further strengthened in singers, orchestra, and chorus, and when landing in New York after a ten-day voyage, it numbered seventy-three,[2] a total soon increased by hiring at least ten more artists locally. Moreover, in addition to its small, non-musical staff, the company included besides soloists, two artistic leaders on the brink of fame, the violinist Luigi Arditi and double bassist Giovanni Bottesini, an orchestra of thirty-two (sometimes enlarged by local recruits), and a small but highly proficient chorus of twenty (four sopranos, three altos, six tenors, and seven basses).[3] Further, it brought its own scenery and a wardrobe of costumes that the *New York Herald* reported to be "worth $30,000."[4] And on opening night, at the city's Park Theatre (capacity 2,300; on Park Row, facing City Hall Park), it proved itself the most complete, best Italian opera company yet to play in the United States.[5]

Teasing New Yorkers, it gave only two performances of opera, on April 15 and 16, and a subsequent concert before departing for a six-week season in Boston. For both staged performances in New York it offered *Ernani*, Verdi's fifth opera but only the second to reach the United States. Six weeks earlier, in a much smaller theater, a local company had produced his fourth, *I Lombardi alla prima crociata* (1843). But where that opera's success had been substantial but soon fading, that of *Ernani* was stupendous and promised to be lasting. A young Manhattan lawyer, George Templeton Strong, failing to get into the second performance, noted in his diary: "House an entire jam; no seats to be had at any price."[6] And he had to wait until June for the company's return.

Opening in Boston's Howard Athenaeum theater with *Ernani* on April 23, the company subsequently presented Verdi's *I Lombardi* (city premiere) and *I due Foscari* (U.S. premiere), Donizetti's *Linda di Chamounix*, Pacini's *Saffo*,

HOWARD ATHENÆUM

FOURTH NIGHT OF THE SECOND AND LAST SEASON

—OF THE—

ITALIAN OPERA COMPANY

FROM HAVANA,

CONSISTING OF 73 PERSONS.

LAST NIGHT OF HERNANI.

☞In compliance with the request of many frequenters of the Opera to witness once more Verdi's Grand Opera of HERNANI, and every other evening of the season being appropriated, it will be produced for the last time, on *Wednesday Evening, May* 19th, 1847. Romeo & Juliet will consequently be withdrawn.

Wednesday Evening, May 19th,

Will be performed, last time in this city, Verdi's Grand Opera, in 4 acts, called

HERNANI!

—OR—

THE CASTILIAN NOBLE!

Dramatis Personae.

HERNANI, the banished - - - - -	Sig. NATALE PERELLI
DON CARLOS, king of Spain - - - - -	LUIGI VITA
DON RUY GOMEZ DE SILVA - - - -	PIETRO NOVELLI
ELVIRA, niece of the bride - - -	Signa. FORTUNATA TEDESCO
GIOVANA, the nurse - - - - -	Signa. TEODOLINDA GERLI
DON RICARDO, officer of the king - - -	Sig. FEDERICO BADIALI
IAGO, officer of Silva - - - - - -	Sig. PIETRO CANDI

Chorus of Ladies and Gentlemen, Mountaineers, Banditti Knights, Servants to Silva, Knights of the King, Followers of the League, Spanish and German Nobles, Pages, Electors, Soldiers, &c. &c.

Tomorrow, Thursday Evening, will be presented for the first time, Verdi's Grand Opera, *THE LOMBARDS AT THE FIRST CRUSADE.*

☞Parquette 50 cents ; Boxes 50 cents ; Second Circle 50 cents.
☞Doors open at 7 o'clock ; the Opera will commence at 1-4 to 8 o'clock.☜
☞Books, containing an English version of the Opera, can be had at the Box Door. Price 12½ cents.

☞ The Choice of Seats will be sold at Public Auction, in the Vestibule of the Athenæum, on THURSDAY MORNING, at 10 o'clock.

CLARK & HATCH, Auctioneers.

Figure 3.1. Playbill for *Ernani*, premiere season in Boston, 1847. The bill's "second" season is merely the extension of the original, subscription run; and Elvira is not "niece of the bride" but of Silva. Reproduced by permission from the Boston Athenaeum. "Hernani," the title of Hugo's underlying play.

Bellini's *Norma* and *Romeo and Juliet* (I Capuleti ed i Montecchi), and, once each onstage and in concert, Rossini's *Mosè in Egitto*. Of them all, *Ernani* roused the greatest excitement. One Bostonian, Samuel Eliot, entered in his *Diary* in the midst of the second week of performances: "I am *going it hard*, glad while the sun shines to make my hay. Monday, *Hernani*, Verdi's beautiful Opera. Tuesday, *Hernani*. Last night Donizetti's *Linda di Chamounix*, a very second rate opera. . . . But the worst opera, I think, would have some charm for me, who have hungered & thirsted too long to refuse even a dry crust, if it had been offered me."[7]

Six years later, the critic for the *Boston Evening Gazette*, William W. Clapp Jr., summarized the importance to Boston's musical life of those *Ernani* performances:

It was on this occasion that Boston first recognized genuine Italian Opera. . . . A superb orchestra led by Arditi and the superlative contrabassist Bottesini, with a good chorus and principals of extraordinary merit, presented Verdi's best opera in a style that absolutely electrified the audience. All the recollections of English opera[8] were effaced by this life-breathing, passionate, and effective performance, and from that hour a new ideal of excellence in operatic affairs became fixed and irrevocable. Such a combination of brilliancy, effect, and vigor, with the sentimental and tender, had never before revealed itself upon the Boston lyric stage, and the excitement produced by this new sensation was commensurate with the marvels that produced it.

The opera itself was interesting from a wild and romantic plot, worked up in a good libretto, and that innate beauty had been most effectively treated by the composer.

So masterly was the orchestration and the introduction of novel, yet most pleasing combinations, modulations, and octaves, with an exquisite skill in use of solo talent in aid of a masterly conceived partition, that, strong as prejudice had been against its composer, this opera instantly commanded admiration, disarmed prejudice, and gave Verdi universal popularity.[9]

Although most of the New York critics, in reviewing their two April performances, had shared Clapp's enthusiasm for the company and opera, one who had not was Richard Grant White of the *Morning Courier and New-York Enquirer*. After praising the singers, he wrote of the composer:

Of the opera we can only say, that it is a pity such singing and such splendid appointments should be lavished on such bad music, without any quality to recommend it but its extravagance, and which is "nothing if not singular." Never was there heard such *stuff*. . . . One cannot sit and listen to it without feeling a strong inclination to murder the composer, or at least to rise up, throw down his hat, and relieve himself by a strong expressing of his feelings . . . [and he proposed for his tombstone] "HE LIKED NOT VERDI."[10]

On the company's return to New York, where it again opened with *Ernani*, the critics promptly fell into argument, not only damning and praising the singers, the opera, the composer, and even the public who esteemed them, but each other. Finally, "A Native Citizen" wrote to the *Herald*, suggesting the critics "write no more":

> I heard "Hernani" . . . before and since the Boston trip. I went the first time, induced to go by the praises of these gentlemen, which however extravagant they appeared in print, were yet verified by the reality. I went the second time of my own volition, and found the second representation equal to the first. Not so with these aforesaid critics. . . . Poor Verdi is no favorite, either, with these "learned Thebans." His melodies, that at the present time in England and on the continent have found access to every heart have too much "color" for them. His music never "comes betwixt the wind and their nobility," without receiving the honor of a broadside.[11] . . . Music, like eloquence, is of the first impression, we feel it instantly or not at all. That the people of New York feel the music of this *troupe*, as they never felt any before, is proved by crowded houses, in the month of June.[12]

In July, after a "season" of twelve performances at the Park Theatre, with *Ernani* sung four times, once more than any other opera, the company departed for Philadelphia, the third of the three cities then said to form jointly the country's "musical capital"—with New Orleans excluded only because outmatched by the three in population almost ten to one and isolated by its distance apart.[13] In Philadelphia, at the Walnut Street Theatre (still in use), the Havana company gave eighteen performances, with five of *Ernani* (city premiere), again more than any other opera, and again with success, though perhaps not so great as in Boston or New York.[14] Returning to New York, the company settled into the Castle Garden Theatre,[15] opening on August 18 with *Ernani* and closing on September 17, also with *Ernani*. In all, it offered twenty-one nights of opera and a concert to display the instrumental skills of Arditi and Bottesini. Of the nine operas presented, Bellini had the most, three, for a total of eight performances; and Verdi, two (*Ernani* and *I due Foscari*), for a total of six, but of all operas, *Ernani* with four was the most frequently played.

Finally, the company went again to Boston for a short season, which, according to Clapp, was not so successful as the first: "Novelty no longer attracted the curious and those eager for a new sensation, while the confidence of control over their audience betrayed the singers into levity and indifferent treatment of the music intrusted to them."[16] And after a single Farewell Concert in New York, the company sailed for Havana on the steamer *Guadalquiver*, having toured for six months and, according to the *Herald*, presented "118 operatic performances."[17]

Yet in New York, despite what might have seemed a surfeit of *Ernani*—ten performances in five months—the public had appetite for more. On November 22, 1847, a company formed locally to inaugurate the new Astor Place

Opera House[18] chose to open with *Ernani*, which it played for five consecutive nights, and the New York critics, far from being bored with the opera, hurried again to hurl their darts at one and all.

In the *Albion*, Henry Cood Watson judged the new company "much inferior" to its predecessor and described its prima donna, Teresa Truffi, as "handsome and well formed, with a noble stage figure, not very youthful, but well matured in her powers. She has some good points and many—very many—faults."[19] White of the *Courier and Enquirer* conversely praised the company and its production, noting that the opera's finale had won an encore, but again assailed the composer. In Verdi he could detect only "beauties of an inferior sort," and urged those who disliked his music to hold their tongues, for Verdi's "poverty of invention, meager effect, and lack of learning would soon work his own destruction. But like a top, if beaten, he will only stand up the longer and hum the louder." Moreover,

> Our chief reason for fault finding is, that Verdi is *not* romantic, is *not* new, but tries to be classic by distorting and elaborating the hackneyed phrases of the feeblest romantic school. At rare times he gives a pleasing imitation of some really great master, but it is so palpably an imitation that we welcome it only as calling to mind something better; witness the tomb scene in *Ernani*, which is too much like the incantation scene in *Robert le Diable*, for the similarity to escape anyone. Verdi's efforts are almost continually apparent. He is determined to be great. He strives for the dignified but attains only the tumid; he would be grand but is only grandiose. He has one contrivance upon which he continually depends for majestic effect. It is to walk up the scale with noisy strides, and then leap down through the seventh in a ponderous staccato. This is very well for once, but we soon surfeit of it, for it is introduced everywhere even in solos. The most striking point in "Ernani, involami" is produced by it. In short, Verdi is a musical coxcomb; but he effects not pretty trappings, and dons a classical toga. Forgetting that he has made it of shred and patches and incongruous remnants, he thinks he resembles a classic statue, when in fact he is more like a Greek scare-crow.[20]

Besides lampooning Verdi as a top and a scarecrow, White sought to reveal how the music sounded to one who revered Handel and Mozart, a view stated with remarkable clarity by lawyer Strong in his diary:

> *Norma* is an opera decidedly worth hearing more than once, and except for the *Giuramento* [Mercadante] and *Sonnambula*, I scarcely know another of the modern Italian operas I've heard that I can say so much for. As a class, they seem to make no pretensions either to harmony or instrumentation, and their melodies (where they're not stolen, as they often are, most audaciously) are languid and weak, and seem to have been cast in the same mold, so that I can't remember them separately, but get the themes of *Lucia* and *Lucrezia* [both Donizetti] and the rest of them all mixed up together in my head—the end of any one air seeming to suit perfectly the beginning of any other.

This isn't the same with Verdi's music, to be sure. His melodies, original or not, have distinction and character. But though they often have a strong dramatic or melodramatic expression, they seem to me to want feeling and *musical* expression. There is a mechanical tone about them, as if they had been elaborated and put together by some music-writing machine. And to compensate for this want of freshness and vital power he, of course, does what all artists whose faculties don't carry them above mediocrity are driven to do—tries to make it up by perpetual intensity, exaggeration, and excitement from beginning to end. He never ventures on the dignity of repose, but puts on all the steam he can raise and keeps up a ceaseless torrent of forcible-feeble emphasis, passion, and vehemence till one is weary of him as of an author who deals only in italics, large capitals, dashes and interjection marks.[21]

Yet, as Strong admits, he found the music effective and memorable; and as history records, the opera was extraordinarily popular, wherever it played. In considering its reception in the United States (see appendix B), let three examples suffice. First, the New York-based Astor Place Company, in its 1850–51 season, which included tours to Boston, Philadelphia, Baltimore, Charleston, and Augusta, Georgia, gave more performances of *Ernani* (20) than of any other opera. Following it were *Lucrezia Borgia* (16), *Lucia di Lammermoor* (16), *Norma* (13), and *La favorita* (11). It is notable, too, that in the company's repertory of fifteen operas, typical of its day, Donizetti had five, Bellini three, Rossini two, and Verdi only one—in part because until the late 1850s, *Ernani* had no competition from Verdi's great trio, *Rigoletto*, *Trovatore*, and *Traviata*. Thus, for almost a decade, for most Americans on the country's East Coast, except those in the three large northeastern cities, *Ernani* was all there was of Verdi onstage.[22]

Second, another touring company, calling itself the New York Opera Company,[23] in 1853–54 took the opera to many cities in Canada and the U.S. Midwest. This tour of fourteen months was the first of such length and the precursor of a sort that would flourish for almost a hundred years. Moreover, the company's city of origin hints at New York's emergence as the country's preeminent musical capital, for the coimpresarios, Rosa DeVriès, a soprano, and Luigi Arditi, formerly the first violinist and codirector of the Havana company, recruited their musicians there. According to Thomas G. Kaufman, who has uncovered much of what we know about this venture, the artists probably numbered about forty, which Kaufman suggests "must have included about six principals plus chorus and orchestra."[24] In Chicago, however, the company grandly advertised itself as offering "a very effective chorus of ladies and gentlemen—the best in the United States of America and desirable even in Europe. . . . The Orchestra is composed of solo performers, and all professors of the highest standing—over 40 in number."[25]

Whatever the true number—and perhaps some local musicians had been added—the company's size compared to the only previous one to play in

Chicago, by then a city of thirty thousand, was immense. In July 1850 a troupe of three or four artists, coming from Milwaukee by ship, had arrived without any chorus or orchestra. Hiring the Rice Theatre's band, perhaps six or eight players, and some local singers who "undertook to perform one or two choruses," the troupe had performed *Sonnambula* to a packed house of the city's leading citizens. The next night, another full house and again *Sonnambula*, but soon after the start of the second act an adjacent building caught fire. The flames crossed to Rice's wooden theater, and though the audience and artists got safely out, in thirty minutes the building "was a heap of ashes."[26] After which, Chicago had no opera until the arrival in October 1853 of the Arditi–DeVriès company.

In all, so far as Kaufman could discover—and there are gaps in the record—this company visited at least twenty-three cities, five of them twice. Some of these, such as Baltimore, Charleston, and Savannah had already heard Italian singers in Italian opera, and for sophisticated New Orleans, Arditi joined forces with another touring group, offering a larger chorus and orchestra, and a greater variety of soloists. But to many cities, the Arditi–DeVriès company offered a first experience, or almost, of Italian opera: Montreal, Toronto, Rochester, Buffalo, Cleveland, Chicago, Milwaukee, Detroit, Saint Louis, and Nashville. Of the twelve operas in the company's repertory, eight were by Donizetti and Bellini, with the most frequently performed: *Norma* (25 times), *Lucia* and *Lucrezia Borgia* (24 each), *Sonnambula* (21), and *Ernani* (11). It was the only Verdi work staged on the tour and received its city premieres in Montreal, Buffalo, Cincinnati, Louisville, New Orleans, St. Louis, and Pittsburgh. In St. Louis, where it opened the season on September 26, 1853, the *Daily Democrat* reported: "With the entertainment generally we were much pleased. The orchestra is full, and in perfect practice. The precision and scrupulous correctness of its performances provoked the admiration of every lover of music. The choruses of *Ernani* gave equal satisfaction. We may particularize the opening chorus as especially well rendered and effective." The critic then went on to complain of the soloists' inadequate acting, adding "we allude to [the entertainment's] discrepancies only to convey an idea of the general character of the troupe."[27] But the opera had a success, for the company later repeated it and, on returning to St. Louis in the spring, played it again.

And for the third example of the opera's reception in the United States, note its record in San Francisco, where for many years touring artists, more often than not, arrived without orchestra or chorus, relying on local musicians to fill their needs. In the years 1851 through 1880, among Verdi's operas, *Ernani* ranked second in number of performances: *Trovatore* (100), *Ernani* (72), *Traviata* (59), *Ballo* (33), and *Rigoletto* (18). Not until 1897 did *Traviata* overtake it, so that it finished the nineteenth century ranking third: *Trovatore* (282), *Traviata* (154), and *Ernani* (150)—still well ahead of *Ballo* (103) and *Rigoletto* (86).[28]

In seeking the roots of this popularity, consider first one that is nonmusical. Clapp, in Boston, had praised the opera's "wild and romantic plot, worked up in a good libretto." And indeed, the opera, based on Victor Hugo's play *Hernani*, is wild, romantic, and with a message. In the preface to his play Hugo defined the Romantic Movement, of which the play is a famous example, as "liberalism in literature." Romanticism in the arts, he asserted, would "not be less popular than in politics. Liberty in Art, liberty in Society." Moreover, the revolution would be led by the young, routing conservatives who "will in vain help each other to restore the old system, literary and social, broken to pieces."[29]

The opera, which takes place in Spain in 1519, puts this message onstage in a story of three men and a woman. The woman and two of the men are young; and the third man, old—and by "young" and "old," both Hugo and Verdi meant no more than nineteen and perhaps forty or forty-five.[30] All three men love Elvira (soprano), niece and ward of the old man, a Spanish grandee mellifluously named Don Ruy Gomez de Silva (bass). One young man, Don Juan of Aragon, has been proscribed by the king of Spain and is living as a bandit under the name "Ernani" (tenor); the other is the king of Spain, Don Carlo (baritone). All three offer Elvira marriage, and her uncle and guardian, against her wish, plans to wed her in the morning, an act both Ernani and the king hope to prevent. On the night before the wedding, as she waits in Silva's castle for Ernani to steal her away, the king in disguise, by threatening her maid, gains entry to her "apartment." When she scorns him, he tries to abduct her, but is stopped by the sudden appearance, through a secret door, of—Ernani! Male rage, taunts, hands to swords, and thrusting herself between the men, Elvira with dagger drawn, threatening, if they do not desist, to kill herself! Silva enters, shocked and shamed to discover two men in Milady's bedroom! The room fills with his retainers (mixed chorus), and a messenger, shown in, astonishes all by addressing the disguised Don Carlo as king. Whereupon Carlo resolves the awkward situation, at least somewhat, by claiming to have come incognito to consult privately with Silva on a political matter (leading Silva to kneel in homage), and with a second fib preserves Elvira's honor by claiming Ernani to be his attendant.

In act 2, another confrontation of principals: in return for Silva's aid in escaping from the king, Ernani pledges to kill himself whenever Silva, by sounding a horn, shall so demand. And he gives Silva his hunting horn, but first, together, they will pursue Don Carlo, who has abducted Elvira. In act 3, in the crypt of the cathedral at Aix-la-Chapelle, before Charlemagne's tomb, Carlo ponders his dreams of greatness, and then enters the tomb or at least its shadows, from which, undetected, he overhears conspirators, led by Silva and Ernani, plotting to kill him. A canon booms, and the crypt fills with dignitaries (outnumbering the conspirators) accompanied by ladies of the court, all come to tell Carlo of his election as Holy Roman Emperor. Emerging from the tomb, Carlo reveals the conspiracy and proposes to execute its leaders, but in response to a plea by Elvira, and desiring to emulate Charlemagne, he instead grants an amnesty. In the same spirit, and to Silva's fury, he gives Elvira to her beloved bandit, whose lands and titles are restored. And in a grand choral finale all praise the new emperor, Charles V.

In the final act Ernani and Elvira are walking in his palace garden while their wedding guests celebrate indoors—and Silva, at first offstage, but continually nearer, repeatedly sounds the horn. Despite the lovers' pleas, Silva is implacable, and Ernani, to redeem his pledge, to satisfy Spanish honor, kills himself. Elvira faints, and the curtain falls (or should) on Silva standing alone, like the last column of a Greek temple amid its ruins.[31]

The message is clear: all the prating about Spanish honor is misplaced loyalty to a feudal, aristocratic code long out of date, and which, for three of the story's characters, destroys their lives. The only one of the four to achieve a useful, happy life is Don Carlo who, as the modern man, transcends those values. Thus, the story allows its audience to revel in nostalgia for the values of days gone by, so colorful and rhetorical, even while dismissing them as oh, so foolish, a message sure to appeal to the young everywhere, and very much to Americans establishing a new egalitarian society.

Of the opera's musical roots to popularity, one was noted at what seems to have been the first public performance in the United States of any of Verdi's music. In May 1846, a year before the arrival of the Cuban company, a soprano, Rosina Pico, in a concert at the Apollo Theater on May 14, sang two arias of Verdi.[32] The first was Elvira's cavatina (opening scene and entrance aria), sung in her room in Silva's castle and in which she longs for Ernani to save her from Silva's horrid embrace: "Ernani! Ernani, involami all'abborrito amplesso."

In what seems to be the earliest critique in the United States of Verdi's music, Richard Grant White for the *Courier and Enquirer* remarked: "The cavatina from Verdi's *Ernani*, though nothing more than pleasing as a composition, offers scope for the exhibition of fine vocalism, which Signora Pico improved: her mode of giving one passage, passing from the upper to the lower extreme of her voice, being wonderfully effective, and bringing down an instantaneous burst of applause."[33]

Thus was noted promptly a thumbprint of Verdi's style, his hitching the outer limits of a singer's vocal range to dramatic purpose, with big jumps on the scale, up and down. Up on the steal-me-away of "Ernani, involami"; down to a guttural snarl on the "aborrito amplesso," the loathsomeness of Silva's embrace. Verdi liked such sudden contrasts, and to singers who would sing the words and not merely seek a beautiful sound he offered drama. Indeed, to such an extent that the opera has been summarized: "A youthful, passionate female voice is besieged by three male voices, each of which establishes a specific relationship with it."[34] Clearly, the New York audience in 1846, though hearing "Ernani, involami" for the first time, instinctively responded to Elvira's surge of love and shiver of loathing. Verdi was not the first to write such music, but he did so more frequently and more dramatically than his predecessors.

Moreover, as the Verdi scholar Julian Budden and others have noted, the opera gains unity by the continual upward leap of its melodies, soaring on strong rhythms that move the music forward.[35] Consider, for example, the chief phrase of the finale to act 3 in which Elvira and ladies of the Spanish court, dignitaries of the Holy Roman Empire, and conspirators just pardoned by Don Carlo, all join in praising the newly elected emperor, Carlo Quinto, Charles V.

The notes, up and down the scale, are punched out in a manner that may have led Strong to write in his diary that although Verdi's melodies "have a strong dramatic or melodramatic expression, they seem to me to want feeling and *musical* expression." Yet the melodies, he added, had "distinction and character." This third act, in Charlemagne's tomb, with two arias for the baritone, a chorus for the conspirators, and a finale with every singer onstage, became very popular in the United States. In 1848 in Philadelphia, another diarist, the merchant Joseph I. Sill, who, like Strong, admired Bellini, privately noted after first hearing *Ernani:* "The music of this opera does not please me, except the finale of the 3rd act, which is very grand."[36] And in Philadelphia that year a visiting company from New York, after presenting *Ernani* three times in March, returned briefly in August to offer twice, as part of a double bill, just the third act.[37]

One of the opera's great virtues is the evenhandedness with which Verdi presents its four characters and the men's chorus (appearing first as bandits and later as conspirators). Each is given several moments of glory, and the first for Silva comes in act 1, when he discovers two men in Elvira's apartment and sings: "Infelice! e tu credevi" (Unhappy man! And you believed her such a beautiful and immaculate lily!). His melody does not leap up the scale, as do those for the younger characters, but slowly, painfully rises, as befits an elderly grandee struggling with disbelief and disappointment.

Later, in the opera's final scene, as Silva demands Ernani's suicide, a good singing actor can make the old man's icy hauteur the incarnation of aristocratic malevolence. One such, who sang the part often in the United States, was Ignazio Marini,[38] and Walt Whitman, who numbered the opera among his favorites, recalled: "De Sylva, the proud old Spaniard—how well it is represented by Marini, a magnificent artist! The haughty attitudes, the fiery breath, the hate, despair, and fiendish revenge—never did we realize an old Spanish hidalgo till we saw Marini play Ruy Gomez de Sylva."[39] So dominating were Marini's performances that a critic could cite the role as "one of the finest, histrionically speaking, on the lyric stage," while dismissing the title role as "not a first rate part for a tenor."[40] And for a number of years in the late 1840s and early 1850s Marini even was given top billing in announcements of the opera.[41]

In the next decade of its history in the country, however, the focus shifted back to tenors, and Whitman, mightily impressed by two of them, put in a poem, "I see where Ernani walking the bridal garden, / Amid the scent of night-roses, radiant, holding his bride by the hand, / Hears the infernal call, the death-pledge of the horn."[42] Still later, in the 1880s when Adelina Patti was singing Elvira in New York, despite her fame and talents, at the close of the third act, critical attention and audience applause focused not on her but on Antonio Galassi, the baritone singing Don Carlo.[43] Small wonder singers of the four vocal categories have been drawn to the opera: If good, they will shine.

By the mid-1880s, however, some of the city's advanced thinkers and cognoscenti, under the impact of Wagner, were beginning to think *Ernani* "old-fashioned."[44] Though the term was the one most often used, by itself it says little, for are not Mozart or Gluck, in adhering to their conventions, also "old-fashioned?" A later critic, Paul Henry Lang, was more specific in his *Critic at the Opera*, where, speaking of *Ernani*, he noted its plain and sometimes crude orchestration, the simple introductions to the arias, and a lack of what he called "motivic unity."

> While an early work . . . it presents something of Verdi as we know him, if rather sketchily and with a strength that is more potential than actual. The building of motivic unity which characterizes the mature works is still undeveloped, only one of the figures of the drama, the King, being fully delineated, and not consistently so; and in contrast to *Rigoletto*, or other later works, the characterization is perhaps interesting but seldom moving. The introductions to the arias merely give the pitch to the singer; they represent a perfunctory vestige of the old "motto aria" beginning, of which Verdi made excellent use in his later operas. Still noticeable is the plain orchestra commentary, serviceable but often awkward, and the crude use of the brasses and percussion can be disconcerting.[45]

The public in 1883, however, still responded to *Ernani* and to what has been described as "the hot vigor of the drama, and the quick cooperation of music in its climacteric moments."[46] And despite the rumbles of disapproval that were beginning to be heard, a critic for the *Times* in 1883, in reviewing a Patti performance, could still call the opera "one of the finest in the whole Italian repertory."[47] Yet others who thought differently were gaining prominence. In the autumn of 1885 an English critic, the Reverend Hugh Reginald Haweis, who wrote music criticism for the *Pall Mall Gazette* and the *Echo*, and had published a much-read book titled *Music and Morals* (1873) as well as *My Musical Life* (1884), was invited to New York by several clubs to speak on a number of subjects including opera.[48] At the Nineteenth Century Club he spoke on Wagner, and according to one who heard him, he assured his audience that the days of Italian opera were numbered; in future, all opera would be Wagnerian in style.[49]

The public and some impresarios disagreed, and for a number of years *Ernani* continued to be given frequently, not only in New York, San Francisco, and the country's larger cities but by touring groups in the smaller ones.[50] Yet in 1903, when New York's Metropolitan Opera, by then the country's premier company, produced *Ernani* for the first time, though the opera did exceptionally well at the box office,[51] it did not unite the critics in praise. One in the *Herald*, in an unsigned review, found "something refreshing" in the evening. "It was a harkening back to the good old days when musical scores had no inconvenient continuity, nor plots troublesome dramatic unities to be preserved; when the prima donna's first entrance might be applauded to the echo, or the tenor's pet aria successfully redemanded; and the large and brilliant audience enjoyed itself in the good old way."[52] Yet the more magisterial Richard Aldrich at the *Times*, though acknowledging that the house was full and the audience enthusiastic, complained: "*Ernani* dates from the earliest years of Verdi's creative activity. . . . It is full of the luxuriant melody of Verdi's early style with the insistent rhythm and the unceasing beat of the orchestra to emphasize it, melody at every opportunity without the remotest connection with the dramatic situation, melody intended to be sung at the gallery from the footlights, and invariably so sung last evening. . . . In 1882 *Ernani* was considered an extremely old-fashioned work, and much water has passed under the bridges since then!"[53]

"Melody," wrote Aldrich, "without the remotest connection with the dramatic situation." Yet anyone examining the score or listening, say, to the opera's finale (a scene for Ernani and Elvira followed by a trio for them and Silva), will discover a flow of melody in which key, tempo, and dynamic continually change to give point to the words and drama. Perhaps familiarity with the opera had deafened the ears of critics to its virtues. Wagner had set a new style of opera, and at the start of the twentieth century he and his works dominated the Metropolitan repertory.[54]

When the Hammerstein Opera Company performed *Ernani* in New York on December 11, 1907, the *Herald* the next morning headlined its unsigned comments: "Good Old *Ernani* Sung Once More. After Five Years New York Operagoers in the Manhattan [opera house] Enjoy Verdi's Old Fashioned Tunes. Receive It With Applause." But further on, the critic's true opinion burst through: "The kind of melodies at which the younger generation of operagoers now turn up their noses were gratefully received with applause, and those who enjoyed it did not mind in the least how hackneyed this music sounded to the musical other half. . . . It [the opera] frankly belongs to another generation of opera and of operagoers."[55]

With that as a death notice, those who claimed to distinguish worth from dross put the opera out of mind. The public, however, still hankered after the "hot drama" and the melodies. Increasingly deprived of productions onstage, it turned to the Victor Talking Machine Company's recordings of the arias and

Figure 3.2. Marcella Sembrich, in costume for Elvira in the Metropolitan production of 1903. Note the style of the costume, more English Edwardian than Spanish sixteenth-century. Photograph courtesy of the Metropolitan Opera Archives.

choruses, of which in 1912 the company found it worthwhile to advertise some forty-five, far more than it offered of most operas.[56]

No doubt, this demonstration of steady support, along with the evident eagerness of singers to sing the opera, in part led to the Metropolitan's revival of it on December 8, 1921, with sumptuous new scenery by Joseph Urban and a starry cast: Rosa Ponselle (Elvira), Giovanni Martinelli (Ernani), Giuseppe Danise (Don Carlo), and José Mardones (Silva). Once again, the audience roared its approval, but Aldrich in the *Times*, complained of the opera much as he had in 1903, adding now of the current singers that they "had not the clearest perception of the style of the work." He scolded Ponselle in particular: "She sacrificed quality to power; and had little conception of the claims of legato, such as should be exemplified, for instance, in "Ernani, involami," whose phrases she dismembered in an apparent attempt at dramatic expression."[57] In the *Herald*, W. J. Henderson made the same observation, calling her singing style "spasmodic," and remarking of the appreciative audience that its "taste has of late been reactionary."[58]

Clearly, Sembrich and Ponselle sang in different styles. Verdi, in his score, nowhere states what kind of soprano, lyric or dramatic, should sing Elvira; he merely asks for a range of A flat below middle C to a C two octaves above and wants the singer to be dramatically effective. Sembrich's voice was lighter than Ponselle's, and she handled coloratura turns and runs with greater elegance, but Ponselle offered greater richness and power.[59] As opera orchestras increased in size, they often played louder, and heavier voices became more usual for the role; and the public, it seems, had less trouble adjusting to this shift from lyric to more dramatic voices than did the critics.

The Metropolitan kept this production in the repertory for eleven performances (three consecutive seasons), and then revived it on December 17, 1928, for an additional four, this time with Ezio Pinza singing Silva. On opening night, according to Henderson, "the house sold out and hundreds of would-be standees" were turned away. "The opera," he added, "happens to serve the present public appetite for violent art." Again, he found Ponselle "more energetic than elegant," and "spasmodic rather than polished," though admitting there was "much temperament in her treatment of the role." Pinza, on the other hand, outsang Ponselle, Martinelli, and Tita Ruffo because "continent" (restrained), offering "smoothness and dignity."[60] As seven years earlier, Henderson seems to have misunderstood the opera. The traits he ascribes to Pinza and Ponselle suit the characters they portray. The elderly Silva should be icily restrained, and the young Elvira more passionate than elegant. After all, though dwelling in the sixteenth century she dares to talk back to a king, to call him to his face un-kingly. Drama first, elegance after; and so in Hugo's play did Sarah Bernhardt act the role.

In all, this 1920s production had fifteen performances at the Metropolitan and four on tour, two in Philadelphia and one each in Brooklyn and Atlanta.

Figure 3.3. Rosa Ponselle, in costume for Elvira in the Metropolitan production of 1921. Photograph courtesy of the Metropolitan Opera Archives.

Figure 3.4. Act 4 designed by Joseph Urban for the Metropolitan Opera production of 1921. Urban, an architect as well as set designer, was noted in the 1920s
for making his sets more substantial than his predecessors, who tended to rely on
painted drops and a few props such as table and chair. Photograph courtesy of the
Metropolitan Opera Archives.

And though successful at the box office, it did not please the leading critics.
Yet the public and singers continued to be fond of the music. In the Metropolitan's Sunday Evening Concerts, in the decade 1924–25 through 1933–34,
soloists of the company sang excerpts from the opera some twenty-seven times,
and WEAF/NBC, a radio station in New York that had its own company and an
active schedule, broadcast a shortened version of the opera at least five times
in the years 1925–32.[61] Thus, though increasingly less often staged, the opera
still was heard.

Alfredo Salmaggi, an Italian-American impresario, who offered audiences
Italian opera at popular prices, revived it at New York's Hippodrome theater
on November 8, 1933. The critic for the *Herald Tribune*, Francis D. Perkins,
greeted it without condescension: "*Ernani*, which is nearing its ninetieth birth-
day, does not include much of Verdi's most perennial music, but still has a
certain vitality and its share of those tunes whose liberal purveyal was one of
Verdi's specialties. Last night's performance was very fair."[62] The unsigned
note for the *Times* merely reported that the opera was "welcomed with curiosity
by the popular audience."[63] Possibly, "curiosity" rather than "anticipation" was
a correct description of the audience's attitude, for by the mid-1930s, mortality
was claiming the elderly, who had happy memories of the opera, while the new

toys of radio and film distracted the young from gaining a similar familiarity. In the United States, at least, by the late 1940s, *Ernani* increasingly was known only to singers, scholars, and Verdi enthusiasts.

In Europe, however, interest in Verdi had revived in the 1920s, swelled into a worldwide Verdi Renaissance that reached the United States in the early 1940s, and accelerated greatly when in June 1950 the Metropolitan Opera Association hired Rudolf Bing, formerly of Glyndebourne and the Edinburgh Festival, to succeed Edward Johnson as general manager. Bing's first new production, introduced on opening night of his first season, 1950–51, was Verdi's *Don Carlo*, followed in two years by *La forza del destino*, and then, even as he offered all the more usual Verdi operas, by *Ernani* (1956), *Macbeth* (1958), and *Nabucco* (1960).

For the *Ernani* revival, Bing offered four great and popular singers, Zinka Milanov, Mario del Monaco, Leonard Warren, and Cesare Siepi, and a world-class conductor, Dimitri Mitropoulos. The last had ideas about the score, and he transferred Silva's lament, "Infelice," from the first act to a point near the end of the second, and following Metropolitan custom, in the short last act inserted, as entertainment for Elvira and Ernani's wedding guests, a "joyous Epithalamium ballet" with music from Verdi's *Les vêpres siciliennes, Un giorno di regno*, and *Macbeth*.[64] Audience and critics alike seemed to enjoy the ballet, but there was some complaint about the shift of the aria, or more specifically, on the shift of the *cantabile* of the aria while leaving its cabaletta in the first act. Howard Taubman of the *Times* wrote: "Dramatic effect is the reason given for this change. One cannot dispute the point on psychological grounds, but one feels that the insertion of the cavatina into the place it now occupies is arguable on musical grounds. The build-up of the act's close is interrupted."[65]

In addition, Mitropoulos in the first two acts cut many bars of chorus as well as a verse from every cabaletta and ten measures from the opera's final trio. Only the third act, Charlemagne's tomb, was left untouched. Presumably, Mitropoulos felt that modern audiences would want the opera to move along faster, and even his tempos, when compared to the old recordings, were often very fast. Whether in this he was following or leading contemporary fashion is hard to tell. Most conductors in the mid-twentieth century took the opera at a faster pace than did their predecessors. And perhaps, in today's fully darkened auditoriums (achieved only with electricity), with the audience's attention more closely focused on the stage, and with life in general conducted at a faster pace, the more leisurely stroll of nineteenth-century opera is truly no longer suitable.

By and large, the critics in their reviews, unlike Clapp in 1847 who thought the story was "worked up in a good libretto," pronounced the story absurd, and the libretto faulty. In addition, the music was scorned as quite unsophisticated, with pounding rhythms continually reinforced by the orchestra's percussion and brass. Taubman sniffed: "We are conditioned and spoiled by the master of the middle and late years; like Verdi, we have outgrown *Ernani*."[66] On the *Herald Tribune*, Lang censured Mitropoulos's conducting: "It was within his power to make this period piece more palatable to modern audiences, yet he emphasized the trivial features."[67] Later, expanding on his thought and comparing Verdi to Wagner, Lang offered as a specific example: "In this particular opera the snare drum needs constant restraint. This most dangerous of instruments can be unleashed in Siegfried's funeral music, where its contribution to the din is magnificent, but in *Ernani* only a *soupçon* is permissible, to avoid accentuating an already harshly accented texture."[68] This sort of comparison to Wagner, usually to Verdi's dispraise, was much heard throughout the 1950s and 1960s, and sometimes led Verdi enthusiasts to murmur to their Wagner cousins a maxim about motes "in thy own eye," or, more bluntly, to retort that surely no music was more vulgar, more overaccented by percussion and brass, more thumped out to pounding rhythms, more dramatically inept than Wagner's elephantine "Ride of the Valkyries."

Taubman later softened his opinion of Verdi, confessing in his 1994 autobiography: "As a young music critic I tended to patronize his music, but as I grew older I learned to appreciate its simplicity and directness and the way in which it spoke unfailingly to the heart."[69] His shift in appreciation mirrored that of many operagoers in the United States as the revival of interest in Verdi permeated the country.

The Metropolitan's 1956 production had seven performances at home (and one in Philadelphia), and though audiences were enthusiastic, the opera did not always fill the house, a failure blamed more on the scenery and costumes than the music. Bing did not reschedule the opera until the 1962 season, when he offered four more top singers: Leontyne Price, Franco Corelli, Cornell MacNeil, and Jerome Hines, and another outstanding conductor, Thomas Schippers. This time, with "Infelice" returned to its proper place and the "Epithalamium" ballet dropped, the critics were more enthusiastic, and the seven performances (again including a nationwide broadcast) sold out, so that two years later Bing scheduled five more, with the same conductor and essentially the same cast or substitutes of equal strength. Then finally, with a cast of Martina Arroyo, Carlo Bergonzi, Sherrill Milnes, and Ruggero Raimondi, and Schippers conducting, Bing opened his 1970–71 season with *Ernani*. When he retired in 1972, having presented the opera twenty-five times in the house, with three national radio broadcasts, millions of opera lovers across the country were again aware of the opera.

But it was seldom staged outside of New York. In the years 1950 to 1972, the old touring companies, such as the Salmaggi and the San Carlo, were slowly dying, stifled after World War II by the rising costs of travel. While the regional companies that seemed destined to take their place in bringing opera to the smaller cities were not yet strong enough (or so they seemed to think) for a costume drama that required passionate singing. Still, in San Francisco, where

Figure 3.5. Leona Mitchell and Luciano Pavarotti in the 1983 Metropolitan production of *Ernani*. Photograph courtesy of the Metropolitan Opera Archives.

Ernani once had been so popular, the resident company opened its 1968 season with a production featuring Leontyne Price and took the opera in the spring to Los Angeles, though not rescheduling it for a second year. In the other large operatic cities, resident companies were slower to produce it: Cincinnati (1975), New Orleans (1977), and Dallas (1982).

Then in 1983, apparently to please the tenor Luciano Pavarotti, the Metropolitan staged a new production of the opera, this time ending act 2 with an aria for Ernani and chorus, "Odi il voto" (Hear my vow, Almighty God!), which Verdi had composed in 1844 for the tenor Nicola Ivanoff (1810–80). Inasmuch as the piece belonged to Ivanoff—paid for in cash—it never became part of the score, but it survived in Verdi's autograph and was remembered. Those who knew its history were happy to hear the florid piece well sung, but its placement injures the opera's drama. In the act's finale, by focusing attention upon Ernani alone (Silva having gone offstage), it spoils the balance between the principals, and by displacing from the finale to an earlier, less impressive position Ernani's pledge to Silva of suicide upon hearing the horn, it deemphasizes the opera's crux, the pledge and, its physical symbol, the horn.[70]

In other respects, also, the production, with twelve performances in the house and eleven on the road, served the opera less well. The staging was perfunctory, the singers often merely standing in a line. When Pavarotti sang, audiences were full and enthusiastic, but he sang less than half the performances (ten in the house and none on the road), and his replacement was disappointing. The role of Elvira needs a soprano who can be effectively dramatic, but the Metropolitan in Leona Mitchell cast one more lyric than dramatic, and she often could not command the passion needed. Unhappily, Sherrill Milnes, singing Don Carlo, was sometimes not in best voice, and his substitute, who in smaller theaters was splendid, in the caverns of the Metropolitan and the auditoriums on tour sounded weak. The conducting, too, was problematic. James Levine, the company's principal conductor, while outstanding in Strauss or Wagner, was never at his best in early Verdi, and his replacement for the tour was young and unexciting.[71] In short, the first ten performances in the home house, the ninth of which was broadcast nationally on radio and recorded for television, went moderately well. But thereafter, the production deteriorated. Audiences, most likely increasingly bored, probably blamed Verdi.

Matching the Metropolitan, the San Francisco Company, in September 1984, staged the opera with Montserrat Caballé, Milnes, Plishka, and Nunzio Todisco (replacing Pavarotti); and as conductor, the Verdi specialist Lamberto Gardelli. Again, apparently, success was moderate—though moderate, be it noted, only modifies, without negating, success; very few operas sell out night after night. A month later, imitating the Metropolitan, the Chicago Lyric Company produced the opera, chiefly for Pavarotti, but again he withdrew, and the substitute was not his equal. But according to the *New York Times* critic Will Crutchfield, the others in the cast, though bearing distinguished names, "made it clear in every possible way that this was just one more quick stop on the international opera circuit." Cuts were made in ensembles, cabalettas were shorn of verses, and the conducting was "with the unyielding drive that is our era's unhelpful gloss on Verdi." Yet the scenery and stage direction would have served "if the individual singing and acting performances had been stronger," but "all four ignored not only hundreds of Verdi's dynamic instructions but, worse, the whole idea that Verdi singing should involve a constant play of pronounced dynamic contrasts. That is no special criticism of these particular artists; it is standard practice. . . . Standard practice was the order of the day."[72] But *Ernani* in its fiery romanticism cannot endure "standard practice"; it must be sung and played with full belief in every wild, romantic word.

Meanwhile, a curious division appeared among critics. While a few were prepared to grant the opera some virtues, others, as in 1847, seemed unable to abide it. For the latter, the irritant seemed to be the opera's success with the public, but in place of scolding the public, they turned their anger onto the singers. One, for example, began a review of a 1965 performance at the Metropolitan: "*Ernani*, on March 11, proved a total shambles, but the audience loved it," and he went on to complain of Corelli "strutting about the stage like an intoxicated peacock."[73] Three years later, in San Francisco, another dismissed the opera as "this potboiler," this "sea of oom-pah-pah," and scolded Price, whose Elvira usually was admired, for "parading around in fancy costumes rather than creating a sympathetic character."[74] Others complained more directly of the opera. In New York it was "so bumpy structurally";[75] in Chicago the roles of Don Carlo and Silva were "dramatically preposterous";[76] and in San Francisco: "Verdi's opera is, of course, a problem in itself: some beautiful music . . . in which a quick carpet of coincidence seems to be unrolled before one mellifluous number after another."[77] The opera's melodies, and the public's liking of them, seems to have enraged these critics. As one wrote: "I suppose distaste for *Ernani* is legitimate: it is the most aggressively popular of the operas, an endless flow of tunes most of which could be danced to without further ado."[78] For such as these, its melody and rhythmic drive condemned the opera.

After the mid-1980s, in the United States, *Ernani* lay unheard for almost ten years, so that a revival in a concert performance in Washington, DC, in November 1996, was declared "a rare presentation."[79] Shortly before that, however, it reappeared onstage in the course of a Verdi cycle undertaken by a small company. On July 12, 1995, the New York Grand Opera, presenting Verdi's operas in chronological order, offered a single, uncut performance of *Ernani* on a stage set up in Rumsey Field in the city's Central Park.[80] The performance had the advantages and disadvantages usual in these park productions, well-coached singers and a full orchestra, but staged out of doors, over microphones, with simple scenery and costumes, yet sung and played with conviction, and led by Vincent La Selva, an outstanding conductor of Verdi. The audience of several thousand evidently found the story not an obstacle and the music delightful.

Two years later, in March 1997, the Sarasota Opera, in its Verdi cycle, offered six performances of *Ernani*. The company's theater seats 1,033, its acoustics are friendly to singers, and its relatively small stage encourages them to react and respond to each other. As a result, relatively unknown singers, who might have little impact in the country's larger theaters, in Sarasota can sound splendid. Led by Victor DeRenzi they sang the opera with passion and without cuts or any insertions, not even of Marini's cabaletta, "Infin che un brando vindice," and almost all the performances sold out.[81] Remarkably, the young bass singing Silva managed to appear older than the young lovers and more haughtily aristocratic. In the final scene his repeated assurances to Elvira that because of her love Ernani must die, "Morrà!" were so pointed and chilling that Silva became not, as sometimes played, a hooded figure in black, hovering on the edge of the scene, but at its center, the dominant figure. In this production there was no "standard practice."[82]

Possibly Sarasota's success with *Ernani* points to where the opera's future in the United States may best lie: not with the country's big companies, with their huge houses needing celebrity voices to fill them and little or no rehearsal time, but with regional companies, in smaller theaters, with younger casts ready to generate excitement by melody and vocal confrontation. For despite the critical disdain, the opera most likely has a future here. It is, after all, a major artifact in the history of Italian Romanticism, has had a continuous performance history here for more than 150 years, and as Bernard Shaw once wrote of its act in Charlemagne's tomb: "Every opera-goer who knows chalk from cheese knows that to hear that scene finely done is worth hearing all the Mephistopheleses and Toreadors that ever grimaced or swaggered."[83] Whether or not the opera as a whole is a masterpiece, as Gabriele Baldini asserts, Julian Budden's more moderate opinion surely is true: "It can still be guaranteed to fill a theatre, even if its heroics strike a modern audience as mildly ridiculous."[84] So long as the vigor and beauty of its melodies continue to attract singers and the public, it likely will be heard.

Chapter Four

I due Foscari

Verdi's sixth opera, *I due Foscari*, based on Byron's verse play *The Two Foscari*, had the bad luck to be brought to the United States in tandem with its predecessor, *Ernani*, and continually to be judged the weaker work or even a failure. Some reasons are clear; among them, a difference between the operas in style and subject, with *Foscari* the less flashy, more introspective, and unusual for its day: no young lovers, no sexual attraction or jealousy, and the chief character an old, old man. Moreover, the Havana company's codirector, Bottesini, stated in a letter to his father that of all the productions taken on tour the orchestra played well only one, *Ernani*;[1] and further, of the company's soloists, the tour's celebrity whom the public adored, Fortunata Tedesco, sang in *Ernani* but not in *Foscari*. Whether the opera might have succeeded under different circumstances is arguable, but it surely would have had a better chance.

The Italian Company of Havana, which had given the opera its trans-Atlantic premiere only three months earlier,[2] had arrived in New York in mid-April 1847, performed *Ernani* twice, and then left for Boston. There it opened at the Howard Athenaeum with *Ernani* on April 23, and on May 10, presented the U.S. premiere of *I due Foscari*. Apparently the opera's soprano, Teresa Rainieri, had succumbed to what one Boston paper called "the prevailing influenza," another, "our east winds and weather changes," and on opening night she sang poorly.[3] On repeating the opera the next night, despite "occasional fits of coughing," she sang better,[4] but even fully recovered she could not match the star quality of the company's prima diva, Tedesco, who was singing repeatedly to frenzied acclaim in *Ernani*.[5] According to a Havana paper that published reports on the tour, during the premiere of *Ernani* one Bostonian, after "having shouted himself hoarse and thrown two bunches and three wreaths of flowers at the feet of the beautiful Fortunata, not having anything more to throw, threw his hat, his gloves and his cane, and no doubt would have thrown himself if he had not been stopped in time."[6]

No such frenzy disturbed performances of *Foscari*, a gloomy story of fifteenth-century Venetian revenge, and Boston's *Daily Evening Transcript* reported: "This opera, which general opinion seems to mark as about equal in faults and beauties, has been brought out with tolerable success. . . . It is a thing to grow upon the musical taste by repeated hearing, and will not 'take' at once, like *La sonnambula*, *Masaniello*, or *Moses in Egypt*." Then the paper quoted at length an unidentified English critic's review of the opera's premiere in London, which stated that Verdi had banished from *Foscari* all "superfluous embellishments which could interrupt the action or weaken the power of the poem which it illustrates. . . . It is clear the composition is an adjunct of the drama, avoiding all that can divert the attention from the march of events, bringing out the passion and feeling with which it abounds."[7] In short, drama undiluted by divertissements.

The *Boston Post*, also in an unsigned article, presented homegrown views:

> Verdi's "lyrical tragedy," *I Due Foscari*, has not produced an equally striking and electrical effect upon its auditors here as *Ernani*, by the same composer, although well given by competent artists in the principal choral and orchestral parts. There is less of brilliancy and quality in the concerted pieces; the ear misses Verdi's glorious unisons, which *Ernani* is replete with, and that intensity of distress and agony required of the Doge, his son [Jacopo], and Lucrezia [Jacopo's wife], tasks the vocalists severely, while it chills and repels the listener to such accumulated horrors. . . . [The review praised] the duet in Jacopo's prison, which reflected that enchantment always given to the senses by the duet in *Ernani*. That, with the trio and quartette [all in act 2], and Jacopo's opening solo [act 1], are the gems of this opera. . . . The choral force has less to do in this opera than usual with Verdi's compositions generally. What they had in charge, however, they executed admirably, and gave out a body of sound worthy of double their number. . . . If we did not know Verdi scored very strongly for his wind instruments, and especially the bass, some idea of too much clangor might suggest itself from the band's execution of some portions of their score. That leading trombone is undoubtedly too sharp and explosive, which the very able leader should correct and subdue, to make the light and shade of his band complete.[8]

In closing, the review stated the company would produce twelve more nights of opera in Boston, "and a choice of parquette boxes for the whole season will be offered at auction this morning, so that all who desire to be numbered among the front three hundred may have an equal chance." But *Foscari*, with two performances of merely "tolerable" success, was not rescheduled. Five years later, the Boston critic W. W. Clapp Jr. summarized the opera's reception in the city: Despite a good performance, it was "too horrible, and the music too somber, for general audiences, so it failed of sensation."[9] This became a frequent complaint of critics in the United States: A story "too horrible, and the music too somber, for general audiences."

In three acts, not four, the opera in many ways differs in style and structure from its immediate predecessors, *Nabucco*, *I Lombardi*, and *Ernani*. Why Verdi chose to shift from a form in which he had found great success to one notably different, he nowhere declared, but from what evolved he plainly was no longer thinking in terms of the earlier operas' headlong, choral, spectacular style in which the protagonists, without much inner life, continually combine or confront each other—a love duet, a plea for mercy, an insult hurled, or an

HOWARD ATHENÆUM

ELVENTH NIGHT OF THE SEASON
—OF THE—

ITALIAN OPERA COMPANY
FROM HAVANA,
CONSISTING OF 73 PERSONS.

Second Night of Verdi's Grand Opera

THE TWO FOSCARI.

Second Night of the PRIMA DONNA

SIGNORA TERESA RAINIERI.

Tuesday Even'g, May 11, 1847,

Will be produced for the 2nd time in the United States, Jose Verdi's Grand
Opera of the

TWO FOSCARI

FRANCISCO FOSCARI, Doge of Venice	- - -	Sig. LOUIS VITA
JACOPO FOSCARI, his Son,	- - - -	Sig. NATALE PERELLI
JACOPO LOREDANO, Member of the Council of " Ten"		Sig. LUIS BATTALINI
BARBARIGO, a Senator,	- - - - -	Sig. FREDERICA BADIALI
FANTI, Member of the Council of " Ten"	- -	Sig. JOSE PIOMONTESI
LUCRECIA CONTARINI, Wife of Young Foscari,		Signora TERESA RAINIERI
PISANA, Friend and confidant of Lucrecia	-	Signorina TEODOLINDA GERLI
SERVANT OF THE DUKE	- - -	Sig. VICINTE LOCATELLI

Chorus of both sexes—Members of the " Council of Ten," Members of the " Junta,"
Lady Attendants of Lucrecia, Venetian Ladies, Populace, Masqueraders
Chief of the Council of Ten, Two Sons of Jacopo Foscari, Knights,
Gondoliers, Sailors, Pages of the Doge, &c. &c.
SCENE, VENICE—TIME, 1457.

☞Parquette Boxes $1 ; Parquette 50 cents ; Boxes 50 cents ; Second Circle 50 cents.
☞ Doors open at 7 o'clock ; the Opera will commence at 1-4 to 8 o'clock.☜
☞Books, containing an English version of the Opera, can be had at the Box Door.
Price 12½ cents.

☞ The Choice of Boxes will be sold at Public Auction, in the Vestibule of
the Athenæum, WEDNESDAY MORNING, at 10 o'clock.
CLARK & HATCH, Auctioneers.

☞ WEDNESDAY— Twelfth Night of the Opera Season.

EASTBURN'S PRESS--18 STATE STREET.

Figure 4.1. Playbill for the opera's second performance in Boston in May 1847.
Note, because of the company's Havana origin, the Spanish form of some names,
such as José Verdi. Photograph courtesy of the Trustees of the Boston Public Library.

aria of remembrance. In that style, gesture, physical and musical, often substitutes for character. With *Foscari*, Verdi sought a style more meditative, one that would better particularize the drama's chief figures.

The story, set in Venice in 1457, is simple, even static. The two Foscari are Francesco, the eighty-four-year-old Doge of Venice (baritone), and his middle-aged son Jacopo (tenor), exiled by the Council of Ten, first to Treviso, then to Candia (Crete), but in 1457 brought back to Venice on new charges of treason, tortured, and awaiting sentence. His father and his wife Lucrezia (soprano) believe him innocent, and she demands justice from the Council, beseeches the Doge to intervene on his son's behalf, and even dares to intrude herself and her children into the Council chamber in a last desperate appeal. On the Council is Loredano (bass), head of another Venetian family, who holds the Foscari responsible for the death of both his father and uncle; and in payment (Venetians being merchants), *two* Foscari men must die. Though Loredano is the opera's villain, Verdi gives him only a few lines, and musically not even an arioso, much less an aria. What caught Verdi's interest in the drama was not the motif of revenge but the conflict between a father's love for his son, his only surviving child, and his duty as Doge to execute the laws of the Council.

The Ten order Jacopo back to Crete in perpetual exile, forbidding his wife and children to join him, and upon boarding the ship he dies. In the Doge's Palace the father, who has steadfastly put duty before affection, on hearing of his son's death, breaks down, and his grief is troubled by the entrance of angry Lucrezia, demanding the Doge avenge Jacopo's death, and implying strongly that he had failed in paternal duty to his son. Wounding him with this charge in the first verse, she stabs him with it again in a second, while throughout the Doge sits silent, his turmoil of emotion appearing in his face and hands (if the singer can act), his long silence increasing the impact of his later outburst.[10] The Council enters and, spurred by Loredano, demands that the aged Doge abdicate, which Francesco does even as a bell begins to toll, proclaiming the election of his successor. The humiliation of such swift dismissal, while unleashing the old man's fury, hastens his death, but not before he leads a finale during which, according to a scholar, Vincent Godefroy, "in a mere thirty bars he springs not to life but to operatic immortality."[11]

As regards the two Foscari, the story essentially is true. The son was exiled to Crete and died there in January 1457. The Doge was overwhelmed at the news, was said to be unable to fulfill the duties of his office, and was forced to abdicate. And two days later, November 1, 1457, he died—commonly said, of a broken heart.[12]

For its era of Italian Romanticism the opera's libretto, with its chief character an old man focused on his inner thoughts, was most unusual. Yet as Godefroy has noted, the plots underlying *Ernani* and *Foscari* share a theme: "The characters of both plays are trapped by the systems in which they live. Hugo's Spanish king and grandees are soaked in the code of ancient chivalry, honour and vengeance. Byron's Venetians are besotted by loyalty to their city-state, to their sacred soil and the immutable laws of its rulers. And in both cases the solitary female stands outside the bounds of protocol, wondering at the hide-bound ways of men."[13] Moreover, *Foscari* touches two other themes frequent in Verdi, the fate of the condemned man (or woman) with no place in society and the rule of the mighty from the shadows, the Council of Ten in Venice or, more openly, the priests in *Aida*. Moreover in two of his earlier operas, *Nabucco* and *Ernani*, are scenes of a sort that Verdi in *Foscari* carried further: the soliloquies for the imprisoned, disoriented Nabucco and for Don Carlo at Charlemagne's tomb.

In *Foscari*, for the first time Verdi used brief musical themes to introduce the main figures in the drama and to accompany them throughout: a suggestion of a slow, purposeful march for the Council of Ten, a plaintive clarinet melody for the imprisoned, tortured Jacopo, a rush of strings up the scale for the agitated Lucrezia, and ten bars of ruminative music for the Doge. He does not develop these themes in any way, and they do not merge, conflict, or lead to action; rather he uses them as tags of identification, suggesting each person's dominant trait. Some people doubtless find his application of them simple-minded. Others approve of two or three, generally those for the Council, Jacopo, or the Doge, and most perhaps find that Lucrezia's forceful, upward scurry of strings that precedes her almost every entrance soon grows tiresome. But then, she has but one thought: Jacopo.

Besides accompanying the Doge with an orchestral theme, Verdi also introduces him vocally in a way unusual for the 1840s. After presenting the Council and Senators in an introductory chorus, in successive scenes he brings on Jacopo and Lucrezia in the conventional style, a bit of recitative, a slow aria, the cantabile, and then the cabaletta. Lucrezia, for instance, begins by declaiming that she will seek justice, not pardon, for Jacopo, sings in a slow aria of her faith in Heaven to protect the innocent, and then, upon hearing of his sentence to exile, soars into fury against the Council. Verdi presents the Doge, though the opera's dominant figure, more briefly and less melodically, yet, despite the seeming musical slight, clothes him with more individuality. After the Doge's ten-bar meditative theme, he enters alone, has a few phrases of recitative on the conflict in his position as father and Doge, sings a slow aria that is as much declamation as song—"O vecchio cor" (Oh, old heart . . . weep for my son, since my eyes have no more tears to shed)—and then moves directly to a duet with Lucrezia in which she vainly urges him to revoke the Council's ruling. Presumably Verdi felt that for a troubled, eighty-four-year-old an elaborate slow aria was appropriate, but a sequent energetic cabaletta, out of character.

It may be helpful here to recall that Shakespeare was Verdi's favorite poet and that in a shorter active life in the theater, barely twenty-five years, Shakespeare, too, frequently changed his style, moving from the rhetorical flourishes of *Titus Andronicus*, through *Macbeth* and the tragedies, on to the romances or tragicomedies of *A Winter's Tale* or *The Tempest*, in which happy endings close a series of strange adventures. And throughout that change Shakespeare gradually tightens his verse, even at times to such brevity that meaning is obscured. In *Titus* (1592), for example, a man faced with a girl in danger of bleeding to death, her tongue cut out and her hands chopped off, discourses for forty-seven lines on her condition, a response more poetic than dramatic. By *Macbeth* (1606), Shakespeare gives greater weight to dramatic needs and his verse is less expansive and more knotted. Verdi, who was thirty-one in the year he composed *Foscari*, had read many of Shakespeare's plays (in French or Italian translation) and was well aware of their shifts in style and structure. In his favorite poet he had a model of an artist changing styles to suit the subject, and in a similar way, quite consciously, he undertook to sharpen the drama of Italian opera. As he honed it, like Shakespeare he often mixed styles, and if in challenging expectations, he sometimes failed to pull the audience along with him, well then, he might try again in a later work.

An example of this occurs in *Ernani* and its successor, *Foscari*. Initially in *Ernani* Verdi denied "old man" Silva a cabaletta to his cantabile "Infelice," but when a leading bass, early in the opera's success, wanted to insert a cabaletta Verdi had composed for him to use in another opera, Verdi acquiesced. But coming to *Foscari* he again denied the "old man" a cabaletta, and this time, partly perhaps because the opera was less often produced, he did not compromise.[14]

An audience's expectations, however, always have a large part in any opera's initial reception, and in Boston in May 1847 all the admired "gems of the opera" were the conventional arias, duets, trios, and quartets. Not included were any of the Doge's solo scenes or even the last act's finale in which the heartbroken Doge, sighing "mio figlio," falls dead—while achieving, for some, "operatic immortality."

At the close of its Boston season, the Havana company returned to New York, where it reopened at the Park Theatre on June 9, 1847, with the local premiere of *Foscari*. The New York critics, a swarm far more numerous, vocal, and often nastier than their Boston colleagues, did not agree on the opera's worth, and while attempting to sting each other sometimes managed to say something about its music. The *Herald*, however, in an unsigned review, as then was custom, merely stressed that Verdi in his musical style differed from Rossini and Donizetti and that "the great feature of the *Two Foscari* is the Doge. . . . The opera seems to have been composed for baritone. The last scene of the first act, in which the Doge resists the supplication of his daughter-in-law, Lucrezia, is excellent." And of the opera's finale the review reported: "We have never seen a better expression of a saint despairing, disgusted, and expiring." In Boston, neither scene had been praised, and the Doge's role ignored in favor of the more musically conventional scenes between Jacopo and Lucrezia. But the New York critic in his final sentences revealed where local audiences were fixing their attention: "Tedesco was seated in a private box, talking with the pretty

Signorina Barili. Both attracted the eyes of the assembly. We understand that Tedesco will appear on Monday next. What a pleasure!"[15]

The *Tribune*, in a review probably written by Charles A. Dana, who usually supported Verdi against detractors, mostly commented on the singers' merits but also added: "An opera of Verdi's is not merely a selection of Solos, Duos, Trios, etc., arranged as is a programme for a Concert, but a composition entire and complete, of which the ground work is as essential as the figures which are inwrought. We have not studied the present piece sufficiently to speak of it discriminatingly."[16]

Others were less respectful. The *Morning Courier and New-York Enquirer*, whose usual critic, Richard Grant White, relished opposing Dana and the *Tribune*, began:

> We cannot bring ourselves to admire Verdi, and we sincerely hope we never may, for then we should cease to love HANDEL and MOZART. The music for this opera seems to us bad beyond all comparison—except with others by the same author. The choruses are almost all unison, and depend for their effect on the singularity and uncouthness of their phrases. . . . Everything in such music is piecemeal and broken; every air, every four bars has its crisis; there is no reserve—none of that mighty power which takes the mind and carries it perforce through a shaded and gradually opening pathway, to some glorious ear-prospect that satisfies the soul—as for instance, in the chorus in the *Messiah*, "and the government shall be," etc., "and his name shall be called wonderful!" . . . Verdi, as we yet have heard him, lacks both power and grace. He has no life, no fire.[17]

To which the *Tribune* (presumably Dana) replied: "The comparison of a modern Italian with Bach, Handel, Beethoven, or even Mozart, may be good enough to show off one's learning, but is ridiculous as criticism. . . . As for *I due Foscari* . . . it may not be a great or very original work, but it will bear comparison in point of originality with the Operas of Rossini, Bellini or Donizetti. . . . Verdi's operas are not mere strings of solos, duets, and choruses, but are considered and coherent wholes, worked up throughout upon a broad ground of harmony." But again he ended by looking forward to performances of *Ernani* and Piccini's *Saffo*, for they "will restore to us that accomplished singer and universal favorite, Tedesco."[18]

Finally, after the third performance of *Foscari*, the *Weekly Mirror* (probably Henry Cood Watson) took aim at the *Tribune*:

> The success of this opera is by no means equivocal; the public feeling is entirely against it, and the critics throw Handel and Mozart, with a dash of Beethoven, so constantly in the teeth of poor Verdi, that they have put him out of countenance, and the very groundlings sneer at him now. *I due Foscari* is certainly a terrible affair—it is the largest mountain producing the smallest

mouse excepting the criticism of it in the *Sunday Mercury.* . . . Verdi is evidently not an educated musician. . . . His scoring exhibits this in its countless outrages upon the commonest theoretical rules. His treatment of the Trombones is perfectly absurd, if it were not for the difference of the clef, we might be tempted to believe that the part had been miscopied from the Piccolo line. His scoring exhibits no relief; his winds instruments are not used as adjuncts to his stringed quartette, which with all good writers is the basis on which all legitimate effects are wrought, but the whole band is brought into constant operation.[19]

Such criticism well describes an older style of operatic orchestration—"stringed quartette" with light, woodwind coloring—but it does not do justice to some of Verdi's new and different sounds. Though American critics perhaps were slow to hear the many suggestive touches of orchestral coloring in *Foscari,* they are there, most famously in the introduction to the prison scene (solo viola over a solo cello), and in the fluttering flute that accompanies Jacopo's greeting to his beloved Venice.

Unhappily for the opera, New York's naysayers fixed its reputation in the Northeast, and when the Havana company journeyed to Philadelphia for a season at the Walnut Street Theatre, eighteen nights of eight operas, it scheduled only one for *Foscari,* presenting the opera's local premiere on July 19, 1847. This followed performances of *Saffo, Ernani,* and *I Lombardi,* the first two with Tedesco, who once again was declared "queen of the corps" and the public's "favorite."[20] Apparently, *Foscari* was not reviewed, and so far as discovered (through 2008), has not had another performance in the city.[21]

Returning to New York to play at the Castle Garden Theatre (capacity 5,000 seated), August 18 through September 17, the company offered a season of nine operas in twenty-one performances, opening and closing with *Ernani,* the opera most frequently given. The tally was *Ernani,* four performances; *Norma* and *Romeo* (Bellini's *I Capuleti*), three; *Sonnambula, Linda di Chamounix, Mosè in Egitto, Barbiere,* and *Foscari,* two; and *Saffo,* one. And for the most part, the critics being on summer vacation, there were no reviews.

Three years later the Havana company returned in still greater strength (104 strong), with Tedesco now merely one of three star sopranos and no longer the brightest. Between mid-April and October it played three separate seasons in New York, followed and interspersed by one each in Boston, Philadelphia, Baltimore, and Charleston. Besides *Ernani* and *Foscari,* it brought two new Verdi operas, *Attila* and *Macbeth,* with *Ernani* still by far the most popular. Of *Foscari* the company offered only three performances, all in New York and in the third season (at Castle Garden, July 8 through September 8), and though the few reviews were mildly favorable, they said little about the music.[22]

The opera suffered a different fate in New Orleans, where the local French company staged its premiere at the Théâtre d'Orléans on March 6, 1851. In

LES DEUX FOSCARI.

GRAND OPERA EN QUATRE ACTES ET SIX TABLEAUX.

PAR MM. SCUDIER FRERES,

MUSIQUE DE G. VERDI.

Représenté pour la première fois sur le Théâtre Français de la Nouvelle Orléans en Février 1851.

DISTRIBUTION:

JACOPO,	MM. DULUC.
LE DOGE,	GENIBREL.
LORÉDAN,	GRAAT.
BARBARIGO,	DEBRINAY.
L'OFFICIER des DIX,	✳✳✳
L'OFFICIER de LORÉDAN,	✳✳✳
UN SERVITEUR,	✳✳✳
LUCRÈCE CONTARINI,	Mad. De VRIES.
PISANA sa suivante,	Mlle. Melanie BLES.

Membres du Conseil des Dix, Sénateurs, Familiers, Dames Vénitiennes, Officiers, Pages, Soldats, Gondoliers, Peuple, etc., etc.

ACTE PREMIER.

1er. Tableau.

Le Théâtre représente une salle du Palais Ducal à Venise, au fond un balcon gothique d'où l'on découvre une partie de la cité et des lagunes au clair de la lune, à droite du spectateur, deux portes; une qui conduit aux appartemens du Doge, l'autre qui mène à la salle du conseil des Dix et aux prisons d'Etat, la scène est éclairée par deux torches de cire soutenues par des supports incrustés dans les murailles.

SCENE I.
Le Conseil des Dix.

PRELUDE ET INTRODUCTION:

Silence ! mystère !
Gardez ce séjour,
Comme un Sanctuaire.
Entourez d'amour.
Cette noble terre,
La nuit et le jour !
Silence mystère.
Qui régnez sur l'eau,
Votre ombre sévère
Promit au berceau,
A Venise entière,
Le sort le plus beau.

FIRST ACT.

First Tableau.

A Hall in the ducal palace in Venice. On the back ground a balcony from which some lagunas and a part of the city can be seen by moonlight. On the right of the public, two doors, one of which opens into the appartments of the Doge, and the other into the Hall of the Council of the Ten, and the State-prisons. Two wax torches resting on props fixed in the wall, light the whole scenery.

SCENE I.
The Conseil of the Ten.

PRELUDE AND INTRODUCTION.

Silence! mystery!
Shield this abode
As a sanctuary;
Day and night,
Encompass with love,
This noble land!
Silence! Mystery!
Who reign on the waters,
Your austere shadow,
Foretold to Venice,
From her very cradle,
The happiest fate;

Figure 4.2. First interior page of the libretto published for the New Orleans premiere of the opera, March 6, 1851. Reproduced by permission from the Williams Research Center, Historic New Orleans Collection (accession no. R.PAM, ML50. V4D4).

that city the popular Verdi opera was not *Ernani*, which had yet to be heard, but *Jérusalem*, Verdi's revision of *Lombardi* to a French text for the Paris Opéra, which favored Grand Opera in Four Acts with spectacular settings and a ballet. Hence, as the libretto for the New Orleans premiere of *Les deux Foscari* reveals, Verdi's three-act lyrical tragedy, which he intended to be a compact, intimate drama, was expanded into an approximation of a Grand Opera, with Four Acts, Six Tableaux, and a ballet. The New Orleans *Bee*, the day before the opening, assured readers that the opera would be presented "with all the accessories of beautiful scenery, magnificent singing and divine acting."[23]

If a libretto from the premiere performance correctly states what was put on the stage, the expansion chiefly was accomplished by the addition of a ballet and the insertion of a third intermission, giving the audience more time for social activities. Act 2 now ended with the quartet in the prison, and the sextet finale to old act 2 now became the separate act 3. The Venetian regatta and Jacopo's departure, the first half of old act 3, now became act 4 with the ballet inserted after the barcarole chorus, leading to the Doge's final scene and death. The ballet was titled *Fête Vénitienne*, but what music was used is not known. Opera ballets, however, were common in New Orleans, dancers were on hand, and most likely something was cobbled together. Whether Verdi's drama gained by these additions is doubtful.[24]

Though the production had five performances and won some critical praise, chiefly for its orchestration and its more conventional arias and ensembles, it did not succeed with the public and was dropped from the repertory.[25] Nevertheless, its soprano, Rosa DeVriès, kept Lucrezia's entrance aria on hand for recitals and sang it at a concert in New York in 1853 and also most likely elsewhere, for she toured frequently.[26] Later, New Orleans heard one more performance of the opera, this time in its original Italian version, staged by the visiting Ghioni/Susini company at the French Opera House on January 19, 1866. Reportedly the audience was thin, and in New Orleans the opera has not been staged since.[27]

Judging by number of performances, *I due Foscari* did best in San Francisco, where it had its premiere on March 23, 1855, but initially drew little attention. After its fifth performance, however, the critic for the *Alta California* suddenly erupted with the kind of praise the opera had achieved nowhere else in the country:

> The opera of *I due Foscari* is less brilliant than *Ernani*, but it is, in our opinion, unrivalled by that or any other work of Verdi known to us, in mingled sublimity and pathos. Francesco Foscari we consider one of the greatest, most impressive figures in the gallery of musical art—an immortal expression of princely and paternal grief. He is in music as the Laocoön in the Sculptor's art—those who have gazed upon the one—those who have listened to the passionate accents of the other—retain forever ineffaceable the memory of their sublime agony.[28]

In all, the opera had five performances in San Francisco in 1855, five more in 1863, and one in 1872, after which, it vanished in the West for more than a hundred years. Meanwhile, on the East Coast, in New York and Boston, it had a brief and somewhat curious revival—three performances—in the years 1863–64. The company, based in New York and led by Max Maretzek, conductor and impresario, was one of American and Italian singers, with a relatively full orchestra (probably about forty), and in these Civil War years, when opera elsewhere was much curtailed, was possibly the country's strongest.[29]

Maretzek, an ebullient Moravian who had come to New York from London in 1849, had soon made himself perhaps the most important impresario in the country. Sometimes called "the Napoleon of opera" or "Maretzek the Magnificent," he was, according to one of his artists, "very handsome and had a vivid and compelling personality." He himself favored, for his efforts to plant an appreciation of opera in the United States, the more ironical title "Don Quixote of Opera." And though in 1855 he personally had preferred Meyerbeer to Verdi, leaving the latter off a list of eleven "good" composers and stating dismissively "even Verdi's [operas] have been hailed with enthusiasm,"[30] by the 1860s after staging the U.S. premieres of *Rigoletto*, *Trovatore*, and *Traviata*, he evidently had changed his mind enough to revive one of the earlier operas. To close a successful season at New York's Academy of Music in the spring of 1863, he mounted *Foscari* for his benefit night, April 15, and the public, with whom he was popular, filled the house (capacity 4,500). The opera at the time was not in the company's repertoire, and Maretzek's choice of it, which he did not explain, surprised many. The *World*, for one, declared the opera "as good as new . . . hitherto unknown to the rising generation of opera-goers." Its reviewer concluded however: "This work is not one to add to Verdi's good name in all respects—being singularly unequal. The music wanders carelessly from sublime ideas to vulgar suggestions. The trial scene is almost burlesqued by the use of hum-drum themes side by side with vigorous and appropriate declamatory rhythms."[31] The *Times*, however, admired "two or three very fine episodes, such for instance as the duet between the soprano and tenor in the second act." Moreover the audience reportedly was responsive, the soloists sang beautifully, and the company, at the close of act 2, presented their leader with a silver tea set, bought presumably with money from their fees and salaries and so, in a sense, a gift from Maretzek to himself. But still, as the *Times* observed: "It was a bright spot in Max's lifetime that he can always look back upon with unalloyed pride and gratification."[32]

The next performance took place in Boston on the last day but one of the company's January 1864 season at the Boston Theatre (capacity 3,140). The revival, however, was quite overshadowed by the season's great excitement, which was the local premiere and subsequent performances of Gounod's *Faust*, for which Maretzek provided a full military band onstage and enlarged the orchestra by the addition of the Mendelssohn Quintette Club and other

musicians. And he gave the season's closing performance, a Saturday matinee, to the seventh performance of *Faust*.[33]

Of *Foscari*, Boston's *Daily Evening Transcript* reported only: The opera, "after an
interval of nearly seventeen years since its first representation in this city, cannot
be counted among the fortunate or successful works of Verdi. Its harrowing scenes
and stormy music, without an instance of good relief, if we may except the tenor
air in the first act and the fine trio in the second, are not calculated for permanent
hold of the lyrical stage." Yet, "The audience to hear it was very large."[34]

Returning to New York, Maretzek opened his season on February 1 and
closed on March 12, 1864, presenting in all twenty-eight performances of fifteen operas, of which *Faust* led with ten; followed by Petrella's *Ione*, three, *Don
Giovanni* and *Norma*, two, and the other eleven, including *Foscari*, one. Notably,
after his benefit Maretzek did not conduct *Foscari* again, leaving it to an assistant, which suggests that the cause of the revival lay less with Maretzek than
with his singers, most likely the soprano Giuseppina Medori, who sang all three
performances to good reviews, or possibly the baritone, Giovanni Bellini, who
had the opera for his benefit night in Boston. Perhaps they, more than the
impresario, sought the revival.[35]

In Europe, though not in England, the opera fared better, and for roughly
thirty years, or until the mid-1870s when pushed aside by Verdi's later works,
it had a steady, quiet success. Perhaps as the scholar Julian Budden has suggested, it did well partly because "it was easy to mount, and therefore often in
demand as an *opera di ripiego*," that is, an opera of expedience, handy for emer-
gencies, such as to replace an opera announced but canceled; handy, because
short, without complicated choral passages or need for spectacular scenery,
and requiring little expense or rehearsal.[36] But there is also evidence that at
least some critics, singers, and audiences found it stirring.[37]

The opera's next revival in the East, another odd one, took place during
a sort of Verdi festival in New York, perhaps the first in the United States, in
which a Signor Angelo[38] in October 1886 pulled together a scratch company
of singers and instrumentalists, hired the Academy of Music, and announced
a season opening with Petrella's *Ione* and thereafter a cycle of Verdi's early
operas: *Luisa Miller*, *I Lombardi*, *I due Foscari*, *Un ballo in maschera*, and *Rigoletto*.
But Angelo ran out of money, and the season closed early, though *Foscari* was
performed on October 27, 1886.[39] Whatever the merits of the performance,
the critics mostly confined their reviews to repeating what by then had hard-
ened into the accepted view of the opera: Questioning any reason for its
"resuscitation," the *Herald* stated (with several inaccuracies): "When the opera
was first produced at Rome, forty-two years ago, the audience gave it the cold
shoulder. The same fate attended its productions in all other countries. And
now, after nearly half a century, what was then considered weak, insipid and
tiresome is simply intolerably bad."[40] In fact, *Foscari* had a successful premiere
season in Rome, in 1844, and thereafter played steadily in Italy. Nevertheless,

the *Tribune* declared, the opera "dates from a sterile period which interrupted a series of brilliant successes and has never won marked popularity either in Italy or out of it." Then, without stopping to explain how or why, it added, "Yet it was found to have the power to hold the attention of an audience of moderate numbers from beginning to end."[41] And the *Times* concluded, the opera "may with safety be allowed to slumber on the shelves of the music shops."[42]

In the United States for the next eighty-two years this was the general opinion. When at a Metropolitan Sunday Evening Concert, on December 22, 1907, the great Italian baritone Riccardo Stracciari sang "O vecchio cor,"—the one time an excerpt of *Foscari* was heard at these concerts, 1883–1946[43]—apparently no one thought to ask why he had chosen such a little-known aria, or what he thought of the opera from which it was taken. A generation later, Francis Toye in 1931 published a study of Verdi's life and works in which he summarized the opera's flaws and virtues, concluding that it was "not a good opera, but it contains a certain amount of music that compels admiration as well as interest." In the libretto he thought the flaws were chiefly those of "of undue compression," especially on the truth of Loredano's belief that the Foscari were responsible for the deaths of his father and uncle. Byron keeps the question open, and even has a scene in which the Doge specifically denies any role in their deaths.[44] Verdi and his librettist F. M. Piave by the omission of that denial and others similar seem to close the case against the Foscari, and too often hustle such bits of explanatory background into a swift phrase or a sentence. Yet the opera, running only 105 minutes, could absorb some slight expansion. But Verdi was less interested in ordering the plot than in setting a scene for a display of emotion, and though the early librettos all included a long "Note" by Piave on the opera's historical background, this soon disappeared.[45] Another fault of the libretto, which Toye does not mention but Julian Budden does, is the continual iteration of the word "innocent," either as a noun or an adjective. If intended by Verdi and Piave as a further tag to Jacopo's character, they overworked it, sometimes turning the genuine pathos of the character, innocent, tortured, and exiled from Venice, into a chafing self-pity.[46]

Yet all these defects and prejudicial opinions were swept away by a production of the opera brought to New York by the Rome Opera Company in midsummer 1968. The company played in the Metropolitan Opera house, Lincoln Center, presenting *Le nozze di Figaro*, in a production by Luchino Visconti; Rossini's *Otello*, with sets by Giorgio de Chirico; and *I due Foscari*, with seemingly no panache except its unfamiliarity. In the United States very few had heard the opera or any part of it, though it had been revived with success in Germany in the 1930s and in Italy in the 1950s. From the Italian performances some tapes were available, but the sound was dreadful, and not until 1978 did a commercial studio recording appear. Happily, by then, a so-called pirated recording, taken from a Rome Opera performance at the Metropolitan, though stamped "Not for Sale," could be bought, and *Foscari* had a reputation, even in the United States, as one of the better of Verdi's early operas.[47]

Figure 4.3. Pier Luigi Pizzi's set for the 1968 Rome production, with the two Foscari, father and son, the Doge and Jacopo. Photograph by the Rome Opera Company.

The Rome Opera's production, at the time it came to New York, was only five months old, having opened to great acclaim in Rome on April 3, 1968. Its setting, by Pier Luigi Pizzi, was simple, a stage sharply focused by enclosing high and blank side and back walls. Within these were three horizontal playing levels, stage floor and two platforms tied by a center stairway: stage level, six steps up to midlevel, and fifteen higher to the top of the back wall where sat the Doge's imposing chair with five Senators in red robes standing to his right with arms folded and five to the left, the Council of Ten. Except for the Senators in dull red, the Doge's gold robe, white cape, and ducal cap, there was nothing specifically Venetian in the set: no gondolas, no gothic arches, no lion of St. Mark. The unbroken, surrounding walls and their dark brown color, repeated in the monochrome backdrop, suited an enclosed, stifling drama, ending unhappily.

The stage direction was similarly simple. At the start the focus was put on the Doge by having the curtain part during the opera's prelude (about two minutes and forty-five seconds), revealing the Doge standing alone, at the foot of the stairway. Then, as a quiet introductory chorus opened the first scene, and the Council of Ten (at the top) and other Senators (at midlevel) took up their positions, the Doge mounted slowly to his seat on the ducal throne. Thereafter, when

Figure 4.4. The 1968 Rome Opera production: The Doge (Mario Zanasi), stripped of his ducal ring and crown, collapses. Photograph by the Rome Opera Company.

acting officially, he either sat on the throne or stood on the steps near it; when acting privately, say, in talking as a father to Lucrezia (duet finale to act 1), he would descend to midlevel, his emotional response to her questions reflected at times by his moving a few steps up or down the stairway, as he answered as Doge or father. If memory serves, after the prelude he never again stood at stage level, toppling as he died from the throne to midlevel.

But all the scenery and staging, though helpful, was minor to the music. Nothing was done to make a short opera longer, or to "improve" on what Verdi had scored. The Rome orchestra played beautifully; the singers sang with understanding and conviction; and the Doge, Mario Zanasi, though not a great baritone, perhaps touched greatness in the role. At the end, his collapse and death while calling for his son was stunning, and in seven swift bars Verdi dropped the curtain.

For the *Times* Raymond Ericson welcomed,

> the chance to hear a neglected, not to say forgotten, Verdi score that for a change, seems worth reviving. *I due Foscari* followed on the heels of the composer's *Ernani*, an opera that had much greater staying powers. If it does not have the stormy dramatic power of its predecessor, *I due Foscari*, has a quality of its own—one that perhaps put off its popularity in early days and yet might win it greater recognition today. This is a kind of concentrated mood; a concern with a single situation, to which Verdi brought the splendor of his melodic writing and some highly expressive but brief orchestral passages. . . . Verdi's treatment is, on the whole, lean, so that the music itself progresses rapidly. There are few choruses, little isolated orchestral writing. The arias and vocal ensembles follow one another swiftly, detailing the character's emotions. A few times one could have done without the traditional cabaletta, or fast section, that follows a slow aria. Yet so much of the vocal writing has the fine lyricism of later Verdi works that the work seems fresh and frequently moving.[48]

Harriet Johnson reported for the *Post*:

> When Francis Toye, Verdi's biographer, dismissed *I due Foscari* as "not a good opera," he arrived at too simple a conclusion. . . . To see this sixth Verdi opera is a far greater emotional than merely historical experience. . . . *I due Foscari* has the big advantage of three cumulative acts, each more powerful than the last, building to a shattering dramatic climax. . . . As the most important character in the opera, the Doge has the most moving music. . . . This was the first of four performances, and a visit is recommended.[49]

At that first performance, the audience was small and by the third act had clustered on the main floor, close to the stage, so that the end of the drama played as if in a small house to an attentive audience in a high state of emotional rapport. By the last performance the audience was much larger, even discounting many returning to hear an opera they thought they might never hear again.[50] Reporting in September for the English magazine *Opera*, the American critic Patrick J. Smith concluded, "The opera, far from being negligible is one of Verdi's strongest early scores. . . . The second act in particular, with the exception of the quartet, is as consistently powerful music as Verdi was capable of at that time: intense and lyric. The opera's personal attraction over, say, *Ernani* . . . is its first-class portrait of the Doge Foscari, which as a Verdian creation ranks only slightly under the later Simon Boccanegra or King Philip as a characterization."[51] Thus, in July 1968, by a production from Rome, was critical opinion in New York on *Foscari* turned right around.

The first company to act was the Chicago Lyric Opera, which, on September 22, 1972, presented as opening night of its season, the Rome production with the same conductor, Bruno Bartoletti, and a new cast featuring Piero Cappuccilli as the Doge. As so far discovered, this was the opera's first performance in Chicago, and apparently it pleased most who heard it, though not the reporter for *Opera*, Roger Dettmer, who dismissed the music as "these Verdian farragos" and had very harsh words for the set and singers. On the other hand, in the same magazine seven years later, in a retrospective article titled "The Lyric at 25," Peter P. Jacobi declared the opera the most memorable of the 1972 season: "*I due Foscari* was a revelation."[52]

Three years later, on May 11, 1975, New York heard a single concert performance of the opera in Town Hall by a semiprofessional group led by Larry Newland, an assistant conductor at the New York Philharmonic. According to the *Times*, the orchestra of fifty-seven members, was "a shining example of how good a community orchestra can be." The singers were not fully adequate, but one, the tenor Herman Malamood, later sang briefly at the Metropolitan, and his excellence as Jacopo overshadowed the Doge. Nevertheless, said the *Times*, "the work is top-drawer early Verdi, full of pulsing arias, stirring ensemble numbers and some novel instrumental touches."[53] The reviewer for the *Daily News* concluded, "This was not a great performance of *I due Foscari* by any means, but it never disguised the considerable worth of the score."[54] By the mid-1970s, apparently the score was now well enough known to be judged on its own, aside from the singers' failings or virtues.

This point was reinforced by another concert performance in New York, this time in Carnegie Hall, on October 20, 1981, and offered by Eve Queler and her Opera Orchestra of New York. She brought together an exceptionally strong cast of Renato Bruson (Doge), Carlo Bergonzi (Jacopo), and Margarita Castro-Alberty (Lucrezia). According to Donal Henahan of the *Times*, the opera "can be turned into a rip-snorting melodrama in which its highly reputed musical nuances are underplayed in favor of traditional Verdian energy and vocal thrust. Whether that is the best way is another question, but certainly Miss Queler's concert version churned up considerable foam, some of it around mouths in the enthusiastic audience. Old-fashioned bellow canto was the order of the evening." But the sometimes hysterical response of the audience interested him less than the ability of the piece to absorb different interpretations. Miss Queler "did not take great pains to bring out the score's intimate qualities, but her robust approach made an interesting evening of it. At least we now know that *I due Foscari* doesn't have to be the deadly bore that Verdi himself once labeled it."[55]

So Verdi once did say. In a letter to his librettist Piave, on July 22, 1848, he wrote: "In subjects which are naturally gloomy if you're not careful you end up with a deadly bore—as for instance *I due Foscari*, which has too unvarying a colour from beginning to end."[56] The remark is much quoted. But it should be qualified. Verdi was very much a man of the present. The opera in hand, on which he was working, was what interested him, and he inclined to dismiss past works as unimportant. In fact, his earlier letters to Piave show him taking a great deal of care over *Foscari;* he liked the subject. Nevertheless, even in the course of composition he worried about the unbroken gloom, and proposed to break it at the start of the third act by introducing the brief scene of the regatta with its chorus urging on the gondoliers. But the break is small compared to the concessions he worked into another intimate drama of father, son, and passionate woman, *Traviata*, which in act 1 offers the popular drinking song, and in act 2, scene 2, Flora's party, songs and dances by the guests. No one argues that these are the finest moments in *Traviata*, but they evidently do satisfy a need for entertainment wanted by a majority of most audiences. With his eye always on the audience Verdi once famously remarked that receipts at the box office were the test of a good opera. "You will object," he wrote to a friend, "what business of yours are the receipts? But they are my business, because they prove that the show was interesting and thus they show us how to go about things in the future."[57]

Following the Rome Opera's production, with success on both sides of the Atlantic, the opera had a surge of productions in Europe, but not in the United States or Canada. Other than Chicago's Lyric Company, the only other to take it up was Opera Hamilton, in Hamilton, Ontario, which staged it in September 1989. A reviewer for *Opera* reported "the setting was brought forward to 1844, the date of the work's composition, to suggest the sinister undertones of a Venice still gorgeous but grown complacently corrupt under an exhausted Austrian politburo." Of course, by 1844 Venice did not have a Doge, and the concept seemed ill-conceived. No matter. "Musically things were happier." And the reviewer closed his piece: "An exciting evening in the opera house. More early Verdi please."[58] Moreover, in 1994 the company revived the production, and though the baritone singing the Doge was a disappointment, "Nevertheless *I due Foscari* was a revival not to be missed."[59]

Why other major or regional companies in the two countries ignored the opera is a mystery. New York's tiny but adventurous Amato Opera, with a theater

Figure 4.5. Vincent La Selva conducting in Central Park, New York, in 2000. Photograph by David Mlotok. Courtesy of the New York Grand Opera Company.

seating only 107, staged eight performances of the opera in March 1991. To explain the historical background in 1457, Anthony Amato added a spoken prologue in which the Doge and Loredano set the scene in English. Then the opera proceeded in Italian. Commented Allan Kozinn for the *Times*, "Given the passions that rule this work, there is much intensity in its music. To a degree, that intensity is tied to the work's orchestration, and some of it is inevitably lost when the work is played by less than a full orchestra. But the company found a reasonable compromise in Linda Fairtile's skillful arrangement, which reduced the orchestral forces to a small wind, brass, and keyboard ensemble, but preserved much of its power and textural beauty."[60]

The following year in Carnegie Hall, Eve Queler and the New York Opera Orchestra returned, after ten years, to *Foscari* in concert performance, and again had a success, this time featuring Vladimir Chernov as the Doge.[61] By then several recordings of the opera were available, and most likely the music was familiar to many in the audience. Perhaps for that reason critics in their reviews did not discuss the music but focused on the singers. Next, on July 19, 1995, Vincent La Selva and the New York Grand Opera, as part of their cycle of Verdi operas presented in chronological order of composition, staged the opera in an outdoor performance in New York's Central

Park. According to the *Times*, though the singing was variable, "as usual, Mr. La Selva over-achieved with his often scrappy orchestra and generally scruffy chorus." And, as usual, he held an audience of several thousand quiet and attentive until the last note.[62]

Today in the United States the opera's reputation stands high with most critics and scholars. For example, Robert Baxter, in reviewing a DVD of it for the *Opera Quarterly* (and summarizing previous recordings and DVDs), stated bluntly: "*I due Foscari* ranks as one of Verdi's most compact and compelling operas."[63] And Julian Budden, writing in 1973, had predicted of *Foscari*, "It may well survive the present Verdi boom more hardily than most."[64] Indeed, in Europe it seems to have done so, and in a brief but acute analysis of the opera to accompany a revival at Covent Garden in 1995, Budden held to his opinion.[65] Moreover, in November 2001, the Rome Opera staged a revival of what was in setting and staging its 1968 production, and again to acclaim.[66]

Why so few companies in the United States have staged the opera is hard to perceive. Relatively easy to mount and able even with reduced orchestra to sound passably well, it would seem ideal for regional companies. True, despite three acts it is relatively short, but that is hardly a great disadvantage. True, it has a complicated political background, but with a historical note in the program and supertitles, that should be compassable. True, it needs singers with strong voices and stage presence, but surely at least for the country's smaller theaters these can be found. And, yes, there is the so-called monotony of tone, unrelieved by dances, drinking songs, or big choral numbers, yet audiences by the thousands in the past fifty years, when given the chance, have responded with enthusiasm to Verdi's concentrated gloom. The music apparently no longer is "too somber for general audiences." So, why does the opera resound so feebly in the United States?[67]

Chapter Five

Attila

When the Italian company of Havana next came on tour to the United States, April–September 1850, it again brought with it *Ernani* and *Foscari*, and, in place of *I Lombardi*, two of Verdi's more recent operas, *Attila* (1846) and *Macbeth* (1847). It was, as before, an extraordinary company, again led by Arditi and Bottesini, and now with an orchestra of fifty, chorus of forty, and with Tedesco only one of three star sopranos and no longer the brightest. It also claimed as its leading bass, Ignazio Marini, not only an outstanding Silva for *Ernani* and Oroveso for *Norma* but the bass for whom Verdi had composed the role of Attila. Maretzek, who was steadily improving New York's Astor Place Company, was moved to describe the visitors as "the greatest *troupe* which had ever been heard in America. Indeed . . . it has seldom been excelled in any part of the Old World."[1] And for the most part, newspapers agreed.

The first of the two new operas to have its U.S. premiere was *Attila*, based on a German Romantic play by Zacharias Werner, *Attila, King of the Huns* (1808). Verdi, however, evidently felt that for Italians at least the opera's protagonist needed no descriptive subtitle. Every literate Italian knew that Attila, the "Scourge of God," the barbarian leader of Asian tribes known collectively as the Huns, in 452 AD had invaded the Western Roman Empire, had sacked and burned the cities, farms, and villages of northern Italy, and forced survivors on the Venetian mainland to flee to the islands of their lagoon. So great was the devastation, so severe the death and misery, that ever after it was said: Grass never grew where his horse had trod. Announcing he soon would march on Rome, he had been confronted at his camp near Mantua by Pope Leo I, leading a Papal embassy in full regalia, and the barbarian Hun reportedly was so impressed by Papal eloquence, majesty, and sacerdotal robes, as well as, according to legend, by a vision of St. Peter and St. Paul in the sky with swords drawn against him, that he had agreed to retreat—and within the year died of a hemorrhage while mounting his latest bride on their wedding night.[2]

On March 17, 1846, the Teatro la Fenice in Venice had introduced the opera, and as the curtains parted after an ominous prelude, those Venetians lucky enough to be in the house for the premiere of a new Verdi opera saw the Huns in camp, celebrating the sack of Aquileia, Rome's port at the head of the Adriatic.[3] A triumphant Attila enters, surrounded by tribal leaders, and then a group of Roman women led by Odabella, captured in arms and fighting. Impressed by her courage, Attila grants her a wish, and when she asks for a sword (resolved to kill Attila to avenge her dead father, brother, lover, and ravaged country), he gives her his. Next, a scene on the Venetian lagoon. First a storm, soon calmed by a musical sunrise, and then refugees from Aquileia coming by boat to the lagoon's islands to found Venice (and the city's boast of later years that it alone of the Western Roman Empire never was conquered by barbarians). Soon, another historical spectacle: Attila in camp near Mantua, met by Pope Leo I and the vision of the saints in the sky, just as Raphael had portrayed the scene in a famous fresco in the Vatican.[4] And in the next act, a barbarian banquet lit by torches, during which Odabella, for a mixture of motives she may not fully understand, betrays her fellow conspirators and saves Attila from poison by knocking a cup from his hand. Whereupon, again attracted to her, he proclaims that she will be his next bride. In the last act Odabella, just married and in a state of emotional confusion, having fled the offstage march to the marriage bed, meets her Roman coconspirators and protests her determination, despite the marriage, to kill Attila. He, entering swiftly and at first seeing only her, asks why she flees one who loves her. But on discovering the two Romans with her, he scents a plot and berates each in turn for ingratitude, for he had dealt honestly with each of them. In the opera's closing quartet, Odabella, giving in to hate, stabs him, and he dies, copying the words of Caesar known to every child—"Et tu, Odabella!"[5]

In adapting the play, Verdi, in a letter to one of his librettists, had admired especially the characters of Attila (whom he heard in his mind as a bass), Odabella (soprano), and the Roman general Ezio (baritone). The last offers to betray to Attila the Roman emperor, Valentinian III, and, when rejected by the more straightforward Hun, joins the conspiracy against him.[6] Ezio (in Latin, Aetius), unlike Odabella, is a historic figure, generally considered the last great Roman general, and in his treasonable maneuvers is presented in the opera with a semblance of truth.[7] The fourth principal, Foresto (tenor), is Odabella's lover, who has survived the sack of Aquileia and leads its refugees to the lagoon islands. When he and Odabella rediscover each other, he joins her plot to kill Attila, but despite some fine music he is the least of the principals.

In its premiere performance the opera seems to have had only a moderate success, perhaps in part because several features, though hardly revolutionary, may have taken the audience by surprise and left it momentarily undecided. Verdi, for the only time in his career gave the title role to a true bass,[8] and though he scored it for a *basso cantante* or high bass, not a *basso profondo* (Pope Leo), many persons believe that a bass of any range cannot color or shade meaning as finely as a baritone or tenor. In the opera's great scene for Attila, for example, he describes a nightmare in which he found himself before the walls of Rome and an old man (Pope Leo) appeared, grabbed him by the hair, and warned him in a voice of thunder to leave God's house untouched. Alarmed by the warning, Attila in his account must move through a variety of emotions, starting with superstitious terror and ending in scorn and resolution, a wider range, say some, than the bass voice can render.[9] Also, though merely an oddity, *Attila* is the only opera in which Verdi set all the scenes out of doors (though one starts in a tent with its front flap open). Besides its barbaric costumes, it is very much an opera "of fields and forests, of lagoons and streams, of winds and clouds and storms and sunrise, of torches and smouldering ruins, of dreams and visions."[10] In this quality it is the extreme opposite of *Traviata*, Verdi's only opera with all scenes set indoors.

Moreover, as some have complained throughout the years, the opera is curiously, even awkwardly constructed. Not in its basic musical form, the five-part *scena*—introduction, recitative, cantabile (slow aria), recitative, and cabaletta (fast aria)—which was typical of its day, but in the final act's sudden shift toward individual characterization rather than the expected vast choral finish. In *Attila*, the prologue and first two acts (ending with the banquet), with texts by T. Solera, the librettist of *Nabucco* and *I Lombardi*, are often spectacular in their settings, offering historical tableaus, and their climaxes frequently are choral and on a vast scale. Whereas the short final act (fifteen minutes), set only in "another part of the forest," with text by F. M. Piave, librettist of *Ernani* and *I due Foscari*, keeps the wedding chorus offstage, brief, and ends the opera—the murder of Attila—with merely a quartet for the four principals. Julian Budden, for one, finds the ending "a theatrical anticlimax . . . a disproportion in scale and an alteration to the fundamental character of the opera."[11] And over the years, at some performances, the abrupt jolt in scale and sudden end has been met with "laughter" or "silence and surprise" (in New York, 1850) or again with "laughter" (London, 1963).[12]

Apparently Solera, who went to Spain before finishing the text, intended to close with a big choral scene celebrating the Roman defeat of the Huns and the triumph of civilization over barbarism, a conclusion in which nineteenth-century Italians might foresee their own ultimate liberation from the Austrian Empire then dominating and occupying much of central and northern Italy. Verdi was not averse to such a patriotic theme, but from the first what had most fired his imagination were the personalities of the principals, and he seems to have been quite happy with the ending he and Piave cobbled together. Which is not surprising, for the steady trend in Verdi's choice and treatment of subjects for his operas was toward the musical characterization of individuals, even those trapped at a triumphal parade. But by the time he composed *Aida*, he was more skilled.

In addition to these particularities of *Attila*, which may have delayed the audience's initial response to it, the premiere had a unique disaster. When at the banquet, as an omen of evil afoot, a wind on cue blew out the onstage torches, something in the guttering materials caused a terrible stink. The next day the critics, besides mocking the accident, found much else in the libretto and music objectionable, but with each performance the public decided more and more vociferously that it liked the opera. No matter that its choral numbers obscured the motivation of the individuals. No matter that Odabella seems "the most unpleasant heroine in all Verdian opera,"[13] or even that by the last act audiences empathize far more with the naive, superstitious Attila than with the vengeful Romans. It was a grand show, full of stirring music, and soon was playing all over Italy and most of Europe. For the next thirty years, among Verdi's operas preceding *Rigoletto*, in number of productions *Attila* probably ranked second only to *Ernani*, and Verdi's first English biographer, Frederick Crowest, writing in 1897 declared it "Verdi's most successful work since *Ernani*."[14]

Yet for reasons not altogether clear it failed utterly in England. According to Benjamin Lumely, the impresario of Her Majesty's Theatre, London, who produced it on March 14, 1848:

> On every side were zeal, talent and good will employed successfully to exe-cute a work which many cities of Italy had pronounced to be Verdi's mas-terpiece. But although Verdi had already commenced to make his way to English favour, and this by means of that vigour and dramatic fire which unquestionably belonged to him, the public displayed an unwonted unanim-ity of sulkiness upon the production of *Attila*. They would have "none of it."[15]

Apparently, music and libretto were equally displeasing. Yet some were enthusiastic. A critic for the *Illustrated London News* declared, "There is a warmth, spirit, and energy in the music which carries away the listener, which excites and inspires. . . . The too frequent use of the drums and the brass instruments is the great fault."[16] But the more influential Henry F. Chorley in the *Athenaeum* raged, "The force of noise can further hardly go. . . . It is some-thing to have touched the limits of the outrageous style. . . . The melodies are old and unlovely . . . and [no Verdi opera] is more devoid of discourse which enchants the ear than this Gothic opera. May we never hear its like again."[17] And the next production in Britain did not occur until 1963, the 150th anni-versary of Verdi's birth.

In the Western Hemisphere *Attila* had its first performance on January 22, 1848, at the Teatro Tacón in Havana. Splendidly produced by the local Italian Company, it pleased both the local critic and the public, and to such an extent that for the fall season, Signor Marty y Torrens, who funded the company, lured from Italy Ignazio Marini, the bass for whom Verdi had composed the title role. And at Marini's first performance in Havana, on November 15, 1848, he turned what had been enthusiasm for the opera into a *furore*. Reported the *Gaceta de la Habana:* "It seems impossible that a voice so mighty as he possesses can be so admirably controlled. . . . We can still hear the hoarse cry of the barbarian who falls to earth. . . . It is not enough to hear Marini, one must also see him."[18]

Whereupon the Havana company, with Marini and a roster of 104 sing-ers, instrumentalists and staff, scheduled the opera for its American tour in 1850. Stopping first in Charleston, South Carolina, from March 26 to April 2, it gave a "season" of four performances, *Norma* (2), *Lucrezia Borgia*, and *Ernani*, each night selling out the Charleston Theatre (capacity 1,200) despite prices advanced to $1, $2, and $20 for private boxes.[19] But in departing for New York, probably for lack of a ship, it elected to go by land, then a difficult journey requiring frequent changes from train to ferry, or even to horse and carriage.[20]

The choice may not have been wise. Though the artists, or some of them, reached New York by April 8, the *Herald* the next day reported, "In consequence of the great fatigue occasioned by a land journey from Charleston, the Havana Italian Opera Company cannot appear for a day or two," and its management has chosen to "postpone the performance until all the vocal and instrumental corps are refreshed and invigorated."[21]

The next day's story announced the first performance would take place on Thursday, April 11, and attributed "the little delay" to the "natural anxiety of the vocalists to be in the very best voice." Yet the reporter stirred a pot of scandal by suggesting that along with troubles caused by the sudden change of climate, "Our free air also affects them. They become very impulsive in it. Being accustomed in Italy and Havana to obey the government and to sing by authority, where our free institutions give them only the law of liberty, they take a little time to enjoy it, to revel in it, and become acquainted with its delicious luxuriousness, so charming to the imagination, and so delicious to its realization. This is all very excusable, if not continued too long."[22] But what were those impulses freed, or revels enjoyed, he did not reveal.

As scheduled, the company opened with *Norma* on April 11 in the newly rebuilt Niblo's Garden Theatre and, as in Charleston, the next night repeated that opera. The critic for the *Herald*, reporting on the two performances was ecstatic: "Thus we have the true Italian opera sure enough. The whole is gloriously perfect and as rich in voices, skill, and all the adjuncts necessary to success as can be found in London or Paris."[23] And for Monday, April 15, the company announced *Attila*, promising repeat performances on Tuesday and Wednesday.

At the premiere, according to the *Morning Courier and New-York Enquirer*, "the house was crowded from top to bottom," and the *Herald* remarked on an audience "remarkable for numbers, beauty and fashion."[24] The *Home Journal* gave the most detailed report of Marini's performance.

> The story aside, we must say, we were delighted with Marini's personation and singing of the part written for him by Verdi. The hero is a magnificent fellow, six feet two, apparently, and athletically developed and proportioned, and his voice would have served any Jupiter we ever dreamed of, on the top of the most windy Olympus. He sings as if he could call up an earthquake at the shortest notice, and his cloak of lion's skin, with the paws sweeping the ground, seems to have a movement like a cloud stirring up the thunder in his lungs. Coarse and prodigal as his beard and other belongings are, Marini is a gentleman savage, withal, and there is a symmetry in his fine limbs and

a good breeding, even in his most violent action, which distinguish him very markedly from what the same part would be in hands of [Federico] Beneventano. The music is written to express overwhelming personal strength and impulses wholly untamed, and it seems to us entirely original, and successful of its kind, storming, bullying, defying, and starting by leaps into rages, from one end of the Opera to the other. There is just one scene where a different action is called for—and, to our thinking, Marini showed himself a master in the giving of it—the progressive degrees, through defiance, terror and submission, with which the barbarian King receives the anathema of the Bishop of the Church of Rome. The death, at the close—where the pulpy and plumptitudinous [Fortunata] Tedesco (Odabella) walks up and kills this tremendous athlete with the smallest possible dab of her nice little sword— was received with a general laugh, and we suggest, that, for the credit of the masculine gender, he should be done for *a la* Holofernes, asleep, or with some show of probability.[25]

Yet not all agreed on the opera's merits. The *Courier and Enquirer* judged "that with the exception of one or two brilliant pieces, it is the most unmitigated, unqualified piece of stupidity both in plot and music, that we ever had the ill-fortune to hear."[26] The weekly *Albion* declared, "*Attila* is a faded patchwork: the borrowed materials are multifarious, but Verdi has so besmeared them that their identification is difficult. The most inveterate air-hunter cannot detect more than one pleasing melody. . . . Signorina Tedesco was in better voice than during her last sojourn among us, and sang really well. Marini was the hero."[27] Even about Tedesco there was no agreement. The *Herald* complained, "Obliged to sing from a score transposed to suit her voice, the leading element of the theme of the composer is lost, and the climax of the music is left to the whole company of vocalists. Though Signorina Tedesco may shine by such means, the composer suffers, because his design is not fully interpreted."[28]

All reports agree, however, that at the opera's second performance the audience was "very slender."[29] Whereupon the company canceled the third performance. Balked of a success with the opera in New York, the company took its production to Boston, where it gave *Attila* its local premiere on May 21 in the Howard Athenaeum. The *Boston Post* admired Marini, "*He* is the opera," and even had a good word for some of the music, "a tenor solo, a duet between tenor and soprano, and the famous trio near the end of the piece." Evidently the trio's fame had preceded the opera to Boston. But best of all, according to the anonymous critic, was Marini recounting Attila's "dream."[30]

The *Evening Transcript*, in its review of the opera, had a greater interest in *Norma*, which even at its second performance drew "a splendid audience and every seat was filled." Apparently *Attila*, despite Marini, did not draw a decent house, and the opera was not performed again east of the Rocky Mountains until 1969.[31]

Seemingly the opera's music was not the cause of banishment, for as will be shown, some of its music remained for years in circulation. Moreover, in San Francisco *Attila* had a continuing success, with productions in 1859, 1862, 1866, and 1872.[32] Following its premiere there, local critics generally ranked it high, and one, while complaining that no libretto either in Italian or English had been made available, was moved by the music alone to write:

> Those grand bursts of harmony that close the different acts, the effect of which is artfully enhanced by the previous declamation and passionate sing- ing of principal personages, wonderfully affects the fancy of the audience. They are like the long role [*sic*] of a stormy sea upon a sandy shore, where the heavy fall of the breakers is incessant. The imagination runs riot in the harmonious uproar; and although the sounds are inarticulate to one who knows not the foreign language that is sung, yet there is a music and a rap- ture in such a union of human voices as there is, according to the poet, by the side of the ocean.[33]

If in San Francisco, why not in New York or Boston? Perhaps the reason lies in contrasting demographics. New York and Boston at the time had a cultural elite made up predominantly of Anglo-Saxon Protestants, many of whom, with a strong streak of Puritanism, viewed the theater with distrust; San Francisco, still in its Gold Rush era, had a more cosmopolitan population and culture. Its opera house was filled with immigrant Italians, French, Spanish, and Germans who outnumbered the Anglo-Saxons, many of whom had left their Puritanism behind. In New York, more clearly than in Boston, society's dictum went out that the opera's libretto was immoral.

The *Home Journal* has the most to say: "The captive warrior-girl, going with a lost reputation, through four acts of intriguing with the barbarian King, becoming his Queen in the last scene, and then stabbing him, and being received on the spot, into the arms of her previous lover. We doubt, whether in English, it would be allowed to keep the stage." And later in that review, the paper stated, "*Attila* was withdrawn from the stage after two representa- tions, and we regret that its moral forbids the expression of a hope for its reproduction."[34] Apparently, in New York as in London, the public would have "none of it."

The Havana company, on its way back to Cuba, stopped to give seasons in Philadelphia (where most Quakers disapproved of theater and music), Balti- more, and Charleston, but in none did it mount the opera.[35] Yet the American impresario, Matetzek, after hiring Marini and most of the company away from its Havana management, in 1854 staged the opera's premiere in Mexico City, where other companies performed it in 1856, 1857, 1861, and 1865.[36]

Meanwhile, even in the United States some of the music, when separated from the stage action, found considerable popularity. At an orchestral concert in New York in December 1850, two members of the Havana troupe, a baritone and a bass sang the duet in which Ezio proposes to Attila, "Avrai tu l'universo, Resti l'Italia a me" (You will have the universe; Leave Italy to me), a duet that in Italy often aroused the greatest excitement. The critic for the *Albion* was unimpressed, lamenting Verdi's "habit of overlaying the richest of instruments, the human voice, with a unison accompaniment of some orchestral instruments." Still, he praised the singers for "giving at the start, a very elevated key-note to the entire performance."[37]

That same month in San Francisco, still nine years before the opera's local premiere, music lovers at a concert heard a trombone fantasy on one of the opera's arias (probably Ezio's "Dagli immortali vertici," his soliloquy on his place in Roman history), and three years later a soprano, tenor, and baritone sang the "famous" trio from the last act, "Te sol, te sol quest'anima," in which Odabella insists to Foresto "You alone my heart loves," while Ezio urges them to stop their cooing and get on with their plans. The next year, 1854, a bass-baritone sang Ezio's aria, which by now was increasingly heard in recitals.[38]

Meanwhile, in New York in 1856, at the Philharmonic Society's fourth and final concert of the year, a baritone sang a scene and aria (probably "Dagli immortali vertici") to such "hurricanes of applause" that he had to repeat it.[39] On the Fourth of July, 1859, Torle's Brass Band, "one of the best we have," played "a fine arrangement of airs" from *Attila*, and the following year the Seventh Regiment Band played a quick-step march drawn from the opera, and a baritone in that year and the next sang (presumably) Ezio's aria.[40] More startling perhaps, a lawyer and amateur baritone, John Ward, in his diary for 1865, records that at the soirees in which he and friends entertained each other with arias, duets, and piano transcriptions of operatic numbers, he sang the baritone aria four times and joined others to sing the trio eight times. Plainly, in New York and San Francisco, at least, some of the opera's music was in the stores, bought by amateurs and professionals, and heard by still others with pleasure.[41]

By 1870, however, when the *Complete Catalogue of Sheet Music and Musical Works* for sale by the country's leading publishers appeared, the vocal numbers available had dwindled to two, Odabella's fierce entrance aria "Allor che i forti corrono" (While your men rush to combat, your women stay in camp, but Italian women fight . . .), offered only with an Italian text, and the trio "Te sol, te sol quest'anima," available in a variety of translations. In addition, however, the publishers offered twelve instrumental arrangements of music from the opera.[42] Yet in the next decade one well-known touring troupe, Clara Louise Kellogg's Concert Company, continued occasionally to offer an excerpt. Kellogg, an American soprano, active from 1861 to 1889 and much praised at home and in Europe, was then at the close of her career, and with three other singers (contralto, tenor, baritone), a violinist, a pianist, and an accompanist (and a Weber concert grand piano) made extensive tours, parts of which in

1881, 1882, 1883, and 1889 played in the towns of Kansas, where dates and programs have been documented.[43]

In 1881 the troupe visited Atchison, Leavenworth, and Topeka and had a success, though charging $2.00 for reserved seats instead of the usual $1.50. Apparently it offered the same program in the three cities, and Kellogg, her tenor, and baritone sang the trio from *Attila*, almost certainly "Te sol, te sol quest'anima." In 1882 and 1883, she scheduled nothing from *Attila*, but in 1889, in a tour that visited eight Kansas cities, she included a duet from the opera and its trio. As her troupe did not include a bass, the duet probably was for soprano and tenor, "Sì, quello io son" (act 1). The local newspapers, preferring to comment on more familiar selections, ignored those from *Attila*.

Kellogg's recitals seemingly were among the last to offer vocal excerpts of the opera, though the trio continued to be heard in Catholic churches where it was fit to new words, "Jesu Dei vivi," and sung usually by professionals hired to lead the choirs. In this disguise it proved so popular that in 1922 the Society of St. Gregory of America, seeking to enforce the Papal *Motu Proprio* of 1903 (ordering a return in Church music to Gregorian chant), took special note of the trio: regardless of words, it was declared "neither fitting nor appropriate."[44] For a time thereafter, at least in some Protestant churches, other arrangements continued to be sung, but for all but a few choristers the trio and its origin were lost to memory. Chiefly what survived was Ezio's aria, which the publisher G. Schirmer had included in his 1904 album of *Celebrated Opera Arias for Baritone*.

Thus as the new century wore on, though Sousa's Band sometimes played selections from *Attila*, including an arrangement of the trio and final quartet, the opera was otherwise all but forgot. It has no entry in the *Collectors' Guide to American Recordings, 1895–1925*, and only one in the early editions of *The Victor Book of the Opera*, an arrangement for band of the final trio. But placed on the reverse side of an "Aida Selections," it could be found only by chance, for the Victor Book had no index or separate listing for *Attila*. Moreover, no artist in the Metropolitan Opera's Sunday Concerts series (1883–1946) sang an excerpt, not even a bass, who might have made a strong showing in Attila's account of his dream.[45] And in Europe the opera fared little better. Its last nineteenth-century production at La Scala had occurred in 1867, raising the total of performances there to eighty-four, and toward the end of the century there were revivals in three smaller Italian theaters and at least two more before 1914.[46] But curiously in Germany, in the early years of the Verdi Renaissance that saw many of his operas revived, *Attila*, though based on a German play, was not among them.

Its first post–World War II revival seems to have been a concert performance in the Venice Festival in 1951, mounted and broadcast on Italian radio to mark the fiftieth anniversary of Verdi's death. Though taped by the Italian company Cetra, the recording was not released in the United States.[47] More decisive in turning the musical world's attention to the opera was a staged production mounted in Florence in December 1962 (anticipating by a month the 150th year of Verdi's birth).[48] This production, with realistic scenery, costumes, and the bass Boris Christoff as Attila, was so successful that companies elsewhere took up the opera.

In London the Sadler's Wells (after 1973, the English National Opera) was one of the first to stage it, on November 26, 1963, offering it in English, as was the company's custom, and in a production that divided opinion. Victor Gollancz, an opera-going publisher, in his *Journey Towards Music*, recorded: "The other night *Attila*, a work full of boring and sometimes laughable crudities (literally laughable: the audience laughed) . . . and people were rushing about in the intervals asking wasn't it all really marvellous?"[49] Most critics judged the Sadler's Wells scenery too skimpy and costumes too severe. One noted that Odabella's "Band of Women," consisted "of only three," and another, who had reveled in the Florence production, complained that the Venetian lagoon, with its storm, sunrise, and founding of Venice, merely "looked like Hackney Marshes in a fog."[50] Yet the *Manchester Guardian* hailed the production as a "great and treasurable" gain to the "London repertory."[51] Though attendance was disappointing, the company revived the production the following year to better reviews.

In the United States the New Orleans Opera Association, on October 9, 1969, in the city's Municipal Auditorium, gave the opera its first performance since the last in San Francisco in 1872.[52] Frank Gagnard, for the New Orleans *Times-Picayune*, found it "worthy of revival," but lamented a libretto that reduced Attila to "a figure in a romantic opera landscape that is as much dominated by the romantic misunderstandings of the soprano and tenor . . . as by the presence of a legendary world terror." As for the production (two performances), he thought it lacked "epic proportion." The young Justino Diaz as Attila, for one, was "more impressive in physical presence than in dynamic thrust." Yet, "the fact exists that the music is independently attractive although not irresistible." He liked particularly "the flinty but lyric" quality of Odabella's entrance aria and the last act ensemble (apparently the final trio), which was "as simple and lovely and persuasive as the group number that ends the third act of *La traviata*."[53]

In a review for *Opera*, Jack Belsom noted that singers were all "singing their roles for the first time" and were initially insecure. "The opera was played on a raked stage with a mosaic floor pattern, abstract drops and an occasional prop. . . . The augmented chorus, still lacking balance in the tenor section, was an asset, but the grotesqueries perpetrated by the ballet [at the banquet] were a major distraction. The opera was sung in three acts, virtually complete save for small cuts in ensembles and repeats of some cabalettas." He wanted more revivals of early Verdi, suggesting *Ernani*, *I Lombardi*, and *I due Foscari*.[54]

New Orleans's partial success with the opera was followed three years later by a production of the Opera Theatre of New Jersey mounted for a single performance in Symphony Hall, Newark, on October 20, 1972. The company's approach to the opera was quite different. Sets and costumes were minimal, and as one reviewer observed, "suggested economy rather than artistic purpose." Further, they were not helped "by a dreary series of projections and some bizarrely miscalculated lighting effects." Yet a critic for the *New York Times* thought the company had done "itself proud with the production."[55] My own memory of the storm, sunrise, and founding of Venice, usually the most disappointing of the scenic spectacles, was of a little steamy mist and gray coloring to the back of the stage while the singers, as if to stay dry, hugged the front. Most of the company's money, it seemed, had gone into rehearsing the orchestra and lesser singers, who played and sang well, and into casting two international stars in the roles of Attila and Odabella, the Metropolitan bass Jerome Hines and the Turkish-Italian soprano Leyla Gencer. Their fans greeted them with rapture, and since no commercial recording of the full opera was yet available in the United States, throughout the audience tape recorders whirred.

Gencer, who was famous for her ability to sustain a soft line with floating pianissimos, not surprisingly made a tour de force out of Odabella's *romanza* "Oh, nel fuggente nuvolo" (Oh, in the fleeting cloud), which she sings alone onstage to open act 1. By then an honored guest in Attila's camp, she soliloquizes in a wood at night, by a stream streaked with moonlight, and in a fleeting cloud sees her dead father's face, which transforms into that of her lover Foresto, whom she believes dead. Haunted by her memories, she appeals to breeze and stream to cease their murmurs so that she may hear the voices of her ghosts. Verdi's accompaniment, featuring flute, English horn, cello, and harp, creates amid the somewhat brassy opera a moment of quiet beauty.

Hines, athletically proportioned and standing six foot six, was physically a stupendous "legendary world terror," though the historic Attila, as described by one who saw him, was "short and squat, broad-chested, a huge beady-eyed head, a wisp of beard, flat-nosed, swarthy complexioned."[56] Hines also had a remarkably fine bass voice, full and sonorous, and even though on this night he may not have been at his best,[57] throughout, the performance was musically exciting, and the audience cheered every number.

Before Newark, Hines had sung Attila only in Buenos Aires (1966), and reportedly in the decade after Newark he told American impresarios that he would go anywhere to sing the role.[58] And so he did, notably to Philadelphia (1978), Edmonton (Canadian premiere, 1978), Memphis (1979), and Chicago (1980). In Philadelphia the critic for the *Inquirer* welcomed the opera as "a reminder of how much intriguing music lies outside the usual operatic choices." In particular, he was impressed by Verdi's orchestral touches not only for Odabella's *romanza* but more generally for the "storm music, sea sounds, and forest murmurs."[59] At Edmonton, a critic for the *Albertan*, was less enthusiastic, concluding that to hear the opera "once was a pleasure and a privilege; more is unnecessary."[60] And after the Chicago premiere a local critic

OPERA THEATRE OF NEW JERSEY

Symphony Hall, 1020 Broad Street, Newark, New Jersey 07102
Friday Evening, October 20, 1972 at 8:00 P.M.

GIUSEPPE VERDI

'attila'

Prologue and three acts
Libretto by Temistocle Solera

Conductor: Alfredo Silipigni
Producer: Hubert L. Fessenden
Staged By Franco Gratale
Sets by: Adewyn Darroll
Lighting by: Martin Abramson
Special Costumes for Madame Gencer and Mr. Hines by:
    Franco Gratale
Co-designed and executed by: Audrey Arnsdorf
Costumes by: Anthony Stivanello

ATTILA . . . . Jerome Hines
EZIO . . . . Cesare Bardelli
ODABELLA. . . . . Leyla Gencer
FORESTO . . . . Nicola Martinucci
ULDINO . . . . Thomas Perri
LEONE . . . . Daniel Bonilla

TIME: 453 A.D.
PLACE: Italy

PROLOGUE
    Scene I: Ruins of Aquileia
    Scene II: An Adriatic Lagoon

ACT I
    Scene I: Forest near Attila's Camp
    Scene II: Attila's Camp

ACT II
    Scene I: Ezio's Camp outside Rome
    Scene II: Banquet in the former ruins of Aquileia

ACT III:
    Forest dividing Ezio's and Attila's Camp

Choreography by: George Tomal
Chorus Master: Anthony Manno
Assistant Conductors: Vincent Scalera, Joan Dornemann
Assistant Stage Director: Richard Getke
Intermission: 12 minutes

GALA TICKET HOLDERS, PLEASE
FOLLOW USHERS INSTRUCTIONS
AT LEFT FRONT OF ORCHESTRA
FOR ADMITTANCE BACKSTAGE.

Figure 5.1. The program for the staged performance in 1972 in Newark, New Jersey (from author's collection).

remarked: "Trouble is, once you strip away the oom-pah music and surface excitement, you are forced to deal with an impossible libretto. . . . There is not one credible figure among the cardboard gallery. The king of the Huns, you are asked to believe, was no blood-thirsty warrior—not *really*—but a kind of hairy marshmallow." He wanted the opera presented in concert so that "an audience could then appreciate what is good about the score without having to worry about its dramatic ineptitude."[61]

In the next twenty years, however, *Attila* was frequently staged as two American basses of the next generation flourished in the role. The elder of these, Justino Diaz, seven years after venturing on it in New Orleans, sang it in Washington (1976), Cincinatti (1979, 1984), and New York (1981). Paul Hume, for the *Washington Post*, described Diaz as "more than a pillar of strength. He looked, moved, acted and sang like a great figure in history. . . . In solo scenes and ensembles, Diaz dominated the action and the sound." The production was "staged very simply, to suggest the somewhat stark surroundings in which the story takes place," and "the lighting was effective." Few might agree with Hume's view of nature's out of doors as "stark surroundings," but "from the roars of approval that burst out after some of the big moments in the piece, the audience seemed to like what it saw and heard."[62] But Andrew Porter for the *New Yorker* spoke harshly of the sets and lighting. "What *Attila* needs first of all is a more bravely picturesque and colorful kind of production than is fashionable today. . . . Spotlights traipsed after the principals, and there seemed to be not quite enough of them to go around: in the fuller ensembles, some of the soloists were lit and others not. The general effect was of murk and gloom . . . particularly ill-suited to an opera that depends so largely on bold color contrasts and scenic splendor."[63]

The other bass, Samuel Ramey, sang Attila in New York (1981, 1985, 2003), San Francisco (1991), and Chicago (2001), even managing on occasion, notably in Venice (1986, 1987), Milan (1991), and London (1993), to nudge aside European basses who also were doing well with the role. But Hines, Diaz, and Ramey were not the only American basses to find success in the opera. In addition, there were Simon Estes (Tulsa, 1982), John Cheek (New York, 1988), and Stephen West (New York, 1996). As this chronicle suggests, there was hardly a year between 1976 and 2003 when the opera was not on the stage somewhere in the United States, and in New York City, where it had been rejected in 1850, it became almost a repertory work, with performances in 1981 (in two seasons), 1985, 1988, 1996 (by two companies), and a concert performance in 2003.[64]

Undoubtedly one reason for the opera's success in the United States was the happy coincidence of a roster of basses who could shine in the role, but another of perhaps equal importance was a particular production that, judging by the number of times it was used, and praised, American audiences in that last quarter of the twentieth century downright liked—it seemed to suit the opera. This production, created in 1980, was a joint project of the Chicago

Friday Evening, March 13 at 8:00 PM

ATTILA

Libretto by Temistocle Solera
(after Zacharias Werner's play, "Attila, König der Hunnen")
Music by Giuseppe Verdi
(By arrangement with Associated Music Publishers, Inc., U.S. agents for G. Ricordi & Co., Milan)

*Conductor: Sergiu Comissiona
Directed by Lotfi Mansouri
Scenery Designed by Ming Cho Lee
Costumes Designed by Hal George
Lighting Designed by Gilbert V. Hemsley, Jr.
Choreography by Margo Sappington (debut)
Chorus Master: Lloyd Walser
Assistant Stage Director: Ronald Bentley
Music Preparation by Diane Richardson
Assistants to Mr. George: David O. Roberts, Peg Schierholz

Cast
(*in order of appearance*)

Attila, King of the Huns . . . . Samuel Ramey

Uldino, a young Breton, Attila's slave . . . . James Clark

Odabella, daughter of the Lord of Aquileia . . . . Marilyn Zschau

Ezio, a Roman General . . . . Richard Fredricks

Foresto, a knight of Aquileia . . . . Enrico DiGiuseppe

Leone, an ancient Roman . . . . Dan Sullivan

Italy, 452 A.D.

ACT I—Scene 1   The ruins of Aquileia

Scene 2   The shores of the Adriatic Sea

Scene 3   A forest near Attila's camp

Scene 4   Attila's camp

INTERMISSION

ACT II—Scene 1   Ezio's camp

Scene 2   Attila's camp

Scene 3   The forest dividing the camps
of the Romans and the Huns

This new production of Attila was made possible by the Gramma Fisher Foundation of Marshalltown, Iowa, through a deeply appreciated joint gift to Lyric Opera of Chicago, New York City Opera, and San Diego Opera.

* A Chair for Conductors has been established by The Fan Fox and
Leslie R. Samuels Foundation, Inc.

Continued on page 20

Figure 5.2. The program for the first performance at the New York City Opera, in 1981 (from author's collection).

Lyric Opera, the New York City Opera, and the San Diego Opera, with its cost underwritten by the Gramma Fisher Foundation of Marshalltown, Iowa.[65] The scenery was designed by Ming Cho Lee who, though born in Shanghai in 1930, studied and made his career almost entirely in the United States, and by 1980 was possibly the country's outstanding designer for opera. The costumes were by Hal George and the lighting was by Gilbert V. Hemsley Jr., but Lee's work, in part because of his choice of a drop curtain, determined the color and style of the costumes and even of the lighting, and the production generally was known by his name. According to the *New Grove Dictionary of Opera*, Lee "has described his sets (he rarely designs costumes) as 'the abstract essence of a dramatic statement.' They are noted for their skeletal but suggestive use of modern materials, especially metals, and their painterly use of lighting to achieve sculptural effects."[66]

Nevertheless, the first bit of scenery the audience saw, while taking seats and during the opera's prelude, was not at all skeletal but an almost exact copy painted on the drop curtain of the Raphael fresco showing Pope Leo confronting Attila in the fields of Mantua. There, sitting calmly on a white palfrey, in white clothing, gold cape, and triple crown, is the pope, while facing him, on a dark horse and in contorted agitation, Attila gazes skyward at the menacing figures of St. Peter and St. Paul. The papal group, cardinals, priests, and attendants, are at rest and confident; the Huns, alarmed by Attila's sudden, odd behavior, all in twisting movement. Whenever down, the colorful, dramatic curtain not only gave the audience something to look at—eight horses, archaic trumpets, horns, banners, staves, swords, crosses, and saints in the sky—but helped to fill out the later, more skeletal presentation of the same scene onstage. It gave the audience a point of view, the same as the composer's, from which to watch and hear the opera.

After the prelude (based on a theme to which Druid seers at the banquet warn Attila against strangers), Lee's drop curtain rose on the ruins of Aquileia in a set more typical of his style: To the front of the stage, an uncluttered, open courtyard allowing room for the large chorus; across the back, a high, semi-ruined city wall pierced by a tall, arched gateway through which billowed smoke and dust from the burning city. Through that swirl of smoke Attila emerged, carried in triumph by his men, and later Odabella, on foot with the captive women, each principal given a highly dramatic entrance. A contrasting scene, equally successful, was the forest near Attila's camp in which Odabella, by a stream streaked with moonlight, sees in a fleeting cloud first her father's face and then her lover's. Lee did not attempt to show stream, forest, or cloud, but instead offered an eight-foot wall of stone, with a hint of trees behind, and the wall showing brightly white in moonlight. The set could hardly be simpler (easy to light, to assemble, or to ship to another city), yet it caught the scene's quiet spirit.

Not every scene was so successful. As often, the founding of Venice, with its storm, sunrise, and refugees arriving by boat, left much to the suspension of

Figure 5.3. Raphael's mural in the Vatican portraying the meeting between Pope Leo I and Attila. Reproduced by permission from the Musei Vaticani.

disbelief. The lighting for the storm and sunrise was a bit disappointing, and—no boats. The refugees came on foot. Perhaps in an era of scenic miracles on television, the storm and sunrise should be played with the curtain down—except that Verdi interspersed the music with remarks by an all-bass "chorus of hermits" (the oxymoron always a butt for jokes) who live on the lagoon's small islands. But might not their voices be heard through the curtain? Which then might rise on the refugees already ashore? In most respects, however, Lee's curtain and sets neatly offered what Porter once had suggested the opera wanted: "A more bravely picturesque and colorful kind of production . . . [for] an opera that depends so largely on bold color contrasts and scenic splendor." Lee's production not only played for five seasons at the New York City Opera but also was used, to general praise, in Chicago, San Francisco, and Tulsa.[67] As Anthony Tommasini for the *Times* wrote of the City Opera's 1996 revival: "Overall, the production provides a chance to hear a solid performance of a seldom-heard and rewarding work."[68]

Yet outside New York, the opera's history in the United States during the twentieth century's last quarter suggests that even when sung by a charismatic bass it often was judged to be an interesting revival but not worth repeating. Of the other cities mentioned, only Chicago and Cincinnati heard it a second season,[69] suggesting perhaps that the opera does not rank among the best of "early Verdi," not the equal, say, of *Nabucco, Ernani,* or *Macbeth.* It no doubt has virtues, but also flaws, the latter seeming neither fatal nor those most frequently cited.

Hasty critics, like one in Chicago, often begin by stating the opera lacks "historical accuracy."[70] In fact, as operas or historical plays go, it does rather well. Attila did invade the Western Empire in 452 AD, did sack Aquileia, driving refugees to islands in the lagoon, did camp outside of Mantua, did parley there with Pope Leo I, did withdraw without marching on Rome, was superstitious and impressed by omens, did marry a lot of women, and did die on a wedding night. So far as anyone knows his character, Verdi's portrait is fairly drawn; so, too, the character of the historical Ezio.[71]

Another frequent complaint is that the characters lack "credibility." As one critic, reviewing a recording of the opera, asked: "Is Attila really the black-voiced black-hearted histrionic villain that [Evgeni] Nesterenko presents. He is the only principal character in the drama who is consistently honorable, trusting and open. . . . He comes closer to tragic nobility than the termàgant Odabella, the deviously politicking Ezio or the weedily ineffective Foresto."[72] Or as Andrew Porter wrote, Verdi's "Attila is a ruthless but greathearted giant ambushed and killed by three treacherous Italians. . . . At the end, instead of feeling that devoted Italian patriots have triumphed, we watch a lion netted by pygmies."[73] Yet if patriotic Italian audiences then and now do not balk at this picture of their ancestors, why should we? Surely this surge of sympathy for Attila is what Verdi intended. He frequently chose subjects in which the main

Figure 5.4. Young-Bok Kim as Attila, Sarasota, 2007. Photograph by Deb Hesser. Courtesy of the Sarasota Opera Company.

character initially is unattractive or socially unacceptable yet at the end inspires sympathy—*Rigoletto, Traviata.*

The libretto's chief flaw is the way motivation and development of character continually are concealed in choral numbers. Midway in the banquet scene, for example, Foresto tells Odabella that Attila's servant Uldino will hand his master a poisoned cup. But first word of the plan is uttered while other soloists and the chorus are singing. And Uldino, who hitherto has seemed quite loyal, explains his change of heart—he is an enslaved Breton, not a Hun—during an ensemble in which his voice is one of five soloists singing over full chorus and orchestra. Even with supertitles, probably few in any audience grasp what is afoot or why, but most, like that early critic in San Francisco who understood not a word, simply let the music, like waves from "a stormy sea," wash over them, until "imagination runs riot in the harmonious uproar."

Even Odabella's character may not be as two-dimensional as often declared. The Italian critic Massimo Mila, in an essay "*Attila,* Verdi's Barbaric Jewel," has much to say about the banquet feast as Verdi's effort to introduce action and character into a huge concerted finale, one that for length and complication is "almost monstrous in its enormity." Mila suggests that Odabella's motive in knocking Uldino's poisoned cup from Attila's hand may not have been solely that she wanted herself to be the cause of the tyrant's death. She may have acted in part because "without it being even clear to herself, the virgin warrior is more attracted to the older leader, than to the immature Foresto. Music is capable of this: it is not perhaps capable of describing an object, as words and drawings do, but long before Doctor Freud, it was already capable of probing with inquisitive lamps the most secret and unmentionable depths of the subconscious."[74]

Once considered, Mila's thought is hard to ignore. Attila clearly is attracted to Odabella; why not she to him? They are alike in courage and equally ruthless. And if Mila is right, then the opera's famous final trio, "Te sol, te sol quest'anima," in which Odabella tries to convince Foresto that she loves him alone becomes still more moving, for she is also trying to convince herself. Is there anything in the music to back up Mila's suggestion? He himself admits there is not, at least not in the banquet's finale. But Julian Budden, writing perhaps even before Mila's essay was published, had this to say about Odabella's *romanza* in the forest outside Attila's camp: "Odabella, meanwhile, has now become Attila's honoured guest. She has accepted her new position so as to have the means of murdering him; but she is unhappy in her dissimulation. Hence the sorrowful G minor melody for violins, not unlike the cello cantilena at the start of act II of *Norma,* which introduces the scene and is woven into the subsequent recitative."[75] Her words do not say as much as Budden hears in the music, but they do declare unhappiness in her position if not in her dissimulation, and as Mila suggests, music can hint at something more. A soprano able to act could find more room in the role for interpretation than most critics allow.

SAN FRANCISCO OPERA

1991 Season
Lotfi Mansouri, General Director

This production was originally funded by the Gramma Fisher Foundation of Marshalltown, Iowa, through a deeply appreciated joint gift to the New York City Opera, the Lyric Opera of Chicago, and the San Diego Opera.
This presentation is sponsored, in part, by generous gifts from Mr. and Mrs. Thomas Tilton and Mr. and Mrs. John C. McGuire.

San Francisco Opera Premiere

Opera in two acts by GIUSEPPE VERDI

Libretto by TEMISTOCLE SOLERA
Based on the play *Attila, König der Hunnen*, by Zacharias Werner

Attila
(in Italian)

Conductor
Gabriele Ferro*

Production
Lotfi Mansouri

Stage Director
Laura Alley*

Set Designer
Ming Cho Lee

Costume Designer
Hal George

Lighting Designer
Joan Arhelger

Choreographer
Kirk Peterson*

Chorus Director
Ian Robertson

Musical Preparation
Susanna Lemberskaya
Kathryn Cathcart
Susan Miller Hult
Philip Eisenberg

Prompter
Philip Eisenberg

Assistant Stage Directors
Paula Suozzi
Sandra Bernhard

Stage Manager
Gretchen Mueller

San Francisco Girls Chorus
Elizabeth Appling, Director

First performance:
Venice, March 17, 1846

CAST
(in order of appearance)

Attila, King of the Huns	Samuel Ramey
Uldino, Attila's Breton slave	Craig Estep
Odabella, daughter of the Lord of Aquileia	Elizabeth Connell
Ezio, a Roman general	Vladimir Chernov* (Nov. 21, 24) Luis Girón May* (Nov. 27, 30; Dec. 3, 6, 8)
Foresto, a knight of Aquileia	Antonio Ordoñez
Leone (Pope Leo I)	Philip Skinner
Huns, Romans, Aquileians, hermits, Druids, priestesses	
Corps de ballet	

*San Francisco Opera debut

TIME AND PLACE: Fifth century A.D.; Italy

ACT I	Scene 1:	At the gates of Aquileia
	Scene 2:	On the banks of the Adriatic lagoons
	Scene 3:	A ruin near Attila's camp
	Scene 4:	Attila's camp outside Rome

INTERMISSION

ACT II	Scene 1:	Ezio's headquarters near Rome
	Scene 2:	Attila's camp outside Rome
	Scene 3:	A ruin near Attila's camp

Supertitles by Christopher Bergen, San Francisco Opera.

Supertitles for this production have been made possible by
the Stanley S. Langendorf Foundation.

Latecomers will not be seated during the performance after the lights have dimmed.

*The use of cameras, cellular phones and any kind of recording equipment
is strictly forbidden.*

The performance will last approximately two and one-half hours.

THURSDAY, NOVEMBER 21 AT **7:30**
SUNDAY, NOVEMBER 24 AT 2:00
WEDNESDAY, NOVEMBER 27 AT **7:30**
SATURDAY, NOVEMBER 30 AT 8:00
TUESDAY, DECEMBER 3 AT 8:00
FRIDAY, DECEMBER 6 AT 8:00
SUNDAY, DECEMBER 8 AT 2:00

*Delta is the official Airline of San Francisco Opera • Lexus is the official automotive sponsor of San Francisco Opera
Kawai is the official piano of the San Francisco Opera. Pianos provided and serviced by R. Kassman*

Figure 5.5. The program for performances in San Francisco, 1991 (from author's collection).

Such nuances, however, will not keep the opera on the stage. Because of its spectacular and choral scenes *Attila* is expensive to mount; and because of its demands on singers, not easy to cast. Yet in the past forty years it repeatedly has shown that revivals well-cast and -staged can delight audiences. The reason is plain. As a critic in San Francisco wrote of its 1991 revival: "This primitive essay in blood-and-guts melodramma . . . is a rip-snorting, razzle-dazzling, oompah-pahing, loosely historical mishmash in which everything is reduced to mellifluous basics." Then he added, "The capacity audience (a local rarity in these days of recession) seemed to love everything."[76]

A New York critic, reviewing a concert performance in 2003, added: "There's no intellectual defense of early Verdi. Either you get it or you don't, and if you have to ask why, you probably aren't going to. *Attila*, which the Opera Orchestra of New York presented at Carnegie Hall on Wednesday night, is full of oompah accompaniments and facile melody. Those of us who adore it say such things with tremendous affection. To make this work as a performer, you have to be naïve enough to believe in this music and sing it as if you meant it."[77]

Despite the opera's problems, it tempts impresarios, for if well done, it will fill the house, as it did for seven performances by the Sarasota Opera in 2007. Moreover, singers, and not only basses, like it for the melodic gems given them individually and together. Costumers like it for the chance to contrast patrician Rome with the less couth barbarians, Christian priests with Druid seers, the Pope against the Hun. And set designers like it for its special effects: the storm, dawn, and founding of Venice, as well as the banquet with its blood-red clouds and wind of evil omen. The opera sits like ripe fruit on a high bough, promising a reward for extra effort. And Lo! The Metropolitan Opera announced it for a house premiere in 2009–10.[78]

Chapter Six

Macbeth

The Italian company from Havana, having come to New York in April 1850 prepared to excite audiences with the U.S. premiere of two Verdi operas, and having failed with the first, *Attila*, promptly went ahead with its second, *Macbeth*. The venture perhaps was riskier, for the play was popular in New York and everyone would have an opinion on how Shakespeare should be handled. In addition, with this opera, his tenth, Verdi had attempted something new in Italian opera of the day—offering in place of romantic youngsters (tenor and soprano) a middle-aged couple (baritone and soprano)[1]—and had sought to underpin the couple's murderous story with a somewhat new style of music—structured less on formal numbers and more on melodic declamation. Dedicating the score to his father-in-law, he wrote, "Here now is this *Macbeth* which I love more than my other operas."[2] And it met with success, playing steadily in Italy and elsewhere for forty years.

The opera, however, has a complication best faced at once. It had its first performance in the Teatro Pergola, Florence, on March 14, 1847, but in 1865, for a production in Paris (sung in French), Verdi revised the score. Here and there, he improved the orchestration; more obviously, he added a ten-minute ballet in the witches' cave, substituted a new aria for Lady Macbeth to open act 2, a new finale for act 3, a new chorus for the Scottish people in act 4, and moved Macbeth's death offstage (as in Shakespeare), ending instead with a hymn of victory for the Scottish people. Though his revision was substantial and added stature to Lady Macbeth, it did not change the opera's basic thrust, to draw the audience into a strongly charged psychological atmosphere of moral disintegration. It had, however, little success in Paris, only fourteen, ill-attended performances, and few elsewhere until the 1930s. Hence, throughout the nineteenth century, the *Macbeth* that most audiences heard was the original version, and in the United States the revision's history did not begin until 1941.[3]

As originally conceived, therefore, the opera came to the United States in the spring of 1850, following its Western Hemisphere premiere at the Teatro Tacón in Havana, on December 19, 1849. The company reportedly had taken special care for the scenery and the mechanical marvels needed for Banquo's ghost and the apparitions in the witches' cave,[4] and the result was a sumptuous musical and scenic success, much praised in Havana's press. One journal, the *Diario de la Marina*, described the opera as "not having cabaletta music [fast arias with high notes] but something more philosophical . . . in a fantastic genre . . . in Meyerbeer's style." The reference was to the latter's *Robert le diable*, which offered the public not only an orgiastic scene of evil spirits but also one in which Robert's father, Satan, calls licentious nuns from their graves to engage in a ghostly dance.[5]

Verdi's "fantastic" scene was his third act in which Macbeth confronts the witches in their cave and demands to know the future, revealed to him by the three apparitions and the procession of Banquo's descendants, the eight kings who will succeed Macbeth. When he faints in despair, a few sylphs descend (at the Florence premiere let down in a boat on pulleys), while the witches sing a soft, lilting appeal. With a few dance steps and mime the sylphs gently fan Macbeth, and as he revives, vanish. He then closes the act with an aria of defiance. In a letter, Verdi directed that the stage throughout the act "must be completely dark,"[6] and for the premiere he planned to use a new magic lantern technique to throw the apparitions onto the back scrim. To that end, he had a special machine, a *fantasmagoria*, made in Milan and brought to Florence, but the local authorities refused in the name of decency to darken the auditorium sufficiently to use it, and so it was sent to the basement where, a critic quipped, it would in time be found and ascribed to "Etruscan origin."[7] In Florence the act was received coolly, though elsewhere it was more successful. But in the history of the opera's reception the witches' cave has always been the problematic act, the most expensive to stage and often declared "too long"—eight kings passing slowly by.[8] Yet in Havana, despite the warning of the *Diario* that *Macbeth*, lacking cabalettas, "does not belong to the public's favorite genre,"[9] the opera's success was real, and lasting. Though the city was without opera for a period, 1851–53, in the following years through 1877, *Macbeth* had six revivals.[10]

After canceling a scheduled third performance of *Attila*, because of a "slender" audience for the second, the company, playing in Niblo's Garden (a wholly enclosed theater) refurbished its finances with good houses for Donizetti's *Lucrezia Borgia* and *La favorita*, and then, as its second novelty of the season, on April 24 offered the U.S. premiere of *Macbeth*, cautiously scheduling only two performances. For both, the house was full. Shakespeare at the time was the country's most performed playwright, the play well-known, and as the *Herald* advised, "No opera is better suited for those who do not understand the Italian language."[11] Yet the play's familiarity was also a hindrance. The *Home Journal* declared the opera "a caricature," comparing Verdi's Macbeth unfavorably to the one recently presented to the New York public by the great English actor William Charles Macready.[12]

The latter's Shakespearian style was one of dramatic force rather than elegant declamation. Macready was harsh-featured, his jaw large and square, and his gestures abrupt; but his voice was rich, compared often to a cello, and even in a whisper could project power. Macbeth was his favorite role, and though he honed his production of the play over the years, in essence it remained the same. The three witches, introduced in semidarkness by thunder and lightning, appeared at center stage, heads together, then separated, and called their farewells. They were men, with staves, torn tunics, scraggly beards, and voices loud, male, and malevolent. The heath was bleak, and Macbeth and Banquo on their entry were preceded by a parade of clansmen, brought to a halt by Macbeth, offstage, calling (with a line not in Shakespeare), "Command they make a halt upon the Heath." According to a surviving prompt book the cry for "Halt!" was repeated "by the prompter and assistants in as many voices as they can summon," and then Macbeth appeared, in a knee-length kirtle, a beret with a badge and feather, and a plaid scarf over his left shoulder. In his right hand he carried a baton, on his left arm a small round shield—the personification of Authority.[13]

Another grand ceremonial scene was Duncan's arrival at Macbeth's castle, set to a royal march. Music was part of the English tradition of presenting the play, and from the 1660s to 1875 most English productions used a score (authorship variously ascribed) titled "Famous Music from *Macbeth*."[14] Macready used this score, which mostly consisted of a reedy, sinister overture, ending with minor chords, a march for Macbeth's troops, another for Duncan, songs and dances for the witches, and an occasional orchestral interlude to cover scene changes. In addition, Macready spiked his production with many rolls of thunder, drums, and trumpet flourishes. There is no reason to think that Verdi knew of this music. He composed his opera before he had seen any Shakespeare play onstage, and his first experience of one occurred only three months after his opera's premiere when he happened to be in London. Learning that Macready was doing *Macbeth* at the Princess's Theatre on Oxford Street, Verdi went, took note of Macready's staging of the procession of kings, and later advised the Teatro San Carlo in Naples to do likewise.[15]

Following Duncan's murder, Macready spoke the colloquy with Lady Macbeth in a piercing whisper, and in order not to stem the rising tension cut the porter scene. The play, in the words of his biographer, was the portrait of "a great general devil-ridden by his imagination,"[16] and it sped to its climax, the duel with Macduff, staged on a rampart of Macbeth's castle. The sword play lasted long and terrified the audience (and sometimes the Macduff). Macready changed expression to match every line. His face took on a startling ferocity, his eyes blazed with fury, he muttered oaths not written, he was supremely "the tyrant at bay."

The biographer, Alan S. Downer, offers an account of the duel, based on the promptbook and compared to contemporary reports:

> Six times the swordsmen rush upon each with a cut and lunge; closely engaged they fight round in a cartwheel six times. Macduff cuts at Macbeth's head, misses, and the force of the blow carried him across stage to the right. Macbeth pursues, they lunge at each other five times, and on the sixth lunge Macduff delivers the death stab.

Macbeth staggers back, catches himself and, with a momentary suggestion of his regal stride, returns only to fall on Macduff's sword in yielding weakness. The spirit fights, but the body sinks in mortal faintness. Thrusting his own sword into the ground, Macbeth raises himself by its help to his knees where he stares full in the face of his vanquisher with a resolute and defiant gaze of concentrated majesty, hate and knowledge, and instantly falls dead.[17]

None of this is in Shakespeare, where Macbeth is killed offstage and denied a heroic, public death. People left Macready's performance stunned by the dramatic force of his Macbeth, pondering "the overthrow of a haunted mind."[18] Writing for the *Brooklyn Daily Eagle* in 1846, Walt Whitman recalled, "We have known the time when an actual awe and dread crept over a large body assembled in the theatre, when Macready merely appeared, walking down the stage, a king. He was a king—not because he had a tinsel gilded crown, and the counterfeit robe, but because he then dilated his heart with the attributes of majesty, and they looked forth from his eyes, and appeared in his walk."[19] And he had played Macbeth in New York in 1826–27, 1843–44, and 1848–49, the last only eleven months before the Havana company brought in Verdi's opera.

The *Tribune*, reviewing the opera's first night, reported:

It was, however an Italian Macbeth from beginning to end—with an Italian Lady Macbeth and Italian witches. . . . In the witch scene, for instance, where "Macbetto" receives the same salutations as our English Macbeth, instead of three witches there are squads of four each [six each in Florence], who deploy backward and forward across the stage, and finally form a hollow square around "Macbetto" and "Banco." . . . The drinking song in the second act, which Signora [Angiolina] Bosio sang twice without satisfying the demands of the audience, is in a rich, gushing strain, that embodies the very spirit of boundless revelry. . . . But we cannot see without prejudice a softened, sentimental Macbeth, with a very amiable, womanly Lady, in place of those whom we have always regarded as among the most grand and terrible creations of mortal brain.[20]

In partial disagreement, the weekly *Albion* complained that Verdi's "Lady Macbeth is a loose, drinking, reckless murderess," and his Macbeth, "a drivelling, pitiful tool." Verdi had "taken a wrong view of the characters" and "his metaphysics are wrongly based." Moreover, "Of melody in the opera there is literally none. It is a series of disconnected phrases. . . . The music of the witches is grotesque, but we see the Polchinelli and the caps and bells peering out through all; the weird, Norse character of Macbeth's witches is no where visible. . . . The finales exceed in unmitigated noise anything we have heard."[21]

Likewise complaining that the leading characters were un-Shakespearian, the critic for the *Evening Mirror* was "outrageously shocked at the dagger scene done into recitative," yet stated further on, "If we were called upon to select the best portions of the music, we should point out the dagger soliloquy and suc-ceeding duet."[22] That conflicted response, seemingly a confusion of feeling, as if the critic thought he *should not* like the opera but rather did, appears in most of the reviews, especially plain when read one after another. The critic for the *Tribune*, for example, before praising the opera, starts out, "In the general char-acter of the music, we were rather agreeably disappointed."[23] His colleague on the *Evening Mirror*, after praising the "unusual care and attention" Verdi took with "the recitatives and their instrumental accompaniments," deplores how in his arias "he revels in his usual outrageous style." Yet, of the opera's *brindisi*, he writes, "The drinking song sung by Lady Macbeth in the banquet scene is very effective and drew down a most tumultuous encore," and later, "the finales to the first and second acts are really tremendous in the power of their vocal and instrumental combination. They took the house by storm." He also praised the chorus and orchestra and concluded, "the opera was magnificently put upon the stage, both as regards scenery and costumes. The witches' cave was a highly effective scene." The *Herald*, too, praised the production's "scenic elegance."[24]

So what was there not to like? Well, George Templeton Strong, a young New York lawyer who adored Mozart and Handel, went to the opening and later wrote in his diary:

> The music is Verdiesque. Screaming unisons everywhere and all the melodies of that peculiar style, the parallel whereof is rope-dancing: first a swing and flourish hanging on by the hands, then a somerset. . . . The unfortunate man is incapable of real melody. . . . His *supernatural* music in this opera is espe-cially comical. . . . The deluded author has no means whatever of expressing *feeling* in music, except by a coarse daubing of *color*. Passion is typified and portrayed by a musical phrase instrumented with the brass; softer emotion by the same phrase written for the oboes and flutes; terror by ditto through the medium of the brasses judiciously heightened with the big drum and the ophicleide.[25]

The *Albion* summarized this view of Verdi for its readers, "We acknowledge for our own part that we expected little, and that we were not disappointed. We felt certain that the subject was too grand for his mental capacity, and we soon found out that he was floundering about helplessly in his endeavors to reach its level."[26]

Closing its short season at Niblo's Garden on May 8, with a performance of *Lucia di Lammermoor*, which reportedly jammed the house and street, the Havana company departed for Boston and the Howard Athenaeum, where in a season of the usual favorites of Bellini and Donizetti, on May 28, it offered a single performance of *Macbeth*. The *Boston Post* did not review it, but according to the *Evening Transcript*, "there was a good but not crowded house." The Mac-beth, sung by Cesare Badiali, "added largely to his reputation by his masterly acting and singing." Yet the paper gave twice the space to the auction of seats for the closing night's *Favorita*.[27] In Boston, the "Athens of America," Verdi's *Macbeth*, though a local premiere, stirred little interest.[28]

Back in New York, the company opened its longer summer season first at the Astor Place Opera House and then, at prices reduced by half to fifty cents, at Castle Garden.[29] There, in a season of 36 performances, the operas most often scheduled were Bellini's *Norma* (6) and *Puritani* (5), Donizetti's *Favorita* (5), and Verdi's *Ernani* (5), and among the less frequent but also of Verdi, *I due Foscari* (3) and *Macbeth* (1). That *Macbeth* had only a single performance is surprising, for earlier the opera had drawn two full houses and some favorable reviews, but perhaps its scenery and contraptions for apparitions made it too expensive to mount in a season at reduced prices; *Foscari* was shorter, less complicated, less costly. Moreover, in the company's two-week closing season in Philadelphia, it performed of Verdi only *Ernani*, still in the United States his only opera to challenge the favorites by Bellini and Donizetti.

In reviewing the U.S. premiere of *Macbeth*, New York's *Sunday Times and Messenger*, after highly praising the sleepwalking scene, had concluded, "The opera is one of Verdi's best, and should be so deemed. It will bear frequent repetitions, or we greatly underrate public taste."[30] Yet after the summer of 1850 it was not heard again in New York or Boston, or for the first time in Philadelphia, for thirteen years, though these three cities at the time, with their proximity and combined populations, were the country's operatic center, their only competitor being New Orleans, the smallest of the four and far distant.

The music of *Macbeth*, however, was not wholly forgotten. At concerts sopranos frequently sang Lady Macbeth's *brindisi* from the banquet scene, which seemingly also had been the first of the opera's music heard in the United States. In New York, on January 15, 1850, three months before the Havana company's premiere of the opera, a soprano, Apollonia Bertucca, had sung the aria at a benefit concert for the French Church of St. Vincent de Paul on Canal Street. The packed audience, some four thousand strong, in the Tabernacle on Broadway, had called for a repeat, which was granted, and which, according to the *Herald*, "was but justice, for never have we heard such difficult music so admirably well sung."[31] Later that year another soprano, Anna Bishop, sang it in English in a pastiche, *Judith*, based loosely on the Biblical story of Judith and Holofernes and set to music taken mostly from *Nabucco* but including the *brindisi*. The show, sung in English and with sumptuous scenery, a ballet, and a military band onstage, played five nights, and the *Morning Express* particularly praised the *brindisi*, "to which she gave a new charm, from the exquisite style in which she rendered it."[32] Sailing to San Francisco in 1854, Bishop again staged *Judith*, now somewhat revised, and again with special praise for the *brindisi*, which she repeated later in two concerts. One critic pointedly suggested that, if sung in context, the aria would have even greater impact,[33] but San Francisco would not hear the complete opera until 1862.

It heard a different excerpt, however, in October 1855, when a tenor in yet another touring company offered Macduff's aria, "Ah, la paterno mano." But the piece passed without comment.[34] Meanwhile, in New York, four months earlier, a soprano, Caterina di Ferrari, had a success with Lady Macbeth's cavatina, or entrance aria.[35] But chiefly it was the *brindisi* that kept memory of the opera alive.

The following year in New York, at least two sopranos sang it, Bertucca repeating her success, and an American, Genevieve Ward, under the name Ginevra Guerrabella.[36] Most likely these reported performances are only a few of others that went unrecorded, for the aria seems to have won considerable popularity, and in those days what was heard in concert usually was attempted at home by amateurs, many of whom were skilled.[37] A sign of that popularity, at least until 1870, is its dual publication as sheet music with Italian or English text, "Si colmi il calice di vino eletto," or "The cup is mantling" [frothing]. It also could be purchased in instrumental arrangements, including one for piano four hands. No other music of the opera fared so well.[38]

Meanwhile, on the West Coast, a tenor, Eugenio Bianchi, and his wife Giovanna, a soprano, who with their Bianchi Opera Company formed San Francisco's first resident company to endure, scheduled the opera for its local premiere on November 18, 1862. Earlier, Eugenio, as part of the Barili touring company, had sung the role of Macduff at the opera's Mexico City premiere on January 10, 1857, and again at its revival there in December, and evidently he liked the opera, though as Macduff his role was relatively small.

For the San Francisco premiere, in which Giovanna sang Lady Macbeth, the Bianchis staged the opera in Maguire's Opera House (capacity 1,700) with an orchestra of twenty-five and a mixed chorus of perhaps thirty.[39] Even so, the orchestra and chorus were only half of what the smaller Italian houses typically employed. In Florence, the Teatro Pergola had a chorus of forty-eight for the opera's premiere, and in Venice, the comparable Teatro la Fenice (capacity 1,500) in 1850, the same year as the opera's premiere in the United States, had a roster for the orchestra of sixty-seven, with its mixed chorus probably numbering at least fifty. Thus, what Verdi's *Macbeth* sounded like in its San Francisco premiere, with chorus and orchestra halved in strength, is conjectural, but from the reviews it had a success. And an anticipatory article in the *Daily Alta California*, presumably based on rehearsals and perhaps memories of performances elsewhere, had reported:

Verdi, in *Macbeth*, has availed himself of the witches to create choruses of peculiar weird-like construction, to set unnatural appearances and disappearances to music, and at the same time, to give a vivid musical picture of the various emotions of the principal characters—Macbeth, Macduff, Banquo, Lady Macbeth, etc. It may appear somewhat strange to hear the soliloquies of the timorous Thane rendered in music—to be entranced with the dulcet strains of Lady Macbeth, stimulating her craven lord to make good the predictions of the weird sisters, but the listener will soon become aware that the composer with rare power, has been faithful to his task. The Witches' Choruses are remarkable for their power and effect. Lady Macbeth exhibits the true tragic muse in the dagger scene, the reading of the letter, and the somnambulic scene, while the *brindisi* at the banquet, is a gem of vocalization, contrasting, with great effect, the more serious part of her *role.* . . . The composition, as an entirety, is strikingly grand, as the finale of the first act, on Duncan's death, will convince all. The principal part is that of Lady Macbeth. . . . The opera will be produced with an entire and enlarged chorus, new scenery and effect; the stage management having been entrusted to Mr. H. Courtaine, whose familiarity with Shakespeare and the Italian lyric drama are such as to assure a correct presentation of the opera.[40]

The next day, after the premiere, the *Daily Evening Bulletin* remarked:

The witch-music—which is a great feature of the opera—especially failed to satisfy expectation, from the imperfect rendering of a feeble female chorus. No doubt the management finds much difficulty in forming an efficient chorus of female voices for a single piece, as in this case, and—as we are perhaps obliged to accept the opera as it is, or dispense with it altogether—we can only lament that the case should be so. Notwithstanding the comparative failure of the witch-music, the opera as a whole was very well received by a crowded and sometimes enthusiastic audience. The stirring finale of the first act met with a storm of applause. Many other passages were very beautiful, and were well received. Among these may be mentioned the drinking song and chorus of the second act and in the fourth act the chorus of Scotch refugees, and air by Macduff. . . . There was also a chorus of witches and a ballet by a sylph (Miss Howard) in the third act, that were very pleasing. The piece unhappily terminates in an abrupt Bowery-stage style, where there is a hacking and hewing of broadswords in the lowest of regular melodramatic mode.[41]

And on the Sunday after the premiere and two succeeding performances, the weekly *Golden Era* summarized its impressions:

We are content. . . . Signora Bianchi's Lady Macbeth was in look, person and action an identity; and her vocalism was superb. Her eminent fitness, physical and facial, for the *role* of the royal murderess, is patent to all who are familiar with her *personnelle* and the historic presentiment of Macbeth's sanguinary and ambitious spouse. The drinking song in the second act, "Fill the Glasses with choicest wine" [though the opera was sung in Italian], was given by the Signora with a dewy deliciousness of musical intonation. The "deranged" scene in the third act [Macbeth at the witches' den] was sublimely wrought, so also was the murder scene, with the leering witches flitting athwart the fitfully flamed window of the castle; weird and unnoted witnesses of the bloody tragedy enacted within. . . . The witch scenes are produced with startling effect. As an entirety *Macbeth* is most engrossing.[42]

These reviews, more detailed on the production than those from Boston or New York, confirm that in the United States the opera on its initial exposure was viewed primarily as a vehicle for Lady Macbeth and as a sort of Gothic horror of weird effects and scenery. In both New York and Boston, Cesare Badiali, a distinguished baritone, had won praise for his Macbeth, but always less notice than his Lady: He had the title role, but she, the spotlight. Yet even in San Francisco, despite good reviews, Giovanna Bianchi could not keep the opera afloat. After four performances in 1862 and one the following year, *Macbeth* disappeared from the stage and was not heard again on the West Coast until 1955.

On the East Coast in the season 1863–64, it had its only revival, and its last until 1941, when Maretzek's company, with a roster of Italian soloists, on October 21, 1863, gave the first of three performances at the Academy of Music (capacity 4,600). On opening night, the *Times* reported, the soprano, Giuseppina Medori, "in the well-known *Brindisi*" was asked to repeat it, which she did, and "the opera was received with so much fervor that it is destined we think, to overcome the old prejudice against operatic versions of Shakespeare's plays." And the critic wrote at length on how "the mere touching of the original situations of the great dramatist is attended—in the minds of Anglo-Saxons—with a certain sense of the ridiculous." Maretzek, regretting the prejudice, confirmed its impact. Though he thought *Macbeth* "perhaps the best" of the four "novelties" he had staged that season, at the box office it had proved "the least attractive."[43]

Moving to Philadelphia for a three-week season in December, he gave the opera its local premiere on the ninth at the city's relatively new Academy of Music, built in 1857 (capacity 2,984) and still in use. The next morning, the *Philadelphia Inquirer* had a short review:

> Great curiosity was excited to witness the manner in which so familiar a tragedy of Shakespeare could be wedded to music. The verbal text follows the original as closely as possible, consistent with the peculiar demands of an opera; and the situation that is best for this purpose. The music is necessarily, to a great extent, declamatory, the occasions for rigid dramatic effects limiting the opportunity of the composer for formal melodies. Nevertheless, Verdi has succeeded, with the skill of great masters, in sustaining the musical interest by the flow of his melodic ideas and the contrasts necessary to sustain interest. The performance was very satisfactory . . . the burden falls entirely on the two principal characters. It was a triumph to satisfy in any sense the taste of those who were impelled constantly to recur to the English of Shakespeare.[44]

Conversely, in Boston the following month, the *Evening Transcript*, reviewing Maretzek's production, concluded: "Excepting the Brindisi, there is not a salient point which commands attention. It is one unbroken series of common-pieces from beginning to end." Later, after extravagant praise for the Lady Macbeth (Giuseppina Medori) and even the Macbeth (Domenico Bellini), the anonymous critic concluded, "The opera as we have said, is a very empty thing as music; but it is a good field for the exhibition of dramatic powers." Yet more important, "Tonight Gounod's *Faust* will be produced for the first time in this city."[45] In the company's two-and-a-half-week season in Boston, *Macbeth* had two performances and *Faust*, fast gaining popularity, seven.

Returning to New York, the company gave one more performance of *Macbeth*, on March 2, and the *Herald* reported:

> There was a select—we might say very select—audience at the Academy of Music last evening. Judging from the small number present, we must conclude that the public do not like Verdi's *Macbeth*; and yet this opera is, like all that the great *maestro* has composed, truly grand. In Boston *Macbeth* was one of the greatest attractions of the season; here it falls flat upon the public ear and goes begging. . . . The audience, though not large, was vastly appreciative and applauding with an energy seldom witnessed when the house is full. All the choice *morceaux* in the opera were encored, the grand finale of the second act rousing those present to enthusiastic applause. Mme. Medori, as Lady Macbeth, was truly artistic. Bellini sang and played the *role* of Macbeth as none but so superior an artist could, and the performance was accordingly a great success. . . . On Saturday a grand matinee with *Faust*.[46]

During that spring "season" in New York, Maretzek offered twenty-eight performances of fifteen operas, of which *Faust* had ten, and the next in number, Petrella's *Jone* (loosely based on Bulwer-Lytton's *Last Days of Pompeii*), three. And in all, during the year 1864, in New York and Brooklyn alone, the Maretzek company would give thirty performances of *Faust*. What did that opera offer the public that *Macbeth* did not? Chiefly, more easy tunes, less declamatory drama, and a happy ending, as Marguerite's soul is "Saved!" Also, in Maretzek's spring production of *Faust* (sung in Italian), he put onstage for the Soldier's Chorus (and possibly also for the fair) a military band, and to his mixed chorus of roughly forty he added the Arion Society's men's chorus of fifty, advertising the combination as "the greatest choral force that has ever been heard in opera."[47] Thus, *Faust* offered a more spectacular, concertlike production, especially as opera houses did not yet fully darken their auditoriums and managers favored encores. In Maretzek's *Faust*, to make use of the military band, the Soldier's Chorus may have been extended by internal repeats before applause as well as encored after. As Clara Louise Kellogg, who sang Marguerite, observed, "The public went to the opera houses to hear popular singers and familiar airs. They had not the slightest interest in a new opera from an artistic standpoint."[48] And so, pushed aside by more popular operas, such as *Norma, Faust,* and *Favorita,* except for a few admirers *Macbeth* in the United States in the 1860s slipped into oblivion.

Until revived in 1941, it surfaces even in excerpts only rarely and then with a shift of focus. Whereas in its first fifteen years in the United States sopranos had kept the opera alive onstage and in recital, after the turn of the century it was the tenors, baritones, and basses who dug out excerpts and sang them. The powerful New York music publisher G. Schirmer, for example, began in 1903 to issue its series of *Celebrated Opera Arias* for soprano, alto, tenor, baritone, and bass. The soprano album of forty-two selections had none from *Macbeth*; but the album for tenor, as one of forty selections, had Macduff's aria, "Ah, la paterna mano"; the album for baritone, Macbeth's "Pietà, rispetto, onore"; and for bass, Banquo's "Come dal ciel precipita." It is doubtful that G. Schirmer did this out of love of Verdi, but, more likely, in response to what it was hearing from vocal teachers and artists.

Moreover, in the Metropolitan Opera's Sunday Evening Concerts, a series that ran from 1883 to 1946, no soprano ever sang an excerpt from the opera, not even the *brindisi*, but the great German bass-baritone Friedrich Schorr in 1927 sang the one excerpt heard, Banquo's aria.[49] The opera at the time was on the cusp of revival in Germany, but Schorr's effort to stir some interest in it at the Metropolitan, if that was his intent, failed.

Meanwhile, in Italy in 1912, the great baritone Mattia Battistini recorded (with piano) Macbeth's aria, "Pietà, rispetto e amore," a rendering that displays some vocal flourishes usual in the nineteenth century but today more often deplored than imitated.[50] Of more consequence for Americans, Enrico Caruso in 1916 recorded (with orchestra) for the Victor company Macduff's aria. This recording had a popular success. So much so that the excited Victor company in a two-paragraph puff in the *Victrola Book of the Opera* (6th ed., 1921) got almost everything wrong, saying the opera had its premiere "in New York in 1848 [wrong]. . . . The opera, which received scant praise in Italy [wrong], and still less in other countries [only partially true], follows closely the familiar Shakespeare tragedy. One of the most interesting airs is the "Paterna Mano" (My Paternal Hand). This however, is one of the numbers written for the Paris version [wrong], as the original work had no part for the tenor [wrong]." No matter, Caruso convinced thousands in the United States that there was more to *Macbeth* than commonly said.[51]

The opera returned to the United States in October 1941, not in an opera house but on Broadway, at the Forty-Fourth Street Theatre (capacity 1,000). The production was staged by the New Opera Company, a group initially formed during the depression of the 1930s to give young American singers another company in which they might gain experience. In the country at the time there were said to be "only about three modest-size companies of any reputation: Chautauqua Opera in Western New York (established 1929); Riverside Opera in California (1932), and Florentine Opera in Milwaukee (1933)."[52]

Moreover, the start of World War II, in 1939, had blocked access for young Americans to the smaller European companies.

The war, however, had brought many European artists to America, including some from the Glyndebourne company in England, among them Fritz Busch who had conducted Glyndebourne's highly successful revival (in Italian) of *Macbeth* in 1938 and 1939. That production, the first in England since 1860,[53] had been born in part by revivals in Germany beginning in 1928 with one at Dresden (in German) with Busch, a chief actor in the Verdi Renaissance in Germany, conducting.[54] In New York on October 24, 1941, he and others formerly at Glyndebourne joined with the New Opera Company to present, with American singers, a *Macbeth*, modeled on the Glyndebourne-Dresden productions and with Busch once again conducting.

As at Glyndebourne, the opera, not just the singers, had an astounding success. Herbert Peyser wrote in the *Musical Courier*, "a large and tensely gripped audience rewarded with a tremendous ovation a feat which ranked unquestionably among the memorable operatic experiences of the community in recent decades."[55] The company gave the opera six performances, and the following year, in the larger Broadway Theatre, which could seat 1,765, gave five more, with Fritz Stiedry, another Glyndebourne artist, conducting. According to Olin Downes of the *Times*, reviewing the second season's opening night,

> The audience last night . . . sat fascinated . . . by the lusty and often superbly imaginative music of the opera. . . . Curious that the work, first produced in 1847, and eighteen years later revised, waited so long for our public to know it. . . . It is a find, in the earlier Verdi manner. To pursue too many comparisons with Shakespeare's drama might be risky. But it remains that the libretto of Piave, so effectively altered and revised by Verdi, is a gold mine of opportunities for the composer, and especially for one of Verdi's imagination and dramatic temperament. By consequence the score seethes with lusty melodies, with frequently prophetic strokes of commentary and characterization, and it often conveys the fantastical atmosphere of the original drama.[56]

As Downes noted, the production was the first in the United States to present Verdi's revision of the opera, scored in 1865 to an Italian text for the Théâtre Lyrique in Paris. The productions in both Glyndebourne and New York, however, declined to follow Verdi's revision in two important instances: Neither included his ten-minute ballet for the witches' cave, though based on scenes supposedly in Shakespeare (in fact interpolated early in the seventeenth century from a play by Thomas Middleton), and both reinserted into the final scene Macbeth's dying aria, "Mal per me," ending "Vile crown, I despise you."[57] Originally Verdi had Macbeth killed onstage, dying with a short, bitter farewell to life and followed by a single-sentence shout of victory from the Scottish people. Curtain. It is an ending that many critics and audiences have found dramatically and musically effective. In Shakespeare, however, Macbeth dies offstage; Macduff reports his death to the army, which gives a shout of victory, accompanied by a trumpet flourish, followed by a speech of noble intentions from Malcolm, the new king, and ending in another trumpet flourish as all exit. Curtain. In his revision Verdi reverted to Shakespeare's plan, killing Macbeth offstage, and on Macduff's report of his death, closed with a hymn of victory by the Scottish soldiers, the Scottish people (women and men, providing a second men's chorus), all led by Malcolm and Macduff. With the voices in four groups and singing at first in response to each other and then together, they close the opera with a large swell of sound. While the insertion of Macbeth's death onstage with "Mal per me" just before the victory hymn seems to some people a happy stroke, preserving a brief, dramatically effective aria, the custom—for so it has become—strikes others as "senseless."[58] It not only ignores Verdi's revision to accord with Shakespeare, but it leaves onstage throughout the hymn a large baritone stretched out and visibly puffing—all that singing and then the duel!

But why should Americans of the 1860s reject the opera and their descendants in the 1940s greet it with enthusiasm? Some reasons are plain; some speculations, plausible. Opera as a form of entertainment had moved slowly away from concert in costume toward drama, a change in taste to which many composers had contributed, notably Gluck, Mozart, Verdi, and Wagner. This shift was impelled in part by the emphasis of the Romantic Age on tragedy, but even more by the gradual introduction into theaters of electricity, a revolution in lighting that took place in the United States in the 1880s.[59] Whereas earlier, because the gas footlights were the best source of light for the singers' faces, they had been all but forced to come downstage to sing their arias (and if applauded to stand there and repeat them); but in the much darkened auditoriums of the future, with the greater possibilities of stage lighting, that march to stage front was no longer necessary. Moreover, the darkness inclined audiences to silence rather than chatter, tended to focus attention on the stage where there was light and movement, and so aided drama without injuring vocal display. What was lost (though another gain for drama) was the frequent encore of arias, the interpolations of popular arias from other operas, and the parading onstage of military bands. The change was slow, and for a long time opera houses continued to be built in the traditional horseshoe, so ideal for social display, the galleries circling a huge chandelier in the auditorium, while onstage the lighting came from a smaller chandelier overhead, the all-important footlights, and some sidelights aided by reflectors. But by the 1940s, the newly built theaters, in place of boxes, had deep galleries cantilevered on steel beams, were shaped more like a truncated slice of pie, and with their spotlights, grids, and dimmer boards offered possibilities onstage that Verdi had imagined but could not realize.

Perhaps, too, by the 1940s Freud and his colleagues had stretched for many people their concept of what a witch might be. To the traditional view of them as satanic tempters, real and substantial, there now was added the idea of them as symbols of inner promptings, real but unsubstantial. That idea, always in the play and opera, was strengthened by the proofs of psychoanalysis. Those who had scoffed at witches as merely the Halloween counterpart of Santa Claus, on these new terms found a way to enter the drama.

Despite the success of the New Opera Company's *Macbeth*, which reverberated across the country, the opera was not staged again in the United States for thirteen years, until the San Francisco Opera company, in its War Memorial Opera House, produced it on October 27, 1955, using most of Verdi's Paris revisions but omitting the new ballet. A company historian found the opera to be, "One of the most interesting novelties in the company history. It revealed, for all its earthy, elementally exuberant, and not displeasing, early Verdiism, pages and pages of strong imagination and pointed ironic touches." The sets were "bare and awesome, nicely suggestive of a dank, barren old castle, with a long curving staircase a recurrent ingredient."[60]

Alfred Frankenstein, a leading critic in the city, reported for the *Chronicle*: "Stage-wise, this was a real triumph, and if one dwells first on the setting it is because such things are unexpected in American opera and immensely welcome. . . . [It was] a setting of vast spaciousness, a setting as notable for its simplicity as its magnificence, as remarkable for its display of artistic imagination as for its practicability. Leo Kerz has designed a long, curved, irregularly gapped staircase and a black saw-toothed architectural framing that remain on stage throughout. Most of the scene changing is done with projections on the cyclorama . . . [and these are] perfectly integrated."[61] The company's annual season then ran five weeks in the autumn followed by a trip to Los Angeles, and after two performances at home it gave one in Los Angeles on November 1, the opera's local premiere.

Planning to revive it in October 1957, the San Francisco company contracted in January with Maria Callas to sing Lady Macbeth, but four days before the season's start, on September 17, she reneged, pleading ill health and wiring that she would not come until October 15, after the opening nights of her two scheduled roles, Lucia and Lady Macbeth. Remonstrance failing, the company announced that she was fired, complained of her behavior to the American Guild of Musical Artists, which ultimately concluded that she was "not wholly justified" in her breach of contract, that is, her reasons were not entirely medical. So the role was taken by Leonie Rysanek who two years earlier had made her U.S. debut in San Francisco as Senta in *Der fliegende Holländer*, and on the opening night of *Macbeth*, October 11, she had a triumph. Again, Frankenstein of the *Chronicle* liked the cyclorama and projections: "In the supernatural prophecy scene of the third act it creates a circle of unimaginably gigantic ghost kings which alone justifies the technique employed." He articulated for many why this sort of setting was so satisfactory: "The score faithfully reflects the ranting, cloak swishing, shrilly pitched Shakespearian dramaturgy of its time. The setting reflects with equal faithfulness, the more restrained, atmospheric and poetic attitude toward Shakespeare which is characteristic of our time. The contrast between the two does not result in inconsistency, it serves rather to underline the tragic ironies of the play and opera."[62] And as in 1955, there were two performances in the home house and one in Los Angeles.

Even as the San Francisco company, considered by many in these years to be second only to the Metropolitan, revived its *Macbeth*, a small company in New York also undertook to stage it, and the New York City Opera presented it on October 24, 1957, at the City Center theater, the former "Mecca Temple" of the Shriners on Fifty-Fifth Street between Sixth and Seventh Avenues. The theater, built in 1924 and seating 2,692, with two large balconies rather than boxes, had been seized by the city in 1942 for nonpayment of taxes, and now housed the City Center of Music and Drama, a project started by the city's mayor, Fiorello H. La Guardia, and dedicated to bringing opera, drama, and ballet to the public at popular prices. For its *Macbeth*, using the 1865 version, the company hired as stage director the distinguished Shakespearian, Margaret Webster, as conductor a young Italian, Arturo Basile, and as choreographer for the Witches' Cave ballet, Robert Joffrey. The singers, though not well-known, proved better than adequate. In all, during the five-week season the production had three performances. Why it was not revived in succeeding seasons is a mystery, for the audiences, though not large, were enthusiastic and the reviews, highly favorable.

Howard Taubman for the *Times* declared, "Flawed though it is, *Macbeth* is a work of genius." The company, "with its limited resources," could not produce a great performance, but "it communicated much of the [opera's] quality and spirit." In using the revised version, at the time the one usually preferred, it even staged the ten-minute ballet in which the witches summon the goddess Hecate to instruct them how to receive Macbeth and his questions on the future. This seemingly was the first staged performance in the United States of Verdi's ballet music, and Taubman judged the dancing as "barely passable."[63] In fact, the ballet was as much mime as dancing—Verdi directed that "Hecate should never dance, but only assume poses"[64]—and in my opinion (having attended two of the three performances) much of it was impressive, not only the movements that Joffrey designed for the evocation and appearance of Hecate, but the music itself. Raw it may be, but it has force. Nevertheless, most subsequent productions in this country of the later version cut the ballet, presumably because it adds ten minutes to the act and more dollars to cost.

Pleased equally with the opera and production, Paul Henry Lang for the *Herald Tribune* wrote a review titled "Verdi and Shakespeare," in which, while ignoring the singers, he pondered the greater question of Verdi's grasp of Shakespeare:

> Some of us now tend to ridicule Verdi's "barrel organ" tunes, but they achieve the very closeness to the audience which Shakespeare enjoyed. . . .

Verdi clearly saw that Shakespeare's motivations are much less severe than those of modern drama, they are purely mental-emotional, always resting on individual causes, and therefore eminently suitable for musical setting. And he realized that in the end the essence of dramatic stylization is to portray a single adventure from a man's experience in such a manner that it will stand for that man's whole life, so that this isolated bit of living becomes an entire life, an entire character. . . . [Verdi realized] that in the life of every man and woman there comes a moment when the driver of his star yields the reins and he is master of his own destiny. It is at these moments that his great, white uncomplicated, yet devastatingly telling melodies appear and with uncanny certainty take command of the situation.[65]

Such a statement of approval from Lang, who was at the time a high priest of musical history and analysis,[66] helped to rescue *Macbeth* from the generally held view in the United States that all of Verdi's "early operas" were inferior, not worth considering. Yet on a more practical level, what mattered most about the City Opera's production was its proof that a small company, of "limited resources" could have a success with the opera. The first other such smaller company to follow the lead was Cincinnati Summer Opera, which staged *Macbeth* in 1960, a local premiere, and again in 1961.[67]

Meanwhile in New York, on March 26, 1958, a group calling itself "The Little Orchestra Society" gave a concert performance of the opera in Carnegie Hall, presenting the revised version but cutting the ballet. The house was packed, in part because the Lady Macbeth, Leonie Rysanek, preceded by good notices from San Francisco, was making her New York debut, and as expected, again had a triumph. So, too, did the opera. Wrote Taubman for the *Times*, "If you want to test the dramatic power of an operatic score, put it on in concert form. . . . Suddenly every one in New York is rediscovering *Macbeth*. The City Center produced it last fall, and the Metropolitan will present it next season. Not bad for an early opera."[68]

Clearly, the Metropolitan's production, if successful, would lift the opera's status still further. In these years no company, not even San Francisco, came close to matching the Metropolitan's annual schedule: roughly, five months in New York with six Tuesday nights during the season in Philadelphia, followed by a two-month tour of major cities mostly in the south and midwest, and during the home season twenty Saturday-afternoon radio broadcasts to a national and international audience estimated at twelve to fifteen million.[69] Moreover, before the production's scheduled opening, on February 5, 1959, it received a tremendous boost of publicity. The company's manager Rudolf Bing had asked Maria Callas to sing Lady Macbeth, and in their negotiations they had arrived at a letter of intent in which they had agreed on the scheduling of her performances of *Macbeth* and *Traviata*. And Bing had announced her acceptance to the press. Then in November, with the season begun, Callas changed her mind, principally about the placement of *Traviata* between performances of

Macbeth, and Bing, with Rysanek in hand, canceled Callas. That day the local radio stations and tabloids, primed by the previous imbroglio in San Francisco, headlined variations of "Bing Fires Callas," all mentioning the new production of *Macbeth.*[70]

By January the furor over Callas had died, and attention shifted to the production, which would be mildly expressionistic in the current German style, for Bing, formerly of Berlin and Glyndebourne, had hired as stage director and designer, Carl Ebert and Caspar Neher, both of whom had worked on the 1931 Berlin production of the opera as well as on Glyndebourne's in 1938 and 1939. Thus, as wits noted, the Metropolitan was offering "a revival of a revival of a revival." But it promised to be sumptuous and exciting, and for those aware of the Verdi Renaissance, it was proof of the latter's continuity and impact.

According to the *Times,* the Metropolitan's scenic shop was preparing for the witches' cave, as symbols of Macbeth's wracked conscience, "a total of 650 monsters' visages, all but partly human, all grotesque and disturbing. . . . They float in mid-air. They seem to come forward in massed formation, and to recede into ever deeper dark. . . . Cunning lighting of greenish pallor produces incredibly weird effects."[71] And for the witches, 150 latex masks; for the soldiers, 65 new shields and spears. Costumes, it later appeared, were in pastel shades, mostly of red, brown, and gray, to contrast with the violence of the action, and costumes, facial makeup, and scenery all shared a chalky white base, unifying all elements. The score to be used was the 1865 revision, reinserting from 1847 Macbeth's death scene, "Mal per me," and omitting the new ten-minute ballet as well as the four-minute episode for sylphs, though Verdi had kept it in the revision.

In performance, two theatrical coups were memorable. For the first act finale, after announcement of Duncan's murder, as the chorus and principals moved stage front, a ten-foot canvas, but stagewide, lowered overhead, depicting in frieze the dead king. Beneath it, the chorus in frozen horror lined the front of the stage, whitened faces turned upward, and while two among them dissembled, all others keened the sacrilege of regicide. Then after the scene in which Banquo is murdered in the park outside the castle, the action moves inside where the Macbeths are, at the very moment of murder, entertaining the court. In the music Verdi moves from the *adagio* of Banquo's aria to the jumpy *allegro brillante* of the banquet, and the lighting went, in a seeming flash, from forest gloom to the hectic overbright banquet hall, strengthening the musical point. The morning after the premiere, the reviews were highly favorable, and Lang of the *Herald Tribune,* calling the production "regal," described the opera as "a great and absorbing music drama, and no one who is lucky enough to hear it will leave the theater without being overwhelmed."[72]

Proclaimed a hit, the opera had six performances in its home house, one in Philadelphia, and a national broadcast, all sung by Rysanek and Leonard Warren, a great baritone in a congenial role. Brought back the next year, it had five

Figure 6.1. The Death of Duncan, act 1 finale. Note the simple costumes and staging: principals (Lady Macbeth, Macbeth with hands raised, and Banquo) backed by the full chorus in lines to swell the sound and overwhelm the audience with their dismay at regicide. Photograph by Louis Mélançon, 1958. Courtesy of the Metropolitan Opera Archives.

performances at home and a broadcast. For this second season, the company, according to the *Herald Tribune*, made some changes in the score, "omitting the duet of Macbeth and Lady Macbeth at the close of the third act and connecting it with the fourth with the Hecate ballet music as a bridge. The battle music was heard as an interlude, but there no visual battling; the curtain rose to reveal Macbeth already defeated and dying."[73]

There was an additional change. Rysanek stepped aside for one performance, allowing her cover, Irene Dalis, to score a surprising success, surprising in part because Dalis was a mezzo-soprano, usually singing such roles as Amneris and Azucena. Yet she had to transpose only one aria down a tone, "La luce langue," and omit only the high D flat in the sleep-walking scene's concluding phrase. Overnight, the Metropolitan's production of *Macbeth* seemed even sturdier: the company had two strong leading ladies.[74]

Two years later, Warren having died, the opera returned with Anselmo Colzani as Macbeth for six performances and a broadcast. Rysanek sang four,

Figure 6.2. The banquet scene, Leonie Rysanek, Leonard Warren, and the ghost of Banquo in the chair (lower left). Photograph by Louis Mélançon, 1958. Courtesy of the Metropolitan Opera Archives.

including the broadcast, and Dalis, two. Then in the spring of 1964 the company offered Cornell MacNeil, another outstanding baritone, for six performances with his Lady alternately sung by Birgit Nilsson, who had opening night, and Dalis, the broadcast. Meanwhile, by the end of that year, two complete recordings of the opera were available: the Metropolitan's production, with Rysanek and Warren (RCA 1959) and the other, with Nilsson and Giuseppe Taddei (London 1964). All in all, the Metropolitan's production was a remarkable artistic and box-office success, in four seasons (six years) twenty-three performances, four broadcasts, and a studio recording by top-notch artists and technicians. Throughout the United States it had a large part in setting *Macbeth* in the public's mind as a repertory opera, one that periodically would return and give pleasure.

In the fall of 1966 the company moved into its new house at Lincoln Center, where the stage was a field of trapdoors, elevators, platforms and whole stages that could rise, sink, or move sideways, to say nothing of the possibilities for projections and lighting. Though the Metropolitan's *Macbeth* had been designed for the old house, which lacked most such devices, there seemed no reason that its concept and sets would not adapt easily to the new.

Six years later, Schuyler Chapin, Bing's successor, revived Bing's production of 1959 in the 1972–73 season, scheduling ten performances at Lincoln Center and seven on tour. But what appeared onstage was a surprise. In the *New Yorker*, Andrew Porter called it "a limp, bloated relic" of the previous production. "The banquet was a drab, glum affair. . . . All the scenic contrasts were flattened by a lighting plot tenebrous from beginning to end, except where the follow spots cast their crude circles of radiance around the principals. No sudden blaze to match the shouts of victory. The appearances of Banquo's ghost were feebly managed (How chilling when it is suddenly there, calmly seated at the table, among the guests; in this version the spectre stalked on amid a flashing of lights.) In the sleepwalking scene, huge gouts of blood splashed all the scenery. The shadow play that opened the battle was rather effective." That conciliatory sentence was almost unique. Porter disliked the casting: "Martina Arroyo's warm, soft-grained voice was ill-suited to her part. . . . In the title role, Sherrill Milnes was dull. He acted as if he knew the story in advance." Nevertheless, Porter concluded, "It was interesting (for once) to hear the 1847 close, rather than the long victory chorus of the 1865 version."[75]

Quite contrary were Gerald Fitzgerald's opinions published in the Metropolitan Opera Guild's *Opera News*, a review that in this instance seemed to speak the opera company's reply to the generally unfavorable comments.

> Last time around, the production retained the cold, stylized, rather bloodless approach of its German originators, director Carl Ebert and designer Caspar Neher. Neither man would have recognized the 1973 version, staged by Bodo Igesz in collaboration with Neil Peter Jampolis, who provided new projections

and additional designs. Igesz and Jampolis scrapped many costumes and all but the essential props and sets from the 1959 mounting. Among the major items missing: hard white lighting (now warm yellows and oranges), a banner depicting Duncan's murder (his corpse is paraded before the horrified court), the banquet chair where Banquo's ghost sat (the vision first flickers among the guests, then appears as a projection high on a front scrim), the staircase where Lady Macbeth wandered as somnabulist (she does it in a courtyard) and the soldiers in pink flannel, bobbing around with wicker shields (steely grays garb the new combatants, who do deadly battle in silhouette, then on a barren field). Other additions: an archway for Macbeth's "Pietà, rispetto, amore" through which the advance of Birnam Wood appears, and projections of a dagger during Macbeth's earlier monologue and some huge, juicy blood drops for the sleepwalking scene.

What did these many changes add up to? The result might be characterized as comprehensive corruption for the better. There was an overall flavor of mid-nineteenth century melodrama to the approach: *Macbeth* now looked the way it sounded. And it all worked, because all was unified, thoroughly thought through. Most important, however, was the new management's decision drastically to revise an old, unidiomatic production.[76]

Igesz and Jampolis had precedent for their point of view. In the summer of 1958, Gian Carlo Menotti had opened his first festival season in Spoleto, Italy, with "a new Macbeth" staged by Luchino Visconti. Wrote one critic: "The opera was set squarely in the Nineteenth Century: a kind of Victorian Gothic revival atmosphere. The ladies wore heavy silks and velvets; and the castle looked like an illustration for a novel of Sir Walter Scott." Another likewise remarked on the costumes, they "followed the taste of Verdi's day, and were sumptuously pictorial." The staging, however, "was direct and uncluttered, in keeping with Visconti's conception of *Macbeth* as an opera of primitive and elemental crudity." Moreover, both noted how swiftly, by use of transparencies, scenes were changed; there were no "long pauses."[77] Perhaps one flaw of the Metropolitan's 1972 revised production was that it followed too much the costumes and colors of Visconti's nineteenth-century concept and too little the fluidity of his staging.

Yet even the costumes and colors were untrue to Verdi's intent, for early in 1847 he had written to the impresario who was mounting the premiere production in Florence: "There's no need to tell you that there mustn't ever be any silk or velvet in the costumes, etc."[78] Seemingly, from this and other letters, he wanted the setting in general to be stark and uncolorful, allowing the witches to merge in and out of darkness and focusing the audience's attention on the two principals rather than on their social background.

These differing views on how to present the opera appeared in productions across the country, stagings that in their extremes inclined either to abstract, timeless settings focusing on the anguish of the two Macbeths or to nineteenth-century melodrama, drenching the landscape and costumes in Scottish fogs,

Figure 6.3. First-act duet for Macbeth and Lady (Warren and Rysanek), in the Metropolitan's first production of the opera. Photograph by Louis Mélançon, 1958. Courtesy of the Metropolitan Opera Archives.

plaids, and blood. Remarkably, whichever tack was taken, the opera seemed to find an appreciative audience.[79]

Moreover, as a part of the Verdi Renaissance in the United States, scholarly interest in the opera continued to mount, and in November 1977, at Centre College, Danville, Kentucky, a three-day international Verdi Congress gathered, the fifth of its kind and devoted entirely to *Macbeth*. Hosted by the recently founded American Institute of Verdi Studies, the Congress later published a *Sourcebook* on the opera, with all the documents, letters, and reviews concerning its composition and early productions, original and revised, as well as a worldwide chronology of performances, 1847–1947, the libretto for the Florence premiere, and the music to numbers that Verdi replaced in his 1865 revision. In addition, the Kentucky Opera Company staged for the congress a performance (in English) of the 1847 version, which so impressed the scholars with its dramatic integrity, its sharper focus on Macbeth, that to some it seemed better than the revision, currently the version usually produced and the one Verdi considered definitive.[80] Thus to the question of what view of the opera a new production should take, abstract or specific to time and place, was added the question of which version to use: 1847, 1865, or, as in the Berlin-Glyndebourne-Metropolitan production, a composite based on the 1865 revision but cutting the new ballet and reinserting the 1847 death aria for Macbeth.

Consequently, when the Metropolitan announced it was retiring its much-revised old production in favor of a new one scheduled for 1982–83, few knew what to expect. As producer, the company hired Peter Hall, famous in London and Glyndebourne for his Shakespeare and Mozart, and he chose to present the 1865 version uncut and unaltered, and to present it, as Porter later wrote, "for a modern audience in a manner observant of its nineteenth-century character."[81] There were seemingly a hundred witches, singers, dancers, and aerialists flying through the sky on broomsticks; many carried stuffed pussycats and rubber bats jiggling on sticks; many wore black, steeply crowned hats, and the prevailing colors in the opening scene were black against an orange sky, bathed in orange moonlight. Unhappily, the orange was the tint of the cheapest Halloween candy and the witches jigging about seemed benign Halloween caricatures. On opening night the audience laughed and booed. After Lady Macbeth (Renata Scotto) read the letter from Macbeth telling of Duncan's coming to the castle, she sat to sing the following rather energetic aria, and instead of rising full of purpose for the cabaletta ("Come, ministers of hell"), dropped to the floor and writhed as if in sexual excitement. In the ballet Hecate was danced by a lady naked except for a G-string, and the apparitions were latex dummies that rose from the cauldron and moved their lips in time to a singer offstage. At the end of that act, when Lady Macbeth appeared, she was costumed as if just dismounted from her horse and sidesaddle, and on the diminutive Scotto the nineteenth-century riding habit with top hat and crop looked comic. The audience tittered. In the sleepwalking scene, she did not walk but squatted on the castle floor beside her candle. As John Rockwell of the *Times* later remarked, she played the role as "a murderous sex kitten," who regresses into "an obsessive child."[82] She was furtive rather than malignant. And because she was a good actress, her portrayal presumably was at Hall's direction. At the curtain calls on premiere night, he was loudly booed. The next morning for the *Times*, Donal Henahan, began, "The quicker said, the better: Peter Hall's *Macbeth* may just be the worst new production to struggle onto the Metropolitan Opera's stage in modern history."[83] Yet audiences at the second performance, according to Porter, received it "with moderate acclaim and no evident hostility." Indeed, the music was reasonably well played and sung, but as Rockwell noted later, the production as a whole "was dismissed as ludicrous."[84]

At its revival in 1984, the number of witches was greatly reduced, all the aerial artists, pussycats, and rubber bats eliminated, and the opening scene's dominant color less orange and more moonlight white. According to Porter, "The once apparently nude Hecate now sports brown briefs . . . and Lady Macbeth is less ready to roll about on the floor." Macbeth, beginning to revive from his faint, no longer tried to lay hands on a sylph, and his 1847 dying aria, "Mal per me," had been inserted before the Victory Hymn. Remarked Porter, "The changes could be deemed improvements had anything but stock dreariness taken their place." He regretted that a worthwhile effort to represent a nineteenth-century production for a modern audience was now "reduced to routine."[85]

Shortly, it got worse. Will Crutchfield for the *Times*, on the production's revival in 1998, reported, "The listless choral work, aimless ballet, low-intensity orchestral playing and excruciatingly tentative stage deportment of almost all concerned . . . hurt this show." He charged the company's management with neglect, adding, "The Met should do better by it or leave it alone."[86]

But even at its best the production was not a good representation of nineteenth-century style, values, and methods. Before the curtain rises, the average operagoer knows that the sleepwalking scene is a high point of the play and opera, and he wants the Lady to walk, not to squat on a castle floor that everyone knows, if real, would be stone cold. Moreover, in nineteenth-century Macready and Verdi, she walks. Similarly, a nude Hecate could not have set foot on either a nineteenth-century or a sixteenth-century stage. Yet audiences for the production even in 1988 (the Metropolitan's last performance until 2007–8) continued reasonably full. Apparently the music carried the show. In all, the Metropolitan, starting in 1959 and ending in 1988, despite its productions' steady decline in sets and staging, gave the opera eighty performances, sixty-four in New York, sixteen on tour, and seven national broadcasts. For the music, a huge exposure.

Meanwhile, an astounding number of productions by other companies, large and small, blossomed around the country, and for each the producer made his choice of score and style of presentation.[87] Most followed a middle course, using the composite version of the score and opening with the witches on a heath, or bare stage, with a castle perhaps on the backdrop; then moving swiftly into the castle, into a hallway bare of furniture and perhaps with a staircase to Duncan's bedroom in the back. Lady Macbeth, in a somewhat timeless garb (costumes with Victorian velvet, ermines, and pearls are expensive), reads Macbeth's letter and sings her aria standing; Duncan arrives, is murdered, and shock registered. And so on, in what might be called a traditional approach in the United States—because apparently more popular and

Figure 6.4. Lady Macbeth (Rysanek) sleepwalking. Photograph by Louis Mélan-çon, 1958. Courtesy of the Metropolitan Opera Archives.

frequent—and inclines more to the abstract than to Victorian Gothic. Moving still further toward the abstract, San Francisco Opera in 1986 presented a severely modernist production by Pier Luigi Pizzi, colored mostly black, white, and red, which the *Chronicle* reported "served Verdi and refracted through him the Shakespearean essence, without tartans or Scottish elements, stone castle, or period costumery."[88] And to open its 1994 season, the company revived the production. Moreover, reflecting its longer schedule as the country's interest in opera steadily grew, in both seasons it gave the opera seven performances.

The companies in Houston and Chicago, in a joint production in 1997, took the modernist style to an extreme. The witches, reported a Houston critic for *Opera*, "are hospital nurses in chartreuse uniforms who later reappear as vamps with tight red leather dresses and a penchant for S&M and Supreme-style dancing. When their prophecies cause Macbeth to faint in terror, they jolt him awake with a car-battery charger." The critic was unimpressed; likewise his colleague in Chicago, and seemingly audiences in both cities, for neither company played the production a second season.[89]

The New York City Opera for its opening night in 1997 ventured on a staging that Bernard Holland for the *Times* called "a modest update." Using the 1865 score but cutting both ballets, it clothed the "men in World War I–ish uniforms and work clothes and women in timeless gowns," an idea that "reflects the composer's insistence on few words and concise action. John Conklin, who also did the costumes, has designed a stage of steel and rivets. There are catwalks, steely stairways and a crane. Geometric quadrilaterals are lighted by neon . . . everything else is black and gloom. Again, the ballroom and battle scenes represent a certain huddling of masses [because of a relatively shallow stage]." On the whole, despite considerable booing at opening night's curtain calls, he thought the production a success.[90]

A visiting critic, Daniel Webster of the *Philadelphia Inquirer*, was less sure, seeing in it "overworked European staging ideas." On the other hand,

> In this stage of aluminum grids and platforms, lines of white light and lowering darkness, the only color is the subdued rose or dark moss of Lady Macbeth's gown. That, at least, places the emphasis where Verdi saw it. By dressing the men in modern military uniforms, whatever flourish period costume might have supplied is removed. At least we are spared an invasion of Nazis. . . . Verdi's witches challenge directors. In this production, they are simply peasant women in earth-colored dress. When Banquo mentions beards [read in the supertitles], the audience giggles because there are none. Since everything is sung on a tilted metal rectangle, the witches become a mass of mainly immobile singers—articulating the text admirably. That stage platform, and the stark objects occasionally placed on it have their moments. The narrow, comfortless metal thrones have high backs that become prison bars when Macbeth sings behind them. The hanging metallic grids and geometrical backdrops chill the scene.[91]

The reviewer for *Opera News* dismissed the set as "a hard-to-beat entry in the ugliness sweepstakes," and the grids as "the underside of stadium bleachers."[92] Still another, for the *Observer*, thought "this approach underscored what is most problematic about the opera: its singleness of mood. All sense of the Macbeths as *individual* monsters was lost in the general murk."[93]

Yet despite the excellence of Lauren Flanigan's Lady Macbeth, the staging of her sleepwalking scene was a disappointment. The director had her crouch on a front corner of the platform, where the light caught only half her face, and for some in the audience she was hard to see. And another scenic miscalculation: During the massed finale of shock following Duncan's murder, his corpse was brought onstage, his body washed, and a white sheet laid over it—a distraction that diminished the music's impact. Yet in nine performances, perhaps because the singing was good, the production on the whole was well received, and in 2001 the company revived it for seven more.

The year 2003 was especially rich in major productions. The Opera Company of Philadelphia imported one along with its stage director, Ralf Långbacka, from the Savonlinna Opera Festival in Finland, where it had played in 1993, 1994, and 1995.[94] In Philadelphia the sets were mostly of brick walls and a few metal platforms. The curtain rose during the opera's prelude on a bare stage except for a huge, monochromatic, green-tinted crown inset with large jewels that did not gleam and human skulls. As the prelude closed, the crown slowly rose, steam swirling from beneath its rim, and witches crept out, thin, scraggy-haired and clothed in greenish gray-white skin costumes, maggots for a sickened host. The 1865 score was used but with both ballets cut, the final victory chorus cut, and in its place the 1847 ending with Macbeth's dying aria. For the sleepwalking scene, Lady Macbeth entered early and awake, walked to a rain barrel, tried to wash her hands, walked off, and reentered asleep. In my opinion, the scene plays better as Verdi wanted, letting the opening bars sound without visual distraction, and allowing the audience to imagine she dreams her hands are spotted. For the end, the gigantic crown slowly came down, the maggots crept under and into it, and the dying Macbeth, reaching toward it, cursed, "Vil corona."[95] Långbacka had provided a strong, clear vision of the opera that left his audience deeply stirred.

That summer the Kirov Opera came to the Metropolitan and as one of six operas offered its *Macbeth*. Again, the stage was mostly bare except for a few props. According to the critic for the *Times*, to denote a scene indoors "a big piece of rusted metal" descended, and on the whole the production "looked as if the Kirov had given [the designer] the lowest budget possible, then left the sets at home."[96] The 1865 score was used, but without the ten-minute ballet, and the opera ended with the victory chorus and Macbeth killed offstage and deprived, as Verdi directed, of his dying aria. The apparition scene opened on a bare stage littered with bodies that writhed and rose to the witches' call. As for the short sylph dance and mime to revive Macbeth, the Kirov cut the sylphs but to their music provided a mime in which Lady Macbeth, entering early, plays blindman's buff with some children who present her with a large shoe box. Opening it, she discovers a dead child (presumably hers), which she shows to Macbeth. Those who liked the scene argued that it fit nicely with Macduff's later line of balked vengeance, "But he has no children," and saw

Figure 6.5. The Sarasota Opera House. Photograph by Greg Parry. Courtesy of the Sarasota Opera Company.

it as yet another trigger to sleepwalking. Others thought it complicated and unnecessary, though agreeing that sylphs are costly and can seem incongruous to the story. They are not in Shakespeare, and perhaps are in Verdi (both versions) only to give the hard-worked Macbeth a four-minute breather.

Perhaps the high point of the year for those who greatly admire the opera was the Sarasota company's productions of the original and revised versions, ten performances of the revision and with them, toward the end of the season, two of the original. Twelve in two months is a lot for a city and county of only 326,000, but the company draws many out-of-towners to its seasons of four or five operas, especially to its productions of rarely performed Verdi. And the visitors came. The *Macbeth*, the most frequently performed opera that year season, sold well, consistently over 90 percent, though unlike Bizet's *Pêcheurs de Perles* (7 performances), not over 100 percent. Privately, Victor DeRenzi, the artistic director and conductor tried to sound disappointed—"After all, Shakespeare *and* Verdi!"[97]

The chance to hear both versions, back to back, drew critics from afar. One from the *Chicago Tribune* reported: "Some listeners, myself included, prefer the original because it keeps the focus on the murdering usurper. The revision

Figure 6.6. Todd Thomas (Macbeth) and Catherine Murphy (Lady Macbeth) in Sarasota Opera's 2003 production of *Macbeth*. Photograph by Deb Hesser. Courtesy of the Sarasota Opera Company.

Figure 6.7. Laurie Seely (Hecate) in Sarasota Opera's 2003 production of *Macbeth*. Photograph by Deb Hesser. Courtesy of the Sarasota Opera Company.

includes an entirely new aria for Lady Macbeth in act II ('La luce langue') and different music for the chorus of Scottish exiles, while removing Macbeth's onstage death aria. Musically it is less consistent in style than the original."[98] DeRenzi, fresh from conducting both versions, agreed. On the other hand, "La luce langue" is psychologically more subtle and musically interesting than the aria it replaces, and though the chorus for Scottish refugees, "Patria oppressa!" is more "hummable" in its original version—Verdi in 1847 gave the audience something to take out of the theater—the revision is more fragmented and yet more impressive musically, a mosaic panel of beautifully balanced phrases and sonorities. Finally, in its original version the opera runs some fifteen minutes shorter than the revision, which if given complete, with three intermissions, takes roughly three and a half hours.

In its staging, much the same for both versions, the Sarasota company offered a solution to one problem that often vexes productions: At the murder of Banquo, accomplished by a large men's chorus of assassins (sometimes as many as thirty), how can Banquo's son Fleance escape from so many killers without making them appear ludicrously inept? At Sarasota, after Banquo finished his aria, he and Fleance strode offstage followed by the murders, and from the wings the dying Banquo cried, "Run, my son"—and the boy, followed by only one man, dashed across an empty stage.

Unlike *Otello* and *Falstaff*, which need not a note changed, *Macbeth* is not perfect, but in the past fifty years in the United States and around the world it has proved its worth in all kinds of productions, in all sizes of theaters. Its misfortune is to exist in versions, a joy for those who like to discourse on small points, but a confusion for operagoers who read of the changes in program notes that are often unclear and sow distrust: Why, if the original was a success, did Verdi revise it? How can it still be undecided whether Macbeth dies onstage or off? Why tell me about the Scottish refugees' chorus that I am *not* going to hear? Better simply to let the music do its work. The opera is sometimes said (most often by the soprano's publicity agent) not to be easy to cast, but over the years a great number of artists have been convincing in the two leading roles. And the opera plays well. Unless very badly produced, it draws an audience into its drama. Yet it will never be as popular as *Aida* or *Otello*, for it has no love story, no leading role for tenor. But then, in Verdi's mind, that's not how he heard *Macbeth*. Which is so much more interesting.

Part Two

Four Operas, Three Resident Companies, 1850–60

Chapter Seven

The Country's Growth Stimulates Opera

As the history of Italian opera in the United States and more particularly of Verdi's operas makes clear, the summer tours in 1847 and 1850 of the Italian company from Havana were crucial. The company not only was chiefly responsible for introducing a new and important Italian composer to the country but even in its performances of familiar Rossini, Bellini, and Donizetti it raised expectations and forced standards higher: better singers, chorus, and orchestra. The touring company of 1850, as its competitor Max Maretzek of New York's Astor Place company later conceded, was simply better than any American company and unmatched by most in Europe.[1]

Moreover, in the summer of 1850 when the Havana company, subsidized by the rich Cuban, Marty y Torrens,[2] opened its long summer season at New York's Castle Garden at fifty cents a seat, it beat all the local companies on price.

The situation was well stated by the *Albion* on the last day of August 1850:

It is uncertain how long this excellent company will remain here; but it is rumoured that they will continue to perform through the greater part of September. They will surely save Mr. Marty's pocket most effectually this summer. Their low prices, however, tell woefully against the establishment of a regular opera in this city; for it must be remembered, that a company permanently located in New York depends upon their success here for existence; our opera house crowded at fifty cents, would not pay half expenses, so that the charge of a dollar is compulsory. The Havana Company does not depend on its success in New York at all. It is engaged for eighteen or twenty months for the Havana Theatre. During that time they perform *two* seasons in Havana, but as Mr. Marty has to pay them every month, he ships them over here to save his expenses between the first and second season. It is a good speculation; the public is gratified by hearing a fine opera, but the resident manager and artists are undersold, and their success rendered more than ever problematical. However much gratified we may be with some of the fine performances of these strangers, we cannot but look upon their advent as a decided injury to the progress of our own music; still we trust that our musical public will rally round our indefatigable and worthy manager Max Maretzek, who is now making preparations for our regular winter campaign, and give him that hearty support which his integrity and energy so richly deserve.[3]

Who can doubt that the article's source was the "worthy" Maretzek. As manager and conductor of the resident Astor Place company, at home he faced strong local competition, especially from a company led by Maurice Strakosch, a pianist, composer and conductor.[4] Then came the Havana company with superior artists and playing a long season at cut prices, and barely would it depart before Jenny Lind, the "Swedish Nightingale," would arrive, accompanied by several outstanding singers and a good conductor, all brought over by P. T. Barnum for a concert tour. And as events proved, the public, excited by Barnum's storm of publicity, succumbed to "Lindomania" and willingly bought tickets priced at $3, to say nothing of prices very much higher that were bid at the periodic ticket auctions, with $125 usually the top bid. But in Philadelphia and Boston the bidding rose to $625 and in Providence, to $650, where the purchaser further distinguished himself by not attending the concert.[5]

Maretzek's answer to Barnum and Lind was to hire Teresa Parodi, who had been singing to acclaim in London, and then, while she was still on the voyage over, to start a rumor that she was not coming because she was about to marry the Duke of Devonshire. When she landed in New York, the "worthy" Maretzek was able to stir another pot of publicity with gasps of surprise and pleasure, amazement at the unfounded story, and promises of exceptional performances with his new and glamorous prima donna. With a Barnum-like flourish, he promptly stopped subscription sales to his season and doubled the price of all remaining tickets. And despite Lind, his 1850–51 season at the Astor Place Opera House did well, with Parodi excelling in the ever-popular *Norma*. But in the spring, while the company was playing in Boston, her contract with Maretzek ran out, and she declined to renew it. Instead, she joined a company organized by Strakosch chiefly to give operatic concerts.[6]

Maretzek was quick to act. His agent in Havana had sent word that with the end of the winter season at the Teatro Tacón, Marty's singers, their contracts fulfilled, were heading for Europe via New York, stopping first in Charleston, South Carolina. Overnight Maretzek closed his Boston season, took his company to Charleston, and while giving performances there succeeded in signing seven of Marty's best singers, including the bass Ignazio Marini, who was splendid in *Norma*, *Ernani*, and *Attila*. With these new stars Maretzek returned to Boston, reopened his interrupted season, and as the scholar Katherine Preston notes, "The Astor Place Company now was a solid troupe with real talent rather than a mediocre company with one shining star."[7]

In one respect Martezek succeeded better than he perhaps had hoped. Not only was he able in following months to hire several more of the Havana company's stars but, for whatever reason, Marty y Torrens did not immediately recruit another Italian company for his Havana theater. For three years, 1851–54, Havana had no Italian season and no Italian company to send on tour to the United States.[8] Instead, in a reversal that Maretzek surely enjoyed, in the fall of 1854 he sent a part of what was now called the Maretzek Company to

Mexico, and on its way back it stopped for a season in Havana during which it presented the Cuban premieres of Verdi's *Luisa Miller* and *I masnadieri*, both with Marini.[9]

But competition in New York was fierce. Both Strakosch and Bernard Ullman[10] put together companies that existed for a time and gave both staged performances and concerts, but Maretzek's was the most solid and the most consistently devoted to opera. Moreover, though he continued to give seasons in several theaters in New York, he mostly played at the Academy of Music, gradually becoming associated with it, though never its exclusive occupant. Not until 1883 when the Metropolitan opened, would New York have an opera house with a resident company such as New Orleans had achieved more than fifty years earlier with its Théâtre d'Orléans and its French company. Nevertheless, though slow in that respect, in the 1850s, New York and not New Orleans became the opera capital of the United States, the hub and recruiting ground of many companies which, following the frontier, toured ever further westward.

With regard to New Orleans, the chief reason for New York's dominance was size and location. The population in New York in that decade was roughly 700,000, and in New Orleans, only 120,000. Moreover, New York had as near neighbors, Boston and Philadelphia, respectively 140,000 and 125,000, which made for easy touring. Whereas New Orleans had no neighboring city of even 30,000 (see appendix C).

Seemingly, either Boston or Philadelphia might have developed a strong resident company to compete with those in New York, for the population of each was slightly larger than in New Orleans, but each, unlike the southern city, had a religious prejudice that hindered the development of opera. But in Catholic New Orleans there was no prejudice against theater or dancing; indeed, the whole city had a passion for dancing, and by 1841 it had "over 80 identifiable ballrooms or sites for dancing." Women even went to Mass on Sunday dressed for the evening ball.[11] Was not the purpose of religion to raise the spirits?

In Puritan Boston, however, there was little dancing and none on Sunday, for many still questioned the propriety of music in almost any form. Some still argued that even in church the psalms should not be sung but merely spoken, for which they cited the prophet Amos, who quotes the Lord as saying: "Take thou away from me the noise of thy songs; for I will not hear the melody of thy viols."[12] Only slowly, and mostly because of the influence of German immigrant musicians, did many Bostonians come to believe that music might have some spiritual value. Theodore Lyman, a Boston visitor in Venice and Trieste in 1816, confessed that "a person of any musical sensibility, on entering one of their theatres, finds himself transported into an ideal world." But he feared that Italian opera "is calculated to produce a character indolent and passive, and is as unfavorable to the lighter powers of genius, as to the great moral and political virtues."[13] That fear lingered in Boston. Recalling how people in the city felt even as late as 1837, the city's historian of music, John Sullivan Dwight, observed, "To have a weakness for a flute or viol, or to sing aught but 'sacred' music, was a thing 'suspect' and leading to temptation." Opera, especially Italian opera, was the "siren" song of debased sensual entertainment. And he pointed directly to the Havana company as the one that introduced it.[14]

Among the Quakers in Philadelphia many shared that prejudice, disapproving, in their pursuit of simplicity, of all music and theater. Consider the case of Samuel N. Lewis, a respected Quaker merchant with an honored wife and nine children, and many good works to his credit. Among his children, his second son, John, had "a weakness for a flute," and would play the instrument with pleasure all his life. Yet, in 1833 Lewis and his wife were "disowned" by their Quaker Philadelphia Monthly Meeting for the Southern District for "having [their] children taught music and dancing and allowing them to attend the theatre."[15] As in Boston, such an attitude, held by a large portion of the general public, hindered the growth of musical institutions, making it easier for New York to take the lead.

The change throughout the country for theaters and music in the years 1800–1860 was very great, especially in the bigger cities where wealth through trade accumulated, and it also was relatively swift, taking place within one generation's memory. One old New Yorker, looking back from 1845 to the turn of the century recalled: "People in New York lived much happier than they do now. They had no artificial wants—only two banks—rarely gave a note—but one small playhouse—no operas, no ottomans, few sofas or sideboards, and perhaps not six pianos in the city."[16]

That "one small playhouse" was the John Street Theatre (1767–98), which with two tiers of boxes, a pit, and a gallery seated in all perhaps 400, and which for many years had an orchestra of "the one Mr. Pelham and his harpsichord, or the single fiddle of Mr. Hewlett."[17] On special occasions the theater might boast a few instruments more, with the splendid maximum perhaps nine. But mostly it was a "playhouse," staging plays without music. Yet on those nights when the manager had singers to offer, the "opera" typically would be a spoken drama—in English—with some songs by the artists, backed by a few musical instruments and a chorus of four or five composed of the actors. Though the format was simple, the performance could be perilous.

After the Revolution patriotism ran high, and members of the audience, in the small house all seated close to the stage, not infrequently called out for "Yankee Doodle" or some similar song, and one night in 1794 the leader of the small orchestra, violinist James Hewitt, "was attacked" because not quick enough "with a popular air when called upon."[18] The theater's historian leaves the attack undescribed, but its usual form was to pelt the musicians with oranges, apples, or bottles. Moreover, two years later, the historian records, "happened one of those riots which tend to throw obloquy on the theatre unjustly."

Two sea captains, doubtless intoxicated, being in one of the stage boxes, called during an overture for Yankee Doodle. The audience hissed them; they threw missiles in the orchestra, and defied the audience, some of whom pressed on the stage and attacked the rioters in conjunction with the peace-officers; one of the latter was injured by a blow from a club. The rioters were dragged from their box, one turned into the street, and the other carried into a dressing room. These madmen afterwards, with a number of sailors, attacked the door of the theatre, and were only secured by the city watch.[19]

Even in New Orleans, where audiences typically were better behaved, the city council in 1804 issued regulations that forbade making "fanciful demands" on the orchestra to play "this or that tune," forbade constant clapping or hissing, and insisted, "No one will be allowed to throw oranges or anything else."[20] But the rule suggests the habit, and though in New Orleans the problem decreased, in New York, among some theaters at least, it worsened, and these became little more than extensions of a tavern, lots of drink with a few skits, songs, and vigorous audience participation. According to a count made of one newspaper's reports, the worst period for riots in theaters was 1833–37, for which the *Commercial Advertiser* reported fifty-two, with the year 1834 the worst, with thirteen.[21] These likely were only the more serious disturbances, and probably most of them occurred in the city's bawdier theaters on Chatham Street. But even in the better-behaved theaters, at the time Verdi's operas began to play, an occasional incident took place, for as late as August 14, 1848, an actor at the Bowery Theatre was pelted from the stage.[22]

Earlier an English visitor, Mrs. Frances Trollope, had toured the country for fifteen months and in 1832 published her sensationally successful *Domestic Manners of the Americans*. She recounted what she had seen in the theaters of Cincinnati, Philadelphia, and New York, deploring the "incessant" spitting, the "mixed smell of onions and whiskey," the nursing of babies in the theater, the snoring of snoozers in the pit, where "the bearing and attitudes of the men are perfectly indescribable; the heels thrown higher than the head, the entire rear of the person presented to the audience, the whole length supported on the benches."[23] American critics, though less caustic, as late as 1846 lamented the continual "music of cracking peanuts," the "buz buz and hum hum of small talk" throughout the performance, "the din of oaths" from the gallery, "the uproarious state of fermentation" in the pit, and "the titter of the impure and dull chatter of her stupid wooer" in the third tier where sat unescorted women plying an ancient trade. Even in 1864, a correspondent for *Dwight's Journal* complained of the behavior of a New York audience.[24]

Yet, at least in the better theaters, improvements gradually were achieved. During the early 1840s in most cities unescorted women increasingly were denied admission, and in many theaters the top tier of boxes, the haunt of prostitutes, was transformed into an open gallery. Meanwhile, as the Revolutionary generation died off, the calls for patriotic numbers dwindled, while smoking and drinking gradually were banished to areas outside the auditorium, lobbies, foyers, and smoking rooms. Meanwhile the quality of singing and orchestral playing slowly improved. People went to the opera for all sorts of reasons, to drink, talk, be seen, and some, even, to hear the music. In 1834 in New Orleans, music lovers who usually attended the French opera went to its American competitor on Camp Street to hear the English singer Mrs. [Elizabeth] Austin, and afterward they insisted that the manager improve his orchestra. One man listed the instruments needed: at least two flutes, two clarinets, two horns, an oboe, and a trombone. He also wanted a new conductor. And soon after, a horn, clarinet, flute, and new conductor were added.[25]

The steady increases in immigration and improvements in transportation also slowly influenced the number and size of the country's theaters and the behavior of their audiences. In 1822, for example, the Park Theatre in New York was the only one in the city to play through the entire winter season, but by 1850, there were six. Similarly, the city's overall seating capacity continually increased. In the twenty years between 1826 and 1847, as one scholar has estimated, it "grew eightfold . . . outstripping population increase in the city by roughly 100 percent." Meanwhile, the country's population steadily rose: in 1820, roughly 9.6 million; in 1840, 17 million; in 1850, 23 million; and in 1860, 31.5 million. And the music-loving portion of the population was increasing at a still faster rate, in part because of the influx of Germans following the failed revolutions in Europe in 1848. According to one survey, in 1850, when the country's population was 23 million, musicians of all kinds numbered 3,550. By 1910, when the population was 92 million, they numbered 139,310. Thus, while population rose fourfold, the number of professional musicians rose by fortyfold.[26]

The arrival of the Germans in significant numbers was perhaps the most important development, for by 1871 the 160,000 Germans living on Manhattan Island were a fifth of the city's population. Even as early as 1850 their influence began to be felt, and German opera, sung in German, began to make a continuous showing. Before then, both *Der Freischütz*, in 1825, and *Fidelio*, in 1839, had premiered in English, and the former had its first production in German in 1845. But no Wagner was performed until *Tannhäuser* in 1859, and Mozart's *Die Zauberflöte*, first heard in English in 1833, was not sung in German until 1862, the same year that *Die Entführung aus dem Serail*, premiered in 1860 in Italian, was first heard in German.

As much as the Italians, the Germans liked their own music, and one of the earliest descriptions of them enjoying it, pre-1850, occurs in *New York by Gaslight*, a series of articles by a newspaper reporter, George G. Foster.

This is Mager's Concert Hall . . . an immense room on the second floor, elaborately and gaudily painted in fresco, with scenes from the Dutch mythology. . . . The floor, on ordinary occasions is filled with rough tables and wooden benches, and partly across one end runs a balconied platform by way of orchestra. Every Sunday night takes place at this establishment a grand German and English concert, vocal and instrumental. Several female singers, with those marvelous guttural alternating voices resembling the compound creaking of a dry grindstone, or the cry of a guinea-hen, are regularly engaged here, and perform in both German and English. The orchestra consists of a gigantic seraphina [an organ with metal reeds and a foot-bellows], two violins, a flute and a fagotto [bassoon], all played by Germans, and of course played well.

These concerts are regularly attended by the respectable German men and women residing in the city, to the number of from twelve to seventeen hundred. . . . There are immense quantities of [Rhine wine and beer] phlegmatically engulphed in the Germanesque oesophagi of the visitors, both male and female. Every thing, however, is carried on in excellent order and there are very seldom any disturbances here. The audience . . . [is] easily pleased and in fact the performances themselves, so far at least as the instrumental music is concerned, are very respectable.[27]

Moreover, in 1847 a group of German men in the city founded the Liederkranz Society primarily to sing German music for male voices, chiefly the hunting songs from Weber's operas, the Prisoners' Chorus from Beethoven's *Fidelio* and works by lesser composers such as Conradin Kreutzer and Carl Friedrich Zelter. The society's events, however, were often as much social as musical occasions, and entire families attended the concerts, festivals, and picnics, at which the men would recite poetry, Goethe or Heine, offer comic impersonations, stage a farce, or even, with the ladies, an operetta. By 1871 there were at least thirteen such male singing societies in the city.[28]

Ultimately, the most important musically, and especially so in opera, was the Arion Society, an offshoot of the Liederkranz and founded in 1854. Thirteen members of the parent society, disgusted with a Liederkranz serving of "a particularly poor and meager supper of red cabbage,"[29] met in the Franz Josef Reich Restaurant and agreed to start a new society. Its musical program was the same, primarily a men's chorus, but it pursued its opportunities more vigorously. In 1859, for example, it furnished both the male and female choruses for the U.S. premiere of *Tannhäuser*, presented in New York's German Stadt Theatre (capacity 2,000),[30] and again a mixed chorus in 1870 for a production of *Der Freischütz*.

Such growth in the music-loving public inevitably led to better equipped theaters, with more and better singers and instrumentalists, and, with "respectable German men and women" in the audiences, to better audience behavior. It also strengthened the touring companies, which in turn forced higher standards in theaters outside the biggest cities, even as the modes of transportation slowly improved and made touring easier. In 1827, for example, the year after the Garcia troupe had presented in New York the country's first season of

Italian opera sung in Italian, stagecoach was still the only form of land travel; there was not one passenger railroad and the longest freight line ran only nine miles;[31] and not until 1852 did a railroad cross the Appalachian Mountains. Until then, roughly speaking, what railroads there were ran from coastal towns inland (to bring freight from the interior to a port), or along the coast only where no large river came down to the sea. There was as yet no steel to build bridges across the wider rivers, and so crossings usually were by ferry or, if the river was shallow, by ford. But in either case, the railroad came to a stop and passengers and freight had to shift into coaches and wagons.

Steamships were common on rivers and inland waterways, but none as yet were oceangoing. The distances were great. On the Mississippi, St. Louis was 800 river miles north of New Orleans, roughly the distance from Paris to Warsaw; Baltimore to Charleston, South Carolina, by land was 770 miles, half again as far as London to Edinburgh; and New York to Boston, 215 miles and, until the Cape Cod Canal opened (1914), much further by water. By stage coach, the trip to Boston required several days, for there was no through railroad until 1849, and then only via Hartford and Springfield, a longer trip than the "shore" line (opened in 1889) via New London and Providence. Before rail, the usual way of travel was to take a steamboat, via Long Island Sound, from New York to Providence, and then coach to Boston. Even New York to Philadelphia in Garcia's decade, was easier by sea than by land, requiring only a voyage along the New Jersey coast and then up the Delaware River. By land, the journey started by steamboat in New York harbor, past Staten Island, up the Raritan River to New Brunswick, New Jersey; by stagecoach from there to Trenton, or some other city on the Delaware River, and then by steamboat down to Philadelphia.[32] In October 1852, to greet the soprano Henriette Sontag who was coming from New York to Philadelphia and crossing New Jersey by the relatively new railroad, a committee chartered a steamboat to meet her at Burlington, New Jersey, and to float down the Delaware while speeches of welcome were spoken, a "splendid collation" was served, "a band played, and German musical societies sang choruses."[33]

As for crossing the ocean, by the early 1840s, steamships had halved the time from Liverpool to New York by sail alone, from four weeks or longer to fourteen and a half days. The scholar Vera Brodsky Lawrence, counting the number of European artists making the trip, has declared 1843 a "watershed" after which a "tidal wave" of virtuosi "began to sweep into the New World."[34] And by 1850, the Collins line, with four ships based in New York, besides being the first to offer bell service to staterooms (Lind crossed to New York on a Collins liner), was making the run in nine and a half days.[35]

As the time and difficulties of touring eased, the companies as well as their repertories grew larger. In 1837 and 1842, the Havana company (not yet managed by Marty) came to New York by sail, and both seasons had a success. Then in 1843 (Marty's first year), the company played first in New Orleans, traveled up the Mississippi by steamboat to Cincinnati and on to Pittsburgh, introducing both cities to Italian opera sung in Italian. It then crossed the Appalachian Mountains by coach, went on to Philadelphia, and afterward to Baltimore, New York, and Washington, DC, before returning to New Orleans. Moreover, in all the cities except New Orleans, it staged the local premiere of *Lucia di Lammermoor.* In all, the tour lasted nine months, during which the company performed only Donizetti and Bellini, chiefly *Lucia, Gemma di Vergy, Norma,* and *I Puritani.* This company, shrunk for the inland tour from its usual fifty or so to thirty, including soloists, chorus, and orchestra, probably swelled its orchestral ranks locally whenever it could. On its later tours, in 1847 it brought a company of 73, and in 1850, one numbering 104.[36]

With railroads improving, by 1849, Maretzek could take his company from New York to Philadelphia at least partway by rail, for both the Hudson and Delaware rivers still had to be crossed by ferry (the Hudson tunnel opened in 1910). But in early days even the rail portion of the journey, from Hoboken to Trenton, was apparently not altogether easy, for as Maretzek later reported:

On the road, we were all excitement, in spite of the discomfort of the railway cars. You are astonished to hear one who has become a citizen of this "glorious" country speaking thus of anything in it. But, my dear Berlioz, I have heard many Americans affirm that New Jersey is no part of this Union. This railroad runs entirely through New Jersey, and I therefore feel completely at liberty to censure it, without at all rendering myself amenable to the censure of a want of due patriotic feeling.[37]

He was not much happier with the same trip on New Year's Day 1856, when he and his leading singers started for Philadelphia at ten a.m. but because of a snow storm did not arrive until eight p.m., "too late for an opera performance." Moreover, as late as 1864 a correspondent for Boston's *Dwight's Journal of Music,* May 14, could write of the "physical and spiritual agonies of a railway passage through New Jersey."[38]

Nevertheless, the railroads did improve, and along with them, together with the increase in the country's population, the country's theaters. In the years 1823 to 1850 the chief step forward, taken often in conjunction with refurbishing and enlarging old theaters, was the substitution of gas for candles and oil. Candles once lit could not be dimmed and not infrequently dropped wax on the audience, a reason why those in the pit, mostly men, often did not remove their hats. Oil, except in large quantities, gave no more light than candles, and often stank. Gas gave good light, did not drip or smell, and, with slow improvements in control, could be dimmed during a performance and eventually even extinguished and relit. But it was also more dangerous. With its introduction, and for lack of safety controls, there were many more fires, with one of the most notable at New York's Park Theatre.[39] To many people in the North and

East, the fifty-year old Park was the country's most venerable theater, but on December 16, 1848, it died when "a file of playbills, hanging at the prompter's entrance to the stage, was accidentally blown or brushed against a burning gas-jet, and almost in an instant the entire wing was in a blaze, and in little more than an hour, the whole interior of the theatre was reduced to ashes."[40]

Nevertheless, at the first use of gas in New York, usually put in the year 1823,[41] it had been hailed as a blessing. Before then the Park was lit by three oil chandeliers, the largest in the auditorium had "ten or twelve" lamps "in a large sheet-iron hoop, painted green, hanging from the ceiling." The other two, for lighting the stage, were half the size and hung on either side.[42] By mid-1825, however, both the Park and a competitor, the Chatham Theatre, had substituted gas for oil and candles. Other theaters moved more slowly, and the historian Krehbiel reports that one in 1845 still boasted of its "thousand candles."[43] But by the mid-1840s, it seems, all the city's new theaters were built with gas for lighting. Palmo's Opera House, which opened in 1844 and housed the first production in the country of a Verdi opera, *I Lombardi*, used gas, and the much larger and more elegant Astor Place Opera House, opening in 1847, had a central chandelier in the auditorium that contained some sixty lamps.[44]

Techniques for dimming them, however, developed only slowly, and sometimes are said not to have been achieved to any great degree until 1855.[45] Even then, any decrease in the auditorium seems to have been only slight, for the audience was still relying on librettos in hand to follow the opera, which the frequent cuts and interpolations often made difficult. As a reporter for the *Boston Musical Times* declared in 1860: "Consequently there is discussion in the auditorium. . . . Some charming daughter, being quicker than the rest of the family, first discovers the place, points it out to paterfamilias, who settles his spectacles and prepares to read; but before he has taken the thumb off the first word, the entire corps operatic has leaped several pages."[46]

Moreover, in addition to better lighting the new and old theaters tried to improve their ambience in other respects. The Park Theatre, for one, in 1840, completely renovated and embellished its interior, presenting a "very neat and attractive appearance," though "externally it continued to wear its old dust and dinginess."[47] Moreover, even in renovation, it was still content not to offer any interior lobby or promenade hall. From the front door and box office a forty-seven-foot hallway led directly to the auditorium, where the managers expected patrons to socialize in their boxes, in the pit, or in the three refreshment rooms, one to each level and all serving liquor. But New York's National Theatre, new that same year, provided not only an interior lobby or hall, where patrons could mingle, but even some retiring rooms for ladies. But the theater was not a success and soon closed.[48]

Gradually, in part because of the improvements, in the Protestant North and East the public's perception of an evening at the opera began to change. Whereas in the 1840s, the Havana company, upon coming to New York, had played in the

Park Theatre or in Niblo's Garden Theatre, both houses more usually offering plays, horse shows, or acrobats, after October 1854, those companies visiting or resident in the city usually played in the far more sumptuous Academy of Music. That house was not the first in the city to be built primarily for opera, but it was the first to prosper, becoming the city's operatic center and enduring as such for thirty years, until supplanted in the mid-1880s by the Metropolitan.

Elsewhere, too, in the 1850s, big opera houses, usually in the Italian horseshoe style, rose in several of the eastern cities, and flaunted themselves as "academies of music." Two of the most notable were the one in Philadelphia, opened in 1857 and still in use, and the other, in Brooklyn in 1861, but replaced, after fire, by the current Academy of Music, which opened in 1908. In Boston, the long-lived Boston Theatre (1854–1925), followed fashion and in 1860 changed its name to Academy of Music, though three years later, the trend's exception, apparently out of nostalgia, it changed back. The shift from "theater" to "opera house," or "academy of music," the latter sounding so charitable of purpose, was not without reason, for still to many people a "theater" was a place of sin and shame.[49]

In the newly populated Midwest and California coast, many of those responsible for their city's opera house did not conceal their enterprise or financial power behind such veils as "academy," but named their opera houses after themselves. Thus, in San Francisco, Thomas Maguire called his elegant structure, which opened in November 1856, Maguire's Opera House, and similarly in Cincinnati in 1859, Samuel Pike, a liquor dealer, called his building Pike's Opera House, and in Chicago, in 1865, a distiller, Uranus Harold Crosby, in trouble with a citizens' committee for dumping waste in the Chicago River, named his pile, which included many studios, several stores, and a restaurant, Crosby's Opera House. But whatever the name, the buildings were large, handsome inside and out, and solid symbols of their cities' desire for culture. And as the frontier moved westward, there were many more, such as the two Tabor houses in Colorado.[50]

First, in 1879, "Silver Dollar" H. W. Tabor built the Tabor Opera House in Leadville, Colorado, a small but finely appointed theater (capacity 880), and then in 1881 he opened the Tabor Grand Opera House in Denver (capacity 1500). The city's *Tribune* rhapsodized, "The Opera house building and the handsome theater in it form one of the broadest pieces of architecture in the West, and almost the perfection of art has been obtained at every point. It is said that one hundred thousand dollars have been spent in the fitting up of the interior of the theater after the walls were plastered, and nearly half of this fortune was expended on the hard woods in which the interior is finished. . . . the stage of the Tabor Opera house is the most perfect in its appointment of any in the country."[51]

And that was not all. The *Denver Tribune* reported further that Tabor's Grand Opera House incorporated several features "to secure the entire comfort of the theater-goers. There are but few theaters in the East that have retiring rooms for ladies even, and when the Academy of Music in Philadelphia was built [1857], the fact that it had rooms in which ladies might arrange their toilets, was hailed as the greatest boon that had ever been given to the theater-goers of the city. The new Opera house not only has spacious rooms, elegantly upholstered, for ladies, but there are also smoking rooms for gentlemen. These rooms open from each of the three foyers."[52] Thus, the new houses provided an experience very different from that of hearing an opera in the 1840s in New York's Palmo's Opera House, with its bare-board seats, or even in the larger, more fashionable, but often unclean Park Theatre, where many of its patrons wherever seated, but especially those in the pit, talked, drank, smoked, and snored in their seats.

The opening of Pike's Opera House in Cincinnati in 1859 was an important event in the establishment of opera in the Midwest, for in the words of one of the city's historians, Cincinnati was "now on the national musical map and would remain there for many years to come."[53] The citizens of the day were conscious and proud of their new position. Cincinnati then was the country's seventh largest city, roughly 160,000, and except for New Orleans, the largest city west of the Appalachian Mountains.[54] Bigger than either Chicago or St. Louis and tied to the East by the Baltimore and Ohio Railroad as well as by the Ohio and Erie canals, it was the main port on the Ohio River (navigable from Pittsburgh to New Orleans) and fast becoming the shipping center of farm products and meats from the Midwest to the East. As the *Cincinnati Daily Commercial* proclaimed: The city was "the emporium of the West," and undergoing a "rapid transition from a backwood settlement to a metropolis in which commerce and the fine arts hold mutual sway."[55]

Newspapers recorded the opening of the new opera house with rapture, extolling every splendid detail, among them a promenade hall, a Grand Hall or ballroom, comfortable seating for two thousand, and "two capacious flights of steps, the entrance to each flight ornamented with life-size statuary."[56] And on the opening night of the first opera season, reportedly three thousand crushed into the house to hear *Martha*. Thereafter the newspaper reported on each day's performance, and in so doing revealed ways in which the public's perception of operagoing was changing.

The inaugural troupe was the Strakosch Italian Opera Company, on tour from New York and led by Maretzek's chief competitor as both impresario and conductor.[57] After the opening night *Martha*, on March 15, 1859, Strakosch in his first week displayed a roster of distinguished soloists of whom the two best-known were Pauline Colson, a Belgian soprano, and Teresa Parodi, whom Maretzek had brought to the country to compete with Jenny Lind. Strakosch's orchestra and chorus, however, were both apparently too thin in numbers for the spacious house, and later praise suggests that he promptly added some local recruits. Initially the chorus was reported to be "lamentably weak in the feminine department," a frequent difficulty for impresarios. And the same reviewer, for *Dwight's Journal*, published in Boston, said of the orchestra that it only was good "as far as it went."[58] But according to the critic for the *Cincinnati Daily Commercial Advertiser*, it numbered "upwards of thirty instruments" and "is, if not so loud, at least as effective as can be desired, most of the performers being fully up to the mark as tip-top soloists."[59]

In the course of a four-and-a-half-week season, the longest yet of any company to present opera in the city "on a daily basis,"[60] Strakosch gave two concerts, one featuring Rossini's *Stabat Mater*, and twenty-three performances of opera. As he had at the time only thirteen operas in his repertory, he was forced to offer seven of them more than once, which ran counter to the well-known desire of American audiences for "novelties," or at least a different opera every night.[61]

The first to repeat, and on a successive night, was *Trovatore*, and in his announcement Strakosch stressed that this second performance would be the opera's "last." The anonymous critic for the *Cincinnati Daily Commercial* strengthened the warning by emphasizing the usual "rule of the management not to repeat a piece."[62] In fact, in his fourth week Strakosch offered *Trovatore* yet again, this time announcing "additional improvements" to the "celebrated Anvil Chorus." To which the critic contributed, "The attraction is Verdi's favorite opera, the *Trovatore* with the original powerful cast."[63] But all the puffery could not fill the house. "Verdi," recorded the critic, "is at a discount, for by far the smallest audience of the season was present. . . . The drain upon the operatic community the two previous evenings was too much, and with even this favorite modern composer as the attraction, a short respite was necessary."[64]

Strakosch earlier had attempted to meet this three-faceted problem of limited repertory, unusually long season, and a large house in a still relatively small city, by claiming that his repeat of *Traviata*, was occasioned only by the "incredible enthusiasm" and "universal desire" to hear "Madame Colson once more in the celebrated character as Violetta." But as an additional lure, he offered a change in cast, or as the critic put it: "Ever awake to the production of novelty, the experienced *improvisario* will present it in a different guise, Brignoli [tenor] being cast for the *role* sustained by Squires at the first representation."[65] Yet for the third of Verdi's operas in the schedule, *Ernani*, which the critic declared "the most finished production of the favorite modern composer," he greeted the impresario's announcement of a single performance more cautiously, inserting into the general rule an allowable exception: "The original rule of the Management, to repeat no opera unless so advertised, will in this case be adhered to." At the season's end, Strakosch had offered only one opera new to Cincinnati, *Robert le Diable*, and had presented it twice. Only *Don Giovanni*, with no change in cast, successfully drew an audience three times in ten days.[66]

In addition to trumpeting his rare change in cast "the experienced *improvisario*" tried yet another way to draw an audience to an opera's repetition—by offering it as a Saturday matinee. In 1859, except in New York, Boston, or Philadelphia, an afternoon performance of an opera on any day was unusual. An opera, typically running longer than a recital or concert, did not fit easily into most people's afternoon schedules, and during daylight hours darkening the auditorium, however seldom, often required blocking window ventilation. Moreover, at all times most of any audience were men, in part because ladies did not attend without an escort; and further, because most men worked at least half a day on Saturdays, afternoon audiences often were sparse. Strakosch, however, pitched his matinees directly to the ladies, scheduling repeats of *Sonnambula* and *Lucia di Lammermoor* on successive Saturday afternoons, inviting the ladies to come unattended, pricing all seats at $1, and making it easy for them to sit in protective groups by having all seats unreserved. The critic at the *Daily Commercial* frothed with excitement: "The grand *matinee* for to-morrow is attracting much attention, and bids fair to inaugurate most successfully this delightful and fashionable amusement. The Strakosch troupe is the very thing to pioneer to a success the *matinee* in this city. When introduced by Thalberg and Vieuxtemps [recitalists], in New York, it was deemed a doubtful experiment, but the convenience of such day entertainments at once became obvious, and it has since been a favorite and permanent institution." And for those who might wonder, he advised, "Of course it is *au fait* for ladies to go unattended, and thus while their husbands, fathers, brothers, or cavaliers, may be immersed in the hum drum toil of daily life, the fair creatures can realize an enchanting day dream of music and poetry. . . . By the way, we will here mention that ladies are not expected, unless they wish it, to appear in full dress at the *Matinee*, which is, in a measure, a sort of social institution, in which both gentlemen and ladies can appear in plain promenade costume." Thus, though as much a convenience for the impresario as for the ladies, the Saturday opera matinee came to Cincinnati; and for the first, *Sonnambula*, according to the critic, an audience of 1,200 turned up with the women outnumbering the men "nine to one." In the 1840s, at any theater in the country, such an audience would have been inconceivable.[67]

By the late 1850s, therefore, the operatic scene in the United States differed greatly from what it had been only twelve years earlier when Verdi's *Lombardi*, *Ernani*, and *Foscari* were first introduced. No longer were most of his operas brought to the country by a touring company from Cuba. Rather, they typically had their Western Hemisphere premieres in New York, presented by a company either resident or recruited there, though by then three of the city's traditional houses for opera had closed, the Park, the Astor Place House, and Castle Garden, which in 1855 became the city's depot for immigrants. That year, Maretzek premiered both *Rigoletto* and *Trovatore*, and the next year *Traviata*, presenting them all at the New York Academy of Music, opened in 1854.

Like *Ernani* in the 1840s, *Trovatore* in the 1850s became instantly popular; *Traviata* had a more troubled start and was briefly banned in Brooklyn, and Boston initially would not have *Rigoletto*, which it considered objectionable, particularly the ending. Note that Strakosch on tour, though he had the first two in his repertory, did not include *Rigoletto*, though it would have been a premiere for Cincinnati. And in New York in the 1860s, the opera would be held up in court as an example of salacious immorality, as told in chapter 11, which closes this second group of Verdi operas to enter the United States: *I masnadieri, Jérusalem, Luisa Miller,* and *Rigoletto*.

Chapter Eight

I masnadieri

In the United States *I masnadieri* is possibly Verdi's least-performed opera. Though the eleventh of his twenty-eight (not counting minor revisions) and completed after *Macbeth*, except for a rare concert performance, it turns up mostly in cycles of his operas. Moreover, in its U.S. premiere, in New York on June 2, 1860, it suffered an artistic disaster—"Of the dead why speak?" wrote one critic.[1] Thereafter, except for nine performances in San Francisco, the last in 1865, *Masnadieri* was not heard again until a concert performance in New York in 1975. Yet initially in Europe and South America it held the stage for several decades. And recently, in the past thirty years, in Europe it has had some notable revivals, confirming that along with some music that is banal, it offers some that is beautiful, some that is dramatic, and one scene that is quite remarkable, a fearful vision of the Last Judgment. Why then do our companies shun it?

Some reasons are clear. It is one of Verdi's longest operas; at roughly two and a quarter hours of music, only *Vespri*, *Forza*, *Don Carlos*, and *Aida* are longer.[2] If Verdi's scenic directions are followed, it needs eight different sets, and even if a generic forest or castle is used twice, scenic costs will be high. In addition, casting is not easy: The opera needs an above-average men's chorus and six strong soloists: Besides the usual quartet, soprano, tenor, baritone, and bass, it needs a second tenor who can hold his own against three principals in the first act's quartet finale, and a second bass who for his single scene, in which he functions somewhat like the Grand Inquisitor in *Don Carlos*, must be imposing in voice and presence. Thus, even a concert performance will be expensive.

Besides these material costs, the opera, based on Schiller's five-act play *Die Räuber* (The Robbers), poses many artistic problems, some of Schiller's making, some of Verdi's. Because conceived by Schiller when he was nineteen and hating the discipline of a military college, the play's plot and tone are wildly, youthfully rebellious and idealistic. Its hero, the university student Karl Moor, disgusted with life and feeling rejected by his father, rants against authority, institutions, even family, and urged on by fellow students agrees to lead them in a life free of society, a homeless life of banditry: hence, the play and opera's title, *The Robbers*. When first produced, in Mannheim in 1782, the play's violent rhetoric—Karl's attacks on Christianity, the state, family, and his all-too-late repentance—roused the audience to frenzy. Today, that violence of language can seem ludicrous, as the Sarasota Opera discovered in 2006, when its initial, quite accurate supertitles caused the audience repeatedly to laugh.[3] Over the years, Verdi's music, too, has caused laughter, notably at a chorus for bandits exulting in the dying croaks of murdered men and the wails of their wives and mothers, all set to a jiggy waltz.[4]

These are the superficial problems. More difficult and essential is the need for both play and opera to make clear to auditors what Schiller and Verdi mean to say. The surface story is clear. Karl/Carlo (tenor), at a German university in the early eighteenth century, has indulged in some student escapades but at heart is deeply fond of his father, Count Moor/Massimiliano (bass), and loves his fiancée Amalia, his father's niece and an orphan. Karl's younger brother, Franz/Francesco (baritone), resents his inferior status, and to gain his father's title and property schemes to estrange his father from Carlo, to marry Amalia himself, and to drive the father to an early death. By trickery he persuades his father and Amalia that Karl has died and persuades Karl by a lying letter that his father, angered by his wild behavior, has disowned him. Franz dominates the two men by playing on their feelings of family obligation, turning each against the other by inflating a falsely induced sense of injury. He is a man—in Coleridge's phrase for Iago—of "motiveless malignity,"[5] a man who in his final scene, even after recounting a nightmare in which he sees himself on Judgment Day denied by God, still cannot bring himself to pray. Like Milton's Satan, he is determined not "To bow and sue for grace with suppliant knee." He is a fully committed revolutionary.[6]

Karl, less committed, is more complicated. Believing himself rejected by his father and unworthy of Amalia, he turns against the world, but unlike Franz he is not by nature evil, and the further he sinks into crime, the more he longs to be free of it, to be his better self. For, like some young idealists, he soon discovers in his revolutionary acts the evil of which he is capable.[7] His extreme reaction to what he conceives to be the world's injustice brings out in his personality streaks of cruelty and social irresponsibility that at first injure only strangers but also ultimately the father and woman he loves, and then himself. In his final scene, after a nervous breakdown brought on by conflicting loyalties, as a sacrifice to his fellow bandits, he kills Amalia, then instantly leaves to submit himself to society as a murderer.

In the play, because Schiller never brings the two brothers onstage together, a single actor can, and sometimes does, take both roles,[8] which may help an audience to grasp Schiller's comparison of evil in man's spirit, evil partial and redeemable or evil whole and damned. The subject is not new. Long before Milton's Satan declared, "Better to reign in hell than serve in heav'n," Homer described men to whom Zeus had given "from the jar of evil only," who had become "outcasts . . . chased by the gadfly of despair over the face of the earth," and "damned by gods and men alike."[9]

In the opera, with Francesco a baritone and Carlo a tenor, a single artist for both is not possible. But Verdi as much as Schiller intended the story, brothers fighting over a woman, property, and a title, to be taken as an allegory personifying a discussion of rebellion against God and man taken too far.

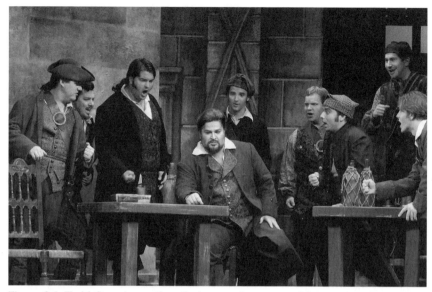

Figure 8.1. Todd Geer (seated) as Carlo, opening scene of *I masnadieri*, Sarasota, 2006. Photograph by Deb Hesser. Courtesy of the Sarasota Opera Company.

In productions of the opera this larger thesis sometimes emerges success-fully. For example, a critic reviewing a performance in English by the Welsh National Opera in March 1977, remarked "The action is as relevant as today's headlines: the management could have billed the work as 'The Urban Gueril-las' without changing a line."[10] But unhappily for the opera, those cast as Carlo and his robbers more often project middle-aged flab than youthful rage.

To help with that larger thesis, Verdi had as librettist his friend Andrea Maf-fei, then the leading Italian expert on Schiller, and together they managed to sprinkle through Carlo's role many indications of his divided self, showing him to be, in the way of the young, both foolishly swift to anger and yet intensely introspective and responsive. In the opening scene, dispensing with the usual introductory chorus, they start with an aria for Carlo, "O mio castel paterno," in whose declamatory introduction he deplores the debased ideals of the day, the lack of heroic leaders, and in the aria expresses his love of home, father, and Amalia. At its close, he receives a long-awaited letter from younger brother Francesco, stating falsely that their father has rejected him, and Carlo in a spasm of despair turns outlaw.

No audience will miss the scene's structure and purpose. To save time, do away with the traditional opening chorus; introduce the lead character in a major aria that shows him loving and idealistic, and then, his illusions of family love shat-tered, his consequent attack on society. But—and this is the flaw that perme-ates the opera—act and reaction happen too fast, and reaction seems overdone.

Modern audiences, thinking one bad letter from home not cause enough for a life of violence and crime, instead of being shocked by the decision, are inclined to laugh. One generation's horror has become another's ho-hum.

At Carlo's next appearance, in act 2, scene 2, a reappearance too long delayed, the structure is reversed and its purpose less clear. The scene opens with the robbers, Carlo's classmates, celebrating the burning of Prague, seen in the background and emphasized by women wailing their way across the back of the stage. The English scholar Julian Budden finds this "a brilliantly effective movement" as "their wailing can still be heard in the distance after the music has subsided."[11] Only after the robbers have described their villainy does Carlo enter, and sending them off, he has his second aria, a *romanza*. Gazing at the sunset, he laments that the beauties of nature and Amalia's love are not for him, whose life is out of joint with all that's good. Though the aria yearns for happiness lost, its dramatic basis is weak. Thus far, Carlo's villainy has only been stated. Prague burns, but the audience has yet to see him commit one crime.

Lastly, the speed with which events unfold in the opera's final scene leaves most in any audience confused and unbelieving. As it opens, Carlo has rescued from imprisonment his dim-sighted, half-starved father, but ashamed of his robber's life has concealed his identity; yet, as his father's rescuer, he asks for the old man's blessing and receives it (duet). Enter robbers to report to Carlo, "Capitano," that Francesco has escaped and disappeared. Carlo, his role as gang leader almost revealed, grows agitated. Enter more robbers with Amalia a captive. She, recognizing Carlo, but unaware of his connection to the robbers, throws her arms around him, calling him "sposo" (bridegroom). Her act astounds the robbers and drives Carlo, his cover blown, into hysteria: "Tear her from my neck! Kill that old man! Kill her too, kill me, kill all of you!" Robbers: "Is he delirious?" Carlo tells Massimiliano that he is indeed his son but also the robbers' leader, stunning Amalia and Massimiliano. Robbers: "Why tell this?" (Though Verdi shifts tone and melody for each new mood or revelation, in the audience only those well-prepared can keep abreast. Carlo's hysteria, for example, goes by in twelve bars of *allegro agitato*—over before the supertitles can be read and absorbed.)

After Carlo's confession, comes the final trio with chorus, which Carlo starts, "Caduto è il reprobo!" (The evildoer has fallen, smitten by God). Amalia insists, "Angel or demon. . . . I will not abandon you," and he cries, "She loves me." They have eight, only eight, bars of happiness with Massimiliano providing a bass line, before the robbers come forward, baring scars suffered following Carlo. By oaths sworn, he belongs to them. Woefully, he agrees, and Amalia declares, "if you cannot break your chains, then kill me." Despite the robbers' protests, he does, stabbing her, and her self-sacrifice frees him to follow his better self to justice, a premonition of the later Romantic Age's cliché, the lost soul saved by the love of a true woman. His last line, predicting society's judgment on him, is "Now to the gallows." And while others rush to support the expiring

Figure 8.2. Final scene of *I masnadieri*, Sarasota, 2006. Carlo (Todd Geer), Amalia (Asako Tamura), Massimiliano (Young-Bok Kim), and the Robbers. Photograph by Deb Hesser. Courtesy of the Sarasota Opera Company.

Amalia, he exits alone, eleven measures before curtain, and so absents himself, the most important character, from the opera's final tableau. Curtain.

Musically, the scene is beautiful as the voices twine above interjections by the robbers; dramatically, it is confusing. Most in any audience will leave the theater asking, Why did he stab her? Why did his earlier vows to Amalia not take precedence over his later to the bandits? Surely he owes more to his father and to his fiancée than to fellow students. And where was he as the curtain fell? The last query arises in part because most in any audience will have their eyes fixed on the dying Amalia and in part because Carlo's final phrase, "Now to the gallows," is drowned by the chorus (and sometimes also by the soprano choosing to die on an unwritten high D flat). But audiences don't leave *Rigoletto* or *Traviata* abuzz with similar questions.

Critics often compare *Masnadieri* to its immediate predecessor *Macbeth*, finding its drama less well handled and its musical forms, especially in the first two acts, more old-fashioned—chiefly too many slow-fast, cantabile-cabaletta arias. All of which is true, but often, too, they miss the grandeur of what Verdi attempted in *Masnadieri*. He and Maffei sought to make an opera of one of the great works of late eighteenth-century German Romantic drama, a play that, chiefly through the force of its language, has periodically found success despite its sprawling structure. In contrast, *Macbeth*, the shortest of Shakespeare's tragedies, is tightly focused on two characters. Though Verdi's reach in *Masnadieri* may have exceeded his grasp, his attempt is intriguing and often beautiful.

The opera had its premiere on July 22, 1847, at Her Majesty's Theatre in London, Verdi's first commission outside of Italy. The occasion was a gala, with the composer conducting, the Swedish soprano Jenny Lind singing Amalia, and Queen Victoria and her consort Prince Albert in the royal box. The queen recorded in her diary that she found the music "very inferior and commonplace,"[12] and evidently others agreed, for in all the opera had only four performances.[13] It was not heard again in England until a single performance in March 1962 by the Philopera Circle in London, when the libretto was deplored, but the music declared, "heady, exhilarating, full of life and energy."[14]

Curiously, after the premiere run of four performances in 1847, Lind, though she had created the role of Amalia, tailored by Verdi to display her ability to decorate a vocal line and to trill, apparently never again sang an aria from it—not even during her 1850–51 tour of the United States, managed by P. T. Barnum, during which she sang ninety-five concerts in fifteen states as well as Washington, DC, and Havana. Though the tenor and baritone on that tour occasionally sang arias from *Oberto* and *I Lombardi*, Lind sang not a note of Verdi.[15] Presumably she felt his music, more passionate and dramatic than then was common, unsuited to her voice.

American excitement over Lind, so cleverly inflated by Barnum, echoes to this day, and journalists often cite it when writing of *I masnadieri*—implying that she and her fame helped to spread the opera abroad. But not so, and even some who heard her declared, against the tide of opinion, that her voice was ill-suited to Italian opera. Walt Whitman wrote: "The Swedish Swan, with all her blandishments, never touched my heart in the least. I wondered at so much vocal dexterity; and they were all very pretty, those leaps and double somersets. But even in the grandest religious airs . . . executed by this strangely overpraised woman in perfect scientific style, let critics say what they like, it was a failure; for there was a vacuum in the head of the performance. Beauty pervaded it no doubt and that of a high order. It was the beauty of Adam before God breathed into his nostrils."[16] In short, little drama, passion, or humanity, and so, unsuited to Verdi. This raises the suspicion that the casting of Lind in the opera's premiere, with Verdi making changes to suit her, did the opera, as opposed to the gala, little good. More than an excellent trill, the Amalia of the opera needs a strong dramatic portrayal.[17]

The earliest reference yet discovered to any of the opera's music sung in the United States occurs in George Templeton Strong's diary, in his entry for March 8, 1856. The young New York lawyer and his wife Ellie had attended a dinner party the previous evening given by their friend Charles Kuhn, a commission merchant on Wall Street. After the party, Strong recorded, "Yesterday we dined with Kuhn; and Ellie, Mrs. Isaac Wright, Kuhn and one Hewitt sang bosh from *Corsaro* and *Masnadieri*."[18]

The first professional performance of an excerpt took place a month later in one of the sixteen concerts offered that winter in Dodworth Hall (capacity 400) by the American pianist Louis Moreau Gottschalk.[19] At the fourteenth of these, an assisting artist, Mrs. Edith G. Bostwick, sang to piano accompaniment Amalia's scene and aria, "Tu del mio Carlo al seno," which opens the opera's second act. Verdi designed this two-part aria to show off Lind's ability first to be wan and pathetic, and then to dazzle with coloratura runs and trills. She sings to the tomb of Carlo's father, whom she believes dead, and envies him for joining Carlo in heaven, though leaving her friendless in grief. But then, on hearing secretly from a family retainer that Carlo still lives, she rockets off "con entusiasmo" into cascades of joy. Though a spectacular piece, in the excitement of Gottschalk's piano fireworks, critics ignored it.[20]

The opera's U.S. premiere took place in New York at the Winter Garden on June 2, 1860. The producer was the conductor and impresario Max Maretzek, whose company then was possibly the country's best, a rank that only the French company in New Orleans could steadily contest. But he was not without competition in the North, and he intended the premiere of a new Verdi opera to cap a New York season in which finally, after great expense, he had outlasted two rivals.[21]

Apparently, in preparation much went wrong. Maretzek postponed the opening twice, and in the end did not conduct the opera himself but left the job to Carl Anschütz, a fine musician but perhaps less familiar with the score. Equally surprising, Maretzek cast the four leading roles not with singers from his own company but from a troupe newly arrived, which had been singing the opera in South America. They seem to have pleased no one, and the New York annalist Joseph Ireland recorded the premiere as "their first and last appearance in New York."[22] The only journal to give *Masnadieri* more than two sentences was the *Spirit of the Times*, whose anonymous critic concluded, it "is not one of Verdi's strong operas. . . . In fact, with the exception of two or three spirited choruses, and an exceedingly clever and thoroughly Verdi-ish finale, there is nothing in the opera that clings to memory."[23] Whereupon Maretzek, after the single performance, claimed ill health, closed the run, and canceled his season in Philadelphia—though some believed the true reason, on evidence of the long season and skimped *Masnadieri*, was that he had run out of money.[24]

San Francisco was the only other city in the United States to hear the opera onstage in the nineteenth century, and again a resident company, after excerpts were sung, attempted it. This time its record was better. The first of its music to be heard, in a concert on October 23, 1858, was a "Grand Duo," most likely "T'abbraccio, O Carlo," in which Amalia, fleeing through woods to escape the evil Francesco, by convenient chance meets Carlo; and together they exclaim that they will nevermore be separated. The singers in San Francisco, an Italian tenor and his wife, Eugenio and Giovanna Bianchi, had arrived from Mexico only eight days earlier, and though unknown were bankrolled to the introductory concert, with an orchestra of some twenty-two, by the local impresario Tom Maguire.[25]

The concert, mostly of selections from Verdi, sold out, gained a highly favorable review in the *Daily Alta California*,[26] and Maguire at once signed the Bianchis for fifteen more concerts. After this, he sent them on tour, starting in Sacramento, where he owned a theater and the state legislature would be sitting. The sixteen San Francisco concerts, all of which reportedly sold out, were sung in a period of fifty-eight days, and starting with the third concert Maguire enlarged the orchestra to thirty or so, and supplied a chorus, costumes, and some minimal scenery. Besides the Grand Duo, repeated twice in the course of the concerts, Signor Bianchi and the chorus in the fourteenth performance presented the opera's opening scene, featuring Carlo's aria, "O mio castel paterno."[27]

The Bianchis' talents were modest but vocally solid. Onstage, Eugenio was said to be "sturdy and rather fussy" and Giovanna, "stout." His voice, however, was exceptionally warm, pure, and sympathetic, and the *Alta California* proclaimed him "the finest tenor we have ever yet heard in California." Her voice apparently was somewhat less appealing, but "she had a gushy style of doing things, and she takes the eyes if not the ears by storm."[28] Backed by Maguire, for almost a year they carried Italian opera, sung in Italian with orchestra and chorus, throughout Northern California. Later, without Maguire and after a sojourn in Australia, they returned to San Francisco, and with their own company produced annual seasons of Italian opera from 1862 until the mid-1870s. Their place in the city's operatic history is large, and they favored Verdi.

Maguire's personal wealth and location, in a faraway city,[29] gave him many advantages over Maretzek, struggling in New York. Owning his own opera house, Maguire could schedule companies as he wished, whereas Maretzek, seeking to play in the Academy of Music, had to negotiate each season with the academy's owners, real estate holders eager to extract the highest rent. Then, too, in San Francisco the competition was not so fierce, or the Bianchis might not have endured so long; and Maguire, in these years, was by far the most powerful impresario in the city, whereas in New York Maretzek regularly faced competing seasons staged by others, chiefly Maurice Strakosch and Bernard Ullman. Finally, audience expectations in San Francisco were not so severe or so ruled by fashion. San Franciscans did not expect always to have a choice of the best—Jenny Lind, for one, never sang in the city—and if they found the entertainment good, they ignored the critics. In sum, talent, audience expectations, and supporting wealth were in a more favorable balance in San Francisco than in many cities of the East, and by 1863, when *Masnadieri* had its premiere in that city, it was more adventurous in opera than Boston, Philadelphia, Chicago, or St. Louis.

On May 29, 1863, at the Metropolitan Theatre, the Bianchi company produced *I masnadieri*. The reviews in subsequent days were all favorable, though not detailed about the music. The *Daily Evening Bulletin* declared, "With a great deal of *noise*, there are many beautiful airs and choruses in the piece. In the absence of a copy of the Italian libretto (not to be found in the city, it appears,) we are unable to particularize the finer passages."[30]

The *Daily Alta California* reported at greater length:

> The California public are familiar with Verdi's compositions, from his *Nabucco*, *Trovatore*, *Traviata*, and *Luisa Miller*. His compositions have been echoed and re-echoed through our hills, valleys and mountains, and no one is more popular. Last evening his opera of *I masnadieri* was presented. . . . We had a glimpse of the beauties of this work on the initial appearance of the Bianchis some years since at Maguire's Opera House, but after hearing the entire work we are somewhat surprised that it has never been presented previously. Few operatic works contain so much melody, or such a number of pleasing and captivating airs. Instead of finding the subject—a tragic one— treated in a ponderous or sombre style, *I masnadieri* is a collection of vocal and instrumental gems rarely equalled in excellence.[31]

That spring and summer of 1863 the opera had eight performances, and the Bianchis revived it for one in 1865, after which it was not heard again anywhere in the United States until 1975. No review suggests that these nineteenth-century San Franciscan audiences saw anything deeper in the opera than the surface melodrama, or that the Bianchis attempted anything more, but a committed performance of the opera, played to a receptive audience, will deliver a moral message, though unstressed and unclear.

Meanwhile, in New York in these years, at least one amateur, John Ward, recorded in his diaries singing unspecified excerpts of the opera during 1865 (six times) and 1867 (four). A lawyer and medical doctor, he was an able singer and pianist, and each winter periodically met with friends to make music.[32] Thus, some of the opera's music was available, but a catalogue of 1870 of what music leading publishers were offering lists only three numbers, each with English text: a duet for Amalia and Massimiliano, another for her and Carlo, and her entrance aria. Also available were four instrumental arrangements of selections.[33]

Thereafter the opera disappeared. No excerpt was sung in the Metropolitan's Sunday Evening Concerts, 1883–1946; none is listed in the *Collectors' Guide to American Recordings, 1895–1925*; the publisher G. Schirmer did not include any in its series of *Celebrated Opera Arias*, 1903 (often reissued); and no account of the opera or any recordings of excerpts appeared in the various editions of *The Victor Book of the Opera*, 1912–36.[34] In the United States the opera was forgotten, even in memory—"Of the dead, why speak?"

In Europe, however, *Masnadieri* still had an occasional staging, and then an important revival in Bremen in 1928. That production was part of the Verdi Renaissance that was mounting in Germany, in which conductors, singers, and impresarios increasingly found Verdi relevant, not only good entertainment but with something to say. After World War II the movement strengthened in the United States, with the Metropolitan leading. In addition to reviving those twelve Verdi operas the company previously had produced, it now brought to its stage and national radio broadcasts five more: *Macbeth* (1959), *Nabucco* (1960), *Vespri Siciliani* (1974), *Stiffelio* (1993), and *I Lombardi* (1993), and by example encouraged smaller companies to mount some of the less familiar operas.[35]

One that did was the Opera Orchestra of New York, which, on February 12, 1975, gave a concert performance of *I masnadieri* in Carnegie Hall. Unhappily for the occasion the singers announced for Carlo and Amalia had to withdraw, and their substitutes hardly had time to rehearse, which may explain in part why the balance between the four principals was somewhat spoiled and why Francesco, the baritone Matteo Manuguerra, so far outshone the others. Raymond Ericson, reviewing for the *Times*, began:

> The revival here of Verdi's early, neglected operas goes on by fits and starts, but it does, fortunately, go on. On Wednesday night it was the turn of *I masnadieri*. . . . The plot defies brief description. . . . The stock characters invite little sympathy, and Verdi's music does not give them enough humanity. This may be the secret behind the work's neglect, because the score in itself is quite effective and entertaining. . . . But nothing is ever so richly textured or deeply felt as in *Trovatore*. It is all lively, surface theatricality, easy to enjoy, easy to forget.
>
> The opera invites the term "ripsnorting," and this was the aspect that Eve Queler, music director of the Opera Orchestra, chose to stress. . . . The evening seemed louder than necessary, since a good deal of the Verdi indications for soft singing and playing were ignored. Yet the energy and precision in the work of the chorus and orchestra could be admired. . . . The cast sang efficiently and sometimes better than that. Two of its members [Carlo and Amalia] were . . . last minute substitutes. The best performance was given by Matteo Manuguerra as Francesco.[36]

Ericson hardly did justice to Manuguerra's success in Francesco's *sogno*, the scene in which he describes his repudiation by God and his inability to pray. Manuguerra held the audience transfixed. And as the following and final scene for the other three characters went well, to those present the entire last act seemed a marvel.[37]

Harriet Johnson for the *Post* stressed the audience's excitement. She concluded, however, that the opera's libretto

> is worse than most. It is vastly inferior to Schiller and to Verdi's *Macbeth*. . . . The music is something else again. While not original in form, it has raw vitality and a rhythmic surge . . . [the opera's structure] is melodious aria followed by a fast caballeta, time after time. There are rousing choruses and a

few concerted pieces. This is without a doubt, a chorus opera. The final trio is a superb piece and there are many other appealing sections. . . . A prime star of the evening was baritone Matteo Manuguerra who stole the show more than once.[38]

Later in that same year the Philips company issued the opera's first complete recording, giving critics an opportunity to expound on the opera's strengths and weaknesses. One who did was Andrew Porter, in *High Fidelity Magazine*, and he made a point of Verdi's scoring pertinent to the drama: "One of Verdi's special devices in this opera is to mark swift, excitable music to be sung softly, to suggest agitation in an 'inner' rather than an obvious way—a repeated *ppp* in the stretta of the soprano/tenor duet, for example. And, more than most tenors who sing the role [of Carlo] Bergonzi has noticed that the rousing cabaletta of his entrance aria carries the indications *sotto voce* and *pp.*"[39]

In the opera's next production in the United States, however, the first to be staged since 1865, it was not the baritone or the tenor who stole the show but the soprano. San Diego Opera, in the city's Civic Theatre in June 1984, as part of its (ultimately incomplete) Verdi cycle[40] gave the opera three performances. As conductor the company hired Richard Bonynge and as Amalia, Bonynge's wife, Joan Sutherland. Only the year before the two had issued the opera's second complete recording,[41] generally thought as good as the first, and so at the moment they were the opera's reigning artists. Donald Dierks of the *San Diego Union* reported of her onstage performance, "There are precious few singers in the world who can, by the greatness of their art, carry a second rate opera and a poor production of it on their backs. Joan Sutherland is such an artist."[42]

His colleague at the *Tribune*, Valerie Scher, agreed, and both deplored the dismal scenery, according to Dierks "platforms and ramps," and stage direction, "more like a meeting of the oratorio society." Yet he felt the music "rising from the pit was not static," and, in Scher's phrase, "at its best, *Masnadieri* transcends its limitations and achieves truly impressive dimensions." Unlike Harriet Johnson in New York, however, Scher judged the music "at its weakest" in the robbers' choruses. "At the emotional heart of the opera," she declared, "is Amalia," a view contrary to most critical opinion, which places the heart in Carlo. Then, comparing Sutherland favorably to Lind, Scher added, "in the elaborate bel canto aria 'Tu del mio Carlo al seno,' probably the best number in the opera, her trills sent thrills of excitement through the audience."[43]

Indeed, they did. But—and in this I suspect Sutherland was much like Lind—her glory dimmed the opera's drama. It was not just that she, the superstar, outshone her colleagues, though that, too, diminished drama, but that she also sometimes changed Verdi's vocal line. In the final trio Amalia twice sings to Carlo "Angel or demon . . . I will not abandon you," each time to a long downward swoop through nine intervals, and then, after a brief start upward, cut short, and then repeated, steadily mounts the scale to an ecstatic B flat.

Sutherland broke the second downward swoop in half, taking the latter half up an octave. The effect was to rob the swoop of energy and to drain some ecstasy from the high B flat. And at the very end, instead of dying silently, as the score directs, she overwhelmed Carlo's "And now to the gallows" with a high D flat, beautifully taken. Small points, but not without their effect on the drama.[44]

Moreover, perhaps because of the reports of dismal scenery, staging, and drama, even with Sutherland the opera sold poorly, requiring the box office for the second and third performance in the hour before curtain to offer tickets at half price.[45] Thus, for impresarios elsewhere, San Diego's experience tended to confirm opinion that, despite some fine music, *Masnadieri* would fail at the box office.

Refusing to be intimidated, the New York Grand Opera, a moderate-sized company, known for its free performances in the city's Central Park, staged the opera on July 14, 1988, the first staged performance in New York in 128 years. The site, the Naumburg Band Shell, precluded all but the simplest scenery and offered only a small stage; hence, the orchestra sat at ground level between the raised stage and the rows of movable park benches. For its season the company was presenting a "Viva Verdi" series of four operas, *Rigoletto*, *Traviata*, *Ballo in maschera*, and, as the novelty, *I masnadieri*.

In favor of a good performance were a full orchestra led by Vincent La Selva, a Verdi specialist, an adequate chorus, and relatively unknown but well-rehearsed singers. Against it, was almost all else: a complicated story, sung in Italian without supertitles, with sound often harshly amplified, and after the first scene in the third act, the weather—thunder, lightning and rain, which sent "the orchestra and singers scurrying away in mid-phrase."[46] After a pause, with two-thirds of the audience gamely remaining, the performance resumed, only to quit in rain ten minutes before the end. Nine years later the same company, on July 2, 1997, in the midst of presenting all of Verdi's operas in order of composition, again staged *Masnadieri*. The site was now the "Summer Stage" erected in Rumsey Field, Central Park, but with the exception of weather, all the previous disadvantages of outdoor performance were on hand. Yet as usual with La Selva's productions, the audience, whether or not it grasped the story, seemed to enjoy the music and stayed to the end.[47]

In San Francisco a smaller company took a different tack. Donald Pippin's Pocket Opera annually offers a season of eight or nine operas sung in English and staged in small auditoriums—"No opera glasses. No supertitles"—with minimal orchestra, chorus, and scenery, and for 1998 it announced two performances of *The Gang of Bandits*. The orchestra of expert players numbered nine, four strings, four woodwinds, and Pippin at the piano. The chorus numbered three, and the singers, though all well-trained, were relatively unknown, and the production was successful enough to be repeated once the following year.[48]

The crux of that success perhaps lay in Pippin's translation of the libretto, summarized in advertisements as: "Carlo—intelligent, idealistic, rebellious, alienated from his family—has gotten into bad company which has steered him onto a steep downward path. His beloved Amalia is more than willing to take him as he is, but can he allow her to become embroiled in a life that he despises but cannot leave?" Note Pippin's emphasis, unlike San Diego's, on Carlo as "the emotional heart of the opera."

Moreover, his translation most likely was helpful, in part because here and there he changed wording to stress important points. In the final scene, for instance, when Carlo reveals to Amalia and his father that he is the band's captain, Verdi has the principals, backed by the chorus, express their shock by repeating eight times "Sventura!" (Misfortune!). Pippin, without changing the vocal lines, makes the horror more specific: "Their leader!" And when the robbers remind Carlo of his vows to them, Verdi has him cry, "È ver, è ver!" (It's true, it's true!). Pippin substitutes, again to Verdi's musical line, "Ah, no escape!" Many such small changes, sung in a small theater, no doubt made the story's events and emotions clearer. Yet the opera remained long (the program stated, two and three-quarter hours, which may have included an introduction by Pippin as well as one intermission), and its record of three performances in two seasons is small compared to his success with Verdi's little known comedy, *Un giorno di regno* (King for a Day), presented first in 1975, and before the century ended five times revived.

Overseas, in that last quarter-century, productions of *Masnadieri* increased, though moderately in number and with equivocal success. The Welsh National Opera in 1977 gave thirteen performances in English in seven cities outside of London, and though the soloists and chorus won praise, audiences, though enthusiastic, were slim. And at year's end, the company dropped the production.[49] La Scala, which had not performed the opera since 1862, mounted it in 1978, and though orchestra and chorus won praise, the soloists did not; and later in the year, new soloists did no better. Yet in France, two years later, a smaller company in Nancy staged "a most winning production of a work too rarely heard."[50] Also in 1980 the Australian Opera Company, playing in Sidney, offered eight performances with Sutherland and Bonynge, and the following March took the opera with other singers and conductor to Canberra and Adelaide. And though success was moderate, subsequent stagings followed in 1987 and 1994.[51]

Finally, one of the more extreme efforts to make the opera relevant occurred on June 1, 2003, in Gelsenkirchen, Germany, in a production (sung in Italian) financed jointly with houses in Lübeck and Liège. Though the house program devoted several essays to the story's basis in Cain and Abel as well as Jacob and Esau, the costumes were vaguely contemporary; the old father was in a modern wheelchair, and the scenery was sparse, dominated for most of the opera by a grand piano center stage. The production made some minor changes in the plot, but mainly it sought to outmatch the textual violence with violence onstage. In the scene in which Francesco threatens Amalia, he attempted to have his way with her atop the piano.[52]

The Gang of Bandits

First Performance: London, 1847
Pocket Opera Premiere

Stage Director	Tim Campbell
Costume Designer	Dana MacDermott
Properties Designer	Jon Wai-Keung Lowe
Orchestra Contractor	Diana Dorman
Stage Manager	Marisa Pugliano

Cast

(in order of appearance)

Carlo..Michael Licciardello
Rolla...Tapan Bhat
Francesco...Ralph Wells
Arminio...Mark Hernandez
Amalia...Elin Carlson
Massimiliano..David Thompson
Moser...Richard Mix
Chorus...Mark D. Lew, Anthony Millette, Andrew Solovay

Pocket Philharmonic

Violin 1	Youngah Suk
Violin 2	Mark Fish
Viola	Stephanie Railsback
Cello	Teressa Adams
Flute	Richard McHenry
Oboe	Margot Golding
Clarinet	Diana Dorman
Bassoon	Alice Benjamin
Piano	Donald Pippin

Length of performance - two and three-quarter hours with one fifteen minute intermission

Figure 8.3. Program for the first performance of Pocket Opera's *The Gang of Bandits*, 1998. Photograph courtesy of Pocket Opera.

Perhaps the opera's grandest production, however, was staged by England's Royal Opera Company at the turn of the century, 1998–2002. Because the company's house at Covent Garden was being rebuilt and furbished, the company staged the opera first in Baden-Baden, Savonlinna, and the Edinburgh Festival, all in 1998, and finally in London in 2002. In Edinburgh, the festival was devoted to all four of Verdi's operas based on Schiller, and as the reviewer for *Opera* noted:

> Seeing *I masnadieri* after having experienced *Don Carlos* on the previous evening, one was often forced to smile. The cardboard characters, the stock situations, the jolly drunken bandits and the regularly trotted-out operatic routines make it seem like a kind of high-powered pantomime.... [In] Elijah Moshinsky's production ... the archaic blood and thunder of the story are embraced with open-eyed relish.... The chorus sings heartily even when blind drunk under the table or bashing the daylights out of each other.... The costumes are almost too traditional for words.... Dmitry Hvorostovsky, as Francesco the wicked brother, is the outstanding figure. He is the original arrogant and overbearing baddie, his richly-coloured tone flowing with prodigious abundance.... His dream scene in act 4, which bids comparison with a whole list of mad scenes, gave a terrifying impression of a bent and deranged mind in a body that looked Neanderthal.... There are some superb moments in *I masnadieri*, and some cheap ones. There are no dull ones. If it is all hokum, then it is magnificent, luxury hokum.[53]

When the production finally reached London, on September 30, 2002, another reviewer for *Opera* noted: "This must be one of the trickiest of all Verdi's operas to bring off.... There is some marvelous music in it: the Mad Scene[54] for baritone, a quartet as adventurous and powerful as the one in *Rigoletto*, consistently beautiful writing for woodwind, and instrumentation that in both its delicacy and violence looks forward to *Boccanegra*. And Schiller's treatment of terrorists seems to grow more, not less 'relevant' as the months pass."[55]

Yet some others thought otherwise. George Hall for *Opera News* declared the production "lacked conviction"; and he disapproved of a change in plot: having Carlo, at the opera's end, "do away with himself."[56] Though seemingly intended to make the ending more immediately comprehensible, it does rob the drama of Carlo's final submission to the society and institutions he had been attacking.

In the four years between the Royal Opera's Edinburgh performances and those in London, Eve Queler of the New York Opera Orchestra lured Hvorostovsky to New York for a concert performance in Carnegie Hall. Surrounding him with a good cast, on March 7, 1999, she produced, according to Paul Griffiths for the *Times*, "a lusty performance." And he added, "With its rollicking chorus of brigands, its ridiculously venomous villain (Francesco) and its melodramatic turns of events, the opera onstage might be hard to take seriously, but in a concert rendering one can forget the characters in favor of the singers."[57]

Yet more recently, the Sarasota Opera Company, as part of its Verdi cycle, gave seven performances of *Masnadieri*, setting the opera in style and scenery as close as possible to Verdi's conception. The performances, always well supported locally, drew many curious Verdi lovers from out of state and overseas, so that the box office, reselling the few tickets turned back, reported for the opera's run a house sold at a rate of 102.63 percent.[58]

The production did well by the opera and made only one change: acts 3 and 4 were played without intermission. The libretto, as always, was the chief problem. The eight changes of scene required time, and several of the pauses within acts took too long, and the audience's attention began to dissipate. And as previously mentioned, the company initially had trouble with supertitles harvesting laughter because of an all-too-literal translation of the lurid text. Better today, it seems, to fudge Francesco's report to Amalia that Carlo, as he lay dying, wrote in blood on his sword (Francesco shows the sword): "Death releases you, Amalia, from our vow; and you should marry Francesco." By the final performance, with some lines translated more blandly and others left blank, the problem seemed mostly solved. Still, laughter erupted twice: at the start of act 3, when Amalia, rushing through the forest to escape Francesco, so conveniently meets Carlo (with no explanation of their later parting), and then in the final scene, though now sounding more like nervous titters, when Carlo stabs her. As she collapsed, with all eyes on her, most likely few in the audience saw Carlo leave the stage or wondered why, and fewer still grasped that she had requested to be killed.[59]

Local critics were enthusiastic: "If you seize this occasion to suspend disbelief, you will come away with a head full of glorious melody," and "It has its moments, including the incredibly robust male choruses."[60] At the same time, they noted the libretto's "baffling tangle" and "unintended moments of hilarity."[61] And all seemed prepared to take the story as straight melodrama, unenriched by any thoughts about rebellion, evil, and their possible consequences.

The production's greatest strengths seemed three: the orchestra's playing, Victor DeRenzi's conducting, and the remarkable balance achieved in the casting of Carlo and Francesco. In the singers' equal artistry, for once they came across as contrasting types of evil, and in that link more important to the drama than Amalia. Perhaps some in the audience took them as more than quarreling brothers, for Francesco's account of his dream, with its occasional foreshadowing of Verdi's *Requiem*, usually stirs deeper thoughts.

But against that possibility and against any popular acceptance of *Masnadieri*, despite its music, is the prevailing culture of our day. The opera is very much a work of the early nineteenth century, peculiarly so, and not only in the musical structure of its first two acts but more essentially in its subject. In our English-speaking world today, not so many read Milton, not even the first

I masnadieri

Giuseppe Verdi

TRAGIC OPERA IN FOUR ACTS, SUNG IN ITALIAN
POETRY BY ANDREA MAFFEI
Based on the play *Die Räuber* by Friedrich Schiller

CONDUCTOR	Victor DeRenzi
STAGE DIRECTOR	Martha Collins
SCENIC DESIGNER	Troy Hourie
COSTUME DESIGNER	Howard Tsvi Kaplan
LIGHTING DESIGNER	James Leitner
WIGS AND MAKE-UP DESIGNER	Georgianna Eberhard
CHORUS MASTER	Roger L. Bingaman
ASSISTANT CONDUCTORS	Lisa Hasson, Richard Cordova
SURTITLE SUPPLIER	Words for Music
SURTITLE TRANSLATOR	Victor DeRenzi

New production created by Sarasota Opera

Cast

AMALIA, an orphan niece of the Count	Asako Tamura
MASSIMILIANO, the Count Moor, regent	Young-Bok Kim
CARLO, Massimiliano's son	Todd Geer
FRANCESCO, Massimiliano's son	Michael Corvino
ARMINIO, chamberlain to the family of the regent	Chad A. Johnson
MOSER, a pastor	Mark Freiman
ROLLA, Carlo's companion	Andrew Bidlack*

* *Studio Artist*

Sarasota Opera Orchestra
Chorus: Sarasota Opera Apprentice and Studio Artists

February 25, 28   March 2, 5M, 8, 11, 18M

Figure 8.4. Program for the premiere of *I masnadieri* at Sarasota, 2006 (from author's collection).

two books of *Paradise Lost*, and have not pondered the Rebellion in Heaven and the ensuing contest between evil and free will. We take less easily than our ancestors to such religious and philosophical speculation. For some of us, evil is no more than a chemical imbalance in the brain, a bit of bad luck. Hence, whether the opera be presented onstage or in concert, with supertitles or in English, in costume or contemporary dress, with elaborate or simplified scenery, "once curiosity has been satisfied," as Porter once wrote, its rank is "likely to be low, perhaps bottom, on anyone's list of Verdi's operas."[62]

Which is our loss, for there is more to the opera than mere melodrama. But that it has defects is undeniable, for as Coleridge noted,

> Schiller has the material Sublime; to produce an effect he sets you a whole town on fire and throws infants with their mothers into the flames, or locks up a father in an old tower. But Shakespeare drops a handkerchief, and the same or greater effects follow.[63]

Chapter Nine

Jérusalem

If number of performances be the measure, then in the United States in the nineteenth century, of Verdi's sixteen operas preceding *Rigoletto*, the most popular, after *Ernani*, was his twelfth, *Jérusalem*.

That popularity, however, had two peculiarities. First, though unmistakably by Verdi, *Jérusalem* is more a French than an Italian opera, being a massive revision of his *I Lombardi alla prima crociata* (1843), one that he created for the Paris Opéra in the style of French grand opera. Set to a wholly new libretto, with an extensive ballet, the knightly crusaders, Christian pilgrims, and principals are no longer Lombards but Frenchmen who sing, *cela va sans dire!* in French. Second, the opera's success in the United States was limited to a single city, New Orleans. Except when taken on tour—at least once to St. Louis and Cincinnati—it was not performed elsewhere, though New Orleans artists on visiting New York and perhaps other cities sang and played excerpts. But after the last performance in New Orleans, in 1890, it was not staged again in this country until 1991. And probably by 1930 most Americans, if aware of it at all, thought it merely a curiosity of Verdi's past, well ignored because inferior to its simpler, more naive original, *I Lombardi*. Yet its record in New Orleans is solid: In addition to frequent performances of excerpts on gala occasions (the last in 1897), in the forty years 1850–90 it had ninety performances.[1]

In 1973, however, the Verdi scholar Julian Budden published his volume on *The Operas of Verdi, from* Oberto *to* Rigoletto, and buried in it was a short chapter on *Jérusalem*. "Buried," because who then cared about *Jérusalem* when even *I Lombardi* was so little heard and little admired? Yet in his remarks Budden directly challenged such thinking: "This and other weaknesses taken into account, *Jérusalem* remains to anyone but an Italian chauvinist the better of the two operas."[2]

His argument was impressive, and in English-speaking countries, and no doubt in others, he stirred interest in the opera. Over the years it had, on occasion, been revived, chiefly in France and Italy, but in the 1990s in Europe it had at least seven successful productions (two in England) and in the United States, four, two onstage and two in concert. The four may seem but a snowflake on a sunny day, but when taken with the multiple recordings of the opera then becoming available, they marked a shift in opinion. An opera, dismissed here for fully a hundred years, began to be heard again.

The differences between the French and the Italian versions of the basic story, good and bad brother reconciled in the Holy Land, are large, and equally so in the music. For the Opéra, where custom required an extended ballet, Verdi composed two, the first a brief *choeur dansé*, in which while the chorus sings dancers taunt their prisoner, Hélène (Giselda), and the second, immediately following, a twenty-two minutes of dance, eighteen numbers without story line.[3] For the premiere, this longer ballet featured seven soloists currently popular in Paris and a corps of six women and six men. But seemingly, it was only moderately successful, as well as expensive to mount, and even in Paris parts soon were cut. In New Orleans, it never was danced.[4]

In addition, Verdi composed a wholly new and lengthy scene for the third act, one that became the crux of the opera, even as he improved much of the orchestration elsewhere. But perhaps the most notable change of the revision was the enhancement of the role for tenor. Gaston, the Frenchman, unlike his counterpart Oronte who does not appear until the second act, has an important part to play in the first, is at the center of the third's new "scene of degradation," as it is often called, and unlike Oronte, survives to sing in the opera's finale. Thus, in composing for the Opéra's leading tenor, Gilbert Duprez,[5] Verdi somewhat dimmed the focus on the evil brother (bass), his crime and redemption, and shifted much of it to Gaston and his alleged crime, his demotion in class and status, and his restoration. In doing so, Verdi created a role in which tenors, if able, will dominate the opera.

Premiered in Paris on November 26, 1847, *Jérusalem* in the succeeding five years achieved thirty-three performances, in terms of the day, a healthy number, though compared to Meyerbeer's *Huguenots* or *Robert le diable* only a moderate success. But because of its demands—scenery, costumes, dancers, and double chorus of pilgrims and crusaders—it was huge and expensive, and even the government-subsidized Opéra, richest of European theaters, began to make cuts.[6] For its 1852 revival, the house presented the opera in three acts, omitting the Crusaders' March, all the dances, and even the opera's closing scene, though as one critic remarked: "if the final curtain falls immediately after the trio, the opera fails its title"; Jerusalem is neither captured nor seen.[7] Nevertheless, whatever the cuts, for a time the opera did well in French-speaking theaters outside of France, notably Antwerp, Brussels, and Ghent, and though data are lacking for the provincial French theaters, Thomas G. Kaufman concludes, "it is safe to assume that its popularity in many French theatres was comparable."[8]

The revision, everyone agrees, tells a more coherent story than *Lombardi*. Of its music, Budden wrote, "with the exception of the uninteresting ballet," nearly all the changes are for the better. "The various numbers, some newly composed, others repositioned and sometimes elaborated, are soldered together by linking passages of far greater significance than the string-accompanied recitative which they replace. The entire opera, as befits one designed for the French stage, is more 'through-composed' than its parent work; and only a sentimentalist could regret the omission of all that was most embarrassingly naïf in the original score."[9] Yet, on that last point, not all agree. The original, say some, has a certain zest, a sincerity, a charm that the greater skill in *Jérsualem* has slightly smothered, always a risk in reforming a work.

In New Orleans, where *Lombardi* had never been staged, no one concerned themselves with such problems. Though undoubtedly excerpts of Verdi had been sung at concerts or played in the city's many ballrooms, not one of his operas had been performed, and the opera audience, predominantly French-speaking, eagerly awaited not the latest work of Verdi but the latest hit from Paris. The city boasted the country's oldest theater primarily devoted to opera, the Théâtre d'Orléans, built in 1819[10] and seating 1,300. Moreover, it housed the country's oldest resident company, usually known simply as the French company to distinguish it from visiting companies that played often in English or Italian. In its initial years the company had struggled to survive but, by 1827, it was showing signs of health, and along with artists imported from Paris had acquired the score of Boieldieu's *La Dame blanche* (1825), an opéra comique, based by its librettist Eugène Scribe on two of Walter Scott's novels, *The Monastery* (1820) and *Guy Mannering* (1815). With its Scottish setting, charming music, and slightly Gothic mystery of the White Lady, it became instantly popular and is still today sometimes played and recorded.[11] Premiered in New Orleans on February 6, 1827, it became the first opera in the city's history to play three nights running, and remained a favorite until the 1880s, by which time it had totaled at home more than ninety performances and had been taken frequently on tour, introduced not only to the cities along the Mississippi and Ohio rivers but to New York, Boston, and Philadelphia.[12]

In the next twenty years, always following the lead in Paris, the French company's repertory grew steadily heavier, more Romantic, and requiring stronger voices, larger orchestras, and a bigger chorus. When the company came on its eighth tour to the Northeast, in 1845, it performed with a conductor (still not usual in the cities visited), an orchestra of forty, a chorus of roughly thirty,[13] and a repertory of French Grand Opera, Rossini's *Guillaume Tell*, Meyerbeer's *Les Huguenots*, Halévy's *La Juive*, and Donizetti's *La Favorite*, all of which had played first in New Orleans and at the time were beyond the skills of northern companies. With reason, critics and audiences in the northeast proclaimed the company the best yet heard.

The people of New Orleans, not surprisingly, were proud of their city's reputation in opera, and looked forward to hearing and judging the latest work from Paris. Anticipating the premiere, on January 24, 1850, the *New Orleans Bee* predicted that the French company would stage the opera with "great care" and described Verdi as "that great master, who, it is said, unites the scientific combination of the German to the inimitable melody and passion of the Italian school"—that "scientific combination" then being a way of saying "increased care in orchestration."[14]

After opening night, the *Daily Picayune* reported: "The new grand opera of *Jérusalem* will prove the great feature of attraction at the opera house for the remainder of the season. The theatre was a perfect 'jam' on the first night of its representation, and everyone speaks of it—music, decorations, scenery, grouping, &c.—in terms of the highest admiration. It is repeated this evening."[15]

The critic for the *Bee*, whose review was longer, began with a disclaimer. The regular critic was in Baton Rouge, and his substitute claimed only to be "a great lover of music," not technically trained. Verdi, coming after Rossini, Bellini, and Meyerbeer, "seems to me to have distanced himself from the style of his predecessors and opened a new way for himself." He has found "a middle ground" between Italian and German styles, and "if I may hazard an opinion, I would say that this music is too noisy, without knowing whether to address that complaint to the maestro or to the interpreters."

Like the enthusiastic audience he greatly admired "the magnificence of the costumes in the first act," and "the dispositions of the Crusaders' army in the valleys of Ramla." But in the final tableau of a distant Jerusalem, he was disappointed; it lacked "perspective." Nevertheless, "All in all, one must see and hear the opera a second time to comprehend and judge; so tonight, I will be there."[16]

His second review was still longer, and he started by telling the story: Roger (bass), for example, was "a bad good-for-nothing who nourished in secret a violent passion for the charming Hélène." The first act, he thought, sparkled with musical beauties, Hélène's *Ave Maria*, an orchestral sunrise, an offstage women's chorus that precedes and in its gentleness contrasts with Roger's aria of fierce self-revelation, the chorus of soldiers drinking, and the act's final chorus as all turn on Gaston (tenor) as the presumed assassin. "I know nothing in all the modern repertoire that makes a more powerful effect than the *stretta* of the finale. . . . It is without doubt the best page of the score."[17]

In later acts, he praised Hélène's excitement on learning that Gaston still lived (the former "Non fu sogno," and now sometimes called the "Polonaise"), her love duet with Gaston, the Pilgrims' Chorus, the scene of degradation, and the final trio, "which worthily crowns the master's work." This is the former "conversion" trio ("Qui posa il fianco"), but now shorn of its violin introduction and obbligato.[18] In the revision, however, the lovers no longer hope for salvation in a better world but despair even as the hermit, who is Roger in disguise, urges them to believe that God will end their trials, restore Gaston's honor, and see justice done. The hermit-Roger can be sure of God's intervention because he knows that it was he, Roger, and not Gaston, who back in Toulouse had tried to murder Hélène's father. But of course at the moment no one else knows the truth, and so for the previous scene of Gaston's "degradation" for his supposed crime the pilgrims, crusaders, townspeople, and all the principals except Roger had gathered in the town square to see Gaston punished.

In that scene, Gaston, as a nobleman, asks that he be killed at once, with his banner unfurled above him. The papal legate, who presides over the ceremony, refuses: tomorrow, execution; today, degradation; Gaston must be stripped of rank and honor, and any claim to nobility or chivalry denied. At the prospect of such "infamie" Gaston breaks down, pleads for instant death, but the Crusader knights and legate are unmoved. The herald, holding up Gaston's helmet to the crowd, declaims, "Behold the helmet of a traitor, of a faithless knight." Gaston cries, "Tu mens, tu mens" (You lie). The knights intone, "no mercy," and with a mace the herald smashes the helmet. The ritual repeats with Gaston's shield and sword, each smashed in turn. Coming down from the scaffold, Gaston furiously turns on his accusers, "Kill me, kill me. What holds you back? I shed my blood for you. In God's presence I will charge you with your crime." The knights and legate chant their righteousness, but the crowd now pleads for Gaston. In all, a highly theatrical scene, and if the tenor and others are up to it, gripping. Those who like to discover "pre-echoes" in opera may want to compare it to the priests' interrogation of Radames (tenor) in *Aida*, where Verdi varies the structure. Questioned three times on his act of treason, Radames three times is silent, while outside the room Amneris, who loves him, wails thrice in despair and fury.

Apparently, on second hearing, the humble critic for the *Bee* liked it all, and so, too, did the people of New Orleans. In a city with a population of only 116,375, between late January and mid-May the opera played fourteen times. And in the next twelve years, until the Civil War closed the theater, it played every season but one, achieving in all fifty-four performances.[19]

Meanwhile, Rosa DeVriès, the soprano who had first sung Hélène in New Orleans and was a favorite there, in visits to New York, in 1850, 1852, and 1853, sang with success excerpts from *Jérusalem*, or perhaps from *I Lombardi*. Her choice of language and score is not clear.[20] Also in New York in 1853 the New Orleans pianist-composer, Louis Moreau Gottschalk, stunned his audiences with a two-piano "Triumphal Fantasie" on themes from *Jérusalem*. So successful was this that on his return in 1855–56, when he gave a series of sixteen concerts, he repeated the now-titled "Grand Triumphal Fantasy" at four of them. Though the two-piano music is lost, a version for one piano exists, and ends with a stirring rendition of the Crusaders' March.[21] In addition, the French Company from New Orleans took the opera (played in three acts) on tour in 1860 to St. Louis and Cincinnati, but perhaps without much success, for in neither city did the opera win a newspaper review.[22]

New Orleans's loyalty to the opera, however, continued strong, and after the war's end, when the Théâtre d'Orléans once again could gather artists and reopen, it soon revived *Jérusalem*. The *Daily Picayune* greeted the return on March 28, 1868, of this "charming opera," and reported: "The play is imposing and grand from beginning to end, and every act contains one of those thrilling scenes which Verdi can bring out so vividly. . . . The scene where Gaston is degraded from the order of knighthood is original and splendid in the extreme, at the same time that it is full of pathetic force. This evening the magnificent opera will be repeated."[23]

Yet by the time of a later revival, in 1888, the opera's decline in critical opinion was becoming apparent:

> The musical portion of the work, after some lengthy discussion and comparison with the later and decidedly better developed ideas of the now great maestro, have been classed as indicative, and in fact, as being altogether representative of what is termed the first period of the author's musical life. There is certainly a quantity of melodious and, at times, gaudy exhibitions of tonal treatment and effect; some virtuosity evident in the harmonic transitions and an occasional masterly indication of the dramatic intelligence, which in his subsequent works earned for him his present title to artistic fame and insured its permanence and lasting effect. It was, in reality, this opera which served as an unquestionable means of deciding the bent of Verdi's genius.[24]

In particular the critic admired "the celebrated trio of the fourth act, which was sung with an effect and *en train* [spirit], such as is not often heard"; and also the choral singing in the "Choeur des Pèlerins." And a treat, unthinkable today but then in keeping with the variety-show style of an evening's musical entertainment: "During an intermission Mons. Moreau gave an exhibition of the various styles and mannerisms of singers, including some among the present troupe, and was heartily applauded after creating more than ordinary amusement."

The most recent revival to date in New Orleans was a series of four performances in the winter of 1891, with the last on February 19. The *Picayune* reported of the first, on January 29: "The chorus, orchestra, and the general ensemble went well, and when the curtain dropped on the last act, it was evident from the applause that *Jérusalem* was one of the season's finer programmes for the remainder of the week."[25]

Closing out the century, a French tenor, Albert L. Guille, who had been singing with success in New Orleans, came to New York for several season at the Metropolitan Opera, and at its Sunday Evening Concert, on January 20, 1892, he sang the tenor's aria "Je veux encore entendre," the only *Jérusalem* excerpt sung at these concerts. As an example of the French company's repertory at the time, Guille in his debut season in New Orleans, 1889–90, sang Manrico in *Trouvère*, Raoul in *Huguenots*, Arnold in *Guillaume Tell* Gaston in *Jérusalem*, Vasco da Gama in *Africaine*, the Duke in *Rigoletto*, Masaniello in *La Musette de Portici*, and the Dauphin in Halévy's *Charles VI*.[26]

In French-speaking Canada, in the Théâtre Français, Montreal, February 6, 1896, L'Opéra français de Montréal gave the opera its Canadian premiere, the first of three performances, with the departure of the Crusaders for the Holy Land (finale to act 1) and the degradation scene particularly admired. And finally, in concerts in New Orleans on January 20 and 27, 1897, the Trio and "Je veux encore entendre" were sung.[27] After which, in the United States

G I U S E P P E   V E R D I ' S

Jérusalem

I N   F R E N C H

San Mateo Performing Arts Center · San Mateo, California
Thursday, July 11, 1991   ·   Saturday, July 13, 1991

Proudly presented by   *Opera Peninsula*

Figure 9.1. Cover page of Opera Peninsula's program for the San Mateo company's 1991 revival of *Jérusalem* (from author's collection).

the opera faded from memory, and for almost a century, apparently even in excerpt, not a note was heard.

Imagine then the astonishment that greeted the announcement by Opera Peninsula, a fledging, two-year old company in San Mateo, California, that it would "proudly" present two performances of *Jérusalem* in the San Mateo Performing Arts Center, "in the original French," on July 11 and 13, 1991. In addition, it staged two anticipatory performances at the nearby Foothill College Main Theatre, and for all four performances it offered an orchestra, led by Robert Feist, of forty-six (twenty-four strings) and a chorus of twenty women and eleven men.

These performances drew Verdi fans from all over the Bay Area, and in the excitement the company's publicity department sometimes overstepped exact truth with statements such as: "The one and only time this four act epic work was performed in the United States was in January, 1850, in New Orleans."[28] But as one of the audience later remarked, "Hardly anyone knew what *Jérusalem* was."[29] Almost without dissent, the production was declared a success. The *San Francisco Chronicle* reported, "a thoroughly creditable and often excellent account," and went on to say:

> Under conductor Robert Feist, Saturday night's performance . . . offered impeccable musical values, including first-rate orchestral playing and vibrant, skillful singing from two of the principals [the soprano and tenor]. If the evening was a bit short on dramatic power, that seemed an acceptable price to pay for a presentation so much richer than what regional opera usually has to offer. . . . In theatrical terms, the production was a definitively shoestring affair. [The] bare set consisted almost entirely of a large, appropriately cruciform slab athwart the stage, with an occasional jeweled curtain to suggest such settings as the Emir of Ramla's tent. The staging . . . was equally minimalist. The chorus, instead of milling about in crowd scenes, spent much of the evening as a ghostly presence behind a scrim.
>
> This simplicity, though probably necessary, was unfortunate, if only because pomp, pageantry and spectacle form such an integral part of French operatic style. The final tableau, in which the dying, repentant villain is redeemed by a glimpse of the Holy City shining in the distance, must be dazzling when staged in the full Parisian manner; on Saturday, a viewer had to imagine most of the gleam.[30]

Later, one Verdi enthusiast in the audience remarked, "the reviewer is a bit too harsh on the production *per se*. Otherwise, I thought he was on line."[31] Another concluded, "the lighting was too bright, amateurish with harsh shadows on the shallow stage; the costuming was minimal, only suggestive of time and place; and the orchestra was adequate, not really up to all the beauties of the score." But despite such disappointments, he counted the production a memorable success, particularly for the tenor who sang Gaston.[32] Suddenly, in the United States, *Jérusalem* was again an opera to be heard.

Two and a half years later, on January 26, 1994, the New York Grand Opera gave the opera its East Coast premiere in a concert performance in New York's Carnegie Hall. The *Times*, while praising the conductor, Vincent La Selva, judged the performance "gallant if imperfect," and remarked of Verdi's reworking of *I Lombardi* that it is "in many ways the stronger of the two versions. History, however, has not agreed."[33] History's judgment, however, was now increasingly questioned. Dale Harris for the *Post*, observed, "To hear *Jérusalem* so soon after the Met staging of *I Lombardi*, new this season, is to gain a valuable insight into the composer's art," and he found the revision's plot "more coherent and interesting."[34]

Notably, the spark for the California and New York premieres, in each case was the conductor, Feist and La Selva, suggesting that the more coherent story and Verdi's orchestral improvements in the revision appealed to them, whereas the Metropolitan's revival of *I Lombardi* (1993–94) apparently was driven by the desire to give a further triumph to the singer Pavarotti. (Some Verdi fans, of course, lamented that the Metropolitan, with its huge resources, had not offered them Pavarotti in *Jérusalem*.)[35]

Three years later, on July 19, 1997, and in New York's Central Park, as part of La Selva's cycle of Verdi's operas presented in order of composition, he gave the opera its first staged performance on the East Coast. But like the performance of *I masnadieri*, which preceded it and is also seldom heard, it went unreviewed.[36]

The following winter, the conductor Eve Queler and her Opera Orchestra of New York offered a concert performance of *Jérusalem* in Carnegie Hall on February 8, 1998. Samuel Ramey had been announced for the role of Roger, but he was indisposed, and the substitute, while gallant, was not his equal. Anthony Tommasini for the *Times* noted that Queler "was working against odds," and judged the performance overall, despite a good tenor and soprano, both making New York debuts, as not one of Queler's "best nights." The "orchestral playing lacked incisiveness" and the chorus, lacking spirit, sang only "capably." He had nothing to say about the worth of the opera.[37]

To date (through 2008), Queler's is the most recent performance of *Jérusalem* in the United States. Nevertheless, though the opera still ranks here (the nineteenth century aside) as one of Verdi's least-often heard, thanks to recordings,[38] it is far better known now than in 1991, when first staged after a sleep of a hundred years. Many people today might agree with the New Orleans critic, writing in 1888, with *Aida* (1871) then known, "It was in reality, this opera [*Jérusalem*] which served as an unquestionable means of deciding the bent of Verdi's genius."[39]

Chapter Ten

Luisa Miller

In the performance history of Verdi's operas in the United States, *Luisa Miller*, his fifteenth, has two claims to uniqueness: It is the only one of his thirty-two operas (counting six revisions as new works) to have had its premiere in Philadelphia, and the only one to have had its first production sung in English. Moreover, another singularity: The Walnut Street Theatre, in which the opera was first heard, is the oldest in the English-speaking world continually in use, and the only site of a nineteenth-century Verdi premiere in the United States still in use.[1] Though its interior has been altered, chiefly by a cantilevered balcony replacing two tiers of wall-clinging boxes, the relatively small space enclosed (capacity 1,088) can still suggest how it might have looked under gaslight on October 27, 1852.

The moving spirit behind the premiere was a soprano, Caroline Richings (1827–82), who, though born in England, was brought as a child to the United States by parents who soon died, and then she was adopted by their friend, the bachelor actor-singer-manager, Peter Richings. Though he, too, had been born in England, beginning in 1821, he made his career in the United States, chiefly in New York and Philadelphia, and in 1852, he began to tour in plays and operas with his daughter.[2] Together, in 1859, they founded the Richings Opera Company, which for many years toured the United States performing operas in English. At the turn of the century, Chicago's leading critic, George P. Upton, said of opera in English that it "did not get a firm foothold until Caroline Richings appeared upon the scene. She was the smartest, brightest, hardest working artist of them all."[3]

At the time of the *Luisa Miller* premiere, however, she was at the start of her career. She had made her operatic debut in February 1852 in Philadelphia as Marie in Donizetti's *Daughter of the Regiment*. The opera was one of a brief season at the Walnut Street Theatre presented by the Seguin Opera Troupe, a small group led by Edward Seguin (bass baritone), which went from city to city, usually employing the local theater's orchestra, chorus, and secondary singers. Besides the *Daughter of the Regiment*, Richings in that season also sang leading roles in *L'elisir d'amore, Sonnambula, Linda di Chamounix,* and *Norma,* all in English.

That October she returned to the theater with her own troupe, consisting apparently only of herself, her father (baritone and business manager), and two others picked from the Seguin troupe, Thomas Bishop (tenor) and a "maestro direttore," William P. Cunnington. Seemingly, as then was custom, for their two-week season they relied on the theater's "stock" company to provide a small orchestra and singers for secondary roles.[4] The repertory, all in English, was *Le postillon de Lonjumeau, Luisa Miller, Florentine* (a world premiere), and *Linda di Chamonix.*

To dispose of the world premiere: The composer was a Mrs. Sheridan Mann, who also had a small role in the troupe's *Linda.* Her opera had two performances and then, in the words of a chronicler of Philadelphia's theater history, "was shelved for ever."[5]

Verdi's opera, in English titled *Louise Muller,* had four performances sung on successive nights, daughter Caroline singing the title role and her adoptive father Peter, her father in the opera, called simply "Miller," or in their version, "Muller." Each performance, as then was custom, was followed by a different one-act farce, often with a slangy title, such as *Bamboozling.* Seemingly, the *Luisa* night was the hit of the short season, for it alone achieved more than two performances. Moreover, the troupe kept the opera in its repertory, bringing it back to Philadelphia in December 1853, and staging it twice in Cincinnati, in 1854 and 1859.[6]

The opera, based on Schiller's early tragedy, *Kabale und Liebe* (Intrigue and Love),[7] is set in the Tyrol in the first half of the seventeenth century, and tells of Luisa, an only child of a retired and widowed soldier and hence middle-class, who loves the local Count's son, and is loved in return. But the Count wants his only son Rodolfo to marry a Duchess and at the suggestion of his steward, Wurm, who himself fancies Luisa, the two compel the girl, in order to save her father's life, to write a letter to Wurm. In the letter dictated by Wurm she is made to say that she loves him and not Rodolfo. And she is sworn, on her father's life, not to reveal the letter's true cause. Wurm has it misdelivered to Rodolfo, who confronts her. Did she write it? The orchestra four times, with chords at double *piano,* tweaks her silence, and after her stammered "Si! . . .," crashes twice double *forte,* with tympani prominent. Rodolfo drinks from a poisoned cup, offers it to her, and she, unknowing, also drinks. On hearing that they both now will die, she feels absolved of her oath and tells him the truth of the letter. Miller enters, and the three have an anguished Trio, after which Luisa expires in the arms of her grieving father. The Count enters, with Wurm, and Rodolfo, with a final effort, stabs Wurm, and the fathers are left, each bereft of his only child. In an operatic period that often gave a happy end to *Romeo and Juliet,* the ending was uncommonly bleak.[8]

How much of Verdi's opera was included in the Richings' adaptation is not clear. No contemporary review reports on it, and a mention of it published eight years later states only that on October 27, 1852, "was produced for the first time, a new opera in three acts, (music by Verdi), founded upon Schiller's *Kabale und Liebe,* translated from the Italian by Miss C. Richings, adapted to the American stage by Mr. Richings, arranged for the orchestra by Mr. Cunnington, D. M., and brought out with all the modern accessories of music and the lyric drama." Then, after four paragraphs on the personal success of Miss Richings, the account concludes with the opera's title unrevealed, no word about its music, and the composer still penned in parentheses.[9]

Some idea of the adaptation, however, may be gleaned from Caroline Richings's debut in New York, only six weeks later, in a production of James Maeder's opera *The Peri* at the Broadway Theatre.[10] This was a more lavish effort, using an enlarged orchestra, double chorus, dancers, and, according to the *Evening Mirror*, boasting over "thirty pieces of music." But it, too, concluded with a farce and musically was easy enough to sing seven nights running. "The character of the music," reported the critic, "is not of a class calculated to produce a *furore*—it has no striking originality and does not startle by any extraordinary effects—there are no terrific crashes of sound—no wild beating of cymbals and thumping of big drums *a la* Verdi." He found Miss Richings's voice accurate but "hard, wiry, unsympathetic," and lacking in power. On the other hand, she was a good actress with an appealing manner. The scenery was much praised, and likely, because typical of the time, without regard to dramatic need she displayed many changes of costume.[11]

The Richings' *Louise Muller* therefore probably offered a selection of arias, duets, simple ensembles, and choruses with vocal difficulties smoothed or omitted and the orchestra's role simplified. Probably also, many passages of music were reduced to spoken dialogue to keep the drama moving and to make the most of both father and daughter's acting ability. Should such an adaptation rank as the opera's U.S. premiere? Some authorities so list it; others do not.[12] Yet it was sung by professionals, to paying audiences, played in at least two cities, and in each at least once revived, and though in 1852 the interpolation of a popular song would not have been unusual, presumably for the most part used Verdi's music.

The opera's premiere in New York, staged by the Max Maretzek Italian Opera Company at the Castle Garden Theatre on July 20, 1854, was more true to the score (though interpolating an aria from Verdi's *Masnadieri*), and sung in Italian.[13] The company, besides soloists imported from Europe, had its own orchestra, chorus, and secondary singers, and in Maretzek, a noted conductor. The New York critics, unlike their Philadelphia colleagues, wrote profusely about the opera, using it to vent their opinions on Verdi in general, and in their disagreements revealing that all were not yet ready to accept Verdi's ideas about what musical drama should be. Among the most detailed reviews, all unsigned, were those in five daily papers, the *Times, Tribune, Herald, Post*, and *Courier and Express*, and the weekly *Albion*, devoted primarily to literature and the arts.[14]

All praised Rodolfo's aria of anguish upon reading Luisa's letter to Wurm— "Even when, in an angelic voice, she said: 'I love you, I love you alone,' Ah, she betrayed me!" The *Albion* reported it was "perhaps the finest aria in the Opera and certainly was *the great hit* of the evening. . . . At the words 'Ah!—mi tradia,' Beraldi fairly seemed to pour out his soul in an extacy [*sic*] of grief. The performance of this entire *morceau* was worthy of any living tenor, and its effect upon the audience was truly electric."[15]

Also generally admired was the Quartet, unaccompanied by orchestra, in which Luisa, brought to the castle to swear that she never loved Rodolfo, sings of her grief; the Duchess (contralto), of her relief that Rodolfo indeed may love her and not the village girl; and the Count (bass) and Wurm (bass), of their scheme's success. The sixty-five bars of *voci sole*, with the unusual combination of voices and wide range for all in pitch and volume, easily can go flat or sharp, which the orchestra on reentry will proclaim—but sung well, it gives its scene a strange and stunning climax. Reviewing opening night, the *Tribune* reported, the "Quartet without accompaniment, which pleased for its piquancy, was re-demanded"; and the *Albion*, it "was rapturously and deservedly encored."[16]

Moreover, all the critics, though without agreement, felt the need to dilate on Verdi's use of orchestral brass. The *Post* remarked: "The noisiness of his instrumentation in the incessant use of his brass instruments, the remarkable and unwarranted use of the crescendo, and, finally, his lack of melody, are the characteristics, which provoke the censure of the musician. It became apparent, last evening, that there had been no improvement, at least, no change, in him in this respect." The *Herald* added a whiff of social disdain to the Post's "censure," saying the opera was "eminently successful, the audience being for the most part of that class with whom the music of this composer is popular."[17]

The *Times* countered: "*Luisa Miller* is unlike any other work by the same composer. It is the offspring of a more matured and sober judgment. The orchestration and the choruses indicate this change more clearly than the solos and the concerted pieces—the latter retaining, not withstanding their increased sobriety, a tone and coloring essentially Verdi-ish." The *Albion* was still more positive: "The most noticeable point in the composition of this Opera, is that it is unlike any thing that Verdi ever wrote. We are constantly compelled to ask ourselves whether this can possibly be by the author of *Lombardi* and *Ernani*, and if so, what has he done with the superabundance of brass he frequently relied on. For this omission, if for nothing else, he deserves great thanks; but apart from this, it is the best instrumented, best scored, and most musician like of the Operas."[18]

The *Courier and Enquirer*, however, judged the alleged improvement a loss. The opera "has all Verdi's mannerisms, with little of the sensuous richness, barbaric pomp and material strength of style which mark some of his earlier compositions. . . . Verdi had written all he had to write when he finished *Ernani* and *I Lombardi*."[19]

Nor could the critics agree on the merits of Verdi's ensembles. The *Post* said: "The excellence of Verdi lies . . . in the beauty of his concerted pieces; they are the sinews of his operas; his quartettes, quintettes and septuors are splendidly wrought up, with a richness of harmony for which we may look to Donizetti in vain. His finales are elaborated with the greatest care, the parts being successively taken up by fresh voices, each with a different melody, but in strict harmony, till the chorus and the orchestra with its inevitable brass unite in the production of an exciting and brilliant, but somewhat 'ad captandum,' [playing to the crowd] climax."[20]

The *Courier* answered: "The concerted music is elaborate enough sometimes, but so barren of genuine and original ideas as to be quite uninteresting." And the *Tribune*, referring to the first act *finale*, complained: "There is, however, in this finale, an immense strain on the voices, and the intensities are not warranted by any interest, thus far created by the plot. A discordance between subject and music is a musical discordance not admissible within the pale of art. The brass here was overwhelming, and should be restrained."[21]

Even about the plot—Schiller's wordy but well-structured drama of lovers living in a despotic state and separated by class—there was no consensus. The *Tribune* declared, "The plot of *Luisa Miller* is not good," and the *Albion*, deploring violence done to Schiller, suggested that Italian composers should "stick to *Mother Goose* stories." Yet the *Times*, though allowing the opera's libretto had "mutilated" the play, felt even so the reduction offered "certain attractions as a lyric play; the plot is simple; the dialogue good, and the catastrophe unexpected and tragic."[22]

The diversity of opinion grew wider still with the reviewers' individual perceptions. Among the more interesting: the *Times* noted, "Unlike the operas of Donizetti, all the morceaux do not fall to one or two favored artists. In *Luisa Miller* there are no less than six leading characters; indeed, for the correct performance of the opera every character must needs be a leading one." The *Tribune* offered, "The plot . . . is simply melodramatic, and its situations where strength is required, are for the most part bloated. The lighter coloring—the vein of Shakespearian comedy—the relaxation of the intensities is wanting." This is a reason, perhaps, that Verdi's *Ballo in maschera* (1859) has proved more popular than *Luisa*. Yet the reviewer ranked Verdi high: "Since Donizetti's death, Verdi is the only man of the Italian opera, who has shown originality and sustained power. It is the fashion to abuse him (as it is with certain persons to abuse everybody who is not a century old), but admitting his faults. . . . He is energetic, not diffuse—seeks after new effects, and is not satisfied with mere sugar, but likes dramatic renderings, though he is called grim for his pains."[23]

Indeed, in all of Verdi's ten operas from *Ernani* to *Luisa*, the leading or most noble character dies, and in many, the deaths are multiple. But in the earlier operas the deaths are eased for audiences by a degree of distance. In *Ernani*, for example, the lovers are as much figures in a historical pageant, to be watched and admired, as vehicles for strong personal identification. Even in Donizetti's *Lucia di Lammermoor*, the lovers die separately, each after a long scene with lovely melodies that serve to soften the death by allowing the audience to revel in gorgeous singing. Lucia even dies offstage, her death merely reported. But the drama in *Luisa Miller* is tighter, the identification with the middle-class Luisa, for most in the audience, stronger, and the two deaths onstage more abrupt and shocking.

A dispute on a structural point, which was an innovation and also crucial to the opera's tone, shows how divided was critical opinion on where Verdi seemed headed with musical drama. The reviewer for the *Tribune* admired "the finale of the first act for one element: it throws overboard memorable melody and deals in dramatic effects." He referred to a short scene, requested by Verdi of the librettist,[24] that follows the quintet and chorus that conventionally would close the act. The Count has come with his archers to arrest Luisa and her father, and the villagers lament the injustice of it. Sung with a grand sweep, the concerted piece seemingly is the act's finale. But instead of the curtain, there follows a short, impassioned dialogue. As in Schiller, Rodolfo threatens to join Luisa in prison. "Fine," says the Count. Rodolfo insists: "Before they take her, I will kill her." "Kill her," says the Count. Desperate, Rodolfo threatens his father *sotto voce* (referring to the unnatural death of the previous Count), "I will tell them all how you gained the title." "Let her go," orders the Count, and the curtain falls as the uncomprehending villagers surround a fainting Luisa.

This declamatory ending to an act, especially following a choral climax, was extraordinary. Writing of it, Verdi scholar Julian Budden, stressed: "Nor is there any operatic model for this type of ending. Verdi had gone far beyond the example of his Italian predecessors in allowing the original drama to dictate his formal ideas."[25]

The *Times* apparently approved of the strange ending, for it declared, "Each of the three acts terminates with a good 'situation'—an indispensible thing in this species of writing." But the *Albion*, after praising the Quintet and chorus, "an admirably constructed *piece d'ensemble*, which was sung with great power and effect," added: "We would suggest to the manager, however, to omit the *Seguito* to this which forms an anti-climax to what precedes. It is, we think, much better to let the curtain descend upon the brilliant ending of the Quintette."[26]

Clearly, Verdi was not yet winning everyone to his ideas of musical form and drama. In the opening scene of *Rigoletto*, composed barely eighteen months later, he would abandon musical convention still further, introducing the Duke and Rigoletto without giving either an entrance aria, presenting them simply as figures in a swiftly moving scene. In the first two acts of *Luisa Miller*, he was not yet so adventurous, but in its third and last, he tied the lyrical moments more closely to the drama, closing the opera with another "seguito" (different from the one in Schiller) that follows a Trio (Luisa, her father, and Rodolfo) that conventionally would have been the finale. In the Trio, as Miller grieves, the lovers sing of how "We will meet in Heaven."

In Schiller, Ferdinand/Rodolfo, who dies much more slowly than Luisa, accuses his father of murder before a crowd of villagers and police officers, and the Count, appalled at seeing his son die, asks forgiveness. Schiller's lines for the father, with stage directions, are: "Not one last look to cheer me in the hour of death? (Ferdinand stretches out his trembling hand to him, and expires). He forgave me! (To the officers) Now, lead on sirs! I am your prisoner." Thus the play ends with reconciliation and a submission to justice.

Verdi's "seguito" after the Trio quite shifts the tone of the ending. The innocent Luisa, for example, unlike the sinful Marguerite in the enormously popular *Faust*, is not given an ascending appeal to angels, "anges purs, anges radieux," that wins her entry to Heaven. Nor does Verdi even allow Rodolfo and Luisa, singing of Heaven, to die in each other's arms. There is no catharsis of Love Triumphant, nor even any reconciliation or submission to justice. Luisa dies in her father's arms, and Rodolfo, as the Count and Wurm enter, with a last surge of life runs his sword through Wurm, and falling dead, tells his father "Look on your punishment." The Count gasps, "Figlio!" and the entering villagers exclaim "Ah!" as the curtain falls on an ending that, for its day, was indeed grim and unusual.

Verdi famously declared, more than once, that an opera's success was proved at the box office,[27] and by that rule New York's premiere production in 1854 was only a moderate success. Apparently, the first of the five performances in New York was well attended, but of the fifth, the *Post* reported, "attendance was better than usual."[28] The *Albion* noted that August's "heat and wet" had cut down on audiences after the first performance, and after the last, declared that for the impresario Maretzek the season had been a financial upset.[29] But besides "heat and wet" other reasons seem likely.

An epidemic of cholera that summer doubtless kept people at home or sent them into the country.[30] The soprano singing Luisa was disappointing.[31] And the costumes, said the *Albion*, "were gaudy and—utterly wrong, out of all character and period, and not suited for the scenes intended to be displayed."[32] This was a frequent complaint. When Maretzek in April 1857 took his production of *Luisa* to Philadelphia, the critic for the *Evening Bulletin* began his review with a discourse on the soprano singing Luisa and the jewelry she wore—Luisa, the village girl. He reported without disapproval that Maretzek, in the potpourri style of opera evenings then common, presented between the second and third acts "the celebrated Scene [for baritone and chorus] from Fioravanti's Comic Opera *La Columella*, representing an Insane Asylum."[33]

Yet he deplored the musical cuts and changes in Verdi's music: in act 1, scene 2, the duet for the Duchess and Rodolfo was dropped, and instead the Duchess sang "the aria from Verdi's *Masnadieri*. It is a good thing, and she sang it well, but it was out of place." Further, "the fine duet [in act 2 between the Count and Wurm] was omitted," and in its place the bass sang "the grand air from Mercadante's *Bravo*." Also omitted was the "grand finale of the second act, the curtain falling very unexpectedly and awkwardly just at the close of the exquisite romance [Rodolfo's aria]." And in the final act the opera apparently ended with the Trio, dropping Verdi's "seguito," the entrance of the Count and Wurm, the stabbing of Wurm, and the final exchange of father and son. After listing many of the opera's best pieces, the critic concluded, the opera "has in it some music as fine as Verdi ever wrote . . . if the parts omitted last night were rendered, we might increase the list of gems."[34]

That was 1857, and the opera next was heard onstage in 1863 when the Bianchi company in San Francisco gave it a local premiere in a production with "the second and third acts considerably cut down from the printed libretto." Such cuts would emphasize the more conventional melodic forms of the first act rather than the drama of the third.[35] In 1886 a company in New York announced a season opening with Petrella's *Jone* and continuing with *I Lombardi, I due Foscari, Luisa Miller,* and *Un ballo in maschera,* but the season closed in debt before reaching *Luisa.*[36] Hence, after 1863 in San Francisco, though vocal excerpts were published with English translations and the tenor's aria "Quando le sere" was remembered and sung, the opera apparently was not staged anywhere in the United States or Canada until the Metropolitan revival in 1929.

Meanwhile in Europe, after initial wide exposure in the 1850s, it had maintained a modest but secure place among Verdi's less frequently heard operas. Arriving in the United States in the early 1850s, it seemingly had come too soon for American musicians or audiences fully to understand and appreciate. No one apparently was willing to let its music tell its tale unassisted. The opera's focus on the tragedy of a middle-class family was seemingly too unrelieved for audiences; its setting, too spare—rural village, minor noble's castle, and a soldier's cottage. The *Times,* noting that the opera did "not in any way depend on scenic effect," had described the settings as of "puritanic simplicity."[37] Verdi's role for the chorus no doubt was likewise disappointing, consisting for the most part of Luisa's village friends. There were no grand choral scenes, such as in *Ernani* when a Holy Roman Emperor, his court, and bandits confront each other at Charlemagne's tomb; no military parades, such as in Gounod's *Faust,* with a chance for an onstage band to march about and double the orchestra; and not even an aristocratic wedding party, as in Donizetti's *Lucia,* with fetching Scottish costumes and a chance for a sword dance. Instead, Verdi offered a straightforward drama, and in the United States the efforts to dress it up for an audience, the soprano's jewels, the interpolated arias, the many cuts, only hurt it more. Hence it vanished, leaving behind an uncertain reputation.

The Metropolitan's production in 1929, if number of performances be the measure, was the least successful of the six Verdi operas then rarely heard that the company revived during the years 1918 through 1935. In this period these were, in order of the number of performances in New York, *Forza* (37), *Falstaff* (16), *Ernani* (15), *Boccanegra* (14), *Don Carlos* (11), and *Luisa Miller* (5). Giulio Gatti-Casazza, the company manager at the time, in his *Memories of the Opera,* quotes Verdi as once advising him: "Read most at-ten-tive-ly [emphasizing each syllable] the reports of the box-of-fice. . . . The theatre is intended to be full, and not empty."[38] And with that as his motto Gatti-Casazza ran the Metropolitan for twenty-seven years, 1908–35. So it seems that, after the first two of four performances of *Luisa* that season, audience response, despite a good cast led by Rosa Ponselle as Luisa and conducted by Tullio Serafin, was tepid.

The New York critics were respectful but with reservations. Olin Downes for the *Times*, after praising the singers and the opera, noted a number of changes that Serafin had made in the score, of which the most important came at the end: "For the last scene, Mr. Serafin alters situation and text so that Rodolfo does not murder Wurm . . . and [his] father does not reappear. The drama is ended with the helpless Miller looking on the death of his daughter and her erstwhile betrothed, while mournful comments of the chorus are heard. Thus curtailed, the opera went forward swiftly, and on the whole in a very effective way." Oscar Thompson for the *Post*, while also citing the cuts and changes, further regretted that the sets were too grand. Citing a production at the Berlin State Opera only the previous year, he felt "the simple, homespun atmosphere of the Berlin production" had suited the opera better.[39] In Philadelphia, where the company took the opera for a single performance, the reviewer for the *Inquirer* was equally admiring and more enthusiastic: "The passionate sincerity of utterance is notable. . . . There is enough wealth of melody to this work to equip a modern composer for life. . . . The wonder is that *Luisa Miller* has slumbered so long. The [unaccompanied] quartet . . . is at once one of the most intricate and most beautiful things the composer ever wrote. . . . Verdi, unlike many composers, has style, not manner; he does not simply imitate himself, and while it would be easy to trace resemblances in *Luisa Miller* to some pages in earlier or later operas, it has an atmosphere of its own."[40]

Nevertheless, the opera seemingly did not pull in the New York audiences, and Gatti, after a single performance in its second season, dropped it. Yet it had an impact, which can be seen in the Metropolitan's Sunday Evening Concerts and in the *Victrola Book of the Opera*. At the concerts, in the years 1883 through 1929, only one excerpt was sung, Rodolfo's "Quando le sere," in 1917; but in the years 1930 through 1937, it was heard five times, and even the Count's aria for bass, "Il mio sangue, la vita darei," once.[41] Further, the RCA Victor Company in its *Book of the Opera*, 1929 edition, for the first time included a synopsis of the opera and offered two recordings of "Quando le sere."[42] Thus the opera and its aria became better known; and, as impresarios planning their seasons have noted, with unfamiliar Italian operas a single well-known aria often will draw the public. People want to hear it sung live and in context.

World War II, for most of the 1940s, closed the country's smaller companies that might have been drawn to the opera, while the larger companies tended to shorten their seasons and restrict their repertory. But in 1960 one of New York's smaller companies, the Amato, staged *Luisa Miller* in Town Hall. The production was simple, orchestra and chorus onstage, with soloists dressed in black period costumes playing on a small space stage front, and without scenery or props. The critic for the *Herald Tribune* found the singers uneven, yet the opera "was revealed once again as a masterpiece whose neglect is as unaccountable as it is shameful." Then he asked: "What holds the work back?" and concluded, "its libretto." Schiller's play "never made much sense, the complications of the plot being so fortuitous that they are more often hilarious than stirring." For him, the music redeemed all faults.[43]

The company then brought the opera in January 1963 to Carnegie Hall, but with less success. Town Hall is small, seating only 1,495, whereas Carnegie Hall seats 2,760, and an intimacy and intensity of performance was lost.[44] As early as 1854, in reviewing Maretzek's production in the cavernous Castle Garden (capacity 5,000), the *Times* had noted that because of the opera's simple scenic demands, "*Luisa Miller* is peculiarly adapted for a good troupe at a small opera house."[45] The final act, after all, but for moments at the start and finish, never has more than three onstage. Nevertheless, the Amato company's two performances gave people a chance to hear the opera whole at a time when no complete recording of it had yet been issued.[46]

In Philadelphia a small company, Rittenhouse Opera, in May 1964 staged three performances in the small Society Hill Playhouse. The production substituted a piano for the orchestra, but offered a full chorus, imaginative scenery and costumes, and an exceptional young tenor. The critic for the *Inquirer* wrote a favorable review, starting with "The opera is one of Verdi's problem works. . . . [It] lacks the beauty and balance that the later operas showed. In their place are echoes of Bellini and of earlier Verdi together with potable bursts of brilliant song and passion. . . . It should be seen to deepen a listener's perspective of Verdi." Besides such specialized listeners, however, the production evidently pleased the public, for the company gave the opera two more performances the following October, again in the Playhouse. At that time another member of the paper's staff declared that he had enjoyed "this pleasant byway in operatic literature." The "minor classic" was "done with taste."[47]

Then, on February 8, 1968, thirty-eight years after the Metropolitan's last effort with the opera, Rudolf Bing, a manager with a background in the Verdi Renaissance,[48] presented a new production of *Luisa Miller*. The cast, led by Montserrat Caballé and Richard Tucker, was strong throughout, and the sets and costumes, though hardly appropriate for the opera, were sumptuous: for a scene in the Count's country castle, a very grand reception hall in Piranesi's exaggerated style; for the outside of the Millers' cottage, a huge, semi-enclosed courtyard; for the inside, a huge, vaulted room, with a side chapel and table and benches enough to seat twenty or more. Nevertheless, though the audience joked about the retired soldier's wealth, the scenes were pretty, left space for the action, and the costumes, though far too grand for the Tyrol, were gorgeous.

One architectural conceit, a frame for the opera, over the years would be cut back and after the 1981–82 season removed altogether. But initially, the audience, on entering the auditorium, saw onstage at either side a tier of boxes, as in a court theater, filled with auditors in nineteenth-century costume

Figure 10.1. Attilio Colonnello's original set for the Metropolitan's *Luisa Miller* (1968), act 1, scene 2, the Count's castle. Note its deliberate touches of nineteenth-century style: overhanging drapes, side boxes for spectators, and prominent line of footlights, providing lighting somewhat too glaring for modern taste and that casts all shadows upright. Photograph by Louis Mélançon, 1967. Courtesy of the Metropolitan Opera Archives.

Figure 10.2. Colonnello's set for act 1, scene 2 as revised, with the overhanging drapes, side boxes, and footlights removed, and with subtler lighting. Photograph by Mélançon, 1990. Courtesy of the Metropolitan Opera Archives.

who flirted, responded to the drama, and sometimes joined in the choruses. Yet these added people proved a distraction, ultimately were dropped, and the boxes removed.

Otherwise the production was a success, and the public came to hear the singers and the music. The views of the New York critics ranged from modified to unrestrained rapture. Harold Schonberg for the *Times* noted, "The vocal parts in *Luisa Miller* are not easy, but neither are they showy. Coloratura is down to a minimum, and last night was even more minimized as several of the singers simplified their roles." And of the music, "It has not been a popular opera in our time. . . . In all truth, *Luisa Miller* is not a strong or especially interesting opera, though it does have the kind of straightforward drama and elemental passions Verdi so delighted in."[49] Contrariwise, Harriet Johnson for the *Post*, declared: "To begin with, *Luisa Miller* is filled with a high order of his genius. It probably only lapsed in popularity because it directly preceded the three aforementioned operas [*Rigoletto*, *Trovatore*, and *Traviata*]. We may not go as far as Francis Toye, Verdi's biographer, when he calls *Luisa Miller* 'one of the most lovable of Verdi's operas,' but there is no doubt (1) of its beauty; (2) that it points the direction to the composer's later style; (3) that it is eminently singable."[50] And Herbert Weinstock, in a review for *Opera*, reported: "The audience's reactions strongly suggest that *Luisa Miller*, the third act of which is a Verdian wonder, may be here to stay."[51]

That spring, after giving the opera a national broadcast in February, the Metropolitan took it on tour, using it to open the brief seasons in Boston, Atlanta, Detroit, and Dallas, and staging it also in Minneapolis and Philadelphia. The production was not cut down. The cast was the same or as good, and the company traveled with an orchestra of ninety-two and a chorus of seventy-eight. In Philadelphia the *Evening Bulletin* said: "The Metropolitan outdid itself yesterday afternoon at the Civic Center with its performance of *Luisa Miller*." In Atlanta, where the opera had its local premiere, the *Constitution* headlined its review: "Met's *Luisa Miller* is Superb Here." Its critic, however, found fault with Richard Tucker for injecting some sobs into "Quando le sere," "by which tenors have always portrayed themselves laboring under strong emotion." But, "The audience loved it."[52]

Apparently not expecting the opera to have such a success, the Met was able to reschedule it only four seasons later, in October 1971, with a new Luisa, Adriana Maliponte. Winthrop Sargeant, for the *New Yorker*, after praising the singers and calling the opera "the most boring in the current repertoire," admitted "the audience applauded everything in sight and sound."[53] And thereafter the Met revived it regularly, in 1978, 1981, 1987, and 1990, for a total of sixty-four performances in the house. Moreover, in each of the six seasons a Saturday afternoon broadcast went out to an audience estimated at twelve to fifteen million.[54] (For the opera's ranking among Verdi works, 1883–2008, see appendix B.)

METROPOLITAN OPERA

Wednesday Evening, January 20, 1982, 8:00–11:20

Subscription Performance

The 38th Metropolitan Opera performance of

GIUSEPPE VERDI

Luisa Miller

Opera in three acts

Libretto by Salvatore Cammarano
after Friedrich Schiller's *Kabale und Liebe*

Conductor:	Nello Santi
Production:	Nathaniel Merrill
Set Designer:	Attilio Colonnello
Costume Designer:	Charles Caine
Associate Designer:	David Reppa
Stage Director:	Paul Mills

Characters in order of vocal appearance:

Miller	Leo Nucci
Luisa	Katia Ricciarelli
Laura	Claudia Catania
Rodolfo	Luciano Pavarotti
Wurm	Richard Vernon
Count Walter	Paul Plishka
Federica	Bianca Berini
A peasant	Luigi Marcella

Chorus Master:	David Stivender
Musical Preparation:	Eugene Kohn and Ubaldo Gardini
Assistant Stage Director:	Lesley Koenig
Prompter:	Ubaldo Gardini

This production of *Luisa Miller* was made possible by a generous and deeply appreciated gift from the late Mrs. John D. Rockefeller, Jr.

The Metropolitan Opera is grateful to The LeVine Foundation, Detroit, Michigan, for its generous gift toward the revival of this production.

Latecomers will not be admitted during the performance.   *Knabe Piano used exclusively.*

Figure 10.3. The Metropolitan Opera's cast in 1982 (from author's collection).

The production, gradually stripped of some excesses and with new costumes (the old, lost in a warehouse fire), wore well. Indeed, in some ways it improved. Though the tenor has the opera's aria, Luisa, as expected of the title role, is the opera's most interesting character and ultimately the one most cherished by the audience. Caballé offered lovely singing, especially in her pianissimos that she could float to the largest auditorium's furthest row, but she was not much of an actress. Some of those who sang the role in subsequent seasons better portrayed the young and vulnerable village girl. Among these was Katia Ricciarelli, who first sang the role in the United States at San Francisco in 1974, with Luciano Pavarotti as Rodolfo, and then at the Metropolitan in 1978 and 1982, with José Carreras and Pavarotti. For many, with her blonde hair, maidenly face and figure, she made the opera, as Toye had said, "loveable." And more recently, according to Anthony Tommasini of the *Times*, a soprano singing with the New York Grand Opera Company in Central Park, distinguished herself in another way: "At one point in the last act, the orchestra pit went dark, forcing the players to stop for several minutes. Ms. [Amelia] D'Arcy, who was kneeling in prayer, just kept praying, so intently that I thought her prayers would be answered and the opera would instead end happily."[55] Meanwhile, in San Francisco in 1982 and 1988, Pocket Opera staged an English version of the opera, and larger companies, singing in Italian, produced it in Chicago in 1986 and Philadelphia in 1989.

With such continual exposure, the opera's standing in the United States steadily rose. It shed the doubtful reputation that had dogged it for more than a century, and gained status as a minor classic that, done with taste, could provide an enjoyable musical evening. Critics and program writers, of course, would continue to dilate on the opera's debts to Donizetti and Bellini, on how it looks backward to *Ernani* and *I Lombardi* and forward to *Rigoletto* and *La traviata*, but the public by the 1990s seemed ready to accept it on its own terms, as an opera with its own particular musical coloring, suited to its story, or as Verdi would have said, its own "tinta." As a Philadelphia critic had observed of the Metropolitan's production in 1929: "Verdi . . . does not simply imitate himself, and while it would be easy to trace resemblances in *Luisa Miller* to some pages in earlier or later operas, it has an atmosphere of its own."[56] And to start the next century, the Metropolitan announced for its 2001 season a new production of the opera.

Chapter Eleven

Rigoletto

As with *Luisa Miller*, so, too, with *Rigoletto:* Verdi's urge to strengthen the opera's drama through a more flexible musical structure than then was common, in some part, delayed popular acceptance. For though today *Rigoletto* in the United States is one of his most popular works—in 125 years at the Metropolitan Opera, 1883–2008, among his works it ranked third (see appendix E)—it has not always stood so high. Indeed, despite quick success in most countries, in the United States, except in New Orleans, it won favor only slowly, hampered in part by its musical structure and by its initial poor production, but most of all by rumors of an immoral plot. In a review following the premiere, on February 19, 1855, at New York's Academy of Music, according to the influential *Albion*, a weekly journal of "arts and literature": "Rumours prejudicial to the morals of *Rigoletto* had been most freely circulated throughout the city, inducing many who would otherwise gladly have heard the new opera, to bide their time until the press should have pronounced its dictum upon the nature of the plot."[1]

But after the premiere, staged by a New York Italian company managed and conducted by Max Maretzek, the press spoke with divided voice. The critic for the *Morning Courier and New-York Enquirer* pronounced, "The opera *Rigoletto* is, to say the least, not one of Verdi's best"; and after a second performance he added, "*Rigoletto* should be withdrawn at once." Yet the critic for the *Times*, on a second hearing, concluded, "The opera improves on acquaintance, and will bear repetition." While the critic for the *Albion*, after a third hearing, pled, "We freely confess that we had not heard enough of *Rigoletto* in three nights, and we are sure that we are uttering the sentiments of many who have seen it more than once. It is too good an Opera to be shelved so soon."[2]

In Italy, after the opera's premiere on March 11, 1851, at the Teatro la Fenice, Venice, some censors, critics, and audiences had protested the opera's lack of morality—an innocent seduced and raped by a lecher, whose life she preserves by substituting for him in her father's plot to kill him—and for a time some cities forced changes on the libretto. Yet the public's delight in the music led to such an extraordinary number of performances that the complaints and changes soon became irrelevant.[3] But not in the United States. Maretzek, no doubt hoping the new opera would prove as instantly and continually profitable as Verdi's *Ernani*, had lowered ticket prices "to popularise the opera" and scheduled five successive performances. But after four, during which audiences in the huge Academy (capacity 4,000), had dwindled from a few thousand to four or five hundred, he canceled the fifth, offering instead Donizetti's

Favorita. In sum, despite considerable critical support *Rigoletto,* on its opening run in New York, failed at the box office.[4]

Taking his company to Boston, Maretzek risked only a single performance, on the second to last night of his season, and for Boston sensitivities cut the final scene, which *Dwight's Journal of Music* called the "absurd . . . revival and singing of the murdered Gilda in the sack." Scheduling the performance for his "benefit" as impresario and conductor, Maretzek drew an appreciative public. The *Boston Evening Transcript* reported one "of the best houses" of the season, but said that *Rigoletto,* "like all the other operas "of Verdi, was "horrible and extravagant in its plot," and "there was altogether too much reliance upon the prompter." And whether because of the plot, the music, or the performance, it concluded, "This opera, as a whole, gave the least satisfaction of any that this troupe has played."[5] Whereupon the enterprising but financially insecure Maretzek dropped it.

After its second performance in New York, the *Albion* critic had declared of its morality: "We hold it to be no worse morally considered, but rather better than that of *Don Giovanni, Lucrezia Borgia, Favorita. . . .* The only real objection in this respect . . . is the superabundance of horrors that prevail with a sort of nightmare effect in the *dénoument.*" To which one who complained of the plot might have answered: In *Don Giovanni* the lecherous Don, at the opera's end, twists, burns, and slowly descends (to the audience's utmost satisfaction) to Hell; whereas in *Rigoletto* the lecherous Duke, though responsible for an innocent's rape and death, walks off happy. And the complainant might have closed, as did the *Times,* "There is no justice, poetic or otherwise; nothing but horrors, horrors."[6]

Moreover, one of Maretzek's purely musical decisions may have spoiled the opera's initial run. Possibly to save time or expense, instead of renting Verdi's orchestration from the publisher Ricordi in Milan, he had used an orchestration "vamped up" from a piano-vocal score. Most newspapers left the arranger unidentified, but *Dwight's Journal* named him: Julius Unger, a violist and frequent conductor of concerts and German operas.[7] All journals but the *Evening Post* found the version unsubtle and noisy. The *Times,* for one, declared the orchestration for the opera's famous quartet, "much too loud, in addition to being common-place." The *Albion* was still more specific: "There is an occasional poverty, baldness, and nakedness of harmony and instrumentation, not characteristic of Verdi. The last, blatant, and obtrusive trombones in the last Quartette are decidedly objectionable, and lead to the suspicion that that portion of the scoring is not Verdi's; if it be, it is very very bad for him." But Verdi did not score trombones for his ever-popular "Bella figlia dell'amore." Likely, therefore, the "much-blamed home scoring," as the *Albion* called it, was equally clumsy elsewhere.[8]

More speculatively, because of fewer contemporary comments, the scene that suffered most from Maretzek's home scoring was the opera's first, set at a ball in the Duke of Mantua's palace during which Verdi introduces to the audience the opera's leading tenor (the Duke) and baritone (Rigoletto), as well as the bass who delivers the father's curse that sets the plot in motion. Verdi structured this introductory scene in a manner unusual for the time, keeping it short (sixteen minutes) and setting it in a fluid style, moving first one person and then another to the fore, much in the way of "close-ups" available later to film and television. But in the 1850s composers typically gave leading singers on their first appearance a full-blown, stand-and-sing double aria, first the lyrical, slower *cantabile* and then the fast *cabaletta*. Yet here, as part of a continually shifting court *festa*, Verdi gave his tenor only a short song, "Questa o quella" (this girl or that . . . no love without freedom), and some gossipy asides to a courtier or to his jester, Rigoletto,[9] most of them delivered while courtiers dance in the background.

To keep these brief exchanges audible, Verdi scored the music for the ball's opening dance, and others that follow, to be played by an *interna banda*, that is, offstage, so that the sound comes *lontana*, from a distance, and at times is to be played *ppp*, very, very softly. For such a *banda interna* the Teatro la Fenice had assembled twenty-four musicians (equally divided between woodwinds and brass). But Maretzek, pandering to a fad then popular with the American public, put onstage a military brass band usually numbering twenty or more (and seemingly with more brass than woodwinds). Apparently, it did not march about (as it would in his production of *Faust*) and presumably it was silent (as Verdi wanted) when the Duke sang "Questa o quella," but on cues for dancing, it frequently struck up. And though the *Tribune* praised Maretzek's coordination of band and orchestra, the balance between them in New York's Academy of Music must have been quite different from their combined or separate sounds heard in the smaller Fenice (capacity 1,500).

Note that Maretzek offered a band of twenty or so onstage against a pit orchestra of forty, which a reviewer later complained was "too weak in stringed instruments, especially for Verdi's operas, where the brass is apt to overlay everything else"; whereas La Fenice had offered a band of twenty-four offstage (scored to play softly), against a pit orchestra of sixty-seven, of which the strings numbered forty-two. These contrasting figures support some of the critical comment.[10]

According to the *Tribune*, "the first scene of the ball-room was brilliant, and an extra blaze of musical splendor was lent to it by the introduction of a military band alternating and coalescing with the well-directed orchestra, led by Mr. Maretzek." The *Herald*, however, reported, "The orchestra is composed of forty performers, who, in conjunction with the brass band, succeeded in making a tremendous noise during the first act. The vocal music was entirely crushed." Quite aside from the visual distraction of the band onstage, probably few in the audience, with the band blaring, heard the Duke and a courtier talk of the middle-class girl whom the Duke currently was pursuing. The critic for the *Tribune*, for one, freely confessed "not to have understood some points of the plot."[11]

Yet in the United States, despite the opera's failure in its opening run, its music, as in Italy, quickly caught the public's fancy. Even in the initial performances the Quartet, the tenor's "La donna è mobile," and the soprano's "Caro nome" were almost always encored. Excerpts were sung in concert halls and on the streets organ-grinders churned out favorite numbers. And soon another impresario, Bernard Ullman, had the opera in rehearsal, with two celebrated sopranos to sing Gilda, Erminia Frezzolini and Anna de LaGrange.[12] His casting, with its emphasis on the soprano role, reflected a view of *Rigoletto* then current among Americans, whether or not they had heard the opera.

Curiously, Victor Hugo, on whose play *Le Roi s'amuse* the opera is based, had stressed in his title the cynical, libertine King, who became in the opera, because of Italian censors, the Duke of Mantua (tenor). Verdi, on the other hand, had first titled the opera *La maledizione* (The Curse), but to appease censors had agreed to *Rigoletto*, yet in both titles he stressed the Duke's jester (baritone). But in the United States initially the character the public took to heart was Gilda.

The Ullman production opened in New York at the Academy of Music on November 4, 1857, with Frezzolini and, as the company proudly advertised (and critics noted), "produced from the original score." Reportedly the production had a success, but Frezzolini fell ill and de LaGrange sang the second performance. The season as a whole was going poorly, and the *Herald* reported another failure at the box office: "*Rigoletto* was admirably done, at an expense of twelve hundred dollars, to an audience which only paid six hundred."[13]

Ullman then took his production with de LaGrange to Philadelphia, staging the opera's city premiere on January 25, 1858, and in a short season of fourteen performances of eleven operas—the public at the time wanted "novelties" or at least a different opera each night—presented only one complete performance and one partial (the final act offered after Rossini's *L'Italiana in Algeri*). The only operas to have two complete performances were *L'Italiana*, *Robert le diable*, and *Trovatore*. Regarding *Rigoletto*, the critic for the *Philadelphia North American and United States Gazette*, to his surprise, was enthusiastic:

> We had been prepared for one of Verdi's most ordinary, not to say unsuccessful efforts, by the tone of criticism with which *Rigoletto* has been greeted elsewhere. We do not agree with this judgment. . . . He has followed the thread of the narrative with music thoroughly adapted to the expression of its situations. . . . It is the especial merit of *Rigoletto* that its strains are of themselves sufficiently full of the progress of the drama, without any of the words of the text. In all respects it is a great lyric play. . . . As regards . . . the exquisite tenor song in the last act "La donna è mobile" . . . [Pietro] Bignardi last evening stood twirling a chair on one leg as he sang it. Not withstanding the remembrance of the street musicians, this solo was vehemently applauded.

Other selections which, like this, had become familiar, through concerts, were received with equal applause, showing conclusively that it only requires familiarity to cause the whole opera to be popular. . . . We may observe, however, that those who attempt to form a judgment respecting [it], should see it at least thrice before doing so.[14]

But outside New York that "thrice" was hard to achieve. Even in Philadelphia, for instance, in the thirty-one years 1858–89 the opera had only ten complete performances, whereas *Ernani* had 19, *Traviata*, 46, and *Trovatore*, 113.[15] In the Midwest, three performances were still harder to hear. The opera had its premiere in Cincinnati in August 1859 and the *Daily Gazette* advised in advance, "Verdi is a great composer—of a poor style of music," and warned, "Verdi lays great stress upon 'body' and 'volume' of instrumentation, and consequently keeps his artists screaming if they would be heard." The opera had a single performance and was not heard again—though the public in Cincinnati was said to like Verdi more than did the local critics—until another single performance in 1873, of which the *Enquirer* reported, "never in the history of opera in this city has there been such an empty house."[16] In Chicago, however, in February 1884, Col. J. H. Mapleson and his touring company, numbering about 115 and one of the best in the country, had a big success with the opera when he presented as Gilda the young American soprano Lillian Nordica. Indeed, it was such a success that the public asked for and received a second performance—yet in all, only two. Further west, in 1884 and 1885, in Kansas City, Missouri, Mapleson had less luck with the opera, in each year announcing a performance of *Rigoletto* and then, chiefly because of casting problems, having to replace it with another. But in Topeka, Kansas, the Topekans forced on him a substitution of *Trovatore*. A local paper, the *Lance*, expressed the public's view: "We regret that *Rigoletto* is to be produced by the company, it is only a one 'part' opera, and does not show the company at its best. We had *Rigoletto* once upon a time, and we pray the Lord will spare us this affliction."[17]

Continually in the opera's first two decades of exposure in the United States its alleged immorality told against it. When Maretzek first revived it for a performance at New York's Academy of Music in 1858, the *Times* greeted it as "perhaps, one of the least attractive of the *maestro's* numerous works." Yet the *Herald*, on a revival in 1861, described it as "one of Verdi's very best works—never sufficiently appreciated here." For that revival Maretzek offered as a conductor Verdi's friend and only pupil, Emanuele Muzio, and as Gilda, a nineteen-year-old American at the start of a long career, the petite (five foot four and 104 pounds) Clara Louise Kellogg. Soprano, conductor, and impresario all had a success at the Academy of Music in Manhattan, but when Maretzek took his company and opera across the river to Brooklyn, though the first two won praise, at the box office he had a failure. The *Brooklyn Daily Eagle* reported: "The audience was small—indeed, perhaps, it was the smallest of the season."

And the critic had begun his review: "The opera was *Rigoletto:* beautiful music wedded to an abominable plot," complaining further, "We are at a loss to know why the duo finale, with the dying Gilda was cut, as also were other portions of the score."[18]

The cut of the final duet was then becoming common, both in Europe and the United States, and seemingly continued so until the end of the century. Apparently, it originated in London, perhaps as early as 1853, in a production with the baritone Giorgio Ronconi and was prompted by audience complaints of indelicacy in stuffing a soprano into a sack. For when Ronconi came from London to Havana in 1857, the final duet initially was cut, and according to the Havana *Gaceta* the custom had been started to spare the sensibilities of English audiences. The Cubans, however, protested, and the duet was restored.[19]

What other cuts were made in London or Havana is not clear. But in the United States, for the opera's Boston premiere, on June 8, 1855, Maretzek had cut not only the "bad" final duet, but according to *Dwight's Journal,* several more of the opera's "good things"; and reviews of its premiere in San Francisco, on June 30, 1860, reveal that in addition to the duet-finale two of the Duke's arias were cut: the lyrical "Parmi veder le lagrime," and its cabaletta "Possente Amor."[20] In much of the twentieth century the former usually was sung, but not the latter. More recently, however, at least one of the latter's two verses has been restored. But as late as 1968 the Metropolitan regularly cut not only both verses of "Possente Amor," but six measures from the Rigoletto-Gilda duet in act 1, scene 2 (often presented as act 2). Today, those favoring such cuts usually argue that the music is in some way inferior, or that it somehow impedes the drama's acceleration, or even simply that the singer needs a rest.[21]

But at least in retrospect the spirited Miss Kellogg, for one, thought even arguments of morality were dubious. In 1861, having sung a highly successful Gilda in New York for Maretzek, she hoped to sing it also on tour. But "Boston would not have *Rigoletto.* It was considered objectionable, particularly the ending. For some inexplicable reason *Linda di Chamounix* was expected to be more acceptable to the Boston public." Some years earlier, however, the Boston weekly *Dwight's Journal of Music* had published an article comparing oratorio to opera and concluded, "The wish has often been expressed by the graver classes of our music-loving Americans, that operas might be presented to them in public performance *musically* only—the dramatic action being omitted. They wish to hear the music, but do not care for or approve of the rest of it. We find this a very natural and reasonable idea on their part." For Boston, Maretzek perhaps found it natural and reasonable not to schedule *Rigoletto.*[22]

Five years later in New York, in a jury trial for libel with Maretzek the plaintiff, the defendants chose *Rigoletto* as their example of an immoral opera. Maretzek claimed that the New York *Sunday Mercury*, at the time said to have the largest circulation (100,000) of any paper in the country, had libeled him in two editorials by printing: "The only apology for an opera presented to the public is such an exhibition as no respectable member of the fair sex could patronize without a sacrifice of both taste and modesty and running the risk of coming in contact with the characters who now make it their rendezvous. . . . [And] to fill up the house, dead-head tickets had been furnished to people whom no decent citizen could wish to see sit beside his wife or daughter. . . . [And] certain it is that the 'scarlet women' have blazed forth in all their glory and shame from parquet, dress-circle, and box." After the suit began, the *Mercury*, searching for the most disreputable opera it could find to serve as an example of Maretzek's perfidy, chose *Rigoletto*, amending its defense to say: "[Maretzek] had permitted to be performed the opera of *Rigoletto*, and that said performance, in its singing, its business, and its plot, was then and there such an exhibition of opera as no respectable member of the fair sex could patronize without then and there sacrificing both taste and modesty."[23]

Maretzek, as an impresario and lessee of the Academy of Music, claimed damages to his business of $20,000. The suit was primarily not about *Rigoletto*, but a fight between the impresario and the *Mercury* over the latter's demand for advertising to be placed in the paper. But this led to a discussion of the custom of distributing free tickets to the press, and finally to the opera. Put on the stand and asked to describe the opera's plot, Maretzek stated: "The Duke of Mantua, is what you call here a 'fast young man.' He has a jester who goes round with him and provides for his amusements. He is a villain, like there is in every plot, and at the end of the piece he is punished. The moral of it is, that his own daughter is the victim of his villainy. That is it, to give it in a few words." Asked to define "a fast young man," Maretzek demurred: "I have only heard it since I came to America; it is not used in London."[24]

In the sparring that followed Maretzek steadily outsmarted the paper's attorney, who seemingly had not heard the opera onstage, had done little homework on it, and never once questioned him about the Duke's happy fate or Gilda's misfortunes. Maretzek throughout stressed Rigoletto, his villainy, his punishment, always avoiding what bothered people most, the display of Gilda's abduction, her entrapment in the Duke's bedroom, and her emergence from it weeping and dishonored in the eyes of herself, her father, and the courtiers. He insisted: "There is nothing immoral on the stage in the whole piece; there is nothing to shock anyone; it has been played in every capital of the theatrical world, and would not shock anybody." And the jury, "after being absent some time," awarded him $1,000.[25]

Nevertheless, though the opera's number of performances remained small compared to other operas by Verdi, much of its music was popular even among those who had not heard or seen the opera onstage. In 1867 for example, one opera lover in New York, John Ward, who was both a lawyer and a doctor and of an evening liked to sing with other amateurs, noted in his diary that he had twice sung selections from *Rigoletto*, at least one of which was the quartet, for which he and three colleagues had rehearsed. Yet he did not list the opera among those he had heard in an opera house. Apparently, as was his custom, he simply had gone to Gustavus Schirmer's music store, at 701 Broadway, and bought the sheet music.[26]

The *Complete Catalogue of Sheet Music and Musical Works, 1870,* a limited but useful compendium of what was available in music stores, lists for *Rigoletto* seven vocal excerpts currently on sale, most of them offered in a variety of keys and with English texts, some of which had no relation to the opera. A popular English version of "La donna è mobile," for instance, began, "Over the summer sea." Not surprisingly, "La donna è mobile" had the most entries, followed by the Quartet and "Caro nome." In addition, the *Catalogue* listed seventy-eight instrumental arrangements of pieces, most of them for piano. Seemingly, these vocal and instrumental numbers from the opera were sung and played in parlors across the country by thousands, who like John Ward, had never experienced the opera onstage as a drama, had never cringed as they heard the Duke's reprise of "La donna è mobile," as he exits from the opera unrepentant, unpunished.[27]

Yet, slowly, the number of performances increased. In New York, where the population could support competing companies and theaters, there were two or three performances almost every year, a record matched only in New Orleans and San Francisco, two cities relatively untouched by Puritan heritage. In New Orleans, for example, where a touring company led by Italians had introduced the opera in 1857, it promptly was translated into French and starting in 1860 had thirteen performances at the French Opera House before the Civil War all but closed that house to opera. Thereafter, and continuing until the house burned in 1919, *Rigoletto,* sung in French, was a staple, achieving in its fifty-nine years at this one house (aside from performances by visiting troupes) a total of 109 performances. But before 1900 among Verdi's operas performed there it steadily lagged behind such favorites as *Le Trouvère, Traviata,* and, even for a time, *Jérusalem.*[28]

Similarly, in San Francisco, where Verdi was popular, following its premiere in 1860, in the decade 1861 through 1870, *Rigoletto,* with ten performances, ranked sixth: behind *Trovatore* (39), *Traviata* (34), *Ernani* (32), *Ballo* (20), and *Nabucco* (11); in the 1870s, again sixth, with five performances, following *Trovatore* (39), *Ernani* (18), *Traviata* and *Ballo* (13 each), and the new *Aida* (12). But in the 1880s, though as yet only fifth, the number of performances greatly increased, to thirty-nine, following *Trovatore* (117), *Traviata* (68), *Ballo* (61), *Ernani* (59), and ahead of *Aida* (36). No doubt that spurt was due in part to the city's growth in population (see appendix C); nevertheless, it gave the public a far greater chance to hear the opera. Finally, in the years 1891 through 1899 the ranking became: *Trovatore* (65), *Aida* (40), *Rigoletto* (29), *Traviata* (27), and *Ernani* (19).[29] Likewise in Philadelphia, after thirty-one years of only ten performances in all (1858–89), the city in the four summer months of 1890 had nine of *Rigoletto,* all staged by the same company. Returning the next year, that company staged five more full performances and the final act paired with *Cavalleria Rusticana*, six times; and in 1892, again in the summer months, five times.[30] Evidently receipts at the box office now were favorable. But why?

The simplest answer seems the best. By the late 1880s an older generation was giving way to a younger one that associated musical theater with the innocent merriment of Gilbert and Sullivan and that had grown up singing the melodies of *Rigoletto*, whether or not to the original text. And now that audience wanted to hear them sung by the best singers of the day. As Clara Louise Kellogg observed of her audiences, "The public went to the opera house to hear popular singers and familiar airs." The opera as drama, if considered at all, was secondary.[31] At the same time, because of the huge immigration in these years of opera-loving Germans and Italians, for whom *Rigoletto* was an old favorite, audiences for the opera were steadily growing. The number of foreign-born Germans in New York, for example, in the years 1880–1900 increased from 218,821 to 305,521, and of Italians, from 13,411 to 145,433; and in the next decade, immigrant Italians numbered 340,765, with first-generation Italian citizens numbering 523,310. By then, city residents of Italian origin were almost one in five of the city's total 4,766,883.

Looked at another way, note the Metropolitan's Sunday Evening Concerts, a program of excerpts sung by the company's artists, which ran continuously (despite gaps in its first decade) from 1883 to 1946. In its first twenty years (with concerts only in fourteen), among excerpts from Verdi's operas, *Rigoletto* tied for first place with *Don Carlo* at twelve each; for *Rigoletto*, eight of the twelve were the Quartet, and for *Don Carlo*, eight were the bass aria "Ella giammai m'amo." But thereafter excerpts from *Rigoletto* took the lead, finishing the sixty-two-year span with a total of 170, followed by *Aida*, 157, and *Forza*, 153.[32]

Similarly, the number of the opera's full performances at the Metropolitan soon began to climb, with a chief stimulant being the arrival of Caruso, who made his house debut singing the Duke on November 23, 1903. The performance was not only the first of the season but the first in a refurbished house, which may explain in part why, though praised, he was not much noticed. The newly painted house and Marcella Sembrich, "an ideal Gilda," got more attention, and the opera itself was passed over as a good choice for opening night, "for the blessed old hurdy-gurdy affair does not require much rehearsal. . . . Stop an Italian tenor in the street and he'll sing 'La donna è mobile.'" But even with Caruso singing, the *Tribune* reported, the aria "was permitted to pass with but a single repetition," which he blamed on "the apathy of the audience."[33] Box holders, following a leisurely dinner, had arrived late, probably after "Questa o quella," and to avoid the crush and confusion of carriages in the streets after curtain, probably left early, thus missing the chilling reprise of "La donna è mobile" and the closing duet for Gilda and Rigoletto.[34]

The description of the opera as "hurdy-gurdy," however, was typical of the view then held by those who supposedly knew best. The critic for the *Times* questioned whether the season should have opened "with a work that has been so far out-grown by public taste as *Rigoletto.*" As the Metropolitan's historian, Irving Kolodin, summarized the attitude: "It is quite clear that the modern concept of a repertory theater had not emerged. *Rigoletto, Lucia,* and *Il Trovatore* were damned as 'old' works whose day had gone, rather than valued as vital expressions that would be welcome in just proportion to other kinds of writing. Wagner was not a unique master, but an 'advanced' writer in whose image future opera would have to be created." As the *Tribune* put it: "*Rigoletto* would not be *Rigoletto* if it were taken out of the old rut of operatic conventionality."[35]

Morover, at the Metropolitan among some of the audience a convention of another sort still ruled. The company's first archivist, Mary Ellis Peltz (1896–1981), could recall being taken as a child to sit in a box and being instructed to follow the lead of the elder ladies. As the music for the third act began, with the Duke singing of his loss of Gilda and then being told by the courtiers that they had locked her in his chamber for his pleasure, the ladies turned their chairs around and sat with their backs to the stage. And in their gesture likely they were not alone.[36]

As for Caruso, in the first quarter of the century, before radio and talking pictures captured the mass public, opera singers were the popular celebrities, and with each new role his success grew. When he first sang Nemorino in *L'elisir d'amore,* the critic for the *Sun* noted, "This part demands something more than good singing. The impersonator of Nemorino must be a good comedian and an interpreter of passionate love. Mr. Caruso disclosed unsuspected humorous powers."[37] Still, his style, his persona, took some getting used to.

The model tenor of the late nineteenth century had been the Polish-Frenchman Jean de Reszke, tall, robust, handsome. Always the aristocrat, whatever the role, he was a gentleman. Not everyone approved. For instance, soprano Clara Louise Kellogg, always in search of context for the role, scorned his appearance in *L'Africaine* when, just after rescue from a foundered vessel, "he appeared in the most beautiful fresh tights imaginable and a pair of superb light leather boots." She felt, "the note of truth" was lacking.[38] Yet the majority of the Metropolitan's audience reveled in de Reszke's style, and gossip delighted to rumor that he was of Polish nobility.

Then came Caruso, short, chubby, and if not ugly at least hardly handsome. Moreover, he drew caricatures that, with a total lack of discrimination, he would hand out to stagehands, reporters, and—well!—to almost anyone. On his first appearance in *Tosca,* the critic for the *Sun* complained: "Mr. Caruso's Cavaradossi was bourgeois. It was difficult to believe in the ardent passion of the aristocratic Tosca for this painter of hack portraits at job prices. His clothes were without distinction and his carriage was less so.[39] The *Times* critic agreed: "He displays him [Cavaradossi] in the first act in a more bourgeois air, with little distinction of bearing and with small intensity of feeling; it is not till the scene of his impending doom in the last that he sounds a note of elemental power in his outpouring of despair and of longing for the love from whom he is to be separated by death. This he did with magnificent eloquence and a nobility of song that deeply stirred the audience, one of the few passages in a performance of the opera remarkable at many points that did stir it, and he yielded to the temptation to repeat the air."[40]

But important as Caruso was to the Metropolitan—in the 1907–8 season he sang 51 of the 122 performances—offstage, in what had started as primarily a business venture with an English company, Gramophone and Typewriter Co., Ltd., he was still more important to the worldwide popularity of opera. In April 1902, in Milan, he made ten recordings of opera arias with piano accompaniment for the company, and the second of these was the Duke's *canzonetta* "Questa o quella." The recordings were technically superior for their day and, to everyone's surprise, proved a financial bonanza. All over Europe people rushed to buy them and to buy gramophones. As the historian and scholar John R. Bolig remarks, "Caruso, almost single-handedly had established public confidence in the fledgling industry."[41] Until then, few important singers could be persuaded to make recordings, for on the detestable machine their voices came through squally and squeaky. Yet somehow it caught Caruso's timbre—partly because he was willing to spend hours stepping closer to or back from the recording horn until the balance was right—and others, seeing his success, followed suit. And as soon as Caruso came to New York, the Victor Talking Machine Company, ancestor of Victor Red Seal Records, contracted with him for more recordings, initially with piano accompaniment, but by 1906 with a small orchestra.[42]

Except for Neapolitan songs, of his first thirty recordings, through 1903, all but five were of operatic numbers, of which two were from *Rigoletto*, "Questa o quella" and "La donna è mobile." In 1906, in New York, he recorded these with orchestra and also that same year, with Antonio Scotti, his first duet, "Solenne in quest'ora" from *Forza del destino*, a marvel that sold steadily for forty-two years.[43] Then in 1908 he recorded two versions of the *Rigoletto* Quartet, each with the baritone Scotti but each with a different mezzo and soprano. With such recordings, he excited an audience of millions, stirring many to want to hear him at least once, in person, onstage, in an opera.

Meanwhile, the plump, good-humored coloratura soprano Luisa Tetrazzini, seeing his success, had recorded with Zonophone Records in 1903 five operatic arias, among them, Gilda's "Caro nome," and then coming to New York in 1908 to sing with Oscar Hammerstein's Manhattan Opera Company, she soon recorded it again with Victor Red Seal Records. A critic for the *Press*, describing her first Gilda in New York, reported of her "Caro nome": "She produced a few beautiful messa di voce effects; she gave a scintillant chromatic scale; she seized with astonishing precision purity and clearness of tone two or three high notes in mezza voce; she obtained a pretty trill on middle D sharp and E; she sang what might be called a slow trill . . . on high B and C sharp," and the audience exploded with rapture. Yet he concluded, "her impersonation of Gilda, on the whole, was not sympathetic or moving."[44]

At a performance some months later, a reviewer for the *Globe and Commercial Advertiser* was enchanted by her. Called upon to repeat the aria, she sang it the second time "even better, with more appealing delicacy, a more enchanting finesse, and she had an entire new set of vocal ornaments for the close."[45] In her musical sophistication, some might say, she had betrayed Verdi's concept of Gilda as an unknowing young girl shut off from the world, but her vocal display was what most in the audience had come to hear, and as a critic raved, "It was not in flesh and blood to listen unmoved."[46]

She sang with the Manhattan company for four seasons as it battled the Metropolitan, 1906–10, paired often with the great singing actor Maurice Renaud, noted especially for his portrayals of Don Giovanni and Rigoletto. Unhappily for him, his voice was one that did not record well, its "rich vibrance," according to one historian, making "phonographs rattle."[47] But for a portion of the audience he increased its appreciation of Verdi's *melodrama*, which is primarily, after all, the story of Rigoletto, not of the Duke or of Gilda. And if he has no excerptible aria to match those of his colleagues, he does have many beautiful duets and powerful dramatic monologues. Even when cast with Nellie Melba or Tetrazzini, Renaud could hold the audience's attention on the drama, and in Hammerstein's last year, 1909–10, *Rigoletto*, with Tetrazzini and Renaud, drew the season's largest audience, confirming a critic's earlier judgment that finally at the Manhattan company, "the opera . . . took its place on the popular list."[48]

When Hammerstein closed his company, the Metropolitan promptly signed both Renaud and Tetrazinni, and though in the winter of 1912 they had sung a *Rigoletto* together, they had not been joined with Caruso, who last had been heard as the Duke in 1910. So, the company's manager Giulio Gatti-Casazza announced a special, all-star, nonsubscription performance for the night of February 6, with Tetrazzini, Caruso, Renaud, and Louise Homer as Maddalena. The critic for the *Sun* observed: "They were together not only in the quartet of which a 'record' would cost a gala price, but they were the quartet of principals who made Verdi's old opera develop unsuspected popularity."[49]

The roughly 3,000 seats from the balcony down through the orchestra promptly sold, leaving for sale on the evening of the performance only the 706 seats in the family circle (the top gallery) and 450 standees (an unusually large number). Shortly after noon two separate lines formed, one for the family circle and one for the standees. As planned, the two lines would be kept separate by winding in different directions around the opera house. But "soon the house was encircled by the patient ones who stood and waited. The winds blew, and the thermometer jeered, but no one went away." Apparently, the gallery seats sold first and without trouble, but after the first fifty standees had got their tickets "the line broke and there was pandemonium. . . . By dint of hard language and wood [night sticks] the amiable and much tried policemen finally built a new line, and Mr. Brown [the teller] opened the window again. Then he did a first class stunt in ticket selling. He sold 400 admissions in twenty minutes."[50]

Applause continually stopped the performance, one critic commenting, "Every high note in *Rigoletto* was like dropping a lighted match into gunpowder. . . . Curtain calls and flowers were taken as a matter of course," and not only at the end of acts but after arias and duets.[51] Seemingly the principals had agreed not to sing encores, but after "La donna è mobile," the applause went on so long that Caruso finally signaled to the conductor that he would sing one more verse, one only. After the Quartet, the singers held firm, and to pass the time as the shouts, cheers, and clapping rolled on, and on, Caruso "thumped himself on the head with Maddalena's tambourine, pretended to shave off his beard with the murderous looking carving knife, and then played a mock game of solitaire with a deck of cards." Finally, sufficient silence restored, "Verdi's old opera" resumed.

One of the curiosities of the evening was the audience. Though familiar faces graced some of the boxes, to older employees the house seemed "full of strangers." For the Metropolitan, it was a new audience, and when taken with the estimated several thousand who failed to get in, a huge one. Though many, no doubt, came only for the all-star cast, the numbers also testified to the opera's hold on the public, its hitherto "unsuspected popularity."[52]

No single performance marks a general acceptance by the American people of *Rigoletto* as one of Verdi's greatest operas, a decision reached gradually during the first decade of the twentieth century, but the performances by the Manhattan company and the Metropolitan's "great, big, three-ring operatic 'hurrah'" with its "pandemonium" were signs of that judgment. Thereafter, people trapped at a bad performance likely blamed the singers, stage director, scenery, or conductor, but not the opera.[53]

A further sign of the opera's improved ranking appears in the records of the San Carlo Opera, a touring company that an Italian immigrant, Fortune Gallo, started in 1913 and continued, with occasional years off, until 1955.[54] In small towns and big cities he offered seats at prices well below those of most companies, and in the larger cities, where he often increased his forces with local recruits, he would provide an orchestra of forty and a chorus of twenty-eight. He usually had well-trained soloists, and in his musical director, Carlo Peroni, an excellent conductor and artistic advisor. Together they typically presented a season of eighteen or twenty operas chosen from a repertory of popular Italian and French works, and on occasion a German one, usually *Lohengrin*. In the company's repertory during its first sixteen years, 1913–14 through 1928–29, when its records are fullest, among operas most frequently performed *Rigoletto* ranked fifth, and among those by Verdi, third, following *Trovatore* and *Aida*.[55]

Contrary to the shift away from encores in the course of an opera, the San Carlo initially encouraged them, and if newspapers reports are accurate, one of the most popular numbers in *Rigoletto* hitherto not much noticed was the Vendetta duet that closes act 2, for Rigoletto and Gilda. But early in the 1930s, as audiences and artists began to think of opera more as drama and less as concert for vocal display, the company adopted a rule against them. Yet audiences sometimes rebelled. In Atlanta in 1934, as applause for the tenor after "La donna è mobile" persisted, the conductor finally signaled a reprise. But the trend was against them.[56]

On May 25, 1944, in New York's Madison Square Garden, Arturo Toscanini, with his National Broadcasting Corp. Chorus and Symphony, gave a benefit concert for the wartime Red Cross. The main feature of the program was act 4 (by Verdi's count, act 3) of *Rigoletto*, and a performance in which Toscanini broke several traditions, not only in playing the act through without any encores, though in a concert performance these were still common, but in his casting of Gilda. In place of the usual coloratura in the Tetrazzini tradition, he cast Zinka Milanov, a dramatic soprano soon known for singing Verdi's heavier soprano roles, such as Aida, Amelia in *Ballo* and *Boccanegra*, and Leonora in *Trovatore* and *Forza*. Verdi nowhere specified a type of soprano for Gilda, but Toscanini, on restudying the score, evidently concluded that the music called for a soprano more dramatic than coloratura.

Because the performance was recorded and promptly put on sale in both the United States and Europe,[57] the breaks with tradition soon were heard around the world. Perhaps the most obvious of them came at the end of the Quartet, where Toscanini had Milanov diverge from the coloratura tradition and sing what Verdi had written. For the final cadence she did not rise, as coloraturas did, to a high A flat followed by a still higher D flat. Instead, she closed an octave lower, moving merely from C to D flat, and so, as one scholar noted, "for the first time in one's life, enabled one to hear the Quartet end on *ppp* (or thereabouts) that the composer intended. . . . It was an entirely different sound from what one was accustomed (in the name of 'singers' operas') to hear."[58]

And there were other changes in sound. Without stinting on the higher, more coloratura-like phrases that Verdi wrote, Milanov, with her weightier voice, was able to enrich Gilda's long legato sighs in the Quartet on such words as "infelice," and "cor tradita." The effect here and elsewhere was, if music were cloth, to substitute for a white lace trim to a weave of heavier material (tenor, baritone, and bass) a fourth intertwining swath of like material and equally strong color. But the performance was only of the last act, a reason its recording has been called Toscanini's "most tantalizing"; and a reason why one critic in reviewing it, though finding the casting "inspired," was led to ask: "Could she have sung 'Caro nome?'" For many, the answer soon became "Yes," as shown by sopranos such as Joan Sutherland and Maria Callas, more dramatic than coloratura.[59]

Another point made by the performance and recording was how well the act played when not stopped by encores. As the conductor-scholar Spike

Hughes noted: "Though for most people the Celebrated Quartet from *Rigoletto* does not begin until the tenor's 'Bella figlia dell'amore,' Verdi's score is, in fact headed 'No. 12. Quartetto' several pages earlier, and it is the bustle and excitement of the Allegro episode [starting with the tenor's "Un di, se ben rammentomi"] leading immediately to it that adds to the dramatic effect of the Quartet proper." Indeed, after the Allegro's bustle, the Quartet proper begins with a sudden promise of repose—its soft solo voice and *pp* accompaniment matching the Quartet's *ppp* ending.[60]

Throughout the act, without encores, Toscanini knit such introductory scenes into their more famous arias and ensembles, so that the act, instead of a succession of famous numbers offset by passages of supposedly less interesting music, became a whole, with greater cumulative punch. Thus Toscanini's fragment confirmed for many that Verdi's old "hurdy-gurdy" opera was in fact a great lyric drama.

Other artists, too, perhaps restudying Verdi as a result of his Renaissance that was gathering strength in all countries, began to see and hear the opera more as a drama; and an example of their new point of view is the first full-length opera recorded on long-playing records by RCA. Made in 1950, this *Rigoletto*, with Renato Cellini conducting Leonard Warren, Erna Berger, and Jan Peerce, was technically, financially, and artistically a huge success, and fifty-six years later still sells. Recorded with Berger, a soprano more lyric than coloratura, with Warren, an outstanding Rigoletto in the Renaud tradition, and without encores, though with many of the traditional small cuts, particularly in act 1, scene 2, it made a strong case for the opera as lyric drama. Yet curiously, though all the leading artists involved at one time or another performed at the Metropolitan, they never had sung a *Rigoletto* together (and never did).[61]

In that same year, however, the Verdi Renaissance came to the Metropolitan with the arrival of Rudolf Bing, who had been part of it in Germany and Austria in the 1930s, in England in the 1940s, and post–World War II at the Edinburgh Festival. He opened his first season, in the fall of 1950, with a new production of *Don Carlo*, which he followed the next year with new productions of *Aida* and *Rigoletto*. The sets and costumes of the latter, designed by Eugene Berman, differed markedly from those they replaced, which dated back forty-eight years to Caruso's debut. It was not just a matter of fresh paint but also, as most critics noted, of style and period. Instead of taking his cue from Mantua's existing medieval castle, Berman followed Hugo, who set the first scene in a hall in the Louvre that "in its architecture, furnishings, and costumes" reflected "the taste of the Renaissance," a more classical and colorful setting. Critics and the audience approved, and Olin Downes in his review for the *Times* put the new point of view first:

> The production of Verdi's *Rigoletto* last night . . . with new scenery and costumes by Eugene Berman and stage direction by Herbert Graf, was one of

Figure 11.1. Eugene Berman's set for act 2 (the lighting less glary in performance) with Rigoletto (Leonard Warren) and Gilda (Hilde Gueden). Later in the scene, Gilda would sing "Caro nome" on the balcony and retire, drawing the curtain in the doorway. Her abductors, in the street to the right (not shown), coming over the wall on the right, would open the door to the yard, run up the stairs into the house, carry her struggling figure out, down, into the street, and away. The action was clear and unhurried, for the distances of the set—up the stairs and so on—fit the music. Photograph by Sedge LeBlang, 1951. Courtesy of the Metropolitan Opera Archives.

the most interesting and exciting interpretations of this work that we have seen. . . . The stage setting is of the period of Hugo's play from which the opera is derived. It is Renaissance, rich and imposing, and far nearer the original conception of Verdi than the ruling of the Italian censor at the time of the *Rigoletto* première permitted. This in itself would not have a determinative upon the dramatic interpretation as a whole, if it were not companioned with such unity of effect by Mr. Graf's stage business.

The groupings of the first act [the court *festa*] added immensely to the dramatic power and contrast of the scene—Marullo and the courtiers, Rigoletto's enemies, clearly delineating, plotting their revenge; the Duke and the Jester in special relations of position and action to each other; the dancing, which was uncommonly well done, and the dancers not curtained off from

Figure 11.2. Berman's set for act 4, at the moment of the quartet, with Warren, Gueden, Richard Tucker (the Duke), and Jean Madeira (Maddalena). Photograph by Sedge LeBlang, 1951. Courtesy of the Metropolitan Opera Archives.

the guests of the occasion, as is frequent, and emerging in the center the ominous figure of the accusing Monterone. The second act was arranged with equal inventiveness and unhackneyed detail.

The scene of the abduction of Gilda was by far the best contrived that we have seen, with the stage all action and purpose, and so well coordinated with the score that for the only time in our experience the chorus of "Zitti, zitti" was not ridiculous but quickening to the pulse. The swift entrance and disappearance of the courtiers carrying Gilda into the Duke's inner chamber [opening act III] is an excellent and legitimate device, which make the more effective what happens afterward between Rigoletto and the courtiers. The stage last night was no mere background for the performances of solo singers. It was an agent of the drama.[62]

Only later, after the scenery and staging, did he judge the principal singers, Leonard Warren, Richard Tucker, and Hilde Gueden, also to be excellent. Gueden, making her debut and presumably nervous, was excused some thinness of tone in her early scenes. But thereafter, according to Louis Biancolli for the *World-Telegram and Sun*, "The voice blossomed into rich flower, every note in its place like a petal. . . . The debate was on last night as to whether Miss Gueden is a coloratura or lyric. My own humble opinion is that she is a lyric soprano who can take coloratura in stride. . . . She took the high E at the end of 'Caro nome' aria—the optional show note of every coloratura. It was a bit cautious and thin, but it was there. As a lyric, she should have left it alone. I might add she acted the part to perfection." If memory serves, in later years she ended the aria as Verdi wrote, on a soft trill an octave lower.[63]

In all Gueden sang twenty-four performances of Gilda at the Metropolitan, alternating frequently with Roberta Peters, whose voice was lighter but who held the same view of the role and who sang, in all, eighty-eight Gildas. This production, one of the best of Bing's tenure at the Metropolitan, 1950–72, served a full quarter-century, through the 1976–77 season. Over the years it was heard on fifteen national broadcasts, and in its first four seasons played on tour in sixteen U.S. and Canadian cities, many of them more than once, and in Toronto four times. In all, in its home house, on tour, in park concerts it played 223 times. For the second half of the nineteenth century it set the style for *Rigoletto* throughout Canada and the United States: to be staged more as a drama than as a "singers' opera." And as a music drama, judged a masterpiece—but it was not always so.[64]

Part Three

Seven Operas Premiered in the Late Twentieth Century

Chapter Twelve

Opera on Tour and the Rise of Regional Companies

Before the country's Civil War, 1861–65, any opera company attempting a tour traveled mostly by water, usually either by sea between the coastal cities (New Orleans to Boston), or if inland, up and down the Mississippi and Ohio rivers (New Orleans to Pittsburgh), making connections when needed (over the Appalachian Mountains) as often by canals or coaches as by railroads. Especially in the South and West, before the war, railroads frequently did not yet connect the larger cities because built primarily not to move people from place to place but to bring produce, coal, wheat, or cotton to market or to port for shipping. Even Chicago, for example, though by 1860 tied to the East by several railroads, was still more of a port on the Great Lakes than a railway hub because as yet no lines ran more than a few miles westward. Similarly, in the South, passage between New Orleans and Mobile, the latter a frequent side-stop for visiting opera stars and companies, was by sea, not railroad; and two inland capital cities, Jackson, Mississippi, and Montgomery, Alabama, still had no rail connection.

Though the war greatly stimulated railroad construction in the North and West and to some extent in the impoverished South, inland waterways nevertheless continued to be much used by people and freight. On the Hudson River, for example, steaming between New York and Albany, a seven-hour run, the *Mary Powell*, launched in 1861, and competing against the New York Central's four-hour train ride, continued in service until 1923. And on Long Island Sound, New York to Boston, before the lock-free Cape Cod Canal opened in 1914, the most important shipping line steamed to Fall River, Massachusetts, from which passengers could take a ninety-minute train ride to Boston.[1] With the canal, the line offered direct overnight service between the two cities and by a journey many considered far more pleasant than the train. In early years the line's two prize ships, the *Bristol* and the *Providence*, each offered 220 staterooms and a total passenger capacity of 840, as well as holds for cargo, and often provided entertainment for the evening's voyage, usually a dance band. In later years, the flagship was the *S. S. Commonwealth*, with 425 staterooms, and despite improved competition from the New Haven railroad, which finally in 1889 opened its "shore" route to Boston by bridging Connecticut's Thames River at New London, the overnight steamer stayed in business until 1937.[2]

Railroads, however, steadily gained dominance, especially in the West and especially after Chicago and San Francisco were joined by the first transcontinental line in 1869. And by 1914, six more lines crossed the plains and mountains from Chicago to the chief cities on the Pacific coast. Meanwhile the country's population, swollen by large families and immigrants, rose from 31 million in 1860, to 76 million in 1900, and to 132 million in 1940, with many of these settling in the Midwest and Far West. After 1865, when expansion west resumed, opera managers and artists, surveying a vast new territory of small towns and cities, saw a chance to earn a living by music, even as those local audiences, longing for a touch of culture in an era before radio or phonograph, were eager to hear sung the latest popular "airs." An Era of Touring Opera, chiefly by railroad, opened.

In another way, too, change came gradually but surely. When in 1852 Caroline Richings, a soprano, and her adoptive father Peter Richings, a baritone, came from New York to Philadelphia to sing several operas, including, in English, the U.S. premiere of Verdi's *Luisa Miller*, they brought with them only two others, a tenor and a "maestro direttore," who probably led and rehearsed the theater's small orchestra. But the orchestra, chorus, scenery, and secondary singers were all provided by Philadelphia's Walnut Street Theatre from its "stock" company, which performed a regular schedule of plays, with or without music, and was ready always to provide backup for celebrated visitors. The company's actors, however, seldom were trained singers, and what they sang usually was kept simple. Hence, for an opera, the smaller roles often were severely cut or dropped altogether, even as the visiting celebrities frequently transposed arias up or down and introduced currently popular songs.

Moreover, "stock" scenery was apt to be generic, a castle, a prison, a garden, or an interior, and so, however cleverly disguised, quite familiar to the audience. On the other hand, principals brought their own costumes—the prima donna was expected to display several, the more gorgeous the better—which might or might not blend with the "stock" players' garb. And for a French or Italian opera, the theater's small orchestra and chorus, sufficient perhaps for a farce or an English ballad opera, might be swollen by local recruits. But in the 1870s and 1880s, these local "stock" companies began to disappear, displaced by touring companies, traveling almost exclusively by rail, with full casts, chorus, orchestra, and even, toward the end of the century, their own scenery.[3]

The Richings, for example, in 1859 reorganized their troupe of four or five artists into an opera company, and after the Civil War began to tour widely, giving opera in English.[4] They were only one of many to do so. Another calling itself the "Cooper Company," after its leader Henry C. Cooper, a violinist, initially offered, with his wife Annie Milner as prima donna, a chorus of twelve and an orchestra of eighteen. In New York's Wallack's Theatre in September 1858, it presented *Lucy of Lammermoor, Elixir of Love, The Sonnambula*, and on the thirteenth, for the first time in the United States, an English version of *Il trovatore*, titled *The Gypsy's Vengeance*.[5] Three weeks later, another small company, Lucy Escott's English Opera Company, offered another version of *Trovatore* in English, *The Troubadour*.[6] Neither company had a success in New York, where audiences, by then used to opera sung in Italian, were sparse, and where the critics scorned the frequent cuts, the simple sets and staging, and the dialogue substituted for recitative.[7] Yet both companies found success in the small towns and cities of the Midwest and Far West where the less sophisticated were grateful for music in any form. Perhaps the oddest of all the vernacular versions of *Trovatore* was that of the New Orleans English Opera Troupe, in which the tenor role of Manrico was sung by a slim-waisted contralto, Georgia Hodson. Exclaimed the critic for the *Alta California:* "That a lady should sing this music at all is wonderful, but to sing as Miss Hodson does, in the original keys, and precisely as a man is 'passing strange.'"[8]

After the nineteenth century, Italian opera in English begin to decline, though even today some important companies, such as the Opera Theatre of St. Louis and the Chautauqua company, sing all operas in English even those as familiar as *Rigoletto* and *Traviata*.[9] But generally speaking, and especially after the arrival in this country in the 1880s of the Gilbert and Sullivan masterworks, *Pinafore, Pirates of Penzance, Patience, The Mikado*, opera in English became increasingly associated with comic opera or, for those seeking romance, with operettas and eventually musical comedies. For these lighter forms of drama in music, even as Verdi and others were writing ever more complicated scores, an orchestra of twenty-six might do, or in many theaters one even smaller.[10] Moreover, a price differential soon appeared; opera in English, usually less expensive to produce, charged less for an evening, and a division in audiences began to appear. Whereas in the 1850s, roughly speaking, there had been a single audience for musical entertainment in whatever form, by the 1890s that was ceasing to be true. There was increasingly an audience for so-called serious opera, typically presented in its original language and needing a large orchestra, large chorus, and roster of well-trained singers, and another for works lighter in spirit, less demanding in forces, and typically sung in English.

To pass from the general to the specific, consider one of the most successful of these nineteenth-century touring companies, the Emma Abbott English Grand Opera company, which in one respect was quite untypical: it survived, year after year, making opera pay, and pay well. Rumor even said that by 1889, Emma Abbott "was the richest woman on the stage," and her wardrobe for that year alone cost "upwards of $45,000," an enormous sum for the day.[11] She herself was acknowledged to be "a fine business-woman," and so too was her husband, Eugene Wetherell, with whom in 1878 she founded the company and who managed its business affairs.[12]

Nevertheless, Abbott, born in 1850 in Chicago and often called "the Illinois songstress," began life poor. Her father, an impecunious music teacher, taught her to sing and to play the guitar, for which she had a flair, and from an early age she accompanied him in recitals given in the lobbies of Illinois hotels. Though these were free to the hotel guests, or apparently to anyone who cared to stop by, the audiences were encouraged to contribute to the musicians' support and often did so liberally, for little Emma was charming and had a voice, as everyone said, that with training was sure to win her fame and fortune. Intensely ambitious and helped by admirers, she scrambled her way to voice teachers, first in Chicago, then in New York, and finally in Italy, where in Milan one night she began the practice of what later became a hallmark of her career. In the middle of a performance of *La Sonnambula*, to the astonishment of the Italians and presumably to please some fellow Americans in the audience, she all of a sudden sang the American hymn *Nearer My God to Thee*. The Milanesi hissed and shouted threats, the manager apologized, the singer then sang some "old Italian love songs," all the while "bowing and kissing her hands to the ladies present," and soon had sufficiently appeased the audience to allow the opera to proceed.[13] But once back in the United States and embarked on her tours, she would sing popular requests—much to the distress of Eastern critics and some of her fellow artists—between acts, at the opera's end, or even in the midst of a performance.[14] Yet for her singing of "Swanee River" or "The Last Rose of Summer," her audiences loved her.

Her voice was "bird-like," but even her adoring biographer, Sadie E. Martin, noted it was "not faultless, being at times shrill almost to unpleasantness, but she sang B flat without an effort, holding it as firmly as she would have done F." Following her sudden death by pneumonia in 1891, at least one New York critic judged her harshly, saying, "Even though the mantle of charity were stretched to the breaking point it could not be made to cover Abbott as an artist . . . In a word, Emma Abbott was the product of the wild and woolly West, and could not possibly have been a success outside the United States."[15]

Chicago papers and those in cities further west were more kind. According to the *Chicago Tribune:* "She was engaged upon the operatic stage about twelve years, and during that time essayed all kinds of roles, heavy and light, in English, French, German and Italian opera, though the style of her action and the capacity of her voice fitted her best for the light roles." One of the latter, important in starting her career, was Marie in *La fille du regiment*, in which she had made a successful debut in London in February 1876 and a year later in New York, both times singing in Italian.[16] But she did not fit comfortably into Italian language companies, and while in England had refused to sing the lead in *Traviata* because she thought Violetta as portrayed was immoral. Dismissed for breaking her contract, she gained a reputation for force of character, and after a year of concert singing founded her opera-in-English touring company.[17]

Her timing was opportune. The first professional opera company to visit Kansas, for example, arrived in 1869, and a scholar of opera in Kansas estimated that for the next twenty years opera "reigned supreme."[18] It garnered copious newspaper attention (sports were not yet fashionable), visiting prima donnas "captured the imagination of the Kansas public and held court backstage or in their hotel rooms," and throughout the state, in the nineteenth century, there were "fifty to a hundred opera houses in regular use."[19] These, as was then usual, booked entertainments of all sorts and opera companies only rarely, but being small, with most seating between 600 and 1,200, they were acoustically kind to singers, and when in 1882 Topeka, the state's leading operatic city, opened a new and splendid "Grand Opera House," it seated only 1,500. The other cities in the state most often visited by troupes or companies were Atchison, Lawrence, Leavenworth, and Wichita. In the course of Abbott's touring career, 1878 to 1891, throughout the West she would inaugurate at least thirty-five opera houses.[20]

She traveled with a company of "about fifty," of which ten, or sometimes fewer, reportedly formed the orchestra; perhaps twenty or twenty-five the chorus; and the balance, soloists and nonsinging personnel in charge of scenery, publicity, train, and other business affairs. By comparison, her chief competitor in Missouri and Kansas in the 1880s was Col. J. H. Mapleson, an English impresario whose company was partially drawn from a London theater, "Her Majesty's Royal Italian Opera House." For many seasons he and "Her Majesty's Opera Company," after presenting seasons in New York and other Eastern cities, would tour, offering "grand opera" in Italian. Traveling through the Midwest and Far West in an eight-car private train, his company, though reduced by nearly a half, still numbered close to eighty-five, "of whom seventy-five were actual performers." The orchestra numbered twenty, double the size of Abbott's, the chorus thirty-five to forty, and he offered sixteen principals, among them stars such as Etelka Gerster, Lillian Nordica, Minnie Hauk, and even at times Adelina Patti.[21]

The two companies' repertories, at least in simple listing, are not greatly different. Abbott typically offered operas such as *Martha, Faust, Carmen, Linda of Chamonix, The Sonnambula, Lucy of Lammermoor,* and of Verdi, *Ernani, Rigoletto, Trovatore,* and *Traviata,* the last made sufficiently moral by portraying Violetta as "the woman who would be good, who appealed to society to aid her, and who sacrificed her love to save a heart-broken father from despair."[22] But apparently in the more demanding operas, the cuts were severe. She also presented lighter works such as *The Chimes of Normandy* and *The Mikado,* and even in the latter, as a reprise of Yum-Yum's song, "The sun whose rays are all ablaze," would introduce a verse or two of "Home Sweet Home."[23] Mapleson omitted the lighter works and generally made fewer cuts in the weightier ones, and his singers did not introduce extraneous ballads or sport costly gowns. In *Trovatore,* for example, in Abbott's production—she sang Leonora—the main feature seems to have been her frequent change of costume.[24] Whereas Mapleson offered as Azucena a world-renowned contralto, Sofia Scalchi; and in *Carmen* (sung in Italian), Minnie Hauk; and in *Faust,* Lillian Nordica. With such stars, his larger orchestra, and larger chorus, his company was acknowledged the better of the two in all respects but one: the "aggregate homeliness" of his chorus. On this point, according to the *Kansas City Daily Journal*, Abbott was excused because she "had only America to select from."[25]

Nevertheless, Abbott won a place for herself in the hearts of her western audiences, and news of her death, following a performance of *Ernani* in Ogden City, Utah, stirred fond memories and much admiration for her determination, exemplary life, and desire to bring opera to the people in their native tongue. She had given the West far more performances than Mapleson, gradually earned a reputation for historically correct costuming for her chorus, if not always for herself; and given pleasure to many by her singing. As a historian later remarked, if not "the Mother of Opera" for the "American Provinces," she was at least its "big sister."[26]

Meantime, of course, many others tried to make touring in the West profitable, but none matched her success. The margin of profit over the costs of travel and production was so close that a snowbound train, a day's mistake in scheduling, or even a slight dip in audience support could tip profit into debt. In the course of his three visits to Kansas City, Missouri, Mapleson had tried to meet the problem by asking for a guarantee of $6,000 for a performance by Adelina Patti, whose fee at the time (to be paid in cash before each performance) was $5,000. Presumably, the house manager was to raise the sum, roughly double the receipts of a sold-out house, by collecting donations from generous citizens. The proposal was rejected, Patti did not sing, and after three seasons of financial loss in Kansas City, and seemingly also in the other cities visited between it and San Francisco, Mapleson soon ended his western tours.[27]

After 1883, both in New York and on tour, Mapleson's chief competitor offering Italian opera sung in Italian had been the Metropolitan's company, which, after a three-month season in the new house, started touring in the winter of 1883–84. And like Mapleson's, its first tour was mostly to Eastern cities: Boston, Brooklyn, Philadelphia, Cincinnati, Washington, and Baltimore, and, slightly further west, St. Louis and Chicago.[28] The manager, Henry E. Abbey, stated that it cost him $7,000 to raise the curtain, and of the first forty-five tour performances not one had earned the figure and only seven had topped $5,000. In Cincinnati, at least, he had a guarantee of $50,000 for thirteen performances, but at the tour's end he was more than $600,000 in debt.[29] By 1904–5, by which time the Metropolitan was acknowledged to be the country's strongest company, it had added to the usual eastern circuit: Minneapolis, Omaha, Kansas City, Salt Lake City, San Francisco, Los Angeles, Dallas, Houston, New Orleans, Atlanta, Birmingham, and Nashville. And because of its undisputed rank it was able to negotiate many more guarantees for an appearance. In 1910, for example, Atlanta citizens raised $50,000 for five performances, and by 1946 in Atlanta the guarantee was $40,500 for three.[30] In later years such guarantees to the Metropolitan increased in amount, for to lure into a visit "the biggest thing that moves except the circus" involved a huge outlay.[31] As a company historian then described: The "current logistics of moving a troupe of 325, with scenery for sixteen operas, 400 trunks and 150 musical instruments in two special passenger trains with nineteen sleepers, plus the baggage train of twenty-nine cars, through the network of American and Canadian railroads to reach sixteen cities in twelve states, would have confounded the masterminds of earlier days."[32] Yet the Met continued touring until 1986, by which time the combination of its weekly radio broadcasts, the improvement of television, and the rise of regional companies in many of the cities visited, made tours redundant and guarantees more difficult to raise. More often now, local support went to the local company.

For the first half of the twentieth century, however, one company offering operas sung chiefly in Italian regularly toured the country and Canada without guarantees, yet managed to stay in business, though with some gaps, from 1913 to 1955. Created by an Italian immigrant, Fortune Gallo, who in 1876 had come to the country at age sixteen with fourteen cents and no English, the San Carlo, which he and briefly his nephew always managed, made thirty-three transcontinental tours, introduced New Orleans to *Forza* in 1920 and to *Otello* (in Italian) in 1924, as well as giving short seasons in other major operatic cities, including San Francisco, Chicago, and New York. At his death in 1970, the *Times* estimated that the company in its first thirty years, when records are fullest, had "played 9,000 times to 19 million people."[33]

His company offered a predominantly Italian and French repertory (see appendix D) at prices generally about a third of the Metropolitan's. In 1918–19, for instance, a good seat at the San Carlo cost $2.00 and at the Metropolitan, $6.00. Moreover, in the depression years of the early 1930s, Gallo offered his cheapest seats at 50¢ and the best at $1.00; and in 1938, when the Metropolitan's top price was $7.00, Gallo's was $1.50. Not surprisingly, he developed a loyal audience, not only on tour but also in the short seasons he presented in New York, Boston, and other large cities. When the company performed well, audiences were apt to applaud tumultuously, for they were inclined to be appreciative, and at the close of a performance in New York of Verdi's *La forza* in October 1921, Manager Gallo was called upon to speak. As reported in *Musical America*, "in his individual way" he said: "You be with me and I will be with you. If you cannot come to-morrow night, send your mother, father, sister or brother. But whoever comes, show appreciation, as you did last season and we will come next season for a longer engagement." And that he would. In 1936–37, his company gave three hundred performances in sixty cities.[34]

Moreover, Gallo sometimes did more than tour. In 1919, in addition to a company on the road, he helped to produce an open-air *Aida* at New York's Sheepshead Bay Speedway, an automobile track with a grandstand, for an audience of some forty-five thousand. The occasion was a benefit to aid earthquake victims in Florence, Italy, and the leading singers came from the Metropolitan,

Chicago Opera, and San Carlo companies, the chorus numbered 300, the ballet 100, and a stage band, 75. Onstage for the triumphal scene were 2,000, as well as horses, oxen, camels, and elephants. According to the *Herald*: "Ordinarily Radames enters in a chariot drawn by two white horses, but last night he was preceded by ten mounted warriors. . . . The animals increased in size as the parade progressed, oxen to camels, to elephants. . . . All the menagerie behaved except the oxen. They shied at the elephant but were led away to stalls before they could mar the regal dignity of the official reception." Though admission was scaled from 50¢ to $3, the performance still managed to cover expenses and to contribute $30,000 to Tuscan relief.[35]

His company also participated in many of the earliest radio broadcasts of opera, such as an *Aida* in 1922 in New York and a *Trovatore* in 1924 in Boston. The latter was astonishing for its day, for its demonstration to listeners outside the theater as well as the audience within of radio's extraordinary speed and power. In the middle of the performance the tenor took ill, and the house manager asked the audience to wait while a message was sent to the "cover" in a nearby hotel. But the man had been listening to the broadcast in his room, and he arrived at the theater before the messenger had left.[36]

Later, in 1931, a nontouring year, Gallo made the "world's first sound picture of a grand opera," an uncut *Pagliacci* that ran for eighty minutes. Though critics judged the music making more successful than the filming, historians rank it as the world's first film of a complete opera in sound, and it played throughout the country as a wonder. But it was not easily made. Filmed on Long Island as a staged production, it ran into difficulties in a scene that called for the soprano to drive off in a donkey cart. Touched on its rump with a switch, the donkey kicked out the buckboard, leaving the soprano shaken and protesting. When the director, after repairs to the cart, reshot the scene, the beast did the same. And a third time, leaving the soprano in tears. According to Gallo, "That was enough for me. With my money pouring out like water from an open faucet, I rushed to the stage" to phone "the Ben-Hur stables." Told to calm down, he described what had happened. And the stableman, after inspecting his animals, reported, "You've got the wrong donkey! You've got Hugo. You should have got Felix!" Gallo never undertook another film.[37]

He was not a musician, though he claimed to play the harmonica and once to have conducted "God Save the King."[38] His singers scorned him as an artist but revered him as a businessman: Though an occasional singer might submit an inflated chit for travel, Gallo always knew the cost of a hotel room, the train fare from one city to the next, and when to use the Canadian railroad in order to avoid tax. In the larger cities, where he often added local recruits, he usually offered an orchestra of at least forty and a chorus of twenty-eight.[39] His weak point was scenery, which by extension or compression had to fit every stage (and he had the measurements of them all). It was always the first item struck by economy, and at times was deplorable: faded, painted sets, and more

than once falling down. In 1934, during a performance of the duel scene in
Gounod's *Roméo et Juliette*, one of Verona's city walls collapsed onto the singers. Their heads poked through the canvas; the house curtain was rung down,
the set rehung, and the opera proceeded.[40] His soloists, however, were well-
trained, and many went on to sing with the Metropolitan. In his best years,
with the aid of his exceptional musical director, Carlo Peroni, Gallo presented
a season of fifteen to twenty operas chosen from a repertory of popular Italian
and French works, occasionally including a German opera, usually *Lohengrin*,
sung in a mixture of languages.[41]

Yet Gallo, without financial angels, made opera pay, chiefly by low wages to
singers. Economic trends, however, were against him. In the 1930s, transportation costs began to rise as did the power of the labor unions. Even after unioniza-
tion in 1937, he managed to negotiate base pay for secondary singers at only $75
a week, for leading tenors and sopranos, $150, and for ballet dancers, $40. Still,
singers were remarkably loyal to him. At the very least he gave them a showcase,
a chance to sing leading roles, and some of them also shared his desire to bring
opera to the American people at prices they could afford to pay. In the San Carlo's thirty-five years it played perhaps to as many as twenty-two million.[42]

Also in the 1930s, both the San Carlo and the Metropolitan began to face
competition from the increasing number of resident companies. The San
Carlo at first suffered more from this than the Metropolitan, which had its
social cachet and guarantees. When in 1913 the San Carlo gave its first performances, as its historian notes, "There were two companies giving lengthy
seasons in New York, the Metropolitan and the Century Opera Company.[43] . . .
There were major companies in Chicago and Boston. There was another major
company in Canada and a touring company, called the National Opera Company, which concentrated on touring the Pacific Coast Within two years, however, the Century, Chicago, Canadian, and National had all gone broke and
the Boston company was disbanded, so Gallo was lucky to have started his company when he did."[44]

By 1946, however, by which time the country's population was nearing 151
million, there were at least forty opera companies in the United States, and
of these twenty-eight in twenty-two cities were resident companies, giving 393
performances in their home houses and 134 elsewhere. The Metropolitan gave
199 performances, the New York City Opera, 73, and the San Francisco Opera,
50. At least three other companies gave 30 or more performances. Among the
primarily touring companies, the San Carlo was the giant, visiting seventy cities
in the United States and Canada, and giving 123 performances. Four others
combined totaled 154.[45]

Newspaper notice of the San Carlo, however, began to decline in the late
1920s and especially so in *Musical America*, which before a change in editors
in 1927–28, had regularly printed reports of performances sent in by "string-
ers" from cities proud to be included on the schedule of the country's major

touring company. The new editor focused the journal more exclusively on New York, Boston, and Philadelphia, and the consequent decline in coverage accelerated in the 1930s, as the number of resident companies began to rise, and the citizens of the smaller cities began to send in reports on what their home company was doing. A visit from the Metropolitan was still news, from the San Carlo, no longer.[46]

Another company that in some ways attempted less than the San Carlo and in others, more, was the "perversely named" Chicago Opera Company, "perversely" because based in New York and commonly known as the Salmaggi Company. Its creator and manager, Alfredo Salmaggi, like Gallo, was an Italian immigrant who created a company that played at low prices, but mostly in large cities. He did not tour in Gallo's fashion, and although presenting the same basic repertory, focused more often on the exceptional performance. He is said to have drawn an audience of eighteen thousand to an *Aida* in Cleveland's stadium in 1931, "twenty thousand with a performance of *Aida* in the Brooklyn Dodgers' Ebbets Field, thirty-three thousand with *Aida* in the Yankee Stadium, and twenty-seven thousand again with *Aida* in the Boston Braves' baseball park." And "forty-five thousand" with an *Aida* in Chicago's Soldier Field. He favored animals, recruited usually from the Ben-Hur Stables, but for the *Aida* in Boston he astonished the crowd with fifty of the city's mounted policemen to lead the Triumphal March. Supplied by the mayor, Michael F. Curley, for costumes as victorious Egyptian warriors they wore bed sheets over their uniforms and turbans wrapped round their heads. Reportedly, Salmaggi gave *Aida* five hundred times, and it seems quite likely.

In performances of it in 1933 in New York's Hippodrome (capacity 5,000), he cast the black soprano Caterina Jarboro in the leading role, the first time an African American "sang a principal role with a mainstream U.S. Company." And the following year he presented an all-black *Aida* at the Hippodrome. Fifteen years later, the National Association for the Advancement of Colored People gave him a citation for his work in integrating opera. In all, with some gaps, his career in producing opera lasted from 1918 until 1971.[47]

Throughout that period, the number of opera performances in the country steadily multiplied, by 1955–56 averaging "nine per day, with an annual total of 3,217 presentations by 544 groups in forty-seven states." Of the 210 operas performed, 65 were from the standard repertory (1,648 performances), and 74 by contemporary American composers (1,143), with Puccini's *La Bohème* (134) the most popular in the standard repertory and Menotti's *Amahl and the Night Visitors* (196) in the contemporary group. Perhaps the most startling figures, no doubt caused in part by the economic surge that followed World War II, revealed an increase in companies of all sizes: In just one year, 1955 to 1956, professional companies rose from 72 to 83; in colleges, from 111 to 167; and in high schools from 43 to 96.[48] In 1998, when the country's population was surging toward 280 million, *Opera America* listed 111 professional companies in the United States and sixteen in Canada, of which over half had been established "after 1970, and a quarter after 1980." In addition, the report listed 186 "affiliate members producing and presenting" opera as well as sixty-three "universities, conservatories and training programs," which in some form staged opera. It also noted that in the decade 1982–92, the U.S. opera audience "grew by almost 25 percent . . . and this trend continued." In 1996–97 "North American professional companies gave 2,397 performances of 456 fully-staged main season and festival productions."[49] With opera production everywhere on the rise, for most towns and cities, its chief provider was no longer the touring company, whether led by an Abbott, Gallo, or Salmaggi, but the local company, whether municipal or regional.

This shift in focus was accompanied by one in the financial underpinning of most companies, a process in which the Metropolitan as the biggest, strongest company (and with the most complete and available records) may serve as a model. As its historian, Irving Kolodin, observed, "The long-term trend . . . was to take ownership out of the hands of the groups that had built the opera house as a place for social display and transfer it to a group interested primarily in the production of opera."[50] Similarly in the cities traditionally relying on touring companies, gradually those who were more interested in producing opera locally, whether in a university, a concert setting, or with a resident company, took control and won local support.

As is well known, the Metropolitan's opera house was built in 1883 by a group of newly rich and socially prominent families, angered because they could not buy boxes in New York's Academy of Music, then the city's leading house for opera and controlled by families with older pedigrees. In essence the plan for the Metropolitan was that the box holders, owning the house, would contract with an impresario to give a season of opera. The impresario's company was his business. He would get the house rent free, but the box holders in return would have their boxes free to all subscription performances, which was most of them. For their first year, 1883–84, the box holders contracted with Henry E. Abbey and he gave a season in the house of sixty-one performances and ten concerts, for which the box holders gave him a guarantee of $60,000. But at the end of the season and the subsequent tour as "the Metropolitan Company" (seventy-six operas and four concerts), Abbey was $600,000 in debt and dropped as a bidder for the next season's contract.[51]

Other impresarios with the Metropolitan did better, including a newly solvent Abbey in a return engagement in 1891–92, and then in 1908 the box holders made a significant change: instead of contracting with an impresario, they hired on salary a general manager who would organize a company linked more closely to the house and continuing year after year. The first such manager was Giulio Gatti-Casazza, 1908–35, who was greatly aided by having on his roster stars such as Caruso and Geraldine Farrar and Antonio Scotti, and under his management the company prospered, building by 1929 a reserve fund of more than $1 million.[52]

Caruso's top fee for a performance in his last year, 1921, was $2,500, only half of what Patti had demanded thirty-five years earlier, but unlike her, by then he had a recording contract with the Victor Company that guaranteed him $100,000 a year or a 10 percent royalty on the sale of his records, whichever was higher. The guarantee was for ten years or life, whichever was shorter, but the royalty would continue after death. His contract was by far the best of the current singers, but Farrar, for one, was also a major movie star, 1915–20, appearing in fourteen films—all silent! Still, the phonograph, radio, and movies, had brought opera into another era, with the first operas on television to come in the late 1930s.[53]

For the Metropolitan, however, and for all other companies, the most jarring experience of the 1930s was the economic depression. Even the mighty Metropolitan, having exhausted its reserve fund in two years, almost quit, as attendance plunged and many box holders refused to pay the annual assessment to keep their house in good repair.[54] On February 25, 1933, a "Committee for Saving Metropolitan Opera" made an appeal, its first by radio, to the general public, and thereafter in the house at "some intermission of every performance," present or past members of the company, including the long-retired Farrar, spoke to the audience. Though no figures were published, the appeal apparently raised about $150,000, of which half was contributed by two foundations, the Juilliard Foundation ($50,000) and the Carnegie Corporation ($25,000). Significantly, the box holders had failed, and the general public, albeit mostly as yet through foundations, had stepped into the financial equation.[55]

The Juilliard Foundation, as chief contributor, spoke with a loud voice, added four of its personnel to the Metropolitan's board of directors as well as its lawyer, Allen Wardwell, to a sort of executive board titled "Opera Management Committee." Wardwell, who personally had only a mild interest in opera, lawyerlike had a strong one in seeing that the intentions of Mr. A. D. Juilliard, expressed in his will, be carried out: "To aid by gift or part of such income at such times and to such extent and in such amounts as the trustees of such [Juilliard] foundations in their discretion deem proper, the Metropolitan Opera Company . . . providing that suitable arrangements can be made with such company so that such gifts shall in no way inure to its monetary profit." In furthering that aim the foundation set forth some preconditions on which further aid might be received: a budget that would have "every promise of operating without a deficit," and "a substantial increase in subscription sales."[56]

In response to the latter, a committee, suggested and chaired by Mrs. August Belmont, strongly backed by Wardwell, was allowed to use the precious name "Metropolitan," and with it founded the Metropolitan Opera Guild to stimulate the sales and attendance generally.[57] In its first year, 1935, it gathered two thousand members.[58] (By 1960 it had nationwide nearly one hundred thousand, had started the magazine *Opera News*, was organizing annual benefit performances "for the production fund," conducting courses on opera for teachers and students in New York schools, and annually contributing to the production company any surplus accumulated from its members, which was often in the hundreds of thousands of dollars.) Then in 1940 came the campaign to buy the house from the box holders and give it to the production company, and Mrs. Belmont, the actress for whom G. B. Shaw had written *Major Barbara*, went on the radio at intermissions of the opera on the Saturday afternoon broadcasts and in a marvelous, quavery, heartrending voice appealed to the general public to "save the opera," to assist in raising the needed million dollars.[59] Whereupon the radio audience (estimated to be fourteen million) put all others to shame, contributing $327,000. Fifteen foundations added $149,482, with Juilliard giving $70,000 and Carnegie, $50,000, and the balance made up by individuals and businesses.[60]

As the nineteenth-century impresario Max Maretzek had railed time and again, New York's Academy of Music, from 1854 to 1883 the city's leading house for opera, did not offer a secure base to any opera company. And why? Because it was primarily a real estate venture run by a board of investors seeking the highest rent possible, along with such perquisites as free seats for box holders for most performances.[61]

Though the initial investors in the Metropolitan's house, chiefly first-tier box holders, had started with the same idea, they gradually transcended, or were pushed to transcend, that purpose and substitute for it support for a resident production company. As Kolodin, the house and company's historian, summarized the event:

When the title of the area designated on the real-estate map of New York City as Block 815 passed to the Metropolitan Opera Association on June 28, 1940, a full cycle had been completed. The property had been bought and the building erected by a group that desired to provide a home for opera, but had no interest in the production of it. Fifty-seven years later, after a slow but perceptible progression, it passed to the control of a group [the Metropolitan Opera Association] interested in the production of opera, but not particularly interested in owning the home for it—save as ownership became a necessary protection of its primary interests.[62]

In the 1943–44 season, when because of World War II there was another plunge in attendance, the company together with the Guild again appealed to the public for assistance, and reaped $316,793. Whereupon, and presumably in recognition of the public's interest, in 1944, for the first time, the Metropolitan Opera Association issued an annual financial statement, giving some details about its operations and problems. With the public's money had come public accountability.[63]

The pattern of the Metropolitan's development was anticipated or followed generally throughout the country as the regional companies developed: Those leading citizens who rallied only to a visit by the Metropolitan company were slowly supplanted by others who saw the future in terms of a resident company supported locally by subscribers and financed increasingly by the local public. Today almost every professional company has its Opera Guild, or counterpart, which may have developed out of volunteer work to ensure the success of a visit from the Metropolitan. For example, in Atlanta, the Junior League women, working for the Metropolitan's 1955 visit, amassed a total of 8,957 hours spent on ticket sales, promotion, publicity, and the sale of advertising for the program.[64] And some of that work and energy now goes into the Atlanta Opera Company. The Annual Field Report for *Opera America, 1997*, which does not claim to account for every guild, reported that in 1988 some forty-seven of them in the United States and Canada logged in 274,300 hours of work for their companies, with the value of these hours estimated to be in excess of $3,766,000. In addition, public support (meaning not contributions by federal, state, or local governments but donations by individuals or foundations) now accounts for almost 50 percent of the budgets for all U.S. and Canadian companies, including the Metropolitan, and provides for these companies a more secure base for producing opera.[65]

Without these developments, the impact of the worldwide Verdi Renaissance, so strong elsewhere, here might well have been less. Note that all seven of Verdi's operas that had their U.S. premieres in the years 1960 to 1978 had them in productions put on by small local companies that, because of their local support—subscribers, patrons, guilds—could afford the risk. Even today none of the big companies, the Metropolitan, the Chicago Lyric, or San Francisco Opera, has mounted Verdi's first opera, *Oberto*, or his second, *Un giorno di regno*, as did the Amato Opera in New York and Pocket Opera in San Francisco. Or consider the record of *Giovanna d'Arco:* premiered by a concert opera group in New York and by another such in Boston, and staged by a small local company in New York and by a startup company in Baton Rouge. Probably none of these performances would have occurred without the smaller company having its own subscription base, guild, and contributions by the public.

Moreover, government in the United States, in various ways, does play a part in support, though minimally by cash contribution. More important, federal and state tax codes allow deductions for gifts to nonprofit organizations, which today include all opera companies. Indeed, opera has become the paradigm of the nonprofit art. Unlike Abbott or Gallo, no one anymore thinks to make a profit on it. And further, in addition to the charitable gift deduction, federal, state, and local governments often exempt opera from entertainment taxes, and even sometimes from real estate taxes. In Canada and most European countries, the governments, through arts councils or departments, make sizable cash contributions to opera companies. That the United States does not, or only rarely and in small grants that tend to disappear in hard times, strikes the others as oddly and peculiarly American. Yet as the statistics collected by

Opera America show, however muddled the system may appear, it seems to be effective, especially in how it keeps the public actively involved.

Opera, no doubt, continues to be a risky business, But as a critic for *Musical America* observed in 1948, in an article titled "A Half-Century of Opera," and reciting some of the changes that had taken place: "History of the past half-century shows that opera has a remarkable tenacity here. Many prophets have foretold its doom, saying year after year that it has no appeal for the younger generation. But the younger generation, as well as the older, keeps on going to it."[66]

Moreover, in the second half of the twentieth century as the operagoing public greatly increased in size, so, too, more particularly did audiences for Verdi's operas, and in that general reappraisal of "old-fashioned" Verdi, the smaller companies had a special role, for it was they who offered audiences the chance to hear even those of his early operas that had never before been staged in the country.

But why should operas that a century earlier had failed to hold the stage, such as *Nabucco, Macbeth*, and *Luisa Miller*, now succeed, with the larger companies as well as with the smaller? And why should productions in the smaller houses with small orchestras, often twenty or less, which a century earlier had been deemed too scratchy, too lacking in violins, too brassy in sound, now be acceptable as a way to experience Verdi and his ideas of opera as drama? In great part, the answer is found in the impact of the Verdi Renaissance that began to seep into the country as early as the 1930s, gathered force during the 1940s with American editions of Werfel's works, Toye's biography, and a stunning production of the hitherto neglected *Macbeth*, and then after 1950 flooded the public with books and articles about the composer as a person as well as analyzing his operas.[67] Wagner who for the century's first forty years had enjoyed almost exclusive critical attention now had to share it, and though to some extent the new may have been simply more exciting than the old, it also proved that Verdi was rewarding to study and exciting to read about both as man and musician.

Moreover, this interest was strengthened by a change in the perception of audiences of operatic history, a change that affected not only Verdi but all composers, and which was spurred in part by the constant improvements in recordings. As Kolodin, the Metropolitan Opera's historian previously quoted, remarked of the audience's attitude in the early 1990s: "The modern concept of a repertory theater had not emerged. *Rigoletto, Lucia*, and *Il trovatore* were damned as 'old' works . . . rather than valued as vital expressions" of a different time and style.[68] But gradually a concept emerged that composers of different periods, customs, and ideas had created masterworks of quite different types, equally good but wholly different, as were, for example, the masterpieces of Gluck, Mozart, Verdi, and Wagner. The history of opera, it seemed, was not a steady progression from good to better, but a record of past achievements built upon concepts that perhaps were no longer viable but could still be of interest for what they once had produced. As the *New York Tribune* of 1847 had written of *Foscari*, which had failed to find an audience: "It may not be a great or very original work, but it will bear comparison in point of originality with the Operas of Rossini, Bellini or Donizetti. . . . Verdi's operas are not mere strings of solos, duets, and choruses, but are considered and coherent wholes, worked up throughout upon a broad ground of harmony."[69]

In rediscovering that truth, audiences in the second half of the twentieth century, excited by Verdi and his ideas of opera as drama, could go to a small theater that was playing a score rearranged for twenty or fewer instruments (see appendix F), and become engrossed in such early works as *Oberto, Un giorno, La battaglia,* and even in one only recently pulled back from oblivion by scholars, *Stiffelio.* The response now was less to the conditions under which the neglected opera was produced than to the voice, however dimly projected, of the composer—that voice unique and still vibrant.

Chapter Thirteen

Oberto

Though Verdi's fifth opera, *Ernani* (1844), by 1848 had established him in the United States as the likely successor to Rossini, Bellini, and Donizetti, and three others of his early operas, *Nabucco, Lombardi,* and *Foscari* had been heard, his first, *Oberto, Conte di San Bonifacio* (1839), did not achieve its U.S. premiere until 1978, a lag of 130 years. Considering how eager audiences were in the mid-nineteenth for "novelties," including new operas,[1] the long delay is surprising, and the cause lies partly in the opera's strangely truncated, early history.

Verdi had composed *Oberto* (as the opera commonly and hereafter is called), in the years 1836–38, but as a composer as yet unknown outside his town in the Po Valley, was unable to persuade any company to mount it until 1839, when the impresario at La Scala, Milan, took it to fill a hole in his spring schedule. After rehearsals began, singers fell ill, and the opera was rescheduled for the fall, with a different cast and some revisions and additions. Premiered on November 17, 1839, it had a substantial success, fourteen performances. The impresario then signed Verdi for three more operas, and the Milanese publisher Giovanni Ricordi, who had bought the rights to *Oberto,* began in December to sell individual numbers and to prepare complete piano and vocal scores. Meanwhile, beyond the Alps, in Paris, the *Revue et Gazette musicale,* published first a note that the opera had won "un grand et légitime succès" in Milan, then that the Parisian publisher Maurice Schlesinger soon would offer seven vocal excerpts for sale, and finally, a long, favorable review from its correspondent in Milan. In Leipzig, the *Allgemeine Musikalishche Zeitung,* in February 1840, published an even more detailed review, illustrating it with music to the *Adagio* of the opera's quartet, and concluding that the opera "had made the fortune of its author."[2]

More productions followed. In January 1840, a company in Turin staged the opera, and then, in October, La Scala revived it, with some further additions and revisions, for seventeen performances. The next year, Genoa and Naples produced it, and on February 1, 1842, in Barcelona, Spain, it became Verdi's first opera to play outside of Italy.[3]

With such a record, *Oberto* perhaps should have survived onstage in Italy for a decade or so while adding more productions in Spain, France, and the German states. But the stunning failure of Verdi's second opera, *Un giorno di regno* (1840)—one disastrous night at La Scala—and the stupendous success of his third and fourth, *Nabucco* (1842) and *I Lombardi alla prima crociata* (1843), obscured *Oberto,* leaving it for most people merely a name in a catalogue.

Seemingly, the opera's only music to reach the United States in the next few years was the tenor aria, "Ciel, che feci!" (Heaven, what have I done!), brought by Lorenzo Salvi, who had sung the role of Riccardo in the Scala premiere and revival, and in the Genoa production. Hired by P. T. Barnum as an assisting artist for Jenny Lind's tour through the South, he joined her company at Louisville, Kentucky, in April 1851. With her at that time were a baritone, Giovanni Belletti, a conductor, Julius Benedict, and a basic orchestra of ten that in the larger cities could grow to fifteen or twenty by the addition of local musicians.[4] Most likely, Salvi brought a vocal score of the *Oberto* aria with him, from which Benedict scored parts for his orchestra. Lind, of course, was the star of the tour, but Salvi was an excellent tenor, especially in Bellini and Donizetti. On several occasions, reviewers, after extolling Lind, praised Salvi for his solo numbers, among them "Spirto gentil" from Donizetti's *La favorita* and "La mia letizia infondere," from Verdi's *I Lombardi*.[5]

Both these arias, however, are songs of a single emotion, whereas "Ciel, che feci!" though titled a *romanza*, is a short *scena* of successive and contrasting moods. In the opera Riccardo, a young medieval knight, rushes onstage, his sword bloody. Provoked to a duel he first had refused because of his challenger's age, he has severely wounded Oberto, whose offstage groans signal death. Riccardo is aghast—"What have I done!"—he has loved, seduced, and abandoned Oberto's daughter (before the opera starts), and then, confronted by her and her father, agreed to marry her. Now he has wounded the father, perhaps killed him. He staggers onstage to a brief orchestral prelude depicting emotional turmoil: "What have I done! Dishonored, guilty, where can I hide? Lord, let the old man live. No, he dies, and his ghost will haunt me. Oh, God! If pray I may, save me, pardon me, per pietà." Onstage and in context, the scene, especially in its closing bars, is moving; in recital, without context, it is hard to make effective. Even twelve years after the opera's premiere, Salvi evidently still liked the piece, but his American audiences preferred his more purely lyric arias to one so dramatic. Though Salvi sang "Ciel, che feci!" in Boston (perhaps twice), in New York at least once, and perhaps also in other cities, no reporter bothered to comment on it. And into that silence, along with its aria, *Oberto* sank, dropping even in excerpt from the American operatic repertory for more than a hundred years.[6]

In Europe, in the mid-nineteenth century, the opera apparently had only one production, in Malta, 1860, but there was talk in Milan, as the opera's fiftieth anniversary approached, November 17, 1889, of a production at La Scala. Verdi, thinking the opera too old-fashioned for contemporary taste, privately protested, and the plan was dropped.[7] But after his death, in 1901, *Oberto* on occasion was revived, usually to commemorate his birth or death, and in 1951, the fiftieth anniversary of death, a performance was broadcast by radio. Even outside of Italy, as the favorable reassessment of Verdi, which had begun in the 1920s, continued to grow, interest in the opera increased.[8]

Figure 13.1. Amato Opera House in 2001, on the Bowery, New York City. Photograph courtesy of Stephen Vogel.

On February 18, 1978, *Oberto* had its United States premiere at the Amato Opera Theatre, in New York. In 1948, Anthony and Sally Amato, husband and wife, had founded a nonprofit organization to present operas, little known and well known, with young singers seeking stage experience. And in its first nine years, mostly in a converted movie theater (capacity 300) on Bleecker Street, the company presented 1,296 performances of 21 operas, attended by an esti-mated 50,000 people, and employing, because of constantly changing casts, some 2,000 young singers. After 1962, larger halls sometimes were rented and semistaged operas mounted with full orchestra, and on two such occasions the company produced a U.S. premiere of a Verdi opera: *Un giorno di regno* and *La battaglia di Legnano*.

After 1962, however, the company more often used its own small theater (capacity 107) on the Bowery. There, with a piano or two, and frequently with six or seven instruments added, Amato, leading from the tiny orchestra pit, would present operas fully staged, with scenery, costumes, and a chorus that could number twenty. For *Oberto* he scheduled ten performances at the Bowery house, with multiple casts and a translation of the libretto for the audience. The musical staff of the *New York Times* ignored the production, but Herbert Kupferberg, a reporter for the *Trib, New York*, went to the opening night and published a review from which the following is taken:

> If New York is the cultural capital of the United States, it isn't only because of the existence of such institutions as the Metropolitan and New York City Operas. It's also because of the enterprise and tenacity of small companies and organizations operating in obscure locations and unlikely surround-ings, powered chiefly by ingenuity and resourcefulness rather than cash and endowments. . . .
>
> Thanks [to such a troupe] I have just participated in . . . the U.S. pre-miere of Verdi's first opera. . . . So what *was* Giuseppe Verdi's first opera? . . . *Oberto, Conte di San Bonifacio.* . . .
>
> The Amato has flourished for some thirty years. . . .[9] It currently operates at a four dollar top, for which it offers well-organized and spirited presenta-tions of both standard operas and rarities. Its only concession to economics is the use of a piano accompaniment rather than an orchestra; otherwise, it has all the essentials—tasteful scenery, good costumes, adroit staging that usu-ally overcomes the restrictions of a postage-stamp floor and sometimes some excellent singing. . . .
>
> In staging *Oberto*, the Amato has scored a brilliant coup. Not that the opera is ever likely to return to the repertory, but as an historical curiosity it is a remarkable piece, with long stretches of what sound like rather tepid Donizettian melodies interspersed with unexpected outbursts of dramatic vigor. The libretto, which is no worse than some that Verdi used in his palm-ier days, is laid in the thirteenth century and has to do with one Leonora, who has been seduced and then spurned by a Count Riccardo. Leonora's father, Count Oberto comes to confront the vile betrayer, who by this time

Figure 13.2. A curtain call (of *Tosca*) at the Amato Opera, with Anthony Amato at the far left. Photograph courtesy of Stephen Vogel.

is engaged to another noblewoman named Cuniza. By the opera's close, Oberto is dead, Riccardo in exile and Leonora mad, with only Cuniza left to pray for heavenly mercy.

As noted, it's an opera that for all its conventionality has its moments, including a splendid act II quartet, a charming duet for the two girls who have become sisters in misery[10] and a supremely dramatic confrontation at the climax of act I in which the miscreant Riccardo's treachery is exposed—a scene that shows the presence of the true Verdi stamp even in his first product.[11]

In Italy, in January 1977, the Teatro Comunale, Bologna, had mounted a production of *Oberto* that the company later took to Parma, Modena, and Reggio Emilia, meanwhile issuing one of the Bologna performances as a recording, the opera's first.[12] Then in 1984 a studio recording was published, with Carlo Bergonzi singing "Ciel, che feci!"[13] In reviewing that recording, an American critic wrote of the opera: "I suspect that what, if anything, distinguished *Oberto* from the many 'Brand X's' [conventional operas] of the 1830s are its moments of rough virility. . . . *Oberto* can be inferred as 'the acorn from which a mighty tree sprang up,' or some other such cliché; viewed in isolation, it's just a typical opera of its time."[14] By the mid-1980s, however, that view was becoming old-fashioned, for by then most scholars and critics, as partisans of the Verdi Renaissance, were extolling the ways in which the opera was *un*typical of its time, notably in how Verdi, rather than seeking to charm his audience with a picture of the drama, sought, however poorly, to excite his audience into sharing the passions of his characters.

Then in March 1985, the San Diego Opera, in what it billed as the opera's "American professional premiere," presented four performances in the city's Civic Theatre (capacity 2,945). Most local critics found the opera "a crushing bore." One, for the *La Jolla Light*, disagreed: "What began as boring homage to early 19th century Italian convention turned out to give opera lovers a substantial taste of Verdi, after all. It took an adventurous spirit both to produce *Oberto*. . . as well as sit through, but, all things considered, it seemed well worth the effort."[15] The naysayers, however, spoke louder and with greater vehemence, especially Martin Bernheimer, critic for the *Los Angeles Times* and also for the British magazine *Opera*.

> Some operas languish for decades, even centuries, in unjust neglect. Others achieve and sustain the oblivion they eminently deserve.
>
> Count among the others, *Oberto, Conte di San Bonifacio*.
>
> When Verdi wrote it in 1839, he was still a lyrical whippersnapper who cranked out music, fast and easy, in a popular, hand-me-down-Bellini manner. At 26, he couldn't tell a decent libretto from a Milanese menu, couldn't distinguish drama from acid indigestion and obviously listened to a lot of bad advice.
>
> No matter. He could manufacture melodies in the best, and worst, organ-grinder traditions. He also could make appreciative use of some hoary operatic conventions that were not yet totally time-dishonored.
>
> But that was hardly enough. . . . Life is so short. And, at 2½ rinky-tink, oom-pah-pah hours, *Oberto* is so long.
>
> The opera simply isn't worth the effort. It creaks along on a preposterous, stilted and static libretto about—what else?—revenge, betrayal and amorous intrigue. . . . It regurgitates lyrical cliches amid primitive harmonies. It bumbles sideways with an orchestration that lends new meaning to the word *naïve*.
>
> Although we have never heard it before, humming along poses no problem. And no challenge.[16]

Bernheimer could claim to echo Verdi's opinion on the opera's revival, and certainly his intemperate language is fun to read. But as criticism, perhaps it fails. A critic, one who sets out to instruct the public, need not like a piece of music, but he should be able to explain to others what in that music appeals to its partisans. In this respect, at least, Bernheimer's total condemnation seems deficient.

Two years later, on July 24, 1986, the New York Grand Opera Company, with a full orchestra conducted by Vincent La Selva, presented *Oberto* as part of a free, open-air season in Central Park. Tim Page of the *New York Times*, hearing more in it than Bernheimer, concluded: "It is, in many ways, a crude work, with a silly libretto and many imperfections, but it is shot through with genius and is recognizably Verdi's from the first slashing phrase." Of the performance he said: "Verdi's power came through."[17]

This was increasingly the view of audiences, or at least of those few thousands who heard the opera on stage. People almost invariably liked the second act better than the first, and many, despite the clumsy libretto and sometimes derivative music, found themselves caught up in the characters and their predicaments as early as the trio leading into the finale of the first act. When La Selva, in July 1994, started his cycle of Verdi's twenty-six operas, *Oberto* to *Falstaff*, in order of composition,[18] the *Times* critic, Alex Ross, wrote:

> Some of his operas are unquestionably better than others. . . . Yet even the most obscure works have something singular and satisfying about them. Such a one is *Oberto*. . . . The composer's fingerprints are unmistakable throughout, and several arias and ensembles are beautifully shaped and controlled almost in the mature Verdi manner. Indeed, with its Bellini-like easeful lyricism and Rossini-like spiritedness, this opera is often more absorbing than some other early Verdi works, even those in which the composer's voice is more recognizable.[19]

The critic for the *New York Observer*, Charles Michener, recorded the spirit of the park performance.

> It was a night of such torpor that even the mosquitoes stayed home. Nonetheless, an audience of many thousands turned up at the Summer-stage in Rumsey Playfield and plunked themselves down on blankets, bleachers, or plastic folding chairs. . . . For this event, admission was free, and the crowd came in everything from Bermuda shorts to tattoos. What they heard was an operatic rarity. . . . But *Oberto* is unmistakably Verdian, a fascinating preview of coming attractions. . . . Already, Verdi had found a way to make opera *surge* with an almost abrasive directness and drive—so powerfully that at the Central Park performance the buzz of a Boeing or the wail of a police siren seemed part of the score.
>
> Despite the heat, an amplification system that made a hash of ensemble singing, costumes that seemed left over from the Marx Brothers' *A Night at the Opera* and a unit set suggestive of ramparts and glades out of Disney cartoon, the performance was vigorously effective. . . . Keeping the whole thing surging was the maestro in front of his shirt-sleeved orchestra—New York Grand Opera's artistic director, Vincent La Selva. A short, portly figure with a musicianly shock of curly gray hair. . . . He seemed oblivious to the heat in white dinner jacket and black tie, and when he appeared on stage to a standing ovation, he still looked fresh.[20]

Then, in 1999, the Opera Theater of Northern Virginia gave *Oberto* its first production in English, three performances at the Thomas Jefferson Community Theater in Arlington. The orchestra, led by John E. Niles, numbered

Figure 13.3. Vincent La Selva conducting outdoors in summer 1984 at Snug Harbor Park, Staten Island, New York. Photograph by John F. Mahoney. Courtesy of the New York Grand Opera Company.

twenty-three; the chorus, fifteen; and the principals, reported Joseph McLellan of the *Washington Post*, were "four fine solo voices." He thought the opera was "still worth knowing—full of lovely *bel canto* melodies and occasional hints of the depth and dramatic power" of Verdi's later operas, and he was especially pleased with the staging, which found "ingenious solutions to the company's budget limitations. Scrims are used imaginatively throughout for symbolic projections (Gothic windows, a luminous cross) to establish scene and mood, and mimed shadows behind the scrims give the action depth, notably in a duel, seen as a shadow play with the lights turning red at the death."[21]

Two years later, to mark the centennial of Verdi's death in 1901, two American companies staged *Oberto*. In San Francisco, Donald Pippin's Pocket Opera alternated two performances of it with three of Verdi's last opera, *Falstaff*, offering a chance to hear the composer's extraordinary growth in a span of fifty-four years. Pippin's productions typically are without sets, using only a few props, sometimes not costumed, but employing professionally trained singers and an orchestra of eight to fifteen, with Pippin leading from a piano. The performances, now in their thirtieth year, are famously idiosyncratic, sometimes with cuts and rearrangements, and with a Pippin translation into idiomatic English designed to present "the spirit of the work rather than word by word, with complete fidelity to the composer's musical intentions."[22]

The other anniversary production, by Florida's Sarasota company, was also put on with *Falstaff*, but sung in Italian, with an orchestra of forty-six and a chorus of twenty-four. The company then was in the midst of its cycle of all thirty-three of Verdi's operas, a count that includes original and revised versions,[23] and its theater (capacity 1,033), with good acoustics, small but adequate stage, and surtitles to provide a translation, was a good size for both operas. Victor DeRenzi, the artistic director, scheduled twelve performances of *Falstaff* and seven of *Oberto*. The latter, unlike the former, did not sell out, but they came close. And a sampling of audience opinion found two comments frequent: "It was better than I had expected," and "By the second act I was gripped."[24] The local music critics divided in their opinions.

John Fleming, for the *St. Petersburg Times*, was succinct:

Proposition: Not every opera by a genius needs to be revived.

Proof: *Oberto*, Verdi's first opera, which premiered in 1839 and now is receiving a rare production. For the most part, it is a primitive affair that could safely have been left in obscurity. . . .

Oberto does contain flashes of the brilliance to come, as in a first-act trio. . . . There are also flashes of the brilliance that came before Verdi, with music that owes a lot to Donizetti and Bellini.[25]

Similarly, Lawrence A. Johnson, for the *South Florida Sun-Sentinel* concluded: "The opera is surprisingly fertile in musical richness for a first attempt, with

Figure 13.4. Kevin Short, in the title role of the Sarasota Opera's production of *Oberto*, winter 2001. Photograph by Deb Hesser. Courtesy of the Sarasota Opera Company.

many duets and ensembles that approach Verdi's familiar rum-ti-tum mode. Unfortunately, *Oberto* is hobbled by an awesomely convoluted story."[26]

Conversely, Richard Storm, for the *Sarasota Herald-Tribune*, though starting cautiously soon burst into enthusiasm:

> One of the problems to be surmounted, particularly in the first act, is the lack of explanation for the actions of the characters, who appear more or less arbitrarily to declare their passions. . . . [But early in act 2, Oberto] challenges Riccardo to a duel.
>
> In a fascinating twist, Riccardo refuses to fight the old man.
>
> In act Two all of this begins to create real dramatic tension. Cuniza [the lady who succeeded Leonora in Riccardo's affections] resolves to give up Riccardo to Leonora, who still loves him despite everything. Oberto, a bit of a despot himself, plans to go ahead with the duel, despite advice to the contrary from nearly everyone on stage.
>
> When he calls Riccardo a coward, Riccardo is torn between shame and rage [the *Adagio* of the quartet][27] while Leonora is torn between her enduring love for Riccardo and her disgust for his actions. Cuniza, however, is no longer torn at all, convincing Riccardo to marry Leonora, assuming that Oberto will then abandon his revenge.
>
> But the old man, in turn, convinces Riccardo to feign agreement to the marriage [starting the *Allegro* of the quartet] while secretly agreeing to the

Figure 13.5. Victor DeRenzi, conductor of Sarasota Opera's *Oberto*, winter 2001. Photograph by Maria Lyle. Courtesy of the Sarasota Opera Company.

duel. The men fight offstage, and Riccardo returns alone, horrified at what he has done. . . .

So, after the creaky cardboard dramaturgy of the first act, we find the beginning of the themes that occupied the mature Verdi for the rest of his life: honor, family, doomed love.

Riccardo's apparently genuine remorse is a fascinating turn, one that brings the climax of the opera into strong focus. . . . [In] the music . . . there are stretches that resemble the style of Donizetti. But there are also wonderful moments that prefigure the mature mastery of later Verdi, particularly the father-daughter duets that expound on the nature of filial duty and love.[28]

Verdi's father-daughter duets are, as everyone knows, a continuing theme throughout his works, often inspiring some of the opera's best music. Beside *Oberto*, they occur in *Nabucco, Giovanna d'Arco, Luisa Miller, Stiffelio, Rigoletto, Simon Boccanegra,* and *Aida*. And a popular speculation of Verdi criticism and biography over the years has been that the powerful father-daughter relationship in his operas was founded, or at least greatly intensified, by the death of his daughter Virginia in August 1838, reinforced by his son's death in 1839, and his wife's in 1840.

Yet because of greater familiarity with *Oberto* and its history, the theory now seems less sure. For within the month after his daughter's death, Verdi was in Milan trying to persuade La Scala to stage *Oberto*, and the opera by then had been ready for production for at least a year. Thus, its intense father-daughter duet in act 1 was composed perhaps as much as a year or more before Virginia's death. It may be, therefore, that the basis for the strong father-daughter duets in so many of his operas lies not in his personal psychic trauma but merely in his strong sense of musical drama: a confrontation of characters with two voices that nicely contrast, soprano and baritone.[29]

Note that all those famous father-daughter duets are for soprano and baritone. And although the vocal score, most programs, and books list Oberto as a role for a bass, the opera has no baritone, and the general lie of Oberto's vocal line is high, much of it in baritone territory. This is why it seems fair to assert, as does this book, that the only title role Verdi composed for bass, true bass, was Attila.[30]

DeRenzi, Sarasota's artistic director, when asked where he ranked *Oberto* after conducting seven performances and rehearsals, concluded, "Not in the first or second rank of Verdi's operas; but as usual with his early works, it plays better onstage than it reads in the score. It's worth an occasional revival. Our audiences seemed to enjoy it, and it drew people from all across the country as well as from Europe."[31]

The next Verdi anniversary year is 2013, the bicentennial of his birth, and already around the United States *verdiani* are on watch for any hint of an *Oberto* production. Meanwhile, those who write in any detail about Verdi should recognize that many of his customary themes, such as honor, doomed love, and a father-daughter relationship began not with his third opera, *Nabucco*, but with his first, *Oberto*. And further, that what to many people is a triumph of his musical style and development—the integration of scene painting, recitative, aria, and action, as attempted in "Ciel, che feci!"—also starts in *Oberto*.

Chapter Fourteen

Un giorno di regno

Like Verdi's first opera, *Oberto*, his second, *Un giorno di regno* (King for a Day), was swept aside by the success of those that soon followed, *Nabucco, Lombardi,* and *Ernani*. But unlike *Oberto, Un giorno* did not enjoy even a moderate run. Rather, though a comedy with a happy ending, it gave him his worst night in the theater. At the premiere at La Scala, Milan, on September 5, 1840, as custom then required of a new opera's composer, he took his seat at the start in the orchestra, between the first double bass and cello, and there, because La Scala then had no orchestra pit (not until the 1907–8 season), he was at floor level in the auditorium, visible to everyone. And thus on view he had to sit throughout the performance while the audience hissed and booed most of the opera's musical numbers.

Most critics saw in the fiasco a chance for sarcasm; the reviewer for the *Figaro* saw deeper:

The near impossibility of finding nowadays a verse comedy which is not utterly insipid, the size of the theatre [capacity about 2,400] which ruins the effect of half-tones and light melodies and the lack of aptitude shown by present-day singers for the comic genre; all this makes it twice as difficult for a new score of this kind to succeed. Add to all this the special circumstances that Verdi was forced to clothe his latest work with gay music just at the time when a cruel and unexpected catastrophe [his wife's death] had struck him in the innermost part of his being, and it will be easily understood how in this his second venture he fell short of the expectations aroused by his first.[1]

La Scala at once canceled all further performances, and did not revive the opera until 2001, the centennial of Verdi's death. Meanwhile, in 1845 in Venice, a smaller house produced it with success, as the following year did one in Rome, and in 1859 one in Naples.[2] After that, *Un giorno* was all but forgotten, as everywhere companies of all sizes and competence hurried to mount later works such as *Ernani, Rigoletto, Trovatore,* and *Traviata*. Even in Italy, for more than a hundred years, it seems, no house staged *Un giorno*—until 1963, when Parma's Teatro Regio revived it to commemorate the 150th anniversary of Verdi's birth.[3]

Before then, however, another production of a different sort but greater importance for the opera had taken place. In 1951, the fiftieth anniversary of

Verdi's death, Italian radio had broadcast a cycle of Verdi's operas (all except *Alzira, Corsaro, Jérusalem,* and *Stiffelio*), and the Italian firm of Cetra began to issue many of these performances as commercial recordings. Of the operas least known at the time, the company offered *I Lombardi, La battaglia di Legnano,* and *Un giorno di regno,* and to the surprise of almost everyone *Un giorno* proved a "hit" of the series.[4] These Cetra recordings of Verdi's early operas, kept in print for many years, helped to nurture the Verdi Renaissance that bloomed in the United States during the second half of the century.

Verdi subtitled his opera "melodramma giocosa," meaning a story set with humor but not so continually comic as a *farsa* or *opera buffa,* or even a *commedia,* such as Rossini's *Il barbiere* (1816). The next year Rossini subtitled his version of the Cinderella story (*La Cenerentola*) "dramma giocoso"—and though that opera has many comic scenes it first is a love story with a happy ending. So, too, is Verdi's *Un giorno.* His immediate model was Donizetti's *L'elisir d'amore* (1832), another love story with comic scenes, yet *Un giorno* in its self-mockery (chiefly in asides to the audience) and in its buffo duets for male voices harks back also to early Rossini. Hence the *Figaro* critic's suggestion that the La Scala audience of 1840 found the opera, in style and story, old-fashioned.

It tells of a French military officer, Cavaliere di Belfiore, a charming playboy, who has agreed to impersonate his friend Stanislaus, the future king of Poland, while the latter secretly hurries from Paris to Warsaw to take the throne. In Belfiore's single day as king, during which he is a guest at the castle of Baron Kelbar, in Brittany, he does several good deeds, chiefly breaking the engagements of two French women to men they do not love and arranging for them to wed the men they do. The younger of the two, Giulietta, an ingénue, has been betrothed by her father, the Baron Kelbar (comic bass), to his elderly, rich friend, "the Treasurer" of Brittany (comic bass), whom Giulietta detests. She prefers, she adores the Treasurer's impecunious nephew, Edoardo (sweet-voiced tenor). The other woman, older and more crucial to the story, is the Baron's niece, a young widow, the Marchesa del Poggio (whose voice, though sharing the ingénue's range, must sound more mature). The Marchesa lives in Paris where she loves the Cavaliere di Belfiore (and he loves her), but despairing of bringing the playboy to the point of marriage, she has engaged to wed a nonentity, with the bond to be tied in the Baron's castle in the same ceremony as Giulietta's to the "Treasurer." And now, to the snobbish Baron Kelbar's intense pleasure, the double wedding will be graced by the presence of the future King of Poland, Stanislaus—except that unknown to the Baron or his guests the true Stanislaus is on his way to Warsaw. From Belfiore's charade in Brittany derives the opera's alternate title, *Il finto Stanislao,* or *The False Stanislaus.*

Both the Marchesa and Belfiore are astonished to see the other on this particular day in Brittany, and their meeting on the morning of the weddings produces in each a cascade of conflicting emotions. She recognizes him but pretends she does not, even as he, to preserve his masquerade, pretends not to know her. As they match wits and machinations, and as the "King" contrives to free Giulietta from the Treasurer to wed her beloved Edoardo, the plot's twists compound and are not always well explained.

For some of the confusions Verdi is responsible. Felice Romani (1788–1865), the librettist of *Norma* (1831) and of *L'elisir d'amore*, in 1818 had derived *Un giorno* from a French play for Adalbert Gyrowetz, whose opera had won a moderate success at La Scala. Since then the libretto had lain in the house archives, and when given to Verdi, twenty-two years later, he cut and rewrote much of it. His aim, as the scholar Roger Parker has shown, was "to involve the audience more directly in the dramatic events; to take away the sheen of objectivity so traditional in opera buffa; to concentrate on character rather than plot."[5] This emphasis on character rather than plot was one of Verdi's chief characteristics and runs steadily through all his operas, increasingly well handled. But in the case of *Un giorno*, though Romani, in 1840, was still Italy's leading librettist and living in not-too-distant Turin, Verdi did not consult him. Perhaps because he sensed, as John Black, an authority on librettists of this period, has remarked: "Romani never liked Verdi's music, presumably realizing—consciously or not—that Verdi's substitution of dramatic thrust for poetry as the stimulus for musical creativity undermined the whole ethos of his work."[6]

The United States premiere of Verdi's *Un giorno*—possibly the first time any of the opera's music was sung[7] in public in this country—took place in New York's Town Hall (capacity 1,495) on June 18, 1960. The Amato Opera Company[8] mounted the opera in a semistaged production and in an "English Adaptation," though with all the musical numbers presented in Verdi's order. The small orchestra, because Town Hall had no orchestra pit, was placed behind a low barrier onstage. Anthony Amato conducted.

The New York critics, hearing the opera in performance for the first time, divided in their opinions. To Francis D. Perkins of the *Herald Tribune*:

> It is far from being an unjustly neglected masterpiece. Still, it showed considerable vitality, and it was interesting to hear it for its illustration of Verdi's style at this early stage of his career. On the whole, it seemed more or less of a conventional early nineteenth-century opera buffa strongly influenced by Rossini and Donizetti. But there are times when the later and better known Verdi is foreshadowed by the style and treatment of the music, and in the melodies and the dramatic force of some of the arias.[9]

John Briggs of the *Times* was more enthusiastic:

> At this stage of his career Verdi was already sure-handed in working up a big ensemble. It is in fact striking to see how much of the essential Verdi already is present. . . . Throughout the score there are interesting hints of things to come in later operas. One of the most striking is the duet [for the two comic

basses] that precedes the first act finale. Here stated in somewhat tentative fashion but unmistakable all the same, is what would appear thirty-one years later as the Grand March from "Aida." Characteristically Verdian turns of phrase, harmonic idiosyncrasies and orchestral figurations abound. But, in addition to its interest as a foreshadowing of the mature Verdi, it is a fine bouncing score in itself. . . . It is to be hoped the work will not go back to the warehouse for another 120 years.[10]

Rather, it was shelved for twelve. Its next American production, May 31, 1972, was a concert performance, again at New York's Town Hall, offered by a group calling itself the Cosmopolitan Young People's Orchestra. Wrote *Times* critic Allen Hughes:

> Since Verdi's *Un giorno di regno* has much delightful music in it, the performance . . . was certainly welcome. . . . The story is a confusing and not very amusing affair . . . [and] libretto confusion for this performance was compounded by an English translation that had been jumbled by the printer into almost total senselessness. . . . The weak element [of the performance] was the orchestra of young people. They played diligently under Stephen Simon's direction, but they simply were not equal to the demands of the score. . . . Despite this, Mr. Simon managed to provide a spirited interpretation and make *Un giorno di regno* sound like a work we should consider hearing more often.[11]

Hughes stressed two problems that sometimes hinder revivals of the opera, especially when undertaken by small or student companies: the libretto's confusions and the difficulties of the score. A literal translation of the text, whether sung, inserted in the program, or flashed in supertitles, will not suffice. Romani's libretto (where not revised by Verdi) is appealingly poetic and not without humor. But written in 1818, it employs an archaic diction that even by 1840 was beginning to sound stilted. Today, to hold an American audience, the opera apparently is better sung in English, in a bold adaptation.

As for the difficulties of the score: if it is not to sound heavy-footed, the orchestra, of whatever size, must have skilled players. Many of the accompaniments to arias, for example, require the strings for long periods to skitter about at high speed, without blurring. The brass and woodwinds must be able to attack with assurance; and all instruments must keep rhythms and tempos clear and precise. Any slurring coarsens the music.

Casting the opera is also a problem, especially for small companies relying on young and inexperienced singers. The widowed Marchesa, for example, has no great vocal challenges, but she must sing with charm, often the last quality a young soprano acquires. Similarly, the two comic bass parts need older men for the musical antics; young men usually lack the necessary physical presence and the veterans' sense of timing.

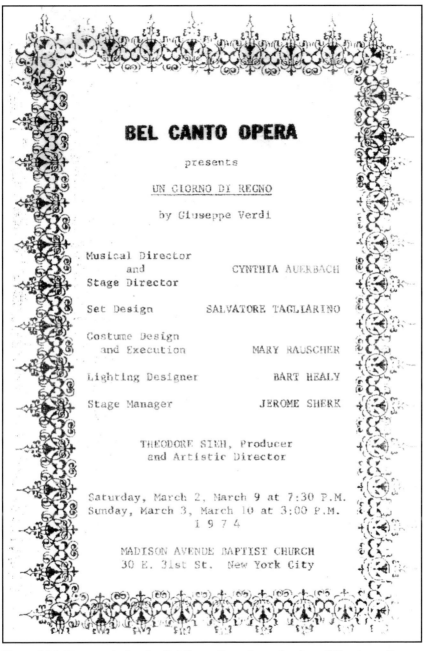

BEL CANTO OPERA

presents

UN GIORNO DI REGNO

by Giuseppe Verdi

Musical Director and Stage Director	CYNTHIA AUERBACH
Set Design	SALVATORE TAGLIARINO
Costume Design and Execution	MARY RAUSCHER
Lighting Designer	BART HEALY
Stage Manager	JEROME SHERK

THEODORE SIEH, Producer
and Artistic Director

Saturday, March 2, March 9 at 7:30 P.M.
Sunday, March 3, March 10 at 3:00 P.M.
1974

MADISON AVENUE BAPTIST CHURCH
30 E. 31st St. New York City

Figure 14.1. Program jacket for Bel Canto Opera's production of *Un giorno di regno*, 1974 (from author's collection).

In March 1974, one of the most enterprising of New York's thirty-five smaller opera companies, Bel Canto Opera, staged four performances of *Un giorno* in a church auditorium (capacity 150), surmounting only some of these problems. Benefiting from New York's extraordinary collection of talent, the company's artistic administrator claimed to have auditioned more than seven hundred singers for the opera and assembled an exceptional cast (including a chorus of five) as well as a rising musical and stage director. On the other hand, as was Bel Canto's custom, the opera was presented in its original language (with a synopsis in the program), and with only a piano accompaniment.[12] Thus, though well performed, Bel Canto's *Un giorno* most likely attracted or pleased only those who were fluent in Italian or had some special interest in the score or singers. Perhaps on average, a hundred people attended each of the four performances, providing an attentive, responsive audience. Critics, however, ignored the production, probably because the opera now was less rare than three others in Bel Canto's schedule for the year: Prokofiev's *La Duenna*, Paisiello's *Il barbiere di Siviglia*, and the American premiere of Saint-Saëns's *Henry VIII*. The *Times*, for example, reviewed the last two, but not *Un giorno*.[13]

In San Francisco, however, Donald Pippin's company—not yet incorporated as Pocket Opera—had a success when it staged a single performance of *King for a Day* (Un Giorno) on August 3, 1975. The occasion was one of Pippin's Sunday-night chamber concerts, the first in which he attempted a full-length opera, and the hall was the backroom (capacity 200–250) of a restaurant, the Old Spaghetti Factory, in North Beach. The singers were professionals, or "professionally trained," the sets were minimal, and the score used was a reduction for chamber orchestra prepared by Pippin: flute, clarinet, trumpet, violin, cello, and Pippin at the piano. The players billed themselves as the New Ravioli Philharmonic, a joke that belied their skills. Pippin provided his own adaptation of the libretto, introduced the opera by an amusing talk rather than by a synopsis in the program, and thereafter, as the opera progressed, often interjected explanations and comments.

The *Oakland Tribune*, in a review by Paul Hertelendy, reported:

Like the (unsuccessful) world premiere, this was a one-night stand, but it's engaging enough to warrant a few repeats. Pippin's translation is brilliant (and quite singable) in threats such as the King's "like a scruffy dirty sandal, I'll hang you on a peg!" A nubile beauty croons to her lover, "Let's Make Love, Not War," with all the coloratura emphasis on the word love. And the castle servants chorus, "We're the vassals of the castle, Oh, it's lucky to be a lackey."

Ultimately, it's no great opera, preceding as it does Verdi's first enduring piece *Nabucco*. The only distinctly Verdian traits are a finnesse [*sic*] in big ensembles and the repeated use of the familiar military canter rhythm (such as in "Di quella pira.") The rest draws on unornamented bel canto, a pronounced Donizettian simplicity, and some Rossinian touches in the bigger

Figure 14.2. Donald Pippin, artistic director of Pocket Opera, San Francisco. Photograph courtesy of Pocket Opera.

ensembles. . . . *King for a Day* is Verdi's Polish joke: not terribly funny, but it's to the point and fulfills its function.[14]

Arthur Bloomfield, for the San Francisco *Examiner*, also praised the adaptation: "Pippin gave lines like 'Enough, Brazen Hussy' an upper-case kind of attention which spotlighted their creaky pomposity. He also brought in refreshing contemporary-isms like 'no fuss, no hassle,' as good a way of translating 'non temer, non temer' as I can think of." And after commenting on Verdi's debt to Donizetti, Bloomfield added, "but there's still something peculiarly Verdian about some of *Giorno's* nervous rhythms and the soaring line he develops now and again in a big ensemble."[15]

Moreover, in the *San Francisco Chronicle*, Robert Commanday found other musical numbers to praise, particularly "one fetching lyric tenor aria" for Giulietta's simpleminded Edoardo to sing about his love for her. The tenor, after announcing to the castle servants (cast principals doubling the roles plus two choristers) that he would tell them of his love "in native tongue," sang in Italian (the only text un-Pippined), offering "Pietoso al lungo pianto," in "a pleasing light voice":

> The performance was tight, excellently paced and professional. Pippin's joking about the modest orchestra aside, the quintet plus Pippin played very well. His re-orchestration—was ingenious and fully self-sufficient—much rather that than a full band of well-meaning volunteer or pick-up players.
>
> And Pippin himself is at least half the show, resembling a puckish Wizard of Oz as he pumps away at the piano, his mouth working at the singers' words. Rarely performed anywhere, *Un Giorno di regno* a la Pippin could run for months if only a way could be found to keep it on the boards.[16]

The way was found by a group of Pippin's admirers who incorporated Pocket Opera, with Pippin artistic manager, and in 1978 the new company presented its first summer season, eight operas on successive Sunday nights in Pippin's adaptations. Of the eight, only two were sung twice that summer: *Così fan tutte* and *King for a Day*. A reviewer for the *Palo Alto Times* felt "much of the finest music in *Un Giorno* comes in its slow ensembles, which would not seem out of place in a more serious context. But there is also some skillful mock-Rossini, particularly the two "buffo" duets for the basses."[17] After this performance Verdi's ancient failure was so renowned in San Francisco that for its repeat, every seat in the Spaghetti Factory was taken an hour before curtain time, and so, because the artists were ready, the show began an hour early.[18]

Three years later, to open an expanded season at a slightly larger house, the On Broadway Theatre (capacity 395), Pocket Opera revived the opera again, this time with a libretto Pippin had polished further.[19] And again, success. After which Pippin performed his adaptation in 1983 (including a live

Figure 14.3. Judith Raddal (center) as Giuletta, Pocket Opera's 1992 production of *King for a Day*. Photograph by Bob Shomler. Courtesy of Pocket Opera.

radio broadcast), 1984, 1989, 1992, and 1999. Thus in San Francisco, for the twentieth-century's final quarter, *Un giorno di regno* became a repertory work.[20]

Meanwhile, other American companies mounted the opera with less success. On June 20, 1981, the San Diego company, as part of an annual Verdi festival,[21] was the country's first major company to try it in a large house, the city's Civic Theatre (capacity 2,945). Making use of a translation by the *New Yorker* critic Andrew Porter, it cast the opera with singers of national, and even international, reputation. But the West Coast's most outspoken critic, Martin Bernheimer of the *Los Angeles Times* (who sent an almost identical review to the English magazine *Opera*), wrote:

> It is a lousy opera. . . . Verdi just plodded along. He came up with simple-minded tunes and did very little with them. He never seemed sure whether he was writing serious music or comic music or caricature music. He settled for banalities, succumbed to empty repetitions and strained for humor.
>
> Much of *Un Giorno di Regno* is pretty, in a straight-forward, innocuous way. Little of it is original or compelling. It remains a trivial curio.
>
> In general, the staging was undeniably swift and fluid and reasonably clever. It also remained gratifyingly free of gimmickry. The cause, nevertheless, was a lost one. . . .
>
> Everyone articulated the graceful English translation with clarity and force.
>
> Still, the lasting impression of this temporary reign was devastatingly simple: little ado about little.[22]

Not everyone who saw the production agreed with Bernheimer,[23] but his voice was loud, twice-published, and, for many, persuasive.

In April and May 1983, in New York, another of the city's small companies, The Bronx Opera, using an adaptation in English gave the work four performances, two in the Bronx and two in Manhattan, the latter in the Hunter College Playhouse (capacity 624).[24] Tim Page, writing for the *Times*, thought the cast and conducting were good, but the orchestra "sounded ragged and often drowned out the vocalists." But he heard more in the music than Bernheimer: "Despite the score's occasional crudity, the music already has the elemental vitality that galvanizes Verdi's mature works."[25]

For ten years, except for Pocket Opera's periodic revivals, the opera rested in obscurity, and then Opera Theatre of Northern Virginia commissioned an English version, *King for a Day*, which to some extent rewrote the libretto, "re-Gallicized the Italianized French names of the characters" and "where possible" based changes on the original French play by Alexandre Duval. Musically, the company offered an orchestra of twenty-five (twelve strings), a piano in place of the score's harpsichord for recitative, and a chorus of twelve. The company's artistic director, John E. Niles, conducted.

Figure 14.4. New York Grand Opera production of *Un giorno di regno* in Central Park, New York, July 13, 1994. Ronald Naldi (Edoardo), Ingrid Zeldin (Giulietta). Photograph by Hal Tiné. Courtesy of New York Grand Opera Company.

The two performances, at the Thomas Jefferson Community Theatre in Arlington, went well. The critic for the *Washington Post*, Joseph McLellan, declared it "a neat little comic opera on the standard subject of people being saved from the wrong marriage." The music, he wrote, was "of high quality, and it shows a virtually unknown side of Verdi." He particularly liked the ensembles, some of the coloratura for the two sopranos, and the duet for the two elderly men, bass-baritones, which "inspired the loudest and most prolonged audience laughter." Moreover, "the orchestra had a strong presence without ever out-balancing the voices." The production "demonstrated" that the opera "is eminently stage-worthy, at least when it is sung in a good English translation."[26]

In contrast, the opera next appeared on July 13, 1994, in New York where Vincent La Selva's Grand Opera Company staged *Un giorno* in Central Park as the second work in his company's eight-year survey, in chronological order, of all Verdi operas. In this instance, however, much was certain to count against the opera: an untranslated text, a lack of surtitles, the open-air setting, and capricious amplification. Unhappily, in addition, the singers proved unequal in talent, and the staging, which might have suited a *farsa*, was too slapstick for a *dramma giocoso*. Allan Kozinn, for the *Times*, reported: "Mr. La Selva and his orchestra did honorably by the work, playing the cheerful, lightweight score with zesty enthusiasm. But it takes more than a solid orchestral performance to make a case for [the opera]. . . . The good news is that Mr. La Selva and his troupe now have *Un Giorno di Regno* behind them. Next Wednesday they move on to the firmer ground of *Nabucco*."[27]

Verdi himself, looking back after *Aida* and the *Requiem*, observed of *Nabucco*, "with this opera it is fair to say my artistic career began"—ignoring *Oberto* and *Un giorno di regno*.[28] Certainly, *Nabucco* is a long step forward. But most critics and scholars today more likely would start Verdi's artistic career with *Oberto*, and see in *Un giorno* not an aberration but a slight advance, if only in crafts-manship. The first work may have more moments of inspiration, but the second is better put together. Verdi scholar Julian Budden, for one, concludes: "In certain respects *Un Giorno di Regno* is an improvement on its predecessor. It contains fewer mistakes of musical grammar, fewer harmonic ineptitudes."[29]

Twenty years after the opera's failure at La Scala, Verdi wrote to a friend: "I haven't looked at *Un giorno di regno* since that time, and it may very well be a bad opera, and yet who knows how many others which are no better have been tolerated or perhaps even applauded."[30]

The opera's history in the United States, somewhat similar to that in Europe,[31] would seem to support a more favorable assessment. Though not a great or even good opera, it is more than "a trivial curio." Aside from interest as Verdi's only comedy other than *Falstaff*, it is "a fine bouncing score." If staged with care—a small theater (as the *Figaro* recommended in 1840); some cuts (chiefly of second verses); a vigorous English adaptation: charming singers and skillful instrumen-talists—*Un giorno*, as Pocket Opera in San Francisco and other companies have shown, can give back an enjoyable evening in the theater.

Chapter Fifteen

Giovanna d'Arco

Of all of Verdi's operas, admired or deplored, possibly none has drawn so many directly contradictory judgments as his seventh, *Giovanna d'Arco*, which had its premiere at La Scala, Milan, on February 15, 1845. Though the audience liked the opera (seventeen performances), the critics sniffed and implied in sum that Verdi was "relatively speaking, a beginner, that he was improving certainly, but that with their guidance he could improve still further."[1] Yet for twenty-five years *Giovanna d'Arco* had a steady success in Italy with productions elsewhere in Europe—a record disparagers often have slighted[2]—and today the disagreements among scholars, critics, and audiences continue, with opinions clashing over the libretto, the music, and the opera's rank among its fellows. In 1940, an English scholar, Dyneley Hussey, declared in a widely read study that the opera's libretto alone "makes it impossible to contemplate a modern revival of the piece."[3] Yet, beginning in 1951 revivals sprouted in Europe, even in England.

The success of many of these led some critics by the mid-1980s to claim that *Giovanna* is an opera of "brilliant patches,"[4] is "swift, shapely, and uncommonly compact,"[5] and one "whose neglect is unaccountable," at least as regards its music.[6] Yet, after a concert performance in New York in 1985, the critic for the *Times* declared: "Even the stoutest partisans of Verdi's early operas do not claim much for *Giovanna d'Arco*, his dramatically naïve and musically crude version of the Joan of Arc story. Most commentators blame the librettist, Temistocle Solera for the work's faults, but that is a little unfair . . . [it] is little more than a contest for three solo voices, a singers' opera of the most blatant sort . . . [and it] is the sort of opera in which the heroine dies in the last act, is brought back in a vision for her final number, then dies again."[7]

Because the complaint of a twice-over death seems a bit unfair, let us begin with Joan's demise, which poses for many people today what they consider to be the opera's greatest blunder: Joan is not tried by French clerics for heresy, convicted, and turned over to English soldiers, and is not burned at the stake. Instead, leading the French to victory in an offstage battle, she is fatally wounded, brought onstage on a litter, revives among friends, and sees the heavens open to reveal the Virgin "who used to speak to me. . . . A golden cloud raises me. . . . Farewell, earth! Farewell, mortal glory. . . . I lift up. . . . Already I glow in the sun!" In Friedrich Schiller's play, *The Maid of Orleans* (1801), on which Temistocle Solera (despite his denials)[8] based his libretto, Joan's final words are: "Light clouds bear me up . . . my heavy armor has become winged raiment. Upwards . . . upwards. . . . Earth is rushing back. Brief is the pain, and joy is everlasting." Verdi's stage direction reads: "She falls; a starry light spreads across the sky. The soldiers lower their flags, and all kneel before her corpse now clothed in glory." Or as managed (with wires) in a 1989 production in England, singing her final bars she floats to heaven.[9]

In the first half of the nineteenth century, when Schiller wrote and Verdi composed, most people knew little about the historical Joan or any details of her trial for heresy. Scholarly research was still meager, and in the literature of the day Schiller's version of Joan's story was a significant account.[10] What concerned most people then, and many today, was her legend: the illiterate, eighteen-year-old farm girl, who in response to mystic voices led French troops to rout the besieging English at Orléans (1429) and opened the way for the Dauphin to be crowned King of France in Rheims Cathedral, both crucial events of the Hundred Years' War. But in the 1840s, she was not yet the patron saint of France, and would not become St. Joan for another eighty years, beatified in 1909 and canonized in 1920. Though a popular heroine in the nineteenth century, she was still to the Church a heretic, and when the opera played in Rome, Palermo, and some other cities, the music was fitted to a different story and the opera titled *Orietta di Lesbo*.[11] In that era, Schiller and Verdi's unhistoric but symbolic treatment of her legend, ending in triumph, perhaps was not so jarring, and in her elevation to heaven, both popular and prophetic.

What they added to her story was a conflict for Joan between her heaven-blessed mission to rescue France and human feelings of love for another person. In Schiller she feels her first hint of love for an English soldier, and in Solera-Verdi, for the Dauphin who, on being crowned, becomes Charles VII; and in both works by momentarily giving way to her feelings she breaks her agreement with her mystic voices: to have their aid in battle she must abjure human love. By wavering, she learns how much she has forsworn, then staunchly resumes her mission.

For most of the twentieth century Bernard Shaw's play *St. Joan* (1923), with its preface discussing the trial for heresy and what Shaw calls her "unconscious Protestantism," has shaped the modern view of Joan. In the preface he states:

> It is hardly surprising that she was judicially burnt, ostensibly for a number of capital crimes which we no longer punish as such, but essentially for what we call unwomanly and insufferable presumption. At eighteen Joan's pretensions were beyond those of the proudest Pope or the haughtiest emperor. She claimed to be the ambassador and plenipotentiary of God, and to be, in effect, a member of the Church Triumphant whilst still in the flesh on earth. She patronized her own king . . . pooh-poohed the plans of generals, leading their troops to victory on plans of her own. . . . As her actual condition was pure upstart, there were only two opinions about her. One was that she was miraculous: the other that she was unbearable.[12]

In the play's Epilogue, Shaw concludes that she was both, but the latter determined her fate: The world is not yet ready to receive God's saints. Neither Schiller nor Verdi touch on Joan's presumption; for them, she is the miraculous Warrior Maid who with Heaven's blessing rallied the French against the English.

The opera is the third of Verdi's four large-scale choral operas to librettos by Solera, following *Nabucco* and *I Lombardi* and preceding *Attila*. In *Giovanna* there are choruses for the Dauphin's courtiers, for the peasants of Joan's farm town, Domrémy, for the voices that only Joan (and the audience) hears— angelic voices from Heaven and of demonic tempters from Hell—for soldiers of the English army, for the crowds outside the cathedral of Rheims, for the Grand Triumphal March at the Dauphin's coronation, and for the crowds gathered to sing a funeral march for Joan. Despite several scenes of simplicity and innocence for Joan, the opera's settings can be as large and spectacular as the production can afford. But on what succeeds musically there is always disagreement. Charles Osborne, in his *Complete Operas of Verdi* (1970), claimed that the last half of the final act "is simply superb," whereas two generations earlier, Francis Toye, in his *Verdi and his Works* (1931), declared that "speaking generally, *Giovanna d'Arco* steadily deteriorates."[13] A critic for the *New York Times* wrote in 1966, "There are arias and set pieces, and the best models are followed, but never is there a flash of the Verdian genius," whereas ten years later one for the *New Yorker* countered: "Every number in the score is filled with life, with feeling. There is no fluently mechanical writing along approved models for easy effect."[14]

Faced with such critical disarray, what are the unopinionated to think? If productions of *Giovanna* were frequent in the United States, we could judge for ourselves, but as they are rare, we lack the opportunity. In the nineteenth century only a few excerpts from the opera were heard, and a full performance did not occur until 1966, done in concert in New York. In all, in the United States, the opera has had only nine productions, five staged, four in concert, and seven of the nine in New York. No doubt, for companies contemplating the opera, all those choruses, costumes, and parades, if fully staged, can be daunting, and also the need for a charismatic soprano, for Joan's voice is the only solo female voice in the opera. Meanwhile there are better and easier operas of Verdi to present.

The first soprano to sing the role, in Milan in 1845, was Erminia Frezzolini, who apparently when young was extraordinary. One admirer wrote: "She was dark; her great liquid eyes, shadowed by long black lashes, exhaled magnetic influences, in which passion melted into love."[15] Another recalled: "At the grand scene of the coronation, she appeared to me like a vision from paradise, in the white costume of a warrior, with the standard of fleur-de-lys which she pressed to her breast."[16] Musically, her voice was exceptional for its even, flexible legato, to which she could add power and brilliance.[17] In her generation, 1840–60, she reigned as Joan. Then, in 1865, Verdi recommended the opera to Teresa Stolz, his future Aida, and at La Scala she made it the hit of the season—seventeen performances, the most that year of any opera.[18] Thereafter *Giovanna* languished until 1951, when Renata Tebaldi carried it from Naples, to Milan (a studio, recorded broadcast) and then to the Paris Opéra, a tour that led to further revivals in England and Europe.[19]

In the United States, the opera's history begins in New York on January 7, 1847, at a farewell concert for the French pianist Henri Herz.[20] Presented in the Tabernacle, on Broadway, the concert preceded by two months the first staging in the country of any Verdi opera (*I Lombardi* at New York's Palmo's Opera House, March 3), and of his music at that time, New Yorkers had heard only an aria from *I Lombardi* and one from *Ernani*. The concert's impresario, Bernard Ullman, surrounded his star with a host of assisting artists, six singers, an operatic chorus, several instrumentalists, and fifteen additional pianists to join Herz in an eight-piano version of Rossini's *William Tell* Overture. Of the singers, all members of a recently formed opera troupe, one was a nineteen-year-old soprano, Clotilda Barili,[21] who with others first sang the "conversion" trio from *I Lombardi* and then alone introduced "a *cavatina* from Verdi's *Giovanna d'Arco*" (presumably Joan's entrance aria, "Sempre all'alba ed alla sera" [Always at dawn and in the evening . . . I pray to you]).[22] With interest focused on Herz, no critic bothered to comment on the Verdi excerpts, and one member of the audience, the lawyer George Templeton Strong, complained of the singers in his diary: "Why *will* they restrict themselves to Verdi, Donizetti, Mercadante, and the like?"[23] He wanted Mozart or Handel.

Nothing more from the opera seems to have been heard until another concert in New York, at Tripler Hall on December 14, 1850, when a currently popular soprano, Teresa Parodi, sang Giovanna's *romanza* of nostalgia for her village, "O fatidica foresta" (Oh, prophetic forest . . . give back the happiness I long for). Again, no critic mentioned the *romanza*, and the audience did not demand an immediate repeat, which it did for Rossini's aria from *Tancredi*, "Di tanti palpiti." At her concert the following week, Parodi dropped the Verdi but sang the Rossini.[24]

Two years later, a reputable but minor soprano, Elisa Biscaccianti, in the eighth of a series of ten concerts in San Francisco, sang Giovanna's cavatina to applause, though not enough to lead her to reschedule the aria in either of two successive concerts. On the other hand, when she sang Bellini's finale to *Sonnambula*, "Ah, non giunge," she immediately had to repeat it twice.[25] Then Frezzolini, coming to New York in 1857, at a joint concert with other artists sang Joan's *romanza*. But despite her fame as the first Joan, she did not have a great success with it.[26] Apparently, Joan's music, when taken out of context, could not stir interest in the opera.

Yet it was not forgotten. Francis Scala, the leader of the U.S. Marine Band, in 1855 made an arrangement for the band of the tenor's entrance aria from its prologue ("Sotto una quercia" [Beneath an oak . . . I seemed to see the Virgin summon me]), and in 1859 he made another of a chorus and trio, perhaps the prologue's finale. He also had in the band's library an arrangement of the opera's overture.[27] During Scala's years with the band (1842–71), from spring to fall it gave weekly Saturday evening concerts, open to the public, on the South Lawn of the White House. Presumably he scheduled these pieces at least once, although as yet dates are undiscovered.[28] The opera's overture, however, made a startling appearance on the inaugural night of opera at the new Brooklyn Academy of Music on January 22, 1861.

The occasion, according to the *Times*, citing a "competent Brooklyn authority," was "the greatest social event of the Nineteenth Century." The just completed Academy (1861–1903), midblock on the south side of Montague Street between Court and Clinton, was a splendid opera house, seating 2,200, and with 12 proscenium boxes, a parquet, dress circle, balcony, and amphitheater (top gallery). The interior was essentially gothic with moorish coloring, featuring bright reds and yellows. The drop curtain portrayed a Temple of Apollo, "in different parts of which are the statues of the four Muses, Melpomene [tragedy], Euterpe [flute playing], Thalia [comedy], and Erato [the lyre]. . . . In the centre is a colossal statue of Apollo, to whom from every corner run men, women, and children, bearing in their arms the votive offerings of humanity to the god of music."[29] And in the audience that night, to grace the Academy's inaugural night of opera, was the wife of the president-elect, Mrs. Lincoln.[30]

The opera company, an experienced troupe calling itself the "Associated Artists" and led by Emanuele Muzio, had scheduled *La traviata* for the opera opening, but as the *Times* explained: "One of the directors of the Academy having become exercised concerning the morality of that performance made such representations to the troupe that they have, greatly to the regret of many who have admired [Pauline] Colson in *La Traviata*, substituted *Il Giuramento*."[31] Hence the honor of inaugurating the new opera house passed to Mercadante.

Except that Muzio, Verdi's friend, only student, and passionate admirer, preceded the opera with a performance of an unscheduled overture. This work, noted the *Times*, "which by the way was an introduction from another opera, *Joana* [*sic*] *d'Arco*, was extraordinarily rendered and much applauded."[32] Thus from the grand occasion Muzio saved a sprig of laurel for Verdi.

Possibly Muzio and his orchestra played the overture on other occasions, though none have been discovered. But the country's leading bandmaster, Patrick S. Gilmore, in the summer of 1875, played an arrangement of it for his wind band with brass in his concerts given at the Hippodrome, or, as he had redecorated it for the summer, Gilmore's Garden. As the season counted 150 consecutive concerts, it seems likely that he repeated it that year and in similar seasons in his Garden in 1876 and 1877.[33] But apparently for about twenty years thereafter no other conductor or company followed his lead, and in the United States the opera even in excerpt was in danger of disappearing. In 1870 a catalogue of sheet music for sale by the country's leading music publishers listed only one aria, "Sempre all'alba ed alla sera," and two undescribed instrumental numbers.[34] Standard opera guides of the late nineteenth century did not mention it or even list it as one of Verdi's early operas, and in the early years of American recordings, roughly 1895–1920, when opera arias and overtures were extremely popular, no artist or orchestra recorded an excerpt.[35]

In 1894, however, John Philip Sousa and his band (sometimes described as a "wind symphony," typically with thirty woodwinds, thirty brass, and three percussion) played an arrangement of the overture, and in the years 1895–1928 revived it in ten seasons, and possibly his success with it encouraged conductors at the Metropolitan Opera's Sunday Concerts to become more adventurous. During World War I, perhaps in part because of prejudice against German music, they frequently had scheduled the overtures to *La forza del destino* and *I vespri siciliani*, and to these Giuseppe Bamboschek in 1920 added the overtures to *La battaglia di Legnano* and *Nabucco*. In 1924, he offered the overture to *Giovanna d'Arco*, which he played again in 1929, as also did conductor Wilfred Pelletier, in 1931.[36]

Then in 1953, in the tradition of Gilmore and Sousa, the Goldman Band, founded and led by Edwin Franko Goldman, in its annual series of some fifty outdoor summer concerts in New York City's parks, played the overture in four concerts, and the following year, in six. Goldman died in 1956, but his son, Richard Franko, who had been his father's associate since 1937, succeeded him, and in 1961 scheduled the overture for three concerts, and the next year, for two; meanwhile, however, he had recommended it to others in his book, *The Band's Music* (1938), and named two music publishers who offered arrangements of it. Hence, it seems possible, perhaps likely, that other bands, too, on occasion played the overture.[37]

Perhaps these slight yet recurring flurries of attention contributed to an emerging opinion, stirred by the Verdi Renaissance, that the overture was one of Verdi's better efforts, and at least one critic has ranked it third, after those to *La forza* and *I vespri siciliani*, though others might propose instead the overture to *Luisa Miller*.[38] The *Giovanna* piece, which runs about eight and a half minutes, has three movements. The first, which is brief, begins softly and builds steadily to crashing, fateful, but rather indeterminate chords, a sort of "once upon a time." The second, the work's gem, is an *andante pastorale* and to be played, by Verdi's direction, *con semplicità*. Introduced by a cadenza for flute, whose sound follows Joan throughout the opera, it presents her as she was in Domrémy and features a flute, clarinet, and oboe, each sounding at first alone and then weaving together in variations on their simple but charming tune. The final movement is all bustle, and marches: Joan the Warrior at the French court where she grows confused and momentarily loses her way. The opera has been described as the portrait of a country girl carried "out of her depth in the Court,"[39] and the overture suggests this theme without revealing its resolution.

A concert group, the American Opera Society, gave *Giovanna* its U.S. premiere on March 1, 1966, in a performance in New York at Carnegie Hall (capacity 2,784). Harold Schonberg, the *Times* critic, scorned the opera but praised the performers:

> Having to listen to *Giovanna d'Arco* in cold blood is a rather pulverizing experience. . . . It is organ grinder music, as often as not, and there is one unforgettable moment where the organ actually goes oom-pah-pah [the demonic voices]. . . . It is possible that *Giovanna d'Arco* can be regarded as a period piece. Let's be kind and do so. The libretto, by the way, looks history in the eye and makes it back down. It deals with Joan of Arc as seen through the eyes of Temistocle Solera. Never a great librettist at best, he outdid himself here. . . . The performance was tidy, and contained two superb characterizations. Teresa Stratas was the Giovanna. She sang with a good deal of personality, with plenty of temperament and some lovely phrasings. . . . Also extremely effective was Sherrill Milnes [Joan's father Giacomo] . . . a really strong baritone, with a secure voice of considerable amplitude, and with a good deal of style.[40]

Harriet Johnson for the *Post* was more enthusiastic than Schonberg about the opera's music, hearing some hints of genius in "the beginning of the Overture, Joan's cavatina, and the duet between Joan and Charles in act 1, and the duet between Joan and her father, Giacomo, in act II." Like Schonberg, she was impressed by Stratas, "though in her most dramatic moments, she forced to the point where her voice lost its beauty and became hard. These places fortunately were few. . . . The young artist is small in size with a mighty temperament, and she used her dramatic gifts to the benefit of Verdi's melodies."[41]

But as so often with this opera, nothing is stated but soon rebutted, and in a review for *Opera*, John Ardoin reported: "The title-role was taken by Teresa Stratas, who made all manner of modification in the part and still sounded mightily uncomfortable. Sherrill Milnes as Joan's father was surprisingly wooden in all respects." And he dismissed the opera as "minor-league Verdi. The libretto is dramatically limp and the music noticeably lacking in back-bone."[42]

With the opera so faintly praised, for another ten years no American company touched it, and equally remarkable in that decade, despite the worldwide revival of interest in Verdi's early operas, only one of the world's leading sopranos, Renata Tebaldi, chose to record either Joan's cavatina or her *romanza*. Amid rarities plucked from such unfamiliar works as *Un giorno di regno*, *Alzira*, *I masnadieri*, and *Il corsaro*, the slighting of *Giovanna*, a title role for sopranos, was startling. As a hundred years earlier, sopranos apparently were not drawn to the music—perhaps for a reason. Both arias lack a brilliant close for the soloist. In the cavatina "sempre all'alba," which Tebaldi favored, after Giovanna prays to the Virgin for a sword, she falls asleep, precluding the usual change of mood and fast aria or even a coda. And the *romanza* of nostalgia, "O fatidica foresta," ends by turning into a duet with the tenor. Of the sixteen "early" operas preceding *Rigoletto*, the only one whose soprano arias were left wholly unexplored was *Oberto*, a fate *Giovanna d'Arco* only just escaped.[43]

Meanwhile, in June 1973, Angel issued the opera's first (and probably still most widely distributed) commercial recording, giving most people their first chance to hear the opera. The cast was glittering, Caballé, Domingo, and Milnes, and the conductor, making his recording debut, James Levine. The critics were hesitant in their praise, and as the years passed, as ever more pirated recordings from live performances became available, it became clear that the Angel recording was far from ideal. The reason, as Andrew Porter suggested in his review, perhaps lay in the conditions of its making. It was rushed, made in ten days. None of the singers had performed the opera onstage, Levine had not conducted it in an opera house, and as the Angel company itself confessed: "There was no resemblance between the sequence of items as they follow each other in the score and their order in the recording plans." The result was a strangely undramatic performance, as the singers and conductor seemed to feel their way into the music, and the opera's scenes did not gather momentum. Levine, in particular, was scolded for his "vulgarity"; a more experienced conductor would have refined the "tawdry" passages, not emphasized them.[44] Nevertheless, the recording drew attention to the opera, and critics, in reviewing other performances, for a time deferentially referred to it.[45]

The opera's U.S. stage premiere took place in Brooklyn on May 15, 1976, at the Academy of Music (capacity 2,121) built in 1908 to replace the old Academy that had burned in 1903. The company was the New York Grand Opera, led by Vincent La Selva, who scheduled three performances. Apparently, because the Giovanna had a cold or some other indisposition on the night of the premiere, much depended on which of the three performances the critic heard. John Rockwell, reviewing the premiere for the *Times*, declared that except for La Selva's conducting the "performance was pretty much a ludicrous travesty." The sets and staging were "just embarrassing," and none of the three principals was "up to the task." In the *Post*, Speight Jenkins (not yet the impresario of the Seattle Opera), though kinder in expression, agreed but rejoiced in the work of La Selva and the orchestra and the opportunity to hear "the blessedly uncut performance."[46]

A month later Andrew Porter wrote in the *New Yorker:* "The first performances were said to be rough. By the third, which I attended, everything conspired to produce a rousing event in which any critical reservations were swept away by the energy and excitement that such music generates when it is executed with spirit. Pyramid Sellers, in the title role, sang with feeling, with force, and with some delicacy. . . . And the Brooklyn Academy itself—New York's only public opera house built on a human scale—played its part in creating

Program
Saturday, May 15, 1976 (8:00pm)/Opera House
Sunday, May 16, 1976 (2:00pm)/Opera House
Friday, May 21, 1976 (8:00pm)/Opera House

Vincent LaSelva
Artistic Director, Conducting

Giuseppe Verdi's

Giovanna d'Arco

Giovanna	Pyramid Sellers
Carlo	Aristides Inchaustegui
Giacomo	Michael Andoor
	(May 15, 16)
	Theodore Lambrinos
	(May 21)
Delil	David Sher
Talbot	James Fleetwood

New York Grand Opera Orchestra
New York Grand Opera Chorus
and Young People's Chorus

Stage Director	Martin Platt
Production Design	Dean Tshetter

These performances are made possible with public funds from the New York State Council on the Arts.

Figure 15.1. Program's title page for the U.S. premiere of *Giovanna d'Arco,* a premiere which at the time the producing company modestly did not claim. Photograph courtesy of the New York Grand Opera Company.

the sort of occasion recorded by the nineteenth-century critics: when a Verdi opera '*muove all'orgasmo pubblico.*'"[47] So, depending on the performance and the critic, a disaster or a triumph.

But not without influence. In the spring of 1978 a recently formed group, Boston Concert Opera, gave the opera its Boston premiere in a single concert performance in New England Life Hall. The artistic director and conductor was David Stockton; the Giovanna, Pamela Hebert; the orchestra, composed of professionals; the chorus, of amateurs; and beyond these facts the performance remains elusive, though regularly listed in the group's publications. Apparently, despite being a Boston premiere no journal reviewed it; the group's archives—Boston Concert Opera died in 1989—have gone missing; and memories, even of the conductor and of a chorus member, have dimmed. Nevertheless, all agree that the performance took place.[48]

Two years later, the San Diego Opera, in the fifth year of its summer Verdi festival and aiming to produce all of his operas, staged *Giovanna* for three performances, with the Italian soprano Adriana Maliponte as Joan and Edoardo Mueller conducting. The local critics wobbled in their views. For Donald Dierks at the *San Diego Union*: The opera "was never more than merely interesting. . . . Actually, it was more than solely instructive. The performance had its beautiful moments." For Andrea Herman in the *Tribune*: The opera "chugs away like a slow locomotive—not being very exciting or particularly inspiring. . . . On the bright side, some stunning dramatic impact was punctuated in act II, Scene 2, inside the cathedral. Giacomo stepped forward and accused his daughter Giovanna of witchcraft, and the ensemble released rich and bold sounds."[49] They disagreed on the soprano: Dierks liked her, Herman did not. A third critic, for the *Los Angeles Times*, temporized: "Her singing often rose to Verdi's demands with power and authority. The voice is big and supple enough to fall in the dramatic soprano category, and while it could not always manage climactic tones without stress and a touch of harshness, it compensated by lyrical singing that floated exquisite pianissimos and frequently conveyed strong emotional impulse."[50]

As for the conductor, Mueller, though generally praised, he perhaps was not praised enough. A noncommercial recording of the second performance suggests that he was a major part of the production's success. He had a light touch, good tempos, infused repeating accompaniments with spirit and bounce, and shaped the scenes dramatically. In performances where most of the audience, hearing the opera for the first time, no doubt thought the libretto a travesty of history, he yet was able to draw them into the musical drama. Every critic lamented the libretto, yet one allowed a word of praise: "It does make a strong statement regarding inner struggle between what the heroine believes to be divine guidance and the realities of mortal existence."[51] And Mueller, like La Selva, was able to close the opera in a mood of exaltation and poignant triumph.[52]

But as Dierks in the *Union* prophesied, "It is not likely that other companies around the country will follow San Diego's lead by producing *Giovanna d'Arco* now that the ice has been broken." Yet he was only partly right. Seven years after La Selva premiered the opera, he returned to it on July 27, 1983, in New York's Central Park. The critic for the *Times*, Edward Rothstein, was enthusiastic:

> Though outdoor performances of opera ordinarily eliminate opportunities for subtlety and suppleness. . . . La Selva at the Central Park Bandshell on Wednesday night did just the opposite. . . . [His] dramatic understanding of the work allowed its broadest gestures to be clearly understood. The simple staged action . . . created a series of effective and sometimes affecting tableaux . . . the music, even at first hearing has a forthright physical energy . . . [and at Joan's death, Juliana] Gondek's control over her lines and Mr. La Selva's supple articulation of the score gave the scene a taut energy. . . . The performance ended at nearly 11 P.M., but much of the audience stayed until the very end, unconcerned by the surrounding darkness of the park, absorbed in the unfolding drama.[53]

Meanwhile, far to the south, in Baton Rouge, Louisiana, a city more known for political than cultural interests, a fledgling company, as its second foray into opera, announced for November 1983 a production of *Giovanna* in English. What drew these gallant souls to such a venture? Even New Orleans, with its long interest in opera, especially French opera, had never staged *Giovanna*, and though the city has in its French Quarter a gilded statue of the Maid, it has no street named for her and does not celebrate her saint's day. Not surprisingly, many people read the announcement of the three staged performances in English with amazement. The critic for the New Orleans *Daily Times-Picayune*, Frank Gagnard, began his review:

> Duty and curiosity pulled one to Baton Rouge's Centroplex Theater last week, rather than any conviction that the Baton Rouge Opera had gained weight and responsibility so soon after entering the world with a threadbare *Aida* last fall. This is not the most buoyant attitude to pack for the opera. But damned if the company didn't mount a dandy show—and with a sickly product to begin with. . . . Designer Donald Dorr kept the scenic elements to a minimum, most of them relevant, and provided at least one memorable stage image: In a handsome tableau behind a scrim upstage, Charles VII was crowned king of France, attended by a banner-toting Joan of Arc, while her father brooded downstage over his decision to denounce Joan as a witch.

Gagnard went on to recite some old opinions about the opera's many faults, countering them with some more modern that praised it. He himself thought the angelic and demonic voices were ridiculous:

Figure 15.2. Edward Perretti (Carlo) and Juliana Gondek (Giovanna) in the New York Grand Opera Company's 1983 production. Photograph by John F. Mahoney Jr. Courtesy of the New York Grand Opera Company.

One ensemble represents, in the jolliest peasant-song lilt, the "seductive" call of demons to a life of pleasure and being pretty. From the opposite side of the wings comes an angelic, harp-supported plea to renounce earthly things. Unfortunately, eternal salvation is depicted in mournful musical measure. Verdi seems to be saying that Joan was indeed schizophrenic, with good reason to be depressed considering dreary alternatives.

Nevertheless, though Gagnard expressed no great love for any of Verdi's early operas, he ranked *Giovanna* high among those he knew.

[It] provided livelier satisfactions, for this listener, than *I Lombardi* in toto, all of *Nabucco* save the celebrated Hebrews' Chorus, and much of the strangely persistent *Ernani*. Even the later *Luisa Miller*, another mysterious Verdi hanger-on, is inferior in its total impact and its parts. *Macbeth* gets silly, too. Perhaps the opera's fatal flaw is that it is ostensibly about Joan of Arc.[54]

Meanwhile in Europe, with the Verdi Renaissance still strong, the number of productions continued to increase. And then, in New York, the only city in the United States to show a continuing interest in *Giovanna*, in 1985 the opera reappeared in a concert performance at Avery Fisher Hall (previously Philharmonic

Avery Fisher Hall

Home of the New York Philharmonic
Lincoln Center for the Performing Arts

Sunday Evening, October 27, 1985, at 7:30

FIRST CONCERT: OPERA-IN-CONCERT

GREAT PERFORMERS AT LINCOLN CENTER
Sponsored by AT&T
presents

GIUSEPPE VERDI

Giovanna d'Arco

("Joan of Arc")

Lyric Drama, in a Prologue and Three Acts

Libretto by Temistocle Solera

Orchestra of St. Luke's and
New York Choral Artists
Richard Bradshaw, *Conductor*

Cast of Characters:

Carlo VII, King of France	Carlo Bergonzi
Giacomo, A Shepherd of Domremy	Sherrill Milnes
Giovanna, His Daughter	Margaret Price
Delil, An Officer of the King	Rick Christman
Talbot, Supreme Commander of the English	Henry Runey

Chorus of Angels, Demons, Villagers, Officers, Sentries, and Soldiers

Orchestra of St. Luke's, Michael Feldman, *Artistic Director*
New York Choral Artists, Joseph Flummerfelt, *Director*

Musical Preparation by Martin Smith

There will be one intermission after Act 1.

This performance by arrangement with
Associated Music Publishers, Inc., U.S. agent for G. Ricordi & Co., Milan.

Series Director for Lincoln Center: William W. Lockwood, Jr.
Associate: Frederick Noonan

Great Performers at Lincoln Center is presented
with the assistance of the New York State Council on the Arts, and the National Endowment for the Arts.

Please make certain the electronic signal on your watch or pager is switched off during the concert.

In consideration of the performing artists and members of the audience, those who must leave before the end of the performance are asked to do so between numbers, not during the performance.
The taking of photographs and the use of recording equipment are not allowed in this building.

Figure 15.3. Program for Avery Fisher Hall concert performance, 1985 (from author's collection).

Hall). Ostensibly organized by Lincoln Center to display the Welsh soprano Margaret Price, who had been touring European houses as Joan, she was backed by Carlo Bergonzi as the Dauphin, Sherrill Milnes as her father, and Richard Bradshaw as conductor. For the *Times*, Donal Henahan deplored the opera and even dared to criticize the visiting diva: "hers is not the warmest or most expressively used soprano—the highest tones tend to be cool in an instrumental style. . . . Never mind. The audience at this performance knew why it had come, and it was not to experience a gripping music drama. It came to hear three important voices in full, early Verdian cry. The ovations would have been as great if Miss Price, Mr. Bergonzi and Mr. Milnes had come out and sung selected pages from the Rome telephone book."[55]

Yet, the evening was disappointing. The ovations might have been still greater if the singers and conductor had worked harder on the opera's drama. Andrew Porter, reviewing the performance, noted that "Milnes sang loudly," and ended an aria, which Verdi directed "should close with a *pianissimo* F sharp on the staff, not a bellowed one an octave higher." Then he added, "Few baritones are prepared to trust Verdi and try for the excitement of very soft, charged, intense singing of vigorous passages—an effect he often called for and counted on—with volume held in reserve for the opening-out moments." In addition, he noted that the opera, one of Verdi's shortest, "was cruelly abridged." Though its music runs only about two hours, Verdi composed it as a prologue and three acts, undoubtedly expecting at least two if not three intermissions. But this performance offered two long acts with one intermission, making large cuts in the two *finales* that no longer ended an act. Porter concluded that though "a shortened version may sometimes be preferable to an underrehearsed full one . . . extensive cuts in a high-priced, metropolitan performance of a rare Verdi opera are unacceptable."[56]

For ten years thereafter *Giovanna* was not heard in the United States, while in Europe, revivals continued to bloom in houses big and small, with celebrity sopranos and unknowns. Then, on August 2, 1995, La Selva and his New York Grand Opera again revived it. The company was now in the second season of its seven-year cycle offering free to the public in Central Park all of Verdi's operas in chronological order. It was La Selva's third staging of *Giovanna*, and before his first, in the Brooklyn Academy of Music in 1976, he had told a reporter: the opera "is interesting stylistically because it looks back to a work like *Nabucco*, yet foreshadows the great works to come," and, most important, "it is full of beautiful music." Twenty-eight years later, he confessed, "I still have a soft spot in my heart for Joan," insisting "You don't have to have a Tebaldi for the role. If the soprano will trust the emotions that Verdi wrote, she'll have a success."[57]

The only paper to send a critic to Central Park was the *Post*, and Dale Harris wrote: "An uneven work, *Giovanna d'Arco* is nevertheless full of interest, especially for lovers of Verdi. The final ensemble is truly stirring. It was here, in fact, that the evening took fire." Though playing as always under poor conditions,

CARNEGIE HALL

1995–96 SEASON

Wednesday Evening, May 8, 1996, at 8:00

OPERA ORCHESTRA
OF NEW YORK

Eve Queler, *Music Director*

GIUSEPPE VERDI

Giovanna d'Arco

Opera in Three Acts
Text by Temistocle Solera

Eve Queler, *Conductor*

**This performance is dedicated with affection and admiration
to the memory of Robert E. Wagenfeld.**

THE CAST
(in order of vocal appearance)

Delil, a French officer	Wright Moore
Carlo VII, King of France	Gegam Grigorian
Giacomo, a shepherd in Dom-Rémy	Carlo Guelfi
Giovanna, daughter of Giacomo	June Anderson
Talbot, the English commander	Eric J. Owens *

Officers of the Court, French and English Soldiers,
Angels, Demons, Villagers, and Nobles

Princeton Pro Musica
Frances Slade, *Music Director*

France, 1429

There will be a single intermission, after the end of Act I.

Libretti are made possible, in part, through the generosity of Rolex Watch, U.S.A.

*Eric J. Owens is the recipient of an award for excellence from
the Seth I. Weissman Young Artists Fund.

This concert is made possible, in part, by the New York State Council on the Arts,
the City of New York Department of Cultural Affairs, and the National Endowment for the Arts.

Figure 15.4. Program for the New York Opera Orchestra's concert performance in
1996 (from author's collection).

outdoors, with amplification, uncomfortable chairs, and without supertitles, La Selva again held an audience to the opera's end.[58]

The following spring, on May 8, 1996, Eve Queler and the Opera Orchestra of New York, performed the opera in Carnegie Hall. Miss Queler has said that most of the requests she receives are for Verdi, and though she has not undertaken a cycle of his operas, she has performed many of the lesser known.[59] Her production of *Giovanna* featured the American soprano June Anderson, who the following month was scheduled to sing the role in a new production at the Royal Opera, Covent Garden, London, and hence at the moment was the reigning Joan. Bernard Holland, of the *Times*, had slight reservations about the singers, even Anderson, whose voice lacked "seductiveness," and whose "attacks are like sharp blows," but he admirably caught the spirit of the performance, which "offered a reasonably honest representation of the good and bad habits *Giovanna d'Arco* carries with it: First there was Eve Queler's orchestra, highly acceptable in quality and character and fast on its feet as well. Musicians trooped all over Carnegie Hall: a triumphal marching band from offstage, brass choirs from the back of the orchestra seats, angelic choirs singing from their balcony roost," and the demonic chorus, if not from the cellar, at least from well below the angels.[60] In short, the evening was good fun, though ultimately perhaps the opera was less stirring than a different view of it might have revealed.

Two years later came the opera's Canadian premiere at a concert performance in Toronto given by Opera in Concert on March 22, 1998, though some purists might argue that this performance, accompanied only by one piano, should not rank as a premiere. Certainly, the loss of Verdi's orchestral touches, such as the flute for Joan, the solo cello beneath the Dauphin's lament for her, and the contrasting wind instruments in the overture's *andante pastorale*, are severe wounds. On the other hand, the soloists were backed by a chorus of thirty-five, and a local critic concluded: "Whatever the inherent silliness of the libretto, the music is impressive . . . the heroine does not perish in the flames, but this performance certainly lit the fires of singers and audience alike."[61]

Finally, to close the twentieth century, in New York on May 13, 1999, the Collegiate Chorale, led by Robert Bass and employing the Orchestra of St. Luke's, gave a concert performance of the opera in Carnegie Hall. Again, angels sang from the balcony and a brass band blared from the back of the hall. Singing Joan was Lauren Flanigan, who reportedly blazed with an intensity that kept attention on her, even when silent. Consciously or not, she acted and reacted with her body, not by gesture, but by presence. As the critic for the *Times* reported, "When she cried out 'Son guerriera' ('I am a warrior'), it seemed as if her fortissimo high notes alone would slice through the French front line." Joan's music "soars and spins throughout a soprano's range. Long-lined heroic melodies must pierce through the full orchestra and chorus. Yet extended passages demand sustained spinto lyricism." And this, too, she offered. The chorus, the Collegiate Chorale, fortified by the Riverside Choral Society, "formed a superchorus of some 250, vastly more than any opera house would employ on this work. It was fun to hear the music sung with such hearty sound and unabashed enthusiasm. . . . But Ms. Flanigan was the center of attention."[62]

Meanwhile in Canada, as if excited by the Concert in Opera performance in 1998, the Canadian Opera Company offered a single concert performance in Toronto on March 18, 2000, with a chorus of forty-two, a full orchestra, and Richard Bradshaw conducting. He had led the severely cut version presented in New York's Avery Fisher Hall in 1985, and seemingly he believed in the work and wanted to return to it. According to the *Toronto Star*, "Palpable excitement and animated orchestral playing was evident early; even the overture was a thriller. . . . A blazing act 3 trio, a moving act 3 family reconciliation duet and a powerhouse deathbed departure were interactive highlights in this successful one-off enterprise that unfortunately is unlikely ever to be repeated."[63]

The critic was too gloomy. In the United States, Vincent La Selva and the New York Grand Opera gave it a concert performance on November 16, 2005, in Carnegie Hall. It was La Selva's fourth turn with the opera, one each decade since the 1970s. He had an orchestra of sixty and a double chorus of more than a hundred as a high school choir from Bethlehem, Pennsylvania, joined the company's regulars. He also had good soloists, and although none of the major local papers bothered to review the performance, they missed an evening exceptional in the way in which the opera's large choral scenes balanced with the more intimate for the principals. The opera, despite the usual complaints, seemed well structured, and the contrast between Joan in the country and Joan losing her way in the great world of the French court was clear. Curiously, the only scene that failed to build its usual intensity was Joan's death, and the reason perhaps was the lack of staging. At its start Joan needs to be seen on a litter, dying, not standing upright in evening dress, and she needs a banner, *her* banner, handed to her by Carlo, before "rapita in estasi" she sighs, "Oh mia bandiera!"[64]

The opera's history through 2008 in the United States raises a question. Why, except for staged productions in San Diego and Baton Rouge, and a concert performance in Boston, has *Giovanna d'Arco* been heard only in New York? It is an opera to which a majority of critics increasingly have warmed. As Anthony Tommasini of the *Times* observed in reviewing the Collegiate Chorale performance in 1999, "If the opera is dramatically two-dimensional, it is rich with stirring choruses, imaginative orchestral writing, and an abundance of arching melodies." In Europe it has had a good number of revivals. Why not in the United States?[65]

Possibly because in Europe, where Verdi and Schiller are more familiar figures in the general culture, opera audiences have a firmer grasp of the conventions within which they lived and worked and are more willing to accept those conventions with their limitations. An opera on Joan of Arc, composed in mid-nineteenth-century style and quite unhistorical in its libretto perhaps seems less strange to Europeans than to Americans. For an impresario in the United States staging the opera against popular knowledge—dammit, she burnt at the stake!—seems as risky as stepping into a bobbing canoe. Yet, all those stirring choruses, orchestral touches, and arching melodies are tempting and, as proved, can make "a dandy show."

Chapter Sixteen

Alzira

The only opera Verdi conceived to be set in the Americas, a conflict between Spanish invaders and the Inca people of Peru, was his eighth, *Alzira*.[1] And whatever its fate in Europe, if for no other reason than the novelty of local color and history, it might have expected to find an audience in the New World. That it did not—only two productions in the nineteenth century, in Peru and Chile, and none at all in North America—today seems the result of an unhappy mix of reasons, notably: a very moderate success in Italy, Spain, and Portugal, where it survived barely twelve years, a reputation of disparagement by its composer that now seems unfairly weighted, and some failures in the work itself, none of which, when the opera is well performed, prove fatal. In short, an opera more interesting than its early reputation would suggest was prematurely put on the shelf, and for roughly a hundred years left unperformed.

Such a tumble for a composer after five successive triumphs is startling, and suggests, at least in the response of audiences and singers to the opera's initial productions, either a misunderstanding of the work or perhaps a prejudice against the composer by some who were eager to see him fall. For both, there is evidence. The reviews of the premiere, in Naples at the Teatro San Carlo, on August 12, 1845, while praising parts of the opera, report the audience's loud displeasure with other parts, particularly with some of the musical forms; and later reviews and coffee shop squibs reveal a delight among many Neapolitans of putting down a foreigner, an "Italian" from the north.[2]

Neapolitan prejudice, however, was not decisive. In Rome (1845), though the opera did better, its structure and music still caused concern, and in Milan (1847), after a single performance at La Scala, it was withdrawn. Thereafter it was staged in Lisbon (1847), Barcelona (1849), Turin (1854), and Malta (1858), and seemingly not again, anywhere, until 1967.[3] Until the 1870s, however, its overture occasionally appeared on Italian concert programs and a cabaletta for the tenor, "Non di codarde lagrime" (No time for cowardly tears) was sometimes interpolated by tenors into other operas.[4] In the United States, throughout the nineteenth century, apparently not a note of *Alzira* was sung, onstage or in concert.

The opera is based on Voltaire's five-act tragedy *Alzire ou les Américaines* (1736), in which a Spanish governor of Peru, about to wed the Inca princess Alzire, is stabbed to death by the bride's Inca betrothed. In the repertory of the Comédie-Française for almost a hundred years, *Alzire* also played in Italy, where it was the source of at least two ballets and five operas.[5] Moreover the librettist, who in 1845 undertook to reduce it for Verdi to a prologue and two acts, was the Neapolitan Salvadore Cammarano, at the time considered the best of Italian librettists. For Donizetti he had created eight operas, notably *Lucia di Lammermoor* (1835) and *Roberto Devereux* (1837),[6] and though *Alzira* was his first work for Verdi, despite the opera's failure, Verdi returned to him for *La battaglia di Legnano* (1849), *Luisa Miller* (1849), and *Il trovatore* (1853).

The story, as Cammarano shrank it for the opera, turns on two acts of clemency, the first in the prologue, and the second at the opera's end. In the prologue, titled "The Prisoner," Inca warriors who have recently captured an elderly Spaniard, Alvaro (bass), are about to kill him, with torture first, when stopped by the unexpected appearance of Zamoro (tenor), a tribal chief. Though he himself has just escaped from a Spanish prison and torture, he is moved by the old man's age, and "noble savage" that he is, orders the prisoner freed: Let him return to Lima to tell his fellow Spaniards of the compassion and nobility of the so-called savages.[7]

The other clement act occurs at the opera's close when the Spanish governor of Peru, Gusmano (baritone), who is Alvaro's son, is about to marry the woman he loves but who does not love him, the Inca princess, Alzira (soprano). She loves Zamoro, but believes him dead. As the wedding guests assemble and as the happy groom and grieving bride take their places for the ceremony, a man disguised as a Spanish soldier steps forward and stabs Gusmano, crying, "It is I, Zamoro. Rejoice faithless woman, drink my blood; and you, Gusmano, learn from me how to die." But Gusmano, dying, recalls true Christianity and as "the noble Christian" forgives his murderer. Further, he publicly reunites the Inca couple, and in a final word from his anguished father, "Figlio," receives the old man's blessing, and dies. All cry a single word, "Spirò" (Dead). Curtain.

A good number of such melodramatic turns of fortune lie between the prologue and the opera's act 2 finale, yet the drama, however mechanical in its reversals of fortune,[8] because of the music, can hold an audience—as recent productions have shown. Almost invariably in performance, even on first hearing, the entire prologue, Alzira's entrance aria, and the first and second act finales win praise, and of the last, the Verdi scholar Julian Budden has written: "The finale of *Alzira* is worthy to be put beside those of *Il trovatore* and *La traviata.*"[9]

Before the opera's premiere in Naples, Verdi, too, seems to have had confidence in his music, for he wrote to his friend Andrea Maffei: "Don't worry, it will not be a *fiasco*. The singers sing it with pleasure, so some of it must be fairly good."[10] After the premiere, which aroused a mixture of cheers and boos, he wrote another friend: "These Neapolitans are fierce, but they applauded. Bishop [a soprano rejected by Verdi for the title role] had prepared for me a faction that would at all costs have liked to cause the downfall of this poor creature. Despite all that, the opera will remain in the repertory and, what is more, will make the rounds like its other sisters."[11]

That was not to be, and one of the more perceptive reviews of the premiere, by Opprandino Arrivabene for the *Gazzetta musicale di Milano*, hints at reasons:

Having heard the music just once, it is difficult to form an opinion . . . [but I am] persuaded that applause for the opera will grow, as it did gradually for *I due Foscari*. The plot, as you know, is based on a not very successful tragedy of Voltaire. Cammarano has done everything in his power to fashion an opera from it . . . but I feel he has not been able to overcome a certain cold monotony that slightly chills even the play. . . . The Sinfonia which Verdi has placed before his opera preserves the two-fold character—savagely warlike and amorous—that informs the drama. In its form the Sinfonia seemed novel and was very much applauded. There was applause for the Prologue . . . and applause for Alzira's cavatina [entrance aria], especially for the soprano who in the cabaletta revealed a bravura that is very rare today . . . [and applause] after the finale of the first act. Moreover, in the last act Zamoro's solo received great applause, as did Gusmano's in the last finale. And so, to great applause, ended this opera, which is very short and in which, it is worth repeating, there are many beautiful passages that doubtless went unnoted because of the sort of detailed work hard to grasp at first hearing. Thus, I believe, a very beautiful insistent string accompaniment that presumably expresses the slumber and amorous dream of Alzira, and a duet between Zamoro and Alzira, will both, in time, win the praise which was not forthcoming at the premiere.[12]

In addition to those numbers Arrivabene mentioned, the others that seemed most often to have pleased in early performances were the more conventional parts of the opera, such as the entrance arias for Zamoro (in the prologue); for Gusmano (in act 1, scene 1); and for Alzira's dream, which immediately follows Gusmano's scene. Three entrance arias, each with a slow cantabile followed by a swifter cabaletta, is a bit unimaginative, even by conventional standards, and Verdi questioned Cammarano on the scheme, but did not insist on a change.[13] And the Neapolitan audience evidently was happy with the sequence; indeed they vociferously applauded the last, Alzira's dream of fleeing in a boat from Gusmano and then being reunited with Zamoro, whom she believes to be dead, in Heaven.

What the Neapolitans emphatically disliked, however, was the duet for Zamoro and Alzira, when he suddenly appears before her, alive. That duet, chiefly because of its unusual musical form, was much criticized and declared a failure; and in seeking to understand why, it is well to remember how different from today or even 1875 was the style in 1845 of staging and singing opera.

Performances then took place under candle or gas chandeliers, but in either case the auditorium remained fully lit; the orchestra, not yet sunk in a pit, sat at floor level with the audience; and the staging throughout was far more like a concert than a modern theatrical performance. Singers, to deliver their arias, came to the front of the stage (in part, to let the footlights illuminate their faces) and usually sang directly to the audience. "I love you," trilled the soprano, not to the tenor but to the audience. Thus, a number that conformed to custom, like Alzira's cabaletta insisting she and Zamoro would be united in heaven, met audience expectations for a chance at vocal display. And with Zamoro still offstage and supposedly dead, the situation did not call for any dramatic interaction.

Verdi, however, by some quirk of nature, from his first opera to his last, sought to create situations that he thought were more theatrically dramatic and to fit them with suitable music. This often put him out of step with convention, and he had to convince audiences that his new artistic guiding principle, his aesthetic, was in some way an improvement on the old, or they would hiss and boo. Inevitably, in the course of his long career he had some works that won out at once, or slowly, and others that lost at once, or slowly. But he never ceased to try—the urge was in him.

Thus when he brought Zamoro into Alzira's chamber, audiences expected a rush of emotion followed by a love duet such as Donizetti had supplied in *Lucia di Lammermoor*. In that opera Cammarano and Donizetti offered as the calm love duet after the emotion of meeting, "Veranno a te" (My sighs will come to you), an eight-line poem, with the last line often repeated. First, the soprano sings it without interruption, then the tenor without interruption, and lastly the two together—five minutes of beautiful music during which the stage action stops, five minutes of song that could be lifted out of context, sold in stores, sung in homes, and sung not as a duet but by a soprano or tenor alone simply as a pretty tune.

Verdi imagined his lovers coming together in a fashion quite different. The initial rush of emotion is more violently expressed, followed by eight measures of extraordinary calm (flute, two oboes, clarinet, and bassoon) in which, in alternating phrases, the couple swears eternal faith. Then, instead of a verse for her, a verse for him, and a verse together, Verdi offers an eight-line poem that they sing together twice in a rush of happiness and that ends with the entrance of Gusmano, and the scene transforms directly into one of anger. Little of Verdi's duet can stand alone as a piece of music, and little makes sense if sung by a single voice. Yet, just because of its interlocking structure, in context it seems more of a duet, in its way, than "Veranno a te." Yet audiences of conservative taste, such as the Neapolitans who viewed *Lucia* (Naples, 1835) as their own, special opera, felt cheated, and they booed.[14]

Another place in the score where Verdi pushed the drama and the music ahead in somewhat similar fashion, but without arousing criticism, occurs in the prologue, in Zamoro's entrance aria. In its first part, the cantabile, he describes to his tribesmen how he survived torture, chiefly by thinking of Alzira and planning revenge on Gusmano, the governor of Peru, and then in the cabaletta he incites his people to rise against the Spanish: "They all shall die." Here, in the cavatina's cabaletta, into what more often in 1845 was a tenor solo, Verdi brought in the chorus, creating a dialogue between the tenor and chorus. More usually the chorus only commented later on the tenor's solo or joined him in a coda. The idea for the dialogue was Verdi's, not the librettist's, and by following his inclination, Verdi tightened the musical pattern and increased the dramatic excitement.[15]

A critic from Rome, after attending the opera's premiere in Naples and perhaps several of its fourteen repetitions,[16] caught a glimpse of Verdi's intent, and commented in his review: "I am persuaded that a soprano and a bass perhaps less valuable as singers but more highly animated could elevate this score to a respectable position."[17] Similarly, in Milan, after a disappointing performance of Verdi's next opera, *Attila*, Alberto Mazzucato, a violinist, composer, writer, and teacher, carried the idea further:

> I am of the opinion that for the music of Verdi a singer with instinct is worth more than a schooled one; by instinct I mean, however, one that tends to combine well with the special kinds of natural gifts that are the life of Verdi's music: an instinct that is similarly impetuous, fiery, and incisive; for Verdi's music . . . a [schooled] singer who is outstanding in breath control, in agility, in the *messa di voce*, in short, outstanding in everything that constitutes difficulties of execution, is not sufficient; instead a bold, brilliant, and vigorous spirit is needed; in a word, one needs what is called a *cantante di slancio*. With this word *slancio* I would not wish anyone to imply *shouting* [grido]. . . . [But in *Attila*] for the four principal roles . . . four performers are needed who are truly endowed with this instinct of *slancio*.[18]

The word is hard to define, but passion is a part of it, also good acting, and response to the others onstage and to the course of the drama. In writing to the soprano who was to sing Lady Macbeth at that opera's premiere Verdi told her, "First of all, the character of the part is resolute, bold, extremely dramatic . . . indeed, I wish the performers to serve the poet better than they serve the composer." Thus, drama first, technical display second. And he assured the soprano about an aria he wanted her to sing "lightly, brilliantly," the *brindisi* in act 2, "I do not recall whether you trill with ease; I have included a trill, but if necessary it can be taken out at once."[19] For Verdi, opera was musical drama, not oratorio or concert.

Meanwhile, another Roman, after hearing *Alzira*, the librettist Jacopo Ferretti, wrote to him offering to remedy defects in the libretto. His letter is lost, but Verdi, in reply, wrote:

> I, too, in Naples, before the opera's premiere, saw these failings, and you cannot imagine how I pondered them! The illness is in the opera's vitals, and retouching the defects would only make them worse. Then . . . how could I do it? I was hoping that the *Sinfonia* and the last *finale* would have vindicated in large part the failures of the rest of the opera, but I see that in Rome they were insufficient . . . and yet they ought not to have been.[20]

Verdi never specified the "failings," but surely a major defect is the vocally diminished presence of Alzira in the final scene. She continues throughout to top the vocal ensemble, but the action shifts entirely to the three men. Gusmano opens the wedding scene with a lovely slow aria expressing his happiness, during which Alzira is allowed only two brief asides to sob her grief; then Zamoro stabs Gusmano, who nobly forgives him in the finale's main section, and the opera ends with the brief exchange between Gusmano and his father, who has the opera's last solo line, his heartbroken "Figlio." Seemingly, the opera should be titled *Gusmano*, for in this final scene, with his redemptive act of forgiveness, he becomes the opera's leading character, the only one who in any way develops (however sudden his growth in stature!), and throughout the finale his is the leading voice. The scene is entirely his, and after *Alzira* Verdi never again in this way displaced a title role.

Even Zamoro, after his bloody act and rhetorical outburst, fades vocally into the background. Though Gusmano unites the lovers, giving them his blessing, there is no happy ending. The music continues to its close at Gusmano's tempo, andante, increasingly *lamentoso* and *morendo*, focused not on the lovers but on the stricken father and dying son.

Disappointed in the opera's failure, convinced that it could not easily be revised, Verdi put it aside, and went on to compose *Attila* and *Macbeth*. Many years later, with *Rigoletto*, *Trovatore*, and *Traviata* playing around the world, he allegedly replied to a query about the value he put on *Alzira*: "Quella è proprio brutta" (That one is really ugly).[21] But just what he meant by the remark, whether musically ugly or something more general, such as box-office failure, is not altogether clear. Moreover, scholars recently have become careful to point out that the remark is "hearsay," that is, the person reporting it did not hear Verdi say it but merely repeats what someone else claims to have heard—evidence routinely rejected by courts.[22] Nevertheless, for the past hundred years journalists unconcerned with judicial rules of evidence have gleefully quoted the statement as Verdi's judgment on the opera.

Verdi also said, in his pre-premiere letter to Maffei: "I would not know how to give an opinion about this opera of mine, because I wrote it almost without being aware of it and without any effort. As a result I would not be very distressed even were it to fail."[23] Again, a remark much quoted by journalists, but in the past thirty years, scholars, doing their part in the Verdi Renaissance, have discovered a number of autograph sketches for scenes in the opera, which reveal that Verdi worked hard to get the music as he wanted it.[24] Hence his proclaimed lack of care begins to seem more likely an effort to be modest, the words of an artist knowing he has tried something unconventional and wanting to shield himself against disappointment. Today most scholars and audiences who have heard *Alzira* onstage think the opera better than its old reputation; in fact, they seem to find, as Verdi had hoped, that its virtues are sufficient to surmount its defects.

It had its premiere in the United States in a concert performance presented by the American Opera Society in Carnegie Hall, New York, on January 17, 1968. That performance had been preceded and presumably inspired by a staged production in Rome on February 12, 1967, which because it was the first in Italy in 113 years had stirred considerable interest. The American critic William Weaver, attending that Roman revival, had reviewed it for *Opera:*

> Now *Alzira* is not *Falstaff*. . . in fact, it is probably one of Verdi's weakest operas; but, all the same, I would say it was well worth reviving, not only because *any* music of Verdi deserves a hearing, but also because it proved a thoroughly pleasant evening. . . .
>
> The opera is all of a piece and, on its own terms (the terms of early Verdi), a dramatically functional work. It is a work written within the conventions that Verdi was later to break free of, but it is written with vigour and brio. . . . The sets and costumes by Danilo Donati and the production by Sandro Sequi were conceived on a grand scale and were carried out effectively. Donati's vast Spanish palaces, his Rousseau-like jungles, his blindingly gold costumes were breath-taking. . . . Visually, this was one of the most fascinating productions seen in Rome in recent years.[25]

In New York the next year, the American Opera Society's concert production, of course, lacked the sumptuous scenery, but in other ways, too, was a disappointment. Though for this U.S. premiere the Society had managed to hire Rome's tenor for Zamoro, its Alzira and Gusmano were less eminent than their Roman counterparts, and all three artists, as if to confirm the opera's bad reputation, sang only loud and louder. Yet Verdi had strewn his score with pleas for *piano, più piano,* and *sotto voce.* Raymond Ericson reviewed the performance for the *New York Times* under a headline "Work That Shamed Author":

> *Alzira* has been called Verdi's worst opera. The composer himself referred to it as "really ugly" and "thoroughly bad." . . . The opera is not a total loss. For one thing, it is short. Even the worst of early Verdi could rise above most of the efforts of his operatic contemporaries. There is always a rhythmic vitality to his scores. When the hurdy-gurdy element is most prevalent, the music's unconscious humor is balanced by strong forward movement.
>
> There are a couple of sturdy well-developed vocal ensembles to bring each of the opera's two acts to a close—a duet for the soprano and the baritone that is of some appeal. But most of the time, the composer seems aimlessly trying to create unusual colors in the orchestra and getting weird ones, or writing arias that are earthbound by awkward harmonic progressions. . . .
>
> Possibly convinced that *Alzira* was weak, the singers in this instance decided to give the music all the vocal power they had. The performance was rough and ready, loud and gusty.[26]

AMERICAN OPERA SOCIETY

Allen Sven Oxenburg, Director

Fifteenth Annual Subscription 1967-1968

• Second Evening •

Giuseppe Verdi (1813-1901)

ALZIRA

Book by Salvatore Cammarano

CONDUCTOR JONEL PERLEA
CHORUS MASTER RICHARD VOGT

ALVARO, Father of Gusmano ⎱ Governors MICHAEL DEVLIN
GUSMANO ⎰ of Peru LOUIS QUILICO
OVANDO, a Spanish Duke SIDNEY JOHNSON
ZAMORO ⎱ GIANFRANCO CECCHELE
⎰ Peruvian Chieftans
ATALIBA ⎰ VERN SHINALL
ALZIRA, Daughter of Ataliba ELINOR ROSS
ZUMA, Sister of Alzira BEVERLY EVANS
OTUMBO, a Warrior FREDERICK MAYER

The American Opera Society Staff

Assistant Conductors	Ethel Evans,	Liaison	Alexander Terry
	Harriet Wingreen	Assistant to Mr. Terry	Michael Mascia
Chorus Manager	Thomas Pyle	Assistant to the Director	Hildegard Stein
Choral Consultant	Margaret Hillis	Secretary	Georgette Heine
Concert Master	Gerald Tarack	Press Representative	Herbert Breslin
Orchestra Manager	Samuel Reiner	Official Piano	The Baldwin

Music by arrangement with Franco Colombo and Teatro dell'Opera di Roma

Figure 16.1. Program for the first U.S. performance (in concert) of *Alzira* (from author's collection).

Harriett Johnson, in the *Post*, was still harsher on "the singers in major roles," and Herbert Weinstock, in *Opera*, echoed the complaint: "Perhaps this noisiness arose out of a wish to compensate for the fact that the score of *Alzira* is something like *Il trovatore* without the magnificent melodies." Remarking that he "felt in two minds" about the concert performance, he took pleasure in the orchestra, the conducting, and the secondary singers and hoped to hear the opera "in a much more relevant reading than this one proved to be."[27]

It is hard today, with multiple recordings of the complete opera available, to realize how wholly ignorant of the music were most who made up the audience for that U.S. premiere. At the time, if memory serves, the only part of the opera recorded was the Overture, which was not easily found, and a vocal score was still rarer. Thus the music fell on ears quite uninformed, except for the few who perhaps had read of the Rome production or knew of Francis Toye's conclusion in his book on Verdi (1931): "To my mind, *Alzira* is the worst of Verdi's operas."[28]

For what it may be worth, what I recall taking from the performance, besides the memory of a moving finale, was a curiosity about many of the minor vocal and orchestral passages. For example, as a prelude to the scene in the cave in the second act, Verdi has an extraordinary sixteen-measure introduction in which a phrase first played by the double bass and cimbasso (a sort of bass trombone or tuba) builds, amid an entwining figure on other instruments, into a double *forte* and then fades away. Toye had called this introduction the opera's "best feature,"[29] so I was waiting for it. Yet on first hearing, like Ericson, I thought it a bit "weird"; but having read Weaver's review of Rome's splendid scenery, I tried to imagine the odd music against a magnificent, dreary cave in dim moonlight. Perhaps then it would be effective. Also, at this first performance in the United States, I was startled by the beauty, noted by Arrivabene at the premiere in Naples, of the introduction to Alzira's cavatina. It begins with muted strings, each group playing its line in unison, and then the female chorus sounding like yet another section of strings softly enters and, most remarkably, reinforces the cellos in the prelude's bottom line. The sound is haunting, and happily it soon became possible to hear it again when later in the year Montserrat Caballé issued her recording of *Verdi Rarities*, including on it Alzira's cavatina and its full introduction. Thus, in this partial way, the opera slowly became better known. Yet the first complete, commercial recording was not released until 1983.[30]

Not until two years later was there a staged performance in the United States. That premiere, seventeen years after the American Opera Society's concert performance, was presented by the Amato Opera Company, in New York, in its small theater on the Bowery, on April 20, 1985. As was Anthony Amato's custom, he offered for each of eight scheduled performances a fully staged production, with an orchestra of piano and six or seven instruments, a chorus of perhaps fifteen or twenty, and four sopranos for Alzira, each to sing two

Figure 16.2. Leading singers in the U.S. stage premiere of *Alzira*, 1985: Mary Maguire, soprano; Edgardo Sensi, tenor; and Joseph Pariso, baritone. Photograph by Moskalenko. Courtesy of the Amato Opera Company.

performances. He also offered, perhaps because the opera was short (roughly ninety minutes of music), a summary in English of Voltaire's five-act *Alzire*. For the *Daily News*, under the headline "Verdi's Worst Worthwhile for 'Curious Opera Buffs,'" Bill Zakariasen reported: "Verdi's music frequently seems a parody of his early 'galley years' style. There's nothing really distinguished in the score, but at least *Alzira* is never dull. Amato's production (especially considering the miniscule size of the theater) is often startlingly impressive, and the action—often overflowing into the audience—unfolds with admirable vigor."[31] Zakariasen barely mentions the reduction of Voltaire's *Alzire*, and I, though attending two of Amato's eight performances, have no memory of it. The opera not the play was the thing, and strangely, in the tiny theater, despite the small forces, it seemed better represented than in concert at Carnegie Hall. The scenery, by Richard Cerullo, was imaginative, and helped the music. Sung and played, as conceived, in a scenic context, it gained impact.[32]

The country's next staged production, a single performance on July 10, 1996, was in New York's Central Park and presented by the New York Grand Opera as eighth in its cycle of Verdi's twenty-eight operas, played in chronological order. These productions, costumed, with simple but suggestive scenery, had the benefit of a full orchestra led by Vincent La Selva, an outstanding conductor of Verdi, but suffered from being out of doors where instrumental sounds dissipate unequally, and over loudspeakers that sometimes hissed or popped. Anthony Tommasini reported for the *Times:*

> *Alzira*, the first offering of the project's third summer, is so little known and unavailable that Mr. La Selva had to have the individual orchestra parts copied by hand from the full score. Yet an audience of 5,000, the police estimated, turned out for this free outdoor performance at Summerstage. People listened appreciatively and surprisingly quietly, applauding the painted backdrop-sets by Massimo Dante, and awarding the performance a hearty standing ovation.
>
> Of course, the event [claimed by the program, because of the full orchestra and all artists paid according to union scale, to be the opera's "first staged professional performance in New York"] was the news here more than the actual performance. It is impossible to truly evaluate operatic voices that are amplified. . . . What the opera is really about is the fight between a Verdi tenor and Verdi baritone over a Verdi soprano as a duet partner. And the music overflows with rousing choral ensembles and beguiling Verdian tunes.[33]

Such appreciative listening, out of doors and to an opera as unfamiliar as *Alzira*, sung in Italian and without supertitles, seemed proof of the music's ability to hold attention. Moreover, the audience was not indulgent to applaud the scenery. One backdrop set a scene in the governor's palace on a loggia, and through wide arches could be seen the Andes, their distant peaks asserting the grandeur of Peru. Note, too, that a critic now could write, without apology, that "the music overflows with rousing choral ensembles and beguiling Verdian tunes." And instead of a headline proclaiming *Alzira* the "worst" of Verdi's operas, it read: "An Evening in the Park/With Rarely Heard Verdi."

Meanwhile, in Europe, though performances continued sparse after Rome's 1967 production, much as in the United States appreciation of the opera's virtues continued slowly to grow. In 1970, as if to rebut Toye's judgment of the opera as Verdi's "worst," Charles Osborne in his widely read survey of Verdi's operas concluded of *Alzira*: "I cannot agree with the conventional view that in *Alzira* and *Il corsaro* Verdi struck rock-bottom. They may be his least successful operas, but I cannot see that they lag so very far behind *Oberto*, *I masnadieri*, *Attila*, and *Aroldo*, in all of which I find much to admire and enjoy."[34]

More European staged productions followed,[35] including an important concert performance at Covent Garden in 1996, part of the Royal Opera's Verdi cycle. By then a critical edition of the opera had been published (1994), and several recordings of the complete opera, commercial and pirated, were in circulation. Andrew Porter reviewed the Covent Garden performance for *Opera:* "Verdi's music *moves*, in both senses of the word. *Alzira* is probably his shortest opera, and the emotional charge is consistently high. . . . A standard soprano-tenor-baritone triangle is given an exotic setting, which Verdi clad with picturesque, exotic harmonies, rhythms and instrumental colours. And he built his numbers with cavalier flouting of the conventions. Groundwork for *Rigoletto* was laid."[36]

In the United States, the Sarasota Opera Company, as part of its Verdi cycle, scheduled six performances of *Alzira* for its season in 2000, and to the company's surprise all six sold out before the first performance. Further, from requests at the box office, it seems likely the house (capacity 1,033) could have sold out a seventh.[37] The production, as is the company's wont, was traditional, and the artistic director and conductor, Victor DeRenzi, produced the opera as Verdi indicated, not only in scenery and staging but also in musical tempos and dynamics.

On two small points he made interesting decisions. Rather than a stage band for the three scenes in which Verdi calls for one,[38] DeRenzi, as is often done, used the pit orchestra for the band's passages but for these greatly reduced the number and range of instruments (no strings; and of the wind and brass, only enough to suggest the melody and harmony). The result was a noticeable change in sonority, suggesting at least a different band and source, as if heard from a distance. The other interesting decision resolved the problem of the score's missing gong.

Verdi's stage direction at the opening of the second act's scene in the desolate cave reads: "The stage remains empty for some time; then Otumbo [an Inca warrior] enters cautiously and strikes a suspended gold shield. At the sound, survivors of the defeated Incas emerge from the back of the cave

Figure 16.3. In the final scene of the Sarasota production (2000), Gusmano welcomes Alzira to their wedding. Zamoro, disguised as a Spanish soldier, stands behind Alzira's right shoulder. Photograph by Frank Atura. Courtesy of the Sarasota Opera Company.

where they have been hiding." But for once, Verdi, though usually precise in his scores about the boomings of cannon and strikings of clocks or gongs, left no instruction. It seems he forgot—perhaps in the pleasure of composing his eerily effective introduction to the scene.

Then, when should the gong be struck? The scene's opening sixteen measures, after which Otumbo starts to sing, are among the opera's most effective, and no musician would spoil them with the bang of a gong. Yet the gong has dramatic purpose, summoning the Incas from the cave's interior. What to do? Both complete recordings, for example, simply omit the gong, as did Rome's staged production in 1967,[39] and perhaps most others since. DeRenzi, however, opened the curtain on the darkened cave to silence, had Otumbo enter and strike the shield, and then, only after a long pause, began the sixteen measures, during which, as Verdi directed, Otumbo and the Incas silently gather.

The result of Sarasota's concern for the music and staging was six remarkably happy evenings in the theater. The audiences seemingly cared not at all about the observance or breaking of musical conventions, were unbothered by the predictability of the romantic triangle, and unperturbed by Alzira's all-but-disappearance in the final scene. They simply gave themselves to the story and reveled in "the rousing choral ensembles and beguiling Verdian tunes."[40]

Figure 16.4. The final trio, Sarasota (2000), as Gusmano pardons Zamoro and urges the Inca couple to live together happily. Alzira, Suzanne Balaes; Zamoro, Matthew Kirchner; and Gusmano, William Andrew Stuckey. Photograph by Frank Atura. Courtesy of the Sarasota Opera Company.

Reviewing opening night, March 11, Florence Fisher for the *Sarasota Herald Tribune*, reported: "The opera makes a surprising dramatic impact." Particularly she liked the savagery of the opening scene in which the Inca tribesmen, in "gorgeous Peruvian-inspired costumes . . . shout their lurid threats against their prisoner."[41] Another reviewer, Chip Ludlow, of the *Venice Gondolier*, was similarly impressed: "In the opening Prologue, the male chorus, singing at full voice, riveted the attention of the audience. The scene was made all the more effective with excellent lighting, the arrival in a canoe of Zamoro, the Incan leader, and the tension built between the captors and Alvaro."[42]

Of the opera's finales, the most excited praise was written by Steven Brown for the *Orlando Sentinel*: "*Trovatore*, for instance, has nothing as eloquent as the end of *Alzira*—in which the baritone, a Spanish colonial governor caught in a love triangle, dies to the strains of a great lament rising from the chorus and principals."[43] John Fleming, for the *St. Petersburg Times*, while praising the production, especially the colorful costumes, noted some of the opera's flaws: "At the center of the music-drama is Gusmano, son of the Spanish governor, whose pursuit of the title character is doomed." Moreover, "Gusmano goes from ruthless cruelty to saintly forgiveness . . . [in] one of the swiftest death-scene conversions in history."[44]

To date, through 2010, no other company in the country has offered a staged production of *Alzira*. But Vincent La Selva and the New York Grand Opera, having concluded their Verdi Cycle in 2001, as their first return thereafter to a Verdi opera, gave it a concert performance in Carnegie Hall on January 31, 2003. The audience was enthusiastic, and though the city's daily newspapers ignored the event, the critic for the *New York Concert Review* praised the performance highly, observing that "*Alzira* is not by any means a sophisticated work, but the composer's craftsmanship and affinity for the voice are already evident."[45] Staged productions, however, are sure to continue rare. Even with the opera's rank raised from "worst" to the more general category of "minor Verdi,"[46] it is still one of the weaker of his twenty-six operas (not counting revisions), and with so many stronger to choose from, what company, with a tight budget, will pick *Alzira?* Yet as the Sarasota and New York Grand Opera companies have shown, when well staged and performed, its Inca costumes and "beguiling tunes" can hold an audience and win applause.

Chapter Seventeen

Il corsaro

Like Verdi's eighth opera, *Alzira*, his thirteenth, *Il corsaro*, failed to hold the stage and even in Italy was not performed for a hundred years (1864–1963), a failure all the more surprising because between the two he had won success with *Attila* and *Macbeth*. Yet as with *Alzira*, his *Corsaro* was dismissed as uninspired, uninteresting, and uniquely even unworthy of him. Writing in 1930, the English critic Francis Toye, probably the dominant voice on Verdi for his generation of English-speaking readers and audiences, declared: "With the exception of *Alzira*, this is the worst opera ever written by the composer." To which he added: "It is perhaps the only opera in which Verdi was definitely, if not deliberately, false to his fine ideals of craftsmanship."[1]

Leaving that last charge to be answered by the sum of this report, consider first the opera's longtime reputation, starting with a statement often made by journalists, as if quoting an authority such as Toye: That *Il corsaro* is the only opera whose premiere and rehearsals Verdi did not attend, making last minute improvements.[2] But the assertion is false, for Verdi did not go to Cairo in 1871 for the premiere of *Aida*—though for the opera's first Italian production he attended rehearsals, took a strong hand, and wrote additional music, none of which he did for *Corsaro*.

Similarly, journalists and program writers often inflate with unduly judgmental implications Toye's comment that Verdi "did not wish to write the opera at all and only did so because of a contract, which, as a matter of fact, he tried to cancel."[3] True, Verdi despised this particular publisher, Francesco Lucca, and in letters to friends aired his dislike, but also true that in the 1840s almost all operas were written to fulfill contracts. That was the method of business. Moreover, buying one's way out of a contract, if the other party agrees, always was and is an acceptable option, and when Verdi's offer to Lucca was rejected, he fulfilled his obligation. In his dealings with the Paris Opéra, for example, he frequently regretted that he had agreed to compose for it, and in the case of *Les vêpres siciliennes* (1854) asked twice to rescind the contract, but was refused.[4] His business tactics concerning some opera are seldom a clue to his views of its music.

As for his staying in Paris rather than going to Trieste for the opera's premiere on October 25, 1848, staging it, and conducting its first three performances, the Triestini perhaps with justice could feel slighted, for that was the custom. On the other hand, Verdi had not composed the opera on commission for Trieste and the city was the publisher's choice. Moreover, 1848 was the "mad and holy" year of revolutions in Europe, with repeated upheavals in Paris, Vienna, and northern Italy where at first dukes were expelled, republics declared, and the Austrian armies of occupation defeated. But by September 17, when the publisher and the impresario in Trieste signed their contract, the Austrians had begun their siege of the upstart Republic of Venice and already had regained Lombardy, Modena, and Verdi's home duchy of Parma. In many Po Valley cities they were ruling by martial law, imposing huge fines on Italian patriots, and driving many into exile. Verdi had multiple reasons for staying in Paris: He was slightly ill,[5] he was enjoying the company of the lady he later married, and he had begun work on a new opera, *La battaglia di Legnano*. Possibly, too, the difficulties and even dangers of travel across northern Italy in October 1848 deterred him. Trieste, though dominated culturally by its many citizens of Italian background, was an Austrian city, the chief port of the Austrian Empire, and perhaps not a comfortable locale for the most patriotic of Italian composers.[6]

Lastly, for many years it was believed that Verdi took no interest in this opera and condemned it in advance, but in 1971 and 1980 two letters unknown to Toye were published that showed the opposite. In the first, to his librettist F. M. Piave, dated August 27, 1846, Verdi said of the libretto: "You want me to give you back *Il corsaro*? That *Corsaro* that I have so longed for, that has cost me so much thought, and that you have set to verse with more care than usual?"[7] In the second, dated October 6, 1848, he replied to the premiere's leading soprano, who had sought advice on how to sing her role. In considerable detail he discussed such points as: "In the duet with the tenor . . . when you come on stage, enter slowly and speak the recitative slowly: the first tempo will be moderato . . . [and] In the final trio . . . take the ¾ in C major at a very moderate tempo and with passion. The last movement should be performed largo, like the trio in *Lombardi*."[8]

The opera's libretto, which Toye called "preposterous," is based on Byron's narrative poem *The Corsair*, first published in 1814 and for forty years immensely popular in Europe,[9] partly no doubt because Byron had died (1824) while aiding the Greeks to win independence from the Turks (1821–32). The opera, like the poem, is set in "the beginning of the nineteenth century," and because of its association with Byron for some in its audiences no doubt carried overtones of the Greeks' revolutionary success. But after the failure of the Italian revolutions of 1848, in which many patriots died, the poem lost its appeal, as, roughly speaking, the Age of Mazzini, with its ideal of a free, united, and republican Italy achieved by local uprisings, gave way to the Age of Cavour, proposing a Kingdom of Italy that the monarchies of Europe might approve and that might be achieved by the gradual expansion of the Kingdom of Sardinia, ruled by the House of Savoy. This shift in spirit, from heroic, regenerative action to cautious diplomacy seeking foreign allies to battle Austria was likely a reason that *Corsaro* even in Italy had only a moderate success. Though conceived in 1846, by its premiere in late 1848 it was, in spirit and mood, already moving out of date.[10]

Both poem and opera are remarkably simple in their narrative structure, and present a typical Byronic hero—"There was a laughing devil in his sneer"—a type much admired in the early Romantic Age. As retold in the opera (with only few changes from the poem), a young man, Corrado (tenor), who has committed some terrible, unspecified crimes and (like Byron) become a social outcast, lives with a pirate band on an island in the Aegean. He bemoans his lot, loves a girl, Medora, whom he leaves to attack a Muslim Pasha (an unhistorical event), is captured, imprisoned, and visited secretly by the Pasha's favorite, Gulnara, whom he saved from death in the assault on the castle. She hates the Pasha, for "Love can flower only in freedom," is smitten with the gallant Corrado, and to free him from prison offers him a knife and a chance to kill the Pasha who is sleeping nearby. Corrado—all his virtues work against him—will not stoop to murder, and declares that his only regret in dying is the loss of the woman he loves, Medora. Gulnara, though now aware that her love is not returned, then murders the Pasha, and Corrado, stating that if he cannot love her, he can at least save her, leads her from the castle. Returning with Gulnara to his island, he discovers Medora surrounded by her maidens on a high cliff overhanging the sea. Thinking him dead, she has taken poison; and during an extended trio for tenor and two sopranos, she dies in his arms. Whereupon Corrado throws himself from the cliff into the sea. Curtain.

Byron describes his hero:

That man of loneliness and mystery,—
Scarce seen to smile and seldom heard to sigh . . .
His soul was changed, before his deeds had driven
Him forth to war with man and forfeit heaven.
Warp'd by the world in Disappointment's school . . .
Fear'd, shunn'd, belied, ere youth had lost her force,
He hated man too much to feel remorse . . .
He knew himself a villain, but he deem'd
The rest no better than the thing he seem'd,
And scorn'd the best as hypocrites who hid
Those deeds the bolder spirit plainly did.[11]

Yet Byron declares, "none are all evil," and grants his hero extraordinary courage and a great capacity for love.

To modern ears, the poem may sound monotonous, as the narrator's voice runs on for fifty-seven long stanzas. The opera conversely gains by turning the scenes described—he said, she said—into confrontations, articulated by contrasting voices. Even so, the opera, like the poem, more than telling a story depicts a favorite Romantic attitude: the misunderstood hero, the social misfit (often an artist), who yet has courage and a heart.

Figure 17.1. Corrado and Medora dying (Enrico di Giuseppe and Christina Andreou), final scene, New York Grand Opera, 1987. Photograph courtesy of the New York Grand Opera Company.

In both poem and opera the story is only lightly sketched, with many details left unexplained: such as Corrado's former crimes, the whereabouts of the two Aegean islands, the gist of the news that starts the expedition against the Muslims, or any reason for Corrado to appear in disguise before the Pasha.

In 1848 Verdi was criticized because the opera was short, only ninety-five minutes of music. Today, that concision seems a virtue, for in musically depicting attitude rather than plot it is as much a vocal tone poem as an opera. In its portrayal of Corrado and his two ladies, it is more akin, say, to Richard Strauss's orchestral tone poem *Don Juan* (1888, based not on Mozart's *Don Giovanni* but on Nicholas Lenau's dramatic poem of 1844),[12] than to the operas Verdi fashioned in the 1850s from the carefully plotted French plays that underlay *Rigoletto* or *La traviata*. Yet, paradoxically the opera seems stronger when staged than if heard in a recording or even in a concert performance.

The first twentieth-century revival, mounted by forces drawn from the conservatory in Venice in 1963, was a concert performance presented in the courtyard of the Doge's Palace. The American critic William Weaver reported:

> Every year at the Venice Conservatory its head, Renato Fasano . . . organizes something called *Le vacanze musicali*, a kind of summer school for advanced students. And at the end of the school, as a kind of final exam, the students perform in public. The voice students of Maestro Giuseppe Pugliese were, this year, given the task of preparing Verdi's *Il Corsaro*, because of the 150th anniversary of the composer's birth. This production, announced in all the Italian papers, naturally aroused great interest, and what might have been a mere students' exercise became an international musical event. . . .
>
> The performance itself (on August 31) could not have been more disastrous. Its deficiencies ordinarily might have been justified on the grounds that this was a non-professional performance, but unwisely, the *Vacanze* had set a quite professional price on the tickets. . . . Apparently the soprano Maria Battinelli had been persuaded to go on, despite a bad cold. She was to sing the important role of Medora, but after croaking a few notes in the first act, she stopped and indicated with gestures, that her voice had gone. There were several minutes of embarrassed silence, while the audience expected some kind of announcement from Maestro Fasano or Maestro Pugliese. Nothing. Was it possible that no one had taken the simple precaution of having understudies (a precaution all the more necessary with young and inexperienced singers)? There were no understudies and no announcements, finally the audience began to shout at the stage, begging the hapless Miss Battinelli to continue somehow, anyhow. Bravely she did, indicating more than singing the music. In the second act, Medora does not appear; but in the third (and last) act, she has an important scene and is part of the trio that concludes the opera. By this time, the girl's voice had gone completely. She came out, tried, but gave up. She sat on the stage with a stole over her throat while the trio was sung by the tenor and the other soprano [Gulnara]. Towards the end, the bells of the campanile striking midnight covered most of the music and

brought the audience's exasperation to the boiling-point. At the end of the opera—something I had never seen in decades of opera-going—there was a fight between members of the audience and members of the orchestra. The police appeared and broke it up.[13]

Thus the opera, at its first hearing in a hundred years, had a true nineteenth-century *fiasco*. Yet Weaver closed: "This is an opera which we should hear again, in a staged version. St. Pancras, please note!"

In petitioning St. Pancras, he was not appealing to the martyred saint, or to the London railroad station named for the church parish in which it stands, but to the opera festival that then periodically took place in nearby St. Pancras Town Hall. And as if in response, on March 15, 1966, a group calling itself "Opera Viva" presented *Corsaro* in a staged performance, the first ever in Britain. Like many who were on hand, Andrew Porter, reviewing it for *Opera*, was excited to italics: Audiences "can welcome the revival . . . not only for the way it illuminates Verdi's progress, not only for its 'historical interest,' but also because, for all the unevenness, it *lives*."

> Take the stretta of *Il corsaro's* second finale [act 2, scene 2, Corrado captured by the Pasha Said]: *um-titty-tum-tum* goes the orchestra, in C major, and the baritone launches a melody which climbs up the scale, a note to a bar with little pushes on the fourth beat. The stalest sort of formula. All set. One's heart sinks. But suddenly, at the second entry, a surprise. The soprano has taken over the tune: C minor; a new running accompaniment in the bass; female chorus adding colour with an unconventional line that drops to two octaves below the soprano. Third entry: sustained accompaniment chords, slightly slackened tempo, and tenor in E flat. Only then, the predicted working-out of the formula, for full ensemble. . . .
>
> One fine example of a conventional effect brought off to perfection is the arrival of Conrad [Corrado] and Gulnare [Gulnara] in the last act: build-up, "excitement ostinato" in the orchestra, cries of "Oh gioia! È lui!", and then an ensemble blaze topped by the two sopranos and tenor in octaves. Nothing could look more ordinary on paper; and on performance it stirred the blood as only fine theatre can.[14]

All at once an opera thought to be without merit became a work of interest, and after its success at St. Pancras, the pace of revivals in Europe began to accelerate. One of the first, as if to make amends, was staged in Venice in March 1971, and led a critic for *Opera* to conclude: "It is a minor work, but there is no denying that it holds the stage perfectly well from beginning to end—which is true of all Verdi's pieces."[15] And it was followed in 1980 by another successful production, this time in Rome. Meanwhile, in 1976, supplementing a succession of privately recorded tapes, a complete, commercial studio recording appeared with a first-rate cast and conductor and the corsair sung by José Carreras.[16] Plainly, some small company in the United States soon would stage the opera.

Its nineteenth-century history in the Western Hemisphere is very slight, a single production in Valparaiso, Chile, in 1852, and an amateur production in Rio de Janeiro in 1855.[17] Even the Italian company in Havana, though introducing many of Verdi's early operas to the New World, did not mount *Il corsaro*; and there were no productions in Mexico, the United States, or Canada.[18]

Even in excerpts the opera hardly existed. Without having made a detailed search of concert or recital performances in the United States, I can report only that in early March 1855 in San Francisco a pianist, Carlotta Patti, in a touring opera company's benefit performance played a fantasy of variations on *Corsaro*. And possibly, touring often in the next fifteen years, she played it elsewhere.[19]

Some of the opera's music evidently also appealed to amateur singers, for at the Fifth Avenue Baptist Church in New York, on December 18, 1856, a group included an aria in their program for the church's benefit. The *Herald* reported: "Every year there are always a certain number of young ladies and gentlemen who are anxious to sing in public without losing their social position. So they get up a fashionable concert by amateurs 'for charitable purposes,' to which as many of the vulgar herd as are willing to invest a dollar each are admitted." The *Tribune* added that the program offered airs "from that wicked opera *La traviata*, from that heathenish tragedy *Semiramide*, and from that desperate drama *Il corsaro*—all in a Baptist Church! What would the man of the Wilderness say to it?" And earlier that year, the New York lawyer George Templeton Strong complained to his diary that at a private evening party, two of the guests had sung "bosh from *Corsaro* and *Masnadieri*."[20]

The interest of amateurs seems to have waned quickly, however, for the *Catalogue of Sheet Music and Musical Works* that records what was in print in the United States in 1870 has only a single entry for *Corsaro*, which appears in a section primarily for piano and titled "Rondos, Fantasies, Variations, etc." But a listing does not mean sales, and for most Verdi operas there are many, many entries of arrangements. Also, the U.S. Marine Band Repertory, 1855 to 1871, had no excerpts from the opera, though of the fourteen operas from *Nabucco* to *Rigoletto*, it had band parts for ten;[21] and no excerpt of the opera ever was sung in the Metropolitan Sunday Evening Concerts, 1883–1946.[22] Not until 1998, with the appearance of the critical edition, was an orchestral score published, and until then even copies of the vocal score were rare. In sum, for most of the twentieth century the average operagoer in the United States knew nothing of the music, and critics and scholars, little more.

The first company to tackle the opera, which required it to make its own orchestral parts from a photo copy of the autograph score, was the newly born Long Island Opera Society, which through one of its four founders, David Lawton, a professor of music at the State University of New York, Stony Brook, had access to the graduate orchestra (of which he was director), a chorus, and a fine concert hall, all without charge. For its first opera, in 1980, the Society produced in a concert performance the original, 1847 version of Verdi's *Macbeth*, and the following year the U.S. premiere of *Il Corsaro*. Lawton later recalled:

> We seized the opportunity to program it, but were concerned that it would be hard to sell out there [Stony Brook is on Long Island's North Shore, about fifty miles from New York City.] We conceived the idea of hiring a big name in order to help sell it, and at the same time, we felt that it would be important for the prestige of our fledgling company to also try to arrange for a repeat performance in a New York venue. The idea of contacting Carlo Bergonzi [at the time a very big name among Verdi tenors] surfaced early on, because he had performed all the Verdi tenor roles except Otello. I just called him up at his Milan apartment. He was delighted to agree to it, gave us a discount on his fee, and agreed to sing a benefit for us later in the year (with John Wustman) [an accompanist]. He then told us to inform Herbert Breslin, his agent in New York. The Breslin firm was furious with us for having gone to him directly, but they honored the verbal arrangements we had made with Bergonzi.[23]

The opera's U.S. premiere accordingly took place at the university's concert hall in Stony Brook on December 12, 1981, followed four days later by a repeat performance in New York City's Town Hall. Of that second performance, John Rockwell reported for the *Times:*

> It cannot be said that the public shows an insatiable desire for these operas [*Alzira* and *Il corsaro*]; Town Hall was not full, and many of those present seemed to have come for Carlo Bergonzi. . . . Still, *Il corsaro,* is by no means negligible. . . . The title role never rises above A in exposed music, and apparently the opera's unpopularity precluded a tradition of interpolated higher notes. This meant Mr. Bergonzi's insecure top was not tested, and he sang superbly, with all his innate beauty of voice, scrupulousness of musicianship, idiomatic sensitivity of phrasing and sumptuous clarity of declamation. The other singers were less well known, but fully honorable.[24]

Rockwell had less kind words for the orchestra and chorus, though he noted that Lawton, who conducted, "has a real feeling for the shape, thrust and flow of Verdi's phrasing." The *Daily News* had a briefer review, hardly more than a report that the performance had taken place, though Lawton again received praise.[25] But neither review noted the pleasure that most of the audience took in the opera. Bergonzi indeed was magnificent; the two sopranos were better than honorable; and some of the music proved beautiful, and some of it theatrically effective. Likely more than one who came out of curiosity to hear one of Verdi's "worst" operas, or merely to revel in Bergonzi, left the hall thinking that *Corsaro* was a viable work that belonged in a theater.[26]

Figure 17.2. David Lawton, professor, scholar, conductor, in 1999. Photograph by Paul Lasurdo. Courtesy of the Music Department, State University of New York, Stony Brook.

The first staged production was mounted by the San Diego Opera as part of its Fifth Verdi Festival in June 1982, and had a moderate success, the company's official history later describing the production as "lackluster," but the singing as "glorious."[27] Donald Dierks for the *San Diego Union* reviewed the first of the three performances:

> During all of the decades that the opera laid idly on the shelf, it was the popular opinion that *Il corsaro* was a hopelessly empty vessel, a work so flawed and uneventful that it was unworthy of the composer. . . . The Francesco Piave libretto, based on a poem by Lord Byron, is admittedly weak, but Verdi's own work never fell below an admirable standard that is not often reached by a host of other composers. Yet, while the title can not be sung in the same breath as *Otello*, of course, nor does it match a dozen or more of Verdi's other operas, but it still has the merits of a number of moving arias and the composer's masterful touch with orchestration. Based upon its own strengths, it deserves occasional productions. The problem with *Il corsaro* may very well be that, although the great Verdi composed it, the opera does not achieve greatness. Had a Boito, or Zandonai, written it, say, it might be in the repertoire, but the probable rational is "why produce *Il corsaro* when so many other Verdi operas are better—and better box office."[28]

Andrew Porter, now reviewing for the *New Yorker*, concluded: "We should be hearing more of *Il corsaro*. While hardly a 'chamber' opera, it would suit a company that cannot muster the larger forces, the spectacle, and the rehearsal time that such a piece as *I Lombardi* calls for. *Il corsaro* is terse."[29]

On that point, however, Dierks touched on a slight awkwardness of the opera that is noticeable in staged productions but less so in concert performances in which the chorus and soloists typically remain onstage whether singing or not. "Since so much of the time lone persons are on stage . . . [the stage director's] work is light. In the one scene where action does take place, however—the battle between the forces of Corrado and Seid—there were too few people involved."[30]

In a staged performance, that imbalance between the one (or few) and the many can be startling. The curtain parts on an empty stage and Corrado enters alone, while from offstage and without orchestral accompaniment, the pirate chorus sings its interjections to his slow aria (a lament for his outcast state); then news arrives, requiring action, and the pirates flock onstage to join their chief in his swift aria promising a fight against the Muslim Pasha. Then chorus exits to one side while Corrado goes out the other to bid goodbye to his love, Medora.

Alone in a room in her tower, she opens the second scene with her *romanza*, and the scene (and act) ends with a duet for her and Corrado, in which he leaves her alone onstage. The third scene (act 2, scene 1) opens with a chorus of women in the Pasha's harem, followed by a full, double aria for Gulnara. By then a pattern seems set, a succession of intimate scenes exploring the inner feelings of a single character. But suddenly we are in a much grander opera: the Pasha Seid (baritone) and his soldiers sing a martial hymn to Allah, the pirates and Muslims fight, and the pirates break off to rescue from fire all the "odalisques from the harem." Meantime, the Muslims regroup, defeat the pirates now burdened with the ladies, Corrado is wounded, bound, and thrown on the floor before the Pasha, and we have a huge choral finale. At least, it should be huge. But if the producer has economized and created a Muslim guard simply by reclothing half the pirates' chorus, in the great fight there will be "too few people involved."

In act 3, scene 1, the pattern of a solo scene and duet repeats, and then the opera concludes with another full-throated finale in which the pirates, who earlier had seemed happy on their island without women, suddenly have them in abundance. These are points of no great concern, for the music sweeps along, but as Dierks noted, the opera, for all of being short and relatively simple in structure, is not entirely free of production problems.

These difficulties as well as others plagued the first staged production on the country's East Coast, a single out-of-doors performance in New York's Central Park on July 30, 1987. The company was the New York Grand Opera, conducted by Vincent La Selva, the site was the Naumburg Bandshell at the north

Figure 17.3. Corrado before Seid (Gabriel Gonzalez, Joshua Benaim), act 2, scene 2, finale, Sarasota Opera, 2004. Photograph by Deb Hesser. Courtesy of the Sarasota Opera Company.

end of the mall, and as the critic for the *Post* observed, "a stringent budget resulted in a woefully stilted production."[31] The bandshell is not large, and the orchestra was seated at ground level in front of the shell's raised stage, thus losing any advantage of the shell's roof, and though voices and orchestra alike were amplified, they tended to sound at times somewhat disjointed.[32] The sets and costumes were simple. The *Times* critic remarked: "The sets consisted of folding screens, wooden beds and a huge ugly assemblage of tilted platforms that served no discernible purpose aside from providing Corrado something from which he could jump to his death. Costumes were colorful and silly. Gulnara's honored role among the harem girls was distinguished by her possessing the wildest hairdo." And the acting sometimes was "unintentionally comic," such as "the toothless second act battle scene between the Corsairs and the Pasha's men."[33] Yet "a large audience attending the free performance filled the bleachers [park benches] and spilled onto the adjacent lawns."

Performances of *Corsaro* in the United States, however, continued rare, partly because the Italian publisher Ricordi, which controlled rental of the score, reported to those requesting orchestral parts that none were available— in which case any company producing the opera had to make its own parts from a copy of the orchestral score, a considerable chore. This obstacle would dissolve in 1998 with the joint publication of a critical edition of the opera by the University of Chicago and Ricordi;[34] but even before then the Opera Theatre of Northern Virginia, making use of parts being prepared in conjunction with the critical edition, mounted a production in May 1996.

The company's aim has been to produce "professional but accessible opera in English," and over the years it has mounted a number of rarely heard operas, including Verdi's *Un giorno di regno* in 1992 and *Oberto* in 1998. For *Corsaro*, staged at the Thomas Jefferson Community Theatre, in Arlington, it offered an English translation by W. Paul Edson, a chorus of twelve, and an orchestra of twenty-four (eleven strings), conducted by John Edward Niles, the artistic director. Apparently this production was the first anywhere of the opera in English and the first to make use of the critical edition.

The critic for the *Washington Post* questioned the value of an English translation when unintelligibly sung, but praised Niles for "shrewd use of limited resources," mentioning in particular the sparse staging, which "relied on diaphanous curtains and mood lighting."[35] According to the *Review*, however, at the end of the opera "Corrado's suicide was a little unclear. . . . He pulled down the draperies which were upstage center and fell into them," which needed the program's synopsis to reveal that he had "flung himself into the sea."[36] But this was a minor matter "in an otherwise well-executed presentation." And both critics agreed with a colleague on the *Northern Virginia Sun*, who concluded: The opera "might lack the passion of an *Aida*, or the dramatic impact of an *Otello*, but it is still a convincing theatrical work, one that has been unjustly ignored."[37]

The next summer, 1997, as part of its cycle of Verdi's operas presented in chron-ological order, La Selva and the New York Grand Opera company again staged the opera, another single performance in Central Park but now at the slightly larger and better equipped Summer Stage in Rumsey Field (an area behind the bandshell). It was not the company's happiest venture, although perhaps not so dire as the *Times* critic reported, who left "after only one act," complaining later of "a lead tenor who consistently deviated from pitch, unlikable strings and all but unlistenable male chorus."[38] Though the critic spoke truth, the tenor and chorus improved, the sopranos were adequate, and the baritone excellent. And seemingly the audience greatly enjoyed an opera that probably few had ever heard before.

Certainly, summer opera in Central Park has its problems, but as John Rock-well once observed in the *Times*, reviewing a production of Puccini's *Trittico*: "The true impact of these performances transcends individual accomplish-ment and, some might argue, music itself. The New York Grand Opera park performances are genuine Volksoper, popular in the way opera used to be before it got all artistic and self-conscious. As an occasion for the sober pre-sentation of Puccinian masterworks, Thursday fell short. As a proof of the still-lively bonds among melodious operatic scores, heartfelt performances and an enthusiastic public, it had its decided charms."[39]

An opportunity to hear *Corsaro* onstage came again when the Sarasota Com-pany, as part of its survey of Verdi's works, announced a production for March 2004, scheduling seven performances, a number that for such a little known opera struck many people as more hopeful than wise. The San Diego company in 1982 had attempted only three. Yet evidently in the twenty-two years, even in the United States where performances were less frequent than in Europe, *Corsaro* had polished its reputation, and the Sarasota house, with surtitles, and a small stage that kept the action focused, seemed ideal for it. And the seven performances sold out at 102.1 percent.[40]

The local critics were not unanimous in their judgments on the work or on the singers, though they all began by citing the opera's history as a fail-ure and retelling old stories (sometimes not updated) about its composition and premiere in Trieste. One even quoted the conductor, Victor DeRenzi, in a statement he likely never uttered: "It was the one opera that he [Verdi] did not attend the world premiere for."[41] After these ritualistic remarks, the crit-ics split in opinion. One thought the two women had the best of "a moderate amount of good music," and were "the most interesting characters"; whereas another was more impressed by the "exceptionally challenging and beautifully rendered duets for the men." About the tenor in the titular role they variously reported: he sang sharp, he sang flat, his voice settled down, he was "exactly what the role demands—a truly heroic tenor of strong, dramatic bearing and romantic charisma."[42] Such disagreements often are rooted in the individual's instinctive response to the recurrent question: Is opera theater or concert? Drama or purely vocal display? If theater, good acting may trump vocal defects.

Figure 17.4. Corrado and Medora (Gabriel Gonzalez, Dara Rahming), act 1 scene 2, at Sarasota, 2004. Photograph by Deb Hesser. Courtesy of the Sarasota Opera Company.

Perhaps the two most acute critics were Lawrence Johnson of the *South Florida Sentinel* and John Fleming of the *St. Petersburg Times*. Johnson wrote: "If not an undiscovered masterpiece, there is much inspired music in *Corsaro*, with fine arias for all four leading characters, an excellent trio and rousing ensemble writing to close acts 2 and 3 . . . [DeRenzi drew] such committed playing from the Sarasota Opera Orchestra that one almost forgot this was a minor Verdi score."[43] Fleming noted why the opera is minor Verdi: "*Il Corsaro* has good tunes, but they never achieve the character development of top-level Verdi." He thought the "opera's finest moment" musically was Corrado alone in prison: "Lighted by a single torch, with solo cello setting the bleak mood."[44] And though the opera as a whole, compared to *Otello*, is surely "a minor Verdi score," Sarasota's audiences loudly approved it.

The production perhaps was at its best in its consistent presentation of Corrado as a man wholly out of sorts with the world, able to find happiness and the best in himself only in his love for Medora and in fighting, the greater the odds the better. Thus DeRenzi, following Verdi's direction, opened the first scene not, as sometimes done, with the pirate chorus lolling on stage and singing to an orchestral accompaniment, but with it offstage, singing unaccompanied, and Corrado entering alone in a mood of self-pity and justification.[45] And because alone, seemingly more complex than Ernani who, in his more conventional opening scene, is surrounded by happy bandits and presented as merely "the tenor in love."[46] Moreover, Corrado does not have his fate imposed upon him by another but generates it within himself. In this he is much like Carlo in *I masnadieri*, a tortured soul who longs, consciously or not, to be his better self. Seemingly the plight of this conflicted character interested Verdi in the mid-1840s, for he conceived both operas in the same period. Indeed, in some respects *Corsaro* is a simpler version of *Masnadieri*, without any wholly evil character like Francesco and hence stripped of the earlier opera's philosophical overtones, the conflict between free will and evil.

Corrado's subsequent scene with Medora reveals his two best qualities in conflict, his ability to love and his courage expressed in his eagerness to fight. Despite his insistence that he will return, his "Farewell" to Medora prefigures his fate, his need to fight will cost him love. And upon his return from prison, when she dies in his arms, he instantly throws himself off the cliff, not like Tosca, stopping on the parapet to pontificate, but without a word. The speed of his self-destruction is shocking, for even as the audience gasps, the curtain falls. Yet, with love lost, would such a man live on?

The production faltered perhaps only in the time needed to change scenes within the acts and in having two intermissions between the three acts instead of the more usual one, achieved by joining acts 1 and 2. DeRenzi himself privately thought these waits too long. Musing later, on what might be an ideal production—except for the chaos it would produce in Verdi's music—he remarked on the speed with which some scenes in their action follow one after another, even overlap, and might be presented as overlapping. For example, at the end of the opening scene, the pirates exit one way to their ship and Corrado exits the other way to bid Medora goodbye. Even at that moment she should be somehow looming onstage, perhaps behind a scrim or on an elevator moving slowly forward, already in the midst of her *romanza* of gloomy premonition, after which he enters, straight from the previous scene.[47] But of course, there is the music, and the need to be practical. Still, in this opera, scene changes should be fast, so that the opera as a whole may deliver its punch with minimum break.

As for the two intermissions between the three acts, both the tenor and baritone need a rest between the finale to act 2 and their lengthy solo scenes in act 3, but Verdi himself recommended playing the first two acts as one: "A final suggestion: let the opera be divided into two acts only. The first act to the end of the finale (to act 2); the second with the trio (act 3). The whole opera will gain in interest, in brevity, in everything."[48] Perhaps after the length of *I masnadieri* he was more than usually conscious of the need for brevity.

Even while the Sarasota run of performances was continuing, Eve Queler and her Opera Orchestra of New York on March 21, 2004, gave a concert performance of the opera in Carnegie Hall, allowing a comparison of the opera onstage and in concert. The orchestras were roughly the same size, in Sarasota fifty-three and in New York fifty-five; the balance, however, was different: in Sarasota twenty-three strings, and in New York thirty-four. Also the size of the chorus differed, in Sarasota twenty-four and in New York, thirty-nine, but Sarasota has the smaller auditorium, seating 1,033 to Carnegie Hall's 2,784. The most notable difference, to my ear, in the orchestral sound in the two auditoriums came in the storm music in the prelude and in the prison scene, where in New York it seemed a touch less scratchy, possibly because of the greater number of strings.

On the other hand, the drama of the opera lost greatly in concert. In the fight scene, there was no distinguishing Muslim from pirate, both wore tuxedos, shared the contemporary hairstyle, and stood rooted to their benches. And Corrado, of course, was not dragged in and thrown at the Pasha's feet. Though Queler had the pirates in the opening scene sing without orchestral accompaniment, they were onstage with the tenor, and their voices did not come from afar. Similarly, at the very end, there was no jump to death; the tenor remained upright before us and no curtain fell. As applause began, the soloists all smiled. Happy ending!

Yet in other ways the concert performance offered several advantages, chiefly to the tenor in the title role. Francisco Casanova had a fine voice,[49] but needed spectacles to see his score and was unfortunately shaped, with small head, hands, feet and large girth. As a corsair onstage he would have been ludicrous; in concert he turned his soliloquy in prison into a tour de force. The auditorium remained lit throughout the performance, allowing the audience to follow the text in the distributed librettos, and to its every twist and turn Casanova gave meaning. Much of what he accomplished might not have projected in a staged performance with the prison lit by a single torch and the prisoner much of the time sitting or lying on his side. But Casanova's artistry and the orchestra's supple accompaniment were powerful, and it was interesting to hear how well the music supported him. The scene evidently has more music to it than most tenors onstage can deliver. Yet over all, as usual with Verdi, the opera has more impact onstage than in concert.

An English critic who saw Sarasota's *Corsaro* was so carried away that he burbled in his report for *Opera Now*, "The opera is entirely worthy of being restored to the standard Verdi repertory."[50] Well, no—though his enthusiasm is proof that *Corsaro*, well performed, can leave an audience eager to hear it again. Meanwhile, its old reputation should be laid to rest, buried in the late twentieth century by the discoveries of scholars and the number of successful productions.

Chapter Eighteen

La battaglia di Legnano

This opera, with its cumbersome title, *The Battle of Legnano*, though praised more often than most of its thirteen predecessors for its musical sophistication, is performed in the United States almost as seldom as Verdi's *I masnadieri*. This is a puzzle, for unlike its fellow, its scenic demands are not great,[1] and though needing a well-rehearsed men's chorus, its musical demands are not insurmountable. Its high notes for the soprano, if beyond reach, can be finessed, and for singers easily tired, some second verses here and there can be cut. Moreover, even uncut, the opera is short, only 107 minutes, including an eight and a half minute overture that has been steadily admired, starting in 1859 with Abramo Basevi, the first Italian critic to attempt a survey of Verdi's operas (through the twentieth, *Aroldo*), and continuing today in Julian Budden's three-volume study of all twenty-eight.[2]

Moreover, the opera throughout is melodic and more carefully orchestrated than its predecessors, the latter improvement generally ascribed to Verdi's experience in composing *Jérusalem* a year earlier for the Paris Opéra, which then had the largest and best opera orchestra in Europe. In addition, *La battaglia*, set in Milan and Como in AD 1176, though unsubtle in its characterizations, has a clear story without loose ends.

Against these virtues, however, can be put what perhaps today strikes most audiences, especially those unfamiliar with European history, as some obvious flaws. First, what battle? Where? Even in Italy, few offhand can name the participants, the year, and the battle's significance. But in its day it was important, and in 1849, when the opera had its premiere in Rome (January 27, 1849), that history had a powerful resonance.

In 1176, the duly crowned Holy Roman Emperor Frederick I, known as "Barbarossa," for a third time brought his German troops across the Alps seeking to put down rebellion in several Italian cities in the Po Valley. In the emperor's view, he was acting to bring peace and order to the Italian peninsula. But he was opposed by the pope, who feared his power, and by several cities led by Milan and Verona, which, though consumed as always with their municipal rivalries, for once united against him as an interfering foreigner. And on May 29, near a small town northwest of Milan, Legnano, "the Lombard League," comprising sixteen towns and cities, in a startling upset defeated the emperor, in their view striking a blow for their ancient municipal liberties.

Almost eight hundred years later, in March 1848, the citizens of Milan in five days of street fighting drove Austrian Emperor Ferdinand I's troops out of

Milan and started a general uprising against the Austrian domination of the duchies and Papal States of northern and central Italy. In 1806, Napoleon had abolished the Holy Roman Empire, but for Italians it continued in the form of the Hapsburg Austrian Empire, which ruled from Vienna.[3] For a time the Austrian rulers and troops were everywhere in retreat, and a united Italian state seemed possible, with most of the revolutionaries eager to establish a republic or some sort of federation of cities and duchies, free of the emperor as well as of the pope's political rule.

As for the pope himself, the revolutionaries were content for him to remain head of the church, a purely spiritual leader, but he, faced with open revolt in Rome, had fled south across the border to Gaeta, where he was protected by the Neapolitan army. There, like the anxious king of Naples, he waited to see if the Austrian army, led by Field Marshal Radetzky, could reassert the Austrian domination of northern and central Italy or whether some compromise would have to be made with the republican revolutionaries. And in that period of uncertainty, of freedom from pope and emperor, when all censorship, even in Rome, was lifted, Verdi, with Salvadore Cammarano as his librettist, composed his most overtly patriotic opera, *La battaglia di Legnano*.[4]

It tells the story of the Lombard cities in 1176 uniting to challenge the Emperor, Barbarossa, but with a huge anachronism: in the opera the soldiers and citizens of Milan, Verona, Brescia, gathering to form the Lombard League, do not cry "Viva Milano" or "Viva Verona," as they did at the time, but, as appropriate for the hopes of 1848–49, "Viva Italia!" And therein perhaps lies one of the opera's problems for audiences today.

Verdi laid on the patriotic fervor heavily, both in the theatrical gestures onstage and in the sentimentality of several scenes. There are of course many choruses for troops assembling and warriors swearing to fight to the death, as well as a stunning theatrical close to the third act, when an outraged husband, Rolando (baritone), thinks he has caught his wife, Lida, in a tryst with his friend, Arrigo (tenor). He confronts them in a tower room of his castle, and as the League's army offstage, with music sounding, marches to battle, he is about to kill Arrigo, who offers no resistance, when instead he suddenly leaves, bolting the door behind him. Locked in the room, Arrigo faces shame, dishonor, infamy if he fails to join his troops. He pulls at the door. Searching for hinges, he finds none. Turning, he sees the balcony and with a cry of "Viva Italia" hurls himself into the river that serves as the castle's moat. (And of course, when the curtain next rises, he has swum to shore, rejoined his troops, and distinguished himself in the fighting.)

Yet it is not just the frequent cries for "Italia" that some people find grating, but the sentimentality with which Verdi and Cammarano drench some of their scenes. Along with the patriotism, for example, there is a constant stress on motherhood, on Italian mothers who nurture patriots and heroes. In the opening scene, Arrigo, in command of troops from Verona, has the opera's first aria,

"La pia materna," in which, before expressing his love for Milan where lives the lady he loves, he thanks his mother's "kindly hand" for nursing his wounds and returning him to health. On the eve of the battle at Legnano, his friend in Milan, Rolando, standing with Lida by their son's cradle, urges her, should she be left a widow, to teach the boy that he is born an Italian and that after God comes "la patria." That same evening, Arrigo, having sworn to fight to the death, sits to pen a letter to his mother, his few remarks accompanied by a distinctive rhythmic figure. As he writes, Lida quietly enters, looking over his shoulder at the letter, and a soft, expressive melody first heard in the Overture and played on woodwinds now sounds above the rhythmic figure—Lida and Arrigo. And Lida, in telling him that because of her marriage (done in the belief that Arrigo had died) they can never be joined, insists that she must live for her son and he, for his mother. Finally, in the last act, as Lida prays for both men to survive, word comes that the battle has been won and the emperor knocked from his saddle "by the Veronese Arrigo."[5] But soon a sound of funereal trumpets disrupts the victory chorus, and Arrigo is brought in on a litter, wounded and dying. He offers his hand to Rolando, who hesitates, and Arrigo, saying it would be a terrible sin to lie with one's dying breath, assures him that Lida is pure: They had never been lovers. Uniting their private story with the public feeling, he insists that dying he cannot tell a lie, and the crowd supports him: "Chi muore per la patria, alma sì rea non ha" (He who dies for his country, such a guilty soul does not have).

On the page, where the eye can linger, such scenes and sentiments may seem maudlin, but played and sung to a melody moving steadily ahead, they become affective. Indeed, in the final scene the melody itself begins to speak, and many in the audience will want more of it than Verdi allows. For, as his wont, he drops the curtain fast.

In Rome, in January 1849, with the pope fled and a Roman Republic about to be declared, the opera had a tremendous success, and at all performances the short, final act was repeated entire. But before the year was out, the Roman Republic had fallen to the French army, called in by the pope, and in the Po Valley the Austrians, under Radetzky, had reestablished themselves, with headquarters in Milan. By which time an opera crying "Viva Italia!" free and united, was banned by authorities, and performances anywhere in Europe became extremely rare. Verdi, believing his music had merit, tried to find another story to fit to it, and Cammarano had his assistant, Emanuele Bardare, write a new libretto called *L'assedio di Arlem* (The Siege of Haarlem), setting the scene in the Netherlands at the time of its revolt against Philip II of Spain. But perhaps because so many were aware of the opera's original story, in this disguise it had little success.[6] Then, Cammarano having died, Verdi tried again with Bardare, but the attempt died aborning, and Verdi, moving ahead to other projects, left the opera to find what way it could.[7]

Ultimately, in 1860, the Italians, led by Garibaldi and Victor Emmanuel of Savoy (king of Piedmont and Sardinia), with France now an ally, managed to drive the Austrians out of most of northern Italy (except for the province of Venice). And performances of *La battaglia* revived. But the opera's initial momentum had been lost. Impresarios, singers, and audiences now wanted *Rigoletto*, *Trovatore*, and *Traviata*. Moreover, *La battaglia* spoke of a dream unfulfilled. Italy had not become a federation of cities or a republic, but a kingdom ruled by the not-too-popular House of Savoy, first from Turin, then from Florence, and finally, after 1870, from Rome. The opera's time had passed.

Yet it had a fitful life. In the 1880s a French translation of its text, titled *La Patrie*, reportedly had a considerable run in French provincial theaters.[8] During World War 1, when Italians again fought Austrians, it had productions in Milan, Florence, Rome, Buenos Aires, and São Paulo, and after World War II it had still more, including a first recording taken from Italian radio in 1951, a premiere in England in 1960, and opening night of the 1961–62 season at Milan's La Scala. Moreover, general opinion following these productions judged the music for its period, pre-*Rigoletto* (1851), to be exceptionally fine. As Budden declared in 1973, "Everything is deliberately made 'interesting'; nothing is repeated without harmonic variation wherever possible. Even the scoring is calculated with greater care than one expects from Verdi at the time. In no opera before *I Vespri Siciliani* [which followed *La traviata* (1853)] does the composer seem so eager to parade his French lessons."[9]

As an example of Verdi's greater care with the orchestration, note the march with which he begins the Overture and which throughout the opera serves as a theme for the Lombard League. It is a compact, chordal tune, only nine measures, to be played *maestoso* (majestically), and if not varied on reappearance could become tiresome. As the opera's first notes heard, it is a call to action, scored only for trumpets, trombones, and a cimbasso (a bass trombone or tuba). Immediately it repeats, but now softly, at higher pitch, played by woodwinds over a sprightly walking bass on strings, and seemingly headed through a series of harmonic variations to a quiet close. Before reaching that close, however, it is overtaken by the theme's opening phrase repeated in aggressive rising steps of a third until dissolving into a cascade of notes that descend into chords played *morendo* (dying). A contrasting theme follows, a soft, expressive melody often associated with Lida (but which she never sings). The woodwinds coil around each other with the melody, gradually breaking down into delicate chordal patterns, all over a distinctive rhythmic accompaniment. But though this theme's function of contrast in the overture is clear enough, there is disagreement (discussed later), about its association. Is it with Lida or Arrigo?

In closing, the march briefly reappears only to be replaced by a wholly new skittering theme that seems to take over altogether, until toward the overture's end it is combined with a statement of the march, whose theme finally sounds alone, *tutta forza*. But even that is not the last of the theme's variations, for in the opening scene, on a street near the walls of Milan, as soldiers from Piacenza, Verona, Brescia, Novara, and Vercelli join those of Milan, with banners flying and women cheering from the balconies, Verdi has the men sing the march "a voci sole," without any orchestral accompaniment at all. A quite different sound.

As the Verdi Renaissance after World War II gathered momentum, the traditional high opinion of the opera's musical virtues seemed confirmed by a succession of recordings. The first to appear was taken from a radio performance in Rome in March 1951, one event of many marking the fiftieth anniversary of Verdi's death. Issued by the Cetra company as a recording, it sold internationally and reawakened interest in the opera.[10] Then pirated recordings of staged performances began to circulate, including one of Milan's opening night in December 1961, which featured a young Franco Corelli as Arrigo.[11] Finally, in 1978, came a well-performed studio recording, available ever since and supplemented by pirated recordings of later live performances.[12] In sum, though onstage performances continued infrequent, the opera's music was more widely heard, and proved, as Budden had said, enjoyable and "interesting." Thus the opera regained some luster.

Its history in the Western Hemisphere, however, is slight: a few performances in the nineteenth century in South America,[13] but none at all in the United States and Canada. Hence, until after World War II, when technological changes in recording—long-playing records, tapes, compact discs—each gave its boost to opera, in the United States the music of *La battaglia* remained generally unknown. The *Complete Catalogue of Sheet Music and Musical Works* showing what twenty-five of the country's leading publishers had in print in 1870 lists nothing for the opera. The U.S. Marine Band, though it had in its library (1855–71) arrangements of excerpts from fifteen of Verdi's operas, had none from *Battaglia*.[14] In 1903 when G. Schirmer, then the country's most active music publisher, started his series of *Celebrated Arias* for soprano, mezzo-soprano, tenor, baritone, and bass, he included no arias from it, though offering some from such rarities of the day as *Nabucco, Attila*, and *Macbeth*.[15] Similarly, the *Collectors' Guide to American Recordings, 1895–1925*, has none for the opera; nor *The Victor Book of the Opera*, whose editions stretch from 1912 to 1938.[16] But, the conductor Giuseppe Bamboschek, on November 21, 1920, at the Metropolitan Sunday Evening Concerts, led a performance of the overture that was, according to the program, for "the first time in America." Still, despite Bamboschek's enterprise, the overture was not rescheduled, or any other of the opera's music heard in the span of the concerts, 1883–1946.[17]

The opera's U.S. premiere, on February 28, 1976, was mounted by the small Amato Opera company in New York as a contribution to the country's bicentennial celebration. For the occasion, the company left its tiny theater (capacity 107) on the Bowery and staged the opera with a full orchestra and chorus of seventeen women and twenty-seven men in the Great Hall (capacity 900) of the Cooper Union, whose building, erected in 1859 and rising five tall stories, covers an entire city block at Astor Place. Its cavernous lecture hall

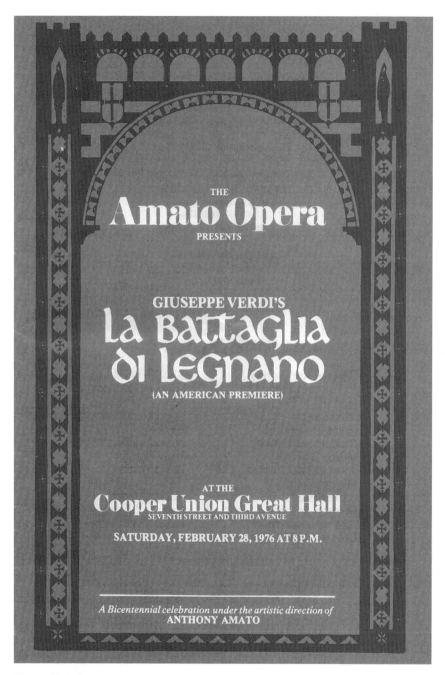

Figure 18.1. The program's jacket for the U.S. premiere of *La battaglia di Legnano*, February 28, 1976 (from author's collection).

— *Saturday, February 28, 1976* —

The Amato Opera presents
The American Premiere of

La Battaglia di Legnano

Music by Giuseppe Verdi
Libretto by Salvatore Cammarano
By arrangement with BELWIN MILLS PUBLISHING CORP.

Director: Anthony Amato
Scenery: Richard Cerullo
Costumes: Ikuko Okaya

CAST

(in order of appearance)

ARRIGO, a Veronese Soldier (*Tenor*) .... Robert Van Valkenburg
ROLANDO, a Milanese General (*Baritone*) .... Gordon Voorhees
THE FIRST CONSUL OF MILAN (*Bass*) .... Carl Barone
LIDA, Rolando's wife (*Soprano*) .... Judith Robinson
IMELDA, Lida's companion (*Mezzo-Soprano*) .... Lois Ann Dunton
MARCOVALDO, a German prisoner (*Baritone*)................. Max Frescoln
A HERALD (*Tenor*) .... Keith Giarosco
THE PODESTA OF COMO (*Bass*) .... Frederick Jahn
FREDERICK BARBAROSSA, the Holy Roman Emperor (*Bass*) ..... John Morgan
ROLANDO'S SON .... John Paul Sparacio

The action takes place in Italy in the year 1176.

PART I

Act One
Scene 1, Milan, at the City Gate
Scene 2, The Garden of Rolando's Estate

Act Two
Council Chamber in City of Como

INTERMISSION (fifteen minutes)

PART II

Act Three
Scene 1, A Vault Beneath the Church of St. Ambrogio in Milan
Scene 2, Lida's Room in Rolando's Castle
Scene 3, Arrigo's Room in a Tower Overlooking the Moat

Act Four
Milan, By the Church

Figure 18.2. Interior page from the U.S. premiere program of *La battaglia*, Amato Opera, 1976 (from author's collection).

in the basement is a New York landmark, the site of many famous speeches, of which the most important, on the evening of February 27, 1860, was delivered by Abraham Lincoln on the topic of slavery, its extension within the United States. He then concluded, "Let us have faith that right makes might, and in that faith let us to the end dare to do our duty as we understand it"; and the speech generally is said to have won for him in May the Republican nomination for president.[18]

Many who gathered in Cooper Union for the opera's premiere were aware of Lincoln's ghost in the hall and appreciated the symbolism of Anthony Amato's timing—almost to the day—in celebrating in that place the Union of States that owed so much to Lincoln. And in the jammed auditorium they vociferously approved. But the hall is not ideal for opera. Its ceiling is supported by rows of pillars, its width is far greater than its depth, its stage is only a dais, and for many seats the reverberation is odd. John Rockwell for the *Times* reported:

> Insofar as one can judge from the score and from Saturday's performance, the opera deserves a better fate. The love scenes have an individuality and passion to match the best of the composer's work of this period. And the big choral passages are really fine, full of Verdi's unique martial conviction. *La battaglia di Legnano* has been dismissed as a pot-boiler akin to Beethoven's *Wellington's Victory*, but that seems fair neither to the composer nor to the excellences of the opera itself.
>
> Unfortunately, those excellences were hardly displayed at their best on Saturday. . . . The Cooper Union stage is wide and shallow, which encouraged stiffly posed tableaux, and its configuration spread out the otherwise decent-sounding orchestra in a way that made coordination between the extremes chancy. The sound is loud and overresonant, such that the many choral scenes were rather overbearing—especially since the singers often confused fervor with yelling. . . . One has to appreciate the communal enthusiasm of Anthony Amato and those working with him for getting the performance onto the stage. This was clearly a special effort.[19]

Harriett Johnson for the *Post* observed of the opera's history:

> Possibly a difficult title and the circumstances of its birth have contributed to its unjustly having fallen into oblivion. By its quality it deserves a performance in one of our Lincoln Center houses. . . . The music is consistently absorbing . . . the final trio is superb as are the two great choruses in Acts I and III. There are also persuasive arias. . . . While Amato's sets and costumes were pretty primitive (skulls painted on the men's shirts) the young singers in leading roles had full-throated voices.[20]

In addition to this celebratory performance in Cooper Union's Great Hall, Amato gave the opera four more performances in his theater on the Bowery, with costumes, scenery, and alternating casts (except for Rolando) but accompanied only by a piano. The experience of the opera in the small house was rather different. Several of the grand choral scenes lost impact, while some of the more intimate scenes of the personal drama gained. One scene, which upon transfer was less effective, takes place in the crypt of Milan's Lombard cathedral, Sant'Ambrogio, where Arrigo joins the Knights of Death, a company sworn to fight to the death (their oaths symbolized by skulls painted on their shirts). The scene had played well amid the vaults and pillars of Cooper Union's basement, and even the music's occasional odd reverberation, had seemed properly authentic. In the small opera house, with only a piano instead of an orchestra, it was less awesome, less eerie. On the other hand, the intimacy of the small house favored the voices, and those scenes devoted to individuals gained balance and power. But the absence of an orchestra was a grievous loss.[21]

The first company to follow the Amato company's lead was Boston Concert Opera, which under the direction of David Stockton, had given the Boston premieres of such operas as Puccini's *Le Villi* and *Edgar*, De Falla's *La vida breve*, and, in the spring of 1978 Verdi's *Giovanna d'Arco*. Curiously, the premiere of *La battaglia* went almost unnoticed by the newspapers, but it was, in the company's style, a full-throated affair with a chorus of sixty-two and an orchestra of forty-four, of which half were strings. Moreover it was presented with a good cast not once but twice, on December 4 and 6, in Jordan Hall (capacity 1,013), one of the city's prestigious halls. The silence with which it was met suggests a failure, either on the part of the Boston critics or in the company's publicity department.[22]

Three years later, the Pittsburgh Opera mounted *La battaglia*, billing it as the first "American fully professional stage premiere." A local critic, analyzing the carefully hedged language surmised that the company's director, Tito Capobianco, had discounted the Amato production in 1976 as "semi-professional," and the little-noted concert performances in Boston as "unstaged." On these terms, he supposed, the production in Heinz Hall (capacity 2,661) was indeed perhaps "the first full-scale staging by a major-league American company."[23] In any case, the company's publicity director did well: newspapers anticipated the production with excited articles and wrote of the premiere as an important social and musical event.

Musically, it was notable for success in some respects and failure in others, about which those who reviewed it expressed themselves with unusual force. To take the failures first. Singers and critics alike objected to Capobianco's staging the opera as if it were taking place in 1848, when Italian republicans united against the Austrians. This shift left the historical Barbarossa, who appears as the climax to one scene, some seven hundred years out of date. As the bass assigned the role remarked, "I hope you are not going to question me about the plot. We know this is a very immature work of Verdi with an immature and senseless

BOSTON CONCERT OPERA

David Stockton, Music Director

LA BATTAGLIA DI LEGNANO

Music by Giuseppi Verdi

Libretto by Salvatore Cammarano

Cast *in order of appearance*
Arrigo, a warrior from Verona, *Tenor* . . . . .Jon West
Rolando, a Milanese officer, *Baritone* . . . . .Andrew Smith
First Consul of Milan, *Baritone* . . . . .Michael Morizio
Second Consul of Milan, *Bariton* . . . . .James Kleyla
Arrigo's squire, *Tenor* . . . . .Mark Jackson
Lida, Rolando's wife, *Soprano* . . . . .Wilhelmenia Fernandez
Marcovaldo, a German prisoner, *Bass* . . . . .Jeffrey Wells
Imelda, Lida's maid, *Soprano* .Cecelia Schieve
A herald, *Tenor* . . . . .Mark Jackson
The Podesta of Como, *Baritone* .James Kleyla
Frederick Barbarossa, *Bass* . . . . .Jeffrey Wells
Chorus of Monks . . . . .Mark Jackson, Michael Morizio,
James Kleyla, Jeffrey Wells

Concert Opera Orchestra and Chorus

David Stockton, Conductor

Jordan Hall

Friday, December 4, 1981

Sunday, December 6, 1981

8:00 P.M.

There will be two intermissions

These performances are funded in part with grants from the Massachusetts Council on the Arts and Humanities (a state agency whose funds are recommended by the Governor and appropriated by the State Legislature), the National Endowment for the Arts, and the Community Services Administration of the City of Boston.

We wish to thank the Eugene F. Fay Trust, the Polaroid Foundation and the New England Conservatory of Music for making possible the special open dress rehearsal for Senior Citizens on Wednesday, December 2.

Figure 18.3. Interior page from the Boston Concert Opera's program for performances of *La battaglia,* 1981 (from author's collection).

libretto." None of this is true, but it shows how unhappy can be the results of a flawed updating.[24]

The usual reason offered for such surgery is a desire to graft onto the opera some modern relevance. But besides stumbling on historical grounds, such shifts in period can also fail for musical reasons. The Welsh National Opera Company, staging the opera's British premiere in 1960, sang it in English and set it in northern Italy during the partisan fighting that followed the collapse of Mussolini's government (1943) and during the German army's slow retreat up the Italian peninsula (1944–45). This shift, with the opera's title reduced to *The Battle*, had the advantage of dropping all reference to the Lombard League and to Barbarossa, with the emperor now merely a German commander. English critics, on the whole were impressed. "Musically," one wrote, "the production was very enjoyable, with lively Welsh choral singing in those grand ensembles, and a beautifully poised account of the heroine Lida."[25] But from the first, some protested the updating, and soon their complaints touched the translation. As the production grew familiar, played on tour and in London, and critics and audiences heard it twice or more, for it was a popular success,[26] the twentieth-century English translation—"Bastard," "Dirty liars," and "After all the hell I've been through"—began to sound awkward, as if "the drama of World War II was being accompanied by out-of-date music."[27] Ultimately critics, and seemingly audiences, too, felt the opera would have played better if left in the period for which Verdi had conceived it. And in the United States, after the Pittsburgh production, many reached the same conclusion.

Another failure in Pittsburgh lay in the lack of balance between the principals. All critics and a full house at each performance agreed that June Anderson as Lida was excellent; unhappily, those singing Rolando and Arrigo were not. The visiting critic from the New York, Donal Henahan of the *Times*, remarked only that the principals were "uneven in quality,"[28] but the local critic, Robert Croan for the *Pittsburgh Post-Gazette*, declared the men's singing "horribly provincial." He also rounded on the chorus as "still raucous and unreliable—particularly the male contingent—in discipline and intonation." And in a shorter review for *Opera News*, he was still outraged, "squally in tone and often undisciplined onstage."[29]

On the other hand the scenery, by John Conklin, was much praised by all, particularly the drop curtain, showing a battle scene that might have been painted by Delacroix or Géricault. Kept down during the overture, toward the latter's closing bars it turned transparent, and through it the audience began to see the chorus assembled in tableau for the opening scene. Moreover, according to Henahan of the *Times*, the scenery, "economically built around six movable pillars, was cleverly lighted."[30] And for the scene in the crypt, for which Amato had provided skulls painted on shirts, the Pittsburgh costume shop carved skulls from styrene foam board that were attached by velcro to the shirts of twenty-four warriors. Conklin had shown with a sample exactly how he wanted the skulls highlighted, and under the clever lighting they glowed.[31]

In another respect, too, the production drew praise. The four acts, unusually uneven in their timing, 33, 15, 38, and 13 minutes, were presented as two, so that the action "unfolded swiftly,"[32] and notably it was accompanied by surtitles projected on a screen below the proscenium, or as the company called its technique (apparently to avoid copyright problems) "Optrans." By whatever name, in 1984 surtitles were still new, used first by the Canadian Opera Company for a performance of *Electra* in Toronto in 1983. Later that year Artpark, in Niagara Falls, had borrowed the titles for its *Electra*, and in the fall, the New York City Opera had introduced them for a production of Massenet's *Cendrillon*. On the whole they were much praised and soon, with improvements, became a fixture in most houses.[33] In sum, the Pittsburgh production, however good or bad its artistry, brought the opera considerable attention, with Henahan declaring: "The score . . . revealed itself as remarkably advanced and sophisticated. Despite the opera's propagandistic aims and attitudes, there is very little banging of the big drum or reliance on cheap tunes. In fact, there is a chamber-music quality to some numbers."[34]

Yet the pace of productions in the United States, always a bit slower than in Europe,[35] did not greatly quicken. On January 12, 1987, Eve Queler's Opera Orchestra of New York gave the opera a concert performance in Carnegie Hall. Despite a cast of "good names," Henahan, for the *Times*, was disappointed. Seemingly, no singer did justice to his or her role, and "the opera's strengths were somewhat obscured by Miss Queler's plodding, uninspiring conducting."[36] Nevertheless, she returned to the opera on November 13, 2001, again in Carnegie Hall, and for this outing the *Times* critic, now Anthony Tommasini, was more enthusiastic: "Here was a seldom-heard Verdi score, presented with as good a cast as any the Met could have assembled." Though he found "the orchestra playing was somewhat listless and unfocused," Queler's company offered a full orchestra numbering fifty-seven and a chorus of fifty. "This is why Ms. Queler has endeared herself to opera fans in New York for more than 25 years."[37]

Meanwhile, on July 30, 1997, the New York Grand Opera Company had given *La battaglia* a staged performance in Central Park as the fourteenth opera in its eight-year cycle of Verdi's twenty-eight, presented in order of composition.[38] Summer park performances, over loudspeakers, have their problems, and on this night, according to *Times* critic, James R. Oestreich, the usual electronic difficulties were compounded by a change in cast. The announced Rolando being indisposed, a substitute "contributed serviceably until his voice collapsed in the third act." On the other hand, Oestreich was impressed by "a splendid performance as Lida by Amelia D'Arcy, a young soprano in her 'professional debut,'" and equally by "Vincent La Selva, the spirit behind the whole rickety enterprise, [who] conducted with a sure hand."[39]

Tuesday Evening, November 13, 2001, at 8:00
Isaac Stern Auditorium

OPERA ORCHESTRA OF NEW YORK

Eve Queler, *Music Director*

GIUSEPPE VERDI

La battaglia di Legnano

Opera in four acts

Libretto by Salvatore Cammarano

Eve Queler, *Conductor*

THE CAST
(in order of vocal appearance)

Arrigo, Veronese captain	. . . . . Francisco Casanova
Rolando, Arrigo's comrade at arms	. . . . . Carlo Guelfi*
Second Consul of Milan	. . . . . Frank Barr
First Consul of Milan	. . . . . Timothy Lafontaine
Lida, Rolando's wife	. . . . . Krassimira Stoyanova
Marcovaldo, a German prisoner	. . . . . Gregory Keil†
Imelda, Lida's servant	. . . . . Carla Wood
A Herald	. . . . . Matthew Walley
Mayor of Como	. . . . . Jason Grant
Federico Barbarossa, Holy Roman Emperor	. . . . . Vitalij Kowaljow‡

Knight of Death; magistrates and leaders of Como; Lida's serving maids; people of Milan; Senators of Milan; soldiers from Verona, Novara, Piacenze, and Milan; and German soldiers:
The Opera Orchestra of New York Chorus,
Prepared by Douglas Martin

The action takes place in Milan and Como in the year 1176.

There will be a pause between Acts I and II, an intermission between Acts II and III, and a pause between Acts III and IV.

Librettos are made possible, in part, through the generosity of Rolex Watch, U.S.A.

*Carlo Guelfi's appearance has been made possible by a generous bequest from Joanne Toor Cummings.

†Vitalij Kowaljow is the recipient of the Harriet Greenfield Young Artists Award for Excellence.

‡Gregory Keil's debut has been funded in part by the Seth I. Weissman Young Artists Fund.

This concert is made possible, in part, by the New York State Council on the Arts, the City of New York Department of Cultural Affairs, and the National Endowment for the Arts, a federal agency. NYSCA

AeroMexico is a generous supporter of Opera Orchestra of New York and its Young Artists Program.

Before the concert begins, please switch off your cell phones and other electronic devices.

25

Figure 18.4. Program for a concert performance of *La battaglia* in Carnegie Hall presented by the Opera Orchestra of New York, 2001 (from author's collection).

Asked ten years later why in the intervening years he had never revived *La battaglia*, La Selva hesitated. "It's a good opera," he began, "but I'm not sure Verdi put his heart in it as he did with *Giovanna d'Arco*." As their titles suggest, *Battaglia* is primarily about patriotism, a concept, whereas *Giovanna*, as Verdi tells her story, is about an individual, a peasant girl on a highly personal mission. Verdi's most popular operas typically are built on characterizations of individuals. Of his twenty-eight, as La Selva counts them, seventeen are titled by the names of their leading characters, to which might be added three more because of their specificity: *Il corsaro*, *Il trovatore*, and *La traviata*.[40] But whatever the title, audiences seem to respond more easily and emotionally to those in which individuals, not ideas, are clearly the center of attention, and most easily to those that keep the significant individuals clearly in focus. In Verdi's *Don Carlos*, for example, though there is much singing about oppression in Flanders and *La liberté*, the opera's focus is steadily on human relations.

In *Battaglia*, Arrigo is, or should be the main character. He opens and closes the opera, appears in the most scenes, and is the only one of the three principals to sing in each act's finale. Yet seemingly, many in any audience do not take him to be the leading character. He is overshadowed not only by the theme of patriotism but also to some extent by Lida. "In casting the opera," La Selva remarked, "a good Lida may be the hardest of the three principals to find. She must be able to handle high Cs and coloratura as well as passionate declamation, and she must be able to shift in and out of these with conviction." Comparing the demands to those that Verdi four years later would ask of Violetta in *Traviata*, he added, "Though sopranos can score a big success with Lida, as some have, she is not quite at the center of the opera."[41] Similarly, neither is Arrigo quite at the center.

To return for a moment to that soft, contrasting theme of the overture, which no principal sings: Is it to be associated primarily with Lida or with Arrigo and his thoughts of his mother? And does it matter? It recurs only once in the opera, for solo oboe and strings, as Arrigo starts to write to his mother and Lida enters noiselessly, *tacitamente*, behind him and over his shoulder reads what he has written. Most critics recently have followed Budden, who in writing about the overture in 1973 stated: "The theme, later to be associated with Arrigo as he sits writing to his mother."[42] Yet in the 1984 Pittsburgh production of the opera, the company cut the women's chorus that in an earlier act introduces Lida to the audience, substituting for the chorus a replaying of the overture's theme, clearly tying it to Lida. The point here is not to urge a view, but to note the uncertainty. When Violetta in *Traviata* sits to write a note to Alfredo, and a solo clarinet plays a theme no one sings, there is no such uncertainty. The instrumental melody expresses Violetta's anguish. But then, Verdi came to *Traviata* four years after composing *La battaglia*.

Others, using different words and examples, have made much the same point. Most often they suggest that the opera's chief defect is a failure to mesh fully the opera's public and private stories, the Lombard League and Lida, Rolando, and Arrigo. The two stories, say some, proceed side by side, but not quite together.[43] Yet the opera's final scene, always a great success with audiences, would seem to contradict that complaint.

Over the years, Italian scholars and critics, on the whole, have been less enthusiastic for the opera than their colleagues in Britain and the United States.[44] That distaste perhaps owes something to a prejudice against any piece written for a patriotic occasion and so seeming to demand approval, as may have happened with the Italian revivals in World War I or even on the Verdi anniversary in 1951. Happily for the opera, that tie to occasion seems to be dissolving. In 1999, an Italian company took it on tour through the smaller cities in the Po Valley; in 2003, the Teatro San Carlo, in Naples, staged it for the first time since 1860; and two years later, in a joint production, it played in Piacenza and Ravenna.[45] Perhaps now, even in Italy, the opera can survive, or fail, solely on its musical and dramatic merits.

In England and the United States, despite its U.S. premiere as part of the country's bicentennial celebration, this has always been true, and as the performances slowly increase, the critics in both countries write of the opera with ever greater approval. After a concert performance by the Royal Opera in London, in June 2000, a critic for *Opera* observed, "There is much more in *La battaglia* than loud cries of 'Viva Italia!'" and he was "especially impressed by the many different ways in which Verdi uses the chorus."[46] Earlier, two American critics for the *Times* had reached that conclusion, and after a concert performance in New York in 2001, still another could state, "This opera is a showcase for singers . . . Lida . . . floating soft, high-lying phrases and summoning ample power in climactic moments . . . is a major Verdi soprano role."[47] And the Verdi scholar Roger Parker declared in 1992 that not only does the overture deserve "revival in today's concert halls," but the opera itself "stands as one of Verdi's most unjustly neglected works."[48]

Possibly, if revived by a major house, in a well-staged production, sung in its nineteenth-century Italian and set with scenery and costumes of the twelfth century, with Barbarossa a colorful, commanding, imperial figure, it might catch the public's fancy. Might, because despite defects, the situations and music for the most part are effective.

Chapter Nineteen

Stiffelio

Among Verdi's operas *Stiffelio*, which immediately preceded *Rigoletto* and was first staged in Trieste in 1850, is in several respects unusual, and in one, unique. To take the last first: Unique, because the only one of Verdi's operas whose orchestral score, in main part, was lost for almost a hundred years, during which time the opera could not be staged or even studied with any assurance that the reader was in touch with what Verdi intended. For its initial decade, however, it had existed in a severely censored form, had played in several theaters, and from that period some vocal scores, librettos, and reviews had come down, enough to give a good idea of how very unusual an opera it was for its day.

Unusual, in that its leading tenor is not a young lover but a middle-aged, married, Protestant minister. Unusual, in that it and *Traviata* are the only operas Verdi conceived to be played in contemporary dress, and unusual because between *Nabucco* and *Falstaff* it is the only opera in which he musically declared the ending happy. And most unusual in its steady focus on a tenet of religious belief, the Christian dogma of forgiveness for sin: how it might be practiced or ignored.

Like most composers, Verdi often had put the Church onstage in choir or procession, massed voices, bells, and colorful cardinals, but in *Stiffelio* he took this core belief of Christianity and portrayed the psychological difficulties of a nineteenth-century Protestant pastor, who discovers his wife has been unfaithful: Can he practice what he preaches? Can he forgive her, both as a minister of God and as a husband?

No opera of the time displayed so bluntly the contrast, some might say the hypocrisy, of professed belief and accepted human behavior. Moreover, in Catholic countries priests do not marry, and in the operatic world, adultery was avenged not by divorce, as Stiffelio offers his wife, but by killing the third party and often the wayward spouse. Even before the premiere in Trieste, religious censors wrote out all references to God, to the Bible, and to the protagonist's role as pastor, so that the minister of God, instead of preaching to his congregation about Jesus forgiving the adulterous woman, became merely a layman speaking to a group of like-minded people about the merits of forgiveness as a general policy. And in Rome, Florence, and other Italian cities, companies staged, without Verdi's approval, a version of the opera, titled *Guglielmo Wellingrode*, which moved the setting from western Austria in the early nineteenth century to Germany in the early fifteenth, with Wellingrode now merely a secular official in a small German state. Nowhere in the nineteenth century did *Stiffelio* play as Verdi intended.

Figure 19.1. The outraged husband Stiffelio (Robert Breault, Chautauqua, 2004) momentarily chooses the sword over forgiveness. Photograph by Marie Ho. Courtesy of the Chautauqua Opera.

After five years of few and highly troubled performances, Verdi asked his publisher, Ricordi, to withdraw the opera, and in its place, using considerable music from *Stiffelio*, he offered a new opera, *Aroldo* (1857), which Ricordi vigorously puffed and pushed. As a result, by the mid-1860s *Stiffelio/Wellingrode* was effectively taken off the operatic market, its score no longer to be had in any form. In all, in any version, it had played only in Italy, Spain, and Portugal.[1]

Meanwhile, Ricordi told any who asked that it no longer had available for hire an orchestral score and parts for *Stiffelio*; moreover, the house had no printed copy of the score, for none (as then was custom) had been published, nor did it have any manuscript copy of the score; and further, it did not have Verdi's autograph orchestral score, for he had taken it back, tearing out the pages he needed for *Aroldo* and presumably destroying the rest. Seemingly, therefore, no complete score existed.[2] Unique among Verdi's operas, *Stiffelio* was "lost."

What was known to remain of the opera, besides reviews of its few early performances, were chiefly some severely censored librettos printed for these performances, some vocal scores similarly censored, and those pages of the *Stiffelio* orchestral autograph that Verdi had transferred directly into the score of *Aroldo*. (Ultimately, scholars were able to set the amount of the old used in the new at 39 percent.)[3] Hence, by 1931, when the English scholar Francis Toye published his influential *Giuseppe Verdi: His Life and Works*, like others he mentioned *Stiffelio* only as a source for the later opera.[4] As a stageable work, it did not exist.

In the substitute *Aroldo*, Verdi tells of a thirteenth-century English knight returning home from a crusade to discover that his wife has committed adultery. Moving the period back six hundred years met the public's desire for the more colorful costumes of yesteryear rather than the drab, Protestant clothing of the day.[5] But of course, in substituting a crusading knight for a minister of God, Verdi cut from the work the crucial conflict between the man's role as a preacher and his feelings as a husband. As *Aroldo*, the opera had an initial wide success—it had its U.S. premiere at New York's Academy of Music on May 4, 1863—but despite some much-admired new music, especially an exciting vocal-orchestral storm in the final act, after some twenty years it departed the stage, reappearing only rarely.[6]

Then in the 1920s, the Verdi Renaissance began, and after World War II, as interest spread, scholars began to remove from his long-familiar scores some of the accretions of faulty tradition and to search for other versions of operas (often with alternative arias), for sketches, and for "lost" works. And in 1968, in the Biblioteca di S. Pietra a Majella in Naples, scholars found two hand-copied manuscripts of orchestral scores: one, of the severely censored *Stiffelio*, and the other, of the unauthorized, *Guglielmo Wellingrode*.[7] These allowed the collation of two orchestral scores with the two existing vocal scores, giving for the first time in a century a relatively certain (though not perfect because based on censored versions of the opera) guide to Verdi's orchestration. Immediately, an opera company in Parma prepared a performing edition of *Stiffelio*, though making some cuts and repositioning one scene, and in December of that same year staged the opera. A performance was recorded, later broadcast in England, and in the United States, at least, sold by a small record company.[8]

Interest in the opera rose, productions elsewhere took place, and seventeen years later in the Österreichische Nationalbibliothek in Vienna scholars found another hand-copied orchestral score of *Stiffelio*, this one seemingly more accurate than that of Naples (though still based on a censored version of Verdi's original score). Promptly, a new performing edition was prepared and the opera staged in Venice in 1985.[9]

Later, in part to assist a Metropolitan production of the opera in New York, scheduled for 1993, Verdi's heirs allowed scholars to examine the autograph manuscripts and sketches of the opera still in their possession, and further corrections could be made. Of these, perhaps the most important was the recovery from an autograph sketch of some original text set by Verdi, which, before the Trieste premiere, had been cut by censors and as rewritten published in the librettos and vocal scores. Thus, although from 1968 onward the opera was perhaps 90 percent correct, in many details it still was not, and the U.S. premiere of the opera in New York in 1976, and productions in Boston 1978,

San Francisco 1979, New York 1980, and Wilmington (Delaware) 1988 were, in a sense, all "works in progress," each incorporating the latest small corrections.

As an example of how a small textual correction could increase a scene's impact, consider the opera's final scene in which Stiffelio, still in emotional turmoil, mounts the pulpit to preach to his congregation. Not knowing what to say, he opens the Bible by chance to St. John's Gospel, chapter 8, and starts to read (or, as those who doubt random chance may prefer, is moved to recite from memory) the story of Jesus and the adulterous woman, ending, "Let him without sin cast the first stone." As Stiffelio begins, Verdi holds the orchestra silent, and the minister's first words sound unadorned and clear. But what are those first words?

The text from which Verdi and his librettist, F. M. Piave, worked was an Italian translation of a French play, *Le Pasteur*,[10] in which the crucial first line reads: "Allora Gesù, volgendosi al popolo assembrato, e mostrando la donna adultera ch'era ai suoi piedi" (Then Jesus, turning to the assembled people, and pointing to the adulterous woman who was at his feet . . .).

This was not heard in Trieste in 1850, where even before the premiere the censors had ruled that the scene could not be in a church, Stiffelio could not be a minister of God, and any mention of God was to be cut. What actually was sung is unsure, for the singers had to be admonished to sing the lines as revised; and for several singers' benefit performances, the scene was dropped.[11] But the censor-approved libretto for Trieste and a vocal score, published in Paris around 1855, with the latter at least setting the scene in a church, has the line read as follows: "Rivolto allor quel Divo al popolo assembrato." But "Rivolto allor quel Divo" (Turned then the godly man), with the opening, unaccompanied words merely "rivolto allor" (turned then) is far less arresting than, "Allor Gesù."

At Parma in 1968 the line was sung as "Rivolto allor quel Divo," and also in a production in Naples (1972) based on the Parma score.[12] But by 1979, when the first studio performance of the opera was recorded in Vienna, the line had improved to: "Rivolto allor Gesù," which, though closer to the original, is still marred by having "Gesù," pushed to third place in the sentence, where it is slightly muffled by the orchestra sounding a chord under the second syllable of "allor." And then a production in Venice in 1985, purportedly following the Viennese manuscript precisely, reverted to the older version: "Rivolto allor quel Divo."[13]

Finally, in 1992, not in Verdi's autograph score of the opera, for even those parts of it discovered in his family's archives lacked the opera's final scene, but in a sketch for that scene, scholars found the line as Verdi had conceived it: "Allor Gesù, rivolto al popolo assembrato mostrò l'adultera ch'era a suoi piedi." Note that Verdi had sharpened the line's effect by shortening the "allora" to "allor" (and several other words as well). In this version, he held the orchestra silent until Stiffelio had uttered the first syllable of the wholly familiar "Gesù." And so it has since been sung.[14]

Figure 19.2. Final scene at Chautauqua, 2004. "Perdonata!" Stiffelio from the pulpit forgives his wife. Photograph by Mark Anderson. Courtesy of the Chautauqua Opera.

In the United States, several opera conductors and impresarios following events in Italy began to think of producing the opera, giving it not only its U.S. but its Western Hemisphere premiere. One of these was Vincent La Selva, the director of the New York Grand Opera Company, one of the city's smaller companies; another was Sarah Caldwell of the Opera Company of Boston, at the time Boston's leading company. But where could either find an orchestral score, or even an old vocal score with which to begin study? Not in any music store.

La Selva, who was destined ultimately to give the opera its premiere, discovered in the archives of the Juilliard School a copy of a vocal score published in Paris, following the opera's production in Venice in 1852.[15] And because he was on the school's faculty, the librarian allowed him to take it home and make a copy. He thus had a start, the vocal lines for singers, but he still lacked any orchestral score and parts. Yet with a burst of incautious confidence in midwinter 1976 he announced a production to be staged in June.

Next, he asked the publisher Ricordi to rent to him copies of the orchestral score used at Parma and copies of parts for the individual orchestral instruments. Ricordi refused to rent to him. No one can be sure of the publisher's reasons, but a possibility leaps to mind: in Ricordi's eyes the New York Grand Opera was a small, local company, and the publisher was hoping that the Metropolitan, the Chicago Lyric, or the San Francisco Opera, would give the opera its American premiere. Or at least, Sarah Caldwell's Opera Company of Boston.

What to do? Happily, La Selva had an acquaintance who had contacts in Italy, and this person, who wishes to remain unnamed, procured and delivered to him a photocopy of the manuscript copy of the *Stiffelio* orchestral score held in the Neapolitan library. Meanwhile, the announced premiere scheduled for June was fast approaching. The singers, soloists and chorus, could study their parts from copies of the vocal score, but the orchestra, as yet without parts, could not rehearse, and to La Selva's dismay, the copy of the manuscript score he had received was difficult to read, a trail of "chicken tracks across the paper." Fortune, however, again placed by his side someone who could help. In his orchestra he had a clarinetist, Arthur Bloom, who was also an expert at deciphering mid-nineteenth-century hand-copied scores, and Bloom with three hired assistants went to work on the score. It took the four of them a month, working full time, to decipher and prepare a conductor's score and make parts for the instrumentalists, but just as rehearsals *had* to begin or the production be canceled, the parts were ready, and the production went ahead. Thus, on June 4, 1976, at the Brooklyn Academy of Music, La Selva and the New York Grand Opera company gave *Stiffelio* its U.S. and hemispheric premiere.[16]

Reviews, with one exception, were favorable and expressed interest in the opera. The most detailed was by Andrew Porter in the *New Yorker*. For example: "The interview between Stiffelius and his wife is the high point. He addresses her in measured Bellinian phrases; the effect is of someone forcing himself to contain fierce emotions within formal utterance. When she replies, her voice is doubled in octaves by clarinet and solo cello, and accompanied only by hollow fifths—an extraordinarily poignant passage. Then an English-horn melody takes over, to express the intensity of feelings that has reduced her speech to little more than a monotone."[17] In the *New York Post*, Speight Jenkins, later the impresario of the Seattle Opera, remarked: "Verdi uses the slow-fast form . . . for most of the big arias and duets in the work; his originality comes in his attempt to characterize each of the three principals as real, suffering people." Of the principals in this production, he thought, as did others, the soprano was "the weakest . . . too pallid. . . . Yet hers was not an unmusical contribution, her pitch was solid; and she got the notes. . . . It is a rare opportunity to hear an unusual Verdi opera, staged and sung with style at a low price."[18]

The disapproving critic, Alan Rich for *New York Magazine*, began by deriding La Selva and the company for pretending "to an intellectual posture by delving into repertory little known." He went on, "I endured two thirds of Verdi's *Stiffelio*; more would have smacked of the suicidal. *Stiffelio* is an interesting failure . . . the plot is weird . . . the sets were somebody's amateurish idea of forced perspective, but merely cockeyed; the costumes were basic bell captain (men) and merely ugly (women)." He devoted his final paragraph to scolding the president of the Academy of Music for renting the house to such as "La Selva's bunch."[19]

Audiences for the two performances, however, were pleased, and in the coming years many who had heard the opera in Brooklyn would ask La Selva to revive it. Apparently, the public did not find the plot "weird," and was willing to overlook some creaky plotting—a wedding ring missing; letters burned unread—in order to empathize with the three principals, "real, suffering people." Verdi was always less interested in plot than character, and in addition to the minister of God, wrestling with his inability to live out his belief, there was the suffering of his wife Lina: Can she come to grips with what she has done? Can she convince her husband, in their crucial third act duet, that even in the brief affair she never ceased to love him, loves him still, and looks for domestic pardon and priestly absolution? In addition, there is the confusion of her father, Stankar, a retired military officer obsessed with family honor. At first he urges her to conceal her adultery, to tell no one, especially not her husband, and throws her wifely letter of confession into the fire. Later, in a burst of passion, he reveals to Stiffelio the seducer's identity, the nobleman Raffaele von Leuthold; and still later, in a duel and always in the name of honor, he kills the man. Should Stankar, too, be pardoned? At the opera's end, as Stiffelio, preaching on the story of Jesus and the adulterous woman, tells his congregation, including Lina, that she is forgiven—*Perdonata!*—God and man's judgment on Stankar is left open. He is not included in the musically joyful, repeated and ringing C-major cry of *Perdonata!*

The next to produce the opera was Sarah Caldwell in Boston, at the Orpheum Theater on February 15, 1978. She reportedly had tried to sign the exceptionally powerful tenor Jon Vickers for the role of Stiffelio, but he, upon reading the score, had declined, in part because Verdi had not given Stiffelio any solo aria in which to express his pain. True enough: though Verdi gave solo scenes of anguish to both Lina and Stankar, he had none for Stiffelio, and for the first time in one of his operas he did not allow the tenor a cadenza. Yet the minister, through his leading part in multiple duets and ensembles, dominates the opera.

Richard Dyer, for the *Boston Globe,* began his review: "Everything about the production of Verdi's *Stiffelio* was a characteristic jumble of the inspired, the respectable and the inexcusably incompetent." The last chiefly was a tenor judged unable to sing the title role effectively. But "The opera itself is an important and uneven work, and it was wonderful to have this opportunity to know it. . . . The last act is magnificent in every way: there is a splendid double aria for the baritone, a thrilling and noble duet for the tenor and soprano (at the climax of which Lina, all human recourse exhausted, turns to her husband and cries, 'Minister, hear my confession!') and a glorious final scene in the church."[20]

The Verdi scholar Julian Budden, who in 1973 had published the first of his three volumes on Verdi's operas had remarked of this closing scene: "What is most striking about this scena finale is its deliberate avoidance of thematic interest. The continuity is maintained chiefly by repetition of pregnant hieratic motifs in the orchestra." That is, as the violins and violas hold quiet chords, the cellos and bassoons repeat a slow thump, thump down half the scale, returning always to the starting note; and later the cellos, joined now by the double-basses, beneath woodwinds holding chords, start in a slow march rhythm, a pattern of plucked strings on each of the first three beats and silence on the fourth, a pattern that suggests—Budden's "pregnant" motif—something more than it sounds. "Its purpose," Budden writes, "becomes clear, when first Stiffelio and then the congregation take up the word 'Perdonata' in a heart-easing cadence. Short as this finale is, it represents a unique solution in all Verdi."[21]

In Caldwell's production, though she evidently paced the scene well, in Andrew Porter's opinion she somewhat spoiled the orchestral effect by having an onstage organist, who had opened the church scene (as Verdi requires), continue to mime away, "in full flight even when the organ was not playing." He thought it "a bad Caldwell idea: the deliberately static, expectant quality of the music—all are waiting to hear on what text Stiffelius will preach—needs to be matched by a motionless scene."[22]

Another bit of Caldwell staging that drew Porter's disapproval was the scene in which Stankar kills the seducer, Raffaele. Verdi, in act 3, scene 1, the scene in which Lina demands the right to confess to her minister-husband, has the killing offstage. Suddenly, into the midst of the Lina-Stiffelio duet, Stankar runs in, bloodied sword in hand, announcing that Raffaele is dead. His startled hearers, seeing the sword, ask: "A duel? A murder?" And he runs off exulting, "An expiation. He who could have revealed our dishonor is now dead." Verdi's staging is very abrupt—Stankar on–off—and the speed of it can leave an audience confused, especially when, as in Boston, the opera is sung in Italian and without subtitles. Moreover, the scene leaves unanswered the question of a duel or a murder, and whether for this religious group there can be a distinction. Verdi does not say, and conflicting views can be argued. Among them, two points seem worth stressing. Stankar, a former soldier, likely offered Raffaele a sword, as he had done in the previous act, and in the Italian translation of the underlying play, from which Verdi first worked, Stankar replies to the question "A murder?" "No, a true duel, an expiation!"[23]

Caldwell's solution to this troublesome scene was to have Stankar onstage stab Raffaele in the back, in front of other people, "a thing," lamented Porter, "he would never have done." The scene is always a problem, and no solution yet offered seems perfect.[24] But whatever the partial failures in the La Selva and Caldwell productions, because of them the opera's reputation in the United States rose.

Two smaller companies thereupon mounted somewhat reduced versions of the opera in 1979 and 1980. First, Pocket Opera, in San Francisco, produced it in an English version prepared by the company's founder and conductor, Donald Pippin. As usual, Pippin led the performance from the piano and offered,

in a theater seating only several hundred, an orchestra of eight or nine players and singers who were professionals or professionally trained. Such a persis-
tently serious opera was a departure for the company, not lending itself easily
to Pocket Opera's usual style of production in which much of the show is the
owlish Pippin, with wit and humor introducing and commenting on the action.
Later, he acknowledged that audience reaction had been "somewhat divided."
But he felt that in a small theater and "clothed in English, *Stiffelio* became truly
contemporary," and he reported that some of his audience, like some of La
Selva's in Brooklyn, had "found it deeply moving, and many claimed that it was
their favorite of all the operas we had done." And in 2003, he revived it.[25]

The other small company production, four performances in December
1980, was sung in Italian by Bel Canto Opera of New York in a Manhattan
high school auditorium, with professional singers and an orchestra of twenty,
including a piano, led by a conductor. (For the "sound" of this reduced orchestra compared to others larger, see appendix F.) Bel Canto offered simple but
realistic scenery along with early nineteenth-century costumes, and though the
orchestra lacked somewhat in musical subtlety, in the small auditorium it effectively made its points. Moreover, the program declared: "Orchestral music published by Barenreiter Verlag, by arrangement with Magnamusic-Baton, Inc., St.
Louis, Missouri." Thus the opera's score, though still open to more small corrections, was now commercially available from more than one publisher. And
yet another step in building an audience for the opera: The Philips company
earlier in 1980 had issued a complete studio recording, the opera's first, with
José Carreras as Stiffelio. In its review, *Opera News* concluded: "Here, after 130
years, is Verdi's intent clearly set forth."[26]

In fact, the discovery in 1985 in the Austrian National Library of a hand-
copied orchestral score of *Stiffelio*, sold by Ricordi in 1852 to the Burgtheater
in Vienna for a production that never took place, revealed a few more corrections, textual and orchestral, that could be made. Whereupon the Teatro la
Fenice, Venice, using a new performing score prepared by an Italian musicologist, mounted a production of *Stiffelio* in its 1985–86 season, alternating it with
performances of *Aroldo*. And an Italian critic reviewing for *Opera* stated: "*Stiffelio* was voted the more successful by the public."[27]

This improved score came to the United States in November 1988 when
OperaDelaware, in Wilmington, mounted a similar production, courtesy of the
Fenice, but sung in English and with some further corrections added. David
Lawton, the conductor for OperaDelaware, upon examining a microfilm of the
Vienna manuscript held by the American Institute for Verdi Studies, in New
York,[28] discovered some mistakes the Italian musicologist had missed. And in
OperaDelaware's program he discussed some of what he had found: "In Lina's
aria in act II, for example, the repeated Trumpet and Trombone E's in the
opening recitative were mistakenly assigned to Clarinets and Bassoons in the
score and parts." A small point perhaps, but trumpets and trombones played

OperaDelaware

44th Season

Presents

November 26, December 2, 3, 1988   8:00 p.m.

STIFFELIO

By Giuseppe Verdi

Libretto by Francesco Maria Piave

(after *Le Pasteur, ou L'Evangile et le Foyer* by
Emile Souvestre and Eugene Bourgeois)
First performed: Teatro Grande, Trieste, November 16, 1850

Critical revision of the Venice version of 1852,
edited by Giovanni Morelli from
the manuscript OA179 in the Nationalbibliothek, Vienna.
Courtesy of Teatro La Fenice, Venice.
English translation: David Lawton and Nicholas Muni

Cast:

Stiffelio (Rodolfo Mueller), an evangelical minister	Noel Espiritu Velasco
Lina, his wife	Susan Marie Pierson
Count Stankar, Lina's father	Mark Rucker
Raffaele von Leuthold, a noble	James Longacre
Jorg, an elderly minister	Del-Bourree Bach
Dorotea and	Carol Andrews
Federico di Frengel, Lina's cousins	Leland Kimball

Three acts
Setting: the nineteenth century

Conductor:	David Lawton
Stage Director:	Nicholas Muni
Chorus Master:	C. Lawler Rogers, Sr.
Producer:	Elizabeth Anfield
Set Design:	Peter Eastman
Costume Design	Cheryl Perkins
Lighting Design:	Michael Lincoln

OperaDelaware is a member of Opera America, American Arts Alliance, Central Opera Service, American Council for the Arts, Greater Wilmington Convention and Vistors Bureau, the Delaware State Chamber of Commerce, Opera for Youth, and the Delaware Theater Association. OperaDelaware is recipient of the first Governor's Award for the Arts (1981).

This production is made possible by the National Endowment for the Arts and the Delaware State Arts Council, a state agency committed to enhancing and supporting the arts in Delaware. The Delaware State Arts Council provides technical and financial assistance to artists and serves as a clearinghouse of information on the arts.

Figure 19.3. Program for OperaDelaware's 1988 production in English (from author's collection).

three times double forte sound quite differently from clarinets and bassoons, and with considerably more impact. Also, "In the cabaletta of Stiffelio's aria in act I a passage for Oboes and Clarinets in unison with Violin II was transcribed as a unison with Violin I." And there were more such corrections. Result: for the Delaware performances "the score and parts now fully correspond with the version of the opera that is preserved in the Vienna manuscript."[29]

The opera house in Wilmington has a small pit, and Lawton had to reduce the orchestra to thirty-five, but because the house seats only about 1,100 and has good acoustics, the sound was full enough. The chorus numbered thirty, and in the small house much of the sung English could be understood. Musically, the drama was gripping.[30]

Scenically, because OperaDelaware's budget was limited, the production was simple, mostly walls of painted canvas. For the offstage scene in which Stankar kills Raffaele, the stage director, Nicholas Muni, turned a canvas wall to advantage, allowing the audience to see the scene in silhouette. And another Muni touch, though of less importance, the final scene, in which Stiffelio preaches on the adulterous woman, was presented as a funeral service for Raffaele. In sum, though most of the audiences for the three performances knew not a note of the music, the production had a memorable success. As a critic for the *New York Times*, who had come to report the event, noted: "To a modern listener, this seems a touching and actually quite religious work."[31]

Soon scholars again took the lead in perfecting the text and score for *Stiffelio.* In the early 1990s, those who were preparing a critical edition (to be published by the University of Chicago Press and Ricordi) and others at the Istituto di Studi Verdiani in Parma asked Verdi's heirs (still living in his house at Sant'Agata, near Busseto) to open their archives to a search for the missing parts of Verdi's autograph score, which the heirs graciously did. And all those parts of the autograph not included by Verdi in his autograph score for *Aroldo* were found except for the opera's final scene. It existed still only as in the copy manuscripts found in the Neapolitan and Viennese libraries (as well as in the piano versions published in the vocal scores). But also found in the Verdi archives were sketches for the final scene, so that its reconstruction, as Verdi must have originally conceived it, became much more certain.[32]

All these new corrections were first heard in a Royal Opera production at Covent Garden, London, on January 25, 1993, and later were incorporated in a vocal score edited by the conductor Edward Downes and published that year.[33] The production's staging had a number of oddities that reduced the opera's impact, of which the most serious involved the final scene. As Andrew Porter reported for *Opera,* "Instead of forgiveness, C-major reconciliation, and happiness, we had a Stiffelio singing his last lines ('*perdonata*') through gritted teeth, staring ahead, not looking with rekindled love at this wife, who tottered forward and apparently expired. While Verdi's music soared through a Happy Ending, the staging—without musical support—sought to suggest a tragedy."[34]

That summer, with the opera's performances steadily increasing in Europe and a production announced by the Metropolitan for October, La Selva and the New York Grand Opera, responding a second time to requests from their audience, repeated from the previous summer a revival for their annual series in Central Park, New York. This time, however, the event was spoiled. "Opera shouldn't have to put up with what happened in Central Park on Wednesday night," wrote the critic for the *Times*. After noting the usual troubles with the sound system, he added:

> Then it rained. The cast, protected by a roof, sang on. A plentiful and immensely cheerful audience stayed, for the most part, either putting up umbrellas or soaking happily in the steady drizzle.
>
> Summerstage's orchestra pit is exposed to the sky, so with the first rain-drops, musicians packed their instruments and looked for shelter. Mr. La Selva, not missing a beat (literally), turned to Plan B: James Besser playing a piano-reduction score on an electronic keyboard.
>
> Mr. Besser's device was loosely covered with plastic; its player, at first at least, was covered with nothing. (One hoped fervently he wasn't touching metal.) Gradually, Mr. Besser—an intrepid player who seemed to relish the calamities around him—was provided with protection, at the end a large Miller Lite café umbrella borrowed from nearby concessionaires. Having made it through act I, Mr. La Selva skipped act II and went straight to the brief finale. By this time, the body microphones were dead, and the stage could offer only a murmured obligato to Mr. Besser's electric piano.
>
> The immediate drama of struggle and survival wholly eclipsed Verdi.[35]

Happily, in 1998 as part of its Verdi cycle in Central Park—presenting all of Verdi's operas in chronological order, 1994–2001—the company staged *Stiffelio* yet again. And the weather allowed Verdi to shine.

The Metropolitan's production of the opera, opening on October 21, 1993, with Placido Domingo as the minister, in eleven performances played to some forty thousand in its home house and through its national radio and television broadcasts introduced the opera to millions across the country. In its program and publicity, the company assured its audiences that it was making use of all the latest scholarly corrections and credited as its source the critical edition being prepared by the University of Chicago Press and Ricordi (published in 2003). Some reviewers made much of this, and in the *New Yorker* Paul Griffiths went so far as to say, "This was effectively the world premiere of the score that Verdi wrote in the summer and fall of 1850."[36] Possibly he exaggerated, for the Covent Garden production in January 1993 had made use of the same sources, and presumably any additional corrections made in the intervening nine months were minor. Still, for the United States, the Metropolitan's score and text were not only an advance on what had been heard before but also set a standard for future productions.

METROPOLITAN OPERA

Thursday Evening, October 21, 1993, 8:00-10:50

METROPOLITAN OPERA PREMIERE

GIUSEPPE VERDI

Stiffelio

Opera in three acts

Libretto by Francesco Maria Piave after the play
Le Pasteur, ou L'Évangile et le foyer
by Émile Souvestre and Eugène Bourgeois.

Conductor:	James Levine
Production:	Giancarlo del Monaco
Set and Costume Designer:	Michael Scott
Lighting Designer:	Gil Wechsler

Characters in order of vocal appearance:	
Jorg, an elderly minister	Paul Plishka
Stiffelio, a minister of the Gospel	Plácido Domingo
Stankar, Lina's father, an elderly colonel	
and count of the Empire	Vladimir Chernov
Dorotea, Lina's cousin	Margaret Lattimore (Debut)
Raffaele, a nobleman of Leuthold	Peter Riberi (Debut)
Federico di Frengel, Lina's cousin	Charles Anthony
Lina, Stiffelio's wife	Sharon Sweet

Chorus Master:	Raymond Hughes
Musical Preparation:	Joan Dornemann, Dennis Giauque, John Keenan, and Steven Eldredge
Assistant Stage Directors:	Catherine Hazlehurst, David Kneuss, and Brad Dalton
Prompter:	Joan Dornemann

This production of *Stiffelio* was made possible by
a generous and deeply appreciated gift from the late Cynthia Wood.

Yamaha is the official piano of the Metropolitan Opera. Latecomers will not be admitted during the performance.

Figure 19.4. Program for the Metropolitan's premiere performance, 1993 (from author's collection).

Figure 19.5. The moody graveyard scene, act 2, designed by Michael Scott for the Metropolitan Opera's production, 1993, with Sharon Sweet as Lina. Photograph by Winnie Klotz, 1997. Courtesy of the Metropolitan Opera Archives.

On the whole the Metropolitan's production was a good one. Domingo was outstanding in a role well suited to his voice and his ability to act, as was also Vladimir Chernov as Stankar. The third principal, Sharon Sweet, perhaps had the voice for Lina, but not the figure. Her pudgy face and startling girth made any adultery seem unlikely and continually interfered with her efforts to act. Gestures seemed effortful; kneeling, hard; getting up, harder—causing some frequenters of the Metropolitan to lament that its casting in these years seemed so often to misfire: two out of three principals, good; and the third seemingly tossed in without thought to fitness for the role. Yet, over all, the opera made a strong impression.[37]

The production had several peculiarities, some of which were primarily scenic. Among them: "The sets," in Martin Mayer's opinion expressed in *Opera*, "are much too big for what is, after all, a domestic opera." Moreover, in an opera unusually full of duets, the production "staged half the opera around a table 40 feet long, with the characters singing at each other over great distances."[38] Many in the audiences noted with amusement that the church in the background of the graveyard in act 2 was (as Verdi directed) gothic, curlicued windows, and dimly colored glass; but the same church inside, in act 3, was English Renaissance with Palladian windows of clear glass. More important, as in London the final scene was strangely misdirected. When Stiffelio, hand on the Bible, tells of Jesus forgiving the adulterous woman, he says, "And the woman, the woman, pardoned rose up," and at that moment, according to Verdi's direction, he is to look at Lina, even as he keeps repeating "perdonata," ending with "God pronounced it." Perhaps at the Metropolitan he did briefly look, but then, as the congregation joyfully repeated "Perdonata," the Metropolitan's stage director, without direction by Verdi, had him come down from the pulpit, go to a side wall and bury his forehead on his arm, turning his back on Lina—even as Verdi's music soared through its C-major Happy Ending. Did he or did he not as husband forgive her? Fortunately, the curtain fell swiftly, and memory of the congregation's joyful cries perhaps convinced the confused in the audience that Lina had achieved human as well as divine pardon.

In the Metropolitan's program, Philip Gossett, the general editor in charge of the critical editions of Verdi's works, concluded his note on the opera with the forthright declaration: "*Stiffelio* is neither early Verdi nor minor Verdi: it is an opera whose dramatic quandaries and musical beauties speak in a particularly poignant way to our modern sensibilities."[39] Paul Griffiths in the *New Yorker* questioned that view:

> The revival of *Stiffelio*, nearly a century and a half after its first, hampered hearing, may be justice coming too late. What the Met offers is, in a certain sense, authentic: here is what Verdi wrote. However, this is authenticity of a uniquely modern sort—an authenticity that places stringent requirements on what's under scrutiny (every quaver, every syllable must be in accord with the composer's original), yet asks for no guarantees from us that we will approach the piece in the same period spirit. History has taught us how to react to *Rigoletto*. . . . But *Stiffelio*, coming to us out of the blue, shows up as acutely alien all the things we casually take as normal: these singsong ensembles driven along by the orchestra, these melodramatic settings (graveyard, church), these arias bound to move from legato to athletics, these cautioning fathers and wayward daughter. . . . The efforts of musicologist, not to be decried, have assembled for us a work; the performers, most of them admirable, have set it in motion. But nobody can tell us what it's for.[40]

Between the contending views, one so sure the opera would appeal to "modern sensibilities," and the other so unsure that we moderns need yet another nineteenth-century opera, at least a sizable portion of the public would seem to have endorsed Gossett's view and found the drama relevant and engrossing. Opera houses seldom revive operas that fail to draw an audience, but Covent Garden revived its 1993 production in 1995 and again in 2007. In 1995 the Los Angeles Opera imported the English production, casting Domingo as the minister; and in 1998 the Metropolitan brought back its 1993 production, giving *Stiffelio* another national broadcast. In 2003, Pocket Opera in San Francisco revived its production in English; in 2004, Chautauqua Opera staged it, also in English (with Lawton conducting); in 2005, Sarasota Opera, in Italian; and in 2010, the Metropolitan again, with another national radio broadcast.[41]

Possibly with the music continually becoming more familiar, more of the public, *pace* Griffiths, is willing with this relatively new opera to respond to the conventions within which it was composed, even as they do with *Rigoletto*, *Trovatore*, and *Traviata*. This ability to meet and enjoy Verdi on his terms, with some understanding of the conventions of his day, is one of the happy results of the Verdi Renaissance. But aside from Verdi, for all composers, audiences today have a more historic view of the repertory than did their great-grandparents who tended to view opera as a progressive art, the new necessarily better, and the old ever more old-fashioned and dated, even Mozart, Gluck, and Monteverdi.

Still, *Stiffelio* has its naysayers, those who find the story's contrivance trite and much of its music trivial. The Parma production of 1968, for example, attempted to improve the score by shifting a brief episode in act 1—Raffaele putting a letter for Lina into a book later requested by Stiffelio—slightly forward.[42] It also omitted altogether Lina's two-versed *allegro* aria, "Perder dunque voi volete," with which she concludes her long scene in the graveyard. True, the faster, concluding aria is not at the same high musical level as its *largo* predecessor, but *Rigoletto*, *Trovatore*, and *Traviata* all have similar concluding arias that sometimes are dropped. Musical conventions do date, and perhaps some cuts are for the better.[43]

In one respect, however, the succeeding three operas clearly improve on *Stiffelio*. Each has a short prelude neatly setting the atmosphere that will pervade the following drama; *Stiffelio*, however, has a ten-minute Overture that from the start, the premiere in Trieste, many have declared too long and, in its tone, misleading. It begins well, featuring a simple but memorable phrase that Lina will sing in the final scene, "Signor, pietà," and this slight introduction is followed by a long, slow, beautiful passage for solo trumpet that in its slightly somber tone nicely sets the color and tone of the coming drama. But then, and for much the greater part of the Overture, Verdi plays variations on some of the opera's more trivial music, suggesting alike to critics and audiences from 1850 forward that a lighthearted drama will follow, perhaps even a comedy.[44]

The opera's first production in Germany, in Cologne in 1973, met the problem head-on and omitted the Overture. The opera thus began with a brief scene for an elderly minister, Jorg (bass), who serves as Stiffelio's conscience, continually recalling him to his ministerial duties and beliefs. The scene presents a seated Jorg onstage alone, reading aloud from the Bible. He closes the book, praying that Stiffelio may continue his evangelical work, but ending with an ominous thought (though expressed in C major as the opera happily will end): "He is coming; his wife with him. May Heaven not let human love dampen his zeal." In all, the scene runs only two and a half minutes, and those in Cologne apparently treated it as a vocal prelude to the opera, setting subject and tone. But so far as discovered, no other company has gone to such an extent. A possible compromise might be to end the Overture after the trumpet solo, giving the opera a brief, *Rigoletto*-like, wholly orchestral prelude. But no company yet has tried it (and purists, of course, would object).[45]

As the twenty-first century advances, no one can be sure whether *Stiffelio* will continue to find an audience, but its record in the previous century's last twenty-five years stirs some thoughts. First, the opera must be unyoked from its history. The scholar's have done their work, and with the publication of the critical edition and the productions and recordings based upon it, *Stiffelio* must stand on its own, no longer claiming novelty or a corrected score to attract an audience.[46]

To that end, it has a virtue in which not all of Verdi's operas share: it plays as effectively in small houses as in large ones. It is not surprising that a Domingo in New York and Los Angeles and a José Carreras in London and Milan can persuade a large audience to empathize with Stiffelio's distress. More surprising perhaps is the opera's success with lesser stars in smaller houses. Yet the Teatro Grande in Trieste, in 1850, seated only about 1,400, and recently in Wilmington, Chautauqua, and Sarasota, in houses of roughly the same size, singers less famous[47] have also been able to stir sympathy for Stiffelio, Lina, and Stankar. Seemingly, a good portion of any audience, upon leaving one of these performances, would echo the *Times* critic, "a touching and actually quite religious work."

Moreover, the opera plays well in English, which not all Verdi's operas do. No doubt it is aided in part by its subject matter: Adultery, and its effect on a husband and a wife and on the community in which they live. Further, it plays well in modern, even colloquial language. Its future therefore may lie more with the country's regional companies, which in their less grand houses can use voices too small for the Metropolitan yet fully able, with an audience sitting closer to the stage, to project the opera's drama.

Lastly, in order of composition, *Stiffelio* followed *Luisa Miller*, which in the past fifty years has had a surge in popularity, and was followed directly by *Rigoletto*. While it may never match the latter in popularity and frequency of performance, it may catch up with the former. It is, after all, the work of a mature artist, pondering a distressing and eternal human problem, and clothing his thoughts in music that at its frequent best is not only highly melodic but remarkably effective and original.

Conclusion

Two questions remain: How much of a change has the Verdi Renaissance of the twentieth century's second half made in Verdi's position in our operatic world? And how much of that change is likely to be permanent? At least for the United States, a rough answer to the first must be: a sizable rise in esteem and performance. And to the second, though more speculatively: at least for the next half century, much of that rise will be permanent.

Before sharpening the argument, however, note the sand on which the thesis builds. Roughly speaking, since Puccini's death in 1926, no composer in any language has caught the public's fancy to the extent of ten operas produced with some regularity. Benjamin Britten has come closest, with perhaps three or four; Richard Strauss, post-1926, added several to his earlier success; and a few other composers such as Berg, Poulenc, and Prokofiev have also contributed one or two to the general repertory. And hence, to some extent because the repertory seems momentarily stuck, impresarios, singers, and audiences have turned to composers of the past, to Verdi, and more recently, to Handel. But let a new composer of genius comparable to Verdi or Handel appear, and in the United States especially if he or she should compose to English librettos, the repertory of a hundred or so operas frequently performed would soon adjust, shrinking old reputations to make way for the new.

Nevertheless, even then I suspect that Verdi will stand high in the general repertory with ten or more of his operas continually or periodically revived—and because of the Verdi Renaissance. The scholarly work that has been done on him in the past half-century, the recordings and DVDs that have made his previously unheard works available to the public, and the success onstage here and there of even the hitherto most ignored of his operas suggest the breadth of his appeal to the public. And the scholarly work and the recordings will last and be available to coming generations and audiences. His position has changed—permanently, I think—from the low regard in which he was held by critics and scholars (but not the public) at the start of the twentieth century to a position in our operatic repertory somewhat like that of Shakespeare in the theater: each is a dominant figure, offering a large number of works, some of which are acknowledged to be masterpieces, some good but flawed, and some of interest only because of their author.

In the early 1930s, as the Verdi Renaissance was starting, the Metropolitan's general manager, Giulio Gatti-Casazza, published his *Memories of the Opera*, and in it remarked: "Out of the thirty odd operas that Verdi wrote, six are indispensable to the repertory, and half a dozen others are periodically revived." But he left his readers to guess which operas he had in mind.[1]

He gave some hints, however, when further in the chapter he added: "Give *Rigoletto* or *La traviata* with a mediocre cast, an impossible orchestra, and you have still a powerful emotional impact. . . . *Aida* with a small orchestra can perhaps be passable. But others of the Verdi operas—*Il trovatore, Rigoletto, La traviata*—they can even be done with dogs!"[2] So, those he mentioned are four of the six Verdi operas "indispensable" to the repertory. What two others had he in mind?

Consider: He was the Metropolitan's general manager for twenty-seven years, 1908–35, and as such, with the comparative wealth of the Metropolitan behind him, he was possibly the most powerful manager or impresario of the twentieth century. Counting the Verdi operas that he scheduled most often in his twenty-seven years, the ranking for the first six goes: *Aida* (192 performances), *Rigoletto* (101), *Traviata* (99), *Trovatore* (84), *Forza* (37), and *Falstaff* (21). And the second "half dozen" he thought should be "periodically revived" are: *Otello* (18), *Ernani* (15), *Boccanegra* (14), *Don Carlo* (11), *Ballo* (10), and *Luisa Miller* (5).

Compare the rankings with those in appendix E, which shows the number of performances of Verdi's works at the Metropolitan, from the first season in 1883–84 through 2008–9. The first four still lead, though their order has slightly changed, but both *Otello* and *Ballo* have moved ahead of *Forza*, and *Don Carlo* has passed *Falstaff*. Moreover, all of these nine operas plus a tenth, *Boccanegra*, have had more than one hundred performances. No other composer has such a record. Further yet, to this first ten must be added *Ernani* and *Luisa Miller* as well as five operas not given at the Metropolitan until the second half of the century, when the impact of the Verdi Renaissance began to impinge: *Macbeth, Vespri siciliani, Stiffelio, Nabucco, I Lombardi*, and to come in 2009–10, *Attila*. In all, eighteen operas.

No other composer has so many: Wagner, eleven; Puccini, ten, Mozart, six; Richard Strauss, six; and Gluck, four. Of course, the Metropolitan is not the country's only company, but with its radio and television broadcasts, and now with its live performances beamed into movie theaters, it dominates our operatic world in two ways. To some extent by its imprimatur it sets the fashion for the public's perception of a composer's worth. People tend to believe that if an opera is presented at the Metropolitan it must have some merit. Conversely, as the previous seven chapters have shown, many small companies on occasion can thrive by presenting what the Metropolitan does not. So what may be the foreseeable future for Verdi's position and operas in the coming half-century?

When asked this question in the context of Gatti's remarks, Victor DeRenzi, the conductor and artistic director of the Sarasota Opera, where he is presenting a cycle of Verdi's operas, concluded that of the thirty-odd, perhaps ten were "indispensable" to the general repertory, another ten merited periodical revival, and a final ten should be reserved for special occasions, such as anniversaries or cycles of the operas.[3] Like Gatti, he did not specify which operas fell into which third, but when pressed to name at least the ten that were "indispensable," he merrily named at least fifteen until stopped and reproved, when he sought an escape by saying: "Of course, it all depends on what singers are available." Nevertheless, for the only-on-special-occasions, he plainly meant works such as Verdi's first two operas, *Oberto* and *Un giorno di regno*, and then perhaps other early works such as *Giovanna d'Arco*, *Alzira*, or *I masnadieri*, the last of which is unusually long, expensive to produce, and difficult to cast. He stressed, however, that in Sarasota's experience, all the operas already performed, including *Oberto*, *Alzira*, and *Masnadieri* had proved stageworthy and had found an appreciative public. As the maxim has it: Verdi plays better onstage than he reads in the score.

As for the future, what Verdi's position in our operatic repertory may be is uncertain, but presently, if number of operas and performances are the measure, he ranks very high: for in the recent past the cumulative Verdi Renaissance—Werfel, Toye, scholars, critics, conductors, impresarios, singers—has achieved a worldwide reappraisal of his works, strongly supported by audiences at the box office. In the United States, as elsewhere, that shift in opinion has been astonishing.

Appendix A

The Operas, Their World, Western Hemisphere, and U.S. Premieres

Opera/World premiere	Western Hemisphere premiere	United States premiere
Oberto November 17, 1839 Milan, Scala	November 17, 1939 Buenos Aires Teatro Colón	February 18, 1978 New York City Amato Opera House
Un giorno di regno, Also known as *Il finto Stanislao* September 1, 1840 Milan, Scala	June 18, 1960 New York City Town Hall	(same)
Nabucco (*Nabucodonosor*) March 9, 1842 Milan, Scala	December 4, 1847 Havana Teatro Tacón	April 4, 1848 New York City Astor Place Opera H.
I Lombardi alla *prima crociata* February 11, 1843	December 1, 1846 Havana Teatro Tacón	March 1, 1847 New York City Palmo's Opera H.
Ernani March 9, 1844 Venice, Fenice	November 18, 1846 Havana Teatro Tacón	April 15, 1847 New York City Park Theatre
I due Foscari November 3, 1844 Rome, T. Argentina	January 2, 1847 Havana Teatro Tacón	May 10, 1847 Boston Howard-Atheneum
Giovanna d'Arco February 15, 1845 Milan, Scala	August 19, 1854 Buenos Aires T. Argentino	March 1, 1966 New York City Carnegie Hall

(cont'd)

Opera/World premiere	Western Hemisphere premiere	United States premiere
Alzira August 12, 1845 Naples, T. San Carlo	January 20, 1850 Lima Teatro Principal	January 17, 1968 New York City Carnegie Hall
Attila March 17, 1846 Venice, Fenice	January 23, 1848 Havana Teatro Tacón	April 15, 1850 New York City Niblo's Garden
Macbeth March 14, 1847 Florence, T. Pergola	December 19, 1849 Havana Teatro Tacón	April 24, 1850 New York City Niblo's Garden
I masnadieri July 22, 1847 London, Her Majesty's Th.	September 7, 1849 Rio de Janeiro T. Sao Pedro	*May 31, 1860* New York City Winter Garden
Jérusalem November 26, 1847 Paris, Opéra	January 24, 1850 New Orleans T. Orléans	(same)
Il corsaro October 25, 1848 Trieste, T. Grande	January 1, 1852 Valparaiso T. Victoria	December 12, 1981 Stony Brook, NY Main Th.
La battaglia di Legnano January 27, 1849 Rome, T. Argentina	August 7, 1864 Santiago. Chile T. Municipal	February 28, 1976 New York City Cooper Union
Luisa Miller December 8, 1849 Naples. T. San Carlo	May 25, 1853 Rio de Janeiro T. Provisorio	October 27, 1852 Philadelphia Walnut St. Th.
Stiffelio November 16, 1850 Trieste, T. Grande	June 4, 1976 Brooklyn, NY Academy of Music	(same)
Rigoletto March 11, 1851 Venice, T. Fenice	February 19, 1855 New York Academy of Music	(same)

Appendix B

The Swift Spread of *Ernani*

A listing by city and date of local premieres to show how *Ernani*, compared to the other sixteen of Verdi's "earlier" operas, *Oberto* through *Rigoletto*, quickly spread throughout the United States, Cuba, Mexico, and Canada in the years 1847 through 1860. Moreover, in most of the larger cities, its local premiere was soon followed by repeat performances, which was far less true of the others, even of *Rigoletto*. Note the number of companies that had *Ernani* in their repertory. The listing is based primarily upon the chronology by Thomas G. Kaufman, to which I have been able to add one or two details. Except for *Ernani*, placed first, the operas are listed in order of world premiere.

City	Theater	Date	Company or leading artist
		Ernani	
New York	Park	April 15, 1847	Havana
Boston	Howard Athenaeum	April 23, 1847	Havana
Philadelphia	Walnut Street	July 14, 1847	Havana
Mexico City	Nacional	May 18, 1850	Barili-Thorn
Charleston	Charleston	April 2, 1850	Havana
Baltimore	Holliday Street	January 23, 1851	NY Astor Place
San Francisco	Adelphi	April 8, 1851	Pellegrini
Augusta, GA	Concert Hall	April 14, 1851	NY Astor Place
Montreal	Royal	June 29, 1853	DeVriès-Arditi
Buffalo	Metropolitan	July 15, 1853	DeVriès-Arditi
Cincinnati	Lyceum	July 27, 1853	DeVriès-Arditi
Louisville	City	August 29, 1853	DeVriès-Arditi
St. Louis	Varieties	September 26, 1853	DeVriès-Arditi
Pittsburgh	Athenaeum	November 28, 1853	DeVriès-Arditi
New Orleans	St. Charles	March 31, 1854	DeVriès-Arditi
Nashville	Adelphi	June 5, 1854	DeVriès-Arditi
Detroit	Metropolitan	November 24, 1859	Strakosch
Cleveland	Academy of Music	October 31, 1859	Strakosch
Chicago	Metropolitan	December 6, 1859	Strakosch
Washington	Washington	March 20, 1860	Strakosch
Mobile	Amphitheater	April 9, 1860	Parodi
Quebec	Music Hall	August 2, 1860	Ghioni

(cont'd)

City	Theater	Date	Company or leading artist

Nabucco

City	Theater	Date	Company or leading artist
New York	Astor Place	April 4, 1848	Astor Place
Boston	Melodeon	June 4, 1848	Astor Place
(a Sunday evening, in concert, presented as "Verdi's Grand Sacred Drama")			
San Francisco	Metropolitan	November 30, 1854	Barili-Thorn
Mexico City	Nacional	November 23, 1856	Maretzek

I Lombardi alla prima crociata

City	Theater	Date	Company or leading artist
New York	Palmo's	March 3, 1847	Sanquirico
Philadelphia	Walnut Street	July 17, 1847	Havana
Boston	Howard Athenaeum	May 20, 1847	Havana
Mexico City	Nacional	July 11, 1852	Maretzek
San Francisco	Metropolitan	May 1, 1855	Barili-Thorn

I due Foscari

City	Theater	Date	Company or leading artist
Boston	Howard Athenaeum	May 10, 1847	Havana
New York	Park	June 9, 1847	Havana
Philadelphia	Walnut Street	July 19, 1847	Havana
New Orleans	Orleans	March 6, 1847	French Th. Co.
San Francisco	American	March 23, 1855	Barili-Thorn

Giovanna d'Arco

City	Theater	Date	Company or leading artist
Mexico City	Nacional	December 23, 1857	Roncari

Attila

City	Theater	Date	Company or leading artist
New York	Niblo's Garden	April 15, 1850	Havana
Boston	Howard Athenaeum	May 21, 1850	Havana
Mexico City	Nacional	August 31, 1854	Maretzek
San Francisco	American	August 18, 1859	Bianchi

Macbeth

City	Theater	Date	Company or leading artist
New York	Niblo's Garden	April 24, 1850	Havana
Boston	Howard Athenaeum	May 28, 1850	Havana
Mexico City	Nacional	January 10, 1857	Roncari

(cont'd)

City	Theater	Date	Company or leading artist
I masnadieri			
Havanna	Teatro Tacón	January 16, 1855	Bottesini
Mexico City	Nacional	December 4, 1856	Fattori
New York	Winter Garden	May 31, 1860	Maretzek
Jérusalem			
New Orleans	Th. Orléans	January 24, 1850	DeVriès
St. Louis	Opera House	June 23, 1860	New Orleans Co.
Cincinnati	National	July 12, 1860	New Orleans Co.
Luisa Miller			
Philadelphia	Walnut St. Th. (in Eng.)	October 27, 1852	Richings
Cincinnati	National	February 24, 1854	Richings
New York	Castle Garden	July 20, 1854	Maretzek
Havanna	Teatro Tacón	December 8, 1854	Maretzek
Rigoletto			
New York	Academy of Music	February 19, 1855	Maretzek
Boston	Boston Theatre	June 8, 1855	Maretzek
Havanna	Teatro Tacón	August 22, 1855	Corrado-Setti
Mexico City	Nacional	November 7, 1856	Fattori
New Orleans	Crisp's Gaiety	May 22, 1857	Corrado-Setti
Philadelphia	Academy of Music	January 25, 1858	Ullman
Vera Cruz	Principal	March 1858	Fattori
Guadalajara	Degollado	May 1858	Fattori
St. Louis	St. Louis Theater	February 16, 1859	Strakosch
Chicago	McVickers	February 26, 1859	Strakosch
Cincinnati	Pike's Opera House	September 2, 1859	Parodi
San Francisco	Maguire's Opera House	July 1, 1860	Lyster
Baltimore	Holliday Street	December 21, 1860	Colson

Note. The six "earlier" operas not represented, *Oberto, Un giorno di regno, Alzira, Il corsaro, La battaglia di Legnano,* and *Stiffelio* did not achieve premieres in Cuba, Mexico, Canada, or the United States until the twentieth century.

Appendix C

Dollar Values and Populations

Dollars

Roughly speaking, a dollar of 1847 retained its full purchasing value until the start of the Civil War in 1860. During the war, it weakened, ending in 1865 as the equivalent of about $1.88. Or, said differently, a person in 1865 would need to spend $1.88 to purchase what $1.00 had bought in 1847. Thereafter, in the twenty-five years until 1890 the dollar slowly recouped, becoming: by 1870, roughly the equivalent of $1.45; by 1880, $1.10; and by 1900, 97¢. Thereafter, it steadily lost in comparative purchasing power: by 1925, being the equivalent of $2.10; by 1950, $2.85; by 1975, $6.45; by 2000, $19.00; and by 2005, $22.00. (The figures are taken, with thanks, from those offered by EH.Net and rounded between the consumer price index [CPI] figure and that of the gross domestic product deflator. EH.Net defines the deflator as "similar to the CPI in that it is a measure of average prices. The 'bundle' of goods and services here includes all things produced in the economy, not just consumer goods and services that are reflected in the CPI.")

The comparisons, at best, are hard to use, and in the world of opera can become almost meaningless. For example: a box seat in the Park Theatre in 1847, then New York's leading theater, usually cost $1 and for an opera was raised to $2. A box seat in 2006 in the center of the parterre boxes at the Metropolitan Opera cost $320 and for one on the side of the parterre $110–50. Plainly, the ratio of $322 (or even of $110) to $2 is much greater than the rounded CPI and deflator figure of 22; and clearly, statisticians do not count many of the costs that underlie the production of an opera.

Populations

Based on figures reported by the U.S. Census Bureau for cities important to opera in the years 1850 to 1900, and including figures for 1950 and estimates for 2003:

City	1850	1900	1950	2003
New York	696,115	3,437,202	7,891,957	8,085,742
Baltimore	169,054	508,957	949,708	628,670
Boston	136,881	560,892	801,444	581,616
Philadelphia	121,376	1,293,697	2,071,605	1,479,339
New Orleans	116,375	287,104	570,445	469,032
Cincinnati	115,435	325,902	503,998	317,361
St. Louis	77,860	575,238	856,796	332,223
Pittsburgh	46,601	321,616	676,806	325,337
Louisville	43,194	304,731	369,129	248,762
Washington, DC	40,001	278,718	802,178	563,384
San Francisco	34,776	342,782	775,357	751,682
Chicago	29,963	1,698,575	3,620,962	2,869,121

Appendix D

The San Carlo
Touring Company

Repertory and Number of Performances,
1913/14 through 1928/29

Based on Cardell Bishop's history of the company (2nd ed., 1980) and on Thomas G. Kaufman's Chronology, and limited to those years because the reports for them were more complete.[1] Even for this limited period, however, neither scholar claims to have discovered every performance. Especially in the South of the United States and in Canada, details often were lacking, causing Bishop to conclude, "There probably will never be a complete history of the San Carlo Grand Opera Company."[2] In its early years, when the Puccini operas were still under copyright, the company, which would have owed a fee, did not sing them. Then for the 1918/19 season, for the benefit of Italian War Relief, the publisher Ricordi donated the fee, and for the first time *Bohème* and *Butterfly* were sung.

Work	Number of Performances
Il trovatore	245
Aida	237
Pagliacci	224
Cavalleria rusticana	215
Rigoletto	210
Carmen	199
Lucia di Lammermoor	177
Madama Butterfly	173
Faust	168

(cont'd)

Work	Number of Performances
La traviata	111
La Bohème	106
Les contes d'Hoffmann	94
Martha	91
Tosca	70
La forza del destino	57
La Gioconda	55
Lohengrin	43
Il barbiere di Siviglia	39
Gioelli della madonna	36
Otello	25
Roméo et Juliette	20
Hänsel und Gretel	16
Thaïs	14
Ballo	6
Amleto (Thomas)	1
Fra Diavolo	1
Salome	1

Appendix E

Number of Performances of Verdi's Operas at the Metropolitan, 1883/84 through 2008/9

Based on statistics posted by the Metropolitan Opera database, www.metopera. org, which includes all performances of operas by the company in its home house, on tour, and concert performances. Though acts of operas from galas or concerts may be found elsewhere in the database, they are not included in the total performance count. That statistic denotes complete performances.

Work	Number of performances
Aida	1103
La traviata	952
Rigoletto	826
Il trovatore	614
Otello	314
Ballo in maschera	287
La forza del destino	230
Don Carlo	190
Falstaff	175
Simon Boccanegra	128
Macbeth	91
Ernani	88

(cont'd)

Work	Number of performances
Luisa Miller	86
Messa di Requiem	49
I vespri siciliani	45
Nabucco	45
Stiffelio	17
I Lombardi alla prima crociata	11
Inno delle Nazioni	1

Note: No other composer has had seventeen operas performed at the Metropolitan (eighteen after *Attila* in 2009–10), or had the first ten of them so frequently performed, reasons for comparing Verdi's place in the repertory to Shakespeare's in the theater. The ranking of other leading composers with the number of operas performed is: Wagner, 11; Puccini, 11 (counting individually each of his three one-act operas, which when performed together are *Il trittico*); and Mozart, 7.

Appendix F

An Arrangement, a Reduction, and the Score as Written

Stiffelio

The preface states that for these early operas I usually define an "arrangement" of the score as one for an orchestra of thirty-two instruments or less and a "reduction" as one of thirty-two or more. The thirty-two is, however, a movable approximation, depending on the opera, the size and conformation of the theater, and the skill of the players. Nevertheless, in an arrangement, though the instruments used may play the tune and give it a little coloring or dramatic punch, the sound to my ear usually is not quite right for Verdi; whereas in a reduction, though there may fewer instruments than he originally scored for, the sound, at least most of the time, is characteristic. To amplify the point, this appendix examines three performances of *Stiffelio*, one accompanied by an arrangement, another by a reduction, and the last by a full orchestra in a large house.

Surely no one thinks that operas should be performed only when accompanied by the exact numbers and type of instruments used in their original performances. Certainly not composers. They hope their works will be staged in theaters of all sizes. Verdi, in his score to *Otello*, in the midst of the second act quartet, noted with an asterisk: "If not possible to achieve a pianissimo, omit the trumpets and trombones. In small theatres it will be better to omit them in any case."[1] When OperaDelaware performed *Otello* in 2001 with an orchestra of forty-seven in a horseshoe-shaped opera house seating about 1,200, with a parquet, parquet circle, and a single surrounding balcony, perhaps few noticed whether trumpets and trombones had been omitted. Plainly, how much one hears depends on the natural acuteness of one's ear, one's experience of the particular opera in theaters of all sizes as well as on recordings, and finally on the success of the production. Most people likely find that when the drama plays well, their ears turn slightly off, and orchestral effects become subliminal, though thereby no less effective. But surely everyone notices some differences caused by the orchestra's size and makeup.

When the Bel Canto company in New York performed Verdi's *Stiffelio* in 1980, in Italian, it was a small but good company performing in a high school auditorium, a wide hall with a single, large balcony, concrete walls and floor, and uncushioned seats.[2] The company had an orchestra of twenty: ten strings, a flute, clarinet, oboe, bassoon, trumpet, three horns, a trombone, and a piano. Within its limitations it did a fine job, but to my ear the music rarely sounded like Verdi, in large part because of the paucity of strings. Verdi, at the time of *Aida*, in writing to a conductor noted that too few strings give "a *shrill, noisy* sound" whereas a goodly number sound "*robust* and *full*."[3] It is an oddity of the strings that doubling their number does not double the volume so much as it doubles the sonority, the lushness, the roundness of tone. Whereas if trombones and tubas are doubled, unless skillfully played they will empty the theater. Thus Bel Canto's effort, though rewarding because the opera then was seldom heard, sounded squeaky in the strings. Further, as often in small theater bands, the individual woodwinds and brass, sometimes entered too abruptly, playing opening notes too loudly, as if trying to make up for their lack of numbers.[4] And then there was the piano. All in all, I suspect the sound was rather like that of Col. Mapleson's touring company in the early 1880s, with an orchestra of twenty, or like the orchestra of twenty-five that New York's Park Theatre in 1825 assembled for the city's first season of Italian opera and that audiences had found so euphonious.[5]

Move now to Chautauqua, New York, where the Chautauqua company, the country's fourth oldest continuous opera company (founded in 1929), was offering *Stiffelio*, in English, as is that company's custom. Its Norton Hall seats 1,365 in a parquet, balcony, and small gallery and has an air of intimacy. The orchestra's pit, however, can seat only thirty-five, and *Stiffelio*, for its premiere at Trieste in 1850 had an orchestra of fifty-six, or close to it,[6] so some reduction of the score was required and furnished by David Lawton, the conductor.

Of Trieste's fifty-six players, thirty-three were strings, including four double basses, which, because of subsequent improvements in design, could be reduced to two, and overall in Lawton's reduction the strings numbered nineteen. The major substitutions occurred in the brass and woodwind sections. At Trieste the woodwinds had numbered nine: two flutes, two oboes, an English horn, two clarinets, and two bassoons. Lawton dropped an oboe and the English horn. "As far as the woodwinds are concerned," he explained, "in most 19th-century operatic scores the second oboe part is pretty much expendable. The few times that it plays by itself instead of doubling another part, it can be covered by a clarinet or flute which otherwise is not playing at that moment." So, he omitted Oboe II and also had a clarinet player double on the English horn, thus saving two seats in the small pit. Nineteenth-century reductions usually reduced the bassoons to one, but Lawton kept the two, "both for the weight they give to the bottom register of [the] woodwind section, and because the two bassoons can be useful in covering some horn parts."[7]

Verdi's brass section for Trieste was standard for the day: four horns, two trumpets, three trombones, and cimbasso (a sort of bass tuba), ten instruments and players. Lawton reduced this to two horns, two trumpets, and one tenor-bass trombone, five instruments and players; thus saving five seats. "Rarely do all four horns play simultaneously," he explained. "Those few places where they do, two of the parts can be played by bassoons. I try to interlace the parts, which improves the blend. For example, if you have a four-part chord, going from top to bottom I might score it as Horn 1/Bassoon 1, Horn II/Bassoon II." Nineteenth-century reductions "often assigned horn part to trumpets in such situations, but I dislike that solution. Trumpets in the low register do not blend at all well with horns. There are some places in *Stiffelio* where there are three independent horn parts playing at once, as for example in the Racconto [Stiffelio's first aria] at the opening of the opera. There the horn players played the top two parts, and the trombone the bottom one. Trombones blend beautifully with horns, and I doubt that anyone would able to tell the difference between this solution and the original orchestration."

Then he added about the brass: "In my reductions the horns sometimes have to cover trombone parts as well, since the trombone section has been so severely reduced. Generally I have the tenor/bass trombone play the cimbasso part, which is usually the true bass of the brass section. Rarely does one have to alter any of the percussion or harp parts, and I didn't here either."

The only place, to my ear, in which the reduction failed to achieve Verdi's aim was in the Adagio introduction for Lina's graveyard aria in the second act. Primarily an evocative string setting for a harrowing, gloomy scene, it needs a lushness of tone, a relish of sound, which the smaller string section could not deliver. Lawton, aware of the problem, explained, "There were exactly enough players to cover all the solo string parts, but only a few left in each section to cover the rest of the string section. Still, all of Verdi's notes were played!"

Such is an example of a good modern reduction for a relatively small company and theater. It is demonstrably more carefully prepared than many in the mid-nineteenth century when some instruments, such as an oboe or multiple cellos, were hard to find, and most likely it was played by more skilled and disciplined musicians, but in other respects it probably sounds somewhat like those of the larger opera orchestras playing in the 1860s.

Yet, even today, perfect conditions for opera are rarely achieved; most productions offer some gains and losses. Consider the Metropolitan's 1993 production of *Stiffelio* with an orchestra larger than that of Trieste, though of course for a much larger house. The Metropolitan can furnish, as needed, an orchestra of a hundred or more, and for *Stiffelio*, the number, though it may have varied slightly from performance to performance, usually was about sixty-five, some eight or so larger than the fifty-six of Trieste. The orchestra sounded splendid, and the introduction to the graveyard scene was ravishing. The singing was good, and those who came to hear Placido Domingo, heard him in a major, congenial impersonation of the Protestant minister who, returning from a trip abroad, discovers his wife has had an adulterous encounter. Yet because of the audience's distance from the stage, for many, the opera itself suffered. Despite its happy ending, it is in other respects rather like *Luisa Miller* or *Traviata*, a somewhat housebound, domestic story—no fields or forests—and few in the audience could see the singers' facial expressions. Moreover, the casting of a very large soprano for the role of Lina, whose adultery drives the story, made the crux of the drama seem improbable.[8] Verdi, with his strong sense of theater, might have preferred the production at Chautauqua.

Orchestral reductions of opera scores will always be with us, and a good thing, too, for many operas play very well in smaller theaters and some, like *Stiffelio*, perhaps even better. Each performance offers a compromise, and as most operagoers recognize, more is not always better, and neither is less.

Notes

Introduction

1. Richard Grant White, *Morning Courier and New-York Enquirer*, April 17, 1847, 4.

2. Vera Brodsky Lawrence, *Strong on Music: The New York Music Scene in the Days of George Templeton Strong, 1836–1875*, vol. 1, *Resonances* (New York: Oxford University Press), 520, quoting Strong's diary entry for December 2, 1848.

3. W. G. Armstrong, *A Record of the Opera in Philadelphia*, 56. William W. Clapp Jr., *A Record of the Boston Stage* (1853; repr., New York: Greenwood Press, 1969), 444–45.

4. Henry A. Kmen, *Music in New Orleans: The Formative Years, 1791–1841* (Baton Rouge: Louisiana State University Press, 1966), music column, 117 and 269, n16; number of performances on tour, 124–26. Boston had a fortnightly *Euterpeiad, Musical Intelligencer*, by 1820, but it was devoted more to a history of music than to current performances.

5. William B. Wood, *Personal Recollections of the Stage, Embracing Notices of Actors, Authors, and Auditors, During a Period of Forty Years* (Philadelphia: Baird, 1855), 307. This actor-manager states that the French company's performance of *Der Freischütz* in Philadelphia, in French, in October 1827, was far better than a local company's effort, in English, on March 18, 1825. The latter, according to Armstrong (*A Record of the Opera in Philadelphia*, 11), was "The first attempt," in Philadelphia, "to produce what is now recognized as opera."

6. John Todd, *The Young Man: Hints Addressed to the Young Men of the United States* (Northampton: J. H. Butler, 1844), 133–34, lists in order the steps to Hell: the confectioner's shop, the beer-shop, the oyster cellar, the billiard-room, the theatre, the brothel. See also the strictures of Thomas Hastings, quoted by Frédéric Louis Ritter, *Music in America*, 2nd ed. (New York: Scribner's, 1890), 165–73.

7. Timothy Dwight, *An Essay on the Stage: In Which the Arguments in Its Behalf, and Those Against It, Are Considered; and Its Morality, Character and Effects Illustrated* (Middletown, CT: n.p., 1824).

8. William Henry Fry, *New York Tribune*, November 10, 1858, 5. Fry was a composer as well as critic. His *Leonora* ranks as the first grand opera composed by an American. It premiered in Philadelphia on June 4, 1845, played eleven more evenings and was revived the following year for four. Although sung to an English text, it was composed in what was then called "the Italian manner," without spoken dialogue and with all the arias and recitatives accompanied by a full orchestra.

9. *Rigoletto*. Max Maretzek vs. Publishers of *Sunday Mercury*, for libel, New York Superior Court. See the sixty-page pamphlet published by Wynkoop and Hallenbeck, New York, 1867. For more on the trial, see chap. 11.

10. *Traviata* banned, see account in chap. 15. On Abbott, see S. E. Martin, *The Life and Professional Career of Emma Abbott* (Minneapolis: J. Kimball, 1891), 37. For more on Abbott, see chap. 12.

11. References to the Verdi Renaissance frequently appear but seldom in any detail. For example, see Stanley Sadie, ed., *The New Grove Dictionary of Opera*, 4:944–45, entry on

Verdi. A more detailed and important because contemporary account appears in the preface to Francis Toye, *Giuseppe Verdi, His Life and Works* (1931; repr., New York: Knopf, 1946). See also George W. Martin, "Franz Werfel and the 'Verdi Renaissance,'" in Martin, *Aspects of Verdi* (1988; repr., New York: Limelight Editions, 1993), 61–77.

12. W. J. Henderson, *New York Sun*, November 23, 1913, 11.

13. Toye, *Giuseppe Verdi*, xi.

14. Marcello Conati, *Interviews and Encounters with Verdi*, trans. Richard Stokes (London: Gollancz, 1984), 323–24. Also, at Trieste, 1902–11, only one performance of *Trovatore*, at Parma, 1904–12, one each of *Rigoletto* and *Aida;* and at Milan's La Scala, 1894–1901, excepting revivals of *Otello* and *Falstaff*, only three of *Rigoletto* and one of *Don Carlos*.

15. Henry Edward Krehbiel, *Chapters of Opera, Being Historical and Critical Observations and Records Concerning the Lyric Drama in New York from the Earliest Days Down to the Present Time* (New York: Henry Holt, 1908), 276, 318, and 361. To trace the relative decline: in 1893–96, Verdi had 42 performances of six operas, and Wagner, 53 of six; and in 1898–1902, 50 of seven operas, and 127 of nine. See also the Metropolitan Archives database at www.metopera.org.

16. Conati, *Interviews and Encounters with Verdi*, 323; and for a popular parody of *Trovatore*, see Harvey Sachs, *Reflections on Toscanini* (New York: Grove Weidenfeld, 1991), 13. Also, Julian Budden, *The Operas of Verdi*, vol. 2, *From Il trovatore to La forza del destino* (London: Cassell, 1978), 66–67.

17. On Toscanini's *Luisa Miller*, see Harvey Sachs, *Toscanini* (Philadelphia: Lippincott, 1978), 84. For the relative importance of these productions and others that followed under Toscanini at La Scala in the mid-1920s, see Toye, *Giuseppe Verdi*, xii–xiii.

18. Henderson, *New York Sun*, November 23, 1913, 11. According to the database www.metopera.org, in Gatti-Casazza's twenty-seven years as general manager, *Otello* and *Falstaff*, though still requiring royalty payments, did better. *Falstaff* had thirty-two performances, twenty-one in house, eight on tour, and three in 1910 in Paris; *Otello* had eighteen in house, ten on tour, and three in 1910 in Paris. For some details on royalty costs in these years, see H. Howard Taubman, *Opera Front and Back* (New York: Scribner's, 1938), 355–56.

19. "Bungling libretto . . . this huge lumbering machine." James G. Huneker, *New York World*, December 24, 1920, 11. See also, unsigned article, *New York Herald*, December 24, 1920, 9: "a forgotten opera . . . machine made." Also Gilbert W. Gabriel, *New York Sun*, December 24, 1920, 5: "legitimate novelty . . . Verdi's most careful, if uninspired, score." And Irving Kolodin, *The Metropolitan Opera, 1883–1966* (New York: Knopf), 293–94.

20. In the United States, Franz Werfel (1890–1945) is best known most likely for the novels: *The Forty Days of Musa Dagh* (1933), *Embezzled Heaven* (1940), and *The Song of Bernadette* (1941). For an extended account of his place in the Verdi Renaissance, see Martin, "Franz Werfel and the 'Verdi Renaissance,'" and Hans Kühner, "Franz Werfel e Giuseppe Verdi," *Verdi Bollettino* 1, no. 3 (December 1960): 1790–804.

21. Franz Werfel, *Verdi, A Novel of the Opera*, trans. Helen Jessiman (New York: Simon and Schuster, 1925; New York: Allen, Towne and Heath, 1947). Review: Edward Goldbeck, "Franz Werfel," *Reflex* 2, no. 3 (March 1928): 33–39. Also, James C. Davidheiser, "Franz Werfel and the Historical Novel, an Analytical Study of *Verdi, Roman der Oper*, *Die Vierzig Tage des Musa Dagh*, and *Das Lied von Bernadette* (PhD diss., University of Pittsburgh, 1972).

22. Agreement is not entire. For example, Sachs writes: "Many Italian music historians consider that production [Toscanini's at La Scala in 1902] to have initiated the 'Verdi Renaissance'" (Sachs, *Toscanini*, 82). A difficulty with that judgment, however, is

that no prominent Italian musician or critic followed Toscanini's lead, and an outstanding Italian critic and scholar of the mid-twentieth century, Massimo Mila (1910–88), has twice rejected the claim. See his preface to *Giuseppe Verdi* (Bari: Laterza, 1958), and his article "L'unità stilistica nell'opera di Verdi," *Nuova Rivista Musicale Italiana* (January/February 1968): 62–75. In the latter he states: "Italian cultural 'highbrows' of the time were ever more inclined to align themselves with the scornful opinions of Verdi's youthful works that dominated French and German circles. The delicate ears of D'Annunzio's Italy were wounded by the brutality of such swift and straightforward masterworks as *Rigoletto* and *Traviata*. . . . Today cultured Italians do not like to be reminded of this repudiation of Verdi's most popular works. When it is discussed there is always someone who, as if to deny responsibility, feigns amazement: 'Verdi? But whoever doubted his greatness?'" And in his preface to *Giuseppe Verdi*, Mila states unequivocally that Werfel's novel was the "official" opening of the Renaissance. For those Americans who may instinctively wonder if an individual who was not a musician is receiving too much praise, there is in American cultural history the comparable figure of Lincoln Kerstein (1907–96). Though not a dancer or musician, by his publications and activities, especially in his role as founder, director, supporter, and chief spokesman of the New York City Ballet Company, he is an essential figure in the history of American dance.

23. Figures are taken from Toye, *Giuseppe Verdi*, xii–xiii. For an account of Fritz Busch in Germany, ending in the demonstration against him organized by the Nazis at a performance of *Rigoletto*, see Gottfried Schmiedel, "Fritz Busch and the Dresden Opera," *Opera* 11, no. 3 (March 1960): 175–81. Toye further reports that records show that in Germany in the 1927–28 season, 135 opera houses reported 1,576 performances of Wagner and 1,513 of Verdi; and at the Vienna Opera in 1930, of a total of 339 performances, 49 were of Wagner and 46 of Verdi. "Ten years earlier any such correlation of Wagner and Verdi in Germany would have seemed frankly incredible."

24. Toye, *Giuseppe Verdi*, xii.

25. Henry Pleasants, *The Agony of Modern Music* (New York: Simon and Schuster, 1960), 142.

26. Igor Stravinsky in his *Poetics of Music, in the Form of Six Lessons* (his Norton lectures at Harvard in 1939–40), trans. Arthur Knodel and Ingolf Dahl (New York: Vintage Books, 1956), 46, 63–64, spoke of the importance of melody and highly praised Verdi, although ranking *Falstaff* below *Rigoletto, Trovatore*, and *Traviata*. Later, he revised that opinion, in Robert Craft, *Conversations with Igor Stravinsky* (Garden City, NY: Doubleday, 1959), 74.

27. Giulio Gatti-Casazza, *Memories of the Opera* (1933, 1937; repr., London: John Calder, 1977), 246.

28. The critical edition is officially titled *The Works of Giuseppe Verdi*, or *WGV*. Its purpose is to provide a scholarly edition of all of Verdi's works, operas and other works, for some of which no printed orchestral scores were available, to explain and settle disagreements among some of the performing materials that were and are in circulation, and to collect in one place all important recent discoveries about the works. Each opera is published in a two-volume set: the orchestral score, with an introduction, and the critical commentary, which takes the opera almost measure by measure. The first two-volume set to appear, in 1983, was *Rigoletto*, listed as volume 17 in Series 1: Operas. The *WGV* is published jointly by the University of Chicago Press and Ricordi (Milan), whose archives hold most of Verdi's autograph scores. Over the years a considerable number of articles have been published on the *WGV*, one of the earliest being David Lawton, "Why Bother with the New Verdi Edition?" in *Opera Quarterly* 2, no. 4 (Winter 1984/85):

43–54. More recently, Philip Gossett, general editor of the *WGV*, published "Scandal and Scholarship: Who Decides How an Opera Should Be Performed?" in *New Republic*, July 2, 2001, 23–32. For an example of how the critical edition can help to make such decisions, see *WGV, Corsaro*, score, xxi–xxii, and critical commentary, 20. And see Gossett, *Divas and Scholars*, a book in which he discusses directly and indirectly the aims of and reasons for a critical edition, with examples drawn from Italian opera 1810–65, Rossini through Verdi's revision of *Macbeth*, for example, 123ff., 142ff., and 278ff.

29. The nine volumes already published on "earlier operas," are *Nabucco, Ernani, Giovanna d'Arco, Alzira, Macbeth, Masnadieri, Corsaro, Luisa Miller,* and *Stiffelio*.

30. Abramo Basevi, *Studio sulle opere di Giuseppe Verdi* (Florence: Tofani, 1859), 159.

31. Perhaps Shakespeare's closest approximation of a monster is Caliban, in *The Tempest*, but even Caliban, like Ariel, is recognizably human. For a good, brief statement of what in this respect Verdi by contrast is *not*, see Leon Botstein, "Wagner and Our Century," *Music at the Turn of Century: A 19th-Century Music Reader,* ed. Joseph Kerman (Berkeley: University of California Press, 1990), 167–80.

32. Will Crutchfield, "Crutchfield at Large," *Opera News* 59, no. 13 (March 18, 1995): 50.

Chapter One

1. The number, in a confusion between season and year, is sometimes misstated. See the published chronology of La Scala (compiled by its archivist Giampiero Tintori and confirmed in a second edition in 1978) in Carlo Gatti's, *Il teatro alla Scala nella storia e nell'arte (1778–1963),* 43. It reports eight performances (starting in March) in the 1842 carnival season and fifty-seven in the autumn season. During the autumn season, *Nabucco* alternated with six other operas, which combined totaled only twenty-nine performances.

2. In Havana, the opera was received "coldly." Critics complained of its vocal difficulties, and even on the opera's revival in 1848–49 the public did not take to it. In the years 1846–49 Havana heard the hemispheric premieres of *Ernani, Lombardi, Nabucco, Foscari, Attila,* and *Macbeth*. Of these, the most popular were *Ernani* and *Attila,* followed by *Lombardi*. See Enrique Rio Prado, *La musica italiana a Cuba, Prime rappresentazioni di Verdi e Morlacchi all'Avana* (Lecce: BESA, 1996).

3. In London in 1846, *Nino;* in 1850, *Anato*. Curiously, in 1857, rival companies there staged *Nabucco,* one as *Nino,* the other as *Anato*.

4. Dwight, "Preface," in *An Essay on the Stage* (pages unnumbered).

5. For example, Boston. See Eugene Tompkins and Quincy Kilby, *The History of the Boston Theatre, 1854–1901* (1908; repr. New York: Benjamin Blom, 2969), 25: "At first the theatre was open only on Monday, Tuesday, Wednesday, Thursday, and Friday evenings, it being against the law to give performances on Saturday evenings, on account of the Puritan Sabbath's beginning at sundown on Saturday." The first Saturday night performance (p. 75) occurred on January 12, 1859. The relaxation, however, was only in custom, not law, for in April 1896 the manager of the Boston Theatre was arrested and fined fifty dollars for allowing Sousa's Band to give a concert in the theater on Sunday. After which, for a time, all Sunday evening concerts and vaudeville shows in Boston were ostensibly for religious or charitable purposes (p. 439). In New York, in December 1907, a judge of the State Supreme Court, unexpectedly upheld a long-ignored "blue law" and forced the cancellation of the Metropolitan Opera's Sunday Evening Concerts on

the eighth and fifteenth. On the seventeenth, the city aldermen passed a law permitting on Sundays "sacred or educational, vocal or instrumental concerts, lectures, addresses, recitations and singing." See lead stories in the *New York Times* and *New York Herald*, on December 8, and following.

6. On the startling increase in the number of musicians in proportion to the country's population, see chap. 7.

7. On the size of La Scala's orchestra, see *Nabucodonosor*, score, xxvi, in *The Works of Giuseppe Verdi*, ed. Philip Gossett et al., Series 1: Operas, critical edition (Chicago: University of Chicago Press; Milan: Ricordi, 1983–) (hereafter references to the critical edition are cited as *WGV* followed by opera title). Verdi calls for twenty-four instruments plus strings, which are not numbered. Probably, however, they numbered at least forty-five, for he scores for six cello. In 1842 La Scala could provide these, and hence La Scala's orchestra, plus an onstage band of at least ten, probably was close to eighty. In 1855 its orchestra numbered "about ninety," see Charles Santley, *Student and Singer: The Reminiscences of Charles Santley* (New York and London: Macmillan, 1892), 78. In 1850, the Teatro la Fenice (capacity 1,500), Venice, seating some eight hundred less than La Scala, had an orchestra of sixty-seven. See *WGV, Rigoletto*, score, xxviii. The Teatro Regio (capacity 1,400), Parma, according to its program, in mounting *Nabucco* in 1984, had an orchestra of sixty-seven, not including the onstage band. But in the United States before the 1850s players and instruments were often scarce. See Ritter, *Music in America*, 204–6, 231; n. 6; and Mark Curtis McKnight, "Music Criticism in the *New York Times* and the *New York Tribune*, 1854–1876" (PhD diss., Louisiana State University, 1980), 30, where a symphony orchestra lacked sufficient cello and an English horn for the *William Tell* overture. In 1856, according to *Dwight's Journal* of May 3, San Francisco lacked a good piano, spoiling a public performance of Mendelssohn's Concerto in D Minor (Irving Sablosky, *What They Heard: Music in America, 1852–1881, from the Pages of "Dwight's Journal of Music"* [Baton Rouge: Louisiana State University, 1986], 173). For the report of Verdi paying the cost of enlarging the La Scala chorus, see Arturo Pougin, *Giuseppe Verdi, Vita Aneddotica, con note ed aggiunte di Folchetto* (Milan: Ricordi, 1881), 34.

8. On the offstage band: Verdi scored for it to play six times during the opera. As then was custom, he left its instruments and scoring to each opera house, to depend on the number and talent of the musicians available. See *WGV, Nabucodonosor*, score, xxvi. Stage bands in the United States were popular and not uncommon. Gounod's *Faust*, for its premiere in Boston, January 14, 1864, had a full military band onstage for the "Soldiers' Chorus." See Tompkins and Kilby, *History of the Boston Theatre, 1854–1901*, 105. In Philadelphia, for the premiere on May 4, 1864, of W. H. Fry's opera *Notre Dame de Paris* (based on Hugo's novel), the production boasted an orchestra of sixty, a large chorus, corps de ballet, a military band of thirty, and a drum corps of ten. See McKnight, "Music Criticism in the *New York Times* and the *New York Tribune*," 210.

9. Author's interview with Sarasota artistic director Victor DeRenzi, September 9, 2001. Sarasota gave the opera fourteen performances, "97 percent sold out."

10. Programs sometimes misstate the relationship of Nabucco and Abigaille. She is not his daughter by blood, but by adoption. She was the child of one of his wives, fathered by one of his slaves. Having executed her parents, Nabucco adopted her. In her moment of self-discovery (recitative to her aria at the start of act 2), she identifies herself as a "child of slaves," who is mistakenly thought by the Babylonian people to be Nabucco's daughter by a slave. For more detail, see Julian Budden, *The Operas of Verdi*, vol. 1, *From* Oberto *to* Rigoletto (London: Cassell, 1973), 94–95.

11. The observation is usually ascribed to Rossini. Its earliest appearance, though without citation, seems to be in Carlo Gatti's *Verdi*, vol. 1 (Milan: Edizioni "Alpes," 1931), 207.

12. *American*, November 30, 1825, p. 2, col. 1. This is the troupe led by Manuel Garcia that played at the Park Theatre, New York, November 29, 1825, through September 30, 1826: seventy-nine performances of nine operas, of which the four most frequently given were Rossini's *Barbiere*, twenty-one; *Tancredi*, sixteen; *Otello*, ten; and Mozart's *Don Giovanni*, ten.

13. Nasal quality, *American*, February 8, 1826, 2: "the female voices, whose music savored rather much of nasal psalmody." Complaints against that quality started early. See Andrew Law, *Musical Primer* (Cheshire, CT: William Law, 1794), from the preface. This part and much else of the preface was dropped in later editions. See also John Sullivan Dwight, "The History of Music in Boston, Including Suffolk County, Massachusetts, 1630–1880," in *The Memorial History of Boston*, vol. 4, *1630–1880*, ed. Justin Winsor (Boston: J. R. Osgood, 1880–81), 415: "Before the year 1800, all that bore the name of music in New England may be summed up in the various modifications of one monotonous and barren type—the Puritan Psalmody." And Ritter, *Music in America* (1883, rev. 1890), 92, 196, 407.

14. *New York Review and Athaeneum Magazine* 11 (February): 230–35.

15. *Le Moqueur*, June 18, 1837: 2–3. The journal, published every Thursday and Sunday, devoted itself to music, opera, and literature. I thank Kathryn Page, curator at the Louisiana State Museum, New Orleans, for finding the article for me.

16. Max Maretzek, *Crotchets and Quavers, or Revelations of an Opera Manager in America* (1855; repr. New York: Da Capo Press, 1966), 18–20.

17. Clara Louise Kellogg, *Memoirs of an American Prima Donna* (New York: Putnam's, 1913), 40.

18. The *Albion, a Weekly Journal of News, Politics, and General Literature*, April 8, 1848, 180. Though the article is not signed, the critic presumably was Henry Cood Watson, see Lawrence, *Strong on Music*, 1:505. On the importance of the *Albion* for its criticism, see Mark N. Grant, *Maestros of the Pen: A History of Classical Music Criticism in America* (Boston: Northeastern University Press, 1998), 10, and for Grant on critic Watson, 16–21.

19. *Albion*, April 15, 1848, 192.

20. *Boston Evening Transcript*, June 5, 1848, 2.

21. On Maretzek's concerts, see Lawrence, *Strong on Music*, 1:569n8.

22. Robert N. C. Bochsa (1789–1856), of Bohemian background, was raised in France, where he became the harpist both to Napoleon and to Louis XVIII. He composed operas, perpetrated forgeries, fled to England, became a conductor, eloped with the wife of Henry Bishop (composer of "Home, Sweet Home"), and turned Anna Bishop (mother of Bishop's three children) into an outstanding operatic soprano. In accomplishing this transformation of a hitherto rather ordinary soprano, Bochsa, who reportedly weighed 300 pounds, perhaps became the model for the extravagantly thin Svengali in George du Maurier's novel *Trilby* (1894). Bochsa died in Sydney, Australia, where he and Bishop were on tour.

23. For the background of *Judith*, see Lawrence, *Strong on Music*, 2:65–66. Lawrence suggests that *Judith* initially "had been concocted for the Latin American tour" that Bishop and Bochsa had completed before coming to New York.

24. *Morning Express*, August 21, 1850, 2, and *Musical Times*, August 31, 1850, 578. See also *New York Herald*, August 21, 1850, 4.

25. See George W. Martin, *Verdi at the Golden Gate: Opera and San Francisco in the Gold Rush Years* (Berkeley: University of California Press, 1993), 65–66. American audiences

in these years craved new operas, "novelties." A critic for the *New York Tribune*, October 17, 1853, in reviewing *I Lombardi*, remarked that the "American desire for change," made consecutive performances of the same work difficult. See also Joseph N. Ireland, *Records of the New York Stage from 1750 to 1860*, 2 vols. (1866–67; repr. New York: Burt Franklin, 1968), 2:148, and Ritter, *Music in America*, 201. No opera in its premiere or first revival in any U.S. city matched the fifty-seven performances of that *Nabucco* in its 1842 fall season at La Scala; or in 1843 at Genoa, thirty-five; or in 1844 at Barcelona, thirty-four. See Roger Parker, "The Exodus of *Nabucco* (1842–44)," in *Studies in Early Verdi, 1832–1844: New Information and Perspectives on the Milanese Musical Milieu and the Operas from* Oberto *to* Ernani (New York: Garland, 1989), 123, 126. In the United States, Gounod's *Faust* (sung in Italian) came close, with an opening season run in New York of thirty-two performances between November 25, 1863, and April 20, 1864. In the same months, another company, with less success, staged the opera in German, also at the Academy of Music. See McKnight, "Music Criticism in the *New York Times* and the *New York Tribune*, 207–9.

26. *Pioneer Magazine*, December 1854, 373. For other San Francisco reviews of *Judith*, see Martin, *Verdi at the Golden Gate*, 275–76nn30–35.

27. George Loder (1816–68) was a conductor, short, with a magnificent beard. He could play the piano, flute, or double bass, and also composed. In San Francisco, in 1852, he founded the city's first Philharmonic Society. In New York, in the late 1840s, he composed a number of opera burlesques, among them *Herr Nanny*, on Verdi's *Ernani*. His lampoons were much admired for his adherence to the mocked composer's style. See Lawrence, *Strong on Music*, 1:135, 589.

28. *Pioneer Magazine*, January 1855, 55. For citations to other enthusiastic reviews of *Nabucco*, see Martin, *Verdi at the Golden Gate*, 278nn21–22.

29. See Martin, *Verdi at the Golden Gate*. Before 1881, for example, in San Francisco, a city passionate for opera, the greatest number of even *non*consecutive performances achieved by any Verdi opera in one year, was thirteen (in 1860, by *Ernani*). Of Verdi's important premieres in San Francisco, *Rigoletto* in its first year, 1860 (when the city had a population of about fifty-seven thousand), had only three performances; *Traviata*, in 1859, four; and *Trovatore*, in 1859 (and for forty years thereafter the city's favorite opera), eleven.

30. San Francisco *Daily Alta California* and *Daily Herald*, December 3 and 5, 1854. Also the *Daily Herald* (steamer ed.), December 9. Fenena's prayer "Oh dischiuso è il firmamento," was translated as "To me the firmament is clouded," see copy in the Morgan Library, New York, GWM Collection #228. Verdi composed two variants of the aria to suit singers' needs, see *WGV, Nabucodonosor*, score, appendixes 4 and 5. The Board of Music Trade's *Complete Catalogue of Sheet Music and Musical Works, 1870* (1871; repr. New York: Da Capo Press, 1973) lists seven vocal selections and twenty-four instrumental arrangements then in print.

31. San Francisco's *Daily Evening Bulletin*, May 26, 1862, 3. Also in Martin, *Verdi at the Golden Gate*, 278n22.

32. Michele Lessona, *Volere è Potere* (Florence: Barbera, 1869), 296–98, quoting an interview with Verdi, the accuracy of which Verdi confirmed in a letter to his friend Opprandino Arrivabene, March 7, 1874 (see Annibale Alberti, ed., *Verdi intimo: Carteggio di Giuseppe Verdi con il Conte Opprandino Arrivabene, 1861–1886* [Milan: Mondadori, 1931], 174).

33. Verdi's Autobiographical Account prepared in 1879 and published as an appendix to the sixth chapter of Pougin, *Giuseppe Verdi, Vita Aneddotica*, 39–46. Verdi dictated the account to his publisher, Giulio Ricordi, on October 19, 1879. For views on the conflicting accounts, see Pierluigi Petrobelli, "From Rossini's *Mosè* to Verdi's *Nabucco*,"

Music in the Theatre: Essays on Verdi and Other Composers, trans. Roger Parker (Princeton: Princeton University Press, 1994), 9–12; Parker, "Verdi and the *Gazzetta Privilegiata di Milano*," in *Studies in Early Verdi*, 17–20; and David R. B. Kimbell, *Verdi in the Age of Italian Romanticism* (Cambridge: Cambridge University Press), 105, who cites Budden, *Operas of Verdi*, 1:92.

34. Toye, in *Giuseppe Verdi*, 206, finds "the fourth act . . . on a distinctly lower level," except for Fenena's aria. Charles Osborne, *The Complete Operas of Verdi* (New York: Knopf, 1970), 60, writes: "Abigaille's last utterances do not have the individuality of Violetta's or Gilda's . . ." whereas "The unaccompanied choral hymn is just right." Against these stands Budden, *Operas of Verdi*, 1:110: "The death of Abigaille is one of the finest numbers of the opera, and it forms yet another of those selectively orchestrated passages which lighten a distinctly heavy score."

35. See *WGV, Nabucodonosor*, score, xviii, quoting the contemporary Italian critic Alberto Mazzucato: "The first two performances closed with the death agony of Abigaille which, although treated with love, did not obtain an effect, as it was a useless prolongation of the action; for this reason the score now ends with the ensemble piece ["Immenso Jehovah"], nor could Verdi more solemnly conclude his fine composition." For the examinations of librettos, see Parker, *Studies in Early Verdi*, 111–41; and Petrobelli, *Music in the Theatre*, for his Postscript, *Studies in Early Verdi*, 30, annotation paragraph entry numbered 2.

36. For reviews of the New York production, see *Dispatch*, October 6, 1860, 5. For reviews in Boston, see *Boston Post*, June 22, 1860, 1: "Mme. Fabbri interpolated a scene at the close to exhibit her dramatic powers in a death scene." Also, *Boston Daily Evening Transcript*, June 21, 1860, 2. Both these reviews show considerable appreciation of the music. But *Dwight's Journal of Music*, after praising Fabbri, and to some extent Verdi, in its review of June 23, 1860, 103, scorned Verdi in the review of June 30, 111: "We trust she [Fabbri] may be heard in music better worth her talent than mere operas of Verdi." See also, Tompkins and Kilby, *History of Boston Theatre*, 82: "The Cortesi Italian Opera Company from Havana gave six performances" in May 1860 and seven in June. The June season opened with *Nabucco* on the twentieth, repeated on the twenty-third.

37. The *Dispatch*, October 6, 1860, 5: "We have a few remarks to make which it strikes us may be unpleasant to Signor Muzio [Emanuele Muzio, a friend of Verdi and his only pupil]. He was upon this occasion the conductor . . . while Muzio on the plea—at least so we are told—that it is the custom in Italy took it upon himself to omit the whole of the last act . . . we see no reason why it should be omitted here after we have once heard and relished it. In short we consider it a wanton impertinence in a conductor who is paid to gratify our tastes to presume to dictate to us upon that which we have once expressed our satisfaction with. We shall not allude to this again, unless Signor Muzio should repeat such a high-handed impertinence." Strangely, the performance is not listed in Gaspare Nello Vetro, *L'allievo di Verdi, Emanuele Muzio* (Parma: Fondazione Casa di Risparmio, 1993), with a chronology by Kaufman that purports to list every performance conducted anywhere by Muzio.

38. See Petrobelli, *Music in the Theatre*, 8–33.

39. See Giuseppe Verdi, *Nabucco*, DVD, Renato Bruson [N], Ghena Dimitrova [A], Dimiter Petkov [Z], Arena di Verona, Maurizio Arena (West Long Branch, NJ: Kultur International Films, 2005).

40. On the opera's record in San Francisco, see Joan Chatfield-Taylor, *San Francisco Opera: The First Seventy-Five Years* [1923–97] (San Francisco: Chronicle Books, 1997); Don L. Hixon, *Verdi in San Francisco: A Preliminary Bibliography, 1851–1899* (privately printed,

1980); and Thomas G. Kaufman, *Verdi and His Major Contemporaries: A Selected Chronology of Performances with Casts* (New York: Garland, 1990).

41. *New York Herald*, May 21, 1860, 1. The review mistakenly states that the performance was "the first time" in the United States. Maretzek's favorite composers: Mozart, Rossini, Meyerbeer, Bellini, Weber, Beethoven, Piccini, Cimarosa, Gluck, Donizetti, and Balfe. See Maretzek, *Crotchets and Quavers*, 206.

42. See George W. Martin, "The Metropolitan Opera's Sunday Evening Concerts and Verdi," *Opera Quarterly* 19, no. 1: 10–27. My analysis of the programs (incomplete records) shows that in the Concerts' sixty-three years some twenty-eight excerpts were offered from *Nabucco*. Fourteen of these were Zaccaria's prayer "Vieni, O Levita! . . . Tu sul labbro." Of these, four were sung by Pol Plançon (thrice in the years 1896–98; once in 1904); by Ezio Pinza (nine times, 1929–40), and by Tancredi Pasero (once, 1933). The overture was played eight times (once, 1920; seven, 1926–40), and the chorus "Va, pensiero" sung only twice (1904–5). In all, the Metropolitan's basses account for sixteen of the twenty vocal excerpts, baritones for two, chorus for two, and sopranos for none. Hence, in common memory during these years, *Nabucco* was primarily an opera for bass. The Metropolitan's Concerts were unique in their longevity and amount of operatic music offered, and perhaps more adventurous in their programs than other series because of the company's constant influx of foreign artists. The celebrity of the artists and their success in the concerts—the imprimatur of the Metropolitan—sometimes led to recordings. For example, in the 1920s a recording of the prayer and another of its sequel, "Del futuro nel buio," by the Metropolitan's bass José Mardones.

43. On the Verdi Renaissance, for more detail, see the introduction, and for more about Werfel, see Martin, "Franz Werfel and the 'Verdi Renaissance,'" in *Aspects of Verdi*, 61–77.

44. Toye, *Giuseppe Verdi*, 206.

45. Introduction to Toye, *Giuseppe Verdi*, by Herbert Weinstock, ix–x. Weinstock himself by 1946 had managed to hear only "ten Verdi operas in more than two decades of opera-going." The critic for the *Chicago Tribune*, George P. Upton, in *The Standard Operas, Their Plots, Their Music, and Their Composers: A Handbook* (Chicago: McClurg, 1889) not only did not include *Nabucco* in the seven Verdi operas he discussed, but he did not even list it in his introductory biography of Verdi, which names seventeen of Verdi's operas from *I Lombardi* to *Otello*. Similarly, in the next generation, the critic for the *New York Tribune*, Henry Edward Krehbiel, in his two books, *Chapters of Opera* (1908) and *More Chapters of Opera* (New York: Henry Holt, 1919), does not mention the opera.

46. A broadcast with the NBC Symphony from Studio 8-H in the NBC building, Rockefeller Center, New York. The concert included a performance of Verdi's rarely heard *Inno delle nazioni*, already performed in the radio broadcast of January 31, 1943. For that first broadcast, Toscanini famously changed a repetition of the hymn's cry from "oh patria" to "oh patria tradita" (my country betrayed). In December of that year the U.S. Office of War Information had made a film of Toscanini and the orchestra performing the *Inno* to use as propaganda, and so successful was the film that it was shown in commercial theaters and, between 1944 and 1957, in whole or in part, twenty-two times on television. Museum of Broadcasting, public letter by Laurence Bergreen, concerning a showing of the film in "Summer Fortnight Festival," August 23 to September 3, 1977.

47. It is difficult now to grasp the fervor with which these events were greeted. Toscanini, the most celebrated of Mussolini's Italian opponents, was in effect recapturing Verdi, and all Italian music, and even all Italians, from years of Fascist domination. The concert was relayed to tens of thousands of people outside La Scala, who heard it over

loudspeakers in the galleria and piazzas near the opera house. It was broadcast throughout Italy and, by short wave radio, to much of the world. The other two Verdi numbers were the overture to *I vespri siciliani* and the *Te Deum.*

48. Since reopening, La Scala has performed the opera in 1946–47, 1958, 1966–67, 1967 (Montreal), 1968, 1986–87, 1987 (Berlin), 1988 (Tokyo), and 1996.

49. This recording, made in Rome, January 18, 1951, was reissued in 2000 by Warner Fonit, 8573 82646-2. It featured Paolo Silveri (N), Caterina Mancini (A), and Antonio Cassinelli (Z), with Pernando Previtali, conductor.

50. Too many to list even partially, but in the 1950s and 1960s they introduced many Americans to the first music heard of operas such as *Giovanna d'Arco, Alzira, Battaglia di Legnano, Luisa Miller,* and even *I vespri siciliani.*

51. "The third," see *San Antonio Express,* January 10, 1960, 12-C, and *Evening News,* March 7, review by Gerald Ashford. The cast was Giuseppe Valdengo (N), Yi-Kwei Sze (Z), Frances Yeend (A), and conductor, Victor Alessandro. The "amateur" chorus, see *Evening News,* March 7, 1960.

52. *San Antonio Express,* March 7, 1960, 3-A. See also, *San Antonio Light,* March 7, 1960, 3. The San Antonio scenery later was used by the New Orleans Opera Company for its city premiere of the opera, October 19, 1978. See the review by Jack Belsom, *Opera,* March 1978, 233. Also, by Frank Gagnard, the *New Orleans Times-Picayune,* October 21, 1978, sec. 3, 8: "*Nabucco* is fun. It is direct and compact and has no waste motion." When Nabucco rode into the Temple, the horse won a burst of applause.

53. *New York Times,* October 25, 1960, 1, and 41. Paul Henry Lang, for the *New York Herald Tribune,* was just as harsh, especially in his "Open Letter to Mr. Bing," November 13, 1960, sec. 4, 1: "The decors . . . were probably the worst seen [recently] in the Met . . . while the stage direction was of the caliber of a high school production." In agreement, Winthrop Sargeant, the *New Yorker,* January 21, 1961, 103–4. Louis Biancolli, for the *World-Telegram,* October 25, 1960, 20, was cautiously more kind.

54. Kolodin, *Metropolitan Opera,* 639. The stage director was Günther Rennert. Opening night, when anticipation ran high, brought a new record at the box office, $91,482 (also, *New York Times,* October 25, 1960, 1). Kolodin concluded, however, "*Nabucco* went its round of the subscription cycle with little evidence of enthusiasm or, even, of appreciation for the effort expended on its preparation."

55. I attended six of the nine performances.

56. See *New York Times,* October 25, 1960.

57. *WGV, Nabucodonosor,* score, xx.

58. Philadelphia, November 29, 1960; Boston, April 17, 1961; Atlanta, May 6; Bloomington, May 15; and Detroit, May 25. For Atlanta, Bloomington, and Detroit, these performances probably were city premieres.

59. Paul Henry Lang, *Critic at the Opera* (New York: Norton, 1971), 136–37. The book's chapters are drawn from his reviews and Sunday articles in the *New York Herald Tribune,* 1954–69.

60. Arthur Bloomfield, *50 Years of the San Francisco Opera* (San Francisco: San Francisco Book Co., 1972), 193.

61. Roger Dettmer, *Opera,* December 1963, 808: Though rather liking the "vividly stylized scenery," he scorned the Metropolitan's "non-period, *haute-*Hallowe'en costumes." The opera's Chicago premiere was on October 4, 1963.

62. A list of post-1967 staged productions in the United States, undoubtedly incomplete, would include: Philadelphia (1969), New York (Grand Opera, 1975, 1979), New Orleans (1978), Miami (1981), San Diego (1981), New York (City Opera, 1981), and

New York (Grand Opera, 1983, 1989), Newark (1990), New York (Grand Opera, Central Park, 1994), Sarasota (1995), Chicago (1998), Cincinnati (2001), Los Angeles (2002), Utah Festival (2003), and North Carolina (Opera Carolina, 2003). These are in addition to the many performances by the San Francisco Opera. Moreover, the Boston Concert Opera offered the opera in 1979; the Philadelphia Orchestra, led by Riccardo Muti, gave three concert performances in Philadelphia (1989) and one in Carnegie Hall, New York (1989). Three other companies have given concert performances in Carnegie Hall, American Opera Society (1968), Opera Orchestra of New York (1984), and New York Grand Opera (1992). After La Scala's visit to Montreal (1967), Canada had performances in Montreal (1992), Toronto (1993), Vancouver (1995), and Montreal (2001).

63. Martin Bernheimer, *Opera*, January 1982, 72, reviewing the San Diego production of *Nabucco* in the previous June, which he reported had "unfortunately" chosen "neither course."

64. *New York Times*, October 11, 1967, 39. Robert Jacobson, though editor of *Opera News*, reviewing here for the English magazine *Opera*, February 1968, 148, liked how La Scala's stage director "moved the large chorus in sweeping patterns," but was disappointed in how "the principals did little more than line up and sing their hearts out."

65. Welsh National Opera, in 1995; Royal Opera, Covent Garden, in 1996; and English National Opera, 1997. For highly unfavorable reviews of the first and second, see *Opera*, November 1995, 1342–45, and June 1996, 706–7.

66. For example, the American soprano, Linda Roark-Strummer, reportedly had sung the role more than 150 times by April 1992, when she sang it in Montreal, after which, she sang it in Verona, Toronto, Vancouver, Santiago, and perhaps elsewhere.

67. Giuseppe Verdi, *Nabucco*, Samuel Ramy, Juan Pons, Maria Guleghina, Metropolitan Opera Orchestra, James Levine, DVD, Deutsche Grammophon B0003850-09; see *Fanfare* July/August 2005. Audience in Manhattan's Central Park, *New York Times*, June 18, 2004, E19.

Chapter Two

1. Richard Grant White, *Morning Courier and New-York Enquirer*, May 15, 1846, 2.

2. Encore, *New York Herald*, May 21, 1846, 1; *New York Evening Mirror*, May 21, 1846, 2: "The great symphony of Beethoven became really tiresome." Strong, *Diary*, May 21, 1846, quoted in Lawrence, *Strong on Music*, 1:368–69. The overtures: Weber's *Der Freischütz* and *Jubilee*, Mozart's *Die Zauberflöte*; the piano concerto, Mendelssohn's in G minor.

3. See George W. Martin, "The Metropolitan Opera's Sunday Evening Concerts and Verdi," *Opera Quarterly* 19, no. 1 (Winter 2003): 16–27.

4. *Morning Courier and Enquirer*, January 8, 1847, 2; *New York Herald*, January 8, 1847, 2; *New York Evening Mirror*, January 9, 1847, 2.

5. On Palmo's Opera House, see description in Lawrence, *Strong on Music*, 1:251–57. Also, Jay Robert Teran, "The New York Opera Audience, 1825–1974" (PhD diss., New York University, 1974), 13–14. Though Rapetti's dates are uncertain, his activities can be traced in Lawrence, *Strong on Music*, vol. 1, especially p. 449; in Howard Shanet, *Philharmonic: A History of New York's Orchestra* (New York: Doubleday, 1975), 67n1; in James Henry Mapleson, *The Mapleson Memoirs: The Career of an Operatic Impresario, 1858–1888*, ed. Harold Rosenthal (New York: Appleton-Century, 1966), 32–33; and in Giovanni Ermengildo Schiavo, *Italian-American History* (1947; repr. New York: Arno Press, 1975), 1:418–19. In the early 1840s Rapetti was possibly the best violinist in the city.

6. On Manuel Garcia and his troupe, and on the Park's orchestra, see Molly Nelson, "The First Italian Opera Season in New York City: 1825–1826" (PhD diss., University of North Carolina at Chapel Hill, 1976), 124–27.

7. *Tancredi, American,* January 5, 1826, 2; *Don Giovanni,* Richard Grant White, "Opera in New York," *Century Illustrated Monthly Magazine,* no. 5 (March 1882), 609.

8. Violins and timpani: *New York Herald,* July 10, 1845, 2; *Anglo-American,* June 21, 1845, 201. On Prévost: *New York Herald,* June 21, 1845, 3: "His beating was full of energy and precision, without any affectation. He has no tin-plate, and we did not hear a single slap throughout the evening—a practice very much in favor with our New York bands, and which cannot be condemned too much."

9. On balance of theater and orchestra, see Charles A. Dana, *New York Tribune,* March 25, 1847, 6.

10. Henry Cood Watson, *Albion,* March 6, 1847, 120.

11. Richard Grant White, *Morning Courier and Enquirer,* March 6, 1847, 2.

12. Walt Whitman, *Brooklyn Daily Eagle,* no "musical connoisseur," December 4, 1846; a "plain man's opinions," April 19, 1847; "its flourishes," etc., December 4, 1846; the review of *Lombardi,* March 6, 1847, 2. All these articles may also be found in Walt Whitman, *The Collected Writings of Walt Whitman: The Journalism,* vol. 2, *1846–1848,* ed. Herbert Bergman (New York: Peter Lang, 2003).

13. See Dana, *New York Tribune,* March 25, 1847.

14. Similarly, Viclinda, married to the good brother and desired by the bad, is the cause of an attempted murder that dominates the end of the first act. In the second, her daughter, Giselda, prays to her in heaven, without a word to the audience about how or when Viclinda died.

15. The final stage picture is explicitly stated in the Ricordi vocal score: "S'apre la tenda, e vedesi Gerusalemme; sulla mura, sulle torri sventolano le bandiere della Croce illuminate dai primi raggi del Sole oriente."

16. For instance, he might have chosen *Nabucco* to revise. He later did add a ballet to *Nabucco* for the opera's premiere season in Brussels, opening on November 29, 1848 (though the music has since disappeared). But he did not rewrite the opera's libretto. See discussion in Martin, *Aspects of Verdi,* 244–46; also *WGV, Nabucodonosor,* xxi.

17. In New Orleans, at the Théâtre d'Orléans and the French Opera House, *Jérusalem* had ninety performances in nineteen seasons, 1849–50 through 1890–91. See Jack Belsom, "Reception of Major Operatic Premieres in New Orleans During the Nineteenth Century" (MA thesis, Louisiana State University, 1972), 121–27, making use of the WPA tabulation of *Opera Performances in New Orleans, 1812–1910.* At least once the New Orleans French company took the opera on tour, playing in St. Louis and Cincinnati in June and July 1860. In addition, the soprano who created the role of Hélène (Giselda) in New Orleans, Rosa DeVriès, visited New York in 1850, 1852, and 1853, when she sang excerpts from *Jérusalem.*

18. Dana, *New York Tribune,* March 25, 1847.

19. The scheduling can be followed in the theater's announcements and brief reviews in the *New York Herald,* April 7 through June 5, 1847. The repertory: *Lucrezia Borgia, Nina* (Paisiello), *Barbiere, Lucia, Lombardi, L'elisir d'amore, Semiramide.* The house for *Lombardi* "not filled," and "to a fair house only," *New York Herald,* May 23, 1847, 2, and May 25, 1847, 2. Rapetti's benefit, May 30, 1847, 2.

20. The Park Theatre, built in 1798 on Park Row facing City Hall, was for fifty years one of the city's most busy and revered theaters. It burned down on December 16, 1848, and was not rebuilt. Descriptions of it vary from R. G. White's horrified backward

glance, "boxes were like pens for beasts," from "Opera in New York," *Century Magazine* 23 (April 1882), 869, to the many more positive accounts. Lawrence, *Strong on Music*, 1:521, reproduces two views of the theater, interior in 1844 (with the boxed beasts exceedingly well-dressed) and exterior as it burned. See also Weldon B. Durham, *American Theatre Companies, 1749–1887* (Westport, CT: Greenwood Press, 1986), 387–410, and Peter G. Buckley, "To the Opera House: Culture and Society in New York City, 1820–1860" (PhD diss., State University of New York at Stony Brook, 1984), 102–25. He quotes at length R. G. White, Washington Irving, and others.

21. *New York Herald*, April 15, 1847, 2.

22. *Albion*, April 17, 1847, 191–92.

23. Prado, *La musica italiano a Cuba*, 24. The hemispheric premiere of *I Lombardi* was at the Teatro Tacón, Havana, December 1, 1846.

24. *Albion*, April 17, 1847, 191–92.

25. Arthur Herman Wilson, *A History of the Philadelphia Theatre, 1835 to 1885* (Philadelphia: University of Pennsylvania Press, 1935), 362–63. The season included *Ernani*, five performances; *Norma*, four; *Sonnambula*, three; *Lombardi*, two; *Saffo, Foscari, Linda di Chamounix*, and *Romeo e Giulietta* (Bellini's *I Capuleti ed I Montecchi*), one. See also Armstong, *A Record of the Opera in Philadelphia*, 54–57.

26. Quoted in Martin Chusid, "Verdi's Early U.S. Premieres," *Opera News*, January 7, 1978, 33.

27. Clapp, *A Record of the Boston Stage*, 444.

28. Charles Durang, "The Stage: History of the Philadelphia Stage, 1749–1855," entry for July 17, 1847. For a description of Durang, actor, dancer, theatre manager, and translator of plays, see Wilson, *History of the Philadelphia Theatre*, vii, 10.

29. Joseph Sill, *Diary*, 1836–54, 10 vols. (Philadelphia, Historical Society of Pennsylvania). Entries in vol. 7 for July 21, 1847, *Sonnambula*, and July 27, *Norma*.

30. Astor Place opera house, see Lawrence, *Strong on Music*, 1:454–57.

31. Maretzek, *Crotchets and Quavers*, 15–16.

32. Dwight, "The History of Music in Boston," 4:426, reports that in 1843 "for the first time" a conductor replaced the violinist as leader of the Academy of Music's orchestra.

33. Strong on *I Lombardi*, December 14, 1848, quoted in Lawrence, *Strong on Music*, 1:520.

34. The other operas and number of performances were *Lucia*, seven; *Gemma di Vergy*, five; *Lucrezia Borgia*, four; *Ernani* and *Il giuramento*, three.

35. Repertory was *Ernani* and *Norma*, three performances; *Linda di Chamounix, Lombardi*, and *Barbiere*, two; *Lucrezia Borgia* and *Lucia*, one.

36. *Albion*, October 22, 1853, 512.

37. *New York Times*, October 18, 1853, 4.

38. For the troubled San Francisco premiere and a review, see Martin, *Verdi at the Golden Gate*, 80–81 and 280n46; and for excerpts sung in California, see opera's entry in the index. The opera's later history in the city can be traced in the various chronologies concerning San Francisco.

39. Ninety performances in nineteen seasons, 1849–50 through 1890–91.

40. Some examples: *Dwight's Journal of Music*, December 8, 1860, in a report from St. Louis, records "La mia letizia" sung in English as "In tears I pine"; and on February 8, 1862, also in St. Louis, Giselda's act 2 "O madre del cielo." For these reports, with the concerts' full programs, see Sablosky, *What They Heard*, 183–87. On February 23, 1883, members of Colonel [James Henry] Mapleson's company gave a concert at the White House, Washington, DC, before President Chester A. Arthur. The program included the

"conversion" trio and is reproduced in Mapleson, *Mapleson Memoirs*, 168. And early in November 1882, Mapleson's chorus at near midnight serenaded his star, Adelina Patti, upon her arrival at the Windsor Hotel, New York City, with "O Signore, dal tetto natio" (Mapleson, *Mapleson Memoirs*, 157).

41. Mapleson, *Mapleson Memoirs*, 302–5.

42. *New York Evening Post*, October 23, 1886, 5.

43. *New York Times*, October 23, 1886, 5, and also unfavorable, *New York Herald*, October 23, 1886, 6. On the collapse of Angelo's season, see Mapleson, *Mapleson Memoirs*, 304n1, quoting at length the *Musical Times*.

44. Joseph Dupuy, in the *Los Angeles Evening Herald*, January 22, 1915, 11. The company's three-week repertory, with number of performances each, was: *Aida, Thais, Lombardi, Rigoletto*, three; *Faust, Trovatore, Ruy Blas, Gioconda, Cavalleria*, and *Pagliacci*, two; *Traviata* and *Lucia*, one.

45. *San Francisco Call*, March 3, 1915, and *Chronicle*, March 3, 1915, 12.

46. *San Francisco Chronicle*, March 9, 1915, 7, and March 12, 1915, 8.

47. See Martin, "The Metropolitan Opera's Sunday Evening Concerts and Verdi." Julian Budden makes clear his dislike of the violin *obbligato* in his chapter on the opera's revision as *Jérusalem:* "There is, fortunately, no solo violin, the 'angelico' arpeggios are played by the much more appropriate flute." See his *The Operas of Verdi*, 1:357.

48. In the Welsh repertory 1956 through 1963. See Richard Fawkes, *Welsh National Opera* (London: Julia MacRae Books, 1986). It was always less popular, however, than the same company's *Nabucco*, which ran for eleven successive years. Some productions, other than those mentioned in the text include: Rome, 1969; Budapest, 1974; London, 1976; New Orleans, 1982; Milan, 1984; Verona, 1984; Milan, 1986; Vancouver, 1986; Lisbon, 1987; Bologna, 1994; Zurich, 1999; and Santiago, 1999.

49. Giuseppe Verdi, *I Lombardi*, with Cristina Deutekom (Giselda), Placido Domingo (Oronte), Ruggero Raimondo (Pagano); conductor, Lamberto Gardelli (Philips CD, cat. no PHI B000942602). Generally, critics greeted the recording with pleasure. But in a review of its reissue on compact discs (*Gramophone*, November 1989), John B. Steane concluded: "I am not convinced that the opera is likely to enjoy a very long run in the theatre of the mind either [i.e., as a recording], for the music is too uneven to give more than intermittent satisfaction. The First act promises well and turns out to be much the best. After that, apart from the famous trio, nothing quite rises to the point of inspiration, and a good deal of it sinks into banality." Perhaps an early sign of reviving interest in the opera in the United States was the inclusion of the trio, with its violin introduction, in the Metropolitan's Farewell Gala to Rudolf Bing, April 22, 1972. The singers were Lucine Amara, Enrico Di Giuseppe, and Cesare Siepi; and violinist, Raymond Gniewek.

50. Andrew Porter, "Musical Events," *New Yorker*, December 16, 1972, 133–34. See also, Allen Hughes, *New York Times*, December 9, 1972, 27; Harriet Johnson, *New York Post*, December 8, 1972, 50.

51. Porter, "Musical Events."

52. Peter G. Davis, *High Fidelity*, July 1972, 89–90.

53. This proposed Verdi cycle, seemingly the first such undertaken in the United States, continued only through March 1985, when its financial underpinnings collapsed. By then, however, it had presented: *Lombardi* (1979), *Traviata* (1979), *Don Carlo* (1979), *Giovanna d'Arco* (1980), *Trovatore* (1980), *Nabucco* (1981), *Un giorno di regno* (1981), *Requiem* (1981), *Corsaro* (1982), *Ballo* (1982), *Aida* (1983), *Masnadieri* (1984), *Boccanegra* (1984), and *Oberto* (1985). Also in a concert on June 28, 1979, the company presented a

number of Verdi's lesser works, such as the *Inno delle nazioni*, the *Ave Maria* (1889), and three of his songs, "Il poveretto," "L'esule," and "Stornello," all sung by Bergonzi. See Donald Dierks, *San Diego Union*, June 29, 1979, 40.

54. Joseph Kerman, "*I Lombardi* in San Diego," *19th-Century Music* 3 (1980): 259–64. He combined this article, the most perceptive and detailed description of the production, with another article to make an essay "Two Early Verdi Operas; Two Famous Terzetti," in *Write All These Down, Essays on Music* (Berkeley: University of California Press, 1994), 288–306. The cast: Cristina Deutekom (G), Carlo Bergonzi (O), Paul Plishka (P), and conductor, Maurizio Arena.

55. *Los Angeles Times*, June 25, 1979, 12.

56. Manuela Hoelterhoff, *Wall Street Journal*, April 9, 1982.

57. Donal Henahan, *New York Times*, April 4, 1982, 60.

58. *New York Times*, January 21, 1986, C12; Aprile Millo (G), Carlo Bergonzi (O), Paul Plishka (P), and conductor, Eve Queler.

59. Millo returned for the seventh performance, January 7, 1994, but thereafter again withdrew.

60. Edward Rothstein, *New York Times*, December 4, 1993, 11.

61. Paul Griffiths, *New Yorker*, "Musical Events, Verdi's Crusades," December 27, 1993, 145–47. Agreeing with Griffiths, Martin Mayer, *Opera*, March 1994, 299.

62. Manuela Hoelterhoff, "Opera: Pavarotti as a Teenage Muslim," *Wall Street Journal*, December 15, 1993.

63. Stephen Hastings, *Opera News* 70, no. 7 (January 2006): 57; Julian Budden, *Opera*, February 2006, 181–82.

64. Ross, "Verdi's Grip," 82–83.

65. This performance was part of the New York Grand Opera's Verdi cycle, giving all his operas in chronological order, all conducted by Vincent La Selva. The cycle began with *Oberto*, July 6, 1994, and closed with *Falstaff*, August 1, 2001, the centennial year of Verdi's death. The *Lombardi* performance was June 28, 1995.

Chapter Three

1. In 1843, in a nine-month tour starting and ending in New Orleans, it played also in Cincinnati, Pittsburgh, Philadelphia, New York, Baltimore, and Washington. See Katherine K. Preston, *Opera on the Road: Traveling Opera Troupes in the United States, 1825–1860* (Urbana: University of Illinois Press, 1993), 115–22, 320–21. For a somewhat lurid account of Marty y Torrens, see John Curtis, "One Hundred Years of Grand Opera in Philadelphia: The First Volume, Section Two (1844–60)" (unpublished typescript, 1920), 372–73.

2. *New York Herald*, April 15, 1847, 2.

3. Preston, *Opera on the Road*, 131–32, 322. Also, Stuart W. Rogers, "The Tremont Theatre and the Rise of Opera in Boston, 1827–1847," *Opera Quarterly* 16, no. 3 (Summer 2000): 390–91, states the orchestra there numbered forty. Also reporting forty, the *Morning Courier and New-York Enquirer*, April 17, 1847, 4.

4. *New York Herald*, April 17, 1847, 2.

5. Park Theatre, "the grand metropolitan theatre of the country," a statement by the contemporary Philadelphian historian Charles Durang, quoted in Wilson, *A History of the Philadelphia Theatre, 1835 to 1855*, 29. On the company's excellence, see *New York Herald*, October 15, 1847, 2.

6. Lawrence, *Strong on Music*, 1:435, quoting Strong's diary entry for April 16, 1847.

7. Rogers, "The Tremont Theatre," 390–91. Samuel Eliot, *Diary*, entry for April 29, 1847. Because the opera is based on Victor Hugo's play *Hernani*, not only the occasional opera company, but many newspapers and operagoers of the time used the play's title for the opera. Verdi did not. See *New York Herald*, April 15, 1847, 2, and September 18, 1847, 2. The practice lingered on, in part because Sarah Bernhardt kept the play alive to the turn of the century, bringing it to New York in 1880 and taking it on tour. As late as 1912, *The Victor Book of the Opera: Stories of Seventy Grand Operas with Three Hundred Illustrations & Descriptions of Seven Hundred Victor Opera Records* (Camden, NJ: Victor Talking Machine Company, 1912), index, included *Hernani* as an alternate title for the opera.

8. English opera at this time was usually either ballad opera, with lots of dialogue and current popular songs often interpolated, or versions of Italian or French operas, often greatly reduced and simplified with extraneous music introduced. Lawrence, *Strong on Music*, 1:15n27 describes Henry R. Bishop's adaptation of Rossini's *Barbiere* as a combination of Rossini's opera, Paisiello's opera, "with a little additional music of his own thrown in for good measure." According to Armstrong, *A Record of the Opera in Philadelphia*, 20, Michael Rophino Lacy's adaptation of Rossini's *Cenerentola*, which restored the fairy godmother and the glass slipper, "was a mere *pasticcio*, being made up from *Cenerentola*, *Armida*, *Maometto*, and *William Tell.*"

9. Clapp, *A Record of the Boston Stage*, 444–45. Also, Dwight, "History of Music in Boston," 4:433.

10. Richard Grant White, *Courier and Enquirer*, April 17, 1847, 4. Cautiously undecided, Henry Cood Watson in the *Albion*, April 17, 1847, 191.

11. The "Native Citizen" was a Shakespearian scholar. King Lear calls Edgar a "learned Theban" when the latter is playing the Fool, act 3, scene 4, line 162; and "betwixt the wind and his nobility" quotes Hotspur describing the staff officer's overrefined sensitivity on viewing the battlefield, *King Henry IV, Part 1*, act 1, scene 3, line 42.

12. *New York Herald*, June 29, 1847, 2.

13. For population figures, see appendix C. For the importance of Boston, Philadelphia, and New York, see Maretzek, *Crotchets and Quavers*, 33.

14. From Durang, "The Stage," whose successive articles on the history of the Philadelphia stage, 1749–1855, appeared in the city's *Sunday Dispatch*, 1854–60 (but never in book form). In vol. 2 (1830–55), 303 (July 14, 1847), Durang states of the Havana company: "There was much excellence in this troupe. They were fine in voice and general dramatic ability." And later (December 19), he refers to *Ernani* as "this fine opera."

15. Castle Garden, if all galleries were in use, could seat some 7,000, but often, apparently, some galleries were not opened. See *Albion*, September 11, 1847, 444. On the company's closing night the *New York Herald* reported an audience of "upwards of 4,000 persons present," and remarked: "The opera of *Hernani* is indeed a magnificent piece of music, and should Verdi, its composer, have written but this partition, it would alone have created him a great maestro" (*New York Herald*, September 18, 1847, 2).

16. Clapp, *A Record of the Boston Stage*, 449.

17. Farewell concert reviewed, *New York Herald*, October 16, 1847, 2; the company departs "yesterday afternoon," October 21, 1847, 2.

18. For a description of the new Astor Place Opera House, see Lawrence, *Strong on Music*, 1:454–56.

19. *Albion*, November 27, 1847, 576. On Henry Cood Watson, see Grant, *Maestros of the Pen*, 16–21.

20. *Morning Courier and Enquirer*, November 23, 1847, 3.

21. Lawrence, *Strong on Music*, 1:520, quoting diary entry for December 2, 1848.

22. The U.S. premieres of the operas were: *Rigoletto*, New York, February 19, 1855; *Trovatore*, New York, May 2, 1855; and *Traviata*, New York, December 3, 1856; and the operas took some months, or even years, to reach the smaller cities. In reviewing *Attila*, the *Albion*, April 20, 1850, p. 188, declared: "The only one to which the public takes kindly is *Ernani*." See appendix B: "The Swift Spread of *Ernani*."

23. The company used several names. In Chicago, it advertised itself as "The Artists' Association." See George P. Upton, *Musical Memories* (Chicago: McClurg, 1908), 227.

24. Thomas G. Kaufman, "The Arditi Tour, The Midwest Gets Its First Real Taste of Italian Opera," *Opera Quarterly* 4, no. 4 (Winter 1986/87): 39–52, 42. As Kaufman notes, Arditi found the role of impresario unpleasant and unrewarding, and his *My Reminiscences* (New York: Dodd, Mead, 1896), 17, gave this tour only two, swift paragraphs.

25. Upton, *Musical Memories*, 227.

26. Ibid., 225–26. Upton talked with a Chicago citizen who had sung in the chorus.

27. The *Daily Missouri Democrat*, September 28, 1853, quoted in Kaufman, "The Arditi Tour," 41–42.

28. See Martin, *Verdi at the Golden Gate*, 254–55, and in the bibliography the chronologies of Don L. Hixon, Thomas G. Kaufman, and Works Progress Administration.

29. A translation of the play and of Hugo's preface to its first edition (1830) may be found in *Three Plays by Victor Hugo, Hernani, The King Amuses Himself, Ruy Blas*, trans. C. Crosland and F. L. Slous (New York: Howard Fertig, 1995).

30. Both Hugo and Verdi specifically set their dramas in the year 1519—when Carlo, as a matter of record, was nineteen and in a period when forty was elderly. The suggestion of the Verdi scholar Gabriele Baldini that the men's ages are Silva, seventy, Carlo, fifty, and Ernani, thirty, is a momentary delusion. See Giovanni Baldini, *Story of Giuseppe Verdi*, trans. Roger Parker (Cambridge: Cambridge University Press, 1980), 75.

31. In the play, both Ernani and Elvira drink poison, die piteously, and Silva, in despair kills himself.

32. *Courier and Enquirer*, May 15, 1846, 2. For the other aria, see chap. 2.

33. *Morning Courier and Enquirer*, May 15, 1846.

34. Baldini, *Story of Giuseppe Verdi*, 74. To which he adds: "Significantly, this ["Ernani, involami"] is her only aria. From now onwards she is exclusively involved in confrontations with the three male voices, contributing to trios, quartets and larger ensembles, but never appearing on her own" (79).

35. Budden, *Operas of Verdi*, 1:148, 150, 152, 153, 156, 166. For a brief account of the opera and its music, see William Ashbrook, "Verdi's Young Blood," *Opera News*, December 24, 1956, 12–14.

36. Sill, *Diary*, 9:285, the entry for "Friday, January 10, 1851."

37. The other half of the double bill was act 2 of Rossini's *Barbiere*. Other performances in Philadelphia of *Ernani* act 3 alone: on April 18, 1874, July 21, 1893, and September 27, 1893. See Philadelphia Opera Chronology, researched by John Curtis, edited by Frank Hamilton, at http://FrankHamilton.org.

38. Although Marini (1811–73) was not the first to sing the role, he was the most admired Silva of his generation, and he had also created the title role of Oberto in Verdi's first opera and would do so in Verdi's ninth, *Attila*. At his request, Verdi had composed for him to use in *Oberto* a cabaletta, "Infin che un brando vindice," which Marini later (seemingly with Verdi's approval) inserted in *Ernani* and sang immediately after the cantabile, "Infelice." For the cabaletta's score and its history, see *WGV, Ernani*, score,

appendix 2 and pp. xxi–xxii. Note the "Afterword," unpaginated but following "Instruments of the Orchestra."

39. Robert D. Faner, *Walt Whitman & Opera* (Carbondale: Southern Illinois Press, 1951; Arcturus Books, 1972), 80, quoting Whitman's essay "The Opera." His four favorite operas were *Lucrezia Borgia, Favorita, Norma,* and *Ernani* (49); for Whitman on the opening chorus of *Ernani,* 217; on Silva's recitative when he discovers "two vile seducers" in Elvira's bedroom, 168–69, and on "Infelice," 188–89.

40. *New York Herald,* November 15, 1853, 4.

41. See playbill for the opera in Boston, May 9, 1851, reproduced in Preston, *Opera on the Road,* 198.

42. Faner, *Walt Whitman & Opera,* 104, quoting Section 3 of "Proud Music of the Storm." The tenors who as Ernani charmed Whitman were Geremia Bettini (p. 61), and Pasquale Brignoli (p. 92).

43. *New York Times,* December 6, 1883, 4.

44. For example, the *New York Tribune,* April 7, 1882, 4: "Verdi's antiquated *Ernani* certainly one of the least admirable of the works which live in the American repertory of this composer's operas." The audience, however, greeted it "with enthusiasm."

45. Lang, *Critic at the Opera,* 137. The book is drawn from Lang's reviews and Sunday articles in the *New York Herald Tribune,* 1954–63.

46. Krehbiel, *Chapters of Opera,* 103–4.

47. *New York Times,* November 24, 1883, 4.

48. *New York Times,* October 4, 1885, 5. Haweis's *Music and Morals* had at least sixteen editions, and though he is forgotten today, he was still an entry in the tenth edition of the *Oxford Companion to Music* (1970).

49. Mapleson, *Mapleson Memoirs,* 251. He heard the speech, and disagreed.

50. In New York in these years it was performed in 1874, 1875, 1882, 1883, 1884, and 1890 (in Brooklyn and in Harlem). And in the 1890s and years following, Sousa's Band, and no doubt others, played selections from the opera, see Paul Edmund Bierley, *The Incredible Band of John Philip Sousa* (Urbana: University of Illinois Press, 2006), 417.

51. It had three performances in the house, and in the week of the first and third it ranked first in box office receipts for regular-priced operas, and in the week of the second, second. It also sold well in its single performance in Philadelphia, see *Philadelphia Record,* December 14, 1903, in Metropolitan Opera Archives, box office receipts and clippings. The opera was not scheduled for another season perhaps because later that year Heinrich Conried replaced Maurice Grau as general manager.

52. *New York Herald,* January 29, 1903, 12.

53. *New York Times,* January 29, 1903, 9. Also disparaging was W. J. Henderson, *New York Sun,* January 29, 1903, 7.

54. See the tables in Krehbiel, *Chapters of Opera,* 362.

55. *New York Herald,* December 12, 1907, 12. *New York Times,* December 12, 1907, 7: "obsolete . . . [but] singers of today still like to sing it."

56. *Victor Book of the Opera,* 79; and the book's ninth edition, third printing in 1938, still advertised recordings of the opera's arias. Olin Downes of the *New York Times,* December 18, 1928, 37, reports how common in homes in past years were recordings of *Ernani* excerpts.

57. *New York Times,* December 9, 1921, 20; also *Globe* (Krehbiel), December 9, 1921, 15; *New York Evening Post* (Henry T. Finck), December 9, 1921, 9.

58. *New York Herald,* December 9, 1921, 11.

59. Krehbiel, *Globe*, December 9, 1921, 15: "Miss Ponselle's characteristics of voice and style are not those with which we have been accustomed to associate the music of Elvira, and her airs were shorn of some of their old-time glitter as well as their essential charm of sustained, well-phrased song. Convenience was also consulted, we fancy, by some transpositions to a lower key."

60. Henderson, *Sun*, December 18, 1928, 33; *New York Times*, December 18, 1928, 37; and *New York Herald Tribune*, December 18, 1928, 22.

61. See Martin, "The Metropolitan Opera's Sunday Evening Concerts and Verdi," 16–27, and Jim McPherson, "Before the Met: The Pioneer Days of Radio Opera, Part 2, the NBC National Grand Opera Company," *Opera Quarterly* 16, no. 2 (Spring 2000): 202–23, 219.

62. Francis D. Perkins, *New York Herald Tribune*, November 9, 1933, 12. For more on Salmaggi, see chap. 12.

63. *New York Times*, November 9, 1933, 27.

64. In act 2, "Infelice" immediately followed Carlo's departure with Elvira and preceded Silva's declaration of hatred for the king, "Vigili pure." A ballet also had been inserted in the Metropolitan's 1920s production of the opera, with music from the ballets of *Les vêpres siciliennes*, *Trovatore*, and *Otello*. Henderson wrote in the *Sun*, December 18, 1928, 33, it was "engaging," used "music composed by Verdi after he had completely abandoned the manner of *Ernani*," and "received the benison of the audience." For a recording of the Mitropoulos, 1950s production, taken from the broadcast on December 29, 1956, see Arkadia CDMP 470.2.

65. *New York Times*, November 24, 1956, 17. The cabaletta referred to is the one Verdi originally composed for the bass Marini to sing in *Oberto*, previously discussed in this chapter.

66. Ibid.

67. *New York Herald Tribune*, November 24, 1956, 6.

68. Lang, *Critic at the Opera*, 138.

69. H. Howard Taubman, *Pleasure of Their Company: A Reminiscence* (Portland, OR: Amadeus Press, 1994), 289.

70. For the score and history of the aria and chorus, see *WGV, Ernani*, score, appendix 3 and p. xxii: "The substitution is easily accomplished. It does change radically the theatrical sense of the Finale, focusing all dramatic and musical interest on the protagonist, and thus modifying the equilibrium between the characters as a whole." See also James Parsons, "Made to Measure," *Opera News*, December 10, 1983, 19–20. In the Metropolitan's revival of *Ernani* in the spring of 2008, it again closed the second act with this aria and chorus.

71. As a young conductor, roughly before he turned fifty in 1993, Levine when conducting Verdi, as the critic Andrew Porter noted, sounds "trapped in a grid of regular bar lines," *Musical Events: A Chronicle, 1980–1983* (New York: Summit Books, 1987), 359. Said differently by Porter in *Music of Three More Seasons, 1977–1980* (New York: Knopf, 1981), 466: "For Wagner, Mr. Levine finds the long breath that often eludes him in Mozart and Verdi." See also Porter on Levine's failings as a conductor of Verdi's *Macbeth*, in the *New Yorker*, February 20, 1984, 111. General opinion, however, guided by the Metropolitan's publicity office, was otherwise. But for critical disapproval of Levine's problematic conducting on his first commercial operatic recording, Verdi's *Giovanna d'Arco* (Angel, SCL 3791), see chap. 15. Also for praise of him, see chap. 10. On Levine's conducting of *Macbeth* when age sixty-four, October 2007, see chap. 6. See also chap. 13. For criticism of

the singers and staging, see Andrew Porter, *Musical Events, 1983–86* (New York: Summit Books, 1989), 67–68.

72. *New York Times,* October 28, 1984, 65. Donato Renzetti conducted.

73. Martin Bernheimer, *Opera,* May 1965, 337–38.

74. Arthur Bloomfield, *Opera,* November 1968, 901–3.

75. Herbert Weinstock, *Opera,* November 1970, 1013–14.

76. Dorothy Samachson, *Opera,* February 1985, 210.

77. Arthur Bloomfield, *Opera,* December 1984, 1356.

78. Martin Mayer, *Opera,* March 1984, 274.

79. Martin Mayer, Opera, April 1997, 424.

80. Author's interview with La Selva, September 18, 2003.

81. Author's interview with DeRenzi, September 19, 2003.

82. I attended the final performance, March 22, when a full house, expecting to be pleased, continually cheered and applauded, and at the close of the third and fourth acts (played without intermission), stood and shouted approval.

83. G. Bernard Shaw, *Shaw's Music: The Complete Musical Criticism in Three Volumes,* ed. Dan H. Lawrence (New York: Dodd, Mead, 1981), 2:724. In Philadelphia, for example, this act alone, was performed on April 18, 1874, July 21, 1893, and September 27, 1893.

84. Baldini, *Story of Giuseppe Verdi,* 70; and Budden, *Operas of Verdi,* 171.

Chapter Four

1. Chusid, "Verdi's Early U.S. Premieres."

2. Western hemisphere premiere of *Foscari,* Havana, January 2, 1847; of *Ernani,* Rio de Janeiro, June 16, 1846, and Havana premiere, November 18, 1846. In the Havana company's 1846–47 season at the Tacón, it performed *Ernani* eighteen times, and *Foscari,* ten. Prado, *La musica italiana a Cuba,* 25–26.

3. East winds, Boston *Daily Evening Transcript,* May 11, 1847; influenza, *Boston Post,* May 13, 1847.

4. *Boston Post,* May 13, 1847.

5. See Clapp, *A Record of the Boston Stage,* 444–45.

6. Prado, *La musica italiana a Cuba,* 26–27, quoting *Il Faro Industrial,* November 6, 1847.

7. Boston *Daily Evening Transcript,* May 11, 1847.

8. *Boston Post,* May 13, 1847. The orchestra's leader, apparently conducting from his chair, or perhaps standing with his violin in hand, was Luigi Arditi.

9. Clapp, *A Record of the Boston Stage,* 447.

10. The English critic Henry F. Chorley (1808–72) wrote a description of this scene, recounting in detail how it was played by the famous Italian baritone Giorgio Ronconi in a production at Covent Garden, June 19, 1847. Henry F. Chorley, *Thirty Years' Musical Recollections* (New York: Knopf, 1926), 210–11. Godefroy quotes the account in full in Vincent Godefroy, *The Dramatic Genius of Verdi: Studies of Selected Operas,* vol. 1 [*Nabucco* through *Traviata*] (London: Gollancz, 1975), 51–52. For how memories of Ronconi's performance lingered on, see Santley, *Student and Singer,* 274.

11. Godefroy, *The Dramatic Genius of Verdi,* 52.

12. Disagreement on the date of the Doge's death: The opera's librettist, F. M. Piave, in the historical note he prepared as a preamble to the text, states October 31, 1457. Giulio Lorenzetti, in the English edition (trans. by John Guthrie) of his *Venice and Its*

Lagoon: Historical-Artistic Guide (1961; repr. Trieste: LINT, 1975), 47, states November 1, 1457. The Encyclopædia Britannnica CD, 1998 standard edition, temporizes: "Oct. 31/ Nov. 1."

13. Godefroy, *The Dramatic Genius of Verdi*, 38.

14. On the inserted cabaletta, see chap. 3.

15. *New York Herald*, June 10, 1847, 2.

16. *New York Tribune*, June 10, 1847, 2.

17. *Morning Courier and New-York Enquirer*, June 10, 1847, 2.

18. *New York Tribune*, June 14, 1847, 2.

19. *American Literary Gazette and New York Weekly Mirror*, June 19, 1847, 77.

20. Durang, "The Stage: History of the Philadelphia Stage," Third Series, 1830–55, 303. In the Historical Society of Pennsylvania's two volumes of clippings, vol. 2, 303.

21. See this book's preface and Frank Hamilton's chronology at http://frankhamilton.org/ph/phcw.pdf. See also Armstrong, *A Record of the Opera in Philadelphia*, 55, and Curtis, "One Hundred Years of Grand Opera in Philadelphia," vol. 1, sec. 2, 376.

22. For a summary account at the close of the tour, see *New York Herald*, September 9, 1850, 1. Performances of *Foscari* were on July 27 and 29, and August 1, 1850; reviews, *New York Herald*, July 29, p. 2; July 30, p. 4; and August 2, p. 3. One critic out of town was N. P. Willis of the weekly *Home Journal*. He earlier had distinguished himself by extravagantly praising Balbina Steffanone, on this tour the brightest of the star sopranos, and yet managed to find a fault: "Her upper lip is unfinished on the inside and—during impassive singing—does not play well upon the teeth." See *Home Journal*, April 20, 1850, 2. Castle Garden, formerly a stone fort at Battery Place on the Hudson, was commonly said to seat five thousand, and, if needed, to be able to crush in another two thousand. Because it was built on a reef in the Hudson, and sat fifty or so feet offshore (the gap was later filled in), it was cooled by river and bay breezes, and hence was a good theater for summer performances.

23. The *New Orleans Bee*, March 5, 1851. This French version of the opera was prepared in Paris by Verdi's French publisher primarily for use in French provincial cities, where the tradition was opera in French. It was not used in Paris where the opera was presented in Italian at the Théâtre des Italiens.

24. The libretto may be found in the Williams Research Center, Historic New Orleans Collection, in New Orleans, and I thank the Center's Reference Associate Sally Spier Stassi who searched for and found it. The six tableaux, stage pictures or important changes of scenery, are: first, a hall in the Doge's palace; second, the Doge's private rooms (ending act 1); third, the state prisons; fourth, the Council of Ten's chamber (the sextet ending New Orleans act 3); fifth, the Old Piazzetta of San Marco (regatta scene and ballet); and sixth, the Doge's private rooms. The libretto has some other slight changes, and substitutes for the librettist Piave the "Scudier Freres"—Verdi's French publishers Léon and Marie Escudier. Because the New Orleans libretto, which offered an English translation alongside the French text, was prepared, published, and sold to accompany the local performances, it seems likely that the announced ballet (to whatever music) was danced. But Jack Belsom, historian of opera in New Orleans, reports of it: "No clue found. It may have been some other Verdi composition, or just as likely something else, or even an arrangement from another opera." Letter to the author, June 24, 2004.

25. For a brief account of the opera's reception, "at most a *success d'estime*," see Jack Belsom's article (misleadingly titled by an editor) "*Macbeth* in New Orleans" in the New Orleans Opera program for the second staging of that opera, December 4 and 6,

1975. Belsom's original title was "Rarely Performed Verdi Opera in New Orleans," and he discussed the local history of *Jérusalem, I due Foscari,* and *Ernani.* Belsom, archivist for the New Orleans Opera Association, confirms that four performances took place, on March 6, 8, 20, and May 17, and probably a fifth, on April 22, because announced in the four leading papers and, though not reviewed (already heard three times), was not reported by any paper to have been canceled. Letter to the author, June 24, 2004. See also the WPA chronicle *Opera Performances in New Orleans, 1812–1919,* 61. The New Orleans *Daily Picayune,* for example, in both the morning and evening editions of April 22, announced for the Orleans Theatre: "The Celebrated Grand Opera of Verdi in four acts The Two Foscari."

26. Rosa DeVriès (1828–89) in a concert in New York, at Niblo's Saloon (auditorium), on February 11, 1853, see *New York Times,* February 12, p. 4. The *New York Herald,* February 11, p. 7, gives her numbers: "Grand Aria from *Foscari,*" "Ah, mon fils" from *Le Prophète,* and "Rondo" from *I Lombardi.*" This concert, shared with a number of artists, is chiefly famous for the U.S. debut of the pianist Louis Moreau Gottschalk.

27. According to Thomas G. Kaufman, author of *Verdi and His Major Contemporaries,* this company led by Angiolina Ghioni (soprano) and Augustino Susini (bass), and directed by Max Strakosch, made two extended tours throughout the East and the Mississippi Valley in 1865–66 and 1866–67. The first and longer tour, of some thirty cities, began in Hartford, went north to Quebec, south to New Orleans, and except for Savannah, Mobile, and New Orleans played only interior towns. Because most of the stops were for shorter periods than in New Orleans and the company sang mostly popular repertory, it seems unlikely that it performed *Foscari* anywhere but New Orleans. But because of a few gaps in its movements and programs, there is no certainty. Author interview with Thomas G. Kaufman, June 7, 2004. It is clear, however, that when the Ghioni/Susini company returned to New Orleans in November 1866, it did not perform *Foscari;* Belsom letter to the author, June 24, 2004. For no performances after January 1866 to date, ibid. Belsom is at present compiling an annal of performances for all the seasons at the French Opera House, 1859–1919, including important traveling companies that appeared there.

28. *Daily Alta California,* June 18, 1855, 2. For a longer account of the opera's history in San Francisco, see Martin, *Verdi at the Golden Gate,* 81–84.

29. In New Orleans, for example, in the first year of the war, the French Opera company, for lack of visiting singers and instrumentalists, was unable to assemble a full company and cut back to presenting operettas, offering among other works a U.S. premiere of Offenbach's *Une Nuit Blanche* (1855). Then, on April 26, 1862, Union forces took the city, and there were no more regular opera seasons until after the war; and even then, for a time, on a reduced scale. Belsom,, "Reception of Major Operatic Premieres in New Orleans During the Nineteenth Century," 158–62.

30. On Maretzek "Napoleon," George G. Foster, *New York by Gaslight and Other Urban Sketches,* ed. Stuart M. Blumin (1850; rept., Berkeley: University of California Press), 159; according to Foster, Maretzek "with his spotless white neckcloth" wielded a "jewel-tipped baton." The baton, true or not, suggests how he was celebrated. "Magnificent . . . personality," Kellogg, *Memoirs,* 40. On "Don Quixote," Maretzek, *Crotchets and Quavers,* iv–vii. His list of "good" composers, ibid., 206: Mozart, Rossini, Meyerbeer, Bellini, Weber, Beethoven, Piccini, Cimarosa, Gluck, Donizetti, Balfe. "Even Verdi's" operas, ibid., 319.

31. *World,* April 15, 1863, 8, and April 16, 1863, 4. It is not clear what the reviewer meant by "trial scene," for there is none. There is a trio and quartet in Jacopo's prison, in which he learns of his sentence from Loredano, and then before the Council of Ten

a formal reading of the sentence (sextet and chorus). Though Verdi and Piave place the scenes in different locales and call only the second a finale, the reviewer perhaps mentally merged the two into one sequence (as some productions have done), or perhaps Maretzek had rearranged or cut scenes. The opera's number most often criticized, as too jaunty for its circumstance, is the quartet in the prison.

32. *New York Times*, April 17, 1863, 4.

33. Boston *Daily Evening Transcript*, January 30, 1864, 2, and advertisements in the *Transcript* for the grand "Farewell Matinee."

34. Ibid.

35. Medori, for one, had sung the role with success at the Teatro San Carlo, Naples, in the winter of 1859. Program for the San Carlo's revival in 2000.

36. Budden, *Operas of Verdi*, 1:179.

37. Among the singers was the English baritone Charles Santley, see his *Student and Singer*, 274. For a record of the opera's productions around the world, see Kaufman, *Verdi and His Major Contemporaries*. Further, at the Teatro San Carlo in Naples, for example, the opera in the years 1845 through 1859 had eighty-seven performances; and in the years 1860 through 1864, fourteen; with the first revival thereafter in 1968. Program for the San Carlo's revival in 2000.

38. For an account of Signor Angelo, see chap. 2.

39. The last of the five Verdi operas scheduled, *Rigoletto*, was not given.

40. *New York Herald*, October 28, 1886, 10.

41. *New York Tribune*, October 28, 1886, 5.

42. *New York Times*, October 28, 1886, 4.

43. For an account of these concerts, see Martin, "The Metropolitan Opera's Sunday Evening Concerts and Verdi," 16–27. In addition, Bierley, in *Incredible Band of John Philip Sousa*, 417, reports some performances of "*Foscari* Selections" in 1902 and 1924. Over the years the band varied in size, but in 1903 it numbered fifty-six, of which thirty-two were woodwinds, nineteen brass, three percussion, a vocal and a violin soloist.

44. Toye, *Giuseppe Verdi*, 221–22. He states: "Loredano's fanatical belief in the poisoning of his father and uncle is never confuted as it is in Byron's tragedy, so that the [opera's] audience is left wondering whether his ruthless vengeance may not, after all, be excused." Even in Byron, Loredano's belief is not "confuted," that is, proved false. Byron merely throws doubt on its basis. Certainly Verdi and Piave could have done as much in a sentence or two. In Byron's scene, act 2, scene 1, line 230, the Doge tells Loredano "I never work'd by plot in council, nor cabal in commonwealth, nor secret means of practice against life by steel or drug. The proof is your existence."

45. This historical note is published in part in Budden, *Operas of Verdi*, 1:176–77; in full in Osborne, *Complete Operas of Verdi*, 96–97; and almost in full in the notes accompanying the recording of the opera by Philips, 6700-105. But where it might be expected to appear, in the vocal score published by Ricordi, it does not.

46. Budden, *Operas of Verdi*, 1:200. He parenthetically suggests that "someone should count up the number of times the word 'innocente' occurs." The challenge remains open. I counted, but quit.

47. Twentieth-century history of the opera: the revivals in Germany are generally said to have started with one in Halle, February 12, 1929. There were several German and Italian radio broadcasts of performances after World War II, and then a staged performance in Venice in 1957, exactly five hundred years after the events portrayed. This production also played in Turin in 1958. Parma staged the opera in 1966, and Rome and Naples in 1968. The "pirated" recording, taken from the Metropolitan stage on July

3, 1968, was issued by MRF, as 26-S. The first commercial, studio recording was Philips, 6700 105 (1978).

48. *New York Times*, July 2, 1968, 35.

49. *New York Post*, July 2, 1968, 55.

50. I attended three of the four performances. Another much impressed by the Rome Opera's performances in New York was the recording reviewer, Henry Fogel, see *Fanfare* January/February 1987, 200–201: "The evening I attended . . . featured one of those moments you carry with you for years afterwards. . . . The sheer beauty and consistency of invention in this opera that most of us had never heard before were striking proof of the genius of Verdi. I've never had another opportunity to see *Foscari*, but have come to know it well through recordings. Repeated rehearings have persuaded me that it stands near the top of Verdi's early operas, deserving of much more attention than it has received." In connection with the Rome Opera's visit, a sixty-three page booklet with essays and many photographs was published, titled *The Rome Opera at Lincoln Center, 22 June–6 July 1968*, ed. Linda Chittarro, and printed by Rizzoli Grafica in Italy.

51. *Opera*, September 1968, 718.

52. Roger Dettmer, *Opera*, December 1972, 1075–76. Jacobi, *Opera*, September 1979, 848–49.

53. Robert Sherman, *New York Times*, May 13, 1975, 28.

54. Bill Zakariasen, *New York Daily News*, May 13, 1975, 49.

55. *New York Times*, October 22, 1981, C20. Also favorable, Harriet Johnson, *New York Post*, October 21, 1981, 23, and P. J. Smith in *Opera*, January 1982, 70.

56. Verdi letter to Piave, July 22, 1848, quoted by Budden, *Operas of Verdi*, 1:179, citing G. Morazzoni, *Verdi: Lettere inedite* (Milan, 1929), 28–29.

57. Verdi letter to Arrivabene, August 29, 1872, Alberti, *Verdi intimo*, 148.

58. Peter Dyson, *Opera*, December 1989, 1468–70.

59. Dyson, *Opera*, April 1995, 422–23.

60. *New York Times*, March 9, 1991, 16.

61. Allan Kozinn, *New York Times*, April 7, 1992, C15. Andrew Porter, *New Yorker*, May 11, 1992. Martin Mayer, *Opera* 43, no. 9 (September 1992): 1045.

62. James R. Oestreich, *New York Times*, July 22, 1995, 14.

63. *Opera Quarterly* 20, no. 2 (Spring 2004): 307–9.

64. Budden, *Operas of Verdi*, 1:201.

65. Julian Budden in "Verdi and his Doges," *Opera*, June 1995, 657–62, published to accompany a revival at Covent Garden with Chernov as Doge. Reviewing the revival, Andrew Porter, in *Opera*, September 1995, 1018–21, was more enthusiastic for the opera than the singers.

66. Rome Opera production, with Renato Bruson as the Doge, November 8, 2001, see *Opera*, April 2002, 452–53.

67. The first U.S. performances in the twenty-first century apparently were one in a concert by the Opera Orchestra of New York in Carnegie Hall on December 13, 2007, and seven staged by the Sarasota Opera in March and April 2008.

Chapter Five

1. Maretzek, *Crotchets and Quavers*, 156.

2. See Gibbon's *The History of the Decline and Fall of the Roman Empire*, 6 vols. (New York: Harper, 1905), vol. 3, chap. 34–35. Also Godefroy, *Dramatic Genius of Verdi*, 1:81–99.

3. Aquileia in 452 AD was the capital of Venetia and Istria and, with a population of almost one hundred thousand, one of the world's largest cities. Outside of Rome, it was the most important commercial, military, and industrial stronghold of the Western Empire, even sometimes called *Roma secunda*. The city held out for more than three months before Attila was able to take it, sack it, and torch it. It was said to have burned for four days, and never fully recovered its former prosperity. See Gibbon, *Decline and Fall of the Roman Empire*, chap. 35; also *The Oxford Classical Dictionary*, 3rd ed. (London: Oxford University Press, 1996).

4. The fresco is in the Room of Heliodorus in the Vatican's *stanze di Raffaello*. Early in composing the opera, Verdi requested a friend in Rome, the sculptor Vincenzo Luccardi, to send him descriptions of the figures in the fresco, especially of their clothing and hairstyles. Letter to Luccardi, February 11, 1846, in Gaetano Cesari and Alessandro Luzio, eds., *Copialettere di Giuseppe Verdi* (Milan, 1913), 441. The site of the famous confrontation is discussed toward the end of the chapter.

5. Suetonius, *Lives of the Caesars*, of which *Julius* is the first of the twelve biographies. But what every child does not know is that, according to Suetonius, Caesar spoke in Greek: *kaí su, téknon* (And you, boy).

6. Cesari and Luzio, *Copialettere*, 437–38, Verdi to Piave, April 12, 1844. Godefroy translates the letter in full (*Dramatic Genius of Verdi*, 1:82–83); Budden, *Operas of Verdi*, 1:246–47, in part.

7. Gibbon, *Decline and Fall of the Roman Empire*, chap. 35. Ultimately, Valentinian had Aetius murdered.

8. The qualification "true" is needed because Verdi in his first opera, *Oberto* (1839), gave the title role to Ignazio Marini, a bass. But consider: *Oberto* has no role for baritone, the quartet of voices being designated soprano, mezzo-soprano, tenor, and bass. But in 1839 the categories of vocal range were far more fluid than today, and the position of baritone especially was ill-defined. Verdi famously preferred the baritone voice (six title roles), and the vocal line he gave to Oberto is high for a bass (see the singer's line in the second act quartet); in fact, much of the time he sounds more like a baritone. In *Attila* the different vocal range and qualities of Ezio (baritone), Attila (high bass), and Pope Leo (low bass) are easily heard; see further on this point in chap. 13.

9. Godefroy, *Dramatic Genius of Verdi*, 1:86. Also, Budden's essay for the 1973 Philips recording of the opera (Philips, 6700 056).

10. Godefroy, *Dramatic Genius of Verdi*, 1:98.

11. For example, Budden, *Operas of Verdi*, 1:248. Godefroy, *Dramatic Genius of Verdi*, 1:98: "The sudden collapse of Attila is too quick." Osborne, *Complete Operas of Verdi*, 142, concludes: "It seems obvious to me that Verdi was on the edge of a nervous breakdown when he wrote this opera."

12. "Laughter," *Home Journal*, April 27, 1850, 2. "Silence." *Courier and Enquirer*, April 17, 1850, 4. "Laughter," Victor Gollancz, *Journey Towards Music* (New York: Dutton, 1965), 75.

13. Budden *Operas of Verdi*, 1:262.

14. Frederick J. Crowest, *Verdi: Man and Musician* (London: John Milne, 1897), 76. Evan Baker summarizes the book's flaws and virtues in his review of it for the *Opera Quarterly* 5, no. 3 (Summer/Autumn 1987): 132–34.

15. Crowest, *Verdi: Man and Musician*, 79, quoting Benjamin Lumley, *Reminiscences of the Opera* (London: Hurst and Blackett, 1864), 214.

16. Quoted at greater length in Crowest, *Verdi: Man and Musician*, 80.

17. Ibid. Chorley, a famous anti-Verdian: see Henry F. Chorley, *Thirty Years' Musical Recollections* (New York: Knopf, 1926) in which in his chapter "Signor Verdi's Operas," 182–86, he states that Gilda's "Caro Nome" is "but a lackadaisical yawn." On page 368,

he heard in the last two acts of *Traviata* (including the Germont-Violetta duet), "little or nothing worth the trouble of singing."

18. Prado, *La musica italiana a Cuba*, 28–30, quoting the *Gaceta* more fully.

19. See W. Stanley Hoole, *The Ante-Bellum Charleston Theatre* (Tuscaloosa: University of Alabama Press, 1946), 40, 55. He reports a company of "more than ninety," and the company's advertisements in the *Boston Daily Evening Transcript*, for example, May 13, 1850, 3, state "The whole company consists of 104 individuals," and name many of them.

20. On travel by railroads, see chap. 7.

21. *New York Herald*, April 9, 1850, 1.

22. *New York Herald*, April 10, 1850, 2. Maretzek, *Crotchets and Quavers*, 158, upon hiring many of the Havana company, complained: "The perfect liberty which they enjoyed in New York, without strict police regulations of either Italy or Havana, soon degenerated into impudence, insolence, and most audacious contempt both for the public who came to listen to, and the management which paid them." But he, too, specifies only rarely, except about the tenor Lorenzo Salvi, see 163–66.

23. *New York Herald*, April 13, 1850, 2.

24. *Morning Courier and New-York Enquirer*, April 17, 1850, 4; and *New York Herald*, April 16, 1850, 1.

25. *Home Journal*, April 27, 1850, 2. Federico Beneventano was a baritone.

26. *Morning Courier and Enquirer*, April 17, 1850, 4.

27. *Albion*, April 20, 1850, 188.

28. *New York Herald*, April 17, 1850, 1. On Tedesco's voice, according to Armstrong, *A Record of the Opera in Philadelphia*, 56, she "was a mezzo-soprano, with a full, strong, luscious voice. She was deficient in method, but quite effective in Verdi's music." Lawrence, *Strong on Music*, 2:16, describes her as a contralto. For her career, see entry in *The New Grove Dictionary of Opera*.

29. "Very slender." *Albion*, April 20, 1850, 188. "Less in numbers." *New York Herald*, April 17, 1850, 1.

30. *Boston Post*, May 23, 1850, 2.

31. *Boston Evening Transcript*, May 23, 1850, 2. For a discussion of how one proves the lack of performances, see the preface.

32. See Martin, *Verdi at the Golden Gate*, 127–51, 208; and on the city's population, 196 and 298n14. According to the federal census of 1860, the population of San Francisco was fifty-seven thousand, though local newspapers put the figure as high as eighty thousand. Most historians favor the lower figure; but measured against either, the opera had a remarkable success (nine performances in thirteen years) in a small city.

33. Martin, *Verdi at the Golden Gate*, 149, quoting the San Francisco *Daily Evening Bulletin*, August 19, 1859, 3.

34. *Home Journal*, April 27, 1850, 2.

35. See *New York Herald*, September 9, 1850, 1, for a summary of the season in New York and the company's travel plans.

36. Kaufman, *Verdi and His Major Contemporaries*, 333, 336. For the Maretzek company's year in Mexico, see Maretzek, *Crotchets and Quavers*, 219–301.

37. *Albion*, December 21, 1850, 608. The admired singers were Federico Beneventano, baritone, and Pietro Novelli, bass; the conductor, Max Maretzek.

38. See Martin, *Verdi at the Golden Gate*, 21, 261n10; 46, 84. What concerts in San Francisco were like is questionable. A correspondent for a Boston journal reported in 1856 that the city still lacked a good piano: see Sablosky, *What They Heard*, 173, quoting report published May 3, 1856.

39. The baritone, one of the 1850 Havana company, was Cesare Badiali. "Applause" *New York Times*, April 22, 1856, 4. *Albion*, April 26, 1856, 200. The program's featured work was Beethoven's Fourth Symphony.

40. Turle's Band, *Dwight's Journal of Music*, July 9, 1859, 118. Quickstep. *New York Times*, March 14, 1860, 7; baritone, Pietro Centemeri, *New York Times*, March 26, 1860, 3; April 6, 1861, 7; April 8, 1861, 4.

41. John Ward, *Diary for 1865*. For more of Ward's musical activities, see Christopher Bruhn, "Taking the Private Public: Amateur Music-making and the Musical Audience in 1860s New York," *American Music* 21, no. 3 (Fall 2003): 264–70. Ward bought his music at Beer and Schirmer's (after 1866, G. Schirmer), 701 Broadway, see diary entry for February 14, 1865. In addition to excerpts from *Attila*, in 1865 Ward also sang numbers from *Masnadieri, Ballo, Nabucco, Lombardi*, and *Aroldo* as well as playing piano transcriptions of parts of *Ernani* and *Trovatore*.

42. *Complete Catalogue of Sheet Music and Musical Works, 1870*, 210.

43. See Harlan Francis Jennings, "Grand Opera in Kansas in the 1880s" (PhD diss., University of Cincinnati, 1978), 42, 89, 93, 104, 137.

44. "Jesu Dei vivi." See Martin, *Aspects of Verdi*, 225. Andrew Porter, in his review of the Washington Opera's 1976 production of *Attila*, noted a transcription of the trio "converted (by William Jones, organist of St. Alban's, Blackburn) into a three-voiced anthem, 'O sacrum convivium.'" See *Washington Post*, December 4, 1976, E1.

45. Sousa's Band, see Bierley, *Incredible Band of John Philip Sousa*, 417; concerts in 1896, 1901, 02, 08, 16, 23, 24. In *Victor Book of the Opera* (1912), 25, by "Kryl's Bohemian Band," led by Bohumir Kryl, cornet soloist. And Martin, "The Metropolitan Opera's Sunday Evening Concerts and Verdi," 16–27.

46. The performances at La Scala were: season of 1846–47, 31 performances; 1849–50, 17; 1851, 22; 1860, 5; 1867, 9; total 84; next performed, May 1975, 4 performances. See Tintori, *Cronologia, opere-balleti-concerti, 1778–1977*, published in Gatti, *Il teatro alla Scala*, index: 32, 35, 36, 40, 43, 136. It was subsequently performed at La Scala in 1991, conducted by Riccardo Muti, with Samuel Ramey as Attila, and published, sound and sight, by Opus Arte OA 3010 D (DVD: 118:16). Note: The sound only recording by Muti, with Ramey and the same cast except for Foresto and Pope Leo was made in a studio in 1989 and issued the next year.

47. An early and perhaps the first commercially recorded vocal excerpt of *Attila* to reach the United States (c. 1965) was the account of the nightmare by Boris Christoff in *Tsars & Kings* (Angel 36172). This soon was followed by Joan Sutherland, *Verdi* (London, OS 25939), singing Odabella's entrance aria, "Allor che i forti corrono," and by Montserrat Caballé, *Verdi Rarities* (RCA, LSC-2995, 1968), singing Odabella's soliloquy, "Oh! nel fuggente nuvolo." The first commercial recording of the complete opera appeared in 1973: Ruggero Raimondi (Attila), Cristina Deutekom (Odabella), Sherrill Milnes (Ezio), and Carlo Bergonzi (Foresto), with Lamberto Gardelli conducting (Philips, 6700 056). Since then many more recordings, including taped performances, have appeared.

48. See review by Harold Rosenthal, *Opera*, February 1963, 91–93.

49. Gollancz, *Journey Towards Music*, 75, and Andrew Porter, reviewing a later Covent Garden production in the *Times Literary Supplement*, February 22, 2002, recalled "open mirth" in 1963.

50. "Only three," *Liverpool Daily Post*, November 27, 1963. "Hackney Marshes," Harold D. Rosenthal, *Opera* 15, no. 1 (January 1964): 59–61.

51. The *Manchester Guardian*, from a clipping, "late" November 1963.

52. The New Orleans Opera Association, founded 1943, performed in the Municipal Auditorium until 1973 when the Theatre for the Performing Arts opened. The Auditorium was a multipurpose hall with a small side for concert and opera, a large side for other events, and the possibility of joining both to make an arena. I thank Jack Belsom, Archivist of the Opera Association, for the explanation.

53. *New Orleans Times-Picayune*, October 11, 1969, 16.

54. *Opera*, March 1970, 219–21. The New Orleans production called the prologue "Act 1" and played Verdi's short act 3 as a third and final scene to the original act 2. The orchestra numbered forty-eight; the conductor was Knud Andersson, at the time the company's resident conductor and music director. Besides Diaz as Attila, Mirna Lacambra sang Odabella; Enzo Sordello, Ezio; and Eugenio Fernandi, Foresto.

55. "Economy," Robert Baxter, *Opera*, February 1973, 132–33. Raymond Ericson, *New York Times*, October 22, 1972, 81.

56. Godefroy, *Dramatic Genius of Verdi*, 1:84, and Gibbon, *Decline and Fall of the Roman Empire*, both quoting Priscus, an Eastern Roman historian and one of an embassy sent from Constantinople to parley with Attila in the latter's headquarters beyond the Danube.

57. Ericson, *New York Times*, October 22, 1972, 81.

58. This remark was widely quoted, and one day John O. Crosby, the founder and leader of the Santa Fe Opera, repeated it to me. Suggestively, I murmured, "Well?' But he, in the midst of his cycle of Richard Strauss operas, just smiled. On a later occasion he told me that what he disliked in Verdi was all "the filler," and I, thinking of Strauss's noodling, just smiled.

59. Daniel Webster, *Philadelphia Inquirer*, April 13, 1978, B, 4. The performances were April 11 and 14. The production was commissioned jointly by the opera companies of Cincinnati, Edmonton (Canada), Philadelphia, and Washington, DC. Like Webster, Budden (*Operas of Verdi*, 1:252) admires some of the storm and sunrise, remarking on how as the storm on the lagoon ends, Verdi simulates the wash of the waters "by chromatic patterns in contrary motion on the lower strings." The four-measure passage is to be played *morendo*.

60. Unidentified critic, *Albertan*, April 29, 1978. On the same date, Clayton Lee, in the *Edmonton Journal*, April 29, 1978, was far more positive, but Peter Calami, for Southam News Services, also in the *Edmonton Journal*, thought the performance failed "musically and dramatically." Besides Hines, the premiere cast included Cristina Deutekom (Odabella), Cornelis Opthof (Ezio), and Ruggero Bondino (Foresto); conductor, Anton Guadagno. Performances were on April 27 and 29, and May 1, 1978. The third was taped and broadcast on May 27 by the Canadian Broadcasting Company, and later won an award for best opera broadcast of that year. The auditorium's seating capacity in 1978 was 2,678. The Edmonton Symphony Orchestra and the Edmonton Opera Chorus played and sang. The opera was given with only a single intermission, the prologue joined to Verdi's act 1, and his acts 2 and 3 joined. The company was founded in 1963. My thanks to Clayton Rodney, Artistic and Production Department assistant.

61. John von Rhein, *Chicago Tribune*, October 27, 1980, 2, 3.

62. *Washington Post*, December 4, 1976, E1.

63. *New Yorker*, January 10, 1977, 79–82.

64. "Two seasons": the New York City Opera, spring, with Ramey; fall, with Diaz. "Two companies": New York City Opera and New York Grand Opera. The latter gave a single performance in Central Park on July 17, 1996, as part of its Verdi cycle of all his operas in chronological order. Valentin Peytchinov sang Attila; Vincent La Selva conducted. Bill Zakariasen, *Chelsea Clinton News*, July 25–31, 1996, 20.

65. Despite its participation in commissioning the production, the San Diego company never staged it. Its Verdi cycle, begun in August 1978 and presented in the summers, continued only through 1982, after which it was canceled for lack of board and financial support. It reportedly sold poorly. See David Gregson, "Nights of Glory: A History of San Diego Opera," in M. L. Hart, *The Art of Making Opera: Two Seasons with San Diego Opera* (San Diego Opera, 1998), 194.

66. Ming Cho Lee's name. Authorities disagree on how to enter him in an index. Some, like *The New Grove Dictionary of Opera*, 4 vols. (London: M acmillan, 1992), list him under "M" and possibly more, like Martin L. Sokol, *The New York City Opera: An American Adventure with the Complete Annals* (New York: Macmillan, 1981) under "L." Reviewers similarly disagree.

67. For approving reviews, see Robert Commanday, *San Francisco Chronicle*, November 23, 1991, C3; in Tulsa, Scott F. Heumann, *Opera* 33, no. 9 (September 1982): 917–18; in Chicago, Donal Henahan, for the *New York Times*, November 6, 1980, C19. The location of the scene in which the Pope confronts Attila is discussed later in the chapter.

68. *New York Times*, March 19, 1996, C16.

69. In Cincinnati, the historian, Eldred A. Thierstein, *Cincinnati Opera: From the Zoo to Music Hall* [1972–95] (Hillsdale, MI: Deerstone Books, 1995), 84, states that at the opera's revival in 1984 "Poor attendance indicated the audience still considered this work a novelty and not a main attraction." The revival, however, successfully "introduced SurCaps to the Cincinnati audience." For more on the history of surtitles, see chap. 18.

70. Phillip Huscher, *Musical America*, April 1981, 37.

71. On "historical accuracy." Many critics, such as Donal Henahan, *New York Times*, July 29, 1985, place the confrontation of the Pope and Attila "at the gates of Rome." And many program writers, such as the author of the San Francisco Opera's program for its 1991 production, set the scene in "Attila's camp outside Rome." Verdi's stage directions do not. His setting for the scene is merely "Attila's camp." Whereas for the following scene, Ezio's camp, he specifically states, "In the distance can be seen the great City of Seven Hills." Thus Ezio's army, camped outside Rome, lies between Attila and the city. In Verdi's lifetime and in Raphael's (and today) the scene of the confrontation was (and is) placed on the northern side of the Po valley, either near modern Peschiera, just north of Mantua, or just east at the conflux of the Mincio and Po rivers. Possibly the urge to place the meeting "at the gates of Rome" is caused by the large arena visible in the background of Raphael's fresco and which people assume is the Colosseum, hence Rome. But Verona, near Peschiera, and the chief Roman city of this area of the Po, has a magnificent Roman arena (still in use). I do not expect my effort at correction to influence anyone, but still: Verdi here is not as inaccurate as many state.

72. Michael E. Oliver, *Gramaphone*, June 1988, discusses what sort of bass voice is best suited to the role of Attila, black Slavic, "the vocal equivalent of a clenched fist," that can convey "a real sense of malign authority," or smooth Italian, "the voice of a gentleman," which can sound too much like the baritone Ezio.

73. *New Yorker*, January 10, 1977, 79–80.

74. Massimo Mila, "Verdi's Barbaric Jewel." The only place that I have as yet discovered this essay on the act 2 finale (the banquet) is in the booklet accompanying the Mondo Musica (MFOH 10151) live recording of the opera's performance at the Teatro la Fenice, Venice, on December 6, 1968. The essay appears in both Italian and English, with Mila apparently his own translator. The recording previously had appeared on other labels; this one seemingly was issued in 1996. Boris Christoff is Attila; Bruno Bartoletti, the conductor.

75. Budden, *Operas of Verdi*, 1:253–54.

76. Martin Bernheimer, *Opera*, March 1992, 332.

77. Anne Midgette, *New York Times*, April 23, 2003, B9, col. 4. The singers who, in this respect, delighted Midgette and the audience were Samuel Ramey and Lauren Flanigan.

78. The premiere with Riccardo Muti conducting (his house debut) took place on February 23, 2010.

Chapter Six

1. Basevi, *Studio sulle opere di Giuseppe Verdi*, 100: Pointedly, on *Macbeth*, "Love is the passion best suited to music." For a translation of Basevi's chapter, see David Rosen and Andrew Porter, eds., *Verdi's* Macbeth: *A Sourcebook* (New York: Norton, 1984), 421–25 (herafter cited as *Sourcebook*). See also Alessandro Gagliardi's review, *Revue et Gazette Musicale*, March 28, 1847, translated in ibid., 379: "What, I ask you, is an opera without a tenor?"

2. Rosen and Porter, *Sourcebook*, 57, in Italian and English. Verdi letter to Antonio Barezzi, March 25, 1847. For Barezzi's reply, see Mary Jane Phillips-Matz, *Verdi: A Biography* (New York: Oxford University Press, 1993), 208.

3. Rosen and Porter, *Sourcebook*, 120n1, and 182–83. Verdi revised the opera to an Italian text, though it was sung in Paris in a French translation. Hence, for the revision's premiere at La Scala, Milan, on January 28, 1874, it was easily put back into Italian, in which it usually is sung today. Despite its failure, Verdi considered it the opera's definitive version, see *WGV, Macbeth*, bk. 1, xi.

4. Prado, *La musica italiana a Cuba*, 36. On the touring company's size: *New York Herald*, April 5, 1850, 1, numbers the orchestra at forty and chorus at fifty. But the company's announcements for its Boston season, for example, the *Boston Daily Evening Transcript*, May 13, 1850, 3, state, "The whole company consists of 104 individuals," naming many, and including a "Chorus of 13 ladies and 18 gentlemen," and an orchestra of "40 distinguished professors."

5. Havana *Diario*, quoted in Prado, *La musica italiana a Cuba*, 36–37. For Verdi's emphasis on the opera's "fantastical genre," see Rosen and Porter, *Sourcebook*, 4, his letter to Alessandro Lanari, May 17, 1846.

6. Rosen and Porter, *Sourcebook*, 67, Verdi letter to Salvatore Cammarano, November 23, 1848.

7. Rosen and Porter, *Sourcebook*, 236. *La Rivista di Firenze*, March 10, 1847.

8. Rosen and Porter, *Sourcebook*, 233, and "too long," 374.

9. Havana *Diario*, quoted in Prado, *La musica italiana a Cuba*, 37.

10. Rosen and Porter, *Sourcebook*, "Chronology," 426.

11. Shakespeare, see Lawrence W. Levine, *Highbrow/Lowbrow: The Emergence of Cultural Hierarchy in America* (Cambridge: Harvard University Press, 1988), 4 and throughout. *New York Herald*, May 1, 1850, 2. Niblo's Garden Theatre (1829–95), at Broadway and Prince Street, was on the site of a former summer theater in a garden setting. This had been replaced in 1827 by an enclosed theater called "Sans Souci," which in turn was replaced two years later by one larger, "Niblo's Garden," named after its manager William Niblo. This burned, but Niblo, "the Napoleon of the theatrical managers," rebuilt and opened a still larger theater on July 30, 1849. Essentially an opera house, it had a capacity of perhaps 3,500. Its decorations were "in the Moorish style" and "one of the most remarkable improvements" were "the seats of the boxes, which are well

cushioned and give comfort to those who find room upon them." See William C. Young, *Documents of American Theater History*, vol. 1, *Famous American Playhouses 1716–1788* (Chicago: American Library Association, 1973), entry 52, quoting the *New York Herald*, July 31, 1849, 1. In 1847 Niblo opened a concert hall, "Niblo's Saloon" (capacity 600), which in 1864 became a theater in which many English operas and operas in English translation were performed. See McKnight, *Music Criticism in the* New York Times *and the* New York Tribune, *1851–1876*, 84 and 223, quoting W. H. Fry, *New York Tribune*, January 15, 1864.

12. *Home Journal*, May 4, 1850, 2.

13. Description of Macready's Macbeth is based chiefly on J. C. Trewin, *Mr. Macready: A Nineteenth-century Tragedian and His Theatre* (London: George Harrap, 1955); Alan S. Downer, *The Eminent Tragedian, W. C. Macready* (Cambridge: Harvard University Press, 1966); and William Archer, *William Charles Macready* (London: Kegan Paul, 1890). For the promptbook, see Downer, 337–38.

14. "Famous Music." Macready's use of it can be traced in Downer, *The Eminent Tragedian*, 318, 322, 324, 329ff. Rosen and Porter, *Sourcebook*, 454–56, discusses its origin and authorship.

15. Rosen and Porter, *Sourcebook*, 67, 144–48, the latter five pages being William Weaver's, essay, "The Shakespeare Verdi Knew."

16. Trewin, *Mr. Macready*, 80.

17. Downer, *The Eminent Tragedian*, 337–38: "The following pages are intended as a running account of what a spectator might have seen at an *ideal* production of Macready's Macbeth. It is based on a promptbook in the Seymour Collection of the Princeton University Library."

18. Trewin, *Mr. Macready*, 80.

19. Walt Whitman, *Brooklyn Daily Eagle*, August 20, 1846, 2, and in *The Collected Writings of Walt Whitman*, 2:25.

20. *New York Tribune*, April 26, 1850, 1.

21. *Albion*, May 4, 1850, 212.

22. *New York Evening Mirror*, April 26, 1850, 2.

23. *New York Tribune*, April 26, 1850, 1.

24. *New York Evening Mirror*, April 26, 1850, 2, and *New York Herald*, April 25, 1850, 1.

25. Strong, diary entry for April 28, 1850, quoted in Lawrence, *Strong on Music*, 2:26–27.

26. *Albion*, May 4, 1850, 212.

27. *Boston Evening Transcript*, May 29, 1850, 2.

28. Boston "best city for a short season," Max Maretzek, *Sharps and Flats*, in *Revelations of an Opera Manager in 19th Century America* (1890; repr. New York: Dover Press, 1968), 41.

29. Castle Garden. New York City acquired Fort Clinton from the federal government in 1824. The fort stood slightly offshore to the west of Battery Place, to which it was attached by a bridge. In 1826 a lessee opened a theater in the fort, now called Castle Garden, which because of its position on the water was cooler in summer than most theaters. In 1854 the small moat was filled in, and the following year the theater-fort was converted into the Emigrant Landing Depot and served as such until 1892 when the depot was shifted to Ellis Island. The most publicized events at Castle Garden were the concerts with Jenny Lind in 1850. Maretzek put the theater's capacity at "more than 5,000 comfortably seated," *Crotchets and Quavers*, 171.

30. *Times and Messenger*, April 28, 1850, 2.

31. *New York Herald,* January 16, 1850, 1.

32. *Morning Express,* August 21, 1850, 2.

33. *Daily Alta California,* September 22, 1854, 2.

34. See Martin, *Verdi at the Golden Gate,* 87. The touring group was known by the name of its leading soprano, Clotilda Barili-Thorn. The tenor was Luigi Comassi.

35. *New York Herald,* June 23, 1855, 4.

36. Bertucca: *New York Times,* October 9, 1856, 4; *New York Herald,* October 9, 1856, 4. Guerrabella: "T. M. W." in *Dwight's Journal of Music,* December 20, 1862, 301.

37. Joseph Ward, *Diary for 1865.* For more of Ward's and other amateurs' musical activities, see Bruhn, "Taking the Private Public," 264–70.

38. See *Complete Catalogue of Sheet Music and Musical Works, 1870,* 237.

39. The size of the orchestra or chorus is seldom revealed, but, for opera performances in 1860, Maguire usually provided an orchestra of twenty-five and a mixed chorus of perhaps twenty-five or thirty. See Martin, *Verdi at the Golden Gate,* 179.

40. *Daily Alta California,* November 18, 1862, 12.

41. *San Francisco Daily Evening Bulletin,* November 19, 1862, 3. Harpists and those who love the harp tend to like the sylph ballet, for only here in the opera does Verdi use it, giving the short diversion a unique sound.

42. *San Francisco Golden Era,* November 23, 1862, 4. For more reviews of the Bianchis' *Macbeth,* see Martin, *Verdi at the Golden Gate,* 247–50.

43. *New York Times,* October 22, 1863, 4. Max Maretzek, *Further Revelations of an Opera Manager in 19th Century America,* ed. and annotated Ruth Henderson (Sterling Heights, MI: Harmonie Park Press, 2006), 60. The other novelties were: Petrella's *Ione;* Peri's *Giuditta;* and Verdi's *Aroldo,* which outranked *Macbeth,* four performances to three.

44. *Philadelphia Inquirer,* December 10, 1863, 4.

45. *Boston Evening Transcript,* January 14, 1864, 2.

46. *New York Herald,* March 3, 1864, 5.

47. See advertisements for performances in the *New York Herald,* for example, February 9, 1864, 7; and a news report, *Herald,* February 9, 1864, 4; and schedule of performances in Maretzek, *Further Revelations of an Opera Manager,* appendix 1, "Performances, 1863–67."

48. Kellogg, *Memoirs,* 81.

49. See Martin, "The Metropolitan Opera's Sunday Evening Concerts and Verdi," 16–27.

50. Nimbus Records, *Battistini, Prima Voce,* NI 7831 (1992). See Will Crutchfield, "Authenticity in Verdi: The Recorded Legacy," *Opera* 36, no. 8 (August 1985).

51. Caruso, Victor Record #88558. Caruso sings the 1865 revision of the aria. In revising, however, Verdi altered only the first five introductory orchestral measures and two notes of the opening recitative. None of the aria. See John Richard Bolig, *Caruso Records: A History and Discography* (Denver: Mainspring Press, 2002), 174.

52. See John Penino, "The New Opera Company: What Did It Accomplish?" *Opera Quarterly* 16, no. 4 (Autumn 2000): 589–610.

53. Paul Rodmell discovered a new date and place for the first performance in England: No longer, Manchester, October 2, 1860 (Rosen and Porter, *Sourcebook,* 437), but Birmingham, on August 27, 1860. See Paul Rodmell, "'Double, Double, Toil and Trouble': Producing *Macbeth* in Mid-Victorian Britain," *Verdi Forum,* nos. 30–31 (2003–4): 37–47. This was a "spontaneous production," a single performance, staged in four weeks, with orchestral parts deduced from a vocal score. It was reviewed, though not very favorably. The more professional Manchester first performance was led by Luigi Arditi, conductor,

with Pauline Viardot as Lady Macbeth. In *My Reminiscences* (New York: Dodd, Mead, 1896), 49–55, Arditi describes the transpositions Viardot requested in the role for the first United Kingdom performance, in Dublin on March 30, 1859. *Dwight's Journal of Music*, May 14, 1859, reprints a review of the premiere from the Dublin *Daily Express*.

54. This performance (in German) starts the Verdi revival of *Macbeth* in Germany. Rosen and Porter, *Sourcebook*, 449n2, cites some statistics on the number of *Macbeth* performances on German stages: 1929–30, eight; 1930–31, twenty; 1931–32, forty-seven; 1932–33, twenty-four; 1933–34, thirty-seven; 1934–35 (six productions), thirty-seven.

55. Herbert F. Peyser, "Verdi's *Macbeth* and Tchaikovsky's *Queen of Spades* Revived," *Musical Courier*, November 15, 1941, 9. The singers were Jess Walters and Florence Kirk. See Spike Hughes, *Glyndebourne: A History of the Festival Opera* (London: Methuen, 1965), 129, for how an initially doubtful audience responded to the opera.

56. *New York Times*, December 3, 1942, 38.

57. "Mal per me." Confirmed by Regina Resnik, e-mail to author, May 21, 2003. She sang one performance as Lady Macbeth, on December 5, 1942, the start of her career. See *New York Times*, December 6, 1942, 78.

58. "Senseless," Marcello Conati, in Rosen and Porter, *Sourcebook*, 238n27.

59. Arguments abound on when electricity first entered theaters as the general source of light. According to Edwin G. Burrows and Mike Wallace, *Gotham, A History of New York City to 1898* (New York: Oxford University Press, 1999), 1149, the Lyceum (1885) was "the first New York playhouse lighted by electricity." Yet they note earlier (p. 1066), that in 1883 Niblo's Garden (1849–95; capacity 3,500) had featured some lighting effects by the Edison Electric Light Company, including "an illuminated model of the new Brooklyn Bridge and chorus girls who flourished electric wands." According to Maretzek, *Sharps and Flats*, 13, the first use of electric light occurred at the premiere of Meyerbeer's *Le Prophète* at Niblo's Garden on November 25, 1853. But he gives no details. Presumably it sought some special effect.

60. Bloomfield, *50 Years of the San Francisco Opera*, 146. The singers were Robert Weede and Inge Borkh.

61. Alfred Frankenstein, *San Francisco Chronicle*, September 29, 1955, 22.

62. Frankenstein, *San Francisco Chronicle*, October 13, 1957, 31.

63. *New York Times*, October 25, 1957, 24.

64. Hecate to be mimed, Rosen and Porter, *Sourcebook*, 90, Verdi letter to Léon Escudier, January 23, 1865. Though Hecate's scenes appear in most editions of Shakespeare's play, since the start of the twentieth century these have been known to be interpolations from Thomas Middleton's *The Witch*. See *Sourcebook*, 454–56. For a detailed discussion of the ballet with costume designs for Hecate, dancing witches, and sylphs for an 1874 production at La Scala, see Knud Arne Jürgensen, *The Verdi Ballets* (Parma: Istituto Nazionale di Studi Verdiani, 1995), 73–92.

65. *New York Herald Tribune*, November 3, 1957, sec. 4, 8.

66. "High priest." Paul Henry Lang had published in 1941 his monumental *Music in Western Civilization* (New York: Norton, 1941), which was much admired, quoted, and used in schools. Also Shanet, *Philharmonic*, 292.

67. Cincinnati premiere, June 23, 1960.

68. *New York Times*, March 27, 1958, 40.

69. Radio audience. See *New York Times* article on the announcer Milton Cross, January 4, 1975, 26.

70. The Metropolitan historian, Kolodin, *Metropolitan Opera, 1883–1966*, 606–8, is kinder to Callas and more severe on Bing. My memory of the fracas, in which both Bing

and Callas continued to speak ill of the other, is that many operagoers by January were fed up with both, and those who had heard Rysanek in Carnegie Hall were quite content that she should sing.

71. Meyer Burger, *New York Times*, January 28, 1959, 34.

72. *New York Herald Tribune*, February 6, 1959, 9.

73. Francis D. Perkins, *New York Herald Tribune*, January 3, 1960, 30.

74. On Irene Dalis: Ross Parmenter, *New York Times*, February 5, 1960, 23; and Jay S. Harrison, *New York Herald Tribune*, February 5, 1960, 8.

75. *New Yorker*, February 10, 1973, 100–102.

76. *Opera News*, March 10, 1973, 23.

77. William Weaver, "Verdi's Twice-Told *Macbeth*," *Saturday Review*, January 31, 1959, 59. This article has a useful account of the opera's major productions in Italy after World War II. Cynthia Jolly, "The Festival of Two Worlds," *Opera*, September 1958, 554–55.

78. Costumes. Verdi letter to Alessandro Lanari, January 24, 1847, Rosen and Porter, *Sourcebook*, 35.

79. The Opera Company of Boston, led by Sarah Caldwell, putting on two quite different productions in 1969 and 1976, seemed to prove that what mattered was not the version used or concept of the opera but simply a good performance of the music. The first presented the original version of the opera, but was generally deplored as underrehearsed. Michael Steinberg for the *Boston Globe*, April 2, 1969, was even harsher: "perfunctory direction, dreary and inept conducting." See also, Nicholas Groth, *Boston After Dark*, April 9, 1969. The 1976 production of the revised version, however, was widely praised. Steinberg, again for the *Globe*, June 3, 1976, 42:1, called it "a remarkable, an impressive evening," even though he wished her "a larger orchestra—with just three basses and hardly more than a dozen violins it really sounds poverty-stricken for Verdi . . . the chorus, too, is small and just a bit scrawny in sound." See also Peter G. Davis, *New York Times*, June 4, 1976, C14, and Robert Baxter, *Opera*, September 1976, 846–47. And in 1986, the Boston Concert Opera performed *Macbeth* with success, see *Globe*, January 21, 1986, 16.

80. For example, Martin Chusid, director of the American Institute of Verdi Studies, in "More about the Performance History of *Macbeth*," *Verdi Newsletter*, no. 13 (1985): 38: "Perhaps the most successful arrangement for modern audiences would be performances of Acts I–III of the revised version together with act IV of the original." That composite, however, would retain the original refugees' chorus, though probably most people today think the revised version is slightly the better. The Kentucky Opera Company later repeated its performance of the original *Macbeth* (in English), in Louisville. A group calling itself the Long Island Opera Society gave a concert performance of the 1847 version in 1980 (see chap. 17). For a comparison of the two versions, see George Badacsonyi, "Verdi's Two 'Macbeths,'" *Opera*, February 1976, 108–13. And see Anne Midgette, *New York Times*, July 14, 2003, E1, for the ending offered by the Kirov Opera.

81. *New Yorker*, December 13, 1982, 176–79.

82. *New York Times*, January 14, 1984, 10.

83. *New York Times*, November 19, 1982, C31.

84. Porter, *New Yorker*, December 13, 1982, 176. Rockwell, *New York Times*, January 14, 1984, 10. And far afield, whether reporting what he saw or merely had heard, a New Orleans critic, Frank Gagnard, in 1994 described the production as "a gaudy fiasco," *New Orleans Times Picayune*, July 31, 1994, D28.

85. Porter, *New Yorker*, February 20, 1984, 111. About conductor James Levine, especially important because since from 1976 to date the chief conductor and music director at the Metropolitan, Porter complained: His "heavy conducting seemed less acceptable

than ever after the alert, precise, colorful account of the score . . . that Riccardo Muti and the Philadelphia Orchestra brought to Carnegie Hall"—in a concert performance on October 11, 1983. The size of orchestra and chorus then were phenomenal: the orchestra had 102 onstage and 26 backstage, and the chorus numbered 185. Though using the score's revised version, Muti cut the Paris ballet, saying in an interview: "When Verdi first wrote the opera, he refused to include ballet music, because he felt it would destroy the continuity of the action. . . . I agree with his first idea, I think it works better." Muti to Allan Kozinn, *Stagebill*, 32, in the evening's program. About Levine's conducting, note that when he returned to *Macbeth* in a new production at the Metropolitan, October 22, 2007, his conducting was much praised, see Anthony Tommasini, *New York Times*, October 24, 2007, E1. Curiously—some might say paradoxically—many conductors seem to do better with Verdi only as they grow older. Cf. Thomas Schippers as a young man conducting *Nabucco*, see chap. 1, and Tullio Serafin as an old man, chap. 15. For comments on Levine as a young man conducting *Macbeth* see chap. 3.

86. *New York Times*, January 9, 1988, E5.

87. For example, the opera's local premiere in New Orleans, November 2, 1967, in a relatively abstract production of bare boards, rear-wall projections, and evocative lighting. Revivals, in much the same style, followed in 1976, 1980, and 1995.

88. Robert Commanday, *San Francisco Chronicle*, November 21, 1986, 82, and on a revival, January 10, 1994, E1.

89. See William Albright, *Opera*, February 1998, 171–73, and vol. 51, no. 3 (March 2000): 297. Another production in this style, which perhaps succeeded musically but not scenically, was the Canadian Opera Company's in Toronto in September 2005: "The unit set was dominated by rows of ornate white settees covered by clear plastic that got progressively more blood-splattered. The stage was populated by 'witches' knitting away—yarn symbolizing destiny, perhaps? The men wore kilts of varying lengths; Lady Macbeth's blonde bombshell wig and extravagant tartan bustle made her look more like a Scottish Barbie doll than a queen." See Joseph K. So, *Opera* 57, no. 1 (January 2006): 45–46. Christopher Hoile, *Opera News* 70, no. 6 (December 2005): 70.

90. *New York Times*, September 13, 1997, 13.

91. Daniel Webster, *Philadelphia Inquirer*, September 13, 1997, D8.

92. James L. Keller, *Opera News*, December 20, 1997, 42.

93. Charles Michener, *New York Observer*, October 6, 1997, 33. Revival, Anthony Tommasini, *New York Times*, October 9, 2001, E5.

94. *Opera*, Festival Issue 1994, 79, and Festival Issue 1995, 77.

95. See David Patrick Stearns, *Philadelphia Inquirer*, March 17, 2003, E3; also March 16, 2003, H1.

96. Anne Midgette, *New York Times*, July 14, 2003, E1.

97. Victor DeRenzi to the author, April 14, 2003. Overall, the season sold at 96 percent, which is high. On New York City Opera sales, Heidi Waleson, *Wall Street Journal*, September 13, 2005, D8, quoting Claudia Keenan Hough, City Opera's director of planning and marketing, that three seasons sold on average in the low 80 percents. Similarly, the Metropolitan, see Joseph Volpe, *The Toughest Show on Earth, My Rise and Reign at the Metropolitan Opera* (New York: Knopf, 2006), 261.

98. John von Rhein, *Chicago Tribune*, April 20, 2003, sec. 7, 10. Several Florida critics also inclined to prefer the original version, mostly on the grounds of greater musical and dramatic unity: John Fleming, *St. Petersburg Times*, April 2, 2003, 6B, and *Opera News*, August 2003, 68; June LeBell, *Longboat Observer*, April 3, 2003, 7C; and Richard Storm, *Sarasota Herald-Tribune*, April 4, 2003, 2B.

Chapter Seven

1. Maretzek, *Crotchets and Quavers*, 156.
2. On Marty, see chap. 3, opening paragraph.
3. *Albion*, August 31, 1850, 416.
4. On Strakosch (1825–87). For his early career in New York as pianist, see Lawrence, *Strong on Music*, 1:512. For his later importance as impresario, see Preston, *Opera on the Road*, 145. He married the contralto Amalia Patti, Adelina's sister, and in the years 1860–68 managed Adelina's career.
5. W. Porter Ware and Thaddeus C. Lockard Jr., *P. T. Barnum Presents Jenny Lind: The American Tour of the Swedish Nightingale* (Baton Rouge: Louisiana State University, 1980), on auction prices, 31, 38; on the orchestra, 48. The orchestra's core of ten consisted of two violins, a cello, a double bass, two flutes, an oboe, a clarinet, a horn, and a trumpet. After the tour with Barnum, Lind sang forty concerts, for a time with the same singers and conductor, mostly in the country's northeastern cities, and with the later concerts managed by her husband, pianist, composer, and conductor Otto Goldschmidt (98, 113). For the Philadelphia bid, see Louis C. Madeira, comp., *Annals of Music in Philadelphia and History of the Musical Fund Society, from Its Organization in 1820 to the Year 1858*, ed. Philip H. Goepp (Philadelphia: Lippincott, 1896; repr. New York: Da Capo Press, 1973), 165.
6. For Parodi leaving Maretzek for Strakosch and Maretzek's maneuvers upon losing his lead soprano, see Preston, *Opera on the Road*, 197–205.
7. Ibid., 208.
8. Prado, *La musica italiana a Cuba*, 39–42. Maretzek, *Sharps and Flats*, 26, states (his memory for dates failing) that Havana was without Italian opera "from 1853 to 1856." He puts the cause to Marty's "pouting." He did not have an easy time with Marty's stars. See *Crotchets and Quavers*, 158.
9. On *Luisa Miller* and *I masnadieri*, see Prado, *La musica italiana a Cuba*, 42–43, 45–46.
10. On Ullman (1817–85), see Preston, *Opera on the Road*, 145.
11. Passion for dancing, Kmen, *Music in New Orleans*, 7–12.
12. Amos, 5:23.
13. Theodore Lyman, writing under the name James Sloan, *Rambles in Italy in the Years 1816–1817* (Baltimore: N. G. Maxwell, 1818), 91, 93. He had been to the Teatro la Fenice, Venice, had heard the castrato Velluti in Mayr's *Lodoiska*, and had been impressed by "the overpowering brilliancy" of Velluti's voice. He added, "In spite, however, of the numberless beauties of the Opera Seria, I must own that to me it appears less suited to the taste of a mixed audience, than the Opera Buffa or comick opera. The latter is seasoned with a species of pleasantry in which the genius of the Italian people appear to delight" (93).
14. Dwight, "History of Music in Boston," 4:437, and "siren," 428, 434. On the influence of the Germans, particularly those who had studied at the Leipzig conservatory, 442.
15. The charge against Lewis: Friends Historical Library, Swarthmore College, to author, February 22, 2001. According to Lewis family memoirs (copies in my possession), though never fully reconciled to his dismissal, he eventually, on his children's urging, began to attend the Episcopal Church. David Grimsted, *Melodrama Unveiled: American Theatre and Culture, 1800–1850* (Chicago: University of Chicago Press, 1968), 29, quotes *An Address on the Subject of Theatrical Amusements, from the Monthly Meeting of Friends Held in New York to Its Members* (New York, 1840), 5, which concluded that plays

encouraged, "a disrelish for that frugality and industry in business, on which even a reasonable degree of success so much depends." On the prejudice against opera and theater in Philadelphia, see Curtis, "One Hundred Years of Grand Opera," vol. 1, sec. 2, 377.

16. Grant Thorburn, *Fifty Years Reminiscences of New York* (New York: Fanshaw, 1845), 28.

17. William Dunlap, *History of the American Theatre*, 2nd ed. (repr., New York: Burt Franklin, 1963), 391.

18. Ibid., 210.

19. Ibid., 302.

20. Kmen, *Music in New Orleans*, 60–61. Seemingly the largest object ever hurled onto a stage in the United States was thrown in Cincinnati at the English actor Macready during a performance of *Hamlet:* a sheep's half carcass. See Buckley, "To the Opera House," 55.

21. Buckley, "To the Opera House, 181.

22. Ireland, *Records of the New York Stage*, 2:504–5.

23. Frances Trollope (1780–1863), *Domestic Manners of the Americans* (Oxford: Oxford University Press, 1985), 110, 230, 300.

24. Grimsted, *Melodrama Unveiled*, 59. Protests against prostitutes in theaters was continual, not only by clergy but by many who loved the theater, starting with Dunlap, *History of the American Theatre*, 1:407–12.

25. Kmen, *Music in New Orleans*, 129.

26. On the city's overall seating capacity and Park Theatre's season, see Buckley, "To the Opera House," 139, 142. In San Francisco, the local impresario and theater manager Thomas Maguire twice enlarged the seating in his theater, first in 1856 and then in 1858, when he increased it from 1,100 to 1,700, see Martin, *Verdi at the Golden Gate*, 109, 117. Increase in musicians, Henry J. Harris, *Musical Quarterly*, April 1915.

27. Foster, *New York by Gaslight*, 157–58. See also, John Koegel, "The Development of the German American Musical Stage in New York City, 1840–1890," in *European Music and Musicians in New York City, 1840–1900*, ed. John Graziano (Rochester, NY: University of Rochester Press, 2006), 149–81.

28. George W. Martin, *The Damrosch Dynasty: America's First Family of Music* (Boston: Houghton Mifflin, 1983), 10.

29. Ibid., 440, n. 3. For similar German singing societies in Boston, see Dwight, "The History of Music in Boston," 4:452–54.

30. On New York's various German Stadt Theatres, see Koegel, The Development of the German American Musical Stage in New York City," 150–51.

31. According to the *Encyclopedia Britannica* (Chicago: Encyclopedia Britannica Press, 1946), vol. 18, "Railroads," 936: "In 1827, the Mauch Chunk railroad in Pennsylvania, 9 mi. long, was built and used in the transportation of anthracite. It was then the longest and most important railroad operating in the United States."

32. On the expansion of railroads, the *Enclycopedia Britannica*; also, *A Maritime History of New York* (WPA project; Garden City, NY: Doubleday, Doran, 1941) for railroads, 219; for steamships, 123, 157, 169, 182.

33. On Sontag, see Madeira, *Annals of Music in Philadelphia*, 165.

34. Lawrence, *Strong on Music*, 1:189.

35. See *A Maritime History of New York*, for railroads, 219; for steamships, 123, 157, 169, 182. Also, Ware and Lockard, *P. T. Barnum Presents Jenny Lind*, 7.

36. For the impact of the 1843 Havana company on Cincinnati, see Larry Robert Wolz, "Opera in Cincinnati: The Years Before the Zoo, 1801–1920" (PhD diss., University of Cincinnati, 1983), 48–53. For subsequent history, see Preston, *Opera on the Road*, 116–29.

37. Maretzek, *Crotchets and Quavers*, 34.

38. "Snow," Maretzek, *Sharps and Flats*, 19. Sablosky, *What They Heard*, 130.

39. Phyllis Hartnoll, ed., *The Oxford Companion to the Theatre*, 4th ed. (New York: Oxford University Press, 1983), 489: "With the introduction of gas, fires in theatres doubled their number in ten years. Some protection was given by glass chimneys, but the open fish-tail burners used for wing-lights were often left without even a wire guard."

40. Park Theatre burns. Ireland, *Records of the New York Stage*, 2:525. It had burned before, on May 25, 1820, and been promptly rebuilt, reopening in September 1821. Ireland writes: "The fire was supposed to have occurred from the wadding of a gun fired during the performance, which probably, lodged in the scenery, and smoldered there unperceived" (ibid., 1:363). After the 1848 fire the theater was not rebuilt: the plot was small and theaters were moving uptown.

41. Krehbiel, *Chapters of Opera*, 4.

42. Description of the Park: Joe Cowell, *Thirty Years Passed Among the Players in England and America* (1844; repr. Hamden, CT: Shoe String Press, an Archon Book, 1979), 57. Later (sometime in the early 1820s) and on p. 61 he replaces the iron hoop with glass chandeliers and "arched and raised" the proscenium, all from his own pocket. Ireland, *Records of the New York Stage*, 1:381, states that the theater was lit by three chandeliers of gas, each "of thirty-five lights." I have followed Cowell, who as an actor, manager, and benefactor of the Park may have had the better knowledge of it.

43. Krehbiel, *Chapters of Opera*, 4.

44. Lawrence, *Strong on Music*, 1:455n46. The chandelier, however, blocked sight lines from the gallery (455–56).

45. Buckley, "To the Opera House," 107.

46. Quoted in Preston, *Opera on the Road*, 170.

47. Ireland, *Records of the New York Stage*, 2:333. Cowell, *Thirty Years Passed Among the Players in England and America*, 57, describes the theater's exterior as he first saw it, in October 1821 (as rebuilt after the 1820 fire) as "the most prison-like-looking place. . . . It is not much better now (1844), but then it was merely rough stone, but now its rough cast, and can boast of a cornice."

48. Buckley, "To the Opera House," 105, and ibid., 105n12, on the new National Theatre's lobby.

49. Tompkins and Kilby, *History of the Boston Theatre, 1854–1901*, 79: the change, on January 2, 1860, "was to bring it in line with the Academies of Music in New York, Brooklyn, Philadelphia and Baltimore, all large theatres, built for opera houses." The change back (98) occurred during a season of opera that began on February 9, 1863. Prejudice against theaters: see Wolz, "Opera in Cincinnati," quoting the *Cincinnati Enquirer*, August 28, 1859, p. 84, on local feeling about theaters and opera houses: "Many persons object to the former, even for an operatic entertainment, and prefer to forego the pleasure of the entertainment, rather than visit a Theatre."

50. On Maguire's, Pike's, Crosby's, and Tabor's opera houses, see entries in Young, *Documents of American Theater History*, vol. 1, *Famous American Playhouses, 1716–1899*.

51. For the *Denver Tribune*, September 4, 1881, see Young, *Documents of American Theater History*, 1:272–81. On the hard woods used by Tabor, see the *Tribune*, which estimates that Tabor "might have saved $30,000 by using cheap woods in the interior construction" (274). On the stage, see *Tribune* (280).

52. Retiring rooms: *Tribune*, quoted in Young, *Documents of American Theater History*, 1:279.

53. Wolz, "Opera in Cincinnati," 82.

54. According to the U.S. Census for 1860, the cities in order of population were: New York, 813,669; Philadelphia, 565,529; Brooklyn, 266,661; Baltimore, 212,418; Boston, 177,840; New Orleans, 168,675; Cincinnati, 161,044; St. Louis, 160,773; Chicago, 112,172; and Buffalo, 81,129.

55. Emporium of the West, *Cincinnati Daily Commercial*, February 23, 1859, quoted in full in Young, *Documents of American Theater History*, 1:177.

56. *Cincinnati Daily Commercial*, February 23, 1859, 1, on the festival opening of Pike's Opera House. See also Young, *Documents of American Theater History*, 1:176–79, who reports, "The Opera House burned on 22 March 1866, was rebuilt in 1867, and burned again on 25 February 1903" (179).

57. Strakosch became active as an impresario in 1857, and besides Cincinnati took his troupe to Chicago in 1859. Later, he managed opera in Paris, 1873–74, and in Rome, 1884–85.

58. Wolz, "Opera in Cincinnati," 82, quoting *Dwight's Journal of Music*, April 23, 1859. The *Cincinnati Daily Commercial*, March 21, 1859, reported of the first *Trovatore* performance: "The weakness on Friday night lay in the choruses, which were deficient in many instances in volume and spirit; on Saturday night, however, this was amply remedied." See chap. 6 for the difficulty in hiring women for the chorus.

59. Orchestra, *Cincinnati Daily Commercial*, March 19, 1859, 1.

60. Wolz, "Opera in Cincinnati," 78: 'Never before and never since [to 1983] has the city been exposed to opera at such length on a daily basis.'

61. "Novelties," see Preston, *Opera on the Road*, 168, 170, and 201. And *Cincinnati Daily Commercial*, April 5, 1859, "of course such an opera [*Don Giovanni*] is usually relied upon for a run, but M. Strakosch, having discovered that we are a novelty-loving community, withdraws it after to-night."

62. *Trovatore* second time, *Cincinnati Daily Commercial*, March 19, 1859, 1.

63. *Trovatore* third time, ibid., April 6, 1859, 1.

64. Ibid., April 9, 1859, 1. Even *Norma* in its second performance drew a notably smaller audience, ibid., March 30, 1859, 1: "It was a repeat to be sure, but who would tire of such a musical treat, presented as that of last night? M'lle Parodi was the Norma, and we question if her superior ever essayed the role." A critic for the *Cincinnati Enquirer*, March 18, 1859, sniffed at the enthusiasm for Verdi: "Whatever may be said against Verdi's noisy music, he is the popular composer after all, and better than any one else, understands how to interpret public taste. . . . It is not surprising that a community like ours, with comparatively little experience, should grow enthusiastic at the sound of his music." Quoted by Wolz, "Opera in Cincinnati," 78.

65. Pasquale Brignoli and Henry Squires. *Cincinnati Daily Commercial*, March 23, 1859, 1. Strakosch's repertory, in order of first performance and with number of performances: *Martha* (1, sung in Italian), *Favorita* (1), *Traviata* (2), *Trovatore* (3), *Sonnambula* (2), *Norma* (2), *Lucrezia Borgia* (1), *Lucia* (2), *Puritani* (1), *Ernani* (1), *Don Giovanni* (3), *Figlia del regimento* (1), *Robert le Diable* (2, sung in Italian), and *Barbiere di Siviglia* (1).

66. On *Ernani*, ibid., April 1, 1859, 1: "The choruses are grand, and the opera throughout is replete with morsels of the choicest melody. It is, indeed conceded as the most finished production of the favorite modern composer." Single performance, ibid.

67. Sigismund Thalberg, virtuoso pianist, to some extent set the style early in 1857 with a series of ten highly successful solo matinees attended almost exclusively by women. See R. Allen Lott, "'Home, Sweet Home' Away from Home," in *European Music and Musicians in New York City, 1840–1900*, ed. Graziano, 71–91. For some operatic "Ladies matinees" in New York later in 1857, but preceding those in Cincinnati by

two years, see Lawrence, *Strong on Music*, 3:63, 68. *Cincinnati Daily Commercial*, March 25, 1859, 1. Advice on dress, ibid., March 26, 1859, 1. Twelve hundred, ibid., April 2, 1859, 1; and nine to one, ibid., March 30, 1859, 1.

Chapter Eight

1. *Albion*, June 9, 1860, 271. The opera had its Western Hemisphere premiere on September 7, 1849, in Rio de Janeiro, playing first in Chile in 1851, in Argentina, Uruguay, and Peru in 1853, in Cuba in 1855, in Mexico City in 1856, and in Colombia in 1858. See Kaufman, *Verdi and His Major Contemporaries*, 352–58.

2. Timings vary, but on average without ballets, *Vespri* runs 2 hours, 53 minutes, and *Don Carlos*, 2 hours, 30 minutes; and with ballets, *Forza*, 2 hours, 40 minutes, and *Aida*, 2 hours, 25 minutes.

3. Author's interviews with Artistic Director Victor DeRenzi and others before and after the final performance on March 18, 2006.

4. In act 3, scene 3.

5. Terence Hawkes, ed., *Coleridge's Writings on Shakespeare* (New York: Capricorn Books, 1959), 171.

6. Milton, *Paradise Lost*, bk. 1, line 111. Andrew Porter, reviewing a production of the opera in London in 2002, noted that Charlotte Brontë in a scene in *Jane Eyre* conceived of Franz as a Fallen Angel. Jane, peeping through a window hears Mary and Diana Rivers reading *Die Räuber* aloud together: "Listen, Diana, Franz is telling a dream" . . . [and Mary exclaimed], "There you have a dim and mighty archangel set before you!" *Times Literary Supplement*, October 11, 2002, 19.

7. If Schiller's development of Carlo's character seems an overheated example of German Romanticism, recall that the French Revolution began with high hopes in 1789, descended in 1792 through the "September massacres" of 1,200 prisoners by a mob, into the Reign of Terror, July 1793 to July 1794. These events, still raw in memory, gave the play much of its force in the early nineteenth century.

8. Single actor, the Glasgow Citizens Theatre at the Edinburgh Festival, summer 1998. Schiller's steady emphasis on the two brothers and their father limits the role of Amalia, and according to the American actor-manager William B. Wood, the play, when performed in Philadelphia in the years 1804–7, failed with ladies in the audience "chiefly from the want of a prominent female character." Wood, *Personal Recollections of the Stage*, 105.

9. Milton, *Paradise Lost*, bk. 1, line 263. Homer, *Iliad*, bk. 24, trans. E. V. Rieu (London: Penguin Books, 1966); cf. lines 615–22, trans. Robert Fagles (New York: Viking Penguin, 1990).

10. Rodney Milnes, *Opera* 28, no. 5 (May 1977): 500.

11. Budden, *Operas of Verdi*, 1:328.

12. Victoria's Diary, quoted by Andrew Porter, *Times Literary Supplement*, October 11, 2002, 19: Her entry continues: "The music is very inferior and commonplace. Lablache acted the part of Maximilian Moor, in which he looked fine, but too fat for the starved old man. Gardoni acted the part of Carlo Moor and was beautifully dressed. Lind sang & acted most exquisitely as Amalia & looked very well & attractive in her several dresses."

13. The most complete collection of English reviews of the premiere run is in Roberta Montemorra Marvin, "Verdi's *I Masnadieri*: Its Genesis and Early Reception" (PhD diss., Brandeis University, 1992), vol. 1, chap. 6. She concludes that opinion in general was

adverse and hesitant, and in part because the opera was "innovative, i.e., that it departed from the traditional expectations associated with Italian opera to a greater degree than modern scholars have recognized" (461). The more important reviews are quoted less copiously in Marvin's introduction to *WGV*, score, pp. xx–xxiii.

14. Andrew Porter, *Opera* 13, no. 5 (May 1962): 334–35.

15. See Ware and Lockard, *P. T. Barnum Presents Jenny Lind.*

16. "Letter from Paumanok," *Evening Post*, August 14, 1851, in *Uncollected Poetry and Prose*, ed. Emory Holloway (New York: Doubleday Doran, 1921), 1:257. The concluding sentence: "I write as I feel; and I feel that there are not a few who will pronounce a Yes to my own confession."

17. See *WGV, I masnadieri*, score, pp. xxx–xxi. Perhaps more accessible, Philip Gossett, *Divas and Scholars: Performing Italian Opera* (Chicago: University of Chicago Press 2006), 70, 165, 323, and notes. In sum: "many changes in Amalia's vocal lines, which were originally much simpler, perhaps because Verdi did not directly know her voice; the changes were introduced during rehearsals to accommodate Lind's style" (70).

18. Lawrence, *Strong on Music*, 2:679.

19. Ibid., 783.

20. *New York Times* and *New York Herald*, both April 24, 1856, 5. The newspapers at this time also were giving considerable space usually devoted to music to the death in Australia of harpist-composer Robert N. C. Bochsa (1789–1856), well-known in New York as Anna Bishop's manager and the creator of a pastiche of Verdi works titled *Judith*. For more on *Judith*, see chap. 1.

21. See Lawrence, *Strong on Music*, 3:341.

22. Ireland, *Records of the New York Stage*, 2:702.

23. *Spirit of the Times*, June 9, 1860, 224. See also *Evening Post*, June 4, 1860, 2.

24. *Spirit of the Times*, June 9, 1860, 224.

25. See Martin, *Verdi at the Golden Gate*, 117–24.

26. *Daily Alta California*, October 24, 1858, 2.

27. Martin, *Verdi at the Golden Gate*, 124.

28. Ibid., 286n20.

29. Ibid., 110–12. See also Lois Foster Rodecape, "Tom Maguire, Napoleon of the Stage," *California Historical Society Quarterly* 20, no. 4 (December 1941); nos. 1, 2, 3 (March, June, September 1942). Maguire, in origin, was a New Yorker, reported variously to have been a carriage driver, a bartender in the Park Theatre, and a hanger-on of Tammany Hall. Arriving in San Francisco in 1849, he ran bars and gambling saloons, built theaters, and because passionate for Italian opera soon had his own opera house, the Metropolitan Theatre, and not long thereafter a chain of others throughout the state. Ultimately, he would build twelve opera houses in California.

30. (San Francisco) *Daily Evening Bulletin*, May 30, 1863, 3.

31. *Daily Alta California*, May 30, 1863, 2. This review, the one above, and another in *Golden Era*, are republished complete in Martin, *Verdi at the Golden Gate*, 250–51.

32. Bruhn, "Taking the Private Public," 264–70. The diaries are at the New-York Historical Society.

33. *Complete Catalogue of Sheet Music and Musical Works, 1870*, 241. The vocal excerpts were "Charles, I die" (Carlo, io muoio), duet for bass and soprano, act 1, scene 3; "What mountains" (Qual mare, qual terra), duet for soprano and tenor, act 3, scene 3; "Yes, in those eyes angelic" (Lo sguardo avea degl'angeli), soprano solo, act 1, scene 3.

34. Martin, "The Metropolitan Opera's Sunday Evening Concerts and Verdi," 16–27.

35. On Verdi Renaissance, see the introduction. Also Martin, "Franz Werfel and the 'Verdi Renaissance,'" in Martin, *Aspects of Verdi*, 61–77.

36. *New York Times*, February 14, 1975, 30.

37. I was present.

38. *New York Post*, February 13, 1975, 30.

39. Philips, 6703 064. Carlo Bergonzi (t), Montserrat Caballé (s), Piero Cappuccilli (b), Ruggero Raimondi (bs), and Lamberto Gardelli, conductor. On Verdi seeking to express "inner" feelings, see Porter, *High Fidelity Magazine* (December 1975): 80–82. Again Milton: "The mind is its own place, and in itself "Can make a heav'n of hell, a hell of heav'n," *Paradise Lost*, bk. 1, line 253.

40. San Diego cycle, see chap. 2.

41. Decca, D273D3, 1983. Other artists were Franco Bonisolli (t), Matteo Manuguerra (b), and Samuel Ramey (bs). Reissued on compact discs, 1993.

42. *San Diego Union*, June 22, 1984, A-21.

43. Ibid., C-1. See also Charles Osborne, *Opera* Festival Issue, Autumn 1984, 110–11.

44. Much of what she changed, perhaps all, can be heard on the recording. Some of the changes seem lovely and appropriate: for example, her decoration to her line that opens act 3. Most of her changes raise the line up an octave.

45. *San Diego Union*, A-21.

46. *New York Times*, July 17, 1988, 39.

47. The performance apparently was not reviewed.

48. Facts taken from the program. The production apparently was not reviewed. I thank the company for putting me in touch with Bay Westlake who furnished a copy of the program and other facts.

49. Reviews in *Opera*: At Cardiff, Rodney Milnes 28, no. 5 (May 1977): 500–501; at Llandudno, Charles Osborne 28, no. 9 (September 1977): 904–5. See also Richard Fawkes, *Welsh National Opera* (London: Julia MacRae Books, 1986), 192–93, 292. The translation was by Stephen Oliver.

50. Charles Pitt, *Opera* 31, no. 4 (April 1980): 382–84.

51. Until the 1994 revival, the reports in *Opera* are so brief as to seem dismissive. See *Opera*, February 1981, 169; June 1987, 667, which refers to the opera as "Verdi's youthful folly"; and January 1995, 553–54: "[The] production, which emphasized rather than glossed over the hiss-the-villain plot, worked surprisingly well as out-and-out melodrama."

52. I thank William Voigtlander who saw the premiere and gave me an account of it as well as its program (62 pages).

53. Raymond Monelle, *Opera* 49, no. 10 (October 1998): 1168–72. See also Ian Brunskill, "Making a Play out of Schiller," *Opera* 49, no. 6 (June 1998): 649–54.

54. As Julian Budden was prompt to point out, in a letter to *Opera* 54, no. 2 (February 2003): 138: "There is no 'Mad Scene for baritone' in the opera. Francesco is merely recounting a dream, certainly with horror, but in full command of his mental faculties."

55. Rodney Milnes, *Opera* 53, no. 12 (December 2002): 1502–3. See also Andrew Porter, *Times Literary Supplement*, October 11, 2002, 19.

56. *Opera News*, January 2003: 83–84. Andrew Porter, *Times Literary Supplement*, October 11, 2002, was generally admiring but declared Hvorostovsky, "a lyric baritone," was "miscast in a dramatic role" and "boomed and banged his beautiful voice into imprecise pitches." And the soprano, Paula Delligatti, in place of trills, could manage only "vague wobbles."

57. *New York Times*, March 10, 1999, E-5.

58. Author's interview with Victor DeRenzi, August 7, 2000.

59. My sampling of opinion during and after the final performance.

60. "Glorious melody," Richard Storm, *Sarasota Herald-Tribune*, February 23, 2006; and "male choruses," John Fleming, *St. Petersburg Times*, March 4, 2006.

61. Lawrence A. Johnson, *South Florida Sun-Sentinel*, March 3, 2006. A similar review by Herman Trotter, *American Record Guide*, July/August 2006, 41, mentions as a difficulty "the multiple scene changes."

62. Reviewing the Royal Opera Company's production, *Times Literary Supplement*, October 11, 2002, 19.

63. Hawkes, *Coleridge's Writings on Shakespeare*, 176.

Chapter Nine

1. *Operatic Performances in New Orleans, 1812–1919* (WPA project, no date), 58–59. Note: the premiere set for January 17, 1850, was shifted to January 24. I thank Jack Belsom, archivist of the New Orleans Opera Association, for identifying excerpts sung on gala occasions. A tally, perhaps incomplete, but indicative, shows for the years 1856–97, the Trio sung five times, not including once as part of act 4 sung entire; the Pilgrims' Chorus, once; the tenor's "Je veux encore entendre," once; and all of act 3 (aria for Hélène and degradation of Gaston), once.

2. Budden, *Operas of Verdi*, 1:344.

3. Jürgensen, *Verdi Ballets*, 15–20.

4. As yet, no reference to the ballet, in whole or part, has been found for any season in any journal. Jack Belsom, letters to the author, November 2006.

5. Gilbert Louis Duprez (1806–96). His stature was small, but his voice, huge; and he is said to be the first tenor to sing a high C from his chest voice, the lowest and supposedly richest of the three male voice "registers," chest, head, and falsetto.

6. The Paris Opéra, the popular name for the Académie Royale de Musique, peformed in the years 1821–73 in the Salle Le Peletier (capacity 1,900). Starting in 1875, it played in the new and more sumptuous Palais Garnier (capacity 2,131). For cuts in the ballet, see Jürgensen, *Verdi Ballets*.

7. Cesari and Luzio, *Copialettere*, 151n1, quoting *La France musicale*.

8. Kaufman, *Verdi and His Major Contemporaries*, 361n41. Outside of Paris, major theaters were in Lyons, Marseilles, Toulouse, Bordeaux, Nantes, Rouen, and Strasbourg. The circuit was important and lucrative for composers.

9. Budden, *Operas of Verdi*, 1:343.

10. The first Théâtre d'Orléans, built in 1815 had burned the following year. The second, opened on November 27, 1819, was chiefly the work of John Davis who, despite his English name, was French, born in Paris, educated there, and continually returned to it, not to London, to recruit his singers and musicians. As a young man he had migrated to Saint-Domingue in the West Indies, and after the revolution there had gone to Cuba and then, in 1809, to New Orleans, where, besides running a number of profitable business, hotels, ball rooms, gambling halls, he built the theater. See Kmen, *Music in New Orleans*, 79–81, on the first theater, and 83–90. on Davis.

11. Recent performances of *La Dame blanche*. For example, a concert performance in Carnegie Hall by the Opera Orchestra of New York in 1992; staged performances at the Opéra-Comique, Paris, in 1997, after which EMI issued a recording (including

dialogue) based on the production; and a staged performance in English in 1998 by the Cincinnati Conservatory of Music.

12. Total performances in New Orleans, Kmen, *Music in New Orleans*, 109; and Belsom, "Reception of Major Operatic Premieres in New Orleans," 13, 16. And on tour, Sylvie Chevalley, "Le Théâtre d'Orléans en Tournée dans les Villes du Nord, 1827–1833," *Comptes Rendus de L'Athénée Louisianais*, March 1955, 27–71. I thank Jack Belsom, archivist of the New Orleans Opera Association, for making me a copy of this hard-to-find article and also of the Mary Grace Swift article cited in the following note.

13. Mary Grace Swift, "The Northern Tours of the Théâtre d'Orléans, 1843 and 1845," *Louisiana History* 26, no. 2 (Spring 1985): 167, 184.

14. *New Orleans Bee*, January 17, 1850. Théâtre d'Orléans capacity, 1,300.

15. *New Orleans Daily Picayune*, January 26, 1850, 2.

16. *L'Abeille de la Nouvelle Orleans* (French ed. of the *Bee*), January 26, 1850, 1.

17. Ibid., January 28, 1850, 1.

18. See chap. 2.

19. See *Operatic Performances in New Orleans, 1812–1919*.

20. Rosa DeVriès. For performances in New York in 1850, see Lawrence, *Strong on Music*, 2:91n1: "a scene from Verdi's *I Lombardi . . .* presumably all in French." For performances in 1852, see *Strong on Music*, 2:259: "gave a brilliant performance of the Rondo from Verdi's *I Lombardi*." Also, the *Morning Courier and New-York Enquirer*, February 8, 1852, 2, describes the excerpt as "the Rondo from *I Lombardi*." But inasmuch as the French vocal score for *Jérusalem* does not use that term, but the Italian vocal score for *I Lombardi* does, perhaps she sang it in Italian. For 1853, see *Courier and Enquirer*, February 12, 1853, 2, and *New York Herald*, February 12, 1853, 4, which do not identify the rondo, but the previous day the *Herald* had announced the program would include the rondo from *I Lombardi*.

21. For the Gottschalk programs, see Lawrence, *Strong on Music*, 2:770–85. For a brief review of the two-piano fantasy, see Sablosky, *What They Heard*, 40. For a recording of the Fantasia for solo piano, see Philip Martin, *Gottschalk Piano Music*, vol. 8, Hyperion Records, 2004, CDA67536. For a child prodigy, later a distinguished concert pianist, playing the Fantasia, see Marta Malinowski, *Teresa Carreño, "by the Grace of God"* (New Haven: Yale University Press, 1940), 9. For Gottschalk's influence on the country, see Madeira, *Music in Philadelphia*, 160–61.

22. The *Missouri Republican, St. Louis*, June 23, 1860, announced the final performance of the French company would be of the "First, Second, and Third Acts of Jérusalem (Il [*sic*] Lombardi)," preceded by a short comic opera. But lacking any review of the *Jérusalem* performance, it is unclear whether act 3, shorn of its ballet, perhaps was joined to act 4 without intermission, or that act 4, or some previous act, was cut. Earlier in the week, the company had performed *La Fille du régiment* twice and *La Favorite* once. Both received favorable reviews.

The *Cincinnati Daily Commercial*, July 11, 1860, announced for the next night "Verdi's Grand Opera in 3 acts, called *Jérusalem;* or *Il* [*sic*] *Lombardi . . .* the performance will commence with Offenbach's Comic Opera in one act, called *La Rose de St. Flour*." Again, no reviews.

23. "Charming opera," *New Orleans Daily Picayune*, March 27, 1868, 2. Review, ibid., March 28, 1868, 2.

24. Ibid., January 28, 1888, 2.

25. Ibid., February 3, 1891, 3.

26. See Martin, "The Metropolitan Opera's Sunday Evening Concerts and Verdi," 16–27, 17, and 26n3, where the records sometimes incorrectly list the tenor's first name, Albert, as Alfred. On Guille's and the French Company's repertory in its 1889–90 season, my thanks to a letter from Jack Belsom, November 26, 2006.

27. Montreal, see Mireille Barrière, *L'Opéra français de Montréal, L'étonnante histoire d'un succès éphémère, 1893–1896* (Montreal: Fides, 2002). Review in *New Orleans Daily Picayune*, January 21, 1897, 3; and I thank Jack Belsom for checking the program for the concert on January 27, 1897.

28. Quotations are from the program and a ticket brochure.

29. Letter from James Keolker, San Francisco author and lecturer on opera, to the author, November 15, 2006.

30. *San Francisco Chronicle*, July 15, 1991, E-2.

31. Letter from Frank Petelka to the author, July 16, 1991.

32. According to the program and ticket brochure, the tenor was Jianyi [Johnny] Zhang, of Taiwan.

33. Bernard Holland, *New York Times*, January 29, 1994, sec. 1, 12.

34. *New York Post*, January 28, 1994, 56. See also Peter G. Davis, *New York*, February 14, 1994, and Leslie Kandell, *Westsider*, February 3–9, 1994.

35. A "triumph" for Pavarotti. He may not have wished to learn the role in French, but also: Gaston, far more than Oronte, must act and move about the stage, and by 1994 Pavarotti was fairly immobile because of weight and arthritis. But to sell out the house he need only to appear and sing.

36. Author's interview, January 17, 2007, with La Selva, who stressed how much more demanding was the role of Gaston than Oronte.

37. *New York Times*, February 10, 1998, E-5.

38. There are several recordings and DVDs of live European performances, some with severe cuts; also a studio recording of the complete opera, including the ballet; and a number of renditions on recitals of the tenor's aria "Je veux encore entendre."

39. *New York Times*, February 10, 1998, E-5.

Chapter Ten

1. The Walnut Street Theatre was built in 1808 at the northeast corner of Nineth and Walnut Streets, then on the western edge of the city. Opening on January 2, 1809, and calling itself "The New Circus," it chiefly offered equestrian and acrobatic shows, such as a chariot race or an exhibition of specially trained horses and riders. At that time, the "circus" had no orchestra seating or stage, for the elliptical arena occupied that space. Then in 1811 the owners bought an additional lot, allowing for a stage at the end of the arena, and while still presenting equestrian shows now added melodramas, patriotic pantomimes, and spectacles, all making use of the stage and the arena. In 1828, when the building adopted the name "Walnut Street Theatre," it was redesigned with the circus ring removed and replaced by orchestra seats, two tiers of balconies (with four boxes overlooking the stage) were laid out in horseshoe style and supported on cast-iron columns, and the stage provided with traps and the latest machinery. The public area also offered a restaurant and a coffeehouse. In 1865 the actor Edwin Booth and his brother-in-law bought the theater and again refurbished it inside and out. In 1920 the two balconies were replaced by a single large one cantilevered from the back wall on steel beams. The most recent refurbishment took place in 1971, restoring inside and

out many of the theater's earlier, elegant touches. In all, from 1809 until now, except for periods of reconstruction, the theater has been in continual use. See an article, "The Exterior Restoration of the Walnut Street Theatre in Philadelphia," by Martin Eli Weil, on file at the Historical Society of Pennsylvania.

2. Peter Richings (1797–1871). For an account of him, see Ireland, *Records of the New York Stage*, 1:387–89. As an actor, he was unequaled as a fop. He was also known for scolding audience members whom he saw kissing. See Joseph Whitton, *Wags of the Stage* (Philadelphia: George H. Rigby, 1902), 19–22. On the adoption, Curtis, "One Hundred Years of Grand Opera in Philadelphia," vol. 1, sec. 2.

3. Caroline Richings (1827–82). According to Durang ("The Stage," 2:361): "She made her *début* as a pianist at a [Philadelphia] Philharmonic Concert in December 1848, playing works by Liszt and Thalberg. Her execution was brilliant and her touch firm and distinct." Thus, before she discovered her voice, she already was a skilled musician. Upton, *Musical Memories*, 137–41. Ireland, *Records of the New York Stage*, 2:605, describes her as "one of the most admired stars in the country."

4. "Stock" company. In the 1840s and 1850s in the United States, most theaters had permanent companies of actors, some of whom could sing, who played a different piece each night. On occasion, visiting celebrities would play the leading roles, say, Hamlet, but the stock company would provide the scenery and secondary actors. A pianist, Benjamin C. Cross, led the company's small orchestra; see Madeira, *Music in Philadelphia*, 139–40. Later, in the 1870s and 1880s, and in part because of the expansion of the railroads, stock companies gradually were supplanted by "touring" companies that would bring into a theater its own scenery, chorus, soloists, and orchestra, and play an extended run of a single show. The last season in which a stock company was employed at the Boston Theatre, for example, was 1884–85. See Tompkins and Kilby, *History of the Boston Theatre*, 313. About *Louise Muller*, Curtis, "One Hundred Years of Grand Opera in Philadelphia," vol. 1, sec. 2, 478, states that Caroline Richings "translated it herself. Peter Richings 'adapted' it to the American stage and Dr. Cunnington arranged the orchestration."

5. Hamilton, *Philadelphia Performance Annals*, http://frankhamilton.org. Curtis, "One Hundred Years of Grand Opera in Philadelphia," vol. 1, sec. 2, 478, adds the opera *Florentine*, was "written expressly" for Caroline Richings, "by one of her ardent admirers."

6. No review in Cincinnati, see Wolz, "Opera in Cincinnati," 67: "Richings and her father, billed only as a well-known comedian, also presented comedy and melodrama during their stay in Cincinnati. The sole cast members listed for the performances were the Richings, though there must have been others. The company did introduce to the city William Vincent Wallace's popular and tuneful *Maritana* and Verdi's *Luisa Miller*." Citing the *Cincinnati Enquirer*, February 22, 1854. In Cincinnati, performances on February 24 and 25, 1854, and on November 22, 1859, see Wolz, "Opera in Cincinnati," 238, 240.

7. Schiller's play, written 1782–83, was first performed in 1784. Initially titled *Luise Müllerin*, he changed the title on the suggestion of a friend, A. W. Iffland, an outstanding actor and director. Iffland had created the role of Franz Moor, in Schiller's *Die Räuber*, the model for the evil brother Francesco in Verdi's *I masnadieri* (1847).

8. Deaths of Luisa and Rodolfo. In the play, Ferdinand/Rodolfo poisons the "cup of lemonade" that Luisa offers him, takes a sip, from which he does not suffer, and then offers the cup to her. She drinks deep and begins to die, tells the truth of the letter, after which he drinks deep. But he dies long after her and only after an angry exchange with his father, whom, as described later in the text, he ultimately forgives.

9. Durang, "The Stage," 2:361.

10. *Evening Mirror*, December 14, 1852, 2.

11. Ibid., 3.

12. Among those who rank it as a premiere: Julius Mattfeld, *A Hundred Years of Grand Opera in New York, 1825-1925* (New York: New York Public Library, 1976), 61; and Kaufman, *Verdi and His Major Contemporaries*, 374. Among those who do not: Robert Sabin, ed., *International Cyclopedia of Music and Musicians*, 9th ed. (New York: Dodd, Mead, 1964), 1238; and Alfred Loewenberg, *Annals of Opera, 1597-1940*, 2nd ed. (Geneva: Societas Bibliographica, 1955), col. 877.

13. *Albion*, July 22, 1854, 344. Not clear which *Masnadieri* aria was interpolated.

14. Though the reviews are unsigned, Lawrence, *Strong on Music*, 2:509-11, identifies some of the critics: *New York Times*, Charles Bailey Seymour; *New York Tribune*, William Henry Fry; *Courier and Enquirer*, Richard Grant White; and *Albion*, Charles Burkhardt.

15. *Albion*, July 22, 1854. The tenor was Pietro Neri-Beraldi (1828-1902). Also known as "Beraldi," he sang mostly in Italy.

16. *New York Tribune*, July 21, 1854, 5; *Albion*, July 22, 1854.

17. *New York Post*, July 21, 1854, 2; *New York Herald*, July 21, 1854, 4.

18. *New York Times*, July 21, 1854, 4; *Albion*, July 22, 1854.

19. *Courier and Enquirer*, July 21, 1854, 2.

20. *New York Post*, July 21, 1854. "Ad captandum": In rhetoric an argument "ad captandum" is one aimed to capture the naive among one's listeners or readers, and has been defined as a kind of seductive casuistry. The term's longer form is "ad captandum vulgus." Curiously, a century later, but also in the *Post* and also in a review of *Luisa Miller*, December 23, 1929, the phrase appears again: "Notable is the circumstance that the opera has no extraneous chorus to make the ad captandum appeal of the anvil, bandit, soldiers' and conspirators' choruses of other Verdi opera."

21. *Courier and Enquirer*, July 21, 1854; *New York Tribune*, July 21, 1854.

22. *New York Tribune*, July 21, 1854; *Albion*, July 22, 1854; *New York Times*, July 21, 1854.

23. *New York Times*, July 21, 1854; *New York Tribune*, July 21, 1854.

24. Verdi, letter to Salvatore Cammarano, May 17, 1848, Cesari and Luzio, *Copialettere*, 470-72. Verdi asks Cammarano to follow Schiller's ending of the scene, which he quotes in full.

25. Budden, *Operas of Verdi*, 1:422. Joseph Kerman, *Opera as Drama* (1956; repr., New York: Vintage Books, 1959), 130, states that in *Luisa Miller* "Verdi first stretched hard the stiff form inherited from Rossini and Donizetti" to model the opera "rather seriously on the play."

26. *Times*, July 21, 1854; *Albion*, July 22, 1854.

27. For example, Verdi, letter to Opprandino Arrivabene, August 29, 1872, Cesari and Luzio, *Copialettere*, 685.

28. *New York Post*, July 29, 1854, 2.

29. *Albion*, August 19, 1854, 392, and August 26, 1854, 404.

30. Cholera, see *New York Post*, July 29, 1854, 1, listing in two and a half columns the recent deaths. And according to Ruth Henderson: That summer Maretzek "contracted cholera . . . as did several other members of the company" (see Maretzek, *Further Revelations of an Opera Manager*, 30).

31. The soprano: *New York Times*, July 21, 1854, 4; *New York Post*, July 27, 1854, 1.

32. *Albion*, July 22, 1854, 344.

33. Philadelphia *Evening Bulletin*, April 3, 1857, 1; and *Public Ledger*, April 3, 1857, 3. To reveal how seriously some in the audience longed for extravagant costuming, see S. E. Martin, *Emma Abbott*, 46, 92, 93, 127.

34. Philadelphia *Evening Bulletin*, April 3, 1857.

35. San Francisco *Evening Bulletin*, May 19, 1863, 3. Quoted complete, with a review, also complete, from the *Daily Alta California*, May 19, 1863, 2, in Martin, *Verdi at the Golden Gate*, 251–52.

36. For more on "Signor Angelo's season," see chap. 4.

37. *New York Times*, July 21, 1854, 4.

38. Gatti-Casazza, *Memories*, 5, and referred to on pp. 14, 51, and 68.

39. *New York Times*, December 22, 1929, 27; *New York Post*, December 23, 1929, 15. Besides the change in the ending, the chief cuts were: second verse of Miller's act 1, scene 1 aria, "Ah! fu giusto"; the first scene in the Count's castle, with his aria, "Il mio sangue" transferred, along with some explanatory dialogue between the Count and Wurm, to the second scene in the second act. Thus, the duet for the Duchess and Rodolfo was dropped and her role, already slight, further reduced.

40. *Philadelphia Inquirer*, January 15, 1930, 8.

41. See Martin, "The Metropolitan Opera's Sunday Evening Concerts and Verdi."

42. *The Victrola Book of the Opera*, 8th ed. (Camden, NJ: RCA Victor Company, 1929), 202–3. The opera and its aria's two recordings were dropped from the 9th ed. (1936).

43. Jay Harrison, *New York Herald Tribune*, May 23, 1960, 10. For more on the Amato Company, see chap. 13.

44. I attended both performances.

45. *New York Times*, December 22, 1929.

46. The first so-called complete recording of the opera, taken from a radio performance on the radio in Rome, February 13, 1951 (the fiftieth anniversary year of Verdi's death), was issued that year by Cetra (in 2000 reissued by Warner Fonit, 8573 82645-2), but the recording had huge cuts, not only of second verses, but of whole numbers, including the unaccompanied quartet. In short, its purpose was to display the tenor, Giacomo Lauri-Volpi (1892–1979). The first truly complete recording was RCA Victor's (LSC 6168) in 1965, with Anna Moffo and Carlo Bergonzi. This was followed by one in 1976 from London Records, with Caballé and Pavarotti; and another in 1980 from Deutsche Grammophon, with Ricciarelli and Placido Domingo. By then, recordings of several live performances were also available.

47. Daniel Webster, *Philadelphia Inquirer*, May 22, 1964, 27; and Clark Larrabee, *Inquirer*, October 30, 1964, 15.

48. For Bing's background in the Verdi Renaissance in Germany and England, see this book's introduction and chapter 6.

49. *New York Times*, February 9, 1968, 54.

50. *New York Post*, February 9, 1968, 57. Toye, *Verdi*, 263: "It still stands, so to say, on its own feet as one of the most loveable of Verdi's operas." Toye also thought, 259, "Verdi himself must be given some credit for what seems to me an exceptionally good libretto." In the English-speaking world for some forty years, Toye's biography was one of the more influential.

51. *Opera*, May 1968, 371.

52. Philadelphia *Evening Bulletin*, June 2, 1968, sec. 5, 2; Jerry Etheridge, *Atlanta Constitution*, May 7, 1968, 15, and for figures on the touring company, ibid., 9.

53. Winthrop Sargeant, *New Yorker*, October 23, 1971, 167–68: "this faded opera," but he praised highly the conducting of James Levine, though adding, "At a few points, he seemed to be driving things. He could do with a little more relaxation." For more on Levine as a conductor of Verdi, see chapters 3, 15, and 6.

54. Radio audience: see the *New York Times* article on the death of the announcer Milton Cross, January 4, 1975, 26.

55. *New York Times,* July 3, 1998, E-1.

56. Philadelphia *Inquirer,* January 15, 1930.

Chapter Eleven

1. *Albion,* February 24, 1855, 91. On the importance of the *Albion* for music criticism in these years, see Grant, *Maestros of the Pen,* 10–12, 337.

2. *Morning Courier and New-York Enquirer,* February 20, 1855, 2, and February 24, 2; *New York Times,* February 22, 1855, 4; and *Albion,* March 3, 1855, 104.

3. *WGV, Rigoletto,* score, intro., xxi, col. 1: "The number of performances *Rigoletto* received during these first years is truly impressive." For examples of censorial changes in Italy, see xxi, col. 2. For a critique of the critical edition expressing modified rapture, see Porter, *Musical Events: A Chronicle, 1983–1986,* 426–28.

4. *New York Herald,* February 20, 1855, 1: "The intention had been, as the public was informed through journals, to 'popularise the opera'"—Parquet, parquet circle and second tier, one dollar, third tier, fifty cents; amphitheatre (fourth tier), twenty-five cents. Also ibid., for the premiere, "the lower part of the house was about one-fourth filled, and the attendance in the third and fourth tiers was very slim." The *New York Tribune,* however, reported "a large audience, not withstanding the counter attraction of the final appearance of Grisi and Mario at the Metropolitan Theatre" (February 20, 1855, 5). A correspondent for *Dwight's Journal of Music,* published in Boston, reported audiences for the last two performances of only "four or five hundred" (March 10, 1855, 180). *Albion,* March 3, 1855, 104.

5. *Dwight's Journal,* June 16, 1855, 87. *Boston Evening Transcript,* June 9, 1855, 2. The cut of the final duet and possible reasons for it are discussed later in the chapter.

6. *Albion,* March 3, 1855; *New York Times,* February 20, 1855, 4.

7. "Vamped up": both the *New York Herald,* February 20, 1855, and the *New York Times,* February 20, 1855, 4, used the phrase. Unger, *Dwight's Journal of Music* 6, no. 23 (March 10, 1855).

8. *Evening Post,* February 20, 1855, 2. *New York Times, February 22,* 1855, 4; *Albion,* March 3, 1855. About trombones in the Quartet: As the text later will state, the popular view of the Quartet is that it starts at "Bella figlia dell'amore," and from there to the end, Verdi did not score for trombones. He does score for them in the introductory part of the Quartet, "Un di, se ben rammentomi." I think the critic here, in talking of "the *last* [emphasis added], blatant, and obtrusive trombones in the last Quartette" is referring to trombones he heard in the "Bella figlia" part, for which Verdi did not score them.

9. People sometimes ask how Rigoletto, who in Hugo's play is called "Triboulet," got his new name. I have no contemporary source to cite, but it seems likely that among the revisions made to please the Venetian censors, which reduced François Premier, King of France, to a nameless Duke of Mantua, the jester's new name was derived from the French verb "rigoler," to jest, to have fun. And people sometimes ask: Was the Duke married? Yes. If the scenic directions for the opening of act 3 (by usual division) in Verdi's orchestral and vocal scores are followed, a portrait of the Duchess hangs on the back wall opposite that of the Duke. Though this is her only appearance in the opera, in Hugo's play the Duke makes a number of brutal references to her while preparing to rape Gilda.

10. "Too weak," *New York Times,* September 4, 1858, 4; *WGV, Rigoletto,* score, xxviii, col. 1.

11. *New York Herald,* February 20, 1855; *New York Tribune,* February 20, 1855, 5.

412 NOTES TO PP. 204–206

12. Frezzolini, who had sung also in Paris and London, in Milan had created the roles of Giselda in *I Lombardi* and Joan in *Giovanna d'Arco*. De LaGrange was an outstanding coloratura soprano with a reputation of being able to act. For a comment on the latter, see *Dwight's Journal*, 6, no. 23 (March 10, 1855). The U.S. premiere's Gilda was Apollonia Bertucca, a soprano of slighter reputation and married to Maretzek.

13. Verdi's orchestration: advertisement in *New York Herald*, November 4, 1857, 7: "original score, obtained in Paris from the composer"; critic noting: *Review and Gazette*, November 14, 1857, 355. Poor box office: *New York Herald*, November 19, 1857, 5.

14. *Philadelphia North American and United States Gazette*, January 26, 1858, 4.

15. Figures based on Hamilton's *Chronology of Opera Performances in Philadelphia*.

16. See Wolz, "Opera in Cincinnati," 85, 136.

17. Chicago: see Ira D. Glackens, *Yankee Diva: Lillian Nordica and the Golden Days of Opera* (1963; repr. New York: Coleridge Press, 1972), 118–20, and 88–89 for an account of her meeting with Verdi in Paris and singing "Caro nome" for him. For Mapleson in Kansas City, see Harlan Francis Jennings, "Her Majesty's Opera Company in Kansas City," *Opera Quarterly* 21, no. 2 (Spring 2005): 227–41. In these years, however, *Rigoletto* always lagged behind *Trovatore* and *Traviata* in Mapleson's scheduling. For example, in the three seasons of 1883 through 1885–86, at New York's Academy of Music the performances numbered *Trovatore* 7, *Traviata* 5, and *Rigoletto* 4, and on tour the gap became wider, *Traviata* 23, *Trovatore* 20, and *Rigoletto*, 12. See John Frederick Cone, *First Rival of the Metropolitan Opera* (New York: Columbia University Press, 1983), appendix 2, 192–227. For Topeka: Jennings, "Grand Opera in Kansas in the 1880s," 115, quoting the *Lance*. The opera's "one part" likely referred to Gilda, because Emma Abbott's touring company (usually about fifty people), with herself in the role, had introduced the opera (with some roles sung in Italian) to the city in March 1884. For the Abbott company, see chap. 12.

18. *New York Times*, September 4, 1858, 4; *New York Herald*, February 28, 1861, 5; *Brooklyn Daily Eagle*, March 6, 1861, 3. Kellogg, *Memoirs*, 27, 33. During these years, 1863 through 1867, in Manhattan and Brooklyn, Maretzek most frequently performed *Faust*, 55 times. Verdi's operas in Maretzek's scheduling ranked, *Trovatore*, 26; *Ernani*, 19; *Ballo*, 13, *Traviata*, 11; *Forza*, 8; and *Rigoletto*, 7. See Maretzek, *Further Revelations of an Opera Manager*, appendix 3, 139–41.

19. Prado, *La musica italiana a Cuba*, 56–58, quoting the *Gaceta*, December 4, 1857. The paper blames the cut directly on London audiences. The opera had its Cuban premiere in Havana on August 22, 1855, where it was given nine times with increasing success. The English baritone Charles Santley, *Student and Singer*, 218, records that the duet was cut in the 1864–65 season in Barcelona: Apparently, the cut was usual in England as late as 1931, for Toye, *Giuseppe Verdi*, 271, states: "Though its customary omission in English theaters may perhaps be justified on grounds of dramatic fitness, [the duet] contains some beautiful music of genuine tenderness, the harmonic treatment of her farewell being particularly felicitous."

20. *Dwight's Journal*, June 16, 1855. California *Daily Evening Bulletin*, July 2, 1860, 3. Quoted more fully in Martin, *Verdi at the Golden Gate*, 185–86; also quoted there, the *Daily Alta California*, July 2, 1860, 2. The fact that Maretzek cut the final duet for the Boston premiere (1855) as well as the Brooklyn premiere (1861) suggests that he never had it in his production, not even in the U.S. premiere in New York (February 19, 1855). But not having yet found a source who so states, I have not dared so to conclude.

21. Traditionally, many small cuts were made in the long sequence of duets in act 2 (act 1, scene 2). Give or take a measure or two, for conductors have many options for starting and ending the cuts, they are: Six measures of Rigoletto-Gilda's "Deh

non parlare," which are three measures of an appealing harmonic sequence played twice (for a critic's rage at the cut, see Spike Hughes, *Famous Verdi Operas* [London: Robert Hale, 1968], 99); the opening thirty-one measures of Rigoletto's "Ah, veglia donna," which are soon repeated in duet with Gilda; six measures toward the end of that duet that are to be sung "sempre pp"; a complicated passage for Gilda and the Duke that precedes the closing of his "È il sol dell'anima"; and some twenty-one measures of the Duke and Gilda's "Addio." I asked the conductor Victor DeRenzi if he knew any reason for these cuts, especially for that of the Rigoletto-Gilda duet, "Deh non parlare," that is to be sung "sempre pp," and which in its sudden decreased volume, harmonic sequence, and vocal line is lovely. He did not, and he ignores it, but thought it might have started as a way to spare singers, tiring at the end of a long duet, from the effort of a soft, delicate passage. Or, he added, in "the age of verismo," a movement starting at the end of the nineteenth century in Italian arts that favored "realism," repetition was scorned. And in agreement, another conductor, John Mauceri, "*Rigoletto* for the 21st century," *Opera* (October 1985): 1135–44. A 1950 RCA recording, with Leonard Warren, Erna Berger, and Jan Peerce, observes these cuts and has been reissued by Preiser Records (2001), 94052.

22. Kellogg, *Memoirs*, 36. *Dwight's Journal of Music* 6, no. 24 (March 17, 1855): 188.

23. *Max Maretzek vs. William Cauldwell and Horace P. Whitney* [publishers of the *Sunday Mercury*], Superior Court of the City of New York (New York: Wynkoop and Hallenbeck, 1867), 1–60. A copy of the trial record is in the New York Public Library.

24. Ibid., 46. In successfully holding the cross-examination to the jester and the Duke, Maretzek followed Victor Hugo's defense of the opera's morality in the latter's preface to his play. Hugo discussed at length the morality of the jester's fate, touched slightly on the King's, and not at all on the girl's. See *Three Plays by Victor Hugo*, trans. by C. Crosland and F. L. Slous (New York: Howard Fertig, 1995), 123–34. But note that Slous, in translating the setting for the first scene, omitted Hugo's direction that the *fête* should have "a little of the character of an orgy."

25. *Max Maretzek v. William Cauldwell and Horace P. Whitney*, 47. Maretzek, under oath, stated some facts about his business: on the number of press tickets issued (forty to fifty regularly), the number of tickets allowed each night to the leading singers (two or three per artist), the size of the company (200–250), the cost of the Academy each night ($250), the cost of putting on opera (about $10,000 a week), methods of operation, and so on. The verdict, ibid., 60.

26. See, Bruhn, "Taking the Private Public," 260–90, 264–70.

27. *Complete Catalogue of Sheet Music and Musical Works, 1870*, 248–49. *Musical World*, May 5, 1855, 8, favorably reviews "Over the Summer Sea."

28. For a brief history, see New Orleans archivist Belsom's article, "Verdi's *Rigoletto* in New Orleans," *New Orleans Opera Association Program*, March 2008, 17, 21. The opera's premiere in New Orleans took place on May 23, 1857, at Crisp's Gaiety Theatre, "at the conclusion of a brief season by the combined forces of the touring Corradi-Setti and Vestvali opera companies." And I extrapolated the statistic of 109 performances at the French Opera House during the years 1860–1919 from *Opera Performances in New Orleans, 1812–1919* (WPA project), which does not include performances by visiting companies that usually sang the opera in either English or Italian.

29. Count based on the chronology of Hixon, *Verdi in San Francisco, 1851–1899*, to which I have been able to make a few slight corrections and additions.

30. Count based on Hamilton's *Chronology of Opera Performances in Philadelphia*.

31. On the "cleansing" influence of Gilbert and Sullivan, see John Philip Sousa, *Marching Along* (Boston: Hale, Cushman and Flint, 1928, repr. 1941), 62. Kellogg, *Memoirs*, 81.

32. See Martin, "The Metropolitan Opera's Sunday Evening Concerts and Verdi," 24, for the list of the twenty Verdi operas from which excerpts were taken, ranked by the number sung or played. Those with a hundred or more are: *Rigoletto*, 170*; Aida*, 157; *Forza*, 153; *Trovatore*, 124; *Traviata*, 119; *Ballo*, 114; and *Don Carlo*, 100.

33. "Ideal Gilda," *New York Tribune*, November 24, 1903, 9. "Hurdy-gurdy," ibid., and *New York Sun*, November 24, 1903, 4. "One repeat," *New York Tribune*, ibid. The critic for the *New York Times*, November 24, 1903, 1, remarked, "Not more times than is usual from tenors of much smaller repute." According to biographer, Stanley Jackson, *Caruso* (New York: Stein and Day, 1972), 107, he usually sang at least three repetitions when touring in South America.

34. "Box holders," *New York Sun*, November 24, 1903, 4.

35. *New York Times*, November 24, 1903, 1. Kolodin, *Metropolitan Opera, 1883–1966*, 129. *New York Tribune*, November 24, 1903, 9.

36. Told by Peltz to Mary Jane Phillips-Matz, the Verdi biographer, who told me, November 17, 2007. As Peltz was born on May 4, 1896 (d. October 24, 1981), she presumably is reporting box-holder behavior in the early years of the new century.

37. *New York Sun*, January 24, 1904, sec. 1, 10.

38. Kellogg, *Memoirs*, 40.

39. *New York Sun*, December 3, 1903, 4. The reviewer, W. J. Henderson reveals his point of view on manners and style by calling Tosca "aristocratic." Her creator, the French playwright Victorien Sardou, whom Puccini followed, starts her in life as a goat girl, a wild savage, and hence her temperament. Nuns took her into their convent and raised her. Cimarosa, the composer, heard her sing and arranged an audition before the pope, who released her from her vows. At the time of the opera, 1800, she is singing at the Teatro Argentina in Rome—behavior most unaristocratic.

40. *New York Times*, December 3, 1903, 6.

41. Bolig, *Caruso Records*, 2, 5. On the first ten recordings, the company managed four different spellings of Caruso's name: Carusso, Caruoso, Carouso, and Caruso (32).

42. Ibid., 5. The Victor Talking Machine Co. had imported and issued in the United States in March 1903 seven of the Gramophone and Typewriter recordings, so that when Caruso arrived in New York in November of that year, he came with an exciting reputation (ibid., 11, 17).

43. Ibid., 18.

44. Tetrazzini singing Gilda: see Cone, *Oscar Hammerstein's Manhattan Opera Company*, 148, 191–92. *New York Press*, January 30, 1908, 5. On the attraction for the public of a coloratura voice, see Metropolitan manager (1910–35) Gatti-Casazza, *Memories*, 170: "Coloratura sopranos are almost in a class by themselves in their pull on the public . . . and I, frankly, do not know any reasoned explanation. When a coloratura succeeds, it is usually a sensational affair. . . . That is the will of the public. I, for example, am left cold by the florid, high voices. The public, however, goes mad when it hears the high notes."

45. Varying the ornamentation, the *Globe and Commercial Advertiser*, December 7, 1908, 7.

46. *Globe and Commercial Advertiser*, January 21, 1908, 7.

47. Julian Morton Moses, *Collectors' Guide to American Recordings, 1895–1925* (1949; repr. New York: Dover Press, 1977), 138.

48. "Largest house," Cone, *Oscar Hammerstein's Manhattan Opera Company*, 269. "Popular list," Krehbiel, *Chapters of Opera*, 370.

49. *New York Sun*, February 7, 1912, 7.

50. Ibid. See also, *New York Herald*, February 7, 1912, 8, and *New York Times*, February 7, 1912, 11.

51. "Every high note," *New York Herald*, February 7, 1912, 8, and *New York Times*, February 7, 1912, 11.

52. "Strangers," *New York Sun*, February 7, 1912, 7.

53. "Hurrah," *New York Herald*, February 7, 1912, 8.

54. For more on the San Carlo Opera Company, see chap. 12. See also appendix D.

55. The ranking is my count of Kaufman's Chronology, see *The San Carlo Opera Company: The First 13 Seasons (1913–1926)*, and appendix D.

56. Vendetta duet: the company had several baritones who could close act 3 with calls for a repeat of its final duet. Perhaps the most distinguished was Vicente Ballester (d. October 3, 1927). See Bishop, *The San Carlo Opera Company, 1913 to 1955: Grand Opera for Profit*, 2nd ed., 2 vols. (Santa Monica: Cardell Bishop, 1980), 1:46, 48, and 120. Atlanta: ibid., 1:156.

57. RCA Victor LM-6041, side 3 of a two-record, long-playing album, *Verdi & Toscanini*. Milanov surprised, Alan Blythe, *Gramophone*, June 1991, reviewing a CD reissue of the album, now GD60276, in which RCA "at this late date insist on labeling act IV" of *Rigoletto*, instead of Verdi's act 3.

58. Spike Hughes, *The Toscanini Legacy* (London: Putname, 1959), 217, a critical study of Arturo Toscanini's performances of Beethoven, Verdi, and other composers.

59. "Tantalizing," ibid., 215. "Caro nome?" Review by James Camner, *Fanfare*, March/April 1981.

60. Hughes, *The Toscanini Legacy*, 216–17. See also, Blythe, *Gramophone*, June 1991.

61. Now as a CD reissued by Preiser Records, 90452. In the accompanying booklet Kurt Malisch states that *Rigoletto* "was not only the first Verdi opera to be recorded in its entirety in 1912—a version by 'Pathé' sung in French—but also the first electric recording of a complete Verdi opera in 1927, which was produced by 'La Voce del Padrone' under the direction Carlo Sabajno. In Germany the first complete recording of a Verdi opera also was *Rigoletto* in 1944, sung in German, with Robert Heger as conductor." The typical cuts were discussed earlier in the chapter.

62. Olin Downes, *New York Times*, November 16, 1951, 21.

63. Louis Biancolli, *World-Telegram and Sun*, November 16, 1951, 21. Like Downes, he stressed first the scenery and costumes.

64. One remarkable deviation from the Berman production took place on December 22, 1951, when in place of Gueden the aging coloratura Lily Pons sang Gilda. See Kolodin, *Metropolitan Opera, 1883–1966*, "She turned up in transparent tights rather than the decorous costume decreed by Berman's décor. No one, apparently, had thought to inspect Pons's costume before she appeared on stage. . . . In any case, her appearances per season soon dwindled to a token one or two" (515).

Chapter Twelve

1. *Maritime History of New York*, for railroads and steamships, 123, 189, 207, and 219. For railroad mileage in Kansas in 1865, 1870, 1880, and 1890, see Jennings, "Grand Opera in Kansas in the 1880s," 6. Expansion of railroads, see the *Encyclopaedia Britannica* (Chicago: Encyclopaedia Britannica Press, 1946), 18, "Railroads," 936; maps in William R. Shepherd, *Historical Atlas*, 8th ed. (New York: Barnes and Noble, 1956), 208, 210; text

and map, R. P. Palmer, ed., *Atlas of World History* (New York: Rand McNally, 1957), 157, 161, 164–65.

2. On the ships, *Maritime History of New York*, 188–90; on the drawbridge at New London, 219.

3. On costumes, see S. E. Martin, *Emma Abbott*, 46, 92, 93, 127. On stock companies, Tompkins and Kilby, *History of the Boston Theatre, 1854–1901*, 313: "The season of 1884–85 proved to be an eventful one for the theatre, for it was the last in which a stock company was regularly engaged, as since that time the actors have been engaged especially for their parts in the productions which have been made, and not for the entire season."

4. On Richings, see opening of chapter 10 on *Luisa Miller*. See also, Preston, *Opera on the Road*, 252. See her appendix D, "English Opera Companies, 1847–1860," for notes on Richings, 368, 370, 371, 372, 375. See also, *New Grove Dictionary of American Music*, 4:40, entry by Dee Baily.

5. First *Trovatore* in English, Preston, *Opera on the Road*, 252. On Cooper, see ibid., 372–74 nn49, 52, 55, and Wolz, "Opera in Cincinnati," 83.

6. On Escott, Preston, *Opera on the Road*, 373–74, nn53, 57. For Escott in San Francisco, see index entries to Martin, *Verdi at the Golden Gate*.

7. Poor reviews, Preston, *Opera on the Road*, 252 and 373n52.

8. Hodson, *Alta California*, July 20, 1859, 2. In greater detail, see Martin, *Verdi at the Golden Gate*, 137 and notes.

9. Opera Theatre of St. Louis (in its program for 2005): "is dedicated to singing in English. In our particular situation we feel it is essential for presenting opera as theater which fully engages the audience." Its repertory, 1976–2005, included of Verdi: *Falstaff*, 1980, 1994; *Othello*, 1999; *Rigoletto*, 1981, 2005; and *La Traviata*, 1979, 1983, 2000. Two smaller companies favoring opera in English are Pocket Opera, San Francisco, and Opera Theatre of Northern Virginia, Arlington.

10. For size of orchestra needed for Gilbert and Sullivan in larger and smaller theaters and what instruments may be dropped or substituted, see Edmond W. Rickett and Benjamin T. Hoagland, *Let's Do Some Gilbert & Sullivan, a Practical Production Handbook* (New York: Coward-McCann, 1940), 154–58.

11. On Abbott, see W. S. B. Matthews, *A Hundred Years of Music in America* (Chicago: G. L. Howe, 1889), 230–32. Also S. E. Martin, *Emma Abbott*, 143, quoting the *Chicago Tribune*; also, 44, 46, 92–93, 173. On S. E. Martin's *Emma Abbott* and opera in Central City, Colorado, a century later, see Porter, *Music of Three More Seasons, 1977–1980*, 426–28.

12. Business woman: S. E. Martin, *Emma Abbott*, 143, Kellogg, *Memoirs*, 275.

13. "Nearer my God to Thee," see S. E. Martin, *Emma Abbott*, 34. Kellogg, *Memoirs*, 274, states the opera as *Faust*.

14. Interpolating songs into opera. Oscar Thompson, *The American Singer: A Hundred Years of Success in Opera* (New York: Dial Press, 1937), 129. Kellogg, *Memoirs*, who seldom has a good word for Abbott, 274: She "did appalling things with her art." And Jennings, "Grand Opera in Kansas in the 1880s," 27. On the generally unfavorable press, Matthews, *A Hundred Years of Music in America*, 252, and S. E. Martin, *Emma Abbott*, 170–71. Specifically in Cincinnati, Wolz, "Opera in Cincinnati," 160, 164, 178, and on the audience's love of Abbott, despite the critics, 182.

15. S. E. Martin, *Emma Abbott*, 18, 24. Deploring Abbott, 171, quoting J. Travis Quigg of *The American Musician*.

16. S. E. Martin, *Emma Abbott*, 149, quoting the *Chicago Tribune*. Debut in *La Fille du régiment*, in *New Grove Dictionary of Opera*, 1:3, entry on Abbott by H. Wiley Hitchcock, correcting dates in Thompson, *The American Singer*, 129.

17. Refuses to sing Violetta. S. E. Martin, *Emma Abbott*, 37. On her force of character, Kellogg, *Memoirs*, 274.

18. "First opera in Kansas": Jennings, "Grand Opera in Kansas in the 1880s," 54; and "reigned supreme": ibid., 146.

19. Ibid., 29.

20. Topeka's new house, Jennings, "Grand Opera in Kansas in the 1880s," 83–84. "Thirty-five opera houses," S. E. Martin, *Emma Abbott*, 98.

21. Abbott's orchestra. Jennings, "Grand Opera in Kansas in the 1880s," 49; but in Cincinnati at least one night, for Gounod's *Romeo and Juliet*, only three instruments, flute, violin, and piano, see Wolz, "Opera in Cincinnati," 161, citing the *Cincinnati Enquirer*, December 10, 1879. Mapleson's orchestra, Jennings, "Her Majesty's Opera Company in Kansas City," 229.

22. Abbott as Violetta, S. E. Martin *Emma Abbott*, 38. Kellogg, *Memoirs*, 70, felt differently about Abbott's interpretation: "The critics said that she was so afraid of allowing it to be suggestive that she made it so, whereas I apparently never thought of that side of it and consequently never forced my audiences to think of it either." And she quoted, without citation, a critic who wrote: "Abbott expects to make *Traviata* acceptable very much as she would make a capon acceptable. She is always afraid of the words. So she substitutes her own." But the quotation does not record the changes.

23. "Home Sweet Home," Jennings, "Grand Opera in Kansas in the 1880s," 27.

24. For a minute description of Abbott's costumes for *Trovatore*, see S. E. Martin, *Emma Abbott*, 46–47: "the most magnificent ever worn in that opera . . . [apparently for Leonora's first appearance]. . . . Strings of pearls and gold-lined beads hung from the throat to the knees . . . [and presumably for the interrupted wedding scene]. . . . The Trovatore 'character gown' or the one bearing the colors and crest of the House of Trovatore is the Lion dress of crimson, white, black and gold, in satin and velvet. The petticoat . . ."

25. Jennings, "Grand Opera in Kansas in the 1880s," 230, citing *Kansas City Evening Star*, February 26, 1884, 4.

26. Thompson, *The American Singer*, 130.

27. Jennings, "Grand Opera in Kansas in the 1880s," 232–33, 239–40.

28. Quaintance Eaton, *Opera Caravan: Adventures of the Metropolitan on Tour, 1883–1956* (New York: Farrar, Straus and Cudahy, 1957), 188–90. Note Eaton's answer to the question, What constituted a touring Metropolitan Opera Company? "In earlier days, the traveling unit may have been called Henry E. Abbey's Italian Grand Opera. . . . But the words 'from the Metropolitan Opera House' were invariably appended" (xiv).

29. To raise the curtain: ibid., 14–15. For discussion of total debt, see Krehbiel, *Chapters of Opera*, 110–11. Abbey pays off final dollar, *Musical Courier*, January 18, 1888, 36, which states this debt totaled $283,000.

30. Atlanta guarantees, Eaton, *Opera Caravan*, 146, 151.

31. Ibid., xiv, quoting Francis Robinson of the Metropolitan staff.

32. Ibid.

33. The chief sources for the San Carlo Opera Company are: The copyrighted typescript history in two volumes by Cardell Bishop, *The San Carlo Opera Company, 1913 to 1955: Grand Opera for Profit*, 2nd ed. (Santa Monica: Author, 1980); Thomas G. Kaufman, *The San Carlo Opera Company: The First 13 Seasons (1913–1926)* (pvt. printing) (See appendix D). Also, Jim McPherson, "Before the Met: The Pioneer Days of Radio Opera, Part 1 an Overview," *Opera Quarterly* 16, no. 1 (Winter 2000), and "Part 3, Cesare Sodero, the Music Man," *Opera Quarterly* 16, no. 3 (Summer 2000). And, to a lesser extent, Fortune

T. Gallo, *Lucky Rooster: The Autobiography of an Impresario* (New York: Exposition Press, 1967). I am extremely grateful to Thomas Kaufman for copies of Bishop's book and of his own 106-page chronology, which, despite its subtitle, which specifies 1913–26, records performances through January 1929.

34. Seat prices, Bishop, *San Carlo Opera Company*, 1:31, 88, 98, 122, 165. Gallo's speech, *Musical America*, October 2, 1926, vol. 46, 11; the three hundred performances: Bishop, *San Carlo Opera Company*, 2:12.

35. The *Aida* spectacular: Bishop, *San Carlo Opera Company*, 1:38; Gallo, *Musical America*, October 2, 1926, 152–53. Gallo and the *American*, August 17, 1919, sec. 1, 10, report an audience of 50,000; the *New York Herald*, August 17, 1919, sec. 1, pt. 2, 7, of 45,000; and the *New York Times*, August 17, 1919, 22, of 30,000. Curiously, no one states the size of the orchestra. The *American*, above, quotes Gallo to say expenses totaled approximately $35,000, receipts $65,000, and that $30,000 was given to the earthquake victims. Shortly after the performance the Speedway was replaced by a commercial housing development.

36. Radio, McPherson, "Before the Met," Part 1:8, 11, and "Part 3, Cesare Sodero," 413. Also, Bishop, *San Carlo Opera Company*, 2:21, 59, 88. See entry on Radio, *New Grove Dictionary of Opera*, 3:1212.

37. The *Pagliacci* movie: Gallo, *Lucky Rooster*, 221–26. Also, Ken Wlaschin, *Encyclopedia of Opera on Screen: A Guide to More Than 100 years of Opera Films, Videos, and DVDs* (New Haven: Yale University Press, 2004), 526. The Ben-Hur Stables specialized in furnishing circus animals to theatrical companies.

38. Harmonica and conducting, Gallo, *Lucky Rooster*, 29, 144, and he claimed, "a good working knowledge of music" (69).

39. On orchestra, Bishop, *San Carlo Opera Company*, 1:27; on chorus, Gallo, *Lucky Rooster*, 144–46: In 1916, in St. Louis, he added sixty-five local recruits to his chorus, one of whom was Helen Traubel. Also, Bishop (1:123), for augmented chorus for a two-week season in San Francisco in 1927.

40. Scenery. *Romeo and Juliet*, Bishop, *San Carlo Opera Company*, 1:158–59. In a 1921 *Forza* (ibid., 54), during the war scene a wall collapsed, which was at least "more logical" than when Alvaro dropped his pistol at center stage (killing the Marquis), and "a puff of smoke floated from the wings at the left." Also from *Forza* in 1935 (119): Alvaro carried into the hospital on a litter, accompanied by a brand-new, brass-buckled 1926 suitcase. And in 1944, in the finale of *Aida*, a kneeling priestess lost her balance, tipped into the tomb, was caught by a sturdy Radames, and pushed back up, with some aid from Aida, without either principal missing a note. See Bishop, *San Carlo Opera Company*, 2:65.

41. Language problems with *Lohengrin*, performed forty-three times in its first sixteen seasons: In 1920–21, sung in Italian, see Bishop, *San Carlo Opera Company*, 1:47; in 1921–22, in English and Italian (56); same season, in English, Italian, French and German (60); in 1925–26, in Italian and German (107); same season, Italian and English (110); and in 1932–33, in German and English (139).

42. Wages, ibid. (2:15). Nineteen million in thirty years, *New York Times*, obituary of Gallo, March 29, 1970, 73. Bishop, *San Carlo Opera Company*, 2:85, quotes with approval an estimate by *Musical America Yearbook* 66 (February 1946), 367, of 16.5 million until then.

43. The Century Company. For a history of its brief existence, see Krehbiel, *More Chapters of Opera*, 176ff.

44. For the failure of the National Opera Company in San Francisco in 1915, see chap. 2. Gallo lucky: Bishop, *San Carlo Opera Company*, 1:5.

45. Francis D. Perkins, "A Half-Century of Opera," *Musical America* 68 (February 1948): 23.

46. Decline in reporting, Bishop, *San Carlo Opera Company*, 1:128, 162.

47. On Salmaggi (1886–1975). The New York Public Library, Performing Arts Branch, Clipping File on "Salmaggi-Chicago Opera Co." Article on Salmaggi, by Gordon Schendel, *Colliers*, October 19, 1946; and obituary, *New York Times*, September 6, 1975. "Perversely," Jim McPherson, "Before the Met, Part 3," 407–26. The Aida performances, Schendel, *Colliers*, October 19, 1946, 32. The NAACP award, *New York Times* obituary.

48. "Opera Conference Meets in New York," *Musical America* 76 (April 1956): 3.

49. *Opera America, Annual Field Report, 1997* (Washington, DC: Opera America, 1998), 23. In the 1998–99 season (25), the ten most frequently produced operas: *Bohème, Butterfly, Carmen, Traviata, Rigoletto, Tosca, Barber, Don Giovanni, Faust, Marriage of Figaro.*

50. Kolodin, *Metropolitan Opera, 1883–1966*, 11.

51. Ibid., 6; Krehbiel, *Chapters of Opera*, 110.

52. Kolodin, *Metropolitan Opera, 1883–1966*, 10–12.

53. Bolig, *Caruso Records*, 13. Farrar's guarantee was $17,000 for ten years, and Scotti's, $6,000 for five. For Farrar's films, see Wlaschin, *Encyclopedia of Opera on Screen*, 230–32.

54. Kolodin, *Metropolitan Opera, 1883–1966*, 30–31.

55. Ibid., 28–29.

56. Ibid., 32.

57. See Eleanor Robson Belmont, *The Fabric of Memory* (New York: Farrar, Straus and Cudahy, 1957), 265–69. In her published account, she gives great credit for support to Cornelius N. Bliss and mentions Allen Wardwell only in passing. No doubt the praise for Bliss was justified, but also it was politic, for his son Anthony was already an outstanding director of the company and soon would become chairman of the board. But in the early 1960s, when I was a director on the board of the Guild, I had several talks with Mrs. Belmont about the trials of starting it, and she said something like this: "The artists on our committee were full of enthusiasm, but had little practical to offer. And the money-bags of Wall Street [her exact phrase] were all for giving up. The only one who consistently and continually supported me was Allen Wardwell, who spoke up at every meeting."

58. Kolodin, *Metropolitan Opera, 1883–1966*, 33. In the Guild in the early 1960s the figure of one hundred thousand members was much touted, perhaps more in hope than in fact. But Kolodin's figure of sixty thousand is too low.

59. Belmont's stage name was Eleanor Robson. She married August Belmont Jr., in 1910, left the stage for him, and named his racehorse "Man-o'-War." See Belmont, *The Fabric of Memory*, 90.

60. Kolodin, *Metropolitan Opera, 1883–1966*, 37.

61. Maretzek, *Crotchets and Quavers*, 332–35; in *Sharps and Flats*, 12–13; and in *Further Revelations of an Opera Manager*, 33, 95.

62. Kolodin, *Metropolitan Opera, 1883–1966*, 37.

63. Ibid., 40.

64. Eaton, *Opera Caravan*, 145.

65. Volunteer work, *Opera America, Annual Field Report*, 35, and contributions from the public, 31.

66. Perkins, "A Half-Century of Opera," 460, concluding sentence.

67. The flood of books was astonishing. Just on Verdi, the man—for books and articles on his music are too numerous to cite—after American editions of Werfel and Toye appeared in the 1940s, American writers published four biographies of Verdi in the

years 1955–63: by T. R. Ybarra in 1955; also in 1955 by E. Abbott, an abridged translation of Carlo Gatti's two-volume life; by Vincent Sheehan in 1958; and by George W. Martin in 1963. And in 1962 appeared an American edition of the Englishman Frank Walker's *The Man Verdi* (New York: Knopf).

    68. Kolodin, *Metropolitan Opera*, 129.

    69. *New York Tribune* (presumably Charles A. Dana), June 14, 1847, 2.

Chapter Thirteen

    1. Desire for novelties, see Preston, *Opera on the Road*, 168, 170, 201; and Ritter, *Music in America*, 20.

    2. Report in *Revue et Gazette musicale*, December 12, 1839, 535; advertisement of publication, December 29, 1839, 588; and review, January 16, 1840, 5. See Marcello Conati, "*L'Oberto, Conte di San Bonifacio*, in due recensioni straniere poco note e in una lettera inedita di Verdi," in *Atti del Congresso #1 Internazionale di Studi Verdiani* (July 1966, pub. 1969), 67–92, for a discussion of the opera's success and significance of these two foreign reports. For translations of excerpts of the reviews in the *Allgemeine* and in Milan's *La Fama*, see William Weaver, *Verdi: A Documentary Study* (London: Thames and Hudson, 1977), 152–53.

    3. It is striking that Antonietta Rainieri-Marini sang the role of Leonora in all the Italian performances, and that her husband, Ignazio Marini, a leading bass of the day, sang in the La Scala premiere and Barcelona productions. The scholar Roger Parker suggests that Rainieri-Marini "was using the work as an *opera di baule*, a piece created for her in which she was assured of some vocal success. It is hard to imagine that she was not the moving force behind each occasion she re-created the role." And he adds, "We can guess that 'singer-patronage' was again involved [in Barcelona], as this time Ignazio Marini, the husband of Rainieri-Marini, repeated his interpretation of Oberto." Parker thus implies that the opera's success, as opposed to the singers', was less than substantial. See, Parker, "'Infin che un brando vindice': from *Ernani* to *Oberto*," *Verdi Newsletter*, no. 12 (1984): 6. To the contrary, Budden, in his discussion of the opera (citing Conati, "*L'Oberto, Conte di San Bonifacio*") summarizes reasons to think that, at least in Milan, the success was real and on the music's merits, see *Operas of Verdi*, 1:51. Also, in his one-volume *Verdi* (New York: Random House-Vintage, 1987), 16, he concludes of the Milan performances: "In fact the opera created a mild sensation." For the casts of the various productions, 1839–42, see Kaufman, *Verdi and His Major Contemporaries*, 265. Kaufman also records performance in Zara, December 1, 1847, and Malta, in March 1860, both without Antonietta or Ignazio Marini.

    4. See Ware and Lockard, *P. T. Barnum Presents Jenny Lind*, 48, 88, 90, 116. Also, C. G. Rosenberg, *Jenny Lind in America* (New York: Stringer and Townsend, 1851), 201, 204. Salvi also had created the role of Edoardo in Verdi's second opera, *Un giorno di regno*, at La Scala, Milan, September 5, 1840. In the early 1850s Salvi sang frequently in the United States; for a favorable review in *I Puritani*, see *New York Times*, January 28, 1852. For a description of his self-regard and imperial business methods, see Maretzek, *Crotchets and Quavers*, 163–67.

    5. Aside from gushings over Lind, newspaper reports and even program announcements are skimpy, but Salvi clearly scheduled "Spirto gentil" more often than other arias. For example, for five concerts in New York, May 7–16, 1851, he sang it in the first and fourth; "Cujus Animam," from Rossini's *Stabat Mater*, in the second; "Ciel, che feci!"

in the third; and an aria from Otto Nicolai's *Il templario* (based on Walter Scott's *Ivan-hoe*) in the fifth. In Boston, for his solo aria he sang "Ciel, che feci!" on June 18, 1851, and possibly again two days later when the program reportedly was repeated (but not reviewed). Again in Boston, on December 1, 1851, he sang a well-known *romanza* from *I Lombardi*, which drew a comment. Reported the *Boston (Morning) Journal* the next day: "The touching and plaintive aria 'La Mia Letizia' . . . was truly one of the gems of the evening, and though not received with boisterous demonstration and applause, yet was duly appreciated by the most discriminating portion of the audience." The aria, though tied to one emotion, develops musically in a way unusual for the time, avoiding the expected reprise of the opening idea in favor of a coda derived from it, and perhaps this unexpected turn left the *un*discriminating *un*appreciative.

6. Loewenberg, *Annals of Opera, 1507–1940*, col. 804, reports a concert performance of *Oberto* in Chicago on an unspecified day in October 1903. But Kaufman, *Verdi and His Major Contemporaries*, 263n, states the event "could not be confirmed by an examination of the Chicago papers for that month." A "scene" of the opera was sung by the Metropolitan Opera Studio (a training group for young singers) sometime before February 1966, when the fact was reported in a single sentence in *Opera* 17, no. 2 (February 1966), 151. The Metropolitan's Archives, however, have no record of *which* scene was sung (though in the circumstance the quartet seems most likely), but in any case it would have been neither staged nor accompanied by an orchestra. Bierley, *Incredible Band of John Philip Sousa*, reports for the year 1893 performances of an unidentified excerpt of *Oberto*, never repeated.

7. Verdi to Arrigo Boito, February 17, 1889: "Try to imagine whether our audience with tastes so different from those of fifty years ago, would have the patience to listen to the two long acts of *Oberto!*" *The Verdi-Boito Correspondence*, ed. Marcello Conati and Mario Medici (Chicago: University of Chicago Press), with a new introduction by Conati, with the English-language edition prepared by William Weaver, 1994), 131. For a list of letters by Verdi expressing his distress at the thought of a revival, see *Verdi's* Falstaff *in Letters and Contemporary Reviews*, ed. and trans. Hans Busch (Bloomington: Indiana University Press, 1997), 324n2.

8. Celebratory performances. For example, in Parma, 1913, hundredth of Verdi's birth; in Busseto and in Buenos Aires, in 1939, hundredth of opera's premiere; and in Milan and Turin, in 1951, fiftieth of Verdi's death. Some of the 1951 radio broadcasts (of all the operas except *Alzira*, *Corsaro*, *Jérusalem*, and *Stiffelio*) also were issued as commercial recordings by the Italian firm of Cetra—though not *Oberto*. Sold internationally, these recordings had an important role in exciting the Verdi Renaissance during the second half of the century.

9. The Amato completed a fifty-third season in May 2001, the centennial of Verdi's death, with sixteen performances of *Falstaff*. For its 2006–7 season it offered six operas, including *Rigoletto*, *La Forza*, and *Falstaff*, for a total of seventy-three performances. Tickets then cost $35; for students, children under twelve, or those over sixty-five, $28. The company, completing sixty-one years (and with Amato turned eighty-eight), gave its final performance, *Le nozze di Figaro*, on Sunday, May 31, 2009. See announcement of closing, *New York Times*, January 13, 2009, C-3, and review of the last performance, *Times*, June 2, 2009, C-1.

10. It is not clear to what music Kupferberg referred by this "charming duet for sisters in misery." Possibly he meant the allegro introduction to the trio that precedes the finale of act 1. For many this is the first number in the opera to rouse interest. There is also a rather brief moment in act 2 when the two women are onstage together, and though each sings of misery, they do not sing together. Or there is a full-blown duet for

them that is not included in the published score but exists in Verdi's hand as an appendix to the autograph manuscript. When it was composed, before or after the premiere, is not clear. It is almost never included in performances and probably was not inserted into Amato's production. It can be heard as an appendix on the Philips recording (454-472-2, 1997) of *Oberto*, with Samuel Ramey (O), Maria Guleghina (L), Violeta Urmana (C), Stuart Neill (R); conductor, Neville Marriner.

11. Kupferberg, the *Trib, New York*, February 23, 1978. The *Trib*, a morning daily paper (except Saturday, Sunday, and holidays) was founded in 1978 by a merger of the *Journal American, Sun*, and *Herald Tribune*. It started publishing January 9, 1978, and ceased April 5, 1978—sixty-two issues.

12. First released in 1977. Reissued by Italia/Fonit Cetra in 1994, with Simon Estes (O), Angeles Gulin (L), Viorica Cortez (C), and Umberto Grilli (R), conductor, Zoltàn Peskó.

13. Orfeo, 1984, with Rolando Panerai (O), Ghena Dimitrova (L), Ruza Baldani (C), Carlo Bergonzi (R); conductor, Lamberto Gardelli.

14. "J. M.," *Fanfare*, July/August 1985, 285. For some contrary opinions, see Budden, *Operas of Verdi*, 1:51.

15. Crushing bore: Donald Dierks, *San Diego Union*, March 11, 1985. See also Valerie Scher, *San Diego Tribune*, March 11, 1985: "The 1839 work is musically moribund, creatively comatose, a long-forgotten footnote in the career of the great composer. Compared to his later masterpieces, *Oberto*, is very nearly dead." A worthy effort: Margaret Rose, *La Jolla Light*, March 14, 1985. Also, *San Diego Reader*, March 14, 1985: "It has some fine moments . . . and it is of great interest to be able to hear the first major work of a master composer in a performance that does it justice."

16. *Los Angeles Times*, pt. 4, March 11, 1985, and *Opera*, June 1985, 645.

17. *New York Times*, July 27, 1986. In the review page includes some criteria for what makes a good conductor of Verdi: "The conductor [La Selva] is an essentialist who lets the melodies flow and breathe but rarely ventures far away from a steady beat. All is energy and propulsion: each aria and ensemble had a clear beginning, middle and end." Cf. chap. 3, n71, and chap. 6, n85.

18. The cycle was completed in the summer of 2001 with park performances of *Aida, Otello*, and *Falstaff*. On January 27, 2001, to mark the hundredth anniversary of Verdi's death, La Selva conducted the *Requiem* in Carnegie Hall, a performance of which the *Times* critic Paul Griffiths, January 29, reported: "Mr. La Selva was the man for the job. Few conductors in the world can have as deep, full and long an experience with Verdi's scores. . . . It is specially remarkable to find a conductor who combines high musical standards with a populism equally true to Verdi's ideals. Like the summer park performances, this *Requiem* found a mixed audience—cognoscenti, children, tourists toting cameras, people prone to clap in the 'wrong' places—united by happiness in being there, enjoying the music and the occasion. And Mr. La Selva did them proud."

19. *New York Times*, July 8, 1994, C3.

20. *New York Observer*, July 18–25, 1994, 19.

21. *Washington Post*, April 9, 1999, C7.

22. Pippin Pocket Opera, after two seasons as a private company, was incorporated as a nonprofit organization with Pippin as artistic director in 1977. Its season can vary greatly, but usually runs from February through June and can be staged in as many as five different theaters in the San Francisco Bay Area. For more on Pocket Opera, see chap. 14.

23. The Sarasota company totals the operas at thirty-three by counting any important revision a separate work. Thus, *Le trouvère* and *Il trovatore* are two operas, though the French title is merely the Italian translated. Nevertheless, for *Le trouvère*, staged at the Opéra in Paris, Verdi made some important changes in the music: chiefly, he revised much of the orchestration, lengthened slightly the final scene, and composed a ballet on themes from the opera, placing it after the soldier's chorus in act 3. The company's Verdi Cycle, running from 1989 to 2013, the latter the bicentennial of Verdi's birth, reached midpoint in 2001. In addition to the two operas scheduled for that year, it also performed the *Requiem*, the *Stabat Mater* and (in concert) the three appendix arias to *Oberto* as well as re-creating the concert Toscanini played at La Scala, February 1, 1901, to commemorate Verdi's death five days earlier. In addition to the operas, the company intends to perform in concert all of Verdi's other works in whatever form.

24. Author's sampling. I was in the opera house for four days in March and talked with many people.

25. *St. Petersburg Times*, March 22, 2001.

26. *South Florida Sun-Sentinel*, March 22, 2001.

27. The quartet for many is the musical high point of the opera, and Budden, in his *Verdi*, 16, calls it "the most obviously Verdian moment in the opera."

28. *Sarasota Herald Tribune*, March 13, 2001.

29. For a discussion of the importance of vocal contrast, see Baldini, *Story of Giuseppe Verdi*, 53, who cites *Nabucco* as the key opera. And Budden, *Operas of Verdi*, 1:34, 147, who cites *Ernani*. Though scholars tend to shun speculation on the importance to Verdi's artistry of his daughter's death (and later, of his son and his wife), journalists, seeking human interest, fly to it. An interesting variation of the speculation appears in Eric A. Plaut's article "Fathers and Daughters in Verdi's Operas." Plaut sees that "the fatal consequence of the father-daughter relationships already appears in *Oberto* . . . [and] therefore precede[s] the years 1838 to 1840." Analyzing Verdi's psyche, he suggests "that his sister was a critical figure for him," arguing with many references to the operas the possible reasons and consequences for Verdi's art. The sister, Giuseppa, was two years younger than Verdi and died at age seventeen. See *Medical Problems of Performing Artists*, March 1986, pp. 30–34.

30. My view that Oberto is more of a baritone than bass—despite the vocal score's designation of him as a bass—is supported by some but contested by others; see the letter of protest in *Opera* 58, no. 7 (July 2007). To my stated point about father-daughter duets, I will add a word about vocal categories. Roughly speaking, in opera in the eighteenth century there were four: soprano, alto, tenor, bass. The designation "baritone" came into use and was commonly understood to be something different from a bass only in the early nineteenth century. I believe therefore that Verdi in *Oberto*, even if he did designate the role for bass, was simply using the terminology then current though already hearing and creating what soon would become known as "the Verdi baritone." For a brief discussion of the vocal category, see the entry "baritone" in *The New Grove Dictionary of Opera*. Also, William Clifford Goold, "The Verdian Baritones: A Study of Six Representative Operas" (PhD diss., University of Kentucky, 1981), 1–7, quotes at length a number of scholars, Henry Pleasants, Julian Budden, Donald Grout, and others, on the emergence of the baritone voice and category. See discussion on this point in chap. 5.

31. DeRenzi to the author, April 29, 2001.

Chapter Fourteen

1. Trans. by Budden, *Operas of Verdi*, 1:71–72, citing Franco Abbiati, *Giuseppe Verdi*, 4 vols. (Milan: Ricordi, 1959), 1:352–53. Weaver, *Verdi: A Documentary Study*, 153–54, translates the review of *La Moda*, September 17, 1840, which puts much of the blame for the "fiasco" on the singers: "Finally, a singer's indifference or negligence, even in an unsuccessful Opera, can also be considered a chief element in its failure."

2. Three smaller theaters: the San Benedetto (Venice), the Teatro Valle (Rome), and the Teatro Nuovo (Naples). The San Benedetto, built in 1756 and several times restored, was torn down in 1951 and replaced by a cinema. Inasmuch as one of the city's larger theaters was La Fenice (capacity 1,500), the San Benedetto, as one of the city's smaller, probably was less than one thousand, and perhaps even less than five hundred. The Teatro Valle (Rome), likewise small, and used primarily for *opera buffa*, by 1860 increasingly staged only spoken drama. The Teatro Nuovo (Naples), by 1880 was turning to plays and variety shows. It lasted until 1935 when, after a fire, it revived as a cinema.

3. The Parma production, using sketches from La Scala's archives, reproduced the opera's 1840 scenery, which the American critic William Weaver reported to be "lovely." He added: "With adequate casting, the work is never less than agreeable, even if it is never first-rate Verdi. There are two surprising things to me, about *Un giorno di regno*. One is that it almost never sounds the least bit like Verdi (it often sounds like Rossini and Donizetti, and even like Bellini); and the other is the work's astonishing self-confidence. It is a completely skilful, professional job." *Opera* 14, no. 12 (December 1963): 825–26.

4. For example, Donald Pippin of Pocket Opera, who (as will be shown) did much for the opera in the United States, described the recording as "the surprise hit of the [Cetra] series. . . . The proof is right there: the opera sparkles from beginning to end." Pippin, "Turning Opera into English," a talk given at the Bocce Café in San Francisco, February 22, 1998. Similarly, Andrew Porter, in a review of the Philips recording of the opera (1974) that offered a glittering international cast, preferred the older, with mostly Italian singers. "The new one lacks any whiff of the theater, of glance and gesture conjured up by the delivery of the music. . . . It is partly a matter of using the words and largely a matter of inflecting the musical phrases more freely, more merrily." Porter, *High Fidelity Magazine*, January 1975, 73–74. The Cetra recording, which cuts most repeats, runs 102 minutes and was reissued by Nuovo Fonit Cetra in 2000. Cast: Renato Capecchi (B), Lina Pagliughi (M), Laura Cozzi (G), Sesto Bruscantini (K), Cristiano Dalamangas (T), Juan Oncina(E); cond. Alfredo Simonetto. The Philips recording, 422 429-2, Ingvar Wixel (B), Fiorenza Cosotto (M), Jessye Norman (G), José Carreras (E), and cond., Lamberto Gardelli.

5. Romani took the story from *Le Faux Stanislas* (Paris, 1808) by Alexandre Vincent Pineu-Duval, and Gyrowetz used the play's title for his opera, *Il finto Stanislao*. For Verdi's changes in the libretto, see Roger Parker, "*Un giorno di regno*, from Romani's Libretto to Verdi's Opera," *Studi Verdiani* (Parma: Istituto di Studi Verdiani, 1983), 2:38–58. Page 40: "Whole scenes are omitted, others added, a good deal of secco recitative is cut and a number of aria or ensemble texts recast or completely rewritten."

6. Black in his article on Romani in *The New Grove Dictionary of Opera*. He also wrote *The Italian Romantic Libretto: A Study of Salvadore Cammarano* (Edinburgh: University Press, 1984).

7. Played but not sung. A choreographer, John Cranko, had used excerpts of the opera's music (reorchestrated by Charles Mackerras) for his Verdi ballet *The Lady and the Fool*, first presented by the Sadler's Wells Ballet (later Royal Ballet) in Oxford, England,

on February 25, 1954. The next year Sadler's Wells, coming to the United States for a five-week season at the Metropolitan Opera House, gave the ballet a New York premiere on September 14, 1955. Soon after, much of the ballet's music (including snippets from *Un giorno*) was made into a suite, recorded by London Records and sold throughout the United States. The ballet entered the repertory of the Stuttgart Ballet in 1961 and of the Royal Danish Ballet in 1971. Complete and in excerpts, its music has been issued on other recordings, see *Fanfare*, November/December 2004, 297.

Also, in 1954, but quite independently, the Metropolitan Opera's choreographer, Zachary Solov, created a Verdi ballet, *Vittorio*, which included music from *Un giorno* (orchestrated by the Metropolitan's assistant conductor Julius Berger). The ballet was used as a curtain raiser for *Salome*, with its premiere on December 15, 1954, and given, in all, six times. See, *Opera News* 19, no. 9 (January 3, 1955): 12–14. And in the Metropolitan's *Ernani* (1956), the conductor, Dimitri Mitropoulos, included a wedding ballet with some music from *Un giorno*. See chap. 3.

8. For a brief history of the Amato Opera, see chap. 13.

9. *New York Herald Tribune*, June 20, 1960, 8.

10. *New York Times*, June 20, 1960, 34.

11. Ibid., June 2, 1972, 29.

12. The Bel Canto company produced operas from 1969 through 1989, opening with *Rigoletto* and closing with Udo Zimmerman's *White Rose* (1967). Mostly it offered operas currently little known, such as Ludwig Spohr's *Zemire und Azore* (1819), which apparently had no performance anywhere between 1885 and Bel Canto's revival in 1980. For a brief history of the company through 1972 and of several of its colleagues in New York, see Harvey E. Phillips, *New York Times*, October 7, 1973, sec. II, 15; and to 1985, George W. Martin, "New York's Smaller Opera Companies, *Opera* 36, no. 9 (September 1985): 1001–5. The company published a *Newsletter*, and the March 1974 issue concerned the production of *Un giorno*. The cast included Stephanie Sundine (Giulietta), Jon Garrison (Edoardo), and Eugene Green (the Treasurer), all of whom had careers in opera, as did Cynthia Auerbach, the production's musical director. Bel Canto's founder and first artistic director and producer was Theodore Sieh.

13. On the Bel Canto audience, author's telephone interview with the production's Giulietta, Stephanie Sundine, July 19, 2001. For reviews of Saint Saëns's *Henry VIII* and Paisiello's *Il barbiere di Siviglia*, see *New York Times*, April 22, 1974, 43, and July 1, 1974, 42.

14. *Oakland Tribune*, August 5, 1975.

15. *San Francisco Examiner*, August 4, 1975.

16. *San Francisco Chronicle*, August 5, 1975, 35.

17. Paul Emerson, *Palo Alto Times*, June 16, 1978. Also C. E. Maves, reviewing the repeat performance, July 25, 1978.

18. Pippin, "Turning Opera into English," February 22, 1998, at the Bocce Café in San Francisco, site of the Old Spaghetti Factory.

19. Marilyn Tucker, *San Francisco Chronicle*, February 15, 1981, Datebook, 38, and February 17, 1981, Datebook, 43.

20. Reviews from 1983: Karen Smith, Palo Alto *Peninsula Times Tribune*, July 19, performance at Marines Memorial Theater in San Francisco (capacity 648); Janet Livingstone, *Berkeley Gazette*, March 31, performance at the Julia Morgan Theatre, Berkeley (capacity 350), opening an eight-week season; and Livingstone, *Berkeley Gazette*, August 17, noting a radio broadcast of the opera on FM-KALW from the stage of the Marines' Memorial Theatre. From 1984: Marilyn Tucker, *San Francisco Chronicle*, and Robert A. Masullo, *Sacramento Bee*, both April 2. In 1999, Pocket Opera produced the opera at the

Florence Gould Theatre of the California Palace of the Legion of Honor (capacity 316), and performances were not reviewed, presumably because critics were more interested in the premiere of Pippin's *Ernani* and the first revival (after 1998) of his *Gang of Bandits* (Verdi's *I masnadieri*). Though some people detest Pippin's productions, more love them, and for sure he has brought many to like opera.

21. The San Diego annual Verdi Festival, opening in August 1978 with performances of the *Requiem* and *Aida*, had financial troubles, canceled its 1983 season, and closed after 1984, though presenting its final production in March 1985 as part of the company's regular season. Typically, the festival offered two operas, one familiar, one less well-known. For its operas performed, see chap. 2.

22. *Los Angeles Times,* June 23, 1981, pt. VI, 1.

23. See review by Donald Dierks, *San Diego Union,* June 22, 1981, A-16, and by Preston Turegand, the *San Diego Tribune,* June 22. The former thought the staging too slapstick "for a piece that has only melodic facility and amusing charm to recommend it," and yet "with all warts and blemishes, the opera is one that any serious opera goer would want to hear." The latter called the production "a pleasant triumph." Both admired Porter's translation.

24. At Lehman College Theatre, the Bronx, on April 29 and 30, 1983; and the Hunter College (now Danny and Sylvia Kaye) Playhouse, Manhattan, on May 6 and 7, 1983. The translators were Mark Herman and Ronnie Apter. For a history of the Bronx Opera company to 1972, see Phillips, *New York Times,* October 7, 1973, II, 15:1; and Martin, "New York's Smaller Opera Companies."

25. *New York Times,* May 12, 1983, C23.

26. *Washington Post,* May 8, 1993; also, Desiree Mays, *Intermission* (June 1993), 18: "The libretto translation is definitely of our time with 1990s puns and humor, but it worked well." The translators were Mark Herman and Ronnie Apter.

27. Allan Kozinn, *New York Times,* July 16, 1994, 12. For a brief account of the New York Grand Opera's cycle of Verdi, see chap. 13.

28. From Verdi's "Autobiographical Account," written at Verdi's home in Sant' Agata at the request of his publisher, Giulio Ricordi. Dated, October 19, 1879.

29. Budden, *Operas of Verdi,* 1:74. For Weaver on the score's "professionalism": see his article "Parma: The Best Verdi Celebration," *Opera* 14, no. 12 (December 1963): 825–26.

30. Verdi, letter to Tito Ricordi, February 4, 1859, Cesari and Luzio, eds., *Copialettere,* 556–57.

31. For example, in the years 1998 through 2004, in Europe the opera was staged or sung in concert at Parma, London, Zurich, Bologna, Buxton, and Milan. A recording preserves the Royal Opera's second concert performances at Royal Festival Hall on June 2, 1999. The first was on May 31. In *Opera* 8 (August 1999), 964, the editor Rodney Milnes wrote: "*Giorno* was in every way so superb a concert performance as almost to persuade you that Verdi's early comedy is better than it actually is. . . . But the energy of the music and the flashes of individual inspiration amidst stock *buffoneria*-by-the-yard—nicely laid-out Sextet, one or two odd harmonic progressions, and that weird arpeggio for trombone and double basses—carry all before them, at least in a performance like this."

Chapter Fifteen

1. Budden, *Operas of Verdi,* 1:206. Opera's South American premiere, in Buenos Aires, August 19, 1854; North American, Mexico City, December 23, 1857.

2. For example, Baldini, *Story of Giuseppe Verdi*, 100, 107: "But if *Giovanna d'Arco* was not a success"; and "After the tepid reception of [the opera] . . ." Also Harold Rosenthal, *Two Centuries of Opera at Covent Garden* (London: Putnam, 1958), 152: the opera "failed in Milan." On its success in Milan, see Walker, *The Man Verdi*, 128. Carlo Gatti, in his *Il teatro alla Scala nella storia e nell'arte (1778–1963): Cronologia complete degli spettacoli e dei concerti a cura di Giampiero Tintori* (Milan: Ricordi, 1964), 123, reports that the opera's "success was good, but not equal to Verdi's preceding operas." It had seventeen performances in the four weeks remaining in the season, and Gatti typically ranked as failures those operas that achieved only three or four. In subsequent years in Milan, the opera had revivals at La Scala in 1858 (7 performances) and 1865 (17), and in three of the city's smaller theaters in 1847, 1851, and 1876. For performances at La Scala, see Tintori, *Cronologia, opere–balletti–concerti, 1778–1977*, in Gatti, ibid., 34, 39, 42. For excerpts of reviews of the premiere, see *WGV, Giovanna d'Arco*, score, intro., xvi–xvii.

3. Dyneley Hussey, *Verdi* (London: J. M. Dent, 1940), 42.

4. Budden, *Operas of Verdi*, 1:223.

5. Andrew Porter, *A Musical Season: A Critic from Abroad in America* (New York: Viking Press, 1974), 83.

6. Alan Blyth, *Opera* 17, no. 7 (July 1966), 598.

7. Donal Henahan, *New York Times*, October 28, 1985, C-15.

8. Solera's denials, Budden, *Operas of Verdi*, 1:205. That Solera started with Schiller's play is perhaps the one point about the opera on which all critics and scholars agree. In Paris, about 1863 and by reprint in 1886–87, vocal scores were published that dropped Solera's name and ascribed the libretto simply as "d'après le drame de Schiller"; see George W. Martin Collection, no. 140 and 141, Pierpont Morgan Library, New York City.

9. The University College London Union Opera at the Bloomsbury Theatre, February 28, 1989, see *Opera* 40, no. 5 (May 1989): 618–19.

10. For example, the French historian Jules E. J. Quicherat did not edit and publish his seminal account of the trial until 1841–49; Jules Michelet did not publish his biography of Joan until 1853; and the first edited, translated account of her trial in English did not appear until 1902.

11. As *Orietta di Lesbo* in Rome, 1845; Palermo, 1847 and 1855; and a vocal score was published under that title in Naples in 1855. See Toye, *Verdi*, 38; and Cecil Hopkinson, *Bibliography of the Works of Giuseppe Verdi, 1813–1901* (New York: Broude Bros., 1978), 2:37. Also, *WGV, Giovanna*, score, intro., xxi–xxii.

12. George Bernard Shaw, *St. Joan*, in *Nine Plays with Prefaces and Notes* (New York: Dodd, Mead, 1935), 983–84, 1026. Shaw based his play (1923) on T. Douglas Murray's edited and translated version (1902) of Quicherat's report of the trial. See Nicholas Grene, *Bernard Shaw: A Critical View* (London: Macmillan, 1984), 134.

13. Osborne, *Complete Operas*, 116; Toye, *Verdi*, 225.

14. Harold C. Schonberg, *New York Times*, March 2, 1966, 47; Andrew Porter, *New Yorker*, June 21, 1976, 99.

15. Pougin, *Verdi*, trans. Matthew, 93.

16. Ibid., 94.

17. Luigi Agostino Garibaldi, *Giuseppe Verdi, nelle lettere di Emanuele Muzio ad Antonio Barezzi* (Milan: Treves, 1931), 329, Muzio to Barezzi, June 16, 1847. See also Mary Ann Smart, "Verdi Sings Erminia Frezzolini," *Verdi Newsletter*, no. 24 (1997): 13–22.

18. Stolz. The opera second to *Giovanna* in number of performances in 1865 was Rossini's *Il barbiere*, 13. See Tintori, *Cronologia, opere–balletti–concerti*, 42.

19. See chronology in Carlamaria Casanova, *Renata Tebaldi, Voice of an Angel* (Dallas: Baskerville, 1995). Her historic studio performance with Carlo Bergonzi and Rolando Panerai for RAI in Milan, May 26, 1951, was recorded and in 2002 issued as a CD by the Istituto Discografico Italiano, IDIS 6363/64.

20. Program in *New York Herald,* January 5, 1847, 3; review January 8, 2; *Albion,* January 9, 1847, 24; *Mirror,* January 9, 1847, 2; *Courier and Enquirer,* January 9, 1847, 2.

21. For a description of Barili, see *Albion,* January 9, 1847, 23, reviewing her in a performance that week of *Linda di Chamounix.* For her extraordinarily talented family (Adelina Patti was a younger half-sister), see Lawrence, *Strong on Music,* 1:425. For her later activities, especially in San Francisco in 1854, see Martin, *Verdi at the Golden Gate,* 67–69.

22. *Mirror,* January 9, 1847, 2: "Signorina Barili sang very sweetly, but the excitement of the stage action seems necessary to bring out her full powers." As there was no orchestra, her aria presumably had piano accompaniment.

23. Lawrence, *Strong on Music,* 1:425.

24. Repeating "Di tanti palpiti," *New York Herald,* December 15, 1850, 3; and announcing it "by general desire" for a concert three days later, see program, *Herald,* December 17, 1850, 5. The review of the first concert in the *Mirror,* December 16, 1850, 2, does not mention the Verdi aria. On Parodi, see chap. 7.

25. See Martin, *Verdi at the Golden Gate,* 35.

26. Frezzolini made her concert debut on October 2, 1857, in a joint appearance with pianist, Sigismond Thalberg, and violinist, Henri Vieuxtemps. She sang four arias of which the first was Joan's *romanza.* The next day the *Herald,* 4 reported: "M'lle Frezzolini sang four pieces—the best were the Polacca ["Non fu sogno"] from the *Lombardi,* and the duet from the *Elisir d'Amore.* Her style is superb, and her success was complete. The Polacca created a positive *furore,* and was vociferously encored: in answer to which M'lle Frezzolini gave the *rondo finale* to the *Sonnambula,* which was the great triumph of the evening." See also *New York Times,* October 3, 1857, 5, reporting her debut "a success," without mentioning any arias. Conversely, in reviewing her performances as Lucrezia in *Lucrezia Borgia* and Zerlina in *Don Giovanni,* the *Albion,* October 3, 1847, 475, and October 10, 1847, 487, was savage: As Zerlina "she seemed to own herself unequal to her task." The critics continued to dispute her qualities, and in their controversy the aria from *Giovanna* went unnoticed. Also, WGV, *Giovanna,* score, intro., xix; and Preston, *Opera on the Road,* 348 nn54–56.

27. See David M. Ingalls, "Francis Scala: Leader of the Marine Band from 1855 to 1871 (MA thesis, Catholic University of America, 1957), 73, 119. Elise K. Kirk, *Music at the White House: A History of the American Spirit* (Urbana: University of Illinois Press, 1986), 130, reports that John Philip Sousa's catalogue in 1885 listed eighteen of Verdi's operas.

28. Kirk, *Music at the White House,* 56, credits Scala with founding the concert series during President John Tyler's administration, 1841–45. The concerts continued until the start of Herbert Hoover's administration in 1929. See Kirk's description of the concert on October 25, 1873, 107, when the Band played an aria from *I masnadieri.*

29. Description, *New York Times,* January 15, 1861, 2. Though the first music heard in the new house was a concert on January 15, at which Rossini's *William Tell* Overture was played, the public seemed to feel that the true opening of the house was the first night of opera.

30. *New York Herald,* January 23, 1861, 6.

31. *New York Times,* January 21, 1861, 8.

32. *New York Times,* January 23, 1861, 6.

33. On Muzio, see Vetro, *L'allevio di Verdi*, with its chronology by Kaufman of all performances conducted by Muzio in the United States, Cuba, Egypt, and Europe. Though Muzio apparently never produced *Giovanna d'Arco* onstage, he did give many concerts in some of which he may have scheduled the overture. Similarly, in Gilmore's summer season of 150 consecutive concerts he may have repeated the overture, which was well received, see *New York Times*, August 22, 1875, 6.

34. *Complete Catalogue of Sheet Music and Musical Works, 1870*, 229.

35. For example, Upton, *The Standard Operas*, and "Notelrac," *Operas: Their Writers and Their Plots* (Philadelphia: Lippincott, 1882); Moses, *Collectors' Guide to American Recordings, 1895–1925*.

36. Bierley, *Incredible Band of John Philip Sousa*, 417. Martin, "The Metropolitan Opera's Sunday Evening Concerts and Verdi," 16–27.

37. The performances of the *Giovanna* overture led by Edwin Franko Goldman were on the following dates: in 1953, on July 11 and 12, and August 15 and 16; and in 1954, on June 28, July 8, 11, 17, and 18, and August 4; in 1955, on July 21 and 22, and August 13 and 14. And those led by Richard Franko Goldman: in 1961, on July 24, and August 12 and 13; and in 1962, on June 30 and July 1. I am grateful to the staff of the Performing Arts Library of the University of Maryland, who searched the years 1953 through 1962 for me. For the entry on the overture in Richard Franko Goldman's book, see *The Band's Music* (New York: Pitman, 1938), 400, 407.

38. Third, see Baldini, *Story of Giuseppe Verdi*, 99. Also Godefroy, *Dramatic Genius of Verdi*, 1:63. And Toye's seminal study of Verdi and his operas, *Verdi*, 225–26.

39. Godefroy, *Dramatic Genius of Verdi*, 68.

40. *New York Times*, March 2, 1966, 47.

41. *New York Post*, March 2, 1966, 58.

42. *Opera* 17, no. 6 (June 1966): 455.

43. For example, Sutherland, Callas, Scotto, and Caballé all offered recordings (variously titled) of "early" Verdi rarities. Among their selections even *Jérusalem* was represented by an aria from its original version, *I Lombardi*, and *Stiffelio*, by an aria from its revision, *Aroldo*. Tebaldi, London Records Stereo, OS 25912.

44. The recording: Angel, SCL3791. Andrew Porter, *High Fidelity Magazine*, June 1973, 64–65. "Vulgarity," John B. Steane, *Gramophone*, November 1989, 979, reviewing the CD reissue of the 1973 recording. "Tawdry": Porter, *High Fidelity Magazine*, June 1973, 65–65. As an example, the overture: Levine plays it in seven minutes ten seconds; Tullio Serafin, older and more experienced, in a recording made in the 1950s, eight and a half minutes, making it sound much better. Serafin, *Verdi Overtures*, Angel S 35676. On Levine, "drives the score and his players and singers too hard," see Harold D. Rosenthal reviewing the recording, *Opera* 24, no. 7 (July 1973): 620–22. For more on Levine conducting early Verdi, see chapters 3 and 6.

45. References to the recording in reviews: see John Rockwell, *New York Times*, May 17, 1976, 41; Speight Jenkins, *New York Post*, May 18, 1976, 19.

46. Ibid. Also scorning the singers but more favorable to the opera, Robert Jacobson, *Opera News*, August 1976, 38–39: "If major houses would take up this early Verdi treasure with the right casting, it could become a repertory staple."

47. *New Yorker*, June 21, 1976, 100.

48. I thank four who uncovered for me such facts as I have on this performance: conductor David Stockton; chorus member Peter J. Wender; director of marketing at the Boston Lyric Opera, Judith McMichael; and head of Reader Services at the Boston Athenaeum, Stephen Nonack.

49. Donald Dierks, *San Diego Union*, June 27, 1980, A21; Andrea Herman, *San Diego Tribune*, June 27, 1980, C-1. The scenery for this production, not much admired in San Diego, in part was borrowed from a Canadian Opera Co. production of Tchaikovsky's *Jeanne d'Arc*. See Dierks, *San Diego Union*, June 27, 1980, A21.

50. Albert Goldberg, *Los Angeles Times*, June 30, 1980, Calendar, Pt. VI, 1.

51. Herman, *San Diego Tribune*, June 27, 1980, C-1. A reviewer for the *Music Journal* 37, no. 4 (July–August 1980): 56, also praised Mueller but found the opera less interesting than the previous year's *I Lombardi*.

52. I thank the Jonas Kamlet Library, Sarasota, for a recording of the second, June 28, 1980, performance.

53. *New York Times*, August 2, 1983, C-13. La Selva recalls the audience as "very large, perhaps 15,000." I was present; the audience was indeed large, and most of it stayed to the end. La Selva drew people to unfamiliar works by opening his four-opera summer season with three that were familiar and popular, building his audience, and then closing with the unknown. The strategy worked; people, having enjoyed *Bohème*, *Traviata*, and *Rigoletto* would return for the fourth opera of which they had never heard.

54. *New Orleans Times-Picayune*, November 15, 1983. I thank Jack Belsom, archivist of the New Orleans Opera for telling me of this production and sending a copy of the review.

55. *New York Times*, October 28, 1985, C-15.

56. Porter, *Musical Events: A Chronicle, 1983–1986*, 444. I was present. Without a vocal score in hand, I could not be sure of what was cut, but probably chiefly choruses, finales, and perhaps even some connecting recitatives in order to allow the principals, with their arias and ensembles, to dominate the opera and evening.

57. La Selva to Raymond Ericson, *New York Times*, May 14, 1976, C-22; and author's interview with La Selva, October 14, 2004.

58. *New York Post*, August 4, 1995, 51. Peter G. Davis, for *New York Magazine*, August 21, 1995, 48–49, also attended and judged the opera "somewhere near the bottom of the Verdi canon," but praised La Selva's "spirited conducting."

59. Queler to the author, at Opera Index dinner, January 11, 2004. For example, in her seasons from 1971/72 through 2005/6, she has presented, *Lombardi* (2), *Foscari* (2), *Masnadieri* (2), *Battaglia* (2), *Nabucco*, *Ernani*, *Attila*, *Corsaro*, *Aroldo*, and *Giovanna d'Arco*.

60. *New York Times*, May 11, 1996, 15.

61. Warren Wilson, *Toronto Globe and Mail*, March 24, 1998, C4. Opera in Concert, which performs at the Jane Mallet Theatre, St. Lawrence Centre for the Arts, is now, 2006–7, in its thirty-third season, having started in 1974.

62. Anthony Tommasini, *New York Times*, May 18, 1999, E-5.

63. Geoff Chapman, *Toronto Star*, March 20, 2000, E-2. See also Urjo Kareda, *Toronto Globe and Mail*, March 20, 2000, R-4. Performance in George Weston Recital Hall (capacity 1,000) and sung in Italian without surtitles.

64. The chief soloists were Maria Knapik, Giovanna; Gustavo Lopez-Manzitti, Carlo; and Fredrick Redd, Giacomo. tenor.

65. Tommasini, *New York Times*, May 18, 1999. In the past two decades in Europe, to name only the larger cities, the opera has had productions in Hamburg, Zurich, London (large and small companies), Berlin, Parma, Bologna, and Genoa. In the United States the Sarasota Opera Company in its Verdi cycle reached *Giovanna d'Arco* in 2010, with a fully staged production and six performances.

Chapter Sixteen

1. To meet the demands of censors Verdi shifted the locale of *Ballo in maschera* to Boston, but he conceived the opera and composed it as set in Stockholm, where many productions now place it.

2. Prejudice, see reviews quoted in *WGV, Alzira*, score, xvii–xix. This edition offers its material, text and quotations, in English and Italian. See also, Walker, *The Man Verdi*, 138–39; Osborne, *Complete Operas of Verdi*, 122–23; and Budden, *Operas of Verdi*, 1:227.

3. Kaufman, *Verdi and His Major Contemporaries*, 327–28.

4. See *WGV, Alzira*, score, xix.

5. Comédie-Française, ibid., xiii. Voltaire, in his preface to the play, quoted in Osborne, *Complete Operas*, 126, begins, "This tragedy, a work of complete fiction . . ." For the operas and ballets, see *WGV, Alzira*, score, xiii.

6. Also: *Belisario* (1836), *L'assedio di Calais* (1836), *Pia de' Tolomei* (1837), *Maria de Rudenz* (1838), *Poliuto* (composed 1838, premiere 1848), and *Maria di Rohan* (1843).

7. Synopses and program notes sometimes state or imply that the Incas know their prisoner is the Spanish governor; hence, in part, their savagery. But nothing in the score so states and the stage directions and text strongly imply the contrary. Zamoro, for instance, "stares at Alvaro, and appears moved by the signs of his venerable age," and addresses him as "old man." If the Incas had recognized him, they more likely would have held him alive in order to wring concessions for his release.

8. On the sudden twists of fortune and emotion, for example, Zamoro freeing Alvaro, then pledging death to the Spaniards; Zamoro and Alzira, disbelief that he's alive, rapture, and then as Gusmano finds them together, masculine rage; in the opera's finale Gusmano's sudden pardon of Zamoro. Meanwhile, in the course of the opera, Zamoro is three times taken prisoner, and freed.

9. Budden, *Operas of Verdi*, 1:241. See also ibid., 230: "Arguably the one moment the music rises to greatness."

10. Verdi to Maffei, July 30, 1845, Cesari and Luzio, *Copialettere*, 431; and *WGV, Alzira*, score, xvi.

11. Verdi to Giuseppina Appiani, August 13, 1845, *WGV, Alzira*, score, xvii. See also, Budden, *Operas of Verdi*, 1:230 for a Verdi letter to Piave (undated): "I hope that later on it will be more appreciated and stay in the repertoire for who knows how long. Then if I'm not mistaken it will go the rounds fairly quickly because I think it makes a stronger effect than *I due Foscari*." Budden, *Operas of Verdi*, cites Abbiati, *Verdi*, 1:566.

12. Quoted at greater length and with comments in *WGV, Alzira*, score, xvi–xvii, citing the *Gazzetta musicale di Milano*, August 17, 1845, 141. Arrivabene first met Verdi in 1836 or 37, as he states in his last letter to Verdi, October 31, 1886, and he became a lifelong friend. See Alberti, *Verdi Intimo*, 333. Arrivabene's review, seemingly unbiased, apparently was based on notes taken at the premiere. See also, Phillips-Matz, *Verdi*, 133–34.

13. On cavatinas, Verdi to Cammarano, May 27, 1845, Cesari and Luzio, *Copialettere*, 430; pleasure in the libretto, *WGV, Alzira*, score, xii–xiv, and *Copialettere*, 429–30. This is Zamoro's second solo double-aria and in its emotions very like his first in the prologue. No other character has *two* such extended scenes, and the tenor needs stamina, making it often the most difficult role to cast. Author's interview with Vincent La Selva, February 20, 2003. In later years the cabaletta, "Non di codarde lagrime," was sometimes sung in *Macbeth* by Macduff as a solo in place of his "La patria tradita," a call and response with Malcolm and the chorus. See *WGV, Macbeth*, score, xxxvii, for discussion and examples.

14. On the conservatism of the Neapolitan audience, see Budden, *Operas of Verdi,* 1:227.

15. Pierluigi Petrobelli, "Thoughts for *Alzira,*" in *Music in the Theater,* 85. He compares Cammarano's libretto, sketched and published, to what Verdi set, and shows how Verdi's changes were improvements.

16. In addition, the opera had five partial performances, WGV, *Alzira,* score, xviii, n76. Whereas, in this same year at the Teatro San Carlo, Verdi's *I due Foscari* had fifty-one performances, ibid., xii.

17. Ibid., xviii, unascribed review published in the Roman periodical *Rivista teatrale.*

18. Quoted in WGV, *Macbeth,* score, xl.

19. Ibid., xvi and xl.

20. Verdi to Jacopo Ferretti, November 5, 1845, Cesari and Luzio, *Copialettere,* 432, and WGV, *Alzira,* score, xviii.

21. Quoted in Cesari and Luzio, *Copialettere,* 432, as Verdi's reply to an inquiry from the Countess Negroni Prati, citing A. M. Cornelio, *Per la storia* (Pistoia, 1904), 29. The latter seems to have been the first to publish the remark.

22. For example, Andrew Porter in a review of the Orfeo complete recording of *Alzira* (C 057 832 H), in *Opus* (December 1984): 43. Also, WGV, *Alzira,* score, xix.

23. See Cesari and Luzio, *Copialettere.*

24. For example, Petrobelli, "Thoughts for *Alzira,*" 75–99, for analyses of the prologue's final aria with chorus and of "the central moment" in the finale to act 1, the point at which Alvaro recognizes Zamoro as the man who saved him from torture and death. And WGV, *Alzira,* score, in its "facsimiles" section has five plates of sketches.

25. *Opera* (April 1967), 289–90. Note Weaver's emphasis on the Roman production's scenic aspects. He considered the conducting, by Franco Capuana, "flaccid," insufficiently "sensitive and energetic," and though the principal singers did better—Virginia Zeani (soprano), Gianfranco Cecchele (tenor), and Cornell MacNeil (baritone)—he granted each only moderate praise. The Jonas Kamlet Library, Sarasota Opera, Sarasota, kindly reproduced for me a tape of this performance, and to my ears, Weaver's strictures on the musical side of the production were a bit harsh.

26. *New York Times,* January 18, 1968, 48. Elinor Ross, Alzira; Gianfranco Cecchele, Zamoro; Louis Quilico, Gusmano; and Michael Devlin, Alvaro; Jonel Perlea conductor.

27. *New York Post,* January 18, 1968, 51. Herbert Weinstock, *Opera* (April 1968), 293.

28. Toye, *Verdi,* introduction by Herbert Weinstock, 229.

29. Ibid.: "Probably the best feature of the opera is the orchestral introduction to Zamoro's arrival at the mountain cave. This, characterized by a clashing of sharps and naturals that looks positively frightening on paper, must have sounded most effective, the prevailing color, too, being admirable."

30. Caballé, *Verdi Rarities,* RCA LSC-2995; and another early recording of an aria, Zamoro's "Irne lungi," on *Carlo Bergonzi, Thirty-One Tenor Arias,* Philips, 432 486-2 (1975). The complete opera: Orfeo (1983): Alzira, Ileana Cotrubas; Zamoro, Francisco Araiza; Gusmano, Renato Bruson; and Alvaro, Jan-Hendrik Rootering; conductor, Lamberto Gardelli. And Philips (2001): Alzira, Marina Mescheriakova; Zamoro, Ramón Vargas; Gusmano, Paolo Gavanelli; conductor, Fabio Luisi. For a survey by two reviewers of three complete recordings, see *Fanfare,* March/April 2002, 190–92.

31. *New York Daily News,* April 23, 1985, 32.

32. For a description of the Amato Company, see chap 13.

33. *New York Times,* July 12, 1996, C21. For what constitutes "a premiere," see discussion in the preface.

34. Osborne, *Complete Operas*, 129. Victor DeRenzi, artistic director of Sarasota Opera, after conducting in successive years rehearsals and staged performances of *Oberto* (2001) and *Alzira* (2000), felt the latter, onstage, was notably the stronger. Author's interview with DeRenzi, July 18, 2003. On the European productions: One of the earliest, oddest, and most surprising performances to follow the Rome 1967 production was a radio concert performance in Berlin sung in German on November 1, 1938 (to honor the 125th anniversary of Verdi's birth [October 10, 1813]). It made some curious cuts and interesting minor additions to the score, and offered as the soprano, a last-minute substitute who reportedly read the score "on sight," the twenty-two-year-old Elisabeth Schwarzkopf. Tapes (though incomplete) of this performance exist, and I thank the Jonas Kamlet Library, Sarasota Opera, Sarasota, for the opportunity to hear one. Some European staged productions were London (1970), the University College Operatic Society; Amsterdam (1980); Parma (1981); and Fidenza (1990).

35. Piero Mioli, *Opera* 32, no. 10 (October 1981): 1058–59.

36. *Opera* 47, no. 9 (September 1996): 1026.

37. Author's interview with Victor DeRenzi, June 26, 2003.

38. *WGV, Alzira*, score, xxiv. The three scenes: act 1, scene 1, at Lima, as the Spanish soldiers enter the plaza, the band plays offstage and is soon joined by the pit orchestra; act 1 finale, as the Inca army approaches, the band plays offstage; act 2 finale, as the wedding guests gather, the band plays onstage, and on the twenty-sixth measure, as the voices enter, is joined by the pit orchestra.

39. The Berlin radio production, November 1, 1938, also omitted the gong in the cave scene, though it added prolonged wedding bells to the final scene.

40. My impression, based on audience behavior and a sampling of audience opinion before and after the final performance. "Beguiling tunes," see *New York Times*, July 12, 1996, C21.

41. *Sarasota Herald-Tribune*, March 14, 2000, 1E.

42. *Venice Gondolier*, March 22, 2000, 2.

43. *Orlando Sentinel*, March 19, 2000, F-3.

44. *St. Petersburg Times*, March 19, 2000, 2B.

45. David La Marche, *New York Concert Review*, Spring 2003, 17. La Marche is the conductor and music administrator for the American Ballet Theatre.

46. "The worst," see Toye, *Verdi*, 229. Budden, "Introductory Essay," to the complete recording of the opera issued in 2001 by Philips (464 628-2), 13: "*Alzira*, like *Il corsaro*, is certainly minor Verdi. But his personal imprint is on every page."

Chapter Seventeen

1. Toye, *Verdi*, 51, 250.

2. For example, Travis Wilds, *Weekly Planet, Sarasota-Manatee* [Florida] 60, no. 22 (March 10–16, 2004).

3. Toye, *Verdi*, 250.

4. Budden, *Operas of Verdi*, 2:179–80. Verdi in 1866 also attempted to cancel his contract with the Opéra for *Don Carlos*, see Martin, *Aspects of Verdi*, 110, 270n15.

5. Illness: summarized in Budden, *Operas of Verdi*, 2:365–66 and notes. See also Stefano Bianchi, "Verdi e Trieste, Verdi a Trieste," *Festival Verdi–2004: Il corsaro* (Reggio Parma Festival, 2004), 80.

6. Though no contemporary critic or any scholar, so far as I have discovered, thinks Trieste an odd choice by the publisher for a Verdi premiere in October 1848, I do. The contract for it, between publisher and opera house, was signed on September 17, a time when the greater the opera's success and the likelihood that it would spark a pro-Italian demonstration, the greater the certainty that the Austrians would immediately shut it down. Even as late as 1880 and 1903, the Austrians in Trieste closed productions of *Ernani* that led to demonstrations, and in 1848 they were far more anxious and inclined to repression. (See Bianchi, "Verdi e Trieste, Verdi a Trieste," 90) Yet the choice, whether or not odd, does not explain why the Triestini greeted the opera so coolly.

7. This letter to Piave has been reprinted many times in part. It is quoted at length in Conati, *Interviews and Encounters*, 318; in the introduction to WGV, *Corsaro*, score, xiii; and in David Lawton, "The Corsair Reaches Port," *Opera News* (June 1982), 16.

8. Though first published in 1906 in an Italian journal, this letter to Barbiere-Nini, singing Gulnara, was not much noted until 1980 when quoted at length in Conati, *Interviews and Encounters*, 319–20; also in WGV, *Corsaro*, score, xx; and in Lawton, "The Corsair Reaches Port," 18.

9. Toye, *Verdi*, 249. The first Italian translation of the poem appeared in prose in 1820 and then one in verse by Guseppe Nicolini, in 1824. The article "Il quadrilatero imperfetto, Vizi e virtú del *Corsaro*," by Giorgio Pagannone, *Festival Verdi–2004*, 50, lists five theatrical renderings of the poem preceding Verdi's: three ballets, in 1826 (very successful, much revived), 1837, and 1843; and two operas, in 1831 (Pacini) and 1847 (Nini); and one opera that followed in 1849 (Cortesi). Apparently, none of the operas had much success. The conductor Luigi Arditi, in his autobiography *My Reminiscences* (New York: Dodd, Mead, 1896), 14, 290, states he composed an opera, *Il Corsaro*, a "Spanish Opera in One Act, performed in the Tacón Theatre, Havana" in 1847. It, too, was based on Byron.

10. Though *Corsaro* had only three performances in Trieste, it found success in Milan's Teatro Carcano and Turin's Teatro Carignano in 1852, and then soon disappeared, with its last nineteenth-century performance in Oporto, Portugal, in 1864. In all, according to Conati's list in *Festival Verdi–2004*, 114–15, it had only eighteen productions, including one in Chile and one by "dilettanti" in Brazil. See also Kaufman, *Verdi and His Major Contemporaries*.

11. Byron, *The Corsair*, canto 1, stanzas 8 and 11.

12. Lenau (1802–50) wrote his epic poem in 1844, though it was not published until 1851. His Don Juan, a sort of Byronic hero, is not a sensualist but an unsatisfied idealist, who in his search for the ideal woman soon is bored and disgusted by his conquests. Finally, despairing of finding the lady and thinking death perhaps an interesting novelty, he allows the son of a man he has murdered to kill him.

13. *Opera* 14, no. 10 (October 1963): 690–92.

14. *Opera* 17, no. 5 (May 1966): 407–8. Of course, not all agreed with Porter. An anonymous critic for the *Observer Weekend Review*, March 20, 1966, remarked: "Now at least we know the worst. . . . Not that it is really all that bad. . . . Only in the third act prison scene, and especially in the original string accompaniment to its opening tenor aria, does Verdi break into a real human world. For the rest, the score is cardboard. . . . Yet at its most perfunctory, Verdi's music rarely lacks a redeeming physical vitality."

15. Alessandro Camuto, *Opera* 22, no. 8 (August 1971): 730–31. This, with the quotation from Porter, *Opera* 17, no. 5 (May 1966): 407–8, "Nothing could look more ordinary on paper; and on performance it stirred the blood," confirm the adage: Verdi plays better onstage than he reads in the score. Discussed in the introduction.

16. Taped recordings of the live performances in Venice and Rome circulated. The first, from the Teatro la Fenice, March 20, 1971, featured A. Gulin (G.), K. Ricciarelli (M.), G. Lamberti (C.), R. Bruson (S.), and Jesus Lopez-Cobos conducting; the second, from the Teatro Eliseo, October 5, 1980, with a less famous cast and Maurizio Rinaldi conducting. The commercial recording, issued in 1976 by Philips (426 118-2), had M. Caballé (G.), J. Norman (M.), J. Carreras (C.), G-P. Mastromei (S), and Lamberto Gardelli conducting. In 2004, following the opera's performance in the Parma Festival that year, Dynamic Recordings issued a CD (468) and a DVD (33468) of the production. The reviewer in *Fanfare* (November/December 2005), despite some doubts about the production thought well of the opera. See also, Budden's review of the production in *Opera* 55, no. 12 (December 2004): 1484–85: "minor Verdi, certainly, but with touches of inspired invention not to be found elsewhere."

17. For the two South American productions, see "Da Trieste a Oporto, La breve corsa del *Corsaro*," by Marcello Conati, *Festival Verdi–2004*, 114–15. See Budden, *Operas of Verdi*, 2:366, for some critics and comments on productions in nineteenth-century Italy.

18. Prado, *La musica italiana a Cuba*, 79n2. As of 1996 he lists nine Verdi operas not yet staged in Havana: *Oberto, Un giorno di regno, Giovanna d'Arco, Alzira, Jérusalem, Il corsaro, La battaglia di Legano, Stiffelio,* and *Simon Boccanegra.*

19. See Martin, *Verdi at the Golden Gate*, 84, 281n53. Carlotta Patti, an elder sister of Adelina Patti, was also a singer but because of lameness more often appeared in concert than in staged productions. She was still touring in 1869–70, when she gave concerts in Detroit on December 1 and 2, 1869, and May 14, 1870 (programs not found).

20. *New York Herald*, December 19, 1856, 5; the program listed "Cavatina from *Il corsaro*," which presumably was Gulnara's double aria, "Vola talor dal carcere." *New York Tribune*, December 19, 1856, 5. Strong, quoted in Lawrence, *Strong on Music*, 2:679.

21. Ingalls, "Francis Scala." Of Verdi's twenty-three operas up to and including *Ballo*, the Marine Band lacked parts for an excerpt from only *Alzira, Jérusalem, Corsaro,* and *Battaglia.*

22. See Martin, "The Metropolitan Opera's Sunday Evening Concerts and Verdi," 16–27.

23. David Lawton, letter to the author, May 9, 2004.

24. *New York Times*, December 17, 1981, C32.

25. *New York Daily News*, December 17, 1981, M18. See also Leighton Kerner, *Opera* 33, no. 6 (June 1982): 627.

26. I was there.

27. Gregson, "Nights of Glory," 193.

28. *San Diego Union*, June 19, 1982, A-23; also, *San Diego Tribune*, June 19, 1982, B6. The papers merged on February 3, 1992. Also, Martin Bernheimer, *Opera*, Festival Issue, Autumn 1982, 114–16: "At the climax, the eponymous corsair was forced to leap into the ocean from a wharf rather than a cliff. It is not quite the same."

29. *New Yorker*, July 19, 1982, 74.

30. *San Diego Union*, June 19, 1982, A-23.

31. Dale Harris, *New York Post*, August 1, 1987, 20.

32. With no knowledge of the craft of amplification, I would guess that there were two separate systems, one for singers, one for orchestra, and they were not blending properly.

33. Michael Kimmelman, *New York Times*, August 1, 1987, 14.

34. A possible reason for Ricordi's reluctance to rent the parts is that it knew better parts, that is, prepared for the critical edition, would soon be available.

35. Pierre Ruhe, *Washington Post*, May 25, 1996, C2.

36. Kelly Jordan, the *Review* (a monthly review of performances in the greater Washington area, published in Alexandria, Virginia, by Terrie Cochran), June 1996.

37. Anja Hauenstein, *Northern Virginia Sun*, May 21, 1996.

38. James R. Oestreich, *New York Times*, August 1, 1997, C16. Oestreich's review, though of the succeeding production, *La battaglia di Legnano*, gives this explanation of why he did not stay at *Corsaro*. I stayed.

39. *New York Times*, July 16, 1989, 45. See also Matthew Gurewitsch, "Opera's Populist," *New York*, August 7, 1995, 58–62.

40. Author's interview with Victor DeRenzi, August 6, 2004. The more than 100 percent can occur when people unable to attend turn in seats for resale for the company's benefit.

41. Wilds, *Weekly Planet, Sarasota-Manatee*, March 10–16, 2004.

42. Women, *Sarasota Herald-Tribune*, March 9, 2004; men's duets, *Pelican Press*, March 18, 2004, 9B; and "heroic tenor," *Pelican Press*.

43. *South Florida Sun-Sentinel*, March 20, 2004.

44. *St. Petersburg Times*, March 13, 2004.

45. In his autograph score, Verdi directed that the curtain part on an empty stage and that the pirates' chorus be sung offstage, unaccompanied. Sometime soon after the premiere, some other person orchestrated the chorus and brought the singers onstage to sing it, presumably to make it easier for them to follow the conductor and to stay on pitch. This orchestration and new stage direction were added to the autograph score and later published in vocal scores, and were used in many performances. But the addition quite changes the sound, appearance, and lonely introspection of Corrado's first aria. For a history of this addition to the score, see *WGV, Corsaro*, score, xxi–xxii, and critical commentary, 20.

46. Budden, *Operas of Verdi*, 1:149.

47. Author's interview with Victor DeRenzi, April 6, 2004.

48. Verdi letter to the soprano Barbieri-Nini, see Conati, *Interviews and Encounters*, 319–20; or *WGV, Corsaro*, scores, xx; or Lawton, "The Corsair Reaches Port," 18.

49. Anne Midgette, *New York Times*, March 26, 2004, E-5: "The tenor . . . showed a ringing tenor and delighted the audience. . . . But what was missing in his voice was a quality of tenderness. It's not that he lacks the musical understanding; it's more a technical failure to support a convincing piano line. For all of their expressiveness, his quiet passages sounded like pale and muffled versions of his full voice. You could call this a quibble, but it constitutes one significant difference between Mr. Casanova and some of the great voices of the past."

50. Tom Rosenthal, *Opera Now*, July/August 2004, 40.

Chapter Eighteen

1. The opera, in four acts, has seven scenes, but Verdi's directions for their settings are mostly generic: for example, "A shady spot . . . a magnificent room . . . a square in Milan, with a church porch in view."

2. The number of operas composed by Verdi varies depending on the number of revisions counted as separate operas, with the possibilities of these usually considered to be seven. For his New York Grand Opera's cycle, Vincent La Selva counted the operas as twenty-eight, adding to the basic twenty-six *Jérusalem* and *Aroldo*, on the ground that these two had their titles changed and were set to a wholly new story. Apparently Bud-

den based his twenty-eight on the same ground. The Sarasota Opera Company, for its cycle of the operas (still in progress), counts them as thirty-three. Basevi, *Studio sulle Opere di Giuseppe Verdi*, 130–31. Budden, *Operas of Verdi*, 1:395.

3. Holy Roman Empire. In Germany in 1803 Napoleon had reduced the number of tiny principalities, palatinates, bishoprics, and imperial cities from 250 to 39 and as one result had secured a Protestant majority in the Diet that elected the Holy Roman Emperor. These changes threatened the hold of the Catholic Hapsburgs on the position and title, and in 1804, Francis II of the Austrian Hapsburgs, following the proclamation of Napoleon as emperor of the French and seeking to ensure for himself some symbol of unity for his complex holdings, had declared himself to be "emperor of Austria." By the treaties following the battle of Austerlitz (December 2, 1805, Napoleon defeating the Austrians and Russians), Napoleon abolished what was left of the Holy Roman Empire in Germany, replacing it with a Confederation of the Rhine from which the Hapsburgs were excluded. Francis II, in reply, abdicated the empty title, becoming the last Holy Roman Emperor. Except for a short break his family had held the title from 1438 until 1806.

4. Cammarano also wrote the librettos for *Alzira*, *Luisa Miller*, and *Trovatore*.

5. The messenger from the battlefield reports that the emperor, knocked from his horse by Arrigo, is either dead or wounded. But program writers sometimes carry that possibility of death into stated fact. But despite the alleged tumble, Barbarossa survived the battle for another fourteen years, until 1190, when he drowned in southern Turkey while on the Third Crusade. For many years, according to legend, he was only asleep, sitting at a table in a cave in central Germany, where his red beard had grown through the tabletop, and upon awaking would restore the power and prestige of the Holy Roman Empire.

6. The record of *L'assedio d'Arlem* is hard to follow, for, apparently, often when staged it was titled (or at least indexed later as) *La battaglia di Legnano*. For an account of efforts to rewrite the libretto, see Luke Jensen, *Giuseppe Verdi & Giovanni Ricordi, with Notes on Francesco Lucca, from* Oberto *to* La Traviata (New York: Garland, 1989), 116–25. Apparently, too, for a revival at La Scala in 1857 that did not take place, the opera with another altered libretto was to be retitled *Lida;* see Gatti, *Verdi*, 1:316, and Abbiati, *Verdi* 1:787.

7. Emanuele Bardare also finished the libretto to *Trovatore* after Cammarano's death. By 1857, when Verdi was busy turning *Stiffelio* into *Aroldo*, he had left *Battaglia* to its fate. One of the opera's problems, as Jensen (*Giuseppe Verdi & Giovanni Ricordi*) makes clear, was that Verdi and his publisher had set the royalty payment for it too high.

8. The chief source for this success in France is a letter from Emanuele Muzio to Verdi in 1886, see Alessandro Luzio, ed., *Carteggi Verdiani*, 4 vols. (Rome: Academia Nazionale del Lincei, 1947), 4:219n1. According to Kaufman, *Verdi and His Major Contemporaries*, 361n41, data from French provincial theaters is hard to find.

9. Budden, *Operas of Verdi*, 1:394, offers some examples of French influence. Also, Kimbell, *Verdi in the Age of Italian Romanticism*, 569–74.

10. The radio performance had Caterina Mancini (Lida), Rolando Panerai (Rolando), Amedeo Berdini (A), and Fernando Previtali as conductor. Issued first by Cetra, it was reissued in 2000 by Warner Fonit, #8573 82644-2.

11. MRF Records-109, with Antonietta Stella (Lida), Ettore Bastianini (Rolando), and Franco Corellia (Arrigo), and Gianandrea Gavazzeni as conductor, taken from the December 7, 1961, performance.

12. Philips, 422 435-2. Katia Ricciarelli (L), José Carreras (A), Matteo Manuguerra (R), and conductor, Lamberto Gardelli. Besides those other recordings mentioned, there have been at least ten more.

13. According to Kaufman, *Verdi and His Major Contemporaries*, these were in Lima (1853), Montevideo (1861), Santiago (1864), and Valparaiso (1865).

14. Ingalls, "Francis Scala."

15. G. Schirmer, *Operatic Anthology: Celebrated Arias, Selected from Operas by Old and Modern Composers* (New York: G. Schirmer, 1904), ed. Max Spicker. This has been reprinted several times; recently, and with some restorations by Glendower Jones, by Joseph Patelson Music House (New York, 1986).

16. Moses, *Collectors' Guide to American Recordings, 1895–1925*. And *Victor Book of the Opera* (1912).

17. Martin, "The Metropolitan Opera's Sunday Evening Concerts and Verdi." Also, *New York Herald*, November 22, 1920, 21, on the overture's premiere, "this event should not pass without record." The concert offered thirteen selections from Verdi and Puccini, see *New York Times*, November 22, 1920, 13. Bamboschek (1890–1969) was general music secretary and conductor at the Metropolitan 1916–29.

18. The title page of the program stated: "A Bicentennial Celebration under the artistic directions of Anthony Amato," and inside, the company thanked the Cooper Union Forum "for its cooperation toward making this production possible." The sense of a bicentennial event, as well as of the opera's "American premiere," was strong. For a detailed account of the Amato company, see chap. 13.

19. *New York Times*, March 1, 1976, 31.

20. *New York Post*, March 1, 1976, 18.

21. I attended both the Cooper Union premiere and the March 14 performance in the opera house.

22. I thank Stephen Nonack, librarian at the Boston Athenaeum, and Judith McMichael, marketing director of the Boston Lyric Opera, for digging out the information on this production. See *Opera News* 46 (March 13, 1982): 32, for a brief note on it: "even unstaged and dressed in evening clothes, a grand *battaglia*." For an article on the demise of Boston Concert Opera, see *Boston Globe*, March 24, 1989, "Living" sec., 39.

23. Robert Croan, *Pittsburgh Post-Gazette*, September 19, 1984, 23.

24. Ibid.

25. William S. Mann, *Opera* 12, no. 1 (January 1961): 52–54.

26. See, Richard Fawkes, *Welsh National Opera* (London: Julia MacRae, 1986), 76–77: "The capacity audience, however, revelled in it and in the spirited choral work, and there were some twenty curtain calls."

27. Desmond Shawe-Taylor, *Opera* 12, no. 7 (July 1961): 468; and Mann, *Opera* 12, no. 1.

28. *New York Times*, September 22, 1984, sec. 1, 33.

29. *Pittsburgh Post-Gazette*, September 21, 1984, and in *Opera News*, December 3, 1984, 43.

30. *New York Times*, September 22, 1984.

31. "Backstage," "Living South Section" of *Pittsburgh Post-Gazette*, September 20, 1984, 18. I thank Jozef Topolski, at the Library of Congress, for alerting me to the article.

32. *New York Times*, September 22, 1984. There were also considerable cuts, chiefly of some second verses, repeats in the act 2 finale, and the women's chorus to introduce Lida's first scene. Gavazzeni at Milan in 1961 also cut this chorus, beginning directly with Lida's recitative. In Pittsburgh, as an introduction to the scene, the orchestra replayed the soft, expressive theme from the overture, associating it with Lida.

33. On the early history of surtitles, see Ezra Schabas and Carl Morey, *Opera Diva, Canadian Opera Company: The First Fifty Years* (Toronto: Dundurn Press, 2000), 166–69. For a discussion, see Donal Henahan, "When Supertitles Fight the Production," *New York Times*, September 30, 1984, sec. 2, 23.

34. *New York Times*, September 22, 1984.

35. The index to *Opera*, for the years 1959–2000 has entries for some thirteen productions in Europe as opposed to three in the United States. For the latter, however, it has no entries for the stagings by the Amato company and the New York Grand Opera or for the concert performance in Boston. Still, the imbalance is clear.

36. *New York Times*, January 14, 1987, C-21. Also, Gary Schmidgal, *Opera News* 51, no. 14 (March 28, 1987): 37–38.

37. *New York Times*, November 19, 2001, E-5.

38. The cycle, which added only two revisions, *Jérusalem* and *Aroldo*, to the basic twenty-six operas, opened with *Oberto* on July 6, 1994, and closed with *Falstaff* on August 1, 2001. See mid-cycle summary by Anthony Tommasini, *New York Times*, July 2, 1997, C-11. The New York Grand Opera company by then had given 133 performances of 41 operas "for some one and a half million people."

39. *New York Times*, August 1, 1997, C-16.

40. The seventeen are: *Oberto, Nabucco, Ernani, due Foscari, Giovanna d'Arco, Alzira, Attila, Macbeth, Luisa Miller, Stiffelio, Rigoletto, Boccanegra, Aroldo, Don Carlos, Aida, Otello, Falstaff.* Moreover, in France, *Traviata* often was titled *Violetta*.

41. Author's interview with La Selva, January 17, 2007. For a possible reworking of the opera with a new title of *Lida*, see Gatti, *Verdi*, 1:316, and Abbiati, *Verdi*, 1:787.

42. Budden, *Operas of Verdi*, 1:395, 411. Also, Osborne, *Complete Operas*, 196.

43. Budden, *Operas of Verdi*, 1:394, 414. Also Kimbell, *Verdi in the Age of Italian Romanticism*, 564.

44. See Budden, *Operas of Verdi*, 1:415, for a brief list of opinions for and against the opera. To his list of critical Italians now should be added Baldini, *Story of Giuseppe Verdi*, 150–53.

45. For a review of the touring company in the Po Valley, see *Opera* 50, no. 6 (June 1999): 706–7. The later Piacenza and Ravenna production (two performances in each, in April 2005) began in an unusual way: Upon entering the theater the audience faced a darkened stage cluttered with debris and apparent corpses, presumably the refuse of a battle. The tableau persisted while first the orchestra, then the conductor entered, and through the gentle theme of the overture. Then, with the reappearance of the march and its more sprightly countertheme, a work crew came onstage to carry off the dead and restore the scene to order. I thank William Voitglander for this account. As in Pittsburgh, the stage setting consisted of five tall towers, which could stand alone or be combined in various positions to suggest different backgrounds.

46. Emanuele Senici, *Opera* 51, no. 9 (September 2000): 1124.

47. Tommasini, *New York Times*, September 22, 1984, 29 and November 19, 2001.

48. Roger Parker, entry on the opera, *The New Grove Dictionary of Opera*. And after a brief but pertinent analysis of the opera's musical style repeating this opinion in his *New Grove Guide to Verdi and His Operas* (Oxford: Oxford University Press, 2007), 123: "In today's climate, in which almost all Verdi's early operas are occasionally revived, *La battaglia* stands as one of Verdi's most unjustly neglected works."

Chapter Nineteen

1. Because of Verdi's ban on further performance, the last in nineteenth-century Italy was at Naples in 1855, and in Spain and Portugal, where Ricordi had a harder time policing productions, at Palma de Mallorca in 1866. On Ricordi's difficulties, see Jensen, *Giuseppe Verdi & Giovanni Ricordi*, 152, 159. Seemingly, the opera found an appreciative

audience in Spain, for, as in Trieste, where it was revived in 1852, it was produced in Barcelona in 1856 and 1860, and in Palma, in 1859 and 1866. As *Guglielmo Wellingrode*, it played in Rome, Florence, Catania, Palermo, and Naples.

2. Conceivably, all these years Ricordi held a manuscript copy in its Milan archives, but if so, it was lost in August 1943 to bombardment and fire in World War II. See Philip Gossett, "New Sources for *Stiffelio*: A Preliminary Report," *Cambridge Opera Journal* (November 1993), 199–222, and *WGV, Stiffelio*, score, xi. Gossett's article was republished in Martin Chusid, ed., *Verdi's Middle Period: Source Studies, Analysis, and Performance Practice* (Chicago: University of Chicago Press, 1997).

3. See *WGV, Stiffelio*, score, xi, n. 3. For the editor Kathleen Kuzmick Hansell's pertinent article "Compositional Techniques in *Stiffelio*: Reading the Autograph Sources," see Chusid, *Verdi's Middle Period*.

4. Toye, *Verdi*, 309–11.

5. Critics and audiences generally complained of the contemporary costumes. For two of the premiere's most outspoken critics on this point, see Quaderni, no. 3, *Stiffelio* (Parma: Istituto di Studi Verdiani, 1968), which republished in full, on the occasion of the opera's first production in Italy since 1855, many reviews of performances in Italy in the early 1850s. Among these, were two reviews of the premiere production: one by the anonymous critic for *Il Diavoletto* (p. 113) and the other by the anonymous critic for *L'Italia Musicale* (p. 118).

6. All the music for the last act of *Aroldo* was new, and besides the storm music the act's *finale*, a trio becoming a quartet, was much admired. On the opera's record of performance, see Hansell, "Compositional Techniques in *Stiffelio*," 97.

7. See Gossett, "New Sources for *Stiffelio*," 203. For Ricordi's difficulties in protecting its scores, see Jensen, *Giuseppe Verdi & Giovanni Ricordi*.

8. The scholar in charge of preparing the score, by whose name this edition is sometimes known, was Rubino Profeta. For a review of the BBC broadcast on October 19, 1969, see Charles Osborne, *Opera* 20, no. 12 (December 1969): 108–9. The record company: MRF–32, with Stiffelio sung by Gastone Limarilli; Lina, by Angeles Gulin; and Stankar, by Walter Alberti; conductor, Peter Maag.

9. The scholar in charge of preparing this edition of the score was Giovanni Morelli. For review of the production, see Alessandro Camuto, *Opera* 37, no. 3 (March 1986): 333–35. The production was successful, and La Fenice revived it in 1988, see idem, *Opera* 39, no. 9 (September 1988): 1070–71.

10. The play, *Le Pasteur, ou L'Évangile et le Foyer* (The Gospel and the Family), by Émile Souvestre and Eugène Bourgeois, apparently had less success in France than in Italy, where it played in translation by Gaetano Vestri under the title *Siffelius!* The Italian text was published by Florilegio Drammatico (Milan: Borroni e Scotti, 1848), vol. VI, anno III.

11. See *WGV, Stiffelio*, score, xxvii, for an account of which of the twelve performances were partial, and xxvi, for the singers admonished to sing the lines as censored.

12. The libretto published with the MRF-32 recording shows by underlining what was cut in Parma: In addition to Lina's fast aria in act 2, twelve lines of dialogue in act 1 between Lina and Stiffelio leading up to his discovery that she has lost, misplaced, or disposed of her wedding ring, and thereafter a line or two here or there. The Naples production, with Mario del Monaco, Angeles Gulin, Giulio Fioravanti, and conductor Oliviero De Fabritiis, used the Parma score and had a considerable success. See *Opera* 24, no. 4 (April 1973): 354. A company, Great Opera Performances, issued a recording, GOP 773, of the performance on January 7, 1973. "The Parma cuts" are discussed toward the chapter's end.

13. Mondo Musica issued a recording, MFOH 10803, of the performance on December 22, 1985, with Antonio Barasorda as Stiffelio, Rosalind Plowright, Brent Ellis, and conductor Eliahu Inbal.

14. See Hansell, "Compositional Techniques in *Stiffelio*," 83–85.

15. Léon Escudier, L. E. 1433, 248 pp (Paris: ca. 1855). For a brief account of the vocal score's publication history, see Hopkinson, *Bibliography*, 2:81, entry 52A (i). The librarian at Juilliard reported by letter to the author, July 10, 2007, that the school still has this copy of the vocal score.

16. Author's interview with La Selva, June 21, 2007; and interview by phone on July 15, 2007, with the acquaintance who wishes to remain unknown. The production had two performances, an orchestra of forty-one, led by La Selva, a chorus of forty-five, and the Brooklyn Academy of Music (capacity 2,121), which Porter in his review, *New Yorker*, June 21, 1976, 100–103, described as "New York's only public opera house built on a human scale."

17. Porter, ibid. Also, Robert Jacobson, *Opera News*, August 1976, 38–39: "The production managed decently enough. . . . The libretto is a patchwork, its characters cardboard and not consistently engaging. La Selva made the most of the big ensembles, whipping up vitality when all else threatened to break down." He praised the tenor, Richard Taylor, and the baritone, Theodore Lambrinos, but the soprano, Norma French, lacked "expansiveness, color, and carrying power."

18. *New York Post*, June 5, 1976, 15.

19. *New York Magazine*, June 21, 1976, 65. The opera company stated its purpose in its program: "Opera has seldom been a profit-making undertaking, and with sky-rocketing costs, it is today in its most difficult age. We cannot withstand exorbitant salaries, nor can we build Hollywood sets, but we believe we can bring you a performance of opera which emphasizes its most valued ingredient: the individual artist performing great music by great composers. With the success of these performances and your support, we hope to continue for many opera-filled seasons."

20. *Boston Globe*, February 17, 1978, 27. Robert Baxter, *Opera* 29, no. 8 (August 1978): 783–84: "a splendid production. . . . No directorial gimmicks here, just an impressive staging that made a convincing statement about Verdi's unconventional but arresting opera." Unlike Dyer, Baxter reported on the second performance, in which a replacement tenor (who had sung the role for La Selva) sang the title role. Andrew Porter, reporting on a still later performance, found the first tenor satisfactory, but closed by hoping one day to hear Vickers sing the role, see Porter, *New Yorker*, March 6, 1978, 106–13.

21. Budden, *Operas of Verdi*, 1:473.

22. Porter, *New Yorker*, March 6, 1978.

23. See Vestri's translation, *Stiffelius!* (Milan, 1848): "No, un duello leale, un'espiazione!"

24. Porter, *New Yorker*, March 6, 1978. On some problems of staging the opera, see George W. Martin, "Verdi's *Stiffelio*, Lost, Found, and Misunderstood," *Opera Quarterly* 13, no. 1 (Autumn 1996): 11–19.

25. Pippin titled his translation, published in 1982, an "English Version," and he based it seemingly on the Parma score, for the brief scene repositioned there is similarly so here; Lina's fast aria in act 2 is cut; and the line from the pulpit is translated as "And then he turned unto the populace." Pippin's often clever rhymes, however, sometimes seem out of place in the story, though perhaps they sang well. Pippin quoted, "Turning

Opera into English," a talk given February 22, 1998, at the Bocce Café, San Francisco, site of the Old Spaghetti Factory.

26. I attended three of the four performances. For an account of the Bel Canto company, see chap. 14. Philips, 422–432, with Sylvia Sass as Lina, Matteo Manuguerra as Stankar, and conductor Lamberto Gardelli. See reviews by John W. Freeman, *Opera News*, October 1980, 42; Andrew Porter, *High Fidelity*, February 1981, 74–75; and Peter G. Davis, *New York Times*, September 14, 1980, 26: "superb . . . in every respect." It restored the brief scene to its original location and included Lina's *allegro* aria.

27. Alessandro Camuto, *Opera* 37, no. 3 (March 1986): 333–35: "La Fenice launched the new season on 1 January with two of Verdi's interesting minor works—*Aroldo* and *Stiffelio*—given on the same day in reverse order chronologically. . . . The theatre's reason for changing the order *vis à vis* dates of composition is that *Stiffelio* is held to be more successful than the revision."

28. For the founding of the American Institute of Verdi Studies in 1976 and the reasons for it, see Porter, *New Yorker*, June 21, 1976.

29. The Wilmington translation was jointly by Lawton and Nicholas Muni, stage director. In addition to his work on *Stiffelio* for this production, Lawton edited the critical edition for *Il trovatore* (1992), for *Macbeth* (2005), and for *Le Trouvère*, not yet officially published but already circulating in a printed score and Commentary.

30. I attended the first performance, on November 26, 1988.

31. Allan Kozinn, *New York Times*, November 28, 1988, sec. 3, 23.

32. See Gossett, "New Sources for *Stiffelio*," and also Gossett, with less detail, in the Metropolitan program for its 1993–94 production. Also Hansell, "Compositional Techniques in *Stiffelio*."

33. Published by the Royal Opera, Covent Garden London, 1993, 272 pages, Downes's preface states that the score was "checked and verified" against the newly discovered parts of Verdi's autograph score and his sketches.

34. *Opera* 44, no. 3 (March 1993): 265–69. Also Jonathan Keates, *Times Literary Supplement*, February 12, 1993, 19. For an unfavorable review, Tom Sutcliffe, *Opera News*, May 1993, 54.

35. Bernard Holland, *New York Times*, July 17, 1993, sec. 1, 12.

36. Paul Griffiths, *New Yorker*, November 15, 1993, 110–12.

37. I attended four of the eleven performances, sitting in different places, and at each found the audience's attention to the drama notable, chiefly, I think, because of Domingo. In a house the size of the Met (capacity 3,800), the opera needs a singer, a presence, of his extraordinary power to project to those in distant rows the minister's interior struggle. On the merits of Sharon Sweet, see Martin Mayer, *Opera* 45, no. 1 (January 1944): 47–48.

38. Ibid.

39. Gossett, Note in the Metropolitan Opera program for the 1993–94 production. That program also offered an article by Andrew Porter in which he discusses the recurrent themes in Verdi, "Family and Fatherland." Equally strong were the articles devoted to the new production in the *Opera News* 58, no. 12 (March 5, 1994). Thus, the Metropolitan's "backup" for the opera was well done.

40. Griffiths, *New Yorker*, November 15, 1993.

41. To which might be added some European productions at Amsterdam (1992), Graz (1994), Madrid (1995), Milan (La Scala, 1995), and Vienna (1996). And the Metropolitan has announced a revival of its production for 2009–10, with Domingo conducting.

42. Osborne, *Complete Operas of Verdi*, 220n1, thinks this repositioning an improvement, Budden thinks it is not, see Budden, *Operas of Verdi*, 1:463.

43. Though the aria is one of those Griffiths deplored for moving too conventionally "from legato to athletics," most productions have included it, or at least one verse of it.

44. For an 1850 review criticizing the length and *buffo* tone of the Sinfonia, see Quaderni, no. 3, *Stiffelio*, 118; and for another complaining of its "too sprightly" tone, see 124. Another complaint, sometimes spoken, is that the lighthearted tunes are taken mostly from the first act and thus too soon repeated. Possibly because Verdi composed the Sinfonia last, as he often did, he made it long because the opera itself was short.

45. The Cologne production, sung in German, opened on October 29, 1972; Istvan Kertész conducted. See the review by Theodore Bloomfield in the *International Herald Tribune*, November 10, 1972, 7, and in *Opera* 24, no. 1 (January 1973): 30.

46. In 2002 Dynamic issued recording 362/1-2, taken from live performances of the opera by the home company of the Teatro Lirico Giuseppe Verdi di Trieste in December 2000. The production was based on the critical edition.

47. The title-role tenors were: in Wilmington, Noel Espiritu Velasco; in Chautauqua, Robert Breault; and in Sarasota, Todd Geer.

Conclusion

1. Gatti-Casazza, *Memories of the Opera*, 246. Gatti-Casazza died in 1940; his book is as he left it in 1933, after most of it had been published in five installments in the *Saturday Evening Post*. He wrote it with the editorial assistance of the *New York Times* critic Howard Taubman, who describes his part in its preparation in the two prefaces to this reprint edition. Before coming to the Metropolitan, Gatti-Casazza, according to Taubman, had served "fifteen years as a director of opera companies in Italy" for "a grand total of forty-two, a record that is perhaps unparalleled in the history of opera."

2. Ibid., 247–48.

3. Author's interview with Victor DeRenzi, April 6, 2004.

Appendix D

1. Bishop, *San Carlo Opera Company*; Kaufman, *San Carlo Opera Company*.

2. Bishop, "Introduction," in *San Carlo Opera Company*, 2.

Appendix F

1. See orchestra score published by the International Music Company, New York City, no. 1150, 243, an asterisk on the trombone line and at the foot of the page: "Se non si può ottenere un pianissimo, si ommettano Trombe e Trombone. Nei piccolo teatri sarà meglio ommetterli addirittura." Or his advice to the first Lady Macbeth: "I do not well recall if you trill with ease; I have included a trill [in the *brindisi*], but if necessary it can be taken out at once." Verdi letter to Barbieri-Nini, January 2, 1847, in Rosen and Porter, *Verdi's* Macbeth: A Sourcebook, 29.

2. Bel Canto's *Stiffelio*, December 6, 7, and 13, 1980, at the Sen. Robert Wagner Junior High School (now Middle School), 220 East Seventy-Sixth Street, New York. The audience for each of the three performances numbered perhaps 150. The Bel Canto company, which usually produced four or five operas a year, opened in 1969 with *Rigoletto* and closed in 1989 with Udo Zimmerman's *White Rose* (1967). For the most part, it presented operas currently little known, typically in the opera's original language and accompanied only by a piano. For a brief history of it through 1972, see Harvey E. Phillips, *New York Times*, October 7, 1973, sec. 2, 15; and to 1985, Martin, "New York's Smaller Companies." The company's founder, first artistic director, and producer was Theodore Sieh.

3. Verdi letter to the conductor Franco Faccio [probably November 29, 1873], trans. Hans Busch in *Verdi's Aida: The History of an Opera in Letters and Documents* (Minneapolis: University of Minnesota Press, 1978), 355–56.

4. See Shanet, *Philharmonic*, 65, for an excellent summary of how musicians in small theater orchestras tended to develop "some good habits and some very bad ones."

5. On Mapleson's touring company, see chapter 12. On the orchestra gathered by the Park Theatre for Garcia's troupe in 1825, see chap. 2.

6. Size of Trieste orchestra, see *WGV*, *Stiffelio*, score, xiv.

7. Quotations here and below, from David Lawton letter to the author, August 16, 2004. On bassoons: Verdi scored *Don Carlos* for four, a reason smaller companies seldom attempt the opera. Even in scores calling for two, they frequently are reduced to one, usually by giving the upper bassoon line to a clarinet. But to a well-tuned ear this may sound odd, improperly balanced. A conductor surely will hear it, but these days, with so many good recordings available, so will some in the audience, many of whom now come to the theater with strong feelings for how certain passages should sound. On hearing something slightly different, though unable to spot the cause, they may be bothered. The Sarasota company, for example, deliberately left productions of *Don Carlos* and *Otello* (four bassoons) to the end of its Verdi cycle, by which time it had enlarged its pit to seat seventy comfortably and eighty crowded. Victor DeRenzi phone call to the author, January 2, 2006.

8. I attended four of the season's eleven performances.

Selected Bibliography

Listed here are works that emphasize the history of Verdi's earlier operas in the United States—*Oberto* through *Rigoletto*. This list does not include those sources, such as critical reviews in newspapers or other journals, used only once or twice or primarily for only one chapter, which are given in full in the notes upon first mention and are not repeated here. Exceptions are made, however, for some sources touching directly on Verdi in the United States. Also several books, though not cited, but relevant to points discussed are included.

Abbate, Carolyn, and Roger Parker, eds. *Analyzing Opera, Verdi and Wagner*. Berkeley: University of California Press, 1989. Eleven essays by different scholars. (See also Gossett; Kerman and Grey.)

Abbiati, Franco. *Giuseppe Verdi*. 4 vols. Milan: Ricordi, 1959.

Alberti, Annibale, ed. *Verdi intimo, Carteggio di Giuseppe Verdi con il Conte Opprandino Arrivabene, 1861–1866*. Milan: Mondadori, 1931.

Armstrong, W. G. *A Record of the Opera in Philadelphia*. 1884. Reprint, New York: AMS Press, 1976.

Arrivabene, Opprandino. See Alberti, *Verdi Intimo*.

Baldini, Giovanni. *The Story of Giuseppe Verdi*. Translated by Roger Parker. Cambridge: Cambridge University Press, 1980.

Basevi, Abramo. *Studio sulle opere di Giuseppe Verdi*. Florence: Tofani, 1859.

Belsom, Jack. "Annals of Performance of the Théâtre d'Orléans (1819–1866) and of the French Opera House (1859–1919)." A work in progress.

———. "History of Opera in New Orleans." *New Orleans Opera Association Program*, October 1983.

———. "New Orleans Hears *Il Trovatore* and *La Traviata* for the First Time." *New Orleans Opera Association Program*, October 1997.

———. "Reception of Major Operatic Premieres in New Orleans During the Nineteenth Century." Master's thesis, Louisiana State University, 1972. (With the author's permission, copies may be had from the Williams Research Center, New Orleans.)

———. "Verdi's *Jérusalem, I due Foscari, Ernani* in New Orleans" (erroneously published as "Verdi's *Macbeth* in New Orleans"). *New Orleans Opera Association Program*, December 1975.

———. "Verdi's *Rigoletto* in New Orleans." *New Orleans Opera Association Program*, March 2008.

Bierley, Paul Edmund. *The Incredible Band of John Philip Sousa*. Urbana: University of Illinois Press, 2006.

Bishop, Cardell. *The Boston National Opera Company and Boston Theatre Opera Company* [1914–18]. Santa Monica: Cardell Bishop, 1981. For chronology, see Kaufman, Thomas G.

———. *The Los Angeles Grand Opera Association, 1924–1934: A Short Career in a Big City*. Santa Monica: Cardell Bishop, 1979.

———. *The San Carlo Opera Company, 1913 to 1955: Grand Opera for Profit*. 2nd ed. 2 vols. Santa Monica: Cardell Bishop, 1980. (For chronology, see Kaufman, Thomas G.)

———. *The Scotti Opera Company* [1919–22]. Santa Monica: Cardell Bishop, 1982. (For chronology, see Kaufman, Thomas G.)

Bloomfield, Arthur. *50 Years of the San Francisco Opera*. San Francisco: San Francisco Book Co., 1972.

Bruhn, Christopher. "Taking the Private Public: Amateur Music-making and the Musical Audience in 1860s New York." *American Music* 21, no. 3 (Fall 2003): 260–90. (Diaries of Gertrude Kellogg, John Ward, William Steinway, George Templeton Strong.)

Buckley, Peter G. "To the Opera House: Culture and Society in New York City, 1820–1860." PhD diss., State University of New York at Stony Brook, 1984. UMI #8513876.

Budden, Julian. *The Operas of Verdi*. Vol. 1, *From Oberto to Rigoletto*. London: Cassell, 1973.

———. *The Operas of Verdi*. Vol. 2, *From* Il Trovatore *to* La Forza del destino. London: Cassell, 1978.

———. *Verdi*. New York: Random House Vintage, 1987.

Cesari, Gaetano, and Alessandro Luzio, eds. *Copialettere di Giuseppe Verdi*. Milan, 1913.

Chatfield-Taylor, Joan. *San Francisco Opera, the First Seventy-Five Years* [1923–97]. San Francisco: Chronicle Books, 1997.

Chevalley, Sylvie. "Le Théâtre d'Orléans en Tournée dans les Villes du Nord, 1827–1833." *Comptes Rendus de L'Athénée Louisianais*. New Orleans (March 1955): 27–71.

Chusid, Martin, ed. *Verdi's Middle Period: Source Studies, Analysis, and Performance Practice*. Chicago: University of Chicago Press, 1997. A collection of thirteen essays by as many scholars along with an introductory essay by Chusid.

Chusid, Martin. "Verdi's Early U.S. Premieres." *Opera News*, January 7, 1978. Also, "Toward an Understanding of Verdi's Middle Period," in his introduction to *Verdi's Middle Period*.

Clapp, William W. Jr. *A Record of the Boston Stage*. 1853. Reprint, New York: Greenwood Press, 1969.

Complete Catalogue of Sheet Music and Musical Works, 1870. 1871. Reprint, New York: Da Capo Press, 1973.

Conati, Marcello. *Interviews and Encounters with Verdi*. Translated by Richard Stokes. London: Gollancz, 1984.

Cone, John Frederick. *First Rival of the Metropolitan Opera*. New York: Columbia University Press, 1983. See its appendix 2 for Mapleson's casts, performances, and cities visited in three seasons, 1883–85.

Cone, John Frederick. *Oscar Hammerstein's Manhattan Opera Company*. Norman: University of Oklahoma Press, 1966.

Cowell, Joe. *Thirty Years Passed Among the Players in England and America*. 1844. Reprint, Hamden, CT: Shoe String Press, 1979.

Cropsey, E. H. "Mr. Crosby's Temple of Art, The Inaugural Season, Chicago, 1865." *Opera Quarterly* 12, no. 1 (Autumn 1995): 79–126.

Crowest, Frederick J. *Verdi: Man and Musician*. London: John Milne, 1897.

Crutchfield, Will. "Authenticity in Verdi: The Recorded Legacy." *Opera* 36, no. 8 (August 1985): 858–66. And, at greater length, as "Vocal Ornamentation in Verdi: The Phonographic Evidence." *19th Century Music* 7, no. 1 (Summer 1983): 3–54.

Curtis, John. "One Hundred Years of Grand Opera in Philadelphia: The First Volume, Section Two (1844–60)"; and "The Second Volume, Section One (1861–76)." Unpublished typescript, 1920. At the Historical Society of Pennsylvania, Philadelphia.

Davis, Ronald L. *A History of Opera in the American West*. Englewood Cliffs, NJ: Prentice Hall, 1965.

De Van, Gilles. *Verdi's Theater: Creating Drama Through Music*. Translated by Gilda Roberts. Chicago: University of Chicago Press, 1998.

Dizikes, John. *Opera in America: A Cultural History*. New Haven: Yale University Press, 1993.

Durang, Charles. "The Stage: History of the Philadelphia Stage, 1749–1855." A series of articles in the Philadelphia *Sunday Dispatch*. First series, 1749–1821, starts in the paper of May 7, 1854; second series, 1822–30, in June 29, 1856; third series, 1830–55, July 8, 1860. Though never published as a book, the Historical Society of Pennsylvania has collected them in two volumes of clippings.

Durham, Weldon B. *American Theatre Companies, 1749–1887*. Westport, CT: Greenwood Press, 1986.

Dwight, John Sullivan. "The History of Music in Boston, Including Suffolk County, Massachusetts, 1630–1880." In *The Memorial History of Boston*. Vol. 4, *1630–1880*, edited by Justin Winsor, 415–64. Boston: J. R. Osgood, 1880–81.

Dwight, Timothy. *An Essay on the Stage: In Which the Arguments in Its Behalf, and Those Against It, Are Considered; And Its Morality, Character and Effects Illustrated*. Middletown, CT, 1824.

Eaton, Quaintance. *The Boston Opera Company*. 1965. Reprint, New York: Da Capo Press, 1980.

———. *Opera Caravan: Adventures of the Metropolitan on Tour, 1883–1956*. New York: Farrar, Straus and Cudahy, 1957. With chronology.

Eliot, Samuel (1821–98). "Diary," 1839–98. Unpublished manuscript in twelve volumes in The Boston Athenaeum's "Samuel Eliot Collection, personal and family papers, 1810–1910."

Fairtile, Linda B. "The Violin Director and Verdi's Middle-Period Operas." In *Verdi's Middle Period: Source Studies, Analysis, and Performance Practice*, edited by Martin Chusid, 413–26. Chicago: University of Chicago Press, 1997.

Faner, Robert D. *Walt Whitman & Opera*. Carbondale: Southern Illinois Press, 1951. Arcturus Books, 1972.

Faulkner, Dewey. "Recordings in Review: The Verdi Centennial." *Yale Review* 89, no. 4 (October 2001): 167–78. A twelve-page summary of alternative versions of Verdi's operas that represents how many listeners judged the operas at the turn of the century.

Foster, George G. *New York by Gaslight and Other Urban Sketches.* Edited by Stuart M. Blumin. 1850. Reprint, Berkeley: University of California Press, 1990.

Freeman, John W. "Carnival Town" Followed by the Repertory of the "New Orleans Opera House Association, 1943–74." *Opera News* 38, no. 22 (April 6, 1974): 12–19.

Garibaldi, Luigi Agostino, ed. *Giuseppe Verdi nelle lettere di Emanuele Muzio ad Antonio Barezzi.* Milan: Treves, 1931.

Gatti, Carlo. *Il teatro alla Scala nella storia e nell'arte (1778–1963): Cronologia completa degli spettacoli e dei concerti a cura di Giampiero Tintori.* Milan: Ricordi, 1964.

———. *Verdi,* vol. 1. Milan: Edizioni "Alpes," 1931.

Gatti-Casazza, Giulio. *Memories of the Opera.* 1933, 1937. Reprint, London: John Calder, 1977.

Glackens, Ira D. *Yankee Diva, Lillian Nordica and the Golden Days of Opera.* 1963. Reprint, New York: Coleridge Press, 1972.

Godefroy, Vincent. *The Dramatic Genius of Verdi: Studies of Selected Operas.* Vol. 1 [*Nabucco* Through *Traviata*]. London: Gollancz, 1975.

Gossett, Philip. "The Composition of *Ernani*." In *Analyzing Opera, Verdi and Wagner,* edited by Carolyn Abbate and Roger Parker, 65–95. Berkeley: University of California Press, 1989.

———. *Divas and Scholars: Performing Italian Opera.* Chicago: University of Chicago Press, 2006.

———. "New Sources for *Stiffelio*: A Preliminary Report." *Cambridge Opera Journal* 5, no. 3 November 1993: 199–222. Also published in Chusid, ed., *Verdi's Middle Period.*

Grant, Mark N. *Maestros of the Pen: A History of Classical Music Criticism in America.* Boston: Northeastern University Press, 1998.

Graziano, John, ed. *European Music and Musicians in New York City, 1840–1900.* Rochester, NY: University of Rochester Press, 2006.

Gregson, David. "Nights of Glory: A History of San Diego Opera." In M. L. Hart, *The Art of Making Opera: Two Seasons with San Diego Opera.* San Diego: San Diego Opera, 1998.

Grimsted, David. *Melodrama Unveiled: American Theatre and Culture, 1800–1850.* Chicago: University of Chicago Press, 1968.

Grossman, F. Karl. *A History of Music in Cleveland.* Cleveland: Case Western University Press, 1972.

Hamilton, Frank. *Chronology of Opera in Philadelphia.* Available at http://frank hamilton.org/ph/phcw.pdf.

Hart, M. L. *The Art of Making Opera: Two Seasons with the San Diego Opera.* San Diego: San Diego Opera, 1998.

Harwood, Gregory W. *Giuseppe Verdi: A Guide to Research.* New York: Garland, 1998.

———. "Verdi's Reform of the Italian Opera Orchestra," *19th Century Music* 10, no. 2 (Fall 1986): 108–34.

The History of Opera in San Francisco. Parts 1 and 2. Monographs xvii and xviii. Works Progress Administration. Project 10677 (1938).

Hixon, Don L. *Verdi in San Francisco: A Preliminary Bibliography, 1851–1899.* Privately printed, 1980.

Hone, Philip (1780–1851). *Diary, 1828–51.* Manuscript at the New-York Historical Society, New York. Parts published in various editions, of which the most useful for this book was *The Diary of Philip Hone, 1828–1851.* Edited by Allan Nevins. 2 vols. New York: Dodd, Mead, 1927.

———. *The Diary of Philip Hone, 1828–1851.* Edited by Allan Nevins. 1927. Reprint, New York: Arno Press, 1970.

Hoole, W. Stanley. *The Ante-Bellum Charleston Theatre.* Tuscaloosa: University of Alabama Press, 1946.

Hopkinson, Cecil. *A Bibliography of the Works of Giuseppe Verdi, 1813–1901.* 2 vols. New York: Broude Bros., 1978.

Hughes, Spike. *Famous Verdi Operas.* London: Robert Hale, 1968.

———. *The Toscanini Legacy.* London: Putnam, 1959. A critical study of Arturo Toscanini's performances of Beethoven, Verdi, and other composers.

Hussey, Dyneley. *Verdi.* London: J. M. Dent, 1940. Master Musicians Series.

Ingalls, David M. "Francis Scala: Leader of the Marine Band from 1855 to 1871." Master's thesis, Catholic University of America, 1957. Copies available from the university's library, Washington, DC.

Ireland, Joseph N. *Records of the New York Stage from 1750 to 1860.* 2 vols. 1866–67. Reprint, New York: Burt Franklin, 1968.

Jennings, Harlan Francis. "Grand Opera in Kansas in the 1880s." PhD diss., University of Cincinnati, 1978. UMI #7901546.

———. "Her Majesty's Opera Company in Kansas City." *Opera Quarterly* 21, no. 2 (Spring 2005): 227–41.

Jensen, Luke. *Giuseppe Verdi & Giovanni Ricordi, with Notes on Francesco Lucca, from Oberto to La Traviata.* New York: Garland Publishing, 1989.

Jürgensen, Knud Arne. *The Verdi Ballets.* Parma: Istituto Nazionale di Studi Verdiani, 1995.

Kaufman, Thomas G. "The Arditi Tour, the MidWest Gets Its First Real Taste of Italian Opera," *The Opera Quarterly,* vol. 4, no. 4, Winter 1986/87.

———. *The Boston National Opera Company (1915–1917).* A chronology. Privately printed.

———. Chronology of the career of Emanuele Muzio as a conductor, much of it in the United States (1858–75). See "Cronologia." In Gaspare Nello Vetro, *L'Allevio di Verdi* Parma: Edizioni Zara, 1993.

———. *The San Carlo Opera Company: The First 13 Seasons (1913–1926).* A chronology of performances with casts. Privately printed.

———. *The Scotti Opera Company.* A chronology. Privately printed.

———. *Verdi and His Major Contemporaries: A Selected Chronology of Performances with Casts.* New York: Garland, 1990.

———. "Wagner vs. Meyerbeer." *Opera Quarterly* 19, no. 4 (Autumn 2003): 644–90. For tables showing comparative number of performances, including those of Verdi, in various periods at leading European houses.

Kellogg, Clara Louise. *Memoirs of an American Prima Donna*. New York: Putnam's, 1913.

Kerman, Joseph. *Opera as Drama*. 1956. Reprint, New York: Vintage Books, 1959.

———. *Write All These Down: Essays on Music*. Berkeley: University of California Press, 1994. Twenty essays on opera, two on Verdi previously published: "Verdi's Use of Recurring Themes" and "Two Early Verdi Operas; Two Famous Terzetti." The two early operas are *Ernani* and *I Lombardi*.

Kerman, Joseph, and Thomas S. Grey. "Verdi's Groundswells: Surveying an Operatic Convention." In *Analyzing Opera, Verdi and Wagner*, edited by Carolyn Abbate and Roger Parker, 153–79. Berkeley: University of California Press, 1989.

Kimbell, David R. B. *Verdi in the Age of Italian Romanticism*. Cambridge: Cambridge University Press, 1981.

Kirk, Elise K. *Music at the White House: A History of the American Spirit*. Urbana: University of Illinois Press, 1986.

Kmen, Henry A. *Music in New Orleans: The Formative Years, 1791–1841*. Baton Rouge: Louisiana State University Press, 1966.

———. "Singing and Dancing in New Orleans: A Social History of the Birth and Growth of Balls and Operas, 1791–1841." PhD diss., Tulane University, 1961. UMI #63-2209.

Kolodin, Irving. *The Metropolitan Opera, 1883–1966*. New York: Knopf, 1966.

Krehbiel, Henry Edward. *A Book of Operas*. New York: Macmillan, 1909.

———. *Chapters of Opera, Being Historical and Critical Observations and Records Concerning the Lyric Drama in New York from the Earliest Days down to the Present Time*. New York: Henry Holt, 1908.

———. *More Chapters of Opera*. New York: Henry Holt, 1919.

Lahee, Henry Charles. *Annals of Music in America: A Chronological Record of Significant Musical Events, from 1640 to the Present Day, with Comments on the Various Periods into Which the Work Is Divided*. Freeport, NY: Books for Libraries Press, 1922.

Lang, Paul Henry. *Critic at the Opera*. New York: Norton, 1971.

Latham, Alison, and Roger Parker, eds., *Verdi in Performance*. Oxford: Oxford University Press, 2001. A collection of essays resulting from a conference on Verdi. In four parts: Staging, Instrumental and Vocal Performances, Ballet, and Editions. Various writers including Andrew Porter, David Rosen, and David Lawton.

Lawrence, Vera Brodsky. *Strong on Music: The New York Music Scene in the Days of George Templeton Strong, 1836–1875*. Vol. 1, *Resonances, 1836–1850*. New York: Oxford University Press, 1988; vol. 2, *Reverberations, 1850–1856*. Chicago: University of Chicago Press, 1995; vol. 3, *Repercussions, 1857–1862*. Chicago: University of Chicago Press, 1999.

Levine, Lawrence W. *Highbrow/Lowbrow: the Emergence of Cultural Hierarchy in America*. Cambridge: Harvard University Press, 1988.

Loewenberg, Alfred. *Annals of Opera, 1507–1940*. 2nd ed. Geneva: Societas Bibliographica, 1955.

Luzio, Alessandro, ed. *Carteggi Verdiani*. 4 vols. Rome: Academia Nazionale del Lincei, 1947.

Madeira, Louis C., ed. *Annals of Music in Philadelphia and History of the Musical Fund Society: From Its Organization in 1820 to the Year 1858*, comp. Philip H. Goepp. Philadelphia: Lippincott, 1896. Reprint, New York: Da Capo Press, 1973.

Madeira, Louis C. *Music in Philadelphia and the Musical Fund Society*. 1896. Reprint, edited by Philip H. Goepp. New York: Da Capo Press, 1973.

Mapleson, James Henry. *The Mapleson Memoirs: The Career of an Operatic Impresario, 1858–1888*. Edited by Harold Rosenthal. New York: Appleton-Century, 1966. See the "Selective Biographical Index" for brief biographies, with dates, of many obscure people working in opera.

Maretzek, Max. *Crotchets and Quavers, or Revelations of an Opera Manager in America*. 1855. Reprint, New York: Da Capo Press, 1966.

———. *Further Revelations of an Opera Manager in 19th Century America*. Edited and annotated by Ruth Henderson. Sterling Heights, MI: Harmonie Park Press, 2006.

———. *Sharps and Flats*. Included as the second part of *Revelations of an Opera Manager in 19th Century America*. 1890. Reprint, New York: Dover Press, 1968. The first part is *Crotchets and Quavers*.

A Maritime History of New York. Works Project Administration project. Garden City, NY: Doubleday, Doran, 1941.

Martin, George W. *Aspects of Verdi*. 1988. Reprint, New York: Limelight Editions, 1993.

———. "The Metropolitan Opera's Sunday Evening Concerts and Verdi." *Opera Quarterly* 19, no. 1 (Winter 2003): 16–27.

———. "New York's Smaller Companies." *Opera* 36, no. 9 (September 1985): 1001–5.

———. *Verdi at the Golden Gate: Opera and San Francisco in the Gold Rush Years*. Berkeley: University of California Press, 1993.

———. "Verdi's *Stiffelio*: Lost, Found, and Misunderstood." *Opera Quarterly* 13, no. 1 (Autumn 1996): 11–19.

Martin, Sadie E. *The Life and Professional Career of Emma Abbott*. Minneapolis: J. Kimball, 1891.

Mattfeld, Julius. *A Hundred Years of Grand Opera in New York, 1825–1925*. New York: New York Public Library, 1976.

Matthews, W. S. B. *A Hundred Years of Music in America*. Chicago: G. L. Howe, 1889.

Mauceri, John. "*Rigoletto* for the 21st Century." *Opera* (October 1985): 1135–44.

McKnight, Mark Curtis. "Music Criticism in the *New York Times* and the *New York Tribune*, 1854–1876." PhD diss., Louisiana State University, 1980. UMI #8103641.

McPherson, Jim. "Before the Met: The Pioneer Days of Radio Opera, Part 1: An Overview." *Opera Quarterly* 16, no. 1 (Winter 2000): 5–23; "Part 2: The NBS National Grand Opera Co.," no. 2 (Spring 2000): 204–23; and "Part 3: Cesare Sodero, the Music Man," no. 3 (Summer 2000): 407–26.

———. "Frances Peralta, the Met's Forgotten Diva." *Opera Quarterly* 17, no. 4 (Autumn 2001): 662–780.

———. "Mr. Meek Goes to Washington: The Story of the Small-Potatoes Canadian Baritone Who Founded America's 'National' Opera." *Opera Quarterly* 20, no. 2 (Spring 2004): 197–267. (Opera in Washington, DC, 1919–36, with annals and list of performers.)

———. "The Savage Innocents: Part 1, King of the Castle Square Opera Company." *Opera Quarterly* 18, no. 4 (Autumn 2002): 503–33.

———. "The Savage Innocents: Part 2, On the Road with *Parsifal, Butterfly*, the *Widow* and the *Girl.*" *Opera Quarterly* 19, no. 1 (Winter 2003): 28–63.

Metropolitan Opera. *Data Base: Archives.* www.metopera.org.

Moses, Julian Morton. *Collectors' Guide to American Recordings, 1895–1925.* 1949. Reprint, New York: Dover Press, 1977.

Mueller, John H. *The American Symphony Orchestra, A Social History of Musical Taste.* Bloomington: Indiana University Press, 1951.

Muzio, Emanuele. *Lettere ad Antonio Barezzi.* See Garibaldi, L. A.

Nelson, Molly. "The First Italian Opera Season in New York City: 1825–1826." PhD diss., University of North Carolina at Chapel Hill, 1976. UMI #77-17,475.

New Grove Dictionary of Opera. Edited by Stanley Sadie. 4 vols. London: Macmillan, 1992.

Norton, Elliot. *Broadway Down East: An Informal Account of the Plays, Players and Playhouses of Boston from Puritan Times to the Present.* Boston: Boston Public Library, 1978.

"Notelrac." *Operas, Their Writers and Their Plots.* Philadelphia: Lippincott, 1882.

Odell, George C. D. *Annals of the New York Stage.* Vols. 1–7. New York: Columbia University Press, 1927–31. Reprint, New York: AMS Press, 1970.

"Opera Performances in New Orleans, 1812–1919." Works Progress Administration in New Orleans. Typescript copy in Louisiana State Museum Library, New Orleans.

Osborne, Charles. *The Complete Operas of Verdi.* New York: Knopf, 1970.

Parker, Roger. *The New Grove Guide to Verdi and His Operas.* Oxford: Oxford University Press, 2007.

———. *Studies in Early Verdi, 1832–1844: New Information and Perspectives on the Milanese Musical Milieu and the Operas from* Oberto *to* Ernani. New York: Garland, 1989.

Penino, John. "The New Opera Company: What Did It Accomplish?" *Opera Quarterly* 16, no. 4 (Autumn 2000): 589–610.

Petrobelli, Pierluigi. *Music in the Theatre, Essays on Verdi and Other Composers.* Translated by Roger Parker. Princeton: Princeton University Press, 1994.

Phillips-Matz, Mary Jane. *Verdi: A Biography.* New York: Oxford University Press, 1993.

Pistone, Danièle. *Nineteenth-Century Italian Opera, from Rossini to Puccini.* Translated by E. Thomas Glasow. Portland, OR: Amadeus Press, 1995.

Porter, Andrew. *Music of Three Seasons, 1974–1977.* New York: Farrar, Straus and Giroux, 1978.

———. *Music of Three More Seasons, 1977–1980.* New York: Knopf, 1981.

———. *Musical Events: A Chronicle, 1980–1983.* New York: Summit Books, 1987.

———. *Musical Events: A Chronicle, 1983–1986.* New York: Summit Books, 1989.

———. *A Musical Season: A Critic from Abroad* [1972–74]. New York: Viking Press, 1974.

Pougin, Arturo. *Giuseppe Verdi, Vita Aneddotica, con note ed aggiunte di Folchetto.* Milan: Ricordi, 1881. Translated from French by James E. Matthew as *Verdi: An Anecdotic History of His Life and Works.* London: Grevel, 1887.

Prado, Enrique Rio. *La musica italiana a Cuba, Prime rappresentazioni di Verdi e Morlacchi all'Avana*. Lecce: BESA, 1996.

Preston, Katherine K. "American Musical Life of the Late Nineteenth Century." *American Music* 21, no. 3 (Fall 2003): 255–59.

———. "Notes from (the Road to) the Stage." *Opera Quarterly* 23, no. 1 (Winter 2007): 103–19.

———. *Opera on the Road, Traveling Opera Troupes in the United States, 1825–1860*. Urbana: University of Illinois Press, 1993.

———. "To the Opera House? The Trials and Tribulations of Operatic Production in Nineteenth-Century America." *Opera Quarterly* 23, no. 1 (Winter 2007): 39–65.

Ritter, Frédéric Louis. *Music in America*. 2nd ed. New York: Scribner's, 1890.

Rodger, Gillian. "Legislating Amusements: Class Politics and Theater Law in New York City." *American Music* 20, no. 4 (Winter 2002): 381–98.

Rogers, Stuart W. "The Tremont Theater and the Rise of Opera in Boston, 1827–1847." *Opera Quarterly* 16, no. 3 (Summer 2000): 363–96.

Rosen, David, and Andrew Porter, eds. *Verdi's* Macbeth: *A Sourcebook*. New York: Norton, 1984.

Rosenthal, Harold. *Two Centuries of Opera at Covent Garden*. London: Putnam, 1958.

Ross, Alex. "Verdi's Grip: Opera as Popular Art." In Ross, *Listen to This*, 188–203. New York: Farrar, Straus and Giroux, 2010.

———. "Verdi's Grip: Why the Shakespeare of Grand Opera Resists Radical Staging." *New Yorker*, September 24, 2001, 82–87.

Sabin Robert, ed. *International Cyclopedia of Music and Musicians*. 9th ed. New York: Dodd, Mead, 1964.

Sablosky, Irving. *What They Heard: Music in America, 1852–1881, from the Pages of "Dwight's Journal of Music."* Baton Rouge: Louisiana State University, 1986.

Santley, Charles. *Student and Singer: The Reminiscences of Charles Santley*. New York and London: Macmillan, 1892.

Schabas, Ezra, and Carl Morey. *Opera Viva, Canadian Opera Company: The First Fifty Years*. Toronto: Dundurn Press, 2000.

Schiavo, Giovanni Ermengildo. *Italian-American History*. 1947. Reprint, New York: Arno Press, 1975.

"Scricci" (John H. Swaby). *Physiology of the Opera*. Philadelphia: Wills P. Hazard, 1852. Reprint, Brooklyn: Institute for Studies in American Music, 1981. Intro., D. W. Krummel. A satiric look at operagoing in Philadelphia in 1852, with *Ernani* the chief opera discussed.

Shanet, Howard. *Philharmonic: A History of New York's Orchestra*. New York: Doubleday, 1975.

Shaw, G. Bernard. *Shaw's Music: The Complete Musical Criticism in Three Volumes*. Edited by Dan H. Lawrence. New York: Dodd, Mead, 1981.

Sill, Joseph (1801–54). "Diary, 1836–1854." 10 vols. Unpublished manuscript at the Historical Society of Pennsylvania, Philadelphia.

Smart, Mary Ann. "'Proud, Indomitable, Irascible'; Allegories of Nation in *Attila* and *Les Vêpres siciliennes*." In *Verdi's Middle Period: Source Studies, Analysis, and Performance Practice*, edited by Martin Chusid, 227–56. Chicago: University of Chicago Press, 1997.

———. "Verdi Sings Erminia Frezzolini." *Verdi Newsletter*, no. 24 (1997): 13–22.

Sokol, Martin L. *The New York City Opera: An American Adventure with the Complete Annals.* New York: Macmillan, 1981.

Sonneck, Oscar G. *Early Opera in American.* 1915. Reprint, New York: Benjamin Blom, 1963.

Strong, George Templeton (1820–75). "Diary, 1835–75." Manuscript at the New-York Historical Society, New York. Parts published in various editions, of which the best for historians of music is Vera Brodsky Lawrence, *Strong on Music: The New York Music Scene in the Days of George Templeton Strong, 1836–1875.* (See separate entry for Lawrence.)

Swift, Mary Grace. "The Northern Tours of the Théâtre d'Orléans, 1843 and 1845." *Louisiana History* 26, no. 2 (Spring 1985): 155–91.

Taubman, H. Howard. *Opera Front and Back.* New York: Scribner's, 1938.

Teran, Jay Robert. "The New York Opera Audience, 1825–1974." PhD diss., New York University, 1974. UMI #75-9708.

Thierstein, Eldred A. *Cincinnati Opera: From the Zoo to Music Hall* [1972–95]. Hillsdale, MI: Deerstone Books, 1995.

Thompson, Oscar. *The American Singer: A Hundred Years of Success in Opera.* New York: Dial Press, 1937.

Tintori, Giampiero. *Cronologia* (of La Scala). See Gatti, Carlo.

Tompkins, Eugene, and Quincy Kilby. *The History of Boston Theatre, 1854–1901.* 1908. Reprint, New York: Benjamin Blom, 1969.

Toye, Francis. *Giuseppe Verdi: His Life and Works.* 1931. Reprint, New York: Knopf, 1946.

Travis, Francis Irving. *Verdi's Orchestration.* Zurich: Juris-Verlag, 1956.

Upton, George P. *Musical Memories.* Chicago: McClurg, 1908.

———. *The Standard Operas, Their Plots, Their Music, and Their Composers: A Handbook.* Chicago: McClurg, 1889.

Vetro, Gaspare Nello. *L'allievo di Verdi, Emanuele Muzio.* Parma: Fondazione Casa di Risparmio, 1993. With a chronology by Thomas G. Kaufman for 1847–79 (pp. 281–333), with many seasons in the United States.

The Victor Book of the Opera: Stories of Seventy Grand Operas with Three Hundred Illustrations & Descriptions of Seven Hundred Victor Opera Records, published in multiple revised editions from 1912 to 1938 initially by the Victor Talking Machine Company and then by the RCA Manufacturing Company.

Walker, Frank. *The Man Verdi.* New York: Knopf, 1962.

Ward, Joseph (1838–96). "Diary, 1864, 1865, and 1867." Unpublished manuscript at the New-York Historical Society, New York. Christopher Bruhn, "Taking the Private Public: Amateur Music-making and the Musical Audience in 1860s New York," *American Music* 21, no. 3 (Fall 2003): 260–90, discusses the reports of several New York diarists, of which the most interesting on Italian opera is Ward.

Ware, W. Porter, and Thaddeus C. Lockard Jr. *P. T. Barnum Presents Jenny Lind: The American Tour of the Swedish Nightingale.* Baton Rouge: Louisiana State University, 1980.

Weaver, William. "The Shakespeare Verdi Knew." In Rosen and Porter, *Sourcebook,* 144–48.

————. *Verdi: A Documentary Study*. London: Thames and Hudson, 1977.

White, Richard Grant. "Opera in New York." *Century Illustrated Monthly Magazine,* March, 686–703; April, 865–82; May, 31–43; June, 193–210.

Whitman, Walt. *The Collected Writings of Walt Whitman: The Journalism*. Vol. 2, *1846–1848*. Edited by Herbert Bergman. New York: Peter Lang, 2003.

Wilson, Arthur Herman. *A History of the Philadelphia Theatre, 1835 to 1885*. Philadelphia: University of Pennsylvania Press, 1935.

Wolz, Larry Robert. "Opera in Cincinnati: The Years Before the Zoo, 1801–1920." PhD diss., University of Cincinnati, 1983. UMI #AAT8323251.

Wood, William B. *Personal Recollections of the Stage, Embracing Notices of Actors, Authors, and Auditors, During a Period of Forty Years*. Philadelphia: Baird, 1855. The period: 1797–1846. Wood, an actor-manager, was the "Late Director of the Philadelphia, Baltimore, Washington, and Alexandria Theatres."

The Works of Giuseppe Verdi. Edited by Philip Gossett et al. Series 1: Operas. Critical edition. Vols. 3, 5, 7, 8, 10, 11, 13, 15, 16, and 17. *Nabucodonosor, Ernani, Giovanna d'Arco, Alzira, Macbeth, Masnadieri, Corsaro, Luisa Miller, Stiffelio,* and *Rigoletto*. Chicago: University of Chicago Press; Milan: Ricordi, 1987, 1985, 2008, 1994, 2005, 2000, 1998, 1991, 2003, and 1983. Each volume consists of an orchestral score with a lengthy introduction and a critical commentary. In Series 3, vol. 1, the press published a score and critical commentary of the *Messa da Requiem,* edited by David Rosen (1990), and in Series 4, vol. 1, of two *Inni,* "Suoria la tromba" and "Inno delle nazioni," edited by Roberta Montemorra Marvin (2007).

WPA, Chronology Projects, see *Opera Performances in New Orleans, 1812–1919;* San Francisco Theatre Research, *The History of Opera in San Francisco;* and also, though not purely a chronology, *A Maritime History of New York* (Garden City, NY: Doubleday, Doran, 1941).

Young, William C. *Documents of American Theatre*. Vol. 1, *Famous American Playhouses, 1716–1899*. Chicago: American Library Association, 1973.

Index

Note: Page numbers in italics indicate illustrations; those with a *t* indicate tables. Descriptors are given parenthetically for most (but not all) composers, playwrights, performers, impresarios, and any music critics whose reviews are treated as evidence in the book.

Eastman Studies in Music

Ralph P. Locke, Senior Editor
Eastman School of Music

Additional Titles of Interest

Berlioz's Semi-Operas: "Roméo et Juliette" and "La damnation de Faust"
Daniel Albright

"Claude Debussy As I Knew Him" and Other Writings of Arthur Hartmann
Edited by Samuel Hsu, Sidney Grolnic, and Mark Peters
Foreword by David Grayson

European Music and Musicians in New York City, 1840–1900
Edited by John Graziano

Good Music for a Free People: The Germania Musical Society in Nineteenth-Century America
Nancy Newman

Janáček beyond the Borders
Derek Katz

Musicking Shakespeare: A Conflict of Theatre
Daniel Albright

Music Speaks: On the Language of Opera, Dance, and Song
Daniel Albright

Of Poetry and Song: Approaches to the Nineteenth-Century Lied
Edited by Jürgen Thym

Opera and Ideology in Prague: Polemics and Practice at the National Theater, 1900–1938
Brian S. Locke

Wagner and Wagnerism in Nineteenth-Century Sweden, Finland, and the Baltic Provinces: Reception, Enthusiasm, Cult
Hannu Salmi

A complete list of titles in the Eastman Studies in Music series, in order of publication, may be found on our website, www.urpress.com.

The operas of Giuseppe Verdi stand at the center of today's operatic repertoire, as they have for more than a century. How the wide appeal and reputation of these operas spread from Western Europe throughout the world is a
story that has long needed to be told. This latest book by noted Verdi authority
George W. Martin details in particular the changing fortunes of Verdi's early
operas in the theaters and concert halls of the United States.

Among the important works whose fates Martin traces are *Nabucco, Attila,
Ernani, Macbeth* (in its original version), *Luisa Miller*, and one of Verdi's immor-
tal masterpieces: *Rigoletto*, denounced in 1860 as the epitome of immorality.

Martin also explores the revival of many of these operas in the 1940s and
onward (including *Macbeth* in its revised version of 1865), and the first American productions—sometimes in small opera houses outside the main circuit—
of some Verdi operas that had never previously managed to cross the Atlantic.
Extensive quotations from newspaper reviews testify to the eventual triumph
of these remarkable works, and reveal the crucial cultural shifts in taste and
expectations from Verdi's day to our own.

"George Martin has done it again. Combining his extraordinary knowledge
of American performances over the past fifty years with a scholar's delight in
exploring the byways of nineteenth-century theatrical life in America, he has
written a book that explores the reception of Verdi's early operas in the United
States, from the first appearance of each through the present. Anyone who
wishes an overview of Verdi's operatic influence in America will be eternally in
his debt."

—Philip Gossett, Robert W. Reneker Distinguished Service
Emeritus Professor of Music, University of Chicago